Logical Symbols

Symbol	Name
$\sim$	Negation sign
$\rightarrow$	Conditional sign
$\wedge$	Conjunction sign
$\vee$	Disjunction sign
$\leftrightarrow$	Biconditional sign
$\bigwedge$	Universal quantifier
$\bigvee$	Existential quantifier
$=$	Identity sign
ι	Descriptive operator

LOGIC

Techniques of Formal Reasoning

Second Edition

LOGIC
Techniques of Formal Reasoning

Second Edition

Donald Kalish

UNIVERSITY OF CALIFORNIA, LOS ANGELES

Richard Montague

LATE OF UNIVERSITY OF CALIFORNIA, LOS ANGELES

Gary Mar

Under the General Editorship of

Robert J. Fogelin

YALE UNIVERSITY

Harcourt Brace Jovanovich College Publishers

Fort Worth Philadelphia San Diego
New York Orlando Austin San Antonio
Toronto Montreal London Sydney Tokyo

ISBN: 0-15-551181-5

Library of Congress Catalog Card Number: 79-91650

Printed in the United States of America

CONTENTS

Preface to the Second Edition

THIS edition, like the preceding one, is an introduction to logic, requiring no prior knowledge of philosophy or mathematics. It does not aim at communicating or justifying results about logical systems but instead at imparting a skill—the ability to recognize and construct correct deductions and refutations. Metamathematical results are sometimes mentioned, but only incidentally and as an aid to understanding.

The subjects treated are the same as in the first edition; they are the sentential calculus, the quantifier calculus, the identity calculus, the description calculus, some automatic proof procedures, and a detailed development of a familiar mathematical theory. The treatment of the latter two subjects remains unchanged, except for the placement of the chapter on automatic procedures. In the present edition, as in the earlier one, the four systems of logic are developed by the simple and intuitive techniques of natural deduction; but here the development is continuous and initially unsupplemented. It is not interrupted, as before, first in the quantifier calculus and then again in the description calculus by the introduction of more sophisticated techniques that require the notions of alphabetic variance, substitution on predicate and operation letters, and interchange, and also by the employment of such techniques to obtain for the sentential calculus and the quantifier calculus derivational procedures that are automatic rather than natural. These more sophisticated notions and techniques are now set forth in a unified fashion after the development by natural deduction of the four systems of logic. Furthermore, the introduction of biconditional derivation (see p. 365) allows proofs obtained by these techniques to be set forth more succinctly and elegantly than in the earlier edition.

There are two comprehensive changes in our treatment of the systems of logic. One is a significant increase in the quantity and quality of the exercises that accompany each section of the first eight chapters, together with an appendix to each of these chapters that contains solutions to many of the exercises. Easier and more graduated exercises than those of the earlier edition will facilitate the reader's understanding, and more difficult exercises will challenge and deepen that understanding. For some of the latter, we give not only a solution but also a description of how it was discovered; see, for example, the solution to exercise 89 on pp. 261–62 and the solution to exercise 82 on pp. 304–5. The other comprehensive change is a more extensive treatment of the invalidity of symbolic arguments obtained by the introduction of models. A problem with models, for an elementary textbook that does not countenance lack of rigor, is that of precisely characterizing truth in a model without introducing the entire Tarskian metamathematical apparatus. This problem has been avoided by employing only models with a finite universe and by precisely defining truth in such a model by means of an expansion comparable to a truth-functional expansion. But in contrast to truth-functional expansions, the method can be extended naturally and easily, and with no loss of rigor, to accommodate operation symbols and the descriptive operator. For invalid arguments whose invalidity cannot be established by a finite model, the method of the earlier edition (that of finding a translation of the symbolic argument into an English argument with true premises and a false conclusion) is still employed. But here, to avoid qualifications about nonextensional contexts of English, the method is limited to translations into the language of the arithmetic of natural numbers. Further, it is supplemented by intuitive but informal explanations that the invalidity of the arguments investigated could not be established by finite models; see, for example, the treatment of argument (7) on pages 288–89.

The most important supplementation within one of the systems of logic occurs in the description calculus. In this edition we not only present a revised exposition of the detailed development of a Fregean theory of descriptions (chapter VI) but also supplement it (chapter VIII) with an equally detailed development, by our system of natural deduction, of a Russellian theory of descriptions and a comparison of the two theories. We depart from Russell by treating the descriptive operator as a primitive symbol rather than as one introduced by a contextual definition; but we capture Russell's intuition and obtain his theorems. Although we do not present here, or elsewhere, a proof that our Russellian theory is *complete*, this fact follows immediately from the eliminability of the descriptive operator. (That is, if we admit among our Russellian models those with infinite as well as finite universe, then every formula is either a theorem of our Russellian theory or false in some such model.)

Our development of the identity calculus has been supplemented by a more extended treatment of numerical conditions and by a wealth of exercises. And our formulation of that calculus is now the customary one. In the earlier edition two elegant rules, representing a single principle (T306, page 275), were taken as primitive, and from these rules the principle of identity and Leibniz' law were derived. Once these familiar and intuitive principles were made available, the primitive rules were never employed again. In this edition, we take as our primitive rules the familiar ones

Our treatment of the quantifier calculus is enhanced mainly by the use of models to demonstrate the invalidity of symbolic arguments. But an understanding of the grammar of the language of that calculus is facilitated by the introduction of grammatical trees to exemplify the generation of symbolic formulas (see, for example, p. 121) and of modified grammatical trees to identify bound occurrences of terms (see, for example, p. 125).

Our treatment of sentential logic has been rewritten and expanded to make the initial presentation of the system of natural deduction more intuitive and understandable. For example, annotations are now employed to indicate how a derivation is concluded as well as how a derivation is initiated, and this supplementation facilitates a discussion of the employment and dispensability of *mixed* derivations (derivations initiated by one method but concluded by another). And the accompanying sections on truth-value analysis now introduce ways to abbreviate truth tables, exercises that should provide entertainment as well as instruction (see, for example, Exercises, Group III, pp. 103–5), an introduction to such topics as normal forms and duality, and a foundation for the subsequent definition of truth in a model.

Symbolic rather than English arguments are the central subject matter of our text, as its title suggests. But here as in the earlier edition arguments of English play a motivating role. We say that an English argument is *valid* (in a particular branch of logic) if and only if it has (within that branch) a valid symbolization. In the earlier edition, in sections titled 'Paradoxical inferences', some intuitively invalid English arguments that appear to have valid symbolizations were considered. Then it was claimed that these English arguments cannot be symbolized and hence do not constitute fallacies, for their symbolizations are blocked by subtle restrictions imposed on the notion of a scheme of abbreviation. This attempt to preserve the adequacy of the characterization of *validity* of English arguments was a step beyond that taken by most, if not all, introductions to classical logic. And it was the point of departure for the profound investigations of the structure of ordinary language by our late colleague Professor Richard Montague (see Montague [4] and Partee [1]). However, this attempt encountered both pedagogical and theoretical difficulties. The pedagogical problems arose because the uninitiated reader could understand neither the formulation of nor the reasons for the subtle impositions on the simple notion of a scheme of abbreviation, and the theoretical problems resulted from the fact that the totality of impositions did not block *all* fallacies. Thus the definition of *validity* of an English argument employed is only an approximate guide to the logic of ordinary language; however, we employ it because the symbolization of English motivates interest in and facilitates an understanding of the symbolic languages, and deepens (even if it does not complete) insight into the structure and logic of English. (See, as an example of the former, Exercises, Group III, on pp. 137–39, and as an example of the latter the treatment of enthymemes in section 9 of chapter IV, on pp. 286–87 of chapter V, and in section 8 of chapter VI.) In place of the paradoxical inference sections of the earlier edition, we recommend as supplements to the material of this text such works as Frege [2], Davis [1], Anderson and Belnap [1], Linsky [1], and Davidson and Harman [1].

The earlier edition was intended to be comprehensible without a teacher. We believe that intention will be more frequently achieved in this edition because of the improved exposition in the earlier chapters and the inclusion in chapters I through VIII of solutions to selected exercises. However, this edition, like the earlier one, is primarily a textbook to be read with an instructor. The comments on the use of the book for semester courses made in the preface to the first edition still apply, except that it is no longer necessary to mention omission of chapter V (for that material now occurs as chapter IX). On the quarter system, as on the semester system, a year course could omit the more sophisticated and mathematical material of chapters IX, X, and XI, covering chapters I through III in the first quarter, chapters IV and V in the second quarter, and chapters VI through VIII in the third quarter. In a year course that included the last three chapters of the text, chapters I through IV should be completed in the first quarter, chapters V through VIII in the second quarter, and chapters IX through XI in the third quarter. If only a one-quarter course is available, an instructor could introduce the additional derivational procedures of chapter VII immediately after either chapter III or chapter IV.

We hope old friends, both colleagues and students, will forgive us for not acknowledging individually each of the many whose useful exercises and insightful suggestions have found their way into, or for practical reasons have been omitted from, the text that follows; we are fully aware of how much our work has benefited from these exercises and suggestions. But we do want to acknowledge individually and extend our thanks to three new friends to whom we are also indebted — to Bill McLane, who sponsored our proposal for a new edition, to Rolf Eberle of the University of Rochester, whose critical comments as reviewer for Harcourt Brace Jovanovich were very useful, and especially to Judy Burke, whose editing of our manuscript resulted in some substantive as well as significant stylistic improvements.

Donald Kalish

Gary Mar

Preface to the First Edition

THE expressions 'logic', 'formal logic', 'symbolic logic', and 'mathematical logic' are in the just acceptation synonyms. They refer to a discipline created by Aristotle, extended by the Stoics, studied by the Scholastics, developed in the esoteric writings of Leibniz, and sent on its modern career in the late nineteenth century. The discoveries of Leibniz and the Stoics, though extensive, were until recently either ignored or misinterpreted, and thus had to be duplicated in the early twentieth century. Presently logic is cultivated as a branch of both philosophy and mathematics.

This book is an introduction to logic, requiring no prior knowledge of philosophy or mathematics. It does not aim at communicating results about logical systems (as do several excellent but more advanced texts), but instead at imparting a skill—the ability to recognize and construct correct deductions. Metamathematical results are indeed sometimes mentioned, but only incidentally and as an aid to understanding.

The logical apparatus introduced in the first seven chapters is essentially that of the first-order predicate calculus with identity and descriptive phrases. The *theorems* of those chapters (with a few exceptions connected with descriptive phrases) are thus standard and well known. (Indeed, the completeness and universal validity of the system has been proved in the publication listed in the bibliography as Montague and Kalish [1].) Some originality, however, may be claimed for the *rules* of the system, which constitute, we think, a closer approximation to everyday and mathematical reasoning than has previously been achieved by any formal system, and which suggest a number of simple and practical strategies for the discovery of proofs. In these chapters heavy emphasis is placed on applications to ordinary language.

To achieve the objective of mirroring everyday reasoning, we have sometimes had to sacrifice economy, though never precision. We have constructed a graduated but unified development of logic from the sentential calculus through the theory of descriptions, steadfastly resisting the temptation to introduce fragmentary though perhaps attractive procedures appropriate to isolated branches of logic. (For instance, sentential logic is not developed by means of truth tables, though they are introduced in an optional section.)

In the last two chapters first-order logic is extended (for the first time, it seems) so as to comprehend arbitrary variable-binding operators and is employed in a fairly detailed development of a familiar mathematical theory. The general theory of variable-binding operators and their definitions was developed in collaboration with Professor Dana Scott and will appear also in the monograph Montague, Scott, Tarski [1].

Although the book is written so as to be comprehensible without a teacher, it is primarily designed for use in a first course in symbolic logic, taught in a department of either philosophy or mathematics. Such a course may occupy either one or two semesters, and be set at any undergraduate level, from freshman to senior. A one-semester course should treat at least the first three, and at most the first seven, chapters, with chapter V probably omitted. A year course could be restricted to the first seven chapters (again with the possible omission of chapter V), in which case all the standard material of elementary logic would be treated, or preferably could cover all nine chapters. In a mathematics department it might be found desirable to begin the second semester with chapter VIII and to extend the mathematical development beyond the limits of chapter IX but along the lines suggested there. Another alternative is to cover the book in two one-semester courses set at different levels, the second semester beginning with chapter V, VI, or VIII. To facilitate this alternative, summaries suitable for reviewing the preceding material are given as appendices to chapters IV and VII. As an additional pedagogical aid a list of special symbols is given at the end of chapter IX (pp. 331 – 32).

The sections and chapter marked with an asterisk, together with the exposition in fine print, may be regarded as optional and can be omitted, in whole or in part, without loss of continuity to the main development.

For historical and bibliographical information we have relied heavily on two works of Alonzo Church, *A bibliography of symbolic logic* and *Introduction to mathematical logic*. For helpful suggestions and discussions we are indebted to Dr. J. D. Halpern and to Professors David Kaplan, Benson Mates, Ruth Anna Mathers, and Dana Scott.

LOGIC
Techniques of Formal Reasoning

Second Edition

Chapter I
'NOT' and 'IF'

LOGIC is concerned with arguments, good and bad. With the docile and the reasonable, arguments are sometimes useful in settling disputes. With the reasonable, this utility attaches only to good arguments. It is the logician's business to serve the reasonable. Therefore, in the realm of arguments, it is the logician who distinguishes good from bad.

Virtue among arguments is known as validity. An argument is valid if it is impossible for its premises to be true and its conclusion false. But this is to speak loosely, and the reasonable do not countenance looseness.

That intuition is not a reliable judge of validity will appear from a few examples.

(1) Suppose that a student, Alfred, satisfies the following conditions. If he studies, then he receives good grades; if he does not study, then he enjoys college; if he does not receive good grades, then he does not enjoy college. Is it correct to draw any conclusion concerning Alfred's academic performance?

It is correct to conclude that Alfred receives good grades. This example is simpler than most of those we shall encounter, yet it is sufficiently complex to puzzle an unschooled intuition. The situation is worse when intuitively plausible premises lead by way of an intuitively valid argument to an obviously false conclusion, as in the next two examples.

(2) Suppose that Alfred, an inhabitant of Berkeley, shaves all and only those inhabitants of Berkeley who do not shave themselves. Does he shave himself or not? The answer is neither. For suppose he shaves himself. Then, since he shaves only those inhabitants of Berkeley who do not shave themselves, he clearly does not shave himself. Suppose, on the other hand, that he does not shave himself. Then, since he is himself an inhabitant of Berkeley and he shaves all inhabitants of Berkeley who fail to shave themselves, he must shave himself. Thus both possibilities lead to absurdity.

(3) Is the following boxed sentence true or false?

The boxed sentence is false.

Again, the answer is neither. For suppose the boxed sentence is true.

Then it is true that the boxed sentence is false. Hence the boxed sentence is false. On the other hand, suppose the boxed sentence is false. Then it is false that the boxed sentence is false. Hence the boxed sentence is true. Thus, if the sentence is true, it is false; and if it is false, it is true.

In the next example, which we owe to St. Anselm, the conclusion is not obviously false but only controversial. To those who believe it, however, the argument should appear blasphemously short.

(4) Even the atheist, who denies that God exists, must be able to conceive of God in order to know what he denies. Suppose that God does not exist. Then the atheist can nevertheless conceive of God as existing and thereby can conceive of something greater than God. But, by definition, God is that than which nothing greater can be conceived. Hence the atheist's supposition leads to contradiction. Therefore God exists.

1. Symbols and sentences. We shall analyze validity in steps. At first we shall restrict ourselves to valid arguments of a very special kind—roughly speaking, those arguments whose validity depends only on the phrases 'it is not the case that' and 'if. . ., then'. We begin by considering sentences that are constructed by means of such phrases.

When the phrase 'it is not the case that' is prefixed to a sentence, say

(1) Socrates is bald ,

the result is a new sentence, in this instance

(2) It is not the case that Socrates is bald .

The sentence (2) is called the *negation* of the sentence (1). Let us adopt the symbol '$\sim$' as an abbreviation for 'it is not the case that'. Further let us use the capital letters 'P' through 'Z' as abbreviations for English sentences; 'A' through 'O' will be reserved for later purposes. For example, we may let 'P' stand for the sentence (1). Then the expression '$\sim$P' becomes an abbreviation for the sentence (2) and is called the *negation* of 'P'.

The phrase 'if. . ., then' is used to combine two sentences, say

(3) Diogenes is a canine

and

(4) Diogenes is carnivorous ,

into a new sentence,

(5) If Diogenes is a canine, then Diogenes is carnivorous .

The sentence (5) is called a *conditional* formed from the sentences (3) and (4). The sentence (3), which is introduced by the word 'if' in (5), is called the *antecedent* of the conditional; the sentence (4), which is introduced by the word 'then', is called the *consequent* of the conditional. Let us adopt the symbol '→', accompanied by a pair of parentheses, as an abbreviation for 'if..., then'. Then, if we let 'Q' stand for the sentence (3) and 'R' stand for the sentence (4), the expression

(6) $(Q \rightarrow R)$

becomes an abbreviation of (5). The expression (6), like the corresponding English sentence, will be called a *conditional* whose antecedent is 'Q' and whose consequent is 'R'.

The relation between a capital letter and the sentence that it abbreviates, unlike that between the symbols '~' and '→' and their English counterparts, is subject to change. By allowing 'P', 'Q', and 'R' to stand for other sentences, we may, for instance, consider '~P' an abbreviation for

It is not the case that the text is readable ,

and (6) an abbreviation for

If snow is white, then Alfred is right

or

If Empedocles is hoary, then Dalmatia is icebound .

Thus, in different contexts, we may ascribe different significance to the capital letters 'P' through 'Z'. The ascriptions will take the form of a *scheme of abbreviation*; such schemes will be discussed more fully in the next section.

Despite the latitude achieved by permitting shifts of abbreviation, it is conceivable that occasions will arise when we shall require more than eleven sentential abbreviations. Therefore, we admit as possible abbreviations for English sentences not only the letters 'P' through 'Z' but also any variant of these letters obtained by adding a numerical subscript, for example, 'P_0' or 'Z_{28}'.

We should mention that the preferred status of English in this book is a matter only of the authors' convenience; the subsequent treatment would apply as well to French, German, or Coptic. Furthermore, our interest will not extend to all sentences of English. We shall arbitrarily avoid questions, commands, and exclamations, leaving their treatment to other logicians. We shall be concerned exclusively with declarative sentences, that is, those sentences that are capable of truth or falsehood. Initially, however, the focus of our attention will be on those declarative sentences of English that are negations or conditionals.

We begin our formal treatment by characterizing a *symbolic language*. Symbols of this language will be *sentence letters*, that is, the capital letters with or without numerical subscripts mentioned above, the *negation* sign '~', the *conditional* sign '→', and parentheses. Loosely speaking, sentences of this language, to be called *symbolic sentences* (in contrast to English sentences), can be characterized as follows: sentence letters are symbolic sentences; negations and conditionals formed from symbolic sentences are symbolic sentences; and nothing other than sentence letters and negations and conditionals formed from symbolic sentences are symbolic sentences.

To be more precise, the class of *symbolic sentences* can be exhaustively characterized as follows:

(1) *Sentence letters, that is, capital letters* 'P' *through* 'Z' *with or without numerical subscripts, are symbolic sentences.*

(2) *The result of prefixing the negation sign* '∼' *to a symbolic sentence is a symbolic sentence.*

(3) *The result of flanking the conditional sign* '→' *by symbolic sentences and enclosing the result in a pair of parentheses is a symbolic sentence.*

With the aid of Greek letters, clauses (2) and (3) admit of the following alternative formulations:

(2′) *If* ϕ *is a symbolic sentence, then so is the result of writing* '∼' *followed by* ϕ.

(3′) *If* ϕ *and* ψ *are symbolic sentences, then so is the result of writing* '(' *followed by* ϕ *followed by* '→' *followed by* ψ *followed by* ')'.

We shall use typographical displays in such a way that (2′) and (3′) will be synonymous, respectively, with the succinct formulations (2) and (3) below. Accordingly, the class of symbolic sentences can be exhaustively characterized as follows:

(1) *Sentence letters are symbolic sentences.*

(2) *If* ϕ *is a symbolic sentence, then so is*

$$\sim\phi \quad .$$

(3) *If* ϕ *and* ψ *are symbolic sentences, then so is*

$$(\phi \rightarrow \psi) \quad .$$

It is evident from the preceding discussion that no symbolic sentence will contain Greek letters; although '∼P' is a symbolic sentence, '∼ϕ' is not. We reserve Greek letters for the purpose of making general statements *about* sentences and, later, for other purposes. Thus, clause (2) in the above succinct formulation is to be regarded as a generalization having, for example, the following assertion among its special cases: if '(P → Q)' is a symbolic sentence, then the result of writing '∼' followed by '(P → Q)' is again a symbolic sentence, that is, '∼(P → Q)' is a symbolic sentence.

The above characterizations of the class of symbolic sentences are called *inductive definitions*, and such definitions are of frequent use in mathematics. Examples from everyday life, however, are available. For instance, the class of Alfred's ancestors can be exhaustively characterized in a similar way:

> The father and mother of Alfred are ancestors of Alfred.
> Any father or mother of an ancestor of Alfred is an ancestor of Alfred.

It should be noted that the characterization is not rendered circular by the fact that in the latter clause 'ancestor' is used to characterize an ancestor of Alfred. This characterization has a consequence, among others, that the father of the mother of the mother of the father of Alfred is an ancestor of Alfred.

Similarly, it is a consequence of our characterization of the class of symbolic sentences that

(7) $$(\sim(\sim P \rightarrow Q) \rightarrow R)$$

is a symbolic sentence: by clause (1), 'P', 'Q', and 'R' are symbolic sentences; by clause (2), then, '$\sim P$' is a symbolic sentence; thus by clause (3), '$(\sim P \rightarrow Q)$' is a symbolic sentence; thus by another application of clause (2), '$\sim(\sim P \rightarrow Q)$' is a symbolic sentence; finally, by another application of clause (3), the expression (7) is a symbolic sentence. We can represent this generation of the sentence (7) by means of a *grammatical tree* that displays its genealogy:

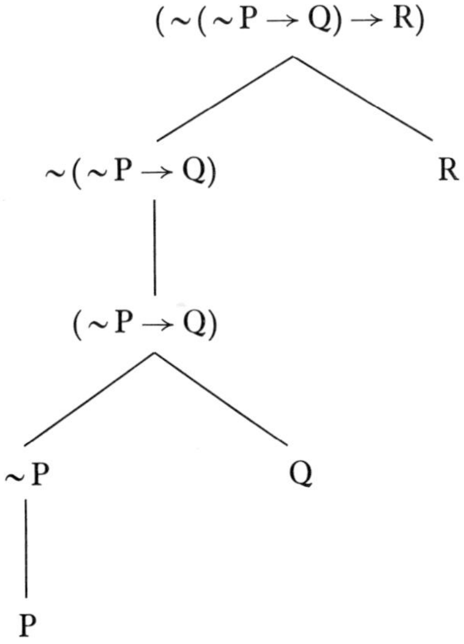

Note that the symbolic sentences mentioned in generating (7) are precisely those that appear in its grammatical tree. Generally, each *initial node* of a grammatical tree is a sentence letter; each *nonbranching node* is of the form

$$\sim\phi \quad ,$$

having the symbolic sentence ϕ as its sole immediate ancestor; each *branching node* is of the form

$$(\phi \rightarrow \psi) \quad ,$$

having the symbolic sentence ϕ as its immediate left ancestor and the symbolic sentence ψ as its immediate right ancestor; and the *top node* is the symbolic sentence whose genealogy is being displayed. Each node of the grammatical tree is generated in accordance with one of the clauses in the characterization of the class of symbolic sentences. Therefore, any expression that can be generated as the top node of a grammatical tree is a symbolic sentence. Indeed, even a stronger claim can be made: it happens that an expression is a symbolic sentence just in case it can be decomposed into a tree; that is, we can reverse the process of generation beginning with the top node and ending with the initial nodes. Thus, to test whether a given symbolic expression is a symbolic sentence we can attempt to decompose it into a grammatical tree.

In the characterization of the class of symbolic sentences, it may seem curious that a pair of parentheses accompanies the '$\rightarrow$'. The function of parentheses is like that of punctuation in written English and becomes conspicuous in the cases of complex sentences. For example, if ϕ and ψ are symbolic sentences, then

(8) $$(\sim\phi \rightarrow \psi)$$

is a conditional whose antecedent is a negation; in contrast

(9) $$\sim(\phi \rightarrow \psi)$$

is a negation of a conditional. For example, in English we distinguish between

(8′) If Alfred does not concentrate, then Alfred will pass

and

(9′) It is not the case that if Alfred concentrates then Alfred will pass .

Similarly, where χ is an additional symbolic sentence, it is important to distinguish between

(10) $$((\phi \rightarrow \psi) \rightarrow \chi)$$

and

(11) $$(\phi \rightarrow (\psi \rightarrow \chi)) \quad .$$

The former is a conditional whose antecedent is a conditional, and the latter is a conditional whose consequent is a conditional. This distinction can be illustrated in English as that between

(10′) If if Alfred concentrates then Alfred will pass, then logic is enjoyable

and

(11′) If Alfred concentrates, then if Alfred will pass then logic is enjoyable .

To drop the inner parentheses of (10) or (11) would obliterate the distinction.

Although parentheses are generally required to prevent ambiguity, no confusion will arise if we omit the outermost parentheses of a sentence, and this we shall do frequently. Thus, for example, (8) and (10) may alternatively be written

$$\sim\phi \rightarrow \psi$$

and

$$(\phi \rightarrow \psi) \rightarrow \chi$$

respectively. Further, when parentheses lie within parentheses, some pairs may for perspicuity be replaced by pairs of brackets. For example,

$$((\phi \rightarrow \psi) \rightarrow \psi) \rightarrow \phi$$

may also be written

$$([\phi \rightarrow \psi] \rightarrow \psi) \rightarrow \phi \quad .$$

EXERCISES

For each of the following expressions, state whether or not it is a symbolic sentence. If an expression is a symbolic sentence, decompose it into its grammatical tree. Exercises 1 and 2 are solved for illustration.

1. $(\sim P \rightarrow (Q \rightarrow P))$

According to clauses (1) and (2) of the characterization of the class of symbolic sentences (p. 4), '$\sim P$' is a symbolic sentence; according to clauses (1) and (3), '$(Q \rightarrow P)$' is a symbolic sentence; thus, according to clause (3) again, No. 1 is a symbolic sentence. The decomposition of No. 1 into its grammatical tree follows.

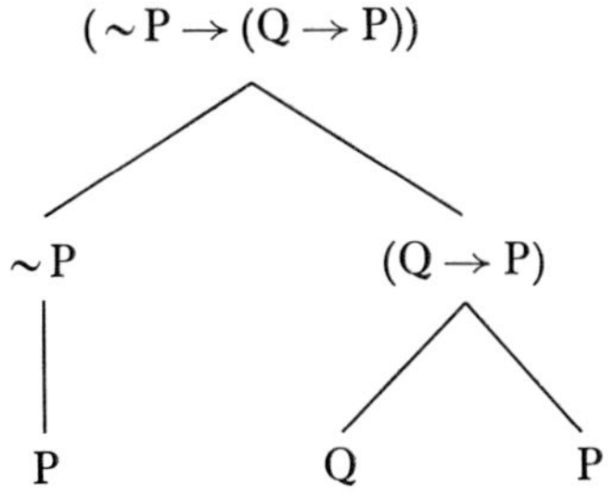

2. $(P \rightarrow Q \rightarrow R)$

Because the characterization of the class of symbolic sentences on page 4 is stipulated to be exhaustive, No. 2, if a symbolic sentence, must result from one of the three clauses of that characterization. Since neither of the clauses (1) or (2) can generate an expression beginning with a parenthesis, clause (3) must yield No. 2. For this to happen, either both 'P' and '$Q \rightarrow R$', or both '$P \rightarrow Q$' and 'R', must be symbolic sentences. But in view of considerations like the foregoing, neither '$Q \rightarrow R$' nor '$P \rightarrow Q$' is, strictly speaking, a symbolic sentence; each fails to be a conditional by virtue of lacking a pair of peripheral parentheses. Hence No. 2 is not a symbolic sentence.

3. $((\sim(\sim P \rightarrow Q) \rightarrow Q) \rightarrow R)$
4. $(\sim(\sim P) \rightarrow Q)$
5. $((P \rightarrow Q) \rightarrow \sim G)$
6. $(\sim((P \rightarrow Q) \rightarrow R) \rightarrow (P \rightarrow \sim Q))$

2. From symbols to English and back. Frequently it will be desirable to *translate* a symbolic sentence into English and perform the reverse process of *symbolizing* an English sentence. We consider first the passage from symbols to English.

As was mentioned earlier, the correlation between sentence letters and the English sentences which they abbreviate is quite arbitrary. Thus the passage from a symbolic sentence to a sentence of English must proceed on the basis of a *scheme of abbreviation*, which will establish such a correlation.

More explicitly, let us understand by an *abbreviation* an ordered pair of sentences, the first of which is a sentence letter and the second an English sentence. A *scheme of abbreviation* is a collection of abbreviations such that no two abbreviations in the collection have the same first member.

For example, the collections

(1)

Q : the lectures are dull
T : the text is readable
P : Alfred will pass

and

S : the lectures are dull
Q : the lectures are dull
T : the text is readable
P : Alfred will pass

are schemes of abbreviation; but the collection

Q : the lectures are dull
Q : the text is readable
P : Alfred will pass

is not. (The two abbreviations whose first member is 'Q' are at fault.)

The process of *literal translation into English on the basis of a given scheme of abbreviation* begins with a symbolic sentence and if successful ends with a sentence of English. The process consists of the following steps:

(*i*) *Restore any parentheses that may have disappeared as a result of applying the informal conventions of the last section.*

(*ii*) *Replace sentence letters by English sentences in accordance with the given scheme of abbreviation; that is, each sentence letter is to be replaced by the English sentence with which it is paired in the scheme.*

(*iii*) *Replace all occurrences of*

$$\sim\phi \quad ,$$

where ϕ *is a sentence, by*

it is not the case that ϕ .

(*iv*) *Replace all occurrences of*

$$(\phi \rightarrow \psi) \quad ,$$

where ϕ *and* ψ *are sentences, by*

(*if* ϕ, *then* ψ) .

For example, under the scheme of abbreviation (1) the sentence

(2) $$Q \rightarrow (\sim T \rightarrow \sim P)$$

becomes in step (i)

$$(Q \rightarrow (\sim T \rightarrow \sim P)) \quad ,$$

in step (ii)

(The lectures are dull → (∼ the text is readable → ∼ Alfred will pass)) ,

in step (iii)

(The lectures are dull → (it is not the case that the text is readable → it is not the case that Alfred will pass)) ,

and in step (iv)

(3) (If the lectures are dull, then (if it is not the case that the text is readable, then it is not the case that Alfred will pass)) .

(The parentheses in sentences such as (3), as in symbolic sentences, serve as marks of punctuation.)

We shall generally wish to be more liberal in translating from symbols to English than the notion of a literal translation will permit. For example, we should like to consider the sentence

(4) Assuming that the lectures are dull, if the text is not readable, then Alfred will not pass

as a translation of (2) on the basis of the scheme (1). Accordingly, we say that an English sentence is a *translation* (or, when a distinction is to be drawn, a *free translation*) of a symbolic sentence ϕ on the basis of a given scheme of abbreviation if it is a stylistic variant of the literal translation of ϕ into English on the basis of that scheme.

Because (4) differs only in style from (3), the former as well as the latter qualifies as an English translation of (2) on the basis of scheme (1).

In the realm of free translations, we countenance looseness. Specifically, we attempt no precise description of *stylistic variance;* in this connection, intuition (here identified with linguistic insight) rather than exact rules must guide the reader. To remove this source of looseness would require systematic exploration of the English language, indeed of what might be called the 'logic of ordinary English', and would be either extremely laborious or perhaps impossible. In any case, we do not consider such an exploration appropriate material for the present book (however, see Montague [4] and Partee [1]).

Although no exact definition of stylistic variance will be offered, we shall not leave the readers entirely to their own devices. Two stylistic variants of

It is not the case that Alfred concentrated

are

Alfred did not concentrate

and

Alfred failed to concentrate .

English idiom provides a number of stylistic variants for

(5) (If Diogenes is a canine, then Diogenes is carnivorous) ,

for example,

(6) Diogenes is carnivorous if Diogenes is a canine ,

(7) Diogenes is carnivorous provided that Diogenes is a canine ,

(8) Diogenes is a canine only if Diogenes is carnivorous ,

(9) Only if Diogenes is carnivorous is Diogenes a canine .

The only difference (apart from the use of parentheses) between (5) and (6) is the order in which the clauses occur. Alternative (7) comes from (6) upon replacement of 'if' by its intuitive equivalent 'provided that'. To see the intuitive equivalence between (5) and (8), the following consideration should be of assistance: to assert that Diogenes is canine only if carnivorous is to deny that Diogenes is a canine and not carnivorous, which is to assert that if Diogenes is a canine, then he is also carnivorous; but this amounts to (5). Alternative (9) comes from (8) by inversion of the order of clauses. (Note that here English idiom also requires an inversion of the word order in the antecedent clause of (5).)

If ϕ and ψ are any sentences, a partial list of stylistic variants of

$$(\text{if } \phi, \text{ then } \psi)$$

is the following:

if ϕ, ψ	ψ if ϕ
provided that ϕ, ψ	ψ provided that ϕ
given that ϕ, ψ	ψ given that ϕ
in case ϕ, ψ	ψ in case ϕ
assuming that ϕ, ψ	ψ assuming that ϕ
on the condition that ϕ, ψ	ψ on the condition that ϕ
ϕ only if ψ	

Further instances of stylistic variance may be obtained by introducing pronouns in place of nouns and by altering word order. Examples of these and other sorts of stylistic variance will be found among the exercises of this and later chapters.

We shall also be interested in the passage from English to symbols. Accordingly, we say that ϕ is a *symbolization* of an English sentence ψ on the basis of a given scheme of abbreviation if and only if ϕ is a symbolic sentence that has ψ as a translation on the basis of that scheme, in other words, if and only if ψ is a stylistic variant of the literal translation of ϕ on the basis of the scheme.

To find a symbolization of a given English sentence on the basis of a given scheme of abbreviation, the reader will find it useful to proceed roughly as follows:

(*1*) *Introduce 'it is not the case that' and '(if . . . , then)' in place of their respective stylistic variants.*

(*2*) *Reverse the steps leading from a symbolic sentence to a literal English translation; that is,*

(*2a*) *replace all parts of the form*

$$(\textit{if } \phi, \textit{ then } \psi) \quad ,$$

where ϕ and ψ are sentences, by

$$(\phi \rightarrow \psi) \quad ;$$

(2*b*) *replace all parts of the form*

$$\textit{it is not the case that } \phi \quad ,$$

where ϕ *is a sentence, by*

$$\sim\phi \quad ;$$

(2*c*) *replace English components by sentence letters in accordance with the scheme of abbreviation; that is, replace each English component by a sentence letter with which it is paired in the scheme of abbreviation;*

(2*d*) *omit peripheral parentheses and replace parentheses by brackets in accordance with the informal conventions of the preceding section.*

EXERCISES

On the basis of the scheme of abbreviation

P : logic is enjoyable
Q : Alfred will pass
R : Alfred concentrates
S : the text is readable
T : Alfred will secure employment
U : Alfred will marry
V : the lectures are exciting

translate the following symbolic sentences into idiomatic English:

7. $P \rightarrow (Q \rightarrow R)$
8. $(R \rightarrow Q) \rightarrow P$
9. $S \rightarrow [P \rightarrow (\sim Q \rightarrow \sim R)]$

On the basis of the scheme of abbreviation above, symbolize the following English sentences. In solving exercises 10–17 (as well as later exercises), the reader may find the following succinct summary a helpful (but not infallible) guide to stylistic variants of conditionals:

(i) replacement in a sentence of 'provided that', 'given that', 'in case', 'assuming that', 'on the condition that' by 'if' yields a stylistic variant of that sentence;

(ii) 'if' (not preceded by 'only') introduces an antecedent, whereas 'only if' introduces a consequent.

Exercise 10 is solved for illustration.

10. Only if Alfred concentrates will he pass, provided that the lectures are exciting.

Sentence No. 10 becomes, in step (1) of the procedure given on pages 11 and 12,

(If the lectures are exciting, then (if Alfred will pass, then Alfred concentrates))

In taking this step we first made minor stylistic changes in accordance with the above summary and replaced 'will he pass' by 'Alfred will pass'; then, in conformity with the discussion on pages 10 and 11, we inverted the order of the component clauses. In step (2a) the sentence becomes

> (the lectures are exciting → (Alfred will pass → Alfred concentrates)) ;

step (2b) is inapplicable; step (2c) leads to

$$(V \rightarrow (Q \rightarrow R)) \quad ;$$

and step (2d) to

$$V \rightarrow (Q \rightarrow R) \quad .$$

11. If Alfred will pass if he concentrates, then logic is enjoyable.

12. Alfred will pass on the condition that if he will pass only if he concentrates then he will pass.

13. If Alfred will pass only on the condition that he concentrates, then logic is enjoyable provided that the lectures are exciting.

14. It is not the case that if Alfred will secure employment provided that logic is enjoyable, then he will marry only if he concentrates.

The following sentences are ambiguous, in the sense that the placement of parentheses in their symbolizations is not uniquely determined. Give all plausible symbolizations of these sentences on the basis of the scheme of abbreviation that appears above.

15. Alfred will pass only if he concentrates provided that the text is not readable.

16. It is not the case that Alfred concentrates if the lectures are not exciting.

17. It is not the case that Alfred will secure employment if he fails to concentrate on the condition that the lectures are not exciting.

3. Derivability and validity of symbolic arguments.

An *argument*, as we shall understand it, consists of two parts: first, a sequence of sentences called its *premises*, and second, an additional sentence called its *conclusion*. An *English argument* is an argument whose premises and conclusion are sentences of English; similarly, a *symbolic argument* is an argument whose premises and conclusion are symbolic sentences. Any group of sentences may constitute an argument if that group is broken down into premises and conclusion—no matter how unrelated the premises and conclusion may seem. Furthermore, 'premise' and 'conclusion' are relative terms; that is, a sentence which occurs as a premise in one argument may be a conclusion in another, and conversely. Ordinarily, we shall present an argument by listing first the premises and then the conclusion, set off by the sign '∴' or the word 'therefore'. Three examples follow:

(1) P $\therefore (P \rightarrow Q) \rightarrow Q$

(2) If Socrates did not die of old age, then the Athenians condemned him to death. The Athenians did not condemn Socrates to death. Therefore, Socrates died of old age.

(3) ∴ If Alfred loves logic, then Alfred loves logic.

Example (3) illustrates that an argument may have an empty sequence of premises (that is, an argument may have no premises at all); however, an argument must have exactly one conclusion.

Intuitively, an English argument is valid if it is impossible for its premises to be true and its conclusion false. Thus it is possible for a valid English argument to have a false conclusion, as in example (2) above. (In the next section, when we define validity for arguments of English, it will be seen that (2) is indeed valid.) In the case of a valid English argument we may be sure only that *if* all the premises are true, then the conclusion will also be true. A valid English argument whose premises are true is often called a *sound* argument. However, only the validity, not the soundness, of arguments is our present concern.

The conclusion of a valid English argument is said to *follow from* its premises. But what follows from given premises is not in general obvious to unschooled intuition, as is illustrated by examples (1)–(4) on pages 1 and 2. Thus, as an aid to intuition, a derivation is often employed to establish the validity of an argument, that is, to show that its conclusion does follow from its premises. A *derivation*, loosely characterized, consists of a sequence of steps, each of which constitutes an intuitively valid argument, that leads from the premises of a given argument to its conclusion. A precise characterization of a derivation for an argument of English would lead to difficulties of analysis which we prefer either not to treat at all or to treat only in connection with stylistic variance. The precise characterization of symbolic sentences given in section 1 obviates these difficulties and makes such sentences easily amenable to the deductive procedures whereby derivations are constructed. We shall therefore confine the application of these deductive procedures to symbolic sentences.

Thus, by a *derivation* we shall understand a sequence of steps that leads from the premises to the conclusion of a symbolic argument. Each intermediate step should be the conclusion of an intuitively valid argument whose premises are among the preceding steps. These intermediate steps are generated in accordance with inference rules. The *inference rules* we shall employ are the following:

Modus ponens (MP):

$$\frac{\begin{matrix}(\phi \rightarrow \psi) \\ \phi\end{matrix}}{\psi}$$

Modus tollens (MT):

$$\frac{\begin{matrix}(\phi \rightarrow \psi) \\ \sim\psi\end{matrix}}{\sim\phi}$$

Double negation (DN), in two forms: $\dfrac{\sim\sim\phi}{\phi}$ $\dfrac{\phi}{\sim\sim\phi}$

Repetition (R): $\dfrac{\phi}{\phi}$

That is, a symbolic sentence ψ is said to follow by *modus ponens* from two other symbolic sentences (the order in which they are listed being irrelevant) if and only if these sentences have the forms

$$(\phi \rightarrow \psi)$$

and

$$\phi \;\; ;$$

a symbolic sentence follows by *modus tollens* from two other symbolic sentences if and only if it has the form

$$\sim\phi$$

and the other sentences have the forms

$$(\phi \rightarrow \psi)$$

and

$$\sim\psi \;\; ;$$

a symbolic sentence follows from another by *double negation* if and only if the two symbolic sentences have the forms ϕ and

$$\sim\sim\phi \;\; ;$$

and a sentence ϕ follows by *repetition* from a symbolic sentence ψ if and only if ϕ and ψ are the same sentence. MP and MT correspond to familiar and intuitively valid forms of reasoning; DN is the intuitively valid principle that a double negative amounts to an affirmative; and the function of the trivial rule R will become clear later. For example, each of the following is an application of the respective rules MP, MT, DN, DN, and R:

$$\frac{P \quad P \rightarrow \sim Q}{\sim Q} \qquad \frac{P \rightarrow \sim Q \quad \sim\sim Q}{\sim P} \qquad \frac{(P \rightarrow Q)}{\sim\sim(P \rightarrow Q)}$$

$$\frac{\sim\sim(P \rightarrow Q)}{(P \rightarrow Q)} \qquad \frac{\sim(P \rightarrow Q)}{\sim(P \rightarrow Q)}$$

Before stating an explicit set of directions for constructing a derivation, let us consider several examples. Suppose we are given the following argument:

(4) $\sim P \rightarrow Q \quad . \quad \sim Q \quad \therefore P \quad .$

A derivation of the conclusion of (4) from its premises may be constructed as follows. We write first the conclusion together with an indication that it is to be established.

1. *Show* P

We may establish 'P' by deriving it directly from the premises of the argument. This form of derivation is known as *direct derivation*. Accordingly, we add the premises.

1. *Show* P
2. $\sim P \rightarrow Q$
3. $\sim Q$

From the second and third lines of the derivation we may infer '$\sim\sim P$' by the inference rule MT, thereby obtaining

1. *Show* P
2. $\sim P \rightarrow Q$
3. $\sim Q$
4. $\sim\sim P$

Applying the inference rule DN to line 4, we obtain the conclusion of the argument:

1. *Show* P
2. $\sim P \rightarrow Q$
3. $\sim Q$
4. $\sim\sim P$
5. P

To indicate that the conclusion has been established, we first *box* lines 2 through 5 (for they have served their purpose) and then *cancel* the occurrence of '*Show*' in line 1. Thus we finally obtain

(5)

1.	~~*Show*~~ P.
2.	$\sim P \rightarrow Q$
3.	$\sim Q$
4.	$\sim\sim P$
5.	P

The derivation of the conclusion of argument (4) from its premises is now *complete.*

It is often convenient, in order to permit a quick decision as to the correctness of a proposed derivation, to include *annotations*, that is, marginal indications of how each step is obtained. Annotations do not, strictly speaking, form part of a derivation. For example, the derivation (5) above, together with annotations, appears as follows:

1.	~~*Show*~~ P	Assertion (Direct derivation)
2.	$\sim P \rightarrow Q$	Premise
3.	$\sim Q$	Premise
4.	$\sim\sim P$	2, 3, MT
5.	P	4, DN

The annotation that accompanies each line is entered along with that line, except for the parenthetical annotation in line 1; that annotation, since it indicates the form of derivation employed in boxing and cancelling, is entered upon boxing and cancelling.

As a second example, consider again argument (1):

(6) $P \quad \therefore (P \rightarrow Q) \rightarrow Q \quad .$

An annotated derivation of the conclusion of (6) from its premise may be constructed as follows. As before, we write first the conclusion together with an indication that it is to be established.

1. *Show* $(P \rightarrow Q) \rightarrow Q$ Assertion

The sentence to be established is a conditional. We may establish a conditional by assuming its antecedent and deriving its consequent. This form of derivation is known as *conditional derivation.* Accordingly we add, as an assumption, the antecedent of the conditional to be established, and include parenthetically in the annotation the type of assumption employed:

1. *Show* $(P \rightarrow Q) \rightarrow Q$
2. $P \rightarrow Q$ Assumption (Conditional derivation)

Now we may add the premise:

1. *Show* $(P \rightarrow Q) \rightarrow Q$
2. $P \rightarrow Q$
3. P Premise

From the second and third lines of the derivation we may infer 'Q' by the inference rule *modus ponens*. (Note that it would be illegitimate to attempt to obtain 'Q' by applying *modus ponens* to lines 1 and 2. To do so would be to beg the question, for we would be using line 1, which is the sentence we are trying to establish.) Thus, we obtain the consequent of the conditional to be established.

1. *Show* $(P \rightarrow Q) \rightarrow Q$
2. $P \rightarrow Q$
3. P
4. Q 2, 3, MP

To indicate that the conclusion of (6) has been established, we first box lines 2 through 4 (for they have served their purpose) and then cancel the occurrence of '*Show*' in line 1. The annotation for this step, which states the form of derivation employed, is entered parenthetically after the annotation that accompanies line 1. Thus we finally obtain

1.	~~*Show*~~ $(P \rightarrow Q) \rightarrow Q$	Assertion (CD)
2.	$P \rightarrow Q$	Assumption (CD)
3.	P	Premise
4.	Q	2, 3, MP

(Here, and often subsequently, we abbreviate 'Conditional derivation' by 'CD'.) The derivation of the conclusion of argument (6) from its premises is now complete.

As a third example, consider the following argument:

(7) $\sim P \rightarrow Q \quad . \quad \sim P \rightarrow \sim Q \quad \therefore P \quad .$

An annotated derivation of the conclusion of (7) from its premises may be constructed as follows. As before, we write first the conclusion together with an indication that it is to be established.

1. *Show* P Assertion

The sentence to be established is not a conditional; thus, it cannot be established by conditional derivation. As an alternative to direct derivation, we may establish the sentence indirectly by assuming its negation and with this assumption deriving a *contradiction*. (A contradiction consists of a pair of sentences, one of which is the negation of the other.) This form of derivation is known as *indirect derivation* and depends for its cogency on the following consideration. To show that an assertion holds, it is sufficient to assume that it does not and to show that a contradiction follows from this assumption; for then the assumption must be mistaken, and hence the assertion must hold. Accordingly, we add '~P' as an assumption for indirect derivation.

    1. *Show* P

    2. ~P   Assumption (Indirect derivation)

Now we may add the premises:

    1. *Show* P

    2. ~P

    3. ~P → Q   Premise

    4. ~P → ~Q   Premise

From lines 2 and 3 of the derivation we may infer 'Q' by the inference rule *modus ponens*; from lines 2 and 4 we may infer '~Q' by the same inference rule. Thus we obtain

    1. *Show* P

    2. ~P

    3. ~P → Q

    4. ~P → ~Q

    5. Q   2, 3, MP

    6. ~Q   2, 4, MP

We have thereby established the conclusion of (7) indirectly, for we have shown that its negation, together with the premises, leads to a contradiction. To indicate this fact, we first box lines 2 through 6 (for they have served their purpose) and then cancel the occurrence of '*Show*' in line 1. The annotation for this step, which states the form of derivation employed in boxing and cancelling, is entered parenthetically after the annotation that accompanies line 1. Thus we finally obtain

    1. ~~*Show*~~ P   Assertion (Indirect derivation)

    2. | ~P   Assumption (Indirect derivation)

    3. | ~P → Q   Premise

    4. | ~P → ~Q   Premise

    5. | Q   2, 3, MP

    6. | ~Q   2, 4, MP

Suppose now that we have certain symbolic premises and wish to derive as a conclusion the symbolic sentence ϕ. We begin by writing

Show ϕ .

We may continue, as indicated by our examples, in one of three ways, each of which has numerous intuitive counterparts in the derivations of mathematics and in the reasonings of law courts and everyday life.

(i) By *direct derivation.* We write next a line that can be established independently (for instance, a premise or a sentence accompanied by a subsidiary derivation) and proceed by inference rules, subsidiary derivations, and citing of premises until we secure ϕ. A direct derivation of ϕ, then, will have the form

(8) *Show* ϕ [Assertion]

.
.
.
ϕ .

(ii) By *conditional derivation*, in case ϕ is of the form

$$(\psi \rightarrow \chi) \quad ,$$

where ψ and χ are symbolic sentences. In this case we write next, as an assumption, the sentence ψ, and proceed by inference rules, subsidiary derivations, and citing of premises until we secure χ. A conditional derivation of

$$(\psi \rightarrow \chi) \quad ,$$

then, will have the form

(9) *Show* $(\psi \rightarrow \chi)$ [Assertion]
ψ [Assumption (Conditional derivation)]
.
.
.
χ .

(iii) By *indirect derivation.* In this case we write next, as an assumption, the sentence

$$\sim\phi$$

and proceed by inference rules, subsidiary derivations, and citing of premises until we secure a symbolic sentence χ and its negation,

$$\sim\chi \quad .$$

Thus an indirect derivation of ϕ will have the form

(10) *Show* ϕ [Assertion]
$\sim\phi$ [Assumption (Indirect derivation)]
.
.
.
χ
.
.
.
$\sim\chi$.

If ϕ is itself a negation, say

$$\sim\psi \quad ,$$

we may assume ψ instead of

$$\sim\sim\psi$$

and proceed as above. In this case the indirect derivation of ϕ will have the form

(11) *Show* $\sim\psi$ [Assertion]
ψ [Assumption (Indirect derivation)]
.
.
.
χ
.
.
.
$\sim\chi$.

In (10) and (11) the order in which the contradiction is listed is irrelevant.

When the derivation of ϕ, accomplished by one of these methods, is complete, we indicate its completion by cancelling the occurrence of '*Show*' in the first line and boxing the remaining lines. Then (8) will become

~~*Show*~~ ϕ [Assertion (Direct derivation)]

.
.
.
ϕ

,

(9) will become

~~*Show*~~ $(\psi \to \chi)$ [Assertion (Conditional derivation)]

ψ
.
.
.
χ ,

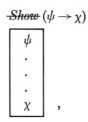

(10) will become

~~*Show*~~ ϕ [Assertion (Indirect derivation)]

$\sim\phi$
.
.
.
χ
.
.
.
$\sim\chi$,

and (11) will become

~~*Show*~~ $\sim\psi$ [Assertion (Indirect derivation)]

ψ
.
.
.
χ
.
.
.
$\sim\chi$.

An example will clarify the use of subsidiary derivations. Suppose that we wish to derive 'P → ([Q → R] → R)' from 'P → Q'. The sentence we wish to derive is a conditional; we therefore start an annotated conditional derivation:

1.	*Show* P → ([Q → R] → R)	Assertion
2.	P	Assumption (CD)

To complete the conditional derivation, we must obtain the consequent of line 1, '$[Q \rightarrow R] \rightarrow R$'. One way of proceeding is to begin with a subsidiary derivation; and since the sentence we wish to establish is a conditional, it is natural to start a conditional derivation:

1.	*Show* $P \rightarrow ([Q \rightarrow R] \rightarrow R)$	
2.	P	
3.	*Show* $[Q \rightarrow R] \rightarrow R$	Assertion
4.	$Q \rightarrow R$	Assumption (CD)

We continue the subsidiary derivation, employing inference rules and the premise (in a way that will be explained more fully later), until we reach the consequent of line 3.

1.	*Show* $P \rightarrow ([Q \rightarrow R] \rightarrow R)$	
2.	P	
3.	*Show* $[Q \rightarrow R] \rightarrow R$	
4.	$Q \rightarrow R$	
5.	$P \rightarrow Q$	Premise
6.	Q	2, 5, MP
7.	R	4, 6, MP

The subsidiary derivation establishing the assertion in line 3 is complete. Thus we may box and cancel to obtain

1.	*Show* $P \rightarrow ([Q \rightarrow R] \rightarrow R)$	
2.	P	
3.	~~*Show*~~ $[Q \rightarrow R] \rightarrow R$	Assertion (CD)
4.	$Q \rightarrow R$	
5.	$P \rightarrow Q$	
6.	Q	
7.	R	

Now the main derivation is complete. Hence we obtain

1.	~~*Show*~~ $P \rightarrow ([Q \rightarrow R] \rightarrow R)$	Assertion (CD)
2.	P	Assumption (CD)
3.	~~*Show*~~ $[Q \rightarrow R] \rightarrow R$	Assertion (CD)
4.	$Q \rightarrow R$	Assumption (CD)
5.	$P \rightarrow Q$	Premise
6.	Q	2, 5, MP
7.	R	4, 6, MP

The foregoing remarks on derivations constitute only an informal introduction. The following is an explicit set of directions for constructing a *derivation* from given symbolic premises:

(1) *If ϕ is any symbolic sentence, then*

$$Show\ \phi$$

may occur as a line. [*Such lines may be accompanied by the annotation 'Assertion'.*]

(2) *Any one of the premises may occur as a line.* [*Annotation: 'Premise'.*]

(3) *If ϕ, ψ are symbolic sentences such that*

$$Show\ (\phi \rightarrow \psi)$$

occurs as a line, then ϕ may occur as the next line. [*Annotation: 'Assumption for conditional derivation' or simply 'Assumption (CD)'.*]

(4) *If ϕ is a symbolic sentence such that*

$$Show\ \phi$$

occurs as a line, then

$$\sim\phi$$

may occur as the next line; if ϕ is a symbolic sentence such that

$$Show\ \sim\phi$$

occurs as a line, then ϕ may occur as the next line. [*Annotation: 'Assumption for indirect derivation' or simply 'Assumption (ID)'.*]

(5) *A symbolic sentence may occur as a line if it follows by an inference rule from* antecedent lines, *that is, preceding lines which neither are boxed nor contain uncancelled 'Show'.* [*The annotation should refer to the inference rule employed and the numbers of the preceding lines involved.*]

(6) *When the following arrangement of lines has appeared:*

$$\begin{array}{l} Show\ \phi \\ \chi_1 \\ \cdot \\ \cdot \\ \cdot \\ \chi_m\ , \end{array}$$

where none of χ_1 through χ_m contains uncancelled 'Show' and either

(*i*) *ϕ occurs unboxed among χ_1 through χ_m,*

(*ii*) *ϕ is of the form*

$$(\psi_1 \rightarrow \psi_2)$$

and ψ_2 occurs unboxed among χ_1 through χ_m, or

(iii) for some sentence χ, both χ and its negation occur unboxed among χ_1 through χ_m,

then one may simultaneously cancel the displayed occurrence of 'Show' and box all subsequent lines. [When we say that a sentence ϕ occurs among *certain lines of a derivation, we mean that one of those lines is either ϕ or ϕ preceded by '~~Show~~'. Further, annotations for clause (6), parts (i), (ii), and (iii) are 'DD', 'CD', and 'ID', respectively, to be entered parenthetically after the annotation for the line in which 'Show' is cancelled.]*

A derivation is said to be *complete* if each of its lines either is boxed or contains cancelled '*Show*'.

A symbolic sentence ϕ is said to be *derivable* from given symbolic premises if, by using only clauses (1)–(6), a complete derivation from those premises can be constructed in which

~~*Show*~~ ϕ

occurs as an unboxed line.

Applications of clauses (1) through (4) are quite straightforward. An annotated derivation of '$(\sim Q \rightarrow \sim P) \rightarrow Q$' from the premise 'P' will illustrate applications of clauses (5) and (6).

1.	*Show* $(\sim Q \rightarrow \sim P) \rightarrow Q$	Assertion
2.	$\sim Q \rightarrow \sim P$	Assumption (CD)
3.	*Show* Q	Assertion
4.	$\sim Q$	Assumption (ID)
5.	P	Premise
6.	$\sim P$	2, 4, MP

Line 6 is justified by an application of clause (5), for line 6 follows from the antecedent lines 2 and 4. The derivation can be continued by an application of clause (6), part (iii); for lines 3–6 have the pattern

Show Q

χ_1

.

.

.

χ_m ,

where none of χ_1 through χ_m contains uncancelled '*Show*' and both 'P' and its negation occur unboxed among χ_1 through χ_m. Thus we may simultaneously cancel the last unboxed occurrence of '*Show*' and box all subsequent lines, to obtain:

1. *Show* $(\sim Q \rightarrow \sim P) \rightarrow Q$
2. $\sim Q \rightarrow \sim P$

3.	~~*Show*~~ Q	Assertion (ID)
4.	$\sim$Q	
5.	P	
6.	$\sim$P	

Now an application of clause (6), part (ii), is possible, for lines 1 – 6 have the pattern

Show $(\sim Q \rightarrow \sim P) \rightarrow Q$

χ_1

.

.

.

χ_m ,

where none of χ_1 through χ_m contains uncancelled '*Show*' and 'Q' occurs unboxed among χ_1 through χ_m. Thus we may again simultaneously cancel the last unboxed occurrence of '*Show*' and box all subsequent lines, to obtain:

1.	~~*Show*~~ $(\sim Q \rightarrow \sim P) \rightarrow Q$	Assertion (CD)
2.	$\sim Q \rightarrow \sim P$	Assumption (CD)
3.	~~*Show*~~ Q	Assertion (ID)
4.	$\sim$Q	Assumption (ID)
5.	P	Premise
6.	$\sim$P	2, 4, MP

A *symbolic argument* is said to be *valid* if its conclusion is derivable from its premises. For example, the argument

$$\sim (Q \rightarrow R) \quad . \qquad P \rightarrow \sim\sim R \quad \therefore \sim P$$

happens to be valid in view of the following derivation:

1.	~~*Show*~~ $\sim$P	Assertion (ID)
2.	P	Assumption (ID)
3.	$P \rightarrow \sim\sim R$	Premise
4.	$\sim\sim$R	2, 3, MP
5.	$\sim(Q \rightarrow R)$	Premise
6.	~~*Show*~~ $Q \rightarrow R$	Assertion (CD)
7.	Q	Assumption (CD)
8.	R	4, DN

A very important feature of the notion given above of a derivation, and one that will be shared by all analogous notions to be introduced subsequently, is that there is a purely automatic procedure for checking the correctness of an alleged derivation from a finite class of premises; more generally, whenever a class of premises is such that one can automatically determine of any sentence whether it belongs to that class, there will be an automatic procedure for determining whether any alleged derivation is indeed a correct derivation from that class of premises. Thus the correctness of derivations, unlike the cogency of everyday reasonings, is removed from the realm of controversy.

EXERCISES, GROUP I

Show by constructing annotated derivations that the following arguments are valid. [Accompanying each exercise is a reference to an example or strategic hint (listed below) which the reader may find useful.]

18. $\sim Q \quad \therefore (P \rightarrow Q) \rightarrow \sim P$ [Example (6)]
19. $P \rightarrow (Q \rightarrow R) \quad . \quad P \rightarrow (R \rightarrow S)$
 $\therefore P \rightarrow (Q \rightarrow S)$ [Example on p. 22]
20. $\sim P \rightarrow Q \quad . \quad P \rightarrow Q \quad \therefore Q$ [Example (7)]
21. $Q \rightarrow \sim R \quad . \quad \sim P \rightarrow R \quad \therefore \sim P \rightarrow \sim Q$
22. $(P \rightarrow Q) \rightarrow R \quad . \quad \sim R \quad \therefore \sim Q$ [Use hint 5]
23. $(R \rightarrow S) \rightarrow P \quad . \quad \sim S \rightarrow Q \quad \therefore \sim P \rightarrow Q$ [Use hint 5]
24. $(Q \rightarrow \sim\sim S) \rightarrow (\sim R \rightarrow \sim S) \quad \therefore S \rightarrow R$ [Use hint 6]
25. $(S \rightarrow P) \rightarrow R \quad . \quad \sim R \quad .$
 $(P \rightarrow Q) \rightarrow (T \rightarrow R) \quad \therefore \sim T$ [Use hints 5 and 6]
26. $(P \rightarrow Q) \rightarrow (T \rightarrow R) \quad . \quad U \rightarrow \sim R \quad .$
 $\sim(S \rightarrow P) \quad \therefore U \rightarrow \sim T$ [Use hints 5 and 6]

In solving exercises 18–26 (as well as later exercises) the reader will find the following *strategic hints* helpful but not infallible. They are intended merely as informal advice and do not have the same status as the official directions for constructing a derivation.

(1) *To derive a conditional, use conditional derivation.*

(2) *To derive anything else, use indirect derivation unless another procedure is immediately obvious.*

(3) *Enter all premises as lines, but not until one or another form of derivation has been commenced.*

(4) *Whenever a sentence follows from antecedent lines by MP or MT, enter that sentence as a line.*

(5) *When using indirect derivation, determine whether any of the antecedent lines is the negation of a conditional; if so, attempt to derive the conditional.*

(6) *When a conditional occurs as an antecedent line and neither MP nor MT is applicable, attempt to derive the antecedent of the conditional.*

To illustrate the utility of hints (2)–(5), we construct a derivation for the following argument:

$$(P \rightarrow Q) \rightarrow Q \quad . \qquad Q \rightarrow P \quad \therefore P \quad .$$

According to hint (2) we begin an indirect derivation:

1.	*Show* P	Assertion
2.	$\sim$P	Assumption (ID)

Next, in accordance with hint (3), we enter the premises:

1.	*Show* P	
2.	$\sim$P	
3.	$(P \rightarrow Q) \rightarrow Q$	Premise
4.	$Q \rightarrow P$	Premise

We then notice that 2 and 4 permit an application of MT, and we follow hint (4):

1.	*Show* P	
2.	$\sim$P	
3.	$(P \rightarrow Q) \rightarrow Q$	
4.	$Q \rightarrow P$	
5.	$\sim$Q	2, 4, MT

Again we apply MT:

1.	*Show* P	
2.	$\sim$P	
3.	$(P \rightarrow Q) \rightarrow Q$	
4.	$Q \rightarrow P$	
5.	$\sim$Q	
6.	$\sim(P \rightarrow Q)$	3, 5, MT

We have now obtained, in our indirect derivation, the negation of a conditional. Thus, following hint (5), we should attempt to derive '$P \rightarrow Q$'; we do this, following hint (1), by conditional derivation:

1.	*Show* P	
2.	$\sim$P	
3.	$(P \rightarrow Q) \rightarrow Q$	
4.	$Q \rightarrow P$	
5.	$\sim$Q	
6.	$\sim(P \rightarrow Q)$	
7.	*Show* $P \rightarrow Q$	Assertion
8.	P	Assumption (CD)

To complete the subsidiary conditional derivation, we must derive 'Q'; thus, by hint (2), we try indirect derivation:

1.	*Show* P	
2.	$\sim$P	

3. $(P \rightarrow Q) \rightarrow Q$	
4. $Q \rightarrow P$	
5. $\sim Q$	
6. $\sim(P \rightarrow Q)$	
7. *Show* $P \rightarrow Q$	
8. P	
9. *Show* Q	Assertion
10. $\sim Q$	Assumption (ID)

It is now obvious how to complete the subsidiary indirect derivation:

1. *Show* P	
2. $\sim P$	
3. $(P \rightarrow Q) \rightarrow Q$	
4. $Q \rightarrow P$	
5. $\sim Q$	
6. $\sim(P \rightarrow Q)$	
7. *Show* $P \rightarrow Q$	
8. P	
9. ~~*Show*~~ Q	Assertion (ID)
10. $\sim Q$	Assumption (ID)
11. P	8, R
12. $\sim P$	2, R

The trivial rule of repetition has been used to place the contradiction of 'P' and '$\sim$P' within the subsidiary derivation of 'Q'. The completion of the subsidiary indirect derivation of 'Q' completes the subsidiary conditional derivation of 'P → Q', whose completion in turn completes the main derivation:

1. ~~*Show*~~ P	Assertion (ID)
2. $\sim P$	
3. $(P \rightarrow Q) \rightarrow Q$	
4. $Q \rightarrow P$	
5. $\sim Q$	
6. $\sim(P \rightarrow Q)$	
7. ~~*Show*~~ $P \rightarrow Q$	Assertion (CD)
8. P	
9. ~~*Show*~~ Q	
10. $\sim Q$	
11. P	
12. $\sim P$	

To illustrate the utility of hint (6), we construct a derivation for the following argument:

$$\therefore [(P \rightarrow \sim P) \rightarrow (\sim P \rightarrow P)] \rightarrow P \quad .$$

Following hints (1) and (2), we obtain:

1.	*Show* $[(P \to \sim P) \to (\sim P \to P)] \to P$	Assertion
2.	$(P \to \sim P) \to (\sim P \to P)$	Assumption (CD)
3.	*Show* P	Assertion
4.	$\sim P$	Assumption (ID)

We now have a conditional in line 2 to which neither MP nor MT can be applied. Following hint (6), we attempt to derive the antecedent of that conditional.

1.	*Show* $[(P \to \sim P) \to (\sim P \to P)] \to P$	
2.	$(P \to \sim P) \to (\sim P \to P)$	
3.	*Show* P	
4.	$\sim P$	
5.	*Show* $P \to \sim P$	Assertion

We start the subsidiary derivation of line 5 in accordance with hint (1) and complete it by employing the rule of repetition:

1.	*Show* $[(P \to \sim P) \to (\sim P \to P)] \to P$	
2.	$(P \to \sim P) \to (\sim P \to P)$	
3.	*Show* P	
4.	$\sim P$	
5.	~~*Show*~~ $P \to \sim P$	Assertion (CD)
6.	P	Assumption (CD)
7.	$\sim P$	4, R

With the antecedent of line 2 now at our disposal, we apply MP to lines 2 and 5:

1.	*Show* $[(P \to \sim P) \to (\sim P \to P)] \to P$	
2.	$(P \to \sim P) \to (\sim P \to P)$	
3.	*Show* P	
4.	$\sim P$	
5.	~~*Show*~~ $P \to \sim P$	
6.	P	
7.	$\sim P$	
8.	$\sim P \to P$	2, 5, MP

We can now complete the subsidiary derivation begun in line 3 by another application of MP, which in turn completes the main derivation.

1.	~~*Show*~~ $[(P \to \sim P) \to (\sim P \to P)] \to P$	Assertion (CD)
2.	$(P \to \sim P) \to (\sim P \to P)$	
3.	~~*Show*~~ P	Assertion (ID)
4.	$\sim P$	

5.	~~*Show*~~ $P \rightarrow \sim P$	
6.	P	
7.	$\sim P$	
8.	$\sim P \rightarrow P$	
9.	P	4, 8, MP

Actually, the two derivations to which our strategic hints led us are unnecessarily complicated. An insight after we reached line 8 of the first derivation would have allowed us to complete it in one additional line, as follows:

1.	~~*Show*~~ P	Assertion (ID)
2.	$\sim P$	Assumption (ID)
3.	$(P \rightarrow Q) \rightarrow Q$	Premise
4.	$Q \rightarrow P$	Premise
5.	$\sim Q$	2, 4, MT
6.	$\sim (P \rightarrow Q)$	3, 5, MT
7.	~~*Show*~~ $P \rightarrow Q$	Assertion (ID)
8.	P	Assumption (CD)
9.	$\sim P$	2, R

Here the subsidiary derivation of line 7 is accomplished in an unusual way. The assumption, line 8, is made in accordance with conditional derivation, but the boxing and cancelling are done in accordance with indirect derivation. This procedure is legitimate; the rules for entering assumptions are separate from the rules for boxing and cancelling.

Similarly, an insight after line 5 in the second derivation would have allowed us to complete it in one less line, as follows:

1.	~~*Show*~~ $[(P \rightarrow \sim P) \rightarrow (\sim P \rightarrow P)] \rightarrow P$	Assertion (CD)
2.	$(P \rightarrow \sim P) \rightarrow (\sim P \rightarrow P)$	Assumption (CD)
3.	~~*Show*~~ P	Assertion (ID)
4.	$\sim P$	Assumption (ID)
5.	~~*Show*~~ $P \rightarrow \sim P$	Assertion (CD)
6.	$\sim P$	4, R
7.	$\sim P \rightarrow P$	2, 5, MP
8.	P	4, 7, MP

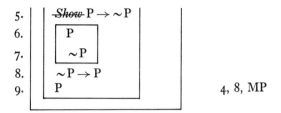

Here the subsidiary derivation for '$P \rightarrow \sim P$' is accomplished without entering an assumption. This procedure is legitimate, for boxing and cancelling in accordance with conditional derivation (clause (6), part (ii)) does not require that an assumption for conditional derivation (clause (3)) be employed. Other mixed forms of derivation are possible and indeed convenient, but in each case the mixture could be avoided at the expense of a few extra lines.

EXERCISES, GROUP II

We shall refer to a derivation as *uniform* if it is completed by the same form of derivation as that by which it is initiated. Thus, a direct derivation is uniform if no assumption follows the assertion line and it is completed by clause (6), part (i); a conditional derivation is uniform if the assertion line is followed by an assumption introduced by clause (3) and it is completed by clause (6), part (ii); and an indirect derivation is uniform if the assertion line is followed by an assumption introduced by clause (4) and it is completed by clause (6), part (iii). If a derivation and all subsidiary derivations within it are uniform, the derivation is *unmixed*; otherwise, it is *mixed*.

27. The validity of the argument

$$\sim(P \rightarrow Q) \rightarrow Q \quad \therefore P \rightarrow Q$$

is established by the following succinct mixed derivation, which begins with an assumption for indirect derivation and is completed by boxing and cancelling in accordance with conditional derivation:

1.	~~*Show*~~ $P \rightarrow Q$	Assertion (CD)
2.	$\sim(P \rightarrow Q)$	Assumption (ID)
3.	$\sim(P \rightarrow Q) \rightarrow Q$	Premise
4.	Q	2, 3, MP

Establish the validity of this argument by means of (a) an unmixed conditional derivation and (b) an unmixed indirect derivation.

28. By means of a four-line derivation, establish the validity of the following argument:

$$\sim(R \rightarrow Q) \quad . \qquad Q \quad \therefore P \quad .$$

4. Validity of English arguments. We shall call an argument whose premises and conclusion are sentences of English an *English argument*. A *symbolization of an English argument on the basis of a given scheme of abbreviation* is a symbolic argument whose premises and conclusion are, respectively, symbolizations on the basis of that scheme of the premises and conclusion of the English argument. A symbolic argument is called simply a *symbolization* of an English argument if there is some scheme of abbreviation on the basis of which it is a symbolization of the English argument. To illustrate, consider again argument (2) of the preceding section:

(1) If Socrates did not die of old age, then the Athenians condemned him to death. The Athenians did not condemn Socrates to death. ∴ Socrates died of old age.

On the basis of the scheme

P : Socrates died of old age
Q : the Athenians condemned Socrates to death ,

we obtain as a symbolization of (1) the symbolic argument

(2) $\sim P \rightarrow Q \quad . \quad \sim Q \quad \therefore P \quad .$

In order to define validity for English arguments we must proceed indirectly, for we have confined the application of deductive procedures to symbolic sentences (see p. 14). Thus an *English argument* is said to be *valid* (in the branch of logic presently under consideration) if and only if it has a symbolization that is valid, that is, whose conclusion is derivable from its premises. (Other branches of logic and wider notions of validity will be considered later.) Argument (1) is valid in view of the symbolization (2) and the derivation

1.	~~*Show*~~ P	Assertion (DD)
2.	$\sim P \rightarrow Q$	Premise
3.	$\sim Q$	Premise
4.	$\sim\sim P$	2, 3, MT
5.	P	4, DN

The reader should note that (1) has other symbolizations; for example, on the basis of the scheme

P : if Socrates did not die of old age, then the Athenians condemned him to death
Q : the Athenians did not condemn Socrates to death
R : Socrates died of old age

the argument

$$P \quad . \quad Q \quad \therefore R$$

is a symbolization of (1); and on the basis of the scheme

P : Socrates did not die of old age
Q : Socrates died of old age
R : the Athenians condemned Socrates to death ,

another symbolization of (1) is the argument

$$P \rightarrow R \quad . \quad \sim R \quad \therefore Q \quad .$$

But neither of the last two symbolizations is valid (as we shall be able to show in the next chapter). In general, the longer the symbolization, the more likely it is to be valid; and among symbolizations of equal length, the likelihood of validity increases as the number of distinct sentence letters decreases.

For another illustration, consider the argument

(3) Free love is justified only if the sex drive is primary. Freud's theory is correct provided that the sex drive is primary. It is not the case that if psychoanalysis is therapeutic, Freud's theory is correct. ∴ Free love is not justified.

On the basis of the scheme

P	:	free love is justified
Q	:	the sex drive is primary
R	:	Freud's theory is correct
S	:	psychoanalysis is therapeutic

we obtain as a symbolization of the argument (3) the symbolic argument

$$P \rightarrow Q \quad . \quad Q \rightarrow R \quad . \quad \sim(S \rightarrow R) \quad \therefore \sim P \quad .$$

Its validity, and hence that of (3), is established by the following derivation:

1.	~~*Show*~~ $\sim P$	Assertion (ID)
2.	P	Assumption (ID)
3.	$P \rightarrow Q$	Premise
4.	$Q \rightarrow R$	Premise
5.	$\sim(S \rightarrow R)$	Premise
6.	Q	2, 3, MP
7.	~~*Show*~~ $S \rightarrow R$	Assertion (CD)
8.	R	4, 6, MP

EXERCISES

Show that the following arguments are valid by constructing symbolizations and deriving the conclusions of the symbolizations from their premises. Indicate the scheme of abbreviation used. (The reader will again find useful the strategic hints given on p. 27.)

29. If Alfred studies, then he receives good grades. If he does not study, then he enjoys college. If he does not receive good grades, then he does not enjoy college. ∴ Alfred receives good grades. (Compare (1), p. 1.)

30. If Herbert can take the apartment only if he divorces his wife, then he should think twice. If Herbert keeps Fido, then he cannot

take the apartment. Herbert's wife insists on keeping Fido. If Herbert does not keep Fido, then he will divorce his wife provided that she insists on keeping Fido. ∴ Herbert should think twice.

31. If Herbert grows rich, then he can take the apartment. If he divorces his wife, then he will not receive his inheritance. Herbert will grow rich if he receives his inheritance. Herbert can take the apartment only if he divorces his wife. ∴ If Herbert receives his inheritance, then Fido does not matter.

32. The standard of living will improve provided that taxes will increase. Business will flourish only if unemployment is not a problem. Business will flourish if the standard of living will improve. ∴ On the condition that taxes will increase, unemployment is not a problem.

33. If business will flourish on the condition that taxes will not increase, then the standard of living will improve. It is not the case that the standard of living will improve. If business does not flourish, then taxes will increase. ∴ Unemployment will be a problem.

34. If Descartes can doubt that he is thinking, then he thinks. If Descartes cannot doubt that he is thinking, then he thinks. If Descartes does not exist, then he does not think. ∴ Descartes exists.

35. If God exists, then He is omnipotent. If God exists, then He is omniscient. If God exists, then He is benevolent. If God can prevent evil, then if He knows that evil exists, then He is not benevolent if He does not prevent it. If God is omnipotent, then He can prevent evil. If God is omniscient, then He knows that evil exists if it does indeed exist. Evil does not exist if God prevents it. Evil exists. ∴ God does not exist.

5. Fallacies. In the directions for constructing a derivation, a number of restrictions appear whose significance is perhaps not immediately obvious. However, if we define a *fallacy* as a procedure that permits the validation of a *false English argument*, that is, an argument whose premises are true sentences of English and whose conclusion is a false sentence of English, then the neglect of any but one of the restrictions would lead to fallacies.

The fallacies involved here are of two kinds—those of begging the question and those of unwarranted assumptions. These kinds of fallacies can be characterized in a rough, informal way, as follows.

When, in deriving something, one uses the assertion that is to be derived, one is said to be guilty of *begging the question*.

Assumptions are useful tools in logical derivations, but they must be employed with caution. Only on special occasions may they be made or inferences drawn from them. The use of assumptions at other junctures is the fallacy of *unwarranted assumptions*. (The reader should observe the difference between the use of *premises*, which is justified by clause (2), and the use of *assumptions*. A premise may be stated at any point in the course of a derivation; there are no restrictions here whose neglect would lead to fallacies.)

In clauses (3) and (4) of the directions for constructing a derivation, it is specified that an assumption may be made only in connection with a line containing uncancelled '*Show*'. Let us examine the consequences of ignoring this restriction, in connection first with clause (3). Consider the argument

> If Schopenhauer was married, then he had a wife.
> ∴ Schopenhauer had a wife.

Here the premise is obviously true, and the conclusion is, as a matter of history, false; hence the argument is false. But by an incorrect use of clause (3), the validity of this argument could be established by means of the following symbolization and accompanying derivation.

(1) $P \rightarrow Q \quad \therefore Q$

1.	~~*Show*~~ Q	Assertion (DD)
2.	$P \rightarrow Q$	Premise
3.	P	Unwarranted assumption (CD)
4.	Q	2, 3, MP

Now let us employ clause (4) incorrectly, again making an assumption in connection with a line not beginning with uncancelled '*Show*'. Consider the false argument

> Snow is white. ∴ Grass is red.

and the following symbolization and derivation:

(2) $P \quad \therefore Q$

1.	~~*Show*~~ Q	Assertion (ID)
2.	P	Premise
3.	$\sim P$	Unwarranted assumption (ID)

In both (1) and (2), then, we have validated false arguments by committing one form of the fallacy of unwarranted assumptions; in neither case was the assumption made in connection with a line containing uncancelled '*Show*'.

The other restriction involved in clauses (3) and (4) is that the assumption be made immediately after the line with which it is connected. It is not yet possible to illustrate the necessity of this restriction; in fact, its neglect will produce no fallacies until our logical apparatus is enlarged by the introduction, in chapter III, of a new form of derivation.

Clause (5) permits us to draw inferences only from *antecedent lines*. This restriction can be violated in two ways—by applying an inference rule to a line containing uncancelled '*Show*' or by applying a rule to a boxed line. Let us illustrate the first violation.

Argument:

Snow is white. ∴ If snow is white, then grass is red.

Symbolization:

$$P \quad \therefore P \to Q$$

Derivation:

1.	~~*Show*~~ P → Q	Assertion (CD)
2.	P	Premise
3.	Q	1, 2, incorrect application of MP

The application of MP is incorrect because at the time it occurred the '*Show*' in line 1 had not been cancelled. Intuitively, we used the conclusion that was to be derived in order to obtain one of the lines in its derivation. Thus we begged the question.

Let us now illustrate the consequences of applying an inference rule to a boxed line.

Argument:

Snow is white. ∴ Grass is red.

Symbolization:

$$P \quad \therefore Q$$

We consider several stages in constructing a derivation corresponding to this symbolization.

(3)	1.	*Show* Q	Assertion
	2.	*Show* Q → P	Assertion
	3.	Q	Assumption (CD)
	4.	P	Premise
(4)	1.	*Show* Q	
	2.	~~*Show*~~ Q → P	
	3.	Q	
	4.	P	
(5)	1.	~~*Show*~~ Q	
	2.	~~*Show*~~ Q → P	
	3.	Q	
	4.	P	
	5.	Q	3, incorrect application of R

The partial derivations (3) and (4) are correctly constructed, but (5) involves an unwarranted use of assumptions. Although the assumption made in line 3 is legitimate, an illegitimate consequence has been drawn from it; for line 3 is boxed in stage (4) and hence no longer available for further inferences.

The derivation (5) can be obtained by another fallacious procedure. From (3) we can proceed legitimately not only to (4), but also to the following partial derivation:

(4′)

1. *Show* Q
2. *Show* Q → P
3. Q
4. P
5. Q — 3, R

Then we might apply clause (6) of the directions for constructing derivations, ignoring the injunction that when an occurrence of '*Show*' is cancelled, *all* subsequent lines must be boxed:

(4″)

1. *Show* Q
2. ~~*Show*~~ Q → P
3. Q
4. P
5. Q — 3, R

From this (incorrect) partial derivation, we might then proceed legitimately to (5). Since line 5 depends on an assumption, it is legitimately available only as long as the assumption is; thus the failure to box line 5 along with lines 3 and 4 in passing from (4′) to (4″) can be construed, like the previous fallacy, as an unwarranted use of an assumption.

In boxing and cancelling by clause (6), the lines to be boxed must be free of uncancelled '*Show*'. Let us consider two examples in which this restriction is violated.

Argument:

Snow is white. ∴ Grass is red.

Symbolization:

P ∴ Q

Derivation:

(6)

1. ~~*Show*~~ Q — Assertion (DD)
2. P — Premise
3. *Show* Q — Assertion

Derivation:

(7)	1. ~~*Show*~~ Q	Assertion (DD)
	2. *Show* Q → P	Assertion
	3. Q	Assumption (CD)

In the derivation (6) we have begged the question, and in (7) we have made unwarranted use of an assumption; in both cases the lines boxed contain uncancelled '*Show*'.

There is another restriction imposed in clause (6). In each of our three forms of derivation certain lines are crucial, and these must occur unboxed. In direct derivation, for instance, the assertion that is to be established must occur in some unboxed line following its initial statement. Let us consider a case in which the crucial line is boxed.

Argument:

Snow is white. ∴ Grass is red.

Symbolization:

P ∴ Q

We consider two stages in constructing a corresponding derivation.

(8)	1. *Show* Q	Assertion
	2. ~~*Show*~~ Q → P	Assertion (CD)
	3. Q	Assumption (CD)
	4. P	Premise

(9)	1. ~~*Show*~~ Q
	2. ~~*Show*~~ Q → P
	3. Q
	4. P

The incomplete derivation (8) is correctly constructed. The passage from (8) to (9), however, fails to satisfy the requirements of clause (6), for the occurrence of 'Q' in line 3 of (8) is boxed. This passage is, moreover, intuitively unsatisfactory; it involves an unwarranted use of an assumption.

We leave to the reader illustrations of the same sort in connection with conditional and indirect derivation.

A third kind of fallacy consists of the misapplication of inference rules. Two such fallacies, bearing a close similarity to our rules MP and MT, have occurred with enough frequency to have acquired names. One is called the *fallacy of affirming the consequent*; as an inference rule, it would appear as follows:

$$\frac{\begin{array}{r}\phi \rightarrow \psi \\ \psi\end{array}}{\phi}$$

The other is called the *fallacy of denying the antecedent*; as an inference rule, it would appear as follows:

$$\frac{\begin{array}{l}\phi \rightarrow \psi \\ \sim\phi\end{array}}{\sim\psi}$$

Consider the argument

> If Caesar committed suicide, then Caesar is dead.
> Caesar is dead. ∴ Caesar committed suicide ,

whose premises are clearly true and whose conclusion, as a matter of history, is false. If the rule corresponding to the fallacy of affirming the consequent were adopted, the validity of this argument could be established by means of the following symbolization and accompanying derivation:

Symbolization:

$$P \rightarrow Q \quad . \qquad Q \quad \therefore P$$

Derivation:

1. ~~*Show*~~ P

2.	$P \rightarrow Q$	
3.	Q	
4.	P	2, 3, Fallacy of affirming the consequent

Again we leave to the reader an illustration of the same sort in connection with the fallacy of denying the antecedent.

6. Theorems. As we stated earlier, it is possible for an argument to have an empty sequence of premises; an example is (3) of section 3. If such an argument is valid and is furthermore symbolic, its conclusion is called a *theorem*. A derivation corresponding to such an argument, which will contain no line justified by clause (2) (the clause that admits premises), will be called a *proof*. Thus a *theorem* is a symbolic sentence derivable from the empty sequence of premises, and its derivation is called a *proof*. The following theorems, some of which are accompanied by proofs, will be useful in subsequent chapters.

T1

1.	~~*Show*~~ $P \rightarrow P$	Assertion (CD)
2.	P	Assumption (CD)

T2

1.	~~*Show*~~ $Q \rightarrow (P \rightarrow Q)$	Assertion (CD)
2.	Q	Assumption (CD)
3.	~~*Show*~~ $P \rightarrow Q$	Assertion (CD)
4.	Q	2, R

T3

1.	~~*Show*~~ $P \rightarrow ([P \rightarrow Q] \rightarrow Q)$	Assertion (CD)
2.	P	Assumption (CD)
3.	~~*Show*~~ $[P \rightarrow Q] \rightarrow Q$	Assertion (CD)
4.	$P \rightarrow Q$	Assumption (CD)
5.	Q	2, 4, MP

T4 and T5 are known as principles of *syllogism*. Their derivations are left to the reader.

T4 $(P \rightarrow Q) \rightarrow ([Q \rightarrow R] \rightarrow [P \rightarrow R])$

T5 $(Q \rightarrow R) \rightarrow ([P \rightarrow Q] \rightarrow [P \rightarrow R])$

T6 and T7 are called principles of *distribution* of '$\rightarrow$' over '$\rightarrow$'.

T6

1.	~~*Show*~~ $(P \rightarrow [Q \rightarrow R]) \rightarrow ([P \rightarrow Q] \rightarrow [P \rightarrow R])$	Assertion (CD)
2.	$P \rightarrow [Q \rightarrow R]$	Assumption (CD)
3.	~~*Show*~~ $[P \rightarrow Q] \rightarrow [P \rightarrow R]$	Assertion (CD)
4.	$P \rightarrow Q$	Assumption (CD)
5.	~~*Show*~~ $P \rightarrow R$	Assertion (CD)
6.	P	Assumption (CD)
7.	Q	4, 6, MP
8.	$Q \rightarrow R$	2, 6, MP
9.	R	7, 8, MP

T7 $([P \rightarrow Q] \rightarrow [P \rightarrow R]) \rightarrow (P \rightarrow [Q \rightarrow R])$

The principle of *commutation:*

T8

1.	~~*Show*~~ $(P \to [Q \to R]) \to (Q \to [P \to R])$	Assertion (CD)
2.	$P \to [Q \to R]$	Assumption (CD)
3.	~~*Show*~~ $Q \to [P \to R]$	Assertion (CD)
4.	Q	Assertion (CD)
5.	~~*Show*~~ $P \to R$	Assumption (CD)
6.	P	Assumption (CD)
7.	$Q \to R$	2, 6, MP
8.	R	4, 7, MP

T9 $(P \to [P \to Q]) \to (P \to Q)$

T10

1.	~~*Show*~~ $([P \to Q] \to Q) \to ([Q \to P] \to P)$	Assertion (CD)
2.	$[P \to Q] \to Q$	Assumption (CD)
3.	~~*Show*~~ $[Q \to P] \to P$	Assertion (CD)
4.	$Q \to P$	Assumption (CD)
5.	~~*Show*~~ P	Assertion (ID)
6.	$\sim P$	Assumption (ID)
7.	$\sim Q$	4, 6, MT
8.	$\sim [P \to Q]$	2, 7, MT
9.	~~*Show*~~ $P \to Q$	Assertion (ID)
10.	P	Assumption (CD)
11.	$\sim P$	6, R

T11 and T12 are the two laws of *double negation.*

T11

1.	~~*Show*~~ $\sim\sim P \to P$	Assertion (CD)
2.	$\sim\sim P$	Assumption (CD)
3.	P	2, DN

T12 $P \to \sim\sim P$

T13 – T16 are known as principles of *transposition.* We shall henceforth omit the annotations 'Assertion' and 'Assumption'.

T13

1.	~~*Show*~~ $(P \to Q) \to (\sim Q \to \sim P)$
2.	$P \to Q$
3.	~~*Show*~~ $\sim Q \to \sim P$

4. $\sim Q$
5. $\sim P$ — 2, 4, MT

T14 $(P \rightarrow \sim Q) \rightarrow (Q \rightarrow \sim P)$

T15 $(\sim P \rightarrow Q) \rightarrow (\sim Q \rightarrow P)$

T16 $(\sim P \rightarrow \sim Q) \rightarrow (Q \rightarrow P)$

T17
1. ~~*Show*~~ $P \rightarrow (\sim P \rightarrow Q)$
2. P
3. ~~*Show*~~ $\sim P \rightarrow Q$
4. $\sim P$
5. P — 2, R

T18 $\sim P \rightarrow (P \rightarrow Q)$

T19 and T20 are known as laws of *reductio ad absurdum.*

T19
1. ~~*Show*~~ $(\sim P \rightarrow P) \rightarrow P$
2. $\sim P \rightarrow P$
3. ~~*Show*~~ P
4. $\sim P$
5. P — 2, 4, MP

T20 $(P \rightarrow \sim P) \rightarrow \sim P$

According to T21 and T22, the denial of a conditional leads to the affirmation of its antecedent and the denial of its consequent.

T21 $\sim (P \rightarrow Q) \rightarrow P$

T22 $\sim (P \rightarrow Q) \rightarrow \sim Q$

T23 is known as *Peirce's law* (after the nineteenth-century American philosopher C. S. Peirce).

T23 $([P \rightarrow Q] \rightarrow P) \rightarrow P$

EXERCISES, GROUP I

36. Prove T4, T7, T15, T18.
37. Prove T20–T23.

In solving exercises 36 and 37, the reader will again find the hints given on page 27 useful.

EXERCISES, GROUP II

38. Construct proofs of T11, T12, and T13 in which the only rule of inference employed is MP.

39. The inference rule

$$\frac{\begin{array}{r}(\sim\phi \rightarrow \sim\psi)\\ \psi\end{array}}{\phi}$$

is a variant of *modus tollens*, to which we shall refer by 'MT*'. Without employing indirect derivation (that is, either clause (4) or clause (6), part (iii) of the directions for constructing a derivation), construct a proof

(a) of T11 in which the only rules of inference employed are MP and MT*,

(b) of T12 in which the only rules of inference employed are MP, MT*, and DN corresponding to T11,

(c) of T13 in which the only rules of inference employed are MP, MT*, and the two forms of DN.

40. Without employing indirect derivation, construct a proof of T19 in which the only rules of inference employed are MP, MT, and MT*. (Exercise 39 establishes that MT is not essential for this exercise.)

(The significance of exercises 38–40 is indicated in the historical remarks of the next section.)

7. Historical remarks. The logic of '$\sim$' and '$\rightarrow$' was first studied by the Stoics in the fourth and third centuries B.C. (see Lukasiewicz [2] and Mates [1]). Its first complete formalization (in a technical sense) occurs in Frege [1]. An extensive investigation into this branch of logic is reported in Łukasiewicz and Tarski [1].

The treatment set forth in the present chapter differs in a marked way from that of Frege and Łukasiewicz. The earlier systems relied on only one form of derivation—direct derivation. The simplicity thus obtained was secured at the expense of postulating certain theorems as axioms. The idea of dispensing with axioms in favor of conditional derivation stems from Gentzen [1] and Jaśkowski [1] and depends on a result obtained independently by Herbrand and Tarski—the so-called *deduction theorem* (see Herbrand [1], [2], and Tarski [1]). Systems of the later variety are said to employ *natural deduction* and, as this designation indicates, are intended to reflect intuitive forms of reasoning.

Other systems of natural deduction may be found in Quine [3], Copi [1], Suppes [1], Hilbert and Ackermann [4], and Mates [2].

Our system could be simplified at the expense of making certain derivations unintuitive. In particular, given our three forms of derivation, all rules of inference other than *modus ponens* are theoretically superfluous; this fact is established by exercise 38 of the preceding section. Further, if we supplement the single rule of *modus ponens* with a variant of *modus tollens*, specifically

$$\frac{\begin{array}{r}(\sim\phi \rightarrow \sim\psi)\\ \psi\end{array}}{\phi}\quad ,$$

then indirect derivation is theoretically superfluous. This fact is established by exercises 39 and 40 of the preceding section and the following consideration: given an indirect derivation of a symbolic sentence ϕ

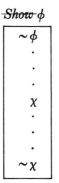

~~*Show*~~ ϕ

$\sim\phi$
.
.
.
χ
.
.
.
$\sim\chi$

and the proof of T19 made available by exercises 39 and 40, one can automatically construct the following direct derivation of ϕ in which no subsidiary derivation is indirect:

~~*Show*~~ ϕ

~~*Show*~~ $\sim\phi \rightarrow \chi$
.
.
.
~~*Show*~~ $\sim\phi \rightarrow \sim\chi$
.
.
.
~~*Show*~~ $\sim\phi \rightarrow \phi$
$\sim\phi$
χ
ϕ
~~*Show*~~ $(\sim\phi \rightarrow \phi) \rightarrow \phi$
.
.
.
ϕ

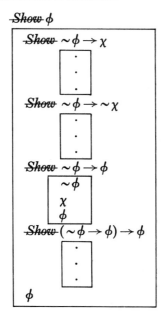

No aspect of the system consisting of two forms of derivation, direct and conditional, and two inference rules, *modus ponens* and the above variant of *modus tollens*, is superfluous.

8. Appendix: solutions to selected exercises.

Section 1

Nos. 3 and 6 are symbolic sentences. Nos. 4 and 5 are not; the former fails to be a symbolic sentence because '$\sim$', in contrast to '$\rightarrow$', does not bring with it a pair of parentheses, and the latter because 'G' is not a sentence letter.

Section 2

7. If logic is enjoyable, then Alfred will pass only if he concentrates.

8. If Alfred will pass provided that he concentrates, then logic is enjoyable. (Compare (10′), p. 7.)

9. If the text is readable, then, provided that logic is enjoyable, Alfred will not pass only if he does not concentrate.

11. $(R \rightarrow Q) \rightarrow P$

12. $[(Q \rightarrow R) \rightarrow Q] \rightarrow Q$

13. 'Only on the condition that' is a stylistic variant of 'only if'; thus we obtain first 'if Q only if R, then P if V', and then '$(Q \rightarrow R) \rightarrow (V \rightarrow P)$'.

14. Note that the sentence is not a conditional; it is symbolized by '$\sim [(P \rightarrow T) \rightarrow (U \rightarrow R)]$'.

To obtain symbolizations of the sentences in exercises 15–17, we first employ parentheses together with sentence letters and negation signs to obtain an unambiguous reading and then follow this with a symbolization.

15. (Q only if R) provided that $\sim S$; $\sim S \rightarrow (Q \rightarrow R)$
    Q only if (R provided that $\sim S$); $Q \rightarrow (\sim S \rightarrow R)$

16. $\sim R$ if $\sim V$; $\sim V \rightarrow \sim R$
    $\sim$(R if $\sim V$); $\sim(\sim V \rightarrow R)$

17. It is not the case that [T if ($\sim R$ on the condition that $\sim V$)];
    $\sim[(\sim V \rightarrow \sim R) \rightarrow T]$
    It is not the case that T if ($\sim R$ on the condition that $\sim V$);
    $(\sim V \rightarrow \sim R) \rightarrow \sim T$
    It is not the case that [(T if $\sim R$) on the condition that $\sim V$];
    $\sim[\sim V \rightarrow (\sim R \rightarrow T)]$
    It is not the case that (T if $\sim R$) on the condition that $\sim V$;
    $\sim V \rightarrow \sim(\sim R \rightarrow T)$
    (It is not the case that T if $\sim R$) on the condition that $\sim V$;
    $\sim V \rightarrow (\sim R \rightarrow \sim T)$

Section 3, Group I

26.

1.	*Show* $U \rightarrow \sim T$	Assertion (CD)
2.	U	Assumption (CD)
3.	~~*Show*~~ $\sim T$	Assertion (ID)
4.	T	Assumption (ID)
5.	$(P \rightarrow Q) \rightarrow (T \rightarrow R)$	Premise

6.	U → ∼R	Premise
7.	∼(S → P)	Premise
8.	∼R	2, 6, MP
9.	~~*Show*~~ S → P	Assertion (CD)
10.	S	Assumption (CD)
11.	~~*Show*~~ P	Assertion (ID)
12.	∼P	Assumption (ID)
13.	~~*Show*~~ P → Q	Assertion (ID)
14.	P	Assumption (CD)
15.	∼P	12, R
16.	T → R	5, 13, MP
17.	R	16, 4, MP
18.	∼R	8, R

This derivation illustrates the utility of hints (5) and (6). The applicability of hint (5) at line 9 is indicated by the premise '∼(S → P)' in line 7; and the applicability of hint (6) at line 13 is indicated by the premise '(P → Q) → (T → R)' in line 5, to which neither MP nor MT is immediately applicable. The subsidiary derivation commenced at line 13 is mixed. Also note that line 18 is required to place the contradiction within the subsidiary derivation of 'P' but that line 10 is not required. (A significantly shorter derivation is possible.)

Section 3, Group II

27. (a)

1.	~~*Show*~~ P → Q
2.	P
3.	~~*Show*~~ Q
4.	∼Q
5.	∼(P → Q) → Q
6.	∼∼(P → Q)
7.	P → Q
8.	Q

(b)

1.	~~*Show*~~ P → Q
2.	∼(P → Q)
3.	∼(P → Q) → Q
4.	~~*Show*~~ P → Q
5.	P
6.	Q

Section 4

Symbolizations for exercises 29–35 on the basis of natural schemes of abbreviation appear as follows; we leave the derivations to the reader.

29. P → Q . ∼P → R . ∼Q → ∼R ∴ Q
30. (P → Q) → R . S → ∼P . T . ∼S → (T → Q) ∴ R
31. P → Q . R → ∼S . S → P . Q → R ∴ S → ∼T
32. Q → P . R → ∼S . P → R ∴ Q → ∼S
33. (∼Q → P) → R . ∼R . ∼P → Q ∴ S
34. P → Q . ∼P → Q . ∼R → ∼Q ∴ R
35. P → Q . P → R . P → S . T → [U → (∼V → ∼S)] .
    Q → T . R → (W → U) . V → ∼W . W ∴ ∼P

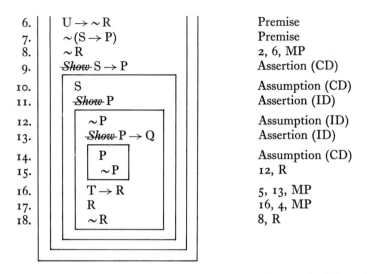

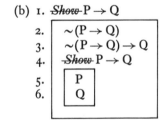

Section 6, Group I

37. T23

1.	~~*Show*~~ $[(P \rightarrow Q) \rightarrow P] \rightarrow P$	
2.	$(P \rightarrow Q) \rightarrow P$	
3.	~~*Show*~~ P	
4.	$\sim P$	
5.	$\sim(P \rightarrow Q)$	2, 4, MT
6.	~~*Show*~~ $P \rightarrow Q$	
7.	P	
8.	$\sim P$	4, R

(This proof of Peirce's law is another illustration of the utility of hint (5).)

Section 6, Group II

38. A proof of T11 using only the inference rule MP can be constructed as follows. (Note that the rule of repetition is eliminated by introducing line 5.)

1.	~~*Show*~~ $\sim\sim P \rightarrow P$	Assertion (CD)
2.	$\sim\sim P$	Assumption (CD)
3.	~~*Show*~~ P	Assertion (ID)
4.	$\sim P$	Assumption (ID)
5.	~~*Show*~~ $\sim\sim P \rightarrow \sim\sim P$	Assertion (CD)
6.	$\sim\sim P$	Assumption (CD)
7.	$\sim\sim P$	5, 2, MP

39. (a) A proof of T11 using only the inference rules MP and MT* and not employing indirect derivation can be constructed as follows. (Note that the rule of repetition is again eliminated, as above.)

1.	~~*Show*~~ $\sim\sim P \rightarrow P$	Assertion (CD)
2.	$\sim\sim P$	Assumption (CD)
3.	~~*Show*~~ $\sim P \rightarrow \sim\sim\sim P$	Assertion (CD)
4.	$\sim P$	Assumption (CD)
5.	~~*Show*~~ $\sim\sim\sim\sim P \rightarrow \sim\sim P$	Assertion (CD)
6.	~~*Show*~~ $\sim\sim P \rightarrow \sim\sim P$	Assertion (CD)
7.	$\sim\sim P$	Assumption (CD)
8.	$\sim\sim P$	6, 2, MP
9.	$\sim\sim\sim P$	5, 4, MT*
10.	P	3, 2, MT*

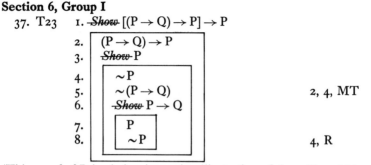

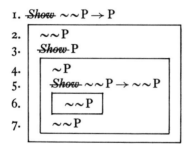

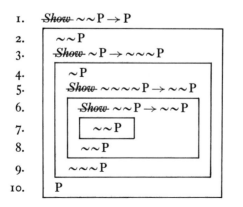

40. A proof of T19 using only the inference rules MP, MT, and MT* and not employing indirect derivation can be constructed as follows:

1.	~~*Show*~~ $(\sim P \rightarrow P) \rightarrow P$	Assertion (CD)
2.	$\sim P \rightarrow P$	Assumption (CD)
3.	~~*Show*~~ $\sim P \rightarrow \sim(\sim P \rightarrow P)$	Assertion (CD)
4.	$\sim P$	Assumption (CD)
5.	~~*Show*~~ $(\sim P \rightarrow P) \rightarrow P$	Assertion (CD)
6.	P	2, 4, MP
7.	$\sim(\sim P \rightarrow P)$	5, 4, MT
8.	P	3, 2, MT*

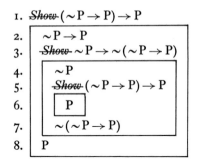

Chapter II

'AND', 'OR', 'IF AND ONLY IF'

1. Symbols and sentences. Let us add to our symbolic language three new symbols, '∧', '∨', and '↔', which symbolize, respectively, 'and', 'or', and 'if and only if'. Each of them, like '→', is used with a pair of parentheses to combine two symbolic sentences, say 'P' and 'Q', into a new symbolic sentence. Thus we obtain as symbolic sentences

(1) (P ∧ Q)
(2) (P ∨ Q)
(3) (P ↔ Q)

If we let 'P' be an abbreviation for 'Socrates is snub-nosed' and 'Q' for 'Socrates is bald', then (1)–(3) are symbolizations, respectively, for

Socrates is snub-nosed and Socrates is bald
Socrates is snub-nosed or Socrates is bald
Socrates is snub-nosed if and only if Socrates is bald .

Symbolic sentence (1) is called a *conjunction* of 'P' and 'Q', which are its *conjuncts*; (2) is called a *disjunction* of 'P' and 'Q', which are its *disjuncts*; and (3) is called a *biconditional* formed from 'P' and 'Q', which are its *constituents*. We will also apply the terms 'conjunction', 'disjunction', and 'biconditional' to English sentences symbolized, respectively, by (1)–(3).

The symbols '∼', '→', '∧', '∨', and '↔' are called *sentential connectives*. The corresponding phrases 'it is not the case that', 'if . . ., then', 'and', 'or', and 'if and only if' are called *phrases of connection*.

Sentence letters, sentential connectives, and parentheses constitute the symbols of the *symbolic language* we now consider. Thus the sentences of our symbolic language consist of sentence letters, negations, conditionals, conjunctions, disjunctions, and biconditionals, and nothing else. To be more explicit, the class of *symbolic sentences* can be exhaustively characterized as follows:

(1) Sentence letters are symbolic sentences.
(2) If ϕ is a symbolic sentence, then so is

$$\sim\phi \quad .$$

(3) If ϕ and ψ are symbolic sentences, then so are

$$(\phi \rightarrow \psi)$$
$$(\phi \wedge \psi)$$
$$(\phi \vee \psi)$$
$$(\phi \leftrightarrow \psi) \quad .$$

Notice that '$\wedge$', '$\vee$', and '$\leftrightarrow$', like '$\rightarrow$', bring with them a pair of parentheses. The ambiguity that would otherwise result is illustrated by the invitation

Bring your spouse or come alone and have a good time .

Here, as in the preceding chapter, the generation of a symbolic sentence by means of clauses (1)–(3) above can be represented by a grammatical tree. Initial nodes of a grammatical tree are sentence letters, obtained by clause (1); nonbranching nodes are negations, obtained by clause (2); and branching nodes are either conditionals, conjunctions, disjunctions, or biconditionals and are obtained by clause (3). For example, the sentence

(4) $$\sim(\sim(P \vee Q) \rightarrow (\sim Q \leftrightarrow P))$$

is generated by the following tree:

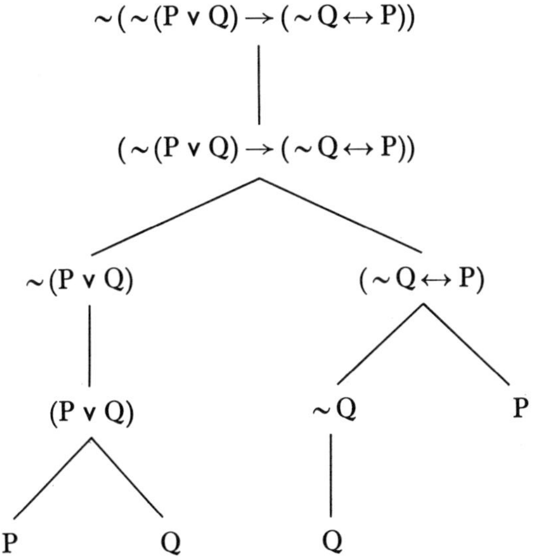

As in chapter I, we shall usually omit the outermost parentheses of a symbolic sentence and sometimes replace parentheses by brackets. In addition, '$\rightarrow$' and '$\leftrightarrow$' will be regarded as marking a greater break than '$\wedge$' and '$\vee$'. Consequently, the parentheses accompanying the latter may be omitted in certain contexts, as in the following examples. The symbolic sentence

$$(P \wedge Q) \rightarrow (R \vee S)$$

becomes

$$P \wedge Q \rightarrow R \vee S \quad ,$$

and

$$(P \vee Q) \leftrightarrow (R \wedge S)$$

becomes

$$P \vee Q \leftrightarrow R \wedge S \quad .$$

Thus we arrive informally at a larger class of symbolic sentences than that provided by clauses (1)–(3) above. In those few cases when it is necessary to draw a distinction, symbolic sentences of the smaller class may be called *symbolic sentences in the official sense.*

EXERCISES

Which of the following are symbolic sentences in the official sense? Exercises 1 and 2 are solved for illustration.

1. $\sim(\sim P \rightarrow (Q \vee R))$

According to clauses (1) and (2) of the characterization of symbolic sentences, '$\sim P$' is a symbolic sentence; and according to clauses (1) and (3), '$(Q \vee R)$' is a symbolic sentence. By clause (3), then, '$(\sim P \rightarrow (Q \vee R))$' is a symbolic sentence; thus, by clause (2), No. 1 is a symbolic sentence in the official sense. The following tree displays graphically the generation of No. 1:

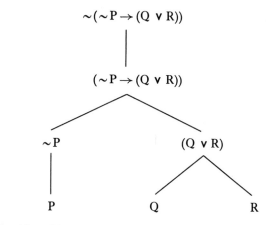

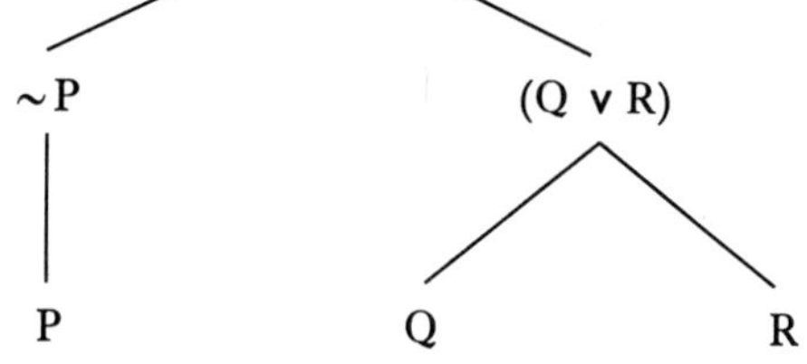

2. $(P \vee (Q \rightarrow R) \wedge \sim P)$

Because the characterization of symbolic sentences given by clauses (1)–(3) is stipulated to be exhaustive, and clauses (1) and (2), together with the fourth part of clause (3), are inapplicable, No. 2, if a symbolic sentence, must be either a disjunction, a conditional, or a conjunction of symbolic sentences. Thus either

$$P$$

and

(5) $$(Q \rightarrow R) \wedge {\sim} P$$

must be symbolic sentences, or

(6) $$P \vee (Q$$

and

(7) $$R) \wedge {\sim} P$$

must be symbolic sentences, or

(8) $$P \vee (Q \rightarrow R)$$

and

$${\sim} P$$

must be symbolic sentences. But (5), (6), and (8) (and, incidentally, (7)) are not symbolic sentences in the official sense, as the reader can easily verify. Thus No. 2 is not a symbolic sentence in the official sense.

3. $((P \leftrightarrow Q) \leftrightarrow ((P \wedge Q) \vee ({\sim} P \wedge {\sim} Q)))$
4. ${\sim}((P \vee Q \rightarrow R) \rightarrow ((P \rightarrow R) \wedge (Q \rightarrow R)))$
5. ${\sim}({\sim}({\sim}{\sim} P \vee Q) \vee R) \rightarrow (P \leftrightarrow (Q \leftrightarrow R))$

From each of the following symbolic sentences obtain a symbolic sentence in the official sense by restoring parentheses omitted by informal conventions. Exercise 6 is solved for illustration.

6. $(P \wedge Q \rightarrow P \vee Q) \leftrightarrow P \vee (Q \wedge R)$

This sentence becomes

$$(((P \wedge Q) \rightarrow (P \vee Q)) \leftrightarrow (P \vee (Q \wedge R))) \quad .$$

7. $Q \vee R \rightarrow (P \wedge R \rightarrow (Q \leftrightarrow R \vee P))$
8. $(P \wedge Q) \vee ({\sim} P \wedge {\sim} Q) \rightarrow ((P \leftrightarrow Q) \leftrightarrow (Q \leftrightarrow P))$
9. $(P \rightarrow Q \vee R) \vee (Q \vee R \rightarrow P) \leftrightarrow (Q \vee R \leftrightarrow P)$
10. ${\sim}(P \vee (Q \wedge R) \rightarrow ((P \vee Q) \wedge (P \vee R) \leftrightarrow P \wedge Q))$

2. Translation and symbolization. The process of *literal translation into English on the basis of a given scheme of abbreviation* begins as before with a symbolic sentence and if successful ends with a sentence of English.

The process consists of the following steps:

(*i*) *Restore any parentheses that may have disappeared as a result of the informal conventions of the last section.*
(*ii*) *Replace sentence letters by English sentences in accordance with the scheme of abbreviation.*
(*iii*) *Eliminate sentential connectives in favor of the corresponding phrases of connection, preserving all parentheses.*

As before, we call an English sentence a *free translation* (or simply a *translation*) of a symbolic sentence ϕ on the basis of a given scheme of abbreviation if it is a stylistic variant of the literal English translation of ϕ based on that scheme.

Let us consider, for example, the scheme of abbreviation

P : Alfred dances with Alice
Q : Alfred dances with Mary
R : Alfred will enjoy the party

and the symbolic sentence

(1) $$P \wedge Q \rightarrow R \quad .$$

In step (i) of the process of literal translation into English, this sentence becomes

$$((P \wedge Q) \rightarrow R) \quad ,$$

in step (ii)

((Alfred dances with Alice ∧ Alfred dances with Mary) → Alfred will enjoy the party) ,

and in step (iii)

(2) (If (Alfred dances with Alice and Alfred dances with Mary), then Alfred will enjoy the party) .

Thus (2) is the literal translation of (1) into English on the basis of the scheme above, and the more idiomatic sentence

(3) Alfred will enjoy the party if he dances with both Alice and Mary ,

being a stylistic variant of (2), qualifies as a free translation of (1) on the basis of the same scheme.

As regards stylistic variance, we persist in our loose practices, giving no exact definition but only a few examples. 'But', 'although', 'even though', 'both . . . and', and sometimes the relative pronouns 'who', 'which', 'that', serve as stylistic variants of 'and'; 'unless', 'either . . .

or', as stylistic variants of 'or'; and 'exactly on condition that', and sometimes 'just in case', as stylistic variants of 'if and only if'. Thus each of

> Alfred slept through class, but he passed ,
> Even though Alfred slept through class, he passed ,
> Alfred, who slept through class, passed

is regarded as a stylistic variant of

> Alfred slept through class and Alfred passed ;

> The needle on the ammeter will deflect unless the battery is dead

as a stylistic variant of

> The needle on the ammeter will deflect or the battery is dead ;

and

> Alfred will be elected exactly on condition that he stand for office ,

> Just in case Alfred stands for office will he be elected

as stylistic variants of

> Alfred will be elected if and only if Alfred stands for office .

It should be noted that 'or', and thus also its stylistic variant 'unless', has two senses in English. When a parent who is attempting to limit a child's consumption of sweets says 'ice cream or cake', the intent is to exclude the option of eating both ice cream and cake; but the host who says 'cream or sugar' is offering to a guest either cream, sugar, or both. For example, in passing from

> The picnic will occur unless it rains

to

> The picnic will occur or it rains ,

'or' is to be understood in the former, *exclusive*, sense if the intent is not to have the picnic if it rains; whereas, in passing from

> Alfred does not pass unless he studies

to

> Alfred does not pass or he studies .

'or' is to be understood in the latter, *inclusive*, sense if studying is considered necessary but not sufficient for Alfred to pass.

As a further illustration of stylistic variance, observe that the phrase 'neither . . . nor' is expressible by means of phrases of connection.

Neither ϕ nor ψ ,

where ϕ and ψ are sentences, has the stylistic variants

(It is not the case that ϕ and it is not the case that ψ)

and

It is not the case that (ϕ or ψ) .

Thus, for example,

(4) Neither Alice nor Mary danced with Alfred

could pass into

(5) It is not the case that Alice danced with Alfred *and* it is not the case that Alfred danced with Mary .

A more idiomatic form of (5), and thus also a stylistic variant of (4), is the sentence

(6) Both Alice and Mary did not dance with Alfred .

The sentence

(7) Not both Alice and Mary danced with Alfred

is sometimes confused with (6) but must be distinguished from it. For (7) has the sentence

(8) It is not the case that Alice danced with Alfred *or* it is not the case that Alfred danced with Mary

as a stylistic variant, and (8) clearly differs in meaning from (5). Thus (7), in contrast to (6), is not a stylistic variant of (4).

It should be emphasized that the *binary* sentential connectives, that is, '$\rightarrow$', '$\wedge$', '$\vee$', '$\leftrightarrow$', may stand only between sentences (or, in later chapters, between formulas). English usage, however, provides other contexts for the corresponding phrases of connection, as in the sentence (3) above,

(9) Socrates is either snub-nosed or bald ,

and

(10) Arcadia lies between Laconia and Achaea .

(3) and (9) have *canonical* stylistic variants, that is, stylistic variants in which phrases of connection operate only on sentences. We have seen this already in the case of (3), and (9) can be expanded into

(Socrates is snub-nosed or Socrates is bald) .

But (10) cannot be similarly treated; it is clearly not synonymous with

> Arcadia lies between Laconia and Arcadia lies between Achaea .

As in chapter I, we say that ϕ is a *symbolization* of an English sentence ψ on the basis of a given scheme of abbreviation just in case ϕ is a symbolic sentence which has ψ as a translation on the basis of that scheme.

To find a symbolization of a given English sentence on the basis of a given scheme of abbreviation, the reader will find it useful to proceed roughly as follows:

(1) *Introduce phrases of connection, accompanied by parentheses and occurring canonically (that is, standing only before or between sentences), in place of their stylistic variants.*

(2) *Reverse the steps leading from a symbolic sentence to a literal English translation; that is,*

(2a) *replace all parts having one of the forms*

it is not the case that ϕ ,
(*if* ϕ, *then* ψ) ,
(ϕ *and* ψ) ,
(ϕ *or* ψ) ,
(ϕ *if and only if* ψ) ,

where ϕ *and* ψ *are sentences, by*

$$\sim\phi \quad ,$$
$$(\phi \rightarrow \psi) \quad ,$$
$$(\phi \wedge \psi) \quad ,$$
$$(\phi \vee \psi) \quad ,$$
$$(\phi \leftrightarrow \psi)$$

respectively;

(2b) *replace English components by sentence letters in accordance with the scheme of abbreviation;*

(2c) *omit parentheses and insert brackets in accordance with the informal conventions of the preceding section.*

EXERCISES

11. On the basis of the scheme of abbreviation

P : Alice will dance with Alfred
Q : Mary will dance with Alfred
R : Alfred will improve his deportment

translate the following symbolic sentence into idiomatic English:

$$([\sim P \wedge \sim Q] \vee R) \wedge (R \leftrightarrow P \wedge Q) \quad .$$

Symbolize each of the following sentences on the basis of the scheme of abbreviation that accompanies it. Exercise 12 is solved for illustration.

12. Errors will decrease in the subject's performance just in case neither motivation is absent nor learning has not occurred. (P : errors will decrease in the subject's performance; Q : motivation is absent; R : learning has occurred)

In step (1) of the informal procedure for symbolizing English sentences (p. 57), we may transform No. 12 into

> (Errors will decrease in the subject's performance if and only if it is not the case that (motivation is absent or it is not the case that learning has occurred)) .

In step (2a) the sentence becomes

> (Errors will decrease in the subject's performance ↔ ~(motivation is absent v ~learning has occurred)) ;

in step (2b),

$$(P \leftrightarrow {\sim}(Q \vee {\sim}R)) \quad ;$$

and in step (2c),

$$P \leftrightarrow {\sim}(Q \vee {\sim}R) \quad .$$

13. Assuming that either logic is difficult or the text is not readable, Alfred will pass only if he concentrates. (P : logic is difficult; Q : the text is readable; R : Alfred will pass; S : Alfred concentrates)

14. Unless logic is difficult, Alfred will pass if he concentrates. (P : logic is difficult; R : Alfred will pass; S : Alfred concentrates)

15. Mary will arrive at 10:30 A.M. unless the plane is late. (P : Mary will arrive at 10:30 A.M.; Q : the plane is late)

16. Assuming that the professor is a Communist, he will sign the loyalty oath; but if he is an idealist, he will neither sign the loyalty oath nor speak to those who do. (P : the professor is a Communist; Q : the professor will sign the loyalty oath; R : the professor is an idealist; S : the professor will speak to those who sign the loyalty oath)

17. If Alfred and Mary are playing dice together, it is the first throw of the game, and Mary is throwing the dice, then she wins the game on the first throw if and only if she throws 7 or 11. (P : Alfred is playing dice; Q : Mary is playing dice; R : Alfred and Mary are playing dice together; S : it is the first throw of the game; T : Mary is throwing the dice; U : Mary wins on the first throw; V : Mary throws 7 or 11; W : Mary throws 7; X : Mary throws 11)

18. If the world is a progressively realized community of interpretation, then either quadruplicity will drink procrastination or, provided that the Nothing negates, boredom will ensue seldom more

often than frequently. (P : the world is a progressively realized community of interpretation; Q: quadruplicity will drink procrastination; R : the Nothing negates; S : boredom will ensue seldom more often than frequently)

The following sentences are ambiguous in the sense that the placement of parentheses in their symbolizations is not uniquely determined. Give all plausible symbolizations of each on the basis of the given scheme of abbreviation. Exercise 19 is solved for illustration.

19. Errors will occur in the subject's performance if and only if motivation is absent or learning has not taken place.

Given the scheme of abbreviation

P : errors will occur in the subject's performance
Q : motivation is absent
R : learning has taken place ,

No. 19 becomes in step (1) either

(Errors will occur in the subject's performance if and only if (motivation is absent or it is not the case that learning has taken place))

or

((Errors will occur in the subject's performance if and only if motivation is absent) or it is not the case that learning has taken place) ;

and in step (2) it correspondingly becomes either

$$P \leftrightarrow Q \vee \sim R$$

or

$$(P \leftrightarrow Q) \vee \sim R \quad .$$

20. If either a war or a depression occurs then neither science nor music and literature will flourish unless the government supports research and provides patronage for artists. (P : a war occurs; Q : a depression occurs; R : science will flourish; S : music will flourish; T : literature will flourish; U : the government will support research; V : the government will provide patronage for artists)

21. Neither Alfred will listen nor Rudolf will listen if Alonzo is talking to either. (P : Alfred will listen; Q : Rudolf will listen; R : Alonzo is talking to Alfred; S : Alonzo is talking to Rudolf)

3. Inference rules and derivability. The *sentential calculus* is that branch of logic which essentially involves the sentential connectives. For a complete formulation of the sentential calculus, we must add to the apparatus of chapter I the following inference rules for the new sentential connectives.

Simplification (S), in two forms: $\dfrac{(\phi \wedge \psi)}{\phi}$ $\dfrac{(\phi \wedge \psi)}{\psi}$

Adjunction (Adj): $\dfrac{\begin{array}{c}\phi\\ \psi\end{array}}{(\phi \wedge \psi)}$

Addition (Add), in two forms: $\dfrac{\phi}{(\phi \vee \psi)}$ $\dfrac{\phi}{(\psi \vee \phi)}$

Modus tollendo ponens (MTP), in two forms: $\dfrac{\begin{array}{c}(\phi \vee \psi)\\ \sim\phi\end{array}}{\psi}$ $\dfrac{\begin{array}{c}(\phi \vee \psi)\\ \sim\psi\end{array}}{\phi}$

Biconditional-conditional (BC), in two forms: $\dfrac{(\phi \leftrightarrow \psi)}{(\phi \rightarrow \psi)}$ $\dfrac{(\phi \leftrightarrow \psi)}{(\psi \rightarrow \phi)}$

Conditional-biconditional (CB): $\dfrac{\begin{array}{c}(\phi \rightarrow \psi)\\ (\psi \rightarrow \phi)\end{array}}{(\phi \leftrightarrow \psi)}$

Thus one symbolic sentence is said to follow from another by *simplification* just in case the former is a conjunct of the latter; a symbolic sentence follows by *adjunction* from two others just in case it is their conjunction; and so on. When

$$(\phi \vee \psi)$$

or

$$(\psi \vee \phi)$$

is inferred from ϕ by Add, the symbolic sentence ψ is called the *added disjunct*.

We display some examples of inferences by our new rules.

Simplification: $\dfrac{\sim P \wedge Q}{\sim P}$ $\dfrac{P \wedge (Q \rightarrow R)}{Q \rightarrow R}$

Adjunction: $\dfrac{\begin{array}{c}\sim P\\ Q\end{array}}{\sim P \wedge Q}$

Addition: $\dfrac{P}{P \vee \sim Q}$ $\dfrac{\sim Q}{P \vee \sim Q}$

(In the left-hand example '$\sim Q$' is the added disjunct; in the right-hand example 'P' is the added disjunct.)

Modus tollendo ponens:

$$\frac{P \vee \sim Q \quad \sim P}{\sim Q} \qquad \frac{P \vee \sim Q \quad \sim\sim Q}{P}$$

Biconditional-conditional:

$$\frac{P \leftrightarrow (Q \vee R)}{P \rightarrow (Q \vee R)} \qquad \frac{P \leftrightarrow (Q \vee R)}{(Q \vee R) \rightarrow P}$$

Conditional-biconditional:

$$\frac{P \rightarrow (Q \vee R) \quad (Q \vee R) \rightarrow P}{P \leftrightarrow (Q \vee R)}$$

We have at our disposal several conventions for dropping parentheses, but they must be used with caution. In particular, when applying inference rules, we must mentally restore omitted parentheses. For example,

(1) $$\frac{P \wedge Q \rightarrow R}{Q \rightarrow R}$$

might seem to be a case of simplification, and

(2) $$\frac{P}{P \vee Q \rightarrow R}$$

a case of addition. But when parentheses are restored according to our conventions, (1) and (2) become respectively

$$\frac{((P \wedge Q) \rightarrow R)}{(Q \rightarrow R)}$$

and

$$\frac{P}{((P \vee Q) \rightarrow R)},$$

which clearly do not constitute applications of our rules. Indeed, the inferences (1) and (2) *should not* fall under our rules. For (1) is comparable to the inference from

> If San Francisco is larger than New York and New York is larger than Los Angeles, then San Francisco is larger than Los Angeles

to

> If New York is larger than Los Angeles, then San Francisco is larger than Los Angeles ,

and (2) to the inference from

Socrates is bald

to

If either Socrates is bald or Socrates is snub-nosed, then Socrates is unmarried .

'Or', as we noticed earlier, has two senses.

ϕ or ψ

may mean either

either ϕ or ψ, but not both ,

or

either ϕ, or ψ, or both .

We select the second sense. This choice is reflected in our adoption of the rule Add; for if the first sense were selected, the inference

Socrates is bald. ∴ Socrates is bald or Socrates is snub-nosed

would lead from truth to falsehood. Though we shall use 'v' in the second sense of 'or', it is clear that the first sense can still be expressed by a combination of 'v', '∼', and '∧':

$$(\phi \vee \psi) \wedge \sim(\phi \wedge \psi) \quad .$$

'If and only if' is a composite of 'if' and 'only if'.

ϕ if and only if ψ

asserts

ϕ if ψ

and

ϕ only if ψ .

This is reflected in our two rules BC and CB, by which the biconditional

$$\phi \leftrightarrow \psi$$

is related to the conditional

$$\psi \rightarrow \phi$$

and its *converse*,

$$\phi \rightarrow \psi \quad .$$

The directions for constructing a *derivation from given symbolic premises* (p. 24) and the definitions of a *complete* derivation (p. 25), of *derivability*

(p. 25), of a *theorem* (p. 40), and of a *proof* (p. 40) are carried over intact from chapter I. However, the interpretation of the phrase 'an inference rule' (which occurs in clause (5) of the directions for constructing a derivation) is extended so as to include our new inference rules (S, Adj, Add, MTP, BC, and CB) as well as MP, MT, DN, and R. Annotations will again be employed, but now only to indicate the introduction of a premise (clause (2)) or the application of an inference rule (clause (5)).

EXERCISES

22. For each of the following inferences, state whether or not it is an application of S, Adj, Add, MTP, BC, or CB.

(a) $$\begin{array}{l} \sim(P \wedge Q) \\ \hline \sim Q \end{array}$$

(b) $$\begin{array}{l} \sim(P \vee Q) \wedge [(R \rightarrow \sim P) \leftrightarrow S] \\ \hline \sim(P \vee Q) \end{array}$$

(c) $$\begin{array}{l} \sim P \wedge Q \rightarrow R \\ \hline \sim P \end{array}$$

(d) $$\begin{array}{l} (R \vee S) \\ Q \leftrightarrow P \\ \hline (R \vee S) \wedge Q \leftrightarrow P \end{array}$$

(e) $$\begin{array}{l} \sim P \\ \sim(Q \leftrightarrow R) \\ \hline \sim[P \wedge (Q \leftrightarrow R)] \end{array}$$

(f) $$\begin{array}{l} R \rightarrow S \\ \hline (R \rightarrow S) \vee (S \rightarrow Q) \end{array}$$

(g) $$\begin{array}{l} P \rightarrow Q \\ \hline P \rightarrow Q \vee R \end{array}$$

(h) $$\begin{array}{l} P \wedge \sim Q \\ \hline (P \vee Q) \wedge (\sim Q \vee R) \end{array}$$

(i) $$\begin{array}{l} \sim(R \vee S) \vee (P \rightarrow S) \\ \sim(P \rightarrow S) \\ \hline \sim(R \vee S) \end{array}$$

(j) $$\begin{array}{l} P \vee \sim(Q \wedge R) \\ \sim P \\ \hline Q \wedge R \end{array}$$

(k) $$\begin{array}{l} (P \vee Q) \rightarrow R \\ \sim P \\ \hline Q \end{array}$$

(l) $$\begin{array}{l} \sim(P \leftrightarrow Q) \\ \hline \sim(P \rightarrow Q) \end{array}$$

(m) $$\begin{array}{l} P \leftrightarrow Q \wedge R \\ \hline Q \rightarrow P \end{array}$$

(n) $$\begin{array}{l} P \wedge Q \rightarrow R \\ R \rightarrow P \wedge Q \\ \hline R \leftrightarrow P \wedge Q \end{array}$$

(o) $$\begin{array}{l} (P \rightarrow Q) \rightarrow R \\ R \rightarrow (Q \rightarrow P) \\ \hline R \leftrightarrow (P \leftrightarrow Q) \end{array}$$

4. Theorems with unabbreviated proofs. It is convenient, in developing the full sentential calculus, to depart from the order of presentation of chapter I. We begin not with derivations involving premises but with proofs of theorems. The first group of theorems primarily concern the connectives '$\sim$', '$\rightarrow$', and '$\wedge$'. T24 is the *commutative law* for '$\wedge$'.

T24

1.	~~Show~~ $P \wedge Q \leftrightarrow Q \wedge P$	
2.	~~Show~~ $P \wedge Q \rightarrow Q \wedge P$	
3.	$P \wedge Q$	
4.	Q	3, S
5.	P	3, S
6.	$Q \wedge P$	4, 5, Adj
7.	~~Show~~ $Q \wedge P \rightarrow P \wedge Q$	
	Similar	
8.	$P \wedge Q \leftrightarrow Q \wedge P$	2, 7, CB

T25 is the *associative law* for '$\wedge$'.

T25 $$P \wedge (Q \wedge R) \leftrightarrow (P \wedge Q) \wedge R$$

Here, as in the case of T24, we prove explicitly only one conditional. The converse can be proved in a similar way, and the biconditional will then follow by CB.

1.	~~Show~~ $P \wedge (Q \wedge R) \rightarrow (P \wedge Q) \wedge R$	
2.	$P \wedge (Q \wedge R)$	
3.	P	2, S
4.	$Q \wedge R$	2, S
5.	Q	4, S
6.	$P \wedge Q$	3, 5, Adj
7.	R	4, S
8.	$(P \wedge Q) \wedge R$	6, 7, Adj

A new informal convention for the omission of parentheses will prove convenient. In a repeated conjunction in which all terms are associated to the left, the internal parentheses may be omitted. For instance,

$$(P \wedge Q) \wedge R$$

becomes

$$P \wedge Q \wedge R \quad ,$$

and

$$([P \wedge Q] \wedge R) \wedge S$$

becomes

$$P \wedge Q \wedge R \wedge S \quad .$$

However, the parentheses of

$$P \wedge (Q \wedge R)$$

may not be omitted. T25 may now be formulated as

$$P \wedge (Q \wedge R) \leftrightarrow P \wedge Q \wedge R \quad .$$

T26, like T4 and T5, is a principle of *syllogism*.

T26 $(P \to Q) \wedge (Q \to R) \to (P \to R)$

T27 is known as the law of *exportation*.

T27

1.	~~*Show*~~ $(P \wedge Q \to R) \leftrightarrow (P \to [Q \to R])$	
2.	~~*Show*~~ $(P \wedge Q \to R) \to (P \to [Q \to R])$	
3.	$P \wedge Q \to R$	
4.	~~*Show*~~ $P \to [Q \to R]$	
5.	P	
6.	~~*Show*~~ $Q \to R$	
7.	Q	
8.	$P \wedge Q$	5, 7, Adj
9.	R	3, 8, MP
10.	~~*Show*~~ $(P \to [Q \to R]) \to (P \wedge Q \to R)$	
11.	$P \to [Q \to R]$	
12.	~~*Show*~~ $P \wedge Q \to R$	
13.	$P \wedge Q$	
14.	P	13, S
15.	$Q \to R$	11, 14, MP
16.	Q	13, S
17.	R	15, 16, MP
18.	$(P \wedge Q \to R) \leftrightarrow (P \to [Q \to R])$	2, 10, CB

T28 $(P \wedge Q \to R) \leftrightarrow (P \wedge {\sim} R \to {\sim} Q)$

T29 is the principle of *distribution* of '$\to$' over '$\wedge$'.

T29 $(P \to Q \wedge R) \leftrightarrow (P \to Q) \wedge (P \to R)$

T30 and T31 are *factor* principles.

T30 $(P \to Q) \to (R \wedge P \to R \wedge Q)$

T31 $(P \to Q) \to (P \wedge R \to Q \wedge R)$

T32 is Leibniz' *praeclarum theorema*.

T32

1.	~~*Show*~~ $(P \to R) \wedge (Q \to S) \to (P \wedge Q \to R \wedge S)$	
2.	$(P \to R) \wedge (Q \to S)$	
3.	~~*Show*~~ $P \wedge Q \to R \wedge S$	
4.	$P \wedge Q$	
5.	$P \to R$	2, S
6.	P	4, S
7.	R	5, 6, MP
8.	$Q \to S$	2, S
9.	Q	4, S
10.	S	8, 9, MP
11.	$R \wedge S$	7, 10, Adj

T33 is a principle of *dilemma.*

T33

1.	~~*Show*~~ $(P \to Q) \wedge (\sim P \to Q) \to Q$	
2.	$(P \to Q) \wedge (\sim P \to Q)$	
3.	~~*Show*~~ Q	
4.	$\sim Q$	
5.	$P \to Q$	2, S
6.	$\sim P$	4, 5, MT
7.	$\sim P \to Q$	2, S
8.	$\sim \sim P$	4, 7, MT

T34, like T19 and T20, is a law of *reductio ad absurdum.*

T34 $\quad (P \to Q) \wedge (P \to \sim Q) \to \sim P$

T35

1.	~~*Show*~~ $(\sim P \to R) \wedge (Q \to R) \leftrightarrow ([P \to Q] \to R)$	
2.	~~*Show*~~ $(\sim P \to R) \wedge (Q \to R) \to ([P \to Q] \to R)$	
3.	$(\sim P \to R) \wedge (Q \to R)$	
4.	~~*Show*~~ $[P \to Q] \to R$	
5.	$P \to Q$	
6.	~~*Show*~~ R	

7.	∼R	
8.	Q → R	3, S
9.	∼Q	7, 8, MT
10.	∼P	9, 5, MT
11.	∼P → R	3, S
12.	R	10, 11, MP
13.	~~*Show*~~ ([P → Q] → R) → (∼P → R) ∧ (Q → R)	
14.	[P → Q] → R	
15.	~~*Show*~~ ∼P → R	
16.	∼P	
17.	~~*Show*~~ P → Q	
18.	P	
19.	∼P	16, R
20.	R	14, 17, MP
21.	~~*Show*~~ Q → R	
22.	Q	
23.	~~*Show*~~ P → Q	
24.	Q	22, R
25.	R	14, 23, MP
26.	(∼P → R) ∧ (Q → R)	15, 21, Adj
27.	(∼P → R) ∧ (Q → R) ↔ ([P → Q] → R)	2, 13, CB

T36 is the law of *contradiction.*

T36

1.	~~*Show*~~ ∼(P ∧ ∼P)	
2.	P ∧ ∼P	
3.	P	2, S
4.	∼P	2, S

T37 shows how to express '→' by means of '∼' and '∧', and T38 how to express '∧' by means of '∼' and '→'. T39 and T40 provide alternative expressions for the negation of a conjunction and of a conditional.

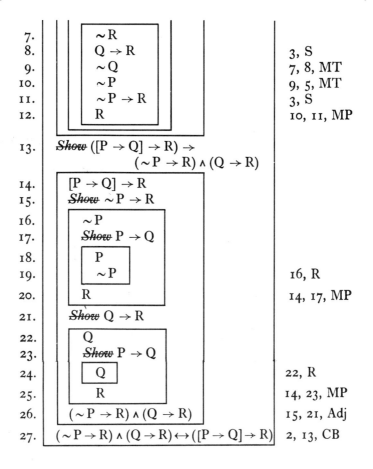

T37

1. ~~*Show*~~ $(P \to Q) \leftrightarrow \sim(P \wedge \sim Q)$
2. ~~*Show*~~ $(P \to Q) \to \sim(P \wedge \sim Q)$
3. $P \to Q$
4. ~~*Show*~~ $\sim(P \wedge \sim Q)$
5. $P \wedge \sim Q$
6. P — 5, S
7. Q — 3, 6, MP
8. $\sim Q$ — 5, S
9. ~~*Show*~~ $\sim(P \wedge \sim Q) \to (P \to Q)$
10. $\sim(P \wedge \sim Q)$
11. ~~*Show*~~ $P \to Q$
12. P
13. ~~*Show*~~ Q
14. $\sim Q$
15. $P \wedge \sim Q$ — 12, 14, Adj
16. $\sim(P \wedge \sim Q)$ — 10, R
17. $(P \to Q) \leftrightarrow \sim(P \wedge \sim Q)$ — 2, 9, CB

T38 $P \wedge Q \leftrightarrow \sim(P \to \sim Q)$

T39 $\sim(P \wedge Q) \leftrightarrow (P \to \sim Q)$

T40 $\sim(P \to Q) \leftrightarrow P \wedge \sim Q$

T41 is the law of *idempotence* for '∧', and T42–T44 will be cited in chapter IX.

T41 $P \leftrightarrow P \wedge P$

T42 $P \wedge \sim Q \to \sim(P \to Q)$

T43 $\sim P \to \sim(P \wedge Q)$

T44 $\sim Q \to \sim(P \wedge Q)$

EXERCISES

23. Prove T28, T29, T34.
24. Prove T38, T44.

In solving these exercises, which essentially involve only '∼', '→', and '∧', the reader will find the following strategic hints, some of which appeared in chapter I, helpful (but not infallible).

(1) *To derive a conditional, use conditional derivation.*

(2) *To derive a conjunction, derive first both conjuncts and then use Adj.*

(3) *To derive a biconditional, derive first the two corresponding conditionals and then use CB.*

(4) *To derive anything else, use indirect derivation unless another procedure is immediately obvious.*

(5) *Whenever a sentence follows from antecedent lines by MP, MT, S, MTP, or BC, enter that sentence as a line.*

(6) *When using indirect derivation, determine whether any of the antecedent lines is the negation of a conditional; if so, attempt to derive that conditional.*

T40 is proved for illustration. We begin the proof by writing '*Show*' followed by the sentence to be proved. This sentence is a biconditional; thus, following (3) and (1) of the foregoing hints, we begin a conditional derivation of one of the corresponding conditionals.

1. *Show* $\sim(P \rightarrow Q) \leftrightarrow P \wedge \sim Q$
2. *Show* $\sim(P \rightarrow Q) \rightarrow P \wedge \sim Q$
3. $\sim(P \rightarrow Q)$

In order to complete the subsidiary conditional derivation we must derive a conjunction; thus, following hints (2) and (4), we begin an indirect derivation of one of its conjuncts.

1. *Show* $\sim(P \rightarrow Q) \leftrightarrow P \wedge \sim Q$
2. *Show* $\sim(P \rightarrow Q) \rightarrow P \wedge \sim Q$
3. $\sim(P \rightarrow Q)$
4. *Show* P
5. $\sim P$

Consideration of the lines now before us and hint (6) lead us to begin next a conditional derivation of the sentence whose negation occurs in line 3, and this can be completed after an application of rule R.

1. *Show* $\sim(P \rightarrow Q) \leftrightarrow P \wedge \sim Q$
2. *Show* $\sim(P \rightarrow Q) \rightarrow P \wedge \sim Q$
3. $\sim(P \rightarrow Q)$
4. *Show* P
5. $\sim P$
6. ~~*Show*~~ $P \rightarrow Q$
7. P
8. $\sim P$ 5, R

We now complete the subsidiary derivation of 'P' and, returning to hints (2) and (4), begin an indirect derivation of '$\sim$Q', which we can complete by employing hint (6) again.

1. *Show* $\sim(P \to Q) \leftrightarrow P \wedge \sim Q$
2. *Show* $\sim(P \to Q) \to P \wedge \sim Q$
3. $\sim(P \to Q)$
4. ~~*Show*~~ P
5. $\sim P$
6. ~~*Show*~~ $P \to Q$
7. P
8. $\sim P$ — 5, R
9. $\sim(P \to Q)$ — 3, R
10. ~~*Show*~~ $\sim Q$
11. Q
12. ~~*Show*~~ $P \to Q$
13. Q — 11, R
14. $\sim(P \to Q)$ — 3, R

Now, following through hint (2), we employ adjunction in order to complete the subsidiary derivation started in line 2.

1. *Show* $\sim(P \to Q) \leftrightarrow P \wedge \sim Q$
2. ~~*Show*~~ $\sim(P \to Q) \to P \wedge \sim Q$
3. $\sim(P \to Q)$
4. ~~*Show*~~ P
5. $\sim P$
6. ~~*Show*~~ $P \to Q$
7. P
8. $\sim P$ — 5, R
9. $\sim(P \to Q)$ — 3, R
10. ~~*Show*~~ $\sim Q$
11. Q
12. ~~*Show*~~ $P \to Q$
13. Q — 11, R
14. $\sim(P \to Q)$ — 3, R
15. $P \wedge \sim Q$ — 4, 10, Adj

To complete the main derivation we derive next the converse of the conditional that occurs in line 2 and then, following through hint (3), employ CB.

1. ~~*Show*~~ $\sim(P \to Q) \leftrightarrow P \wedge \sim Q$
2. ~~*Show*~~ $\sim(P \to Q) \to P \wedge \sim Q$
3. $\sim(P \to Q)$
4. ~~*Show*~~ P

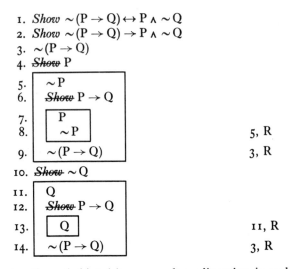

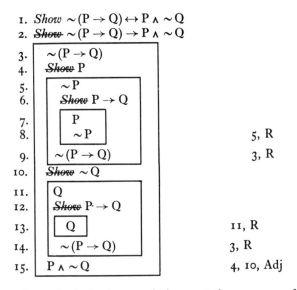

5.	$\sim P$	
6.	~~*Show*~~ $P \rightarrow Q$	
7.	P	
8.	$\sim P$	5, R
9.	$\sim (P \rightarrow Q)$	3, R
10.	~~*Show*~~ $\sim Q$	
11.	Q	
12.	~~*Show*~~ $P \rightarrow Q$	
13.	Q	11, R
14.	$\sim (P \rightarrow Q)$	3, R
15.	$P \wedge \sim Q$	4, 10, Adj
16.	~~*Show*~~ $P \wedge \sim Q \rightarrow \sim (P \rightarrow Q)$	
17.	$P \wedge \sim Q$	
18.	~~*Show*~~ $\sim (P \rightarrow Q)$	
19.	$P \rightarrow Q$	
20.	P	17, S
21.	Q	19, 20, MP
22.	$\sim Q$	17, S
23.	$\sim (P \rightarrow Q) \leftrightarrow P \wedge \sim Q$	2, 16, CB

5. Abbreviated derivations. It will be useful, from time to time, to append to the directions for constructing a derivation what we shall call *abbreviatory clauses;* we shall thus arrive at a more comprehensive class of derivations, called *abbreviated derivations,* which will be constructed on the basis of clauses (1) – (6) along with the new clauses. Abbreviatory clauses must satisfy two conditions. In the first place, they must be theoretically dispensable; that is to say, whenever a conclusion can be derived from a class of premises by means of an abbreviated derivation, it must also be derivable from the same premises by means of some *unabbreviated derivation* (a derivation constructed on the basis of clauses (1) – (6) alone). In the second place, abbreviated derivations must share the important characteristic of unabbreviated derivations pointed out earlier: there must be an automatic procedure for checking the correctness of an abbreviated derivation (at least when membership in the class of premises is automatically decidable).

For the sentential calculus we shall adopt only two abbreviatory clauses, (7) and (8), which, when adjoined to clauses (1) – (6), will constitute the directions for constructing an *abbreviated derivation,* or, as we shall henceforth say, a *derivation.* The fact that clauses (7) and (8) satisfy the two conditions mentioned above will be fairly obvious but will not be established in a formal way.

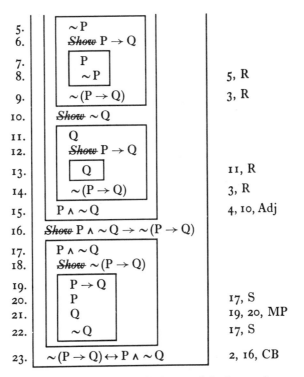

For clause (7) we must introduce a new notion. By an *instance* of a symbolic sentence ϕ we shall understand any symbolic sentence obtained from ϕ by replacing sentence letters uniformly by symbolic sentences. (The replacement is *uniform* just in case all occurrences of a sentence letter are replaced by the same sentence.)

For example, T2,

$$Q \rightarrow (P \rightarrow Q) \quad ,$$

has as an instance

$$Q \rightarrow ({\sim} R \rightarrow Q) \quad .$$

In this case, we have replaced 'P' by '$\sim$R' and 'Q' by 'Q' itself. We may indicate this replacement diagrammatically as follows:

$$\begin{array}{cc} Q & P \\ \hline Q & {\sim}R \end{array} \quad .$$

Other instances of T2, together with an indication of the replacements by which they were obtained, are:

(1) $\quad {\sim}R \rightarrow (Q \rightarrow {\sim}R) \quad ; \qquad \begin{array}{cc} Q & P \\ \hline {\sim}R & Q \end{array}$

(2) $\quad P \rightarrow ([R \rightarrow T] \rightarrow P) \quad ; \qquad \begin{array}{cc} Q & P \\ \hline P & R \rightarrow T \end{array}$

(3) $\quad Q \vee P \rightarrow ([P \rightarrow Q] \rightarrow Q \vee P) \quad ; \qquad \begin{array}{cc} Q & P \\ \hline Q \vee P & P \rightarrow Q \end{array}$

(4) $\quad Q \rightarrow (P \rightarrow Q) \quad ; \qquad \begin{array}{cc} Q & P \\ \hline Q & P \end{array}$

(5) $\quad P \rightarrow (Q \rightarrow P) \quad ; \qquad \begin{array}{cc} Q & P \\ \hline P & Q \end{array}$

As a further example, T26,

$$(P \rightarrow Q) \wedge (Q \rightarrow R) \rightarrow (P \rightarrow R) \quad ,$$

has as an instance

$$([S \rightarrow T] \rightarrow T) \wedge (T \rightarrow S) \rightarrow ([S \rightarrow T] \rightarrow S) \quad ,$$

obtained by the replacement

$$\begin{array}{ccc} P & Q & R \\ \hline S \rightarrow T & T & S \end{array} \quad .$$

The relation 'ϕ is an instance of ψ' is intended to apply only to symbolic sentences. (This accords with our previous decision to apply deductive procedures only to symbolic sentences.)

It is because of clause (7) that theorems are important. Having proved a theorem, we may then use it in a later derivation without repeating its proof. Indeed, we may use as well any of its instances, for their proofs could be obtained by a simple procedure of replacement from the original proof.

(7) *If ϕ is an instance of a theorem already proved, then ϕ may occur as a line.* (*Annotation: the number of the theorem of which ϕ is an instance, sometimes together with a diagrammatic indication of the replacement involved.*)

For example, clause (7) provides the justification for lines 3 and 5 in the following abbreviated derivation.

1.	~~Show~~ $([P \to Q] \to Q) \wedge (Q \to P) \to P$	
2.	$([P \to Q] \to Q) \wedge (Q \to P)$	
3.	$([P \to Q] \to Q) \wedge (Q \to P) \to ([P \to Q] \to P)$	$T26\left(\frac{P}{P \to Q}\ \frac{Q}{Q}\ \frac{R}{P}\right)$
4.	$[P \to Q] \to P$	2, 3, MP
5.	$([P \to Q] \to P) \to P$	T23
6.	P	4, 5, MP

It is often convenient to compress several steps into one, omitting some lines that an unabbreviated derivation would require. Such compression will be allowed only when no clauses other than (2) (premises), (5) (inference rules), and (7) (instances of previously proved theorems) are involved, and is legitimized by clause (8).

(8) *A symbolic sentence may occur as a line if it is the last in a succession of steps and each step in the succession is either an antecedent line or can be justified by one of clauses* (2), (5), *or* (7). (*The annotation should determine the succession of steps leading to the line in question. This can be done by indicating, in order of application, the antecedent lines, the premises, the inference rules, and the previously proved theorems employed. Also, in connection with the rule Add, the added disjunct should be indicated whenever there is a chance of ambiguity; and when an instance of a previously proved theorem is involved, the relevant replacement, if not obvious, should be indicated.*)

For example, clause (8) provides the justification for line 5 in the following abbreviated derivation.

1.	~~Show~~ $(P \to Q) \to (R \wedge P \to R \wedge Q)$	
2.	$P \to Q$	
3.	~~Show~~ $R \wedge P \to R \wedge Q$	
4.	$R \wedge P$	
5.	$R \wedge Q$	4, S, 2, MP, 4, S, Adj

The omitted lines are, in order:

i.	P	(4, S)
ii.	Q	(i, 2, MP)
iii.	R	(4, S)

Line 5 follows from (ii) and (iii) by Adj. Clause (8) also provides the justification for lines 3, 4, and 5 in the derivation accompanying the following argument:

$$(Q \rightarrow P) \rightarrow P \quad . \quad P \rightarrow Q \quad \therefore Q$$

1.	~~*Show*~~ Q	
2.	$\sim Q$	
3.	$\sim P$	2, 2nd premise, MT
4.	$Q \rightarrow P$	2, T18$\left(\frac{P \quad Q}{Q \quad P}\right)$, MP
5.	P	4, 1st premise, MP

An unabbreviated derivation of the conclusion from the given premises can be obtained by inserting in the abbreviated derivation the omitted lines, along with a subsidiary derivation of the instance of the theorem employed. The following is an example of such a derivation.

1.	~~*Show*~~ Q	
2.	$\sim Q$	
3.	$P \rightarrow Q$	Premise
4.	$\sim P$	2, 3, MT
5.	~~*Show*~~ $\sim Q \rightarrow (Q \rightarrow P)$	
6.	$\sim Q$	
7.	~~*Show*~~ $Q \rightarrow P$	
8.	Q	
9.	$\sim Q$	6, R
10.	$Q \rightarrow P$	2, 5, MP
11.	$(Q \rightarrow P) \rightarrow P$	Premise
12.	P	10, 11, MP

Abbreviated derivations, unlike unabbreviated derivations, require as an essential part their annotations—at least those annotations given in connection with clause (8). For without an indication of omitted steps, it would be impossible, even for the simple logical system now under consideration, to give an automatic procedure for checking the correctness of an abbreviated derivation.

EXERCISES

Corresponding to the following argument, two abbreviated derivations are given.

(6) $\sim P \rightarrow R \quad . \quad P \rightarrow Q \quad . \quad Q \rightarrow R \quad \therefore R$

(7)

1. ~~*Show*~~ *R*
2. $\sim R$
3. $\sim Q$
4. $\sim P$
5. R

(8)

1. ~~*Show*~~ *R*
2. $P \rightarrow R$ 2nd premise, 3rd premise, Adj, T26, MP
3. R 2, 1st premise, Adj, T33$\left(\frac{P \quad Q}{P \quad R}\right)$, MP

25. Annotate the derivation (7).

26. Construct an unabbreviated derivation corresponding to (6), using indirect derivation. (Consider (7) and its annotations.)

27. Construct an unabbreviated derivation corresponding to (6), using direct derivation. (Consider (8).)

Show, by constructing derivations in which at least one step is justified either by clause (7) or by clause (8), that the following arguments are valid.

28. $(P \rightarrow Q) \rightarrow R \quad . \quad \sim P \quad \therefore R$

29. $(P \rightarrow Q) \rightarrow R \quad . \quad Q \quad \therefore R$

(The reader should attempt two-line derivations in each case and may find T18 and T2 useful.)

6. Theorems with abbreviated proofs. Many of the remaining derivations of this chapter are considerably simplified by the addition of clauses (7) and (8) to the directions for constructing a derivation.

Now we consider theorems primarily concerned with 'v' as well as '~', '→', and '∧'. T45 shows how to express 'v' in terms of '~' and '→', and T46 shows how to express '→' in terms of '~' and 'v'. Clause (8) is used in the proof of T45.

T45

1.	~~Show~~ $P \vee Q \leftrightarrow (\sim P \rightarrow Q)$	
2.	~~Show~~ $P \vee Q \rightarrow (\sim P \rightarrow Q)$	
3.	$P \vee Q$	
4.	~~Show~~ $\sim P \rightarrow Q$	
5.	$\sim P$	
6.	Q	5, 3, MTP
7.	~~Show~~ $(\sim P \rightarrow Q) \rightarrow P \vee Q$	
8.	$\sim P \rightarrow Q$	
9.	~~Show~~ $P \vee Q$	
10.	$\sim(P \vee Q)$	
11.	~~Show~~ $\sim P$	
12.	P	
13.	$P \vee Q$	12, Add
14.	$\sim(P \vee Q)$	10, R
15.	$P \vee Q$	8, 11, MP, Add
16.	$P \vee Q \leftrightarrow (\sim P \rightarrow Q)$	2, 7, CB

T46 $(P \rightarrow Q) \leftrightarrow \sim P \vee Q$

T47 is the law of *idempotence* for 'v'.

T47

1.	~~Show~~ $P \leftrightarrow P \vee P$	
2.	~~Show~~ $P \rightarrow P \vee P$	
3.	P	
4.	$P \vee P$	3, Add
5.	~~Show~~ $P \vee P \rightarrow P$	
6.	$P \vee P$	
7.	~~Show~~ P	
8.	$\sim P$	
9.	P	6, 8, MTP
10.	$P \leftrightarrow P \vee P$	2, 5, CB

T48 and T49, like T33, are principles of *dilemma*.

T48

1.	~~Show~~ $(P \vee Q) \wedge (P \rightarrow R) \wedge (Q \rightarrow S) \rightarrow R \vee S$	
2.	$(P \vee Q) \wedge (P \rightarrow R) \wedge (Q \rightarrow S)$	
3.	~~Show~~ $\sim R \rightarrow S$	
4.	$\sim R$	
5.	$(P \vee Q) \wedge (P \rightarrow R)$	2, S

6.	$Q \to S$	2, S
7.	S	5, S, 4, MT, 5, S, MTP, 6, MP
8.	$R \vee S$	T45$\left(\frac{P \quad Q}{R \quad S}\right)$, BC, 3, MP

T49

1.	~~*Show*~~ $(P \vee Q) \wedge (P \to R) \wedge (Q \to R) \to R$	
2.	$(P \vee Q) \wedge (P \to R) \wedge (Q \to R)$	
3.	R	T48$\left(\frac{P \quad Q \quad R \quad S}{P \quad Q \quad R \quad R}\right)$, 2, MP, T47$\left(\frac{P}{R}\right)$, BC, MP

T50 is a principle of *composition.*

T50

1.	~~*Show*~~ $(P \to R) \wedge (Q \to R) \leftrightarrow (P \vee Q \to R)$	
2.	~~*Show*~~ $(P \to R) \wedge (Q \to R) \to (P \vee Q \to R)$	
3.	$(P \to R) \wedge (Q \to R)$	
4.	~~*Show*~~ $P \vee Q \to R$	
5.	$P \vee Q$	
6.	R	5, 3, Adj, T49, MP
7.	~~*Show*~~ $(P \vee Q \to R) \to (P \to R) \wedge (Q \to R)$	
8.	$P \vee Q \to R$	
9.	~~*Show*~~ $P \to R$	
10.	P	
11.	R	10, Add, 8, MP
12.	~~*Show*~~ $Q \to R$	
13.	Q	
14.	R	13, Add, 8, MP
15.	$(P \to R) \wedge (Q \to R)$	9, 12, Adj
16.	$(P \to R) \wedge (Q \to R) \leftrightarrow (P \vee Q \to R)$	2, 7, CB

T51 $(P \vee Q) \wedge (P \to R) \wedge (\sim P \wedge Q \to R) \to R$

T52 $(P \to R) \wedge (\sim P \wedge Q \to R) \leftrightarrow (P \vee Q \to R)$

The following forms of inference, each corresponding to a theorem proved by now, will appear frequently in what follows:

Form I

(1) $\phi \rightarrow \psi$
(2) $\sim\phi \rightarrow \psi$

ψ (1), (2), Adj, T33 $\left(\frac{\text{P} \quad \text{Q}}{\phi \quad \psi}\right)$, MP

Form II

(3) $\phi \vee \psi$
(4) $\phi \rightarrow \chi$
(5) $\psi \rightarrow \chi$

χ (3), (4), Adj, (5), Adj, T49 $\left(\frac{\text{P} \quad \text{Q} \quad \text{R}}{\phi \quad \psi \quad \chi}\right)$, MP

Form III

(6) $\phi \rightarrow \chi$
(7) $\psi \rightarrow \chi$

$\phi \vee \psi \rightarrow \chi$ (6), (7), Adj, T50 $\left(\frac{\text{P} \quad \text{Q} \quad \text{R}}{\phi \quad \psi \quad \chi}\right)$, BC, MP

We shall refer to these three forms jointly as inferences by *the derived rule of separation of cases*, and we shall employ 'SC' to indicate their use. More explicitly, we shall abbreviate the lengthy annotations above by 'SC' together with the numbers of the antecedent lines involved. Thus, for example, the second form becomes:

(3) $\phi \vee \psi$
(4) $\phi \rightarrow \chi$
(5) $\psi \rightarrow \chi$

χ (3), (4), (5), SC

Illustrations of the first and third forms of SC are provided by the following derivations.

Argument:

$$\text{P} \rightarrow \text{Q} \quad . \quad \sim\text{P} \rightarrow \text{R} \quad . \quad \text{R} \rightarrow \text{Q} \quad \therefore \text{Q}$$

Derivation:

1. ~~*Show*~~ Q
2. $\sim\text{P} \rightarrow \text{Q}$ 2nd premise, 3rd premise, Adj, T26 $\left(\frac{\text{P} \quad \text{Q} \quad \text{R}}{\sim\text{P} \quad \text{R} \quad \text{Q}}\right)$, MP
3. Q 1st premise, 2, SC

Argument:

$$\therefore\ \sim P \vee Q \rightarrow (P \rightarrow Q)$$

Derivation:

1. ~~*Show*~~ $\sim P \vee Q \rightarrow (P \rightarrow Q)$

2.	$\sim P \rightarrow (P \rightarrow Q)$	T18
3.	$Q \rightarrow (P \rightarrow Q)$	T2
4.	$\sim P \vee Q \rightarrow (P \rightarrow Q)$	2, 3, SC

Another useful form of inference is called *the derived rule of conditional-disjunction* and is justified by T45:

(8) $$\frac{\sim \phi \rightarrow \psi}{\phi \vee \psi}$$ (8), T45, BC, MP

We shall henceforth replace the annotation 'T45, BC, MP' by the abbreviation 'CD'. An illustration is provided by the following proof.

1. ~~*Show*~~ $(P \rightarrow Q) \rightarrow \sim P \vee Q$

2.	$P \rightarrow Q$	
3.	~~*Show*~~ $\sim\sim P \rightarrow Q$	
4.	$\sim\sim P$	
5.	Q	4, DN, 2, MP
6.	$\sim P \vee Q$	3, CD

T53 is the *commutative* law for 'v'.

T53 $\quad P \vee Q \leftrightarrow Q \vee P$

The *associative* law for 'v':

T54 $\quad P \vee (Q \vee R) \leftrightarrow (P \vee Q) \vee R$

As in a conjunction, internal parentheses may be omitted from a repeated disjunction in which all terms are associated to the left. Thus T54 becomes

$$P \vee (Q \vee R) \leftrightarrow P \vee Q \vee R \quad .$$

T55 is the *distributive law* for '→' over 'v'.

T55 $\quad (P \rightarrow Q \vee R) \leftrightarrow (P \rightarrow Q) \vee (P \rightarrow R)$

T56 $\quad (P \rightarrow Q) \rightarrow (R \vee P \rightarrow R \vee Q)$

T57 $\quad (P \rightarrow Q) \rightarrow (P \vee R \rightarrow Q \vee R)$

T58 $\quad (P \rightarrow Q) \vee (Q \rightarrow R)$

The law of the *excluded middle:*

T59 $P \vee \sim P$

T60, like T50, is a principle of *composition.*

T60 $(P \rightarrow R) \vee (Q \rightarrow R) \leftrightarrow (P \wedge Q \rightarrow R)$

T61 and T62 are laws of *distribution.*

T61 $P \wedge (Q \vee R) \leftrightarrow (P \wedge Q) \vee (P \wedge R)$

T62 $P \vee (Q \wedge R) \leftrightarrow (P \vee Q) \wedge (P \vee R)$

T63 – T66 are known as *De Morgan's laws*, after the nineteenth-century logician, Augustus De Morgan; T67, a corollary of T66, will play an important role in chapter IX.

T63 $P \wedge Q \leftrightarrow \sim(\sim P \vee \sim Q)$

T64 $P \vee Q \leftrightarrow \sim(\sim P \wedge \sim Q)$

T65 $\sim(P \wedge Q) \leftrightarrow \sim P \vee \sim Q$

T66 $\sim(P \vee Q) \leftrightarrow \sim P \wedge \sim Q$

T67 $\sim P \wedge \sim Q \rightarrow \sim(P \vee Q)$

T68 and T69 provide redundant but useful forms of expression.

T68 $P \leftrightarrow (P \wedge Q) \vee (P \wedge \sim Q)$

T69 $P \leftrightarrow (P \vee Q) \wedge (P \vee \sim Q)$

We come now to theorems which primarily concern '$\leftrightarrow$'. All but T78, T80, T94, and T95 (which are included because of their unintuitive character) will be found extremely useful in what follows.

T70 $Q \rightarrow (P \wedge Q \leftrightarrow P)$

T71 $\sim Q \rightarrow (P \vee Q \leftrightarrow P)$

T72 $(P \rightarrow Q) \leftrightarrow (P \wedge Q \leftrightarrow P)$

T73 $(P \rightarrow Q) \leftrightarrow (P \vee Q \leftrightarrow Q)$

T74 $(P \leftrightarrow Q) \wedge P \rightarrow Q$

T75 $(P \leftrightarrow Q) \wedge Q \rightarrow P$

T76 $(P \leftrightarrow Q) \wedge \sim P \rightarrow \sim Q$

T77 $(P \leftrightarrow Q) \wedge \sim Q \rightarrow \sim P$

T78 $(P \rightarrow [Q \leftrightarrow R]) \leftrightarrow ([P \rightarrow Q] \leftrightarrow [P \rightarrow R])$

T79 $(P \rightarrow [Q \leftrightarrow R]) \leftrightarrow (P \wedge Q \leftrightarrow P \wedge R)$

T80	$(P \leftrightarrow Q) \vee (P \leftrightarrow \sim Q)$
T81	$(P \leftrightarrow Q) \leftrightarrow (P \rightarrow Q) \wedge (Q \rightarrow P)$
T82	$(P \leftrightarrow Q) \leftrightarrow \sim([P \rightarrow Q] \rightarrow \sim[Q \rightarrow P])$
T83	$(P \leftrightarrow Q) \leftrightarrow (P \wedge Q) \vee (\sim P \wedge \sim Q)$
T84	$P \wedge Q \rightarrow (P \leftrightarrow Q)$
T85	$\sim P \wedge \sim Q \rightarrow (P \leftrightarrow Q)$
T86	$([P \leftrightarrow Q] \rightarrow R) \leftrightarrow (P \wedge Q \rightarrow R) \wedge (\sim P \wedge \sim Q \rightarrow R)$
T87	$\sim(P \leftrightarrow Q) \leftrightarrow (P \wedge \sim Q) \vee (\sim P \wedge Q)$
T88	$P \wedge \sim Q \rightarrow \sim(P \leftrightarrow Q)$
T89	$\sim P \wedge Q \rightarrow \sim(P \leftrightarrow Q)$
T90	$\sim(P \leftrightarrow Q) \leftrightarrow (P \leftrightarrow \sim Q)$
T91	$P \leftrightarrow P$
T92	$(P \leftrightarrow Q) \leftrightarrow (Q \leftrightarrow P)$
T93	$(P \leftrightarrow Q) \wedge (Q \leftrightarrow R) \rightarrow (P \leftrightarrow R)$
T94	$(P \leftrightarrow [Q \leftrightarrow R]) \leftrightarrow ([P \leftrightarrow Q] \leftrightarrow R)$
T95	$(P \leftrightarrow Q) \leftrightarrow ([P \leftrightarrow R] \leftrightarrow [Q \leftrightarrow R])$
T96	$(P \leftrightarrow Q) \leftrightarrow (\sim P \leftrightarrow \sim Q)$
T97	$(P \leftrightarrow R) \wedge (Q \leftrightarrow S) \rightarrow ([P \rightarrow Q] \leftrightarrow [R \rightarrow S])$
T98	$(P \leftrightarrow R) \wedge (Q \leftrightarrow S) \rightarrow (P \wedge Q \leftrightarrow R \wedge S)$
T99	$(P \leftrightarrow R) \wedge (Q \leftrightarrow S) \rightarrow (P \vee Q \leftrightarrow R \vee S)$
T100	$(P \leftrightarrow R) \wedge (Q \leftrightarrow S) \rightarrow ([P \leftrightarrow Q] \leftrightarrow [R \leftrightarrow S])$
T101	$(Q \leftrightarrow S) \rightarrow ([P \rightarrow Q] \leftrightarrow [P \rightarrow S]) \wedge ([Q \rightarrow P] \leftrightarrow [S \rightarrow P])$
T102	$(Q \leftrightarrow S) \rightarrow (P \wedge Q \leftrightarrow P \wedge S)$
T103	$(Q \leftrightarrow S) \rightarrow (P \vee Q \leftrightarrow P \vee S)$
T104	$(Q \leftrightarrow S) \rightarrow ([P \leftrightarrow Q] \leftrightarrow [P \leftrightarrow S])$
T105	$P \wedge (Q \leftrightarrow R) \rightarrow (P \wedge Q \leftrightarrow R)$

Each of the following theorems is an occasionally useful biconditional corresponding to a conditional listed in chapter I. The number of the corresponding conditional (and in some cases that of its converse) is indicated in parentheses.

T106	$(P \rightarrow [Q \rightarrow R]) \leftrightarrow ([P \rightarrow Q] \rightarrow [P \rightarrow R])$	(T6, T7)
T107	$(P \rightarrow [Q \rightarrow R]) \leftrightarrow (Q \rightarrow [P \rightarrow R])$	(T8)
T108	$(P \rightarrow [P \rightarrow Q]) \leftrightarrow (P \rightarrow Q)$	(T9)
T109	$([P \rightarrow Q] \rightarrow Q) \leftrightarrow ([Q \rightarrow P] \rightarrow P)$	(T10)
T110	$P \leftrightarrow \sim\sim P$	(T11, T12)
T111	$(P \rightarrow Q) \leftrightarrow (\sim Q \rightarrow \sim P)$	(T13)
T112	$(P \rightarrow \sim Q) \leftrightarrow (Q \rightarrow \sim P)$	(T14)
T113	$(\sim P \rightarrow Q) \leftrightarrow (\sim Q \rightarrow P)$	(T15)
T114	$(\sim P \rightarrow P) \leftrightarrow P$	(T19)
T115	$(P \rightarrow \sim P) \leftrightarrow \sim P$	(T20)

Some additional laws of distribution and other corollaries of earlier theorems will be useful in chapter VII; thus we list them here.

T116	$(P \wedge Q) \vee (R \wedge S) \leftrightarrow (P \vee R) \wedge (P \vee S) \wedge (Q \vee R) \wedge (Q \vee S)$
T117	$(P \vee Q) \wedge (R \vee S) \leftrightarrow (P \wedge R) \vee (P \wedge S) \vee (Q \wedge R) \vee (Q \wedge S)$
T118	$(P \rightarrow Q) \wedge (R \rightarrow S) \leftrightarrow$ $(\sim P \wedge \sim R) \vee (\sim P \wedge S) \vee (Q \wedge \sim R) \vee (Q \wedge S)$
T119	$(P \vee \sim P) \wedge Q \leftrightarrow Q$
T120	$(P \wedge \sim P) \vee Q \leftrightarrow Q$
T121	$P \vee (\sim P \wedge Q) \leftrightarrow P \vee Q$
T122	$P \wedge (\sim P \vee Q) \leftrightarrow P \wedge Q$
T123	$P \leftrightarrow P \vee (P \wedge Q)$
T124	$P \leftrightarrow P \wedge (P \vee Q)$
T125	$(P \rightarrow Q \wedge R) \rightarrow (P \wedge Q \leftrightarrow P \wedge R)$

EXERCISES

30. In the following derivation, which is a proof of T83, list with annotation all lines omitted by the use of clause (8) in lines 12–17.

1. ~~*Show*~~ $(P \leftrightarrow Q) \leftrightarrow (P \wedge Q) \vee (\sim P \wedge \sim Q)$
2. ~~*Show*~~ $(P \leftrightarrow Q) \rightarrow$ $(P \wedge Q) \vee (\sim P \wedge \sim Q)$
3. $P \leftrightarrow Q$
4. ~~*Show*~~ $\sim (P \wedge Q) \rightarrow$ $\sim P \wedge \sim Q$

5.	$\sim(P \wedge Q)$	
6.	~~Show~~ $\sim P$	
7.	P	
8.	$P \wedge Q$	3, BC, 7, MP, 7, Adj
9.	$\sim(P \wedge Q)$	5, R
10.	$\sim P \wedge \sim Q$	3, BC, 6, MT, 6, Adj
11.	$(P \wedge Q) \vee (\sim P \wedge \sim Q)$	4, CD
12.	~~Show~~ $P \wedge Q \rightarrow (P \leftrightarrow Q)$	
13.	$P \wedge Q$	
14.	$P \leftrightarrow Q$	13, S, T2, MP, 13, S, $T2\left(\frac{Q\ P}{P\ Q}\right)$, MP, CB
15.	~~Show~~ $\sim P \wedge \sim Q \rightarrow (P \leftrightarrow Q)$	
16.	$\sim P \wedge \sim Q$	
17.	$P \leftrightarrow Q$	16, S, T18, MP, 16, S, $T18\left(\frac{P\ Q}{Q\ P}\right)$, MP, CB
18.	$(P \leftrightarrow Q) \leftrightarrow (P \wedge Q) \vee (\sim P \wedge \sim Q)$	12, 15, SC, 2, CB

Of the preceding theorems, prove

31. T55, T60–T62;
32. T63, T64, T68, T69;
33. T70 – T73;
34. T78 – T80;
35. T86, T87, T90, T95;
36. T97 – T100.

In solving exercises 31–36 (as well as later exercises), the reader will find the following strategic hints helpful (though again not infallible).

(*1*) *To derive a sentence*

$$\phi \vee \psi \rightarrow \chi \quad ,$$

derive first

$$\phi \rightarrow \chi$$

and

$$\psi \rightarrow \chi \quad ,$$

and then use SC (Form III).

(*2*) *To derive*

$$\phi \rightarrow \psi \quad ,$$

where ϕ *is not a disjunction, use conditional derivation.*

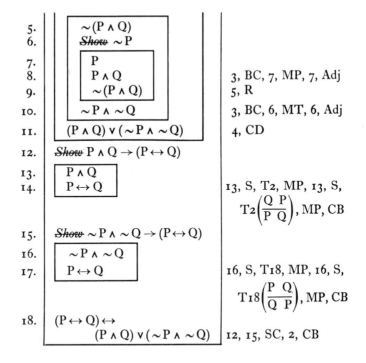

(3) *To derive a conjunction, derive first both conjuncts, and then use Adj.*

(4) *To derive*

$$\phi \vee \psi \quad ,$$

derive first

$$\sim\phi \rightarrow \psi$$

and then use CD.

(5) *To derive a biconditional, derive first the two corresponding conditionals, and then use CB.*

(6) *To derive a sentence* χ *when*

$$\phi \vee \psi$$

is an antecedent line, derive first

$$\phi \rightarrow \chi$$

and

$$\psi \rightarrow \chi \quad ,$$

and then use SC (Form II).

(7) *To derive anything else, use either indirect derivation or separation of cases (Form I).*

(8) *If a disjunction occurs as an antecedent line to which MTP is not applicable, as an alternative to (6) above, derive the negation of one of the disjuncts.*

Two proofs of T58 are given for illustration. We employ strategic hint (4) first. Thus after writing the initial assertion line, we enter immediately another assertion line and begin the indicated conditional derivation.

1. *Show* $(P \rightarrow Q) \vee (Q \rightarrow R)$
2. *Show* $\sim(P \rightarrow Q) \rightarrow (Q \rightarrow R)$
3. $\sim(P \rightarrow Q)$

Now by employing theorems of chapter I we can quickly complete the subsidiary derivation initiated in line 2.

1. *Show* $(P \rightarrow Q) \vee (Q \rightarrow R)$
2. ~~*Show*~~ $\sim(P \rightarrow Q) \rightarrow (Q \rightarrow R)$
3. | $\sim(P \rightarrow Q)$
4. | $Q \rightarrow R$ 3, T22, MP, T18 $\left(\frac{P\ \ Q}{Q\ \ R}\right)$, MP

And we complete the main derivation by employing CD.

1. ~~*Show*~~ $(P \rightarrow Q) \vee (Q \rightarrow R)$
2. | ~~*Show*~~ $\sim(P \rightarrow Q) \rightarrow (Q \rightarrow R)$
3. | | $\sim(P \rightarrow Q)$
4. | | $Q \rightarrow R$
5. | $(P \rightarrow Q) \vee (Q \rightarrow R)$ 2, CD

Next we obtain a proof of T58 by separation of cases (the second alternative of strategic hint (7)). Here after writing the initial assertion line, we introduce one of the cases and then make the appropriate assumption.

1. *Show* $(P \rightarrow Q) \vee (Q \rightarrow R)$
2. *Show* $Q \rightarrow (P \rightarrow Q) \vee (Q \rightarrow R)$
3. Q

And this can be completed quickly by now familiar principles.

1. *Show* $(P \rightarrow Q) \vee (Q \rightarrow R)$
2. ~~*Show*~~ $Q \rightarrow (P \rightarrow Q) \vee (Q \rightarrow R)$
3. Q
4. $(P \rightarrow Q) \vee (Q \rightarrow R)$ — 3, T2, MP, Add

Next we introduce the other case together with the appropriate assumption.

1. *Show* $(P \rightarrow Q) \vee (Q \rightarrow R)$
2. ~~*Show*~~ $Q \rightarrow (P \rightarrow Q) \vee (Q \rightarrow R)$
3. Q
4. $(P \rightarrow Q) \vee (Q \rightarrow R)$
5. *Show* $\sim Q \rightarrow (P \rightarrow Q) \vee (Q \rightarrow R)$
6. $\sim Q$

And again this case can be completed quickly.

1. *Show* $(P \rightarrow Q) \vee (Q \rightarrow R)$
2. ~~*Show*~~ $Q \rightarrow (P \rightarrow Q) \vee (Q \rightarrow R)$
3. Q
4. $(P \rightarrow Q) \vee (Q \rightarrow R)$
5. ~~*Show*~~ $\sim Q \rightarrow (P \rightarrow Q) \vee (Q \rightarrow R)$
6. $\sim Q$
7. $(P \rightarrow Q) \vee (Q \rightarrow R)$ — 6, T18 $\left(\frac{P\ \ Q}{Q\ \ R}\right)$, MP, Add

We now complete the main derivation by employing SC in Form I.

1. ~~*Show*~~ $(P \rightarrow Q) \vee (Q \rightarrow R)$
2. ~~*Show*~~ $Q \rightarrow (P \rightarrow Q) \vee (Q \rightarrow R)$
3. Q
4. $(P \rightarrow Q) \vee (Q \rightarrow R)$
5. ~~*Show*~~ $\sim Q \rightarrow (P \rightarrow Q) \vee (Q \rightarrow R)$
6. $\sim Q$
7. $(P \rightarrow Q) \vee (Q \rightarrow R)$
8. $(P \rightarrow Q) \vee (Q \rightarrow R)$ — 2, 5, SC

The decision to base the cases in the above derivation on 'Q' and '$\sim$Q' required some insight or some trial and error. Generally, any formula and its negation may be the basis for Form I of separation of cases; and for some theorems in subsequent chapters considerable insight may be required for a judicious choice of the cases to be employed in obtaining a proof.

7. Arguments. The definitions of an *argument*, a *symbolic argument*, and an *English argument* (p. 13), and of a *valid symbolic argument* (p. 26) and a *valid English argument* (p. 33), remain unchanged. Thus, for example, to establish the validity of the English argument

> Either life is a dangling conversation and silence speaks more eloquently than words, or life is a dangling conversation and we do not measure out our lives with coffee spoons. If we do not measure out our lives with coffee spoons, then life is not a dangling conversation. Therefore, silence speaks more eloquently than words

we first introduce a scheme of abbreviation

P : life is a dangling conversation
Q : silence speaks more eloquently than words
R : we measure out our lives with coffee spoons ;

next we pass to a symbolization of the argument on the basis of the scheme

$$(P \wedge Q) \vee (P \wedge \sim R) \quad . \qquad \sim R \rightarrow \sim P \quad \therefore Q \quad ;$$

and then we establish the validity of the symbolization by means of a derivation, such as

1.	~~*Show*~~ Q	
2.	$(P \wedge Q) \vee (P \wedge \sim R)$	Premise
3.	$\sim R \rightarrow \sim P$	Premise
4.	~~*Show*~~ $\sim(P \wedge \sim R)$	
5.	$P \wedge \sim R$	
6.	P	5, S
7.	$\sim P$	5, S, 3, MP
8.	Q	4, 2, MTP, S

(Strategic hint (8) on p. 84 suggested the introduction of the assertion in line 4 of the above derivation.)

EXERCISES, GROUP I

Show by constructing derivations that the following arguments are valid. (Accompanying each exercise is a reference to a strategic hint (listed on pp. 83–84) or theorem which the reader may find useful.)

37. $(P \rightarrow Q) \rightarrow R \quad . \quad S \rightarrow (\sim Q \rightarrow T) \quad \therefore\ R \vee \sim T \rightarrow (S \rightarrow R)$ [Hint 1, T2]
38. $P \leftrightarrow \sim Q \wedge S \quad . \quad P \wedge (\sim T \rightarrow \sim S) \quad \therefore\ \sim Q \wedge T$ [Hint 3]
39. $P \wedge Q \rightarrow R \vee S \quad \therefore\ (P \rightarrow R) \vee (Q \rightarrow S)$ [Hint 4, T40]
40. $P \vee Q \leftrightarrow P \wedge Q \quad \therefore\ P \leftrightarrow Q$ [Hint 5]
41. $\therefore\ (P \leftrightarrow [P \rightarrow Q]) \rightarrow Q$ [Hint 7, T21]
42. $(P \rightarrow Q) \vee (R \rightarrow S) \quad \therefore\ (P \rightarrow S) \vee (R \rightarrow Q)$ [Hints 4, 8]

EXERCISES, GROUP II

Show that the following arguments are valid by constructing symbolizations and deriving the conclusions of the symbolizations from their premises. Indicate in each case the scheme of abbreviation used. (Before symbolizing Nos. 43–46, the reader should review the remarks concerning symbolizations made on pp. 33–34.)

43. If Alfred's prayers are answered if he believes in God, then God exists. Alfred does not believe in God unless this is the best of all possible worlds. This is not the best of all possible worlds. Therefore if God does not exist, then everything is permitted.

44. If Alfred orders champagne, then so does Alonzo; and if Kurt orders champagne, then so does Alfred. Either Alfred or Kurt, but not both Alonzo and Kurt, orders champagne. Therefore both Alfred and Alonzo, but not Kurt, order champagne.

45. If Alfred is a lover of logic who organizes his time, then he enjoys Mozart in the morning or whiskey at night, but not both. If he enjoys whiskey at night, then either he enjoys Mozart in the morning and organizes his time, or he does not enjoy Mozart in the morning and does not organize his time, or else he is not a lover of logic. Alfred enjoys whiskey at night provided that he both enjoys Mozart in the morning and organizes his time. Therefore Alfred is a lover of logic only if he does not organize his time.

46. Either it is not the case that Alfred pays attention and does not lose track of the argument, or it is not the case that he does not take notes and does not do well in the course. Alfred neither does well in the course nor loses track of the argument. If Alfred studies logic, then he does not do well in the course only if he does not take notes and does pay attention. Therefor Alfred does not study logic.

8. Truth-value analysis of sentences. Inability to construct a derivation corresponding to a given symbolic argument is not conclusive evidence that no such derivation exists. The question naturally arises whether there is an automatic method of testing a symbolic argument for validity. For symbolic arguments of the sentential calculus there is such a method. Its presentation requires some new notions.

A symbolic sentence, like an English sentence, may have one of two *truth values*, truth (T) or falsehood (F). We may consider arbitrary *assignments* of truth values to sentence letters; such an assignment correlates with each sentence letter either T or F. Given an assignment A, we may determine the *truth value of* an arbitrary symbolic sentence ϕ *with respect to* A by the following rules:

(1) If ϕ is a sentence letter, then the truth value of ϕ is the truth value correlated with ϕ by A.

(2) If ϕ is

$$\sim\psi \quad ,$$

where ψ is a symbolic sentence, then the truth value of ϕ is T if that of ψ is F and is F if that of ψ is T.

(3) If ϕ is

$$(\psi \rightarrow \chi) \quad ,$$

where ψ, χ are symbolic sentences, then the truth value of ϕ is F if that of ψ is T and that of χ is F; otherwise, the truth value of ϕ is T.

(4) If ϕ is

$$(\psi \wedge \chi) \quad ,$$

where ψ, χ are symbolic sentences, then the truth value of ϕ is T if the truth values of ψ and χ are both T; otherwise, the truth value of ϕ is F.

(5) If ϕ is

$$(\psi \vee \chi) \quad ,$$

where ψ, χ are symbolic sentences, then the truth value of ϕ is F if the truth values of ψ and χ are both F; otherwise, the truth value of ϕ is T.

(6) If ϕ is

$$(\psi \leftrightarrow \chi) \quad ,$$

where ψ, χ are symbolic sentences, then the truth value of ϕ is T if ψ and χ have the same truth value; otherwise, the truth value of ϕ is F.

It can be concluded on the basis of the rules (1)–(6) that, with respect to an assignment A, every symbolic sentence has one of the two truth values T or F, but not both. Thus we may restate the rules succinctly as follows. Given an assignment A:

(1) A sentence letter has the value correlated with it by A.

(2) A negation has the value T if and only if the sentence negated has the value F.

(3) A conditional has the value F if and only if its antecedent has the value T and its consequent has the value F.

(4) A conjunction has the value T if and only if both conjuncts have the value T.

(5) A disjunction has the value F if and only if both disjuncts have the value F.

(6) A biconditional has the value T if and only if its constituents have the same value.

This summary of the rules is displayed by the following tableau:

ψ	χ	$\sim\psi$	$(\psi \rightarrow \chi)$	$(\psi \wedge \chi)$	$(\psi \vee \chi)$	$(\psi \leftrightarrow \chi)$
T	T	F	T	T	T	T
T	F	F	F	F	T	F
F	T	T	T	F	T	F
F	F	T	T	F	F	T

A *tautology* is a symbolic sentence whose truth value is T with respect to every possible assignment. For instance,

(1) $$\mathrm{P} \rightarrow \mathrm{P}$$

is a tautology. For consider any assignment A. It will correlate with 'P' either T or F. In neither case can the antecedent of (1) have the value T and the consequent the value F. Hence, by rule 3, the value of (1) is always T.

In deciding whether a symbolic sentence is a tautology, it is convenient to construct a *truth table*. The following is a truth table for the sentence '$(\mathrm{P} \rightarrow \mathrm{Q}) \leftrightarrow \sim(\mathrm{P} \wedge \sim\mathrm{Q})$'.

P	Q	$\sim$Q	P $\rightarrow$ Q	P $\wedge\sim$Q	$\sim$(P $\wedge\sim$Q)	(P $\rightarrow$ Q) $\leftrightarrow\sim$(P $\wedge\sim$Q)
T	T	F	T	F	T	T
T	F	T	F	T	F	T
F	T	F	T	F	T	T
F	F	T	T	F	T	T

Given an arbitrary assignment A, the table can be regarded as an abbreviation of the following considerations:

If A correlates T with both 'P' and 'Q' (first row), then (by rule 2) the value of '$\sim$Q' with respect to A is F, that of 'P $\rightarrow$ Q' is (by rule 3) T, that of '$P \wedge \sim Q$' is (by rule 4) *F*, hence (by rule 2) that of '$\sim(P \wedge \sim Q)$' is *T*, and hence (by rule 6) the value of '$(P \rightarrow Q) \leftrightarrow \sim(P \wedge \sim Q)$' is *T*.

If *A* correlates *T* with 'P' and *F* with 'Q' (second row), then the value of '$\sim Q$' is *T*, that of '$P \rightarrow Q$' is *F*, that of '$P \wedge \sim Q$' is *T*, and hence that of '$\sim(P \wedge \sim Q)$' is *F*, and hence that of '$(P \rightarrow Q) \leftrightarrow \sim(P \wedge \sim Q)$' is *T*.

If *A* correlates *F* with 'P' and *T* with 'Q' (third row), then, similarly, the value of '$(P \rightarrow Q) \leftrightarrow \sim(P \wedge \sim Q)$' is *T*.

If *A* correlates *F* with both 'P' and 'Q', then the value of '$(P \rightarrow Q) \leftrightarrow \sim(P \wedge \sim Q)$' is again *T*.

Since in all cases the value of '$(P \rightarrow Q) \leftrightarrow \sim(P \wedge \sim Q)$' is *T*, this sentence is a tautology.

In general, to construct a complete truth table for a given symbolic sentence proceed as follows. Provide a column for each component of the sentence, including the sentence itself. Arrange the components in order of increasing complexity, placing all sentence letters to the left of a double line. To the left of the double line, construct a row for each possible combination of truth values. (If there are n sentence letters, there will be 2^n rows.) Proceed to the right in each row, filling in truth values for the sentences heading the columns, on the basis of previous entries and the rules on page 88. The sentence is then a tautology just in case its table contains nothing but '*T*' in the final column.

Truth tables can be abbreviated. In the top row of the table, rather than entering a separate column for each component of a given sentence, we may simply enter the given sentence itself together with a column under each occurrence of a sentence letter and connective. Thus, an abbreviation of the above truth table together with the initial truth assignments to its sentence letters appears first as

(P	$\rightarrow$	Q)	$\leftrightarrow$	$\sim$	(P	$\wedge$	$\sim$	Q)
T		*T*			*T*			*T*
T		*F*			*T*			*F*
F		*T*			*F*			*T*
F		*F*			*F*			*F*

Next we fill in the truth values in the columns of the table that correspond to the component sentences of the given sentence, considering these components in increasing order of complexity. Here a grammatical tree can be a helpful guide to a correct order of steps. The nodes of the grammatical tree are numbered successively as they enter into the generation of the tree. Alternative numberings are possible; we need only be sure that all ancestral nodes to a given node are numbered before that node can enter into the numbering. Thus, the abbreviated table constructed with the aid of a numbered grammatical tree finally appears as

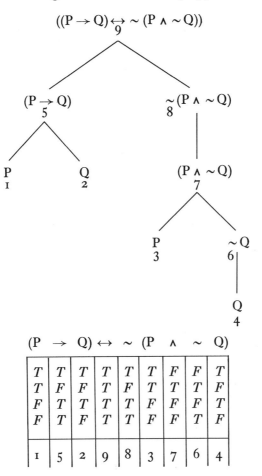

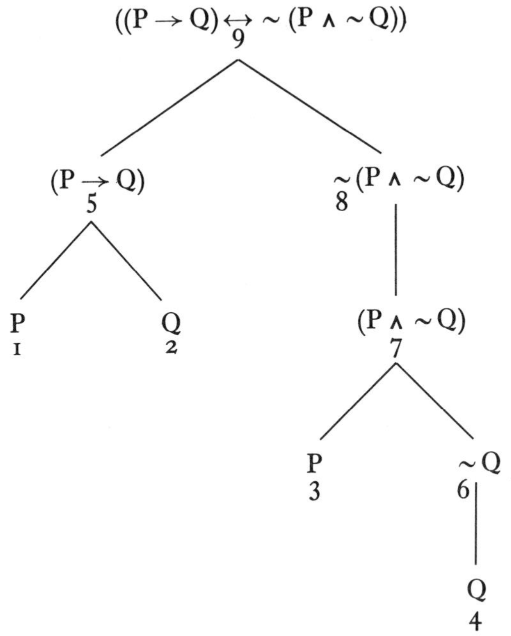

(P	→	Q)	↔	~	(P	∧	~	Q)
T	*T*	*T*	*T*	*T*	*T*	*F*	*F*	*T*
T	*F*	*F*	*T*	*F*	*T*	*T*	*T*	*F*
F	*T*	*T*	*T*	*T*	*F*	*F*	*F*	*T*
F	*T*	*F*	*T*	*T*	*F*	*F*	*T*	*F*
1	5	2	9	8	3	7	6	4

The numerals beneath each column of the abbreviated truth table indicate the order in which the columns were filled. The last column to be filled gives the truth value of the given sentence for each assignment of truth values to its sentence letters. The truth values in columns corresponding to initial nodes are determined by the various truth value assignments; truth values in columns corresponding to noninitial nodes are determined by the truth values in the column or columns corresponding to the nodes that are the immediate ancestor or ancestors of the given node. Thus, column 5 is obtained from columns 1 and 2 and the rule for '→'; column 6 is obtained from column 4 and the rule for '~'; column 7 is obtained from columns 3 and 6 and the rule for '∧'; column 8 is obtained from column 7 and the rule for '~'; and finally column 9 is obtained from columns 5 and 8 and the rule for '↔'.

It happens that a sentence is a theorem of the sentential calculus if and only if it is a tautology. (This fact will not be proved here; part of it will be proved in chapter IX.) Thus truth tables provide an automatic test for validity in case of symbolic arguments without premises.

EXERCISES, GROUP I

Determine by means of truth-value analysis which of the following sentences are tautologies. Exercises 47–50 are solved for illustration.

47. (P → Q) v (Q → R) [T58]

No. 47 is a tautology. To demonstrate this it is not necessary to construct a complete or abbreviated truth table. Generally, to demonstrate that a symbolic sentence ϕ is a tautology, it is sufficient to show the assumption that it is not a tautology leads to a contradiction; that is, to assume that ϕ has the value *F* for some assignment and to show that this assumption leads to an assignment of truth values incompatible with rules (1)–(6). We apply this *reductio ad absurdum* procedure to No. 47, with the aid of the following table.

(P	→	Q)	v	(Q	→	R)
T	*F*	*F*	*F*	*F*	*F*	
4	2	5	1	5	3	

The numerals in this table indicate the order in which steps are taken. On the assumption that No. 47 is not a tautology, we initially assign to it the truth value *F* (step 1). The rule for 'v' then requires that both disjuncts of No. 47 be assigned *F* (steps 2 and 3). With these assignments made, the rule for '→' requires that *T* be assigned to 'P' and *F* to 'Q' (steps 4 and 5). (In step 5 we entered the letter '*F*' under both occurrences of 'Q', for rule (1) requires that a sentence letter be assigned a unique truth value.) The table now reveals (as indicated by the link) that we have contradicted the rule for '→', for we have assigned *F* to a conditional whose antecedent has been assigned *F*. This contradiction demonstrates that No. 47 is a tautology.

48. (P ∧ Q → R) → (P → R)

No. 48 is not a tautology. In order to demonstrate this it is sufficient to give, rather than a complete or abbreviated table, one row in which No. 48 has the truth value *F*. Such a row can be expeditiously obtained by attempting the *reductio* procedure introduced in the preceding exercise. When applied to a sentence that is not a tautology, this procedure leads to an assignment of truth values to the sentence letters of the given sentence compatible with rules (1)–(6). We thereby obtain a row of an abbreviated table in which the sentence has the truth value *F*. The following row of an abbreviated table, in which No. 48 has the truth value *F*, is obtained by the *reductio* procedure.

(P	∧	Q	→	R)	→	(P	→	R)
T	*F*	*F*	*T*	*F*	*F*	*T*	*F*	*F*
4	6	7	2	5	1	4	3	5

Here the numerals indicate the order of steps in the *reductio* procedure. On the assumption that No. 48 is not a tautology, we initially assign to it the truth value *F* (step 1). The rule for '→' then requires that the antecedent of No. 48 be assigned *T* (step 2) and its consequent be assigned *F* (step 3). The consequent of No. 48 is again a conditional; thus its antecedent is assigned *T* (step 4) and its consequent *F* (step 5). As before, once a sentence letter is assigned a value, we enter this assignment under all its occurrences. The antecedent of No. 48 is also a conditional. It has been assigned the value *T* (step 2) and its consequent *F* (step 5); thus by the rule for '→' its antecedent must be assigned *F* (step 6). Finally, the rule for '∧', together with truth assignments made in steps 4 and 6, requires that 'Q' be assigned *F* (step 7). All the above assignments are in accordance with rules (1)–(6); thus No. 48 is not a tautology, for we have found a row in its truth table in which it has the truth value *F*.

49. (P → Q) ∧ (Q → P) → (P ↔ Q)

No. 49 is a tautology. To demonstrate this we begin the *reductio* procedure.

(P → Q)	∧	(Q → P)	→	(P ↔ Q)
T	*T*	*T*	*F*	*F*
4	2	5	1	3

At step 5 no contradiction to the rules has been obtained, and no further assignments are required by the rules. Thus, the *reductio* procedure must be supplemented to include cases. That is, we choose an arbitrary sentence letter which has not already received an assignment, say 'P', and consider the cases in which it is first assigned *T* and next assigned *F*. These are the only two alternatives according to rule (1).

(case 1) P: *T*

(P	→	Q)	∧	(Q	→	P)	→	(P	↔	Q)
T	*T*	*T*	*T*	*T*	*T*	*T*	*F*	*T*	*F*	*T*
6		7		7		6		6		7

We initiate case 1 by assigning 'P' the truth value *T* (step 6). Given this and previous assignments, the rule for '→' requires that 'Q' (on the basis of its leftmost occurrence) be assigned the truth value *T*. However, this assignment contradicts the rule for '↔', for we have now assigned *F* to a biconditional (step 3) both of whose constituents have been assigned *T* (steps 6 and 7). (This contradiction is indicated by the link.)

(case 2) P: *F*

(P	→	Q)	∧	(Q	→	P)	→	(P	↔	Q)
F	*T*	*F*	*T*	*F*	*T*	*F*	*F*	*F*	*F*	*F*
6		7		7		6		6		7

We initiate case 2 by assigning 'P' the truth value *F* (step 6). Given this and previous assignments, the rule for '→' requires that 'Q' (on the basis of its second occurrence) be assigned the truth value *F*. However, this assignment contradicts the rule for '↔', for we have now assigned *F* to a biconditional (step 3) both of whose constituents have been assigned *F* (steps 6 and 7). (This contradiction is indicated by the link.) Since both cases lead to a contradiction of rules (1)–(6), we have demonstrated that No. 49 is a tautology.

50. (P ∧ Q) ∨ (~P ∧ Q) → (P ↔ Q)

No. 50 is not a tautology. To demonstrate this we may again employ the *reductio* procedure to obtain a row in the truth table for No. 50 in which that sentence has the value *F*.

(P ∧ Q)	∨	(~P ∧ Q)	→	(P	↔	Q)
	T		*F*		*F*	
	2		1		3	

At step 3 no contradiction to the rules has been obtained, and no further assignments are required by the rules. Thus, here too we pass to cases.

(case 1) P: *T*

(P	∧	Q)	∨	(~	P	∧	Q)	→	(P	↔	Q)
T	*T*	*T*	*T*	*F*	*T*	*F*	*T*	*F*	*T*	*F*	*T*
4	7	8		5	4	6	8		4		8

(case 2) P: *F*

(P	∧	Q)	∨	(~	P	∧	Q)	→	(P	↔	Q)
F	*F*	*T*	*T*	*T*	*F*	*T*	*T*	*F*	*F*	*F*	*T*
4	5	8		6	4	7	8		4		8

Notice that case 1 leads to a contradiction of the rules, as is indicated by the link; however, case 2 leads to a row in the truth table for No. 50 in which that sentence has the truth value *F*. Thus case 2 has established that No. 50 is not a tautology.

In general, the *reductio* procedure is initiated by assigning *F* to a given sentence. Given this assignment, make all assignments to components of the sentence, beginning at the left, which are required by rules (1)–(6). Then make all assignments required by the latter assignments and continue until either there is obtained an assignment to the sentence letters of the given sentence that does not contradict rules (1)–(6) (in which case the sentence is not a tautology) or it is determined that no such assignment can be obtained (in which case the sentence is a tautology). Sometimes the *reductio* procedure cannot be completed in a single row. If so, pass to cases. These cases can be based on the assignment of *T* and then *F* to any sentence letter not already assigned a truth value (for definiteness, always take the leftmost). This process must eventually terminate, for there are a finite number of sentence letters in any given sentence. As before, enter assignments required by rules (1)–(6) and take cases within cases if necessary. If one of the cases (or subsidiary cases) leads to an assignment for which the given sentence has the value *F*, the sentence is not a tautology. If all the cases (and subsidiary cases) lead to a contradiction of rules (1)–(6), then the initial assumption has been reduced to an absurdity and the sentence is a tautology. (The reader should recognize that the *reductio* procedure can be more tedious than the construction of a complete truth table when cases are involved. For example, four cases would be required to demonstrate by the *reductio* procedure that '$(P \wedge Q) \vee (\sim P \wedge \sim Q) \leftrightarrow (P \leftrightarrow Q)$' is a tautology. Indeed, for most exercises the reader will soon be able to dispense with all tables in favor of mental computation or insight to ascertain whether or not a symbolic sentence is a tautology.)

51. $(P \wedge Q \rightarrow R) \rightarrow (Q \rightarrow R)$
52. $(P \rightarrow R) \rightarrow (P \vee Q \rightarrow R)$
53. T61, T66, T73, T78, T94
54. The converse of T32 and the converse of T93

EXERCISES, GROUP II

We can generalize the definitions of *conjunction* and *disjunction*: by the *conjunction* or *disjunction* of the sentences $\phi_1, \ldots, \phi_n$ we shall understand the sentences

$$\phi_1 \wedge \ldots \wedge \phi_n$$

or

$$\phi_1 \vee \ldots \vee \phi_n$$

respectively. (In case n is 1, both these sentences reduce to ϕ_1.)

By a *basic sentence* we understand either a sentence letter or the negation of a sentence letter. We say that a sentence is in *conjunctive normal form* (abbreviated 'CNF') if it is a conjunction of disjunctions of basic sentences and in *disjunctive normal form* (abbreviated 'DNF') if it is a disjunction of conjunctions of basic sentences. Symbolic sentences ϕ and ψ are said to be *equivalent* if the biconditional

$$\phi \leftrightarrow \psi$$

is a theorem. Symbolic sentences ϕ and ψ are said to be *tautologically equivalent* if the truth value of ϕ is the same as that of ψ with respect to every possible assignment. It follows from the fact that a sentence (of the sentential calculus) is a theorem if and only if it is a tautology that ϕ and ψ are equivalent just in case ϕ and ψ are tautologically equivalent.

55. Consider the following truth table for a symbolic sentence ϕ:

P	Q	R	ϕ
T	*T*	*T*	*T*
T	*T*	*F*	*F*
T	*F*	*T*	*F*
T	*F*	*F*	*T*
F	*T*	*T*	*T*
F	*T*	*F*	*F*
F	*F*	*T*	*T*
F	*F*	*F*	*F*

Find a symbolic sentence in DNF that is tautologically equivalent to ϕ. (Hint: each row of the truth table that contains a '*T*' in the last column will yield one of the disjuncts of the sentence in DNF; each of these disjuncts is a conjunction of basic sentences.)

56. Given any symbolic sentence (of the sentential calculus), formulate a general procedure for finding a tautologically equivalent sentence in DNF.

Consider the truth tables for a conjunction and a disjunction of 'P' and 'Q'.

P	Q	P ∧ Q	P ∨ Q
T	*T*	*T*	*T*
T	*F*	*F*	*T*
F	*T*	*F*	*T*
F	*F*	*F*	*F*

In this table interchange '*T*' and '*F*' to obtain

P	Q	P ∧ Q	P ∨ Q
F	*F*	*F*	*F*
F	*T*	*T*	*F*
T	*F*	*T*	*F*
T	*T*	*T*	*T*

Note that in the latter table 'P ∧ Q' has the value *F* just in case both 'P' and 'Q' have the value *F*, and 'P ∨ Q' has the value *T* just in case both

'P' and 'Q' have the value *T*. Thus the truth rules for conjunction and disjunction have been interchanged. This observation suggests that

$$P \lor Q$$

and

$$P \land Q$$

are tautologically equivalent, respectively, to

$$\sim(\sim P \land \sim Q)$$

and

$$\sim(\sim P \lor \sim Q) \quad .$$

More generally, given a symbolic sentence ϕ whose connectives are among '$\sim$', '$\land$', and '$\lor$', the *dual* of ϕ comes from ϕ by interchanging every occurrence of '$\land$' and '$\lor$' and every occurrence of a sentence letter and its negation. It happens that ϕ is always tautologically equivalent to the negation of the dual of ϕ; and hence the negation of ϕ is tautologically equivalent to the dual of ϕ. For example, the dual of

$$\sim Q \land (\sim P \lor Q)$$

is

$$Q \lor (P \land \sim Q) \quad ,$$

and the negation of the former is tautologically equivalent to the latter.

57. Find a symbolic sentence in CNF that is tautologically equivalent to the symbolic sentence ϕ in exercise 55. (Hint: put the negation of ϕ in DNF and then consider the dual of that DNF sentence.)

58. Given any symbolic sentence (of the sentential calculus), formulate a general procedure for finding a tautologically equivalent sentence in CNF.

59. (a) Find a symbolic sentence that is tautologically equivalent to '$P \land Q$' and contains just the sentence letters 'P' and 'Q' and the connectives '$\sim$' and '$\lor$'.

(b) Do the same for '$P \land Q$' and the connectives '$\sim$' and '$\rightarrow$'.
(c) Do the same for '$P \lor Q$' and the connectives '$\sim$' and '$\land$'.
(d) Do the same for '$P \lor Q$' and the connectives '$\sim$' and '$\rightarrow$'.
(e) Do the same for '$P \rightarrow Q$' and the connectives '$\sim$' and '$\land$'.
(f) Do the same for '$P \rightarrow Q$' and the connectives '$\sim$' and '$\lor$'.
(g) Do the same for '$P \leftrightarrow Q$' and the connectives '$\sim$' and '$\land$'.
(h) Do the same for '$P \leftrightarrow Q$' and the connectives '$\sim$' and '$\lor$'.
(i) Do the same for '$P \leftrightarrow Q$' and the connectives '$\sim$' and '$\rightarrow$'.

(Exercise 59 establishes that every symbolic sentence of the language of chapter II is tautologically equivalent (and hence equivalent) to a sentence of the language of chapter I. Hence every theorem of chapter II can be expressed in the language of chapter I.)

60. Let us introduce *Sheffer*'s *stroke* '|' as a new binary sentential connective. If ϕ and ψ are symbolic sentences, then so is

$$(\phi \mid \psi) \quad .$$

The tableau that displays the truth rule for the new connective is

ϕ	ψ	$(\phi \mid \psi)$
T	*T*	*F*
T	*F*	*T*
F	*T*	*T*
F	*F*	*T*

Thus we may read '(P | Q)' as 'not both P and Q'.

(a) Find a symbolic sentence that contains only the sentence letter 'P' and the binary connective '|' that is tautologically equivalent to '$\sim$P'.

(b) Find a symbolic sentence that contains only the sentence letters 'P' and 'Q' and the binary connective '|' that is tautologically equivalent to 'P $\rightarrow$ Q'.

(c) Do the same for 'P $\wedge$ Q'.

(d) Do the same for 'P $\vee$ Q'.

(e) Do the same for 'P $\leftrightarrow$ Q'.

61. Let us introduce the *joint denial connective* '$\downarrow$' as a new binary sentential connective. If ϕ and ψ are symbolic sentences, then so is

$$(\phi \downarrow \psi) \quad .$$

The tableau that displays the truth rule for the new connective is

ϕ	ψ	$(\phi \downarrow \psi)$
T	*T*	*F*
T	*F*	*F*
F	*T*	*F*
F	*F*	*T*

Thus we may read '(P $\downarrow$ Q)' as 'neither P nor Q'.

(a) Find a symbolic sentence that contains only the sentence letter 'P' and the binary connective '$\downarrow$' that is tautologically equivalent to '$\sim$P'.

(b) Find a symbolic sentence that contains only the sentence letters 'P' and 'Q' and the binary connective '$\downarrow$' that is tautologically equivalent to 'P $\rightarrow$ Q'.

(c) Do the same for 'P $\wedge$ Q'.

(d) Do the same for 'P $\vee$ Q'.

(e) Do the same for 'P $\leftrightarrow$ Q'.

(Exercises 60 and 61 establish that we could have developed our sentential logic, with a gain in elegance but with a loss in perspicuity, with just one sentential connective. The Sheffer stroke and the joint denial connectives are the only binary connectives that are by themselves sufficient for this purpose.)

9. Truth-value analysis of arguments. A symbolic sentence ϕ is *tautologically implied* by other symbolic sentences just in case there is no assignment of truth values with respect to which each of the latter sentences has the truth value T while ϕ has the truth value F. It happens (but will not be proved) that a symbolic argument is valid in the sentential calculus if and only if its conclusion is tautologically implied by its premises.

In the case of symbolic arguments with finitely many premises, truth tables are convenient for determining tautological implication. Consider, for example, the argument

(1) $\quad \mathrm{P} \rightarrow \mathrm{Q} \quad . \quad \mathrm{P} \rightarrow \sim \mathrm{Q} \quad \therefore \sim \mathrm{P}$

The following is a truth table for this argument:

P	Q	~P	~Q	P → Q	P → ~ Q
T	*T*	*F*	*F*	*T*	*F*
T	*F*	*F*	*T*	*F*	*T*
F	*T*	*T*	*F*	*T*	*T*
F	*F*	*T*	*T*	*T*	*T*

The table can be regarded as an abbreviation of the following considerations. Let A be an arbitrary assignment. If A correlates T with both 'P' and 'Q' (first row), then the value of '~ P' with respect to A is F, and that of '~ Q' is F, that of 'P → Q' is T, and that of 'P → ~ Q' is F. The other rows have a similar meaning, and the four rows exhaust all possible cases. We observe that in all cases in which the premises of (1) all receive the value T (rows 3 and 4), the conclusion also receives the value T. Thus the conclusion of (1) is tautologically implied by its premises, and hence (1) is valid.

In general, to construct a truth table for a given symbolic argument proceed as follows. Provide a column for each component of the premises and the conclusion, including these sentences themselves. Arrange the components in order of increasing complexity, placing all sentence letters to the left of a double line. To the left of the double line, construct a row for each possible combination of truth values. Proceed to the right in each row, filling in truth values for the sentences heading the columns, on the basis of previous entries and the rules on page 88. The conclusion of the argument is tautologically implied by its premises just in case there is no row in which the premises all have the value T and the conclusion has the value F.

Since a symbolic argument is valid in the sentential calculus just in case its conclusion is tautologically implied by its premises, truth tables provide both an automatic test for validity and a method of showing invalidity in the case of symbolic arguments with finitely many premises.

The truth-table method of showing invalidity applies directly only to symbolic arguments. The reader will recall that an English argument is valid in the sentential calculus just in case it has a symbolization whose conclusion is derivable from its premises (within the sentential calculus). Hence, to show the invalidity of an English argument within this branch of logic, it is necessary to show that no symbolization of it is valid. Using truth tables, we may be able to show that various particular symbolizations are invalid, but without more precise information about the notion of a symbolization (in particular, about the notion of stylistic variance, on which it depends) we shall be unable to establish general assertions about all possible symbolizations of a given argument. Thus, although it would be desirable to develop a test of validity for arguments expressed in idiomatic English, this does not seem possible without a more detailed analysis of the notion of stylistic variance than we care to undertake.

EXERCISES, GROUP I

Test each of the following arguments for validity using truth-value analysis. If an argument is valid, construct a derivation of its conclusion from its premises. Nos. 62 and 63 are solved for illustration.

62. $(P \rightarrow Q) \wedge R \quad . \quad \sim R \vee P \quad \therefore Q$

No. 62 is valid. To demonstrate this it is not necessary to construct a complete truth table. Generally, to demonstrate that a symbolic argument is valid, it is sufficient to show that the assumption it is not valid leads to a contradiction; that is, to assume that the premises of the argument have the value *T* and its conclusion *F* and to show that this assumption leads to an assignment of truth values incompatible with rules (1)–(6) given on page 88. This technique is a generalization of the *reductio ad absurdum* method introduced in the preceding section (pp. 94–95). We can apply the *reductio* procedure to No. 62 with the aid of the following table.

(P	→	Q)	∧	R	.	~	R	∨	P	∴ Q
F	*T*	*F*	*T*	*T*		*F*	*T*	*T*	*F*	*F*
4	2	1	1	3		5	3	1	4	1

Numerals in the above table indicate the order in which steps are taken. On the assumption that No. 62 is not valid, we initially assign its premises *T* and its conclusion *F* (step 1). (In step 1 we enter '*F*' under both occurrences of 'Q', in accordance with rule (1).) The rule for '∧' then requires that both conjuncts of the first premise be assigned *T* (steps 2 and 3). The rule for '→' then requires that 'P' be assigned *F*, for we have assigned *T* to a conditional whose consequent has been assigned *F* (step 4). Next the rule for '$\sim$' requires that *F* be assigned to '$\sim$R' (step 5). The table now reveals (as indicated by the link) that we have contradicted the rule for '$\vee$', for we have assigned *T* to a disjunction each of whose disjuncts has been assigned *F*. This contradiction demonstrates that No. 62 is valid. (The derivation is left to the reader.)

63. $\sim P \leftrightarrow Q \quad . \quad R \rightarrow P \vee Q \quad \therefore P \vee \sim R$

No. 63 is invalid. In order to demonstrate this it is sufficient to give, rather than a complete table, one row in which the premises of No. 63 have the value *T* and its conclusion *F*. Such a row can be expeditiously obtained by attempting the *reductio* procedure introduced in the preceding exercise.

$\sim P \leftrightarrow Q$.	$R \rightarrow P \vee Q$	$\therefore P \vee \sim R$
T F T T	*T T F T T*	*F F F T*
4 2 1 5	7 1 2 6 5	2 1 3 7

Here the numerals indicate the order of steps in the *reductio* procedure. All the above assignments are in accordance with rules (1)–(6); thus No. 63 is invalid, for we have found a row of its truth table in which its premises have the value *T* and its conclusion *F*.

In general, the *reductio* procedure for the truth-value analysis of arguments is initiated by assigning the truth value *T* to each of the premises of a given argument and the value *F* to its conclusion. Given this assignment, make all assignments to the components of the sentences, beginning on the left, which are required by the rules (1)–(6). Then make all assignments required by these latter assignments, and continue until either there is obtained an assignment to the sentence letters of the given argument that does not contradict rules (1)–(6) (in which case the argument is invalid) or it is determined that no such assignment can be obtained (in which case the argument is valid). Sometimes the *reductio* procedure cannot be completed in a single row. If so, pass to cases (see p. 95). If one of the cases (or subsidiary cases) leads to an assignment for which all the premises have the value *T* and the conclusion *F*, the argument is invalid. If all the cases (and subsidiary cases) lead to a contradiction of rules (1)–(6), then the initial assumption has been reduced to an absurdity and the argument is valid.

64. $P \rightarrow \sim R \quad . \quad Q \vee P \rightarrow R \vee Q \quad . \quad \sim Q \quad \therefore \sim P$

65. $\sim S \vee P \vee Q \quad . \quad \sim Q \rightarrow \sim R \quad . \quad P \rightarrow R \wedge S \quad \therefore Q$

66. $\sim(P \leftrightarrow Q) \quad . \quad R \rightarrow P \vee \sim Q \quad \therefore P \vee \sim R$

67. $\sim P \rightarrow Q \vee R \quad . \quad R \rightarrow (Q \rightarrow \sim P) \quad . \quad Q \rightarrow R \quad \therefore \sim P \leftrightarrow Q$

EXERCISES, GROUP II

Although we cannot establish in a clear-cut way the invalidity (within the sentential calculus) of arguments expressed in idiomatic English, we can at least, if they are invalid, establish the invalidity of any one of their symbolizations. Together with each of the arguments 68–72 below we give an *interesting* symbolization, that is, one that appears to reflect to a maximal degree the logical structure of the argument it symbolizes. Such a symbolization will be one that is as long as possible and, among those of maximal length, one which uses the smallest possible number of different sentence letters. For each of the symbolizations below, either derive its conclusion from its premises or show by the method of truth tables that it is invalid. In finding derivations, the reader will again find helpful the hints made on pages 83–84. (Nos. 68 and 69 correspond to an example on page 1.)

68. If Alfred studies, then he receives good grades; if he does not study, then he enjoys college; if he does not receive good grades, then he does not enjoy college. Therefore Alfred studies.

$$P \rightarrow Q \quad . \quad {\sim}P \rightarrow R \quad . \quad {\sim}Q \rightarrow {\sim}R \quad \therefore P$$

69. If Alfred studies, then he receives good grades; if he does not study, then he enjoys college; if he does not receive good grades, then he does not enjoy college. Therefore Alfred enjoys college.

$$P \rightarrow Q \quad . \quad {\sim}P \rightarrow R \quad . \quad {\sim}Q \rightarrow {\sim}R \quad \therefore R$$

70. Alfred will marry either Alice or Mary, but not both. If he marries Alice but not Mary, then he is fortunate. If he does not marry Alice but marries Mary, he is also fortunate. Therefore Alfred is fortunate.

$$(P \vee Q) \wedge {\sim}(P \wedge Q) \quad . \quad P \wedge {\sim}Q \rightarrow R \quad . \quad {\sim}P \wedge Q \rightarrow R \quad \therefore R$$

71. Alfred passes just in case he is both intelligent and industrious, and he is intelligent. Alfred is industrious if and only if he both is intelligent and does not pass, provided that he does not succumb to temptation. Therefore Alfred succumbs to temptation.

$$(R \leftrightarrow P \wedge Q) \wedge P \quad . \quad {\sim}S \rightarrow (Q \leftrightarrow P \wedge {\sim}R) \quad \therefore S$$

72. If Alfred enjoys the music just in case the music is classical, then he enjoys Mozart; but he does not enjoy Mozart. Therefore it is not the case that if Alfred enjoys the music then the music is classical.

$$([P \leftrightarrow Q] \rightarrow R) \wedge {\sim}R \quad \therefore {\sim}(P \rightarrow Q)$$

Give an interesting symbolization of each of the following arguments, and for each symbolization either derive its conclusion from its premises or show by the method of truth tables that it is invalid.

73. If God is willing to prevent evil but unable to do so, he is impotent. If God is able to prevent evil but unwilling to do so, he is malevolent. Evil exists if and only if God is either unwilling or unable to prevent it. God exists only if he is neither impotent nor malevolent. Therefore if God exists, evil does not exist.

74. Caesar went to England, and either Pompey went to Spain or Crassus marched against the Parthians. It is not the case that

both Caesar went to England and Crassus was not killed by the Parthians. If Caesar went to England and Cicero denounced Catiline, then Pompey did not go to Spain. If Cicero did not denounce Catiline, then Crassus marched against the Parthians. Therefore Caesar was murdered on the Ides of March, 44 B.C.

75. If neither an adequate social life nor a comfortable income can replace Alfred's love of logic, then, provided that he has normal intelligence, he can expect nothing better than an instructorship. An adequate social life can replace Alfred's love of logic just in case a comfortable income can replace his love of logic. Therefore either an adequate social life can replace Alfred's love of logic or he can expect nothing better than an instructorship.

EXERCISES, GROUP III

We conclude our treatment of truth-value analysis of sentential logic with four problems that should provide entertainment as well as instruction.

76. According to ancient legends the Oracle at Delphi was infallible. The Oracle, it appears, was once asked whether any of the triumvirate of Pompey, Caesar, and Crassus would be assassinated. The Oracle gave a two-sentence reply:

> More than one of the triumvirate will be assassinated.
> Crassus will be assassinated and either Caesar will not be assassinated or Pompey will be assassinated, if and only if, Pompey will not be assassinated and either Crassus or Caesar will be assassinated.

Needless to say, these pronouncements left the ancients baffled. Assuming that the Oracle is infallible, who among the triumvirate will be assassinated? (Hint: construct a (partial) truth table for the second pronouncement.)

77. When Sancho Panza was governor of Barataria, the following case came before him for decision. A certain manor was divided by a river upon which was a bridge. The lord of the manor had erected a gallows at one end of the bridge and had enacted a law that whoever would cross the bridge must first swear whither he or she were going and on what business; if he or she swore truly, he or she should be allowed to pass freely; but if he or she swore falsely and did then cross the bridge, he or she should be hanged forthwith upon the gallows. One man, by coincidence named 'Alfred', coming up to the other end of the bridge from the gallows, swore when his oath was required: 'I go to be hanged on yonder gallows', and thereupon crossed the bridge. The vexed question whether the man should be hanged was brought to Sancho Panza, who was holding court in the immediate vicinity and who was of course obligated to uphold the law as enacted by the lord of the manor.*

---

* Adapted from Alonzo Church, *Introduction to Mathematical Logic*, vol. 1 (Princeton: Princeton University Press, 1956), p. 105.

Given the scheme of abbreviation

P : Alfred crosses the bridge
Q : Alfred is hanged on the gallows
R : the oath to which Alfred swore is true
S : the law is obeyed ,

the data of the situation are expressed in the three sentences

(2) $R \leftrightarrow P \wedge Q$
(3) P
(4) $S \rightarrow (Q \leftrightarrow P \wedge \sim R)$

By means of a derivation demonstrate that the law cannot be obeyed in this situation, that is, derive the sentence '$\sim S$' from the sentences (2), (3), and (4). Note that to replace (4) by the sentence

(5) $S \rightarrow (P \wedge \sim R \rightarrow Q)$

would not sufficiently represent the data, for we must suppose that it is as much a violation of the law to hang an innocent person as it is to let a guilty one go free. Demonstrate by means of truth-value analysis the insufficiency of (5); that is, demonstrate that the argument with (2), (3), and (5) as premises and '$\sim S$' as conclusion is invalid.

78. Alfred, Kurt, and Rudolf are suspected of civil disobedience. They testify under oath as follows.

Alfred: Kurt is guilty and Rudolf is innocent.
Kurt: If Alfred is guilty, then so is Rudolf.
Rudolf: I am innocent but at least one of the others is guilty.

Assuming that one is guilty if and only if not innocent, answer the following questions:

(a) Can everyone's testimony be true?
(b) The testimony of one of the suspects follows from that of another. Which from which?
(c) Assuming that everyone is innocent, who committed perjury?
(d) Assuming that everyone's testimony is true, who is innocent and who is guilty?
(e) Assuming that the innocent told the truth and the guilty told lies, who is innocent and who is guilty?

79. Alfred is kidnapped for ransom, but it is soon ascertained that the funds available to ransom a logician are insufficient to make the project remunerative. Alfred's kidnappers decide to allow him a chance to escape. Their leader, a sporting woman, states: 'One of the two doors before you leads to certain death and the other to freedom. You can leave by either door. To help you in making a decision, one of my two assistants will stay with you and will respond with the word 'true' or with the word 'false' to any one sentence which you wish to utter. I must warn you, however, that one of my assistants is completely truthful while the other always lies.' The leader then leaves, believing that she has

given Alfred at least a sporting chance and smiling because she has relieved herself of making the critical decision. Alfred is smiling, too, for what was only a sporting chance in the mind of a kidnapper was a certainty for a quick-witted logician. Alfred asserted his sentence, and got his one response; he then walked through one of the doors knowing that it led to his freedom. What sentence did Alfred assert? Explain by truth-value analysis how he knew that the sentence would obtain for him his freedom.

A solution to the exercise can be systematically discovered as follows. Let us say Alfred desires the response to his sentence to be such that the assistant (truth teller or liar) will respond with the word 'true' if the left door leads to freedom and with the word 'false' otherwise. To construct such a sentence, let us introduce the following scheme of abbreviation

P : the assistant who remains is a truth teller
Q : the left door leads to freedom

and discover a truth table for the sentence Alfred should utter with the aid of the following tableau:

P	Q	Desired response	Alfred's sentence
T	*T*	'true'	*T*
T	*F*	'false'	
F	*T*	'true'	*F*
F	*F*	'false'	

In the first two columns we list all possible truth assignments to 'P' and 'Q'; in the third column we list the responses Alfred desires to obtain by his sentence; in the fourth column we enter the truth value of Alfred's sentence. For example, if the assistant is truthful (that is, 'P' has the value *T*) and answers 'true', then in row 1 Alfred's sentence should have the value *T*. However, if the assistant is a liar (that is, 'P' has the value *F*) and answers 'true', then in row 3 Alfred's sentence should have the value *F*. Upon completing the fourth column, we have reduced the problem to that of finding a sentence having the fourth column as its truth table, a procedure familiar to the reader who has solved exercises 55 and 56 at the end of section 8.

10. Historical remarks. What is now called the sentential calculus has been designated variously the 'calculus of equivalent statements' (MacColl [1]), the 'Aussagenkalkül' (Schröder [1]), the 'propositional calculus' (Russell [2]), and the 'theory of deduction' (Russell [3]).

The sentential calculus was first investigated by the Stoics (see Łukasiewicz [1] and Mates [1]). Its modern development was adumbrated by Leibniz (see Couturat [1] and [2]), in Boole [1] and [2], De Morgan [1], Peirce [1], and MacColl [1], but properly begins with Frege [1]. Its fullest development, based on the ideas of Frege, occurs in Whitehead and Russell [1].

Besides the system of symbols used here, which is due to Tarski, there are two other principal systems. The notation that is most frequent in the literature is that of Whitehead and Russell [1]; its symbols are the following:

'$\sim$' for '$\sim$'
'$\supset$' for '$\rightarrow$'
'$\cdot$' for '$\wedge$'
'$\vee$' for '$\vee$'
'$\equiv$' for '$\leftrightarrow$' .

(To indicate grouping, Whitehead and Russell use, along with parentheses, a complicated system of dots.)

A much more economical notation is that of Łukasiewicz [1]. The essential feature is the placement of sentential connectives. A binary connective is placed *before*, rather than *between*, the two sentences which it connects. Thus, using our symbols '$\sim$' and '$\rightarrow$', we would write

$$\rightarrow \sim P \rightarrow QR$$

for

$$(\sim P \rightarrow (Q \rightarrow R)) \quad ,$$

and

$$\rightarrow\rightarrow \sim PQR$$

for

$$((\sim P \rightarrow Q) \rightarrow R) \quad .$$

The advantage of Łukasiewicz' notation is that it makes unnecessary special symbols for grouping, such as parentheses.

The notion of an instance of a theorem and the principle that an instance of a theorem is again a theorem occur more or less explicitly in Frege [3], Couturat [3], and Russell [2].

The method of truth tables occurs informally in Frege [1], and explicitly in Peirce [2]. The assertion that a symbolic argument is valid in the sentential calculus if and only if its premises tautologically imply its conclusion was first established in Post [1].

Our formulation of the sentential calculus admits of a certain simplification, at the expense of detracting from its intuitive character. We could, as in chapter I, dispense with indirect proof and replace the four inference rules of that chapter by two, *modus ponens* and a variant of *modus tollens;* further, we could replace the primitive inference rules introduced in the present chapter by the following rules, which embody in some sense 'definitions' of '$\wedge$', '$\vee$', '$\leftrightarrow$' in terms of '$\sim$' and '$\rightarrow$':

$$\frac{(\phi \wedge \psi)}{\sim(\phi \rightarrow \sim\psi)} \qquad \frac{\sim(\phi \rightarrow \sim\psi)}{(\phi \wedge \psi)}$$

$$\frac{\phi \vee \psi}{(\sim\phi \rightarrow \psi)} \qquad \frac{(\sim\phi \rightarrow \psi)}{(\phi \vee \psi)}$$

$$\frac{(\phi \leftrightarrow \psi)}{((\phi \rightarrow \psi) \wedge (\psi \rightarrow \phi))} \qquad \frac{((\phi \rightarrow \psi) \wedge (\psi \rightarrow \phi))}{(\phi \leftrightarrow \psi)}$$

The observation made at the end of section 5, that there is no automatic procedure which, in the absence of annotations, will permit a decision as to the correctness of an abbreviated derivation, holds in the sentential calculus only when infinitely many premises are permitted. It can be shown, however, that even when the class of premises, though allowed to be infinite, is required to be decidable (that is, loosely speaking, such that it can automatically be decided of any given sentence whether it is a member of the class), it is not generally possible to formulate an automatic test for a correct abbreviated derivation from that class of premises without recourse to annotations. In abbreviated derivations of the quantifier calculus (that is, the system of chapters III and IV), annotations are indispensable even when only finitely many premises are involved.

The story of exercise 77 is slightly modified from the original as given by Miguel de Cervantes (1615); it appears in Church [3]. The story of exercise 78 is due to Keisler and is a slight modification of its appearance in Kleene [2]. The story of exercise 79 is an old logical puzzle; it appears in Kemeny [1] and is discussed in Gardner [1].

11. Appendix: list of theorems of chapters I and II.

T1	$P \rightarrow P$
T2	$Q \rightarrow (P \rightarrow Q)$
T3	$P \rightarrow ([P \rightarrow Q] \rightarrow Q)$
T4	$(P \rightarrow Q) \rightarrow ([Q \rightarrow R] \rightarrow [P \rightarrow R])$
T5	$(Q \rightarrow R) \rightarrow ([P \rightarrow Q] \rightarrow [P \rightarrow R])$
T6	$(P \rightarrow [Q \rightarrow R]) \rightarrow ([P \rightarrow Q] \rightarrow [P \rightarrow R])$
T7	$([P \rightarrow Q] \rightarrow [P \rightarrow R]) \rightarrow (P \rightarrow [Q \rightarrow R])$
T8	$(P \rightarrow [Q \rightarrow R]) \rightarrow (Q \rightarrow [P \rightarrow R])$

T9	$(P \rightarrow [P \rightarrow Q]) \rightarrow (P \rightarrow Q)$
T10	$([P \rightarrow Q] \rightarrow Q) \rightarrow ([Q \rightarrow P] \rightarrow P)$
T11	$\sim\sim P \rightarrow P$
T12	$P \rightarrow \sim\sim P$
T13	$(P \rightarrow Q) \rightarrow (\sim Q \rightarrow \sim P)$
T14	$(P \rightarrow \sim Q) \rightarrow (Q \rightarrow \sim P)$
T15	$(\sim P \rightarrow Q) \rightarrow (\sim Q \rightarrow P)$
T16	$(\sim P \rightarrow \sim Q) \rightarrow (Q \rightarrow P)$
T17	$P \rightarrow (\sim P \rightarrow Q)$
T18	$\sim P \rightarrow (P \rightarrow Q)$
T19	$(\sim P \rightarrow P) \rightarrow P$
T20	$(P \rightarrow \sim P) \rightarrow \sim P$
T21	$\sim(P \rightarrow Q) \rightarrow P$
T22	$\sim(P \rightarrow Q) \rightarrow \sim Q$
T23	$([P \rightarrow Q] \rightarrow P) \rightarrow P$
T24	$P \wedge Q \leftrightarrow Q \wedge P$
T25	$P \wedge (Q \wedge R) \leftrightarrow (P \wedge Q) \wedge R$
T26	$(P \rightarrow Q) \wedge (Q \rightarrow R) \rightarrow (P \rightarrow R)$
T27	$(P \wedge Q \rightarrow R) \leftrightarrow (P \rightarrow [Q \rightarrow R])$
T28	$(P \wedge Q \rightarrow R) \leftrightarrow (P \wedge \sim R \rightarrow \sim Q)$
T29	$(P \rightarrow Q \wedge R) \leftrightarrow (P \rightarrow Q) \wedge (P \rightarrow R)$
T30	$(P \rightarrow Q) \rightarrow (R \wedge P \rightarrow R \wedge Q)$
T31	$(P \rightarrow Q) \rightarrow (P \wedge R \rightarrow Q \wedge R)$
T32	$(P \rightarrow R) \wedge (Q \rightarrow S) \rightarrow (P \wedge Q \rightarrow R \wedge S)$
T33	$(P \rightarrow Q) \wedge (\sim P \rightarrow Q) \rightarrow Q$
T34	$(P \rightarrow Q) \wedge (P \rightarrow \sim Q) \rightarrow \sim P$
T35	$(\sim P \rightarrow R) \wedge (Q \rightarrow R) \leftrightarrow ([P \rightarrow Q] \rightarrow R)$
T36	$\sim(P \wedge \sim P)$
T37	$(P \rightarrow Q) \leftrightarrow \sim(P \wedge \sim Q)$

T38	$P \wedge Q \leftrightarrow \sim(P \rightarrow \sim Q)$
T39	$\sim(P \wedge Q) \leftrightarrow (P \rightarrow \sim Q)$
T40	$\sim(P \rightarrow Q) \leftrightarrow P \wedge \sim Q$
T41	$P \leftrightarrow P \wedge P$
T42	$P \wedge \sim Q \rightarrow \sim(P \rightarrow Q)$
T43	$\sim P \rightarrow \sim(P \wedge Q)$
T44	$\sim Q \rightarrow \sim(P \wedge Q)$
T45	$P \vee Q \leftrightarrow (\sim P \rightarrow Q)$
T46	$(P \rightarrow Q) \leftrightarrow \sim P \vee Q$
T47	$P \leftrightarrow P \vee P$
T48	$(P \vee Q) \wedge (P \rightarrow R) \wedge (Q \rightarrow S) \rightarrow R \vee S$
T49	$(P \vee Q) \wedge (P \rightarrow R) \wedge (Q \rightarrow R) \rightarrow R$
T50	$(P \rightarrow R) \wedge (Q \rightarrow R) \leftrightarrow (P \vee Q \rightarrow R)$
T51	$(P \vee Q) \wedge (P \rightarrow R) \wedge (\sim P \wedge Q \rightarrow R) \rightarrow R$
T52	$(P \rightarrow R) \wedge (\sim P \wedge Q \rightarrow R) \leftrightarrow (P \vee Q \rightarrow R)$
T53	$P \vee Q \leftrightarrow Q \vee P$
T54	$P \vee (Q \vee R) \leftrightarrow (P \vee Q) \vee R$
T55	$(P \rightarrow Q \vee R) \leftrightarrow (P \rightarrow Q) \vee (P \rightarrow R)$
T56	$(P \rightarrow Q) \rightarrow (R \vee P \rightarrow R \vee Q)$
T57	$(P \rightarrow Q) \rightarrow (P \vee R \rightarrow Q \vee R)$
T58	$(P \rightarrow Q) \vee (Q \rightarrow R)$
T59	$P \vee \sim P$
T60	$(P \rightarrow R) \vee (Q \rightarrow R) \leftrightarrow (P \wedge Q \rightarrow R)$
T61	$P \wedge (Q \vee R) \leftrightarrow (P \wedge Q) \vee (P \wedge R)$
T62	$P \vee (Q \wedge R) \leftrightarrow (P \vee Q) \wedge (P \vee R)$
T63	$P \wedge Q \leftrightarrow \sim(\sim P \vee \sim Q)$
T64	$P \vee Q \leftrightarrow \sim(\sim P \wedge \sim Q)$
T65	$\sim(P \wedge Q) \leftrightarrow \sim P \vee \sim Q$
T66	$\sim(P \vee Q) \leftrightarrow \sim P \wedge \sim Q$

T67	$\sim P \wedge \sim Q \rightarrow \sim(P \vee Q)$
T68	$P \leftrightarrow (P \wedge Q) \vee (P \wedge \sim Q)$
T69	$P \leftrightarrow (P \vee Q) \wedge (P \vee \sim Q)$
T70	$Q \rightarrow (P \wedge Q \leftrightarrow P)$
T71	$\sim Q \rightarrow (P \vee Q \leftrightarrow P)$
T72	$(P \rightarrow Q) \leftrightarrow (P \wedge Q \leftrightarrow P)$
T73	$(P \rightarrow Q) \leftrightarrow (P \vee Q \leftrightarrow Q)$
T74	$(P \leftrightarrow Q) \wedge P \rightarrow Q$
T75	$(P \leftrightarrow Q) \wedge Q \rightarrow P$
T76	$(P \leftrightarrow Q) \wedge \sim P \rightarrow \sim Q$
T77	$(P \leftrightarrow Q) \wedge \sim Q \rightarrow \sim P$
T78	$(P \rightarrow [Q \leftrightarrow R]) \leftrightarrow ([P \rightarrow Q] \leftrightarrow [P \rightarrow R])$
T79	$(P \rightarrow [Q \leftrightarrow R]) \leftrightarrow (P \wedge Q \leftrightarrow P \wedge R)$
T80	$(P \leftrightarrow Q) \vee (P \leftrightarrow \sim Q)$
T81	$(P \leftrightarrow Q) \leftrightarrow (P \rightarrow Q) \wedge (Q \rightarrow P)$
T82	$(P \leftrightarrow Q) \leftrightarrow \sim([P \rightarrow Q] \rightarrow \sim[Q \rightarrow P])$
T83	$(P \leftrightarrow Q) \leftrightarrow (P \wedge Q) \vee (\sim P \wedge \sim Q)$
T84	$P \wedge Q \rightarrow (P \leftrightarrow Q)$
T85	$\sim P \wedge \sim Q \rightarrow (P \leftrightarrow Q)$
T86	$([P \leftrightarrow Q] \rightarrow R) \leftrightarrow (P \wedge Q \rightarrow R) \wedge (\sim P \wedge \sim Q \rightarrow R)$
T87	$\sim(P \leftrightarrow Q) \leftrightarrow (P \wedge \sim Q) \vee (\sim P \wedge Q)$
T88	$P \wedge \sim Q \rightarrow \sim(P \leftrightarrow Q)$
T89	$\sim P \wedge Q \rightarrow \sim(P \leftrightarrow Q)$
T90	$\sim(P \leftrightarrow Q) \leftrightarrow (P \leftrightarrow \sim Q)$
T91	$P \leftrightarrow P$
T92	$(P \leftrightarrow Q) \leftrightarrow (Q \leftrightarrow P)$
T93	$(P \leftrightarrow Q) \wedge (Q \leftrightarrow R) \rightarrow (P \leftrightarrow R)$
T94	$(P \leftrightarrow [Q \leftrightarrow R]) \leftrightarrow ([P \leftrightarrow Q] \leftrightarrow R)$
T95	$(P \leftrightarrow Q) \leftrightarrow ([P \leftrightarrow R] \leftrightarrow [Q \leftrightarrow R])$

T96	$(P \leftrightarrow Q) \leftrightarrow (\sim P \leftrightarrow \sim Q)$
T97	$(P \leftrightarrow R) \wedge (Q \leftrightarrow S) \rightarrow ([P \rightarrow Q] \leftrightarrow [R \rightarrow S])$
T98	$(P \leftrightarrow R) \wedge (Q \leftrightarrow S) \rightarrow (P \wedge Q \leftrightarrow R \wedge S)$
T99	$(P \leftrightarrow R) \wedge (Q \leftrightarrow S) \rightarrow (P \vee Q \leftrightarrow R \vee S)$
T100	$(P \leftrightarrow R) \wedge (Q \leftrightarrow S) \rightarrow ([P \leftrightarrow Q] \leftrightarrow [R \leftrightarrow S])$
T101	$(Q \leftrightarrow S) \rightarrow ([P \rightarrow Q] \leftrightarrow [P \rightarrow S]) \wedge ([Q \rightarrow P] \leftrightarrow [S \rightarrow P])$
T102	$(Q \leftrightarrow S) \rightarrow (P \wedge Q \leftrightarrow P \wedge S)$
T103	$(Q \leftrightarrow S) \rightarrow (P \vee Q \leftrightarrow P \vee S)$
T104	$(Q \leftrightarrow S) \rightarrow ([P \leftrightarrow Q] \leftrightarrow [P \leftrightarrow S])$
T105	$P \wedge (Q \leftrightarrow R) \rightarrow (P \wedge Q \leftrightarrow R)$
T106	$(P \rightarrow [Q \rightarrow R]) \leftrightarrow ([P \rightarrow Q] \rightarrow [P \rightarrow R])$
T107	$(P \rightarrow [Q \rightarrow R]) \leftrightarrow (Q \rightarrow [P \rightarrow R])$
T108	$(P \rightarrow [P \rightarrow Q]) \leftrightarrow (P \rightarrow Q)$
T109	$([P \rightarrow Q] \rightarrow Q) \leftrightarrow ([Q \rightarrow P] \rightarrow P)$
T110	$P \leftrightarrow \sim\sim P$
T111	$(P \rightarrow Q) \leftrightarrow (\sim Q \rightarrow \sim P)$
T112	$(P \rightarrow \sim Q) \leftrightarrow (Q \rightarrow \sim P)$
T113	$(\sim P \rightarrow Q) \leftrightarrow (\sim Q \rightarrow P)$
T114	$(\sim P \rightarrow P) \leftrightarrow P$
T115	$(P \rightarrow \sim P) \leftrightarrow \sim P$
T116	$(P \wedge Q) \vee (R \wedge S) \leftrightarrow (P \vee R) \wedge (P \vee S) \wedge (Q \vee R) \wedge (Q \vee S)$
T117	$(P \vee Q) \wedge (R \vee S) \leftrightarrow (P \wedge R) \vee (P \wedge S) \vee (Q \wedge R) \vee (Q \wedge S)$
T118	$(P \rightarrow Q) \wedge (R \rightarrow S) \leftrightarrow$ $(\sim P \wedge \sim R) \vee (\sim P \wedge S) \vee (Q \wedge \sim R) \vee (Q \wedge S)$
T119	$(P \vee \sim P) \wedge Q \leftrightarrow Q$
T120	$(P \wedge \sim P) \vee Q \leftrightarrow Q$
T121	$P \vee (\sim P \wedge Q) \leftrightarrow P \vee Q$
T122	$P \wedge (\sim P \vee Q) \leftrightarrow P \wedge Q$
T123	$P \leftrightarrow P \vee (P \wedge Q)$

T124 $P \leftrightarrow P \wedge (P \vee Q)$

T125 $(P \rightarrow Q \wedge R) \rightarrow (P \wedge Q \leftrightarrow P \wedge R)$

12. Appendix: solutions to selected exercises.

Section 1

No. 3 is a symbolic sentence. Nos. 4 and 5 are not; the former fails to be a symbolic sentence because '$(P \vee Q \rightarrow R)$' lacks a pair of parentheses, and the latter because the '$\rightarrow$' fails to bring with it a pair of parentheses.

7. $((Q \vee R) \rightarrow ((P \wedge R) \rightarrow (Q \leftrightarrow (R \vee P))))$
10. $\sim((P \vee (Q \wedge R)) \rightarrow (((P \vee Q) \wedge (P \vee R)) \leftrightarrow (P \wedge Q)))$

Section 2

11. Neither Alice nor Mary will dance with Alfred unless he will improve his deportment, but Alfred will improve his deportment if and only if both Alice and Mary will dance with him.

To obtain symbolizations of the remaining sentences of these exercises, we first employ parentheses together with sentence letters and negation signs to obtain a reading, and follow this with a symbolization.

13. Assuming that either P or $\sim Q$, R only if S; $P \vee \sim Q \rightarrow (R \rightarrow S)$
14. Unless P, R if S; $P \vee (S \rightarrow R)$
15. In this sentence 'unless' is to be understood in the exclusive sense. Thus, 'P unless Q' may pass into '$(P \vee Q) \wedge \sim(P \wedge Q)$'.
16. Assuming that P, Q; but if R, neither Q nor S; $(P \rightarrow Q) \wedge [R \rightarrow \sim(Q \vee S)]$
17. In the sentence 'Alfred and Mary are playing dice together' the word 'and' is not used as a phrase of connection; however, the word 'or' in the sentence 'Mary throws 7 or 11' has such a use. Thus, in symbolizing No. 17 we may not use the sentence letters 'P' and 'Q', but we may use either 'V' or both 'W' and 'X'. On the basis of the given scheme, we can obtain two symbolizations of No. 17:

If R, S, and T, then U if and only if V; $(R \wedge S) \wedge T \rightarrow (U \leftrightarrow V)$
If R, S, and T, then U if and only if (W or X); $(R \wedge S) \wedge T \rightarrow (U \leftrightarrow W \vee X)$

18. If P, then either Q or, provided that R, S; $P \rightarrow Q \vee (R \rightarrow S)$
20. If (either P or Q), then (neither R nor [S and T]) unless (U and V); $(P \vee Q) \rightarrow \sim(R \vee [S \wedge T]) \vee (U \wedge V)$

If (either P or Q) then (neither R nor [S and T]), unless (U and V); $[(P \vee Q) \rightarrow \sim(R \vee [S \wedge T])] \vee (U \wedge V)$
(Other alternative readings are less plausible.)

21. (Neither P nor Q) if either R or S; $R \vee S \rightarrow \sim(P \vee Q)$
Neither P nor (Q if either R or S); $\sim(P \vee [R \vee S \rightarrow Q])$
Neither (P if either R or S) nor (Q if either R or S); $\sim[(R \vee S \rightarrow P) \vee (R \vee S \rightarrow Q)]$

(Although the third reading is less plausible than the former two, its symbolization and that of the second reading will be derivable one from the other within the system of logic to be introduced in the next section.)

Section 3

22. The inferences (b), (f), (i), and (n) are applications, respectively, of S, Add, MTP, and CB. None of the other inferences is *an* application of one of the inference rules in question.

Section 5

28.

1.	~~*Show*~~ R	
2.	R	T18, premise 2, MP, premise 1, MP

Section 6

30. The unabbreviated lines that correspond to lines 12–14 are given below; those for lines 15–17 are left to the reader.

12.	~~*Show*~~ $P \wedge Q \rightarrow (P \leftrightarrow Q)$	
13.	$P \wedge Q$	
13.1	Q	13, S
13.2	$Q \rightarrow (P \rightarrow Q)$	T2
13.3	$P \rightarrow Q$	13.1, 13.2, MP
13.4	P	13, S
13.5	$P \rightarrow (Q \rightarrow P)$	$\mathrm{T2}\left(\frac{Q\ \ P}{P\ \ Q}\right)$
13.6	$Q \rightarrow P$	13.4, 13.5, MP
14.	$P \leftrightarrow Q$	13.3, 13.6, CB

Section 7, Group I

37. $(P \rightarrow Q) \rightarrow R \quad . \quad S \rightarrow (\sim Q \rightarrow T) \quad \therefore R \vee \sim T \rightarrow (S \rightarrow R)$

1.	~~*Show*~~ $R \vee \sim T \rightarrow (S \rightarrow R)$	
2.	$R \rightarrow (S \rightarrow R)$	$\mathrm{T2}\left(\frac{Q\ \ P}{R\ \ S}\right)$
3.	~~*Show*~~ $\sim T \rightarrow (S \rightarrow R)$	
4.	$\sim T$	
5.	~~*Show*~~ $S \rightarrow R$	
6.	S	
7.	$\sim Q \rightarrow T$	2nd premise, 6, MP
8.	Q	4, 7, MT, DN
9.	$P \rightarrow Q$	T2, 8, MP
10.	R	1st premise, 9, MP
11.	$R \vee \sim T \rightarrow (S \rightarrow R)$	2, 3, SC

39. $P \wedge Q \rightarrow R \vee S \quad \therefore (P \rightarrow R) \vee (Q \rightarrow S)$

1.	~~*Show*~~ $(P \rightarrow R) \vee (Q \rightarrow S)$	
2.	~~*Show*~~ $\sim(P \rightarrow R) \rightarrow (Q \rightarrow S)$	
3.	$\sim(P \rightarrow R)$	
4.	$P \wedge \sim R$	T40$\left(\frac{P\ \ Q}{P\ \ R}\right)$, BC, 3, MP
5.	~~*Show*~~ $Q \rightarrow S$	
6.	Q	
7.	S	4, S, 6, Adj, 1st premise, MP, 4, S, MTP
8.	$(P \rightarrow R) \vee (Q \rightarrow S)$	2, CD

41.

1.	~~*Show*~~ $[P \leftrightarrow (P \rightarrow Q)] \rightarrow Q$	
2.	$P \leftrightarrow (P \rightarrow Q)$	
3.	~~*Show*~~ $P \rightarrow Q$	
4.	P	
5.	$P \rightarrow Q$	2, BC, 4, MP
6.	~~*Show*~~ $\sim P \rightarrow Q$	
7.	$\sim P$	
8.	$\sim(P \rightarrow Q)$	2, BC, 7, MT
9.	$P \rightarrow Q$	3, R
10.	Q	3, 6, SC

42. $(P \rightarrow Q) \vee (R \rightarrow S) \quad \therefore (P \rightarrow S) \vee (R \rightarrow Q)$

1.	~~*Show*~~ $(P \rightarrow S) \vee (R \rightarrow Q)$	
2.	~~*Show*~~ $\sim(P \rightarrow S) \rightarrow (R \rightarrow Q)$	
3.	$\sim(P \rightarrow S)$	
4.	$P \wedge \sim S$	T40$\left(\frac{P\ \ Q}{P\ \ S}\right)$, BC, 3, MP
5.	~~*Show*~~ $R \rightarrow Q$	
6.	R	
7.	~~*Show*~~ $\sim(R \rightarrow S)$	
8.	$R \rightarrow S$	
9.	S	6, 8, MP
10.	$\sim S$	4, S
11.	$P \rightarrow Q$	7, premise, MTP
12.	Q	4, S, 11, MP
13.	$(P \rightarrow S) \vee (R \rightarrow Q)$	2, CD

Section 7, Group II

Symbolizations for exercises 43–46 on the basis of natural schemes of abbreviation appear as follows; we leave the derivations to the reader.

43. $(Q \rightarrow P) \rightarrow R \quad . \quad \sim Q \vee S \quad . \quad \sim S \quad \therefore \sim R \rightarrow T$
44. $(P \rightarrow Q) \wedge (R \rightarrow P) \quad . \quad (P \vee R) \wedge \sim(Q \wedge R) \quad \therefore (P \wedge Q) \wedge \sim R$
45. $P \wedge Q \rightarrow (R \vee S) \wedge \sim(R \wedge S) \quad . \quad S \rightarrow [(R \wedge Q) \vee (\sim R \wedge \sim Q)] \vee \sim P \quad .$
    $R \wedge Q \rightarrow S \quad \therefore P \rightarrow \sim Q$
46. $\sim(P \wedge \sim Q) \vee \sim(\sim R \wedge \sim S) \quad . \quad \sim S \wedge \sim Q \quad .$
    $T \rightarrow [\sim S \rightarrow (\sim R \wedge P)] \quad \therefore \sim T$

Section 8, Group II

55. A DNF sentence tautologically equivalent to ϕ is

$$(P \wedge Q \wedge R) \vee (P \wedge \sim Q \wedge \sim R) \vee (\sim P \wedge Q \wedge R) \vee (\sim P \wedge \sim Q \wedge R) \quad .$$

This DNF sentence can be obtained from the truth table for ϕ. Each disjunct is correlated with a row in the table for which ϕ has the value *T*. Each disjunct is a conjunction of sentence letters or negations of sentence letters in ϕ. A sentence letter enters into such a conjunction if the sentence letter is assigned *T* in the correlated row of the table; the negation of a sentence letter enters into such a conjunction if the sentence letter is assigned *F* in the correlated row of the table.

57. A CNF sentence tautologically equivalent to ϕ is

$$(\sim P \vee \sim Q \vee R) \wedge (\sim P \vee Q \vee \sim R) \wedge (P \vee \sim Q \vee R) \wedge (P \vee Q \vee R) \quad .$$

This CNF sentence can be obtained by forming the dual of a DNF sentence tautologically equivalent to the negation of ϕ. (To form a DNF sentence, see the solution to No. 55 above.)

59. Tautological equivalences for exercises (a)–(f) can be summarized in the following table. The symbolic sentence at the top of each column is tautologically equivalent to each of the symbolic sentences in its column. Symbolic sentences in the table contain only the connectives listed on the left.

	$P \rightarrow Q$	$P \wedge Q$	$P \vee Q$
$\sim, \rightarrow$		$\sim(P \rightarrow \sim Q)$	$\sim P \rightarrow Q$
$\sim, \wedge$	$\sim(P \wedge \sim Q)$		$\sim(\sim P \wedge \sim Q)$
$\sim, \vee$	$\sim P \vee Q$	$\sim(\sim P \vee \sim Q)$	

60. (a) '$\sim P$' is tautologically equivalent to '$(P|P)$'.
    (b) '$P \rightarrow Q$' is tautologically equivalent to '$(P|(Q|Q))$'.
    (c) '$P \wedge Q$' is tautologically equivalent to '$((P|Q)|(P|Q))$'.
    (d) '$P \vee Q$' is tautologically equivalent to '$((P|P)|(Q|Q))$'.

Section 9, Group I

Nos. 64 and 66 are valid, but Nos. 65 and 67 are invalid. No. 67 may require cases.

Section 9, Group II

On the basis of natural schemes of abbreviation, Nos. 73, 74, and 75 pass into the following symbolizations, each of which is invalid. Nos. 73 and 74 may require cases.

73. $P \wedge {\sim}Q \rightarrow R$. $Q \wedge {\sim}P \rightarrow S$. $T \leftrightarrow {\sim}P \vee {\sim}Q$. $U \rightarrow {\sim}(R \vee S)$ $\therefore U \rightarrow {\sim}T$

74. $P \wedge (Q \vee R)$. ${\sim}(P \wedge {\sim}S)$. $P \wedge T \rightarrow {\sim}Q$. ${\sim}T \rightarrow R$ $\therefore U$

75. ${\sim}(P \vee Q) \rightarrow (R \rightarrow S)$. $P \leftrightarrow Q$ $\therefore P \vee S$

Section 9, Group III

78. On the basis of the scheme

P : Alfred is innocent
Q : Kurt is innocent
R : Rudolf is innocent

and the assumption that one is guilty if and only if not innocent, the testimonies of Alfred, Kurt, and Rudolf can be symbolized as follows:

Alfred: ${\sim}Q \wedge R$
Kurt: ${\sim}P \rightarrow {\sim}R$
Rudolf: $R \wedge ({\sim}P \vee {\sim}Q)$.

(a) Yes, everyone's testimony can be true. This can be demonstrated by assigning *T* to each of the above symbolic sentences and obtaining an assignment to the sentence letters that does not contradict the rules (1)–(6).
(b) Rudolf's testimony follows from Alfred's.
(c) Assuming that everyone is innocent (that is, 'P' ,'Q', and 'R' all have the value *T*), Alfred and Rudolf committed perjury.
(d) Assuming that everyone's testimony is true, Alfred and Rudolf are innocent but Kurt is not.
(e) Assuming that the innocent told the truth and the guilty told lies, Alfred and Rudolf are guilty but Kurt is innocent. This can be demonstrated by assigning *T* to each of the following symbolic sentences:

$P \leftrightarrow {\sim}Q \wedge R$
$Q \leftrightarrow ({\sim}P \rightarrow {\sim}R)$
$R \leftrightarrow R \wedge ({\sim}P \vee {\sim}Q)$.

Chapter III
'ALL' and 'SOME'

1. Variables, quantifiers, formulas. Not all intuitively valid English arguments can be reached by the procedures of chapters I and II. For example, the validity of

(1) All persons are mortal. Socrates is a person. ∴ Socrates is mortal

and

(2) All Communists are Marxists. Some Communists are American. ∴ Some Marxists are American ,

unlike that of the arguments in chapters I and II, depends on the meaning of the words 'all' and 'some'.

Before investigating the logic of such words, we must engage in grammatical considerations. Of *sentences* we have already spoken. A *sentence of English* is an expression of English that is either true or false. An *English name* is a word or group of words that purports to designate (at least within a given context) a single object. For example, 'Socrates', 'David Hume', '7', '7 + 5', and 'the author of *Waverley*' are names respectively designating Socrates, David Hume, 7, 12, and Sir Walter Scott. A *variable* is a lower-case italicized Latin letter, with or without a numerical subscript. For example, 'a', 'b', 'x', 'y', 'a_1', 'y_3', 'z_2' are variables.

Using variables, we can construct expressions that closely resemble but fail to be sentences of English. For instance, the expression

(3) x is bald ,

unlike

(4) Socrates is bald

and

(5) Samson is bald ,

is neither true nor false and hence is not a sentence.

Although we cannot ascribe truth or falsehood to (3), we can make other assertions about it. For instance, we can assert that a particular object, such as Socrates or Samson, *satisfies* (3); this amounts to asserting (4) or (5). Or we can say that every object, or at least one object, satisfies (3); these assertions amount respectively to

(6) For each x, x is bald

and

(7) There is an object x such that x is bald .

Expressions (6) and (7), although not completely idiomatic, can nevertheless, like their more idiomatic counterparts 'Everything is bald' and 'Something is bald', be construed as sentences of English; in fact, (6) is false and (7) is true. We have thus discovered three ways of converting (3) into a sentence: by replacing its variable 'x' by an English name, by prefixing the phrase 'for each x', or by prefixing the phrase 'there is an object x such that'.

We shall abbreviate 'for each' by '$\wedge$' and 'there is an object...such that' by '$\vee$'. The symbols '$\wedge$' and '$\vee$' are known respectively as the *universal quantifier* and the *existential quantifier*. A quantifier may be written before any variable to form a *quantifier phrase*, which is *universal* or *existential* according to the quantifier used. The English counterparts of quantifier phrases, that is, expressions of the form

for each α

or

there is an object α such that ,

where α is a variable, are called *phrases of quantity*.

By a *formula of English* we shall understand either a sentence of English or an expression containing occurrences of variables that becomes a sentence of English when some or all of these occurrences are replaced by English names. Expression (3) above, as well as each of the following, is a formula of English:

David Hume is human ,
a loves b ,
(8) there is an object y such that x loves y ,
(9) $x + y = z$,
if x is a person, then x is mortal .

To see, for example, that (8) is a formula, we need only replace the variable 'x' by 'Romeo'; and to see that (9) is a formula, we may replace the variables 'x', 'y', and 'z' by the names '2', '3', and '4'.

In symbolic abbreviations, we shall henceforth employ not only sentence letters but also *name letters* and *predicate letters*. The former are to be capitals from 'A' through 'E', with or without numerical subscripts; the latter are to be capitals from 'F' through 'O', with or without numerical subscripts. 'P' through 'Z', with or without numerical subscripts, continue in their role as sentence letters. A name letter will serve as an abbreviation for an English name; for example, the name 'Socrates' may be abbreviated by the letter 'A'. A predicate letter accompanied by a variable will serve as an abbreviation for a formula of English containing only that variable. (Abbreviations for formulas of English with more than one variable will be introduced in the next chapter.) For example, the formula '*x* is bald' may be abbreviated by 'F*x*'. Given this abbreviation, we may replace '*x* is bald' in (6) and (7) above by 'F*x*' to obtain 'For each *x*, F*x*' and 'There is an object *x* such that F*x*'. We may then replace phrases of quantity in the latter expressions by quantifier phrases to obtain

$$\bigwedge x \mathrm{F} x$$

and

$$\bigvee x \mathrm{F} x \quad ,$$

which will serve, respectively, as symbolizations of (6) and (7). Further, if we let 'A' abbreviate 'Socrates', we obtain (by replacing '*x*' by 'A' in 'F*x*')

$$\mathrm{FA} \quad ,$$

which will serve as a symbolization of (4), that is, of 'Socrates is bald'.

More generally, the *symbolic language* with which we are now concerned contains the following symbols:

(1) the sentential connectives;
(2) parentheses;
(3) the quantifiers, that is, '⋀' and '⋁';
(4) variables, that is, italicized lower-case Latin letters with or without numerical subscripts;
(5) name letters, that is, capital letters 'A' through 'E' with or without numerical subscripts;
(6) sentence letters, that is, capital letters 'P' through 'Z' with or without numerical subscripts;
(7) predicate letters, that is, capital letters 'F' through 'O' with or without numerical subscripts.

We shall refer to variables and name letters as *symbolic terms*.

Loosely speaking, the formulas of our symbolic language can be characterized as follows: sentence letters standing alone and predicate letters followed by a symbolic term are symbolic formulas; sentential compounds of symbolic formulas are symbolic formulas; quantifier phrases followed by a symbolic formula are symbolic formulas; and nothing else is a symbolic formula. To be more precise, the class of *symbolic formulas* can be exhaustively characterized as follows:

(*1*) *Sentence letters are symbolic formulas.*

(*2*) *The result of writing a predicate letter followed by a symbolic term is a symbolic formula.*

(*3*) *If* ϕ *is a symbolic formula, then so is*

$$\sim\phi \quad .$$

(*4*) *If* ϕ *and* ψ *are symbolic formulas, then so are*

$$(\phi \rightarrow \psi) \quad ,$$

$$(\phi \vee \psi) \quad ,$$

$$(\phi \wedge \psi) \quad ,$$

$$(\phi \leftrightarrow \psi) \quad .$$

(*5*) *If* ϕ *is a symbolic formula and* α *is a variable, then*

$$\bigwedge\alpha\phi \quad ,$$

$$\bigvee\alpha\phi$$

are symbolic formulas.

Clause (5) leads not only to '⋀*x*F*x*', but also to seemingly meaningless combinations such as '⋀*x*P'. It would be artificial to exclude the latter possibilities; their meaning will be explained in due course.

Some further terminology will be useful. We shall refer to the collection of formulas obtained by means of clauses (1) and (2) as *atomic formulas*; thus, an atomic formula is a symbolic formula in which neither a sentential connective nor a quantifier occurs. The result of prefixing one or more universal quantifier phrases to a symbolic formula is called a *universal generalization* of that formula; similarly, one forms *existential generalizations* of a symbolic formula. For example, '⋀*x*(F*x* ∧ G*y*)' and '⋀*x*⋀*y*(F*x* ∧ G*y*)' are universal generalizations, and '⋁*x*(F*x* ∧ G*y*)' and '⋁*y*⋁*x*(F*x* ∧ G*y*)' are existential generalizations, of '(F*x* ∧ G*y*)'; further, '⋁*y*⋀*x*(F*x* ∧ G*y*)' is an existential generalization of a universal generalization of '(F*x* ∧ G*y*)'.

Symbolic formulas, like the symbolic sentences of the preceding chapters, are generated by grammatical trees. Here the initial nodes of a grammatical tree are atomic formulas, nonbranching nodes are reached by clauses (3) and (5), and branching nodes by clause (4) of the characterization of symbolic formulas. For example, the formula

$$(10) \qquad \bigvee x(\bigvee x(Fx \vee Gy) \rightarrow \bigwedge y(Fx \vee \bigvee z Gy))$$

is generated by the following tree:

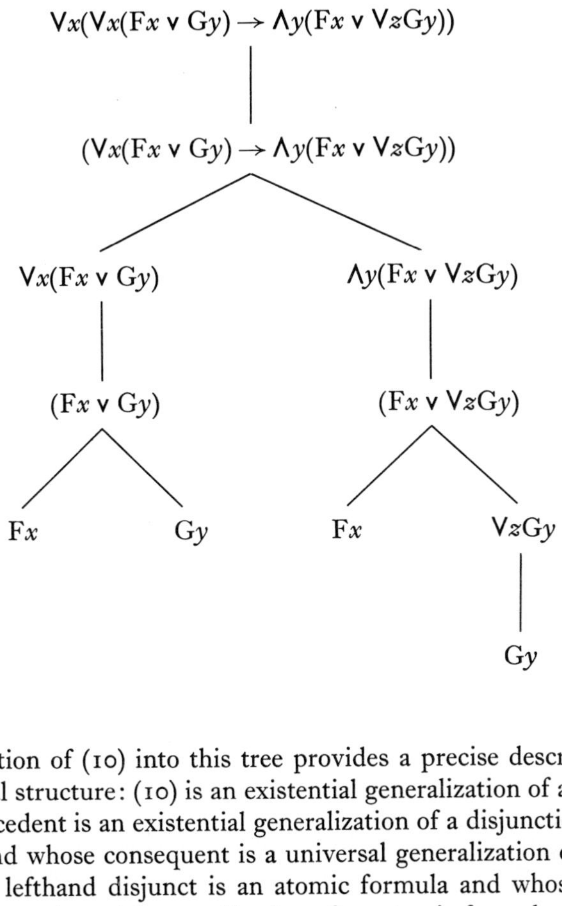

Decomposition of (10) into this tree provides a precise description of its grammatical structure: (10) is an existential generalization of a conditional whose antecedent is an existential generalization of a disjunction of atomic formulas and whose consequent is a universal generalization of a disjunction whose lefthand disjunct is an atomic formula and whose righthand disjunct is an existential generalization of an atomic formula.

EXERCISES

For each of the following expressions, state whether or not it is a symbolic formula. If an expression is a symbolic formula, describe its grammatical structure (perhaps with the aid of a grammatical tree).

Exercises 1 and 2 are solved for illustration.

1. $\bigwedge z(\bigwedge x \bigvee y(Fx \vee Gy) \rightarrow Hz)$

According to clause (2), 'Fx', 'Gy', and 'Hz' are symbolic formulas; thus according to clause (4), '$(Fx \vee Gy)$' is a symbolic formula, and according to clause (5), first '$\bigvee y(Fx \vee Gy)$' and then '$\bigwedge x \bigvee y(Fx \vee Gy)$' are symbolic formulas. By clause (4) again, '$(\bigwedge x \bigvee y(Fx \vee Gy) \rightarrow Hz)$' is a symbolic formula, and according to clause (5) again, No. 1, is a symbolic formula. No. 1 is generated by the following grammatical tree:

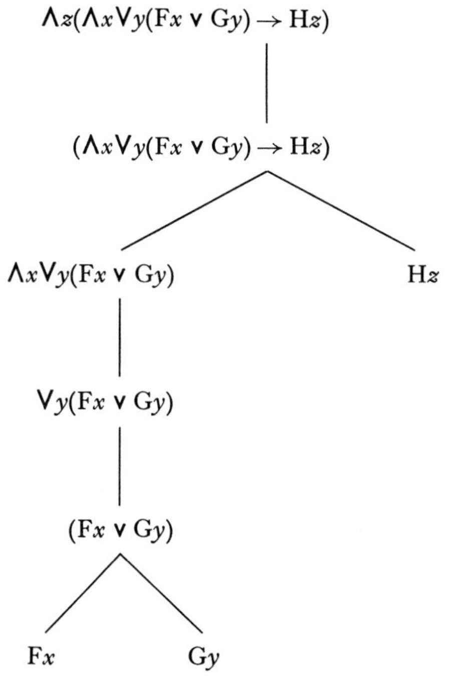

Reading the grammatical tree from its top to its initial nodes gives us the grammatical structure of No. 1: it is a universal generalization of a conditional whose consequent is an atomic formula and whose antecedent is a universal generalization of an existential generalization of a disjunction of two atomic formulas.

2. $\bigwedge x Fx \vee \bigwedge y Gy$

This could be a symbolic formula only of the kind introduced by clause (5), for it is not a sentence letter (clause (1)), it is not a predicate letter followed by a symbolic term (clause (2)), its first symbol is not a negation sign (clause (3)), and its first symbol is not a left parenthesis (clause (4)). But clause (5) is applicable only if what follows the quantifier phrase '$\bigwedge x$' is a symbolic formula; that is, only if '$Fx \vee \bigwedge yGy$' is a symbolic formula, and, strictly speaking, this is not the case, as another review of clauses (1)–(5) would reveal. Thus No. 2 is not a symbolic formula. (What is missing from No. 2 is a pair of parentheses, in either of two places; both '$(\bigwedge xFx \vee \bigwedge yGy)$' and '$\bigwedge x(Fx \vee \bigwedge yGy)$' are symbolic formulas.)

3. $((\bigwedge x(Fx \rightarrow Gx) \wedge FA) \rightarrow GA)$
4. $\sim(\sim\bigwedge x \sim Fx \vee Gy)$
5. $(Fxy \rightarrow Gyx)$
6. $\bigwedge a(Hx \leftrightarrow Gy)$
7. $\bigvee\bigwedge x(Hx \leftrightarrow Gx)$
8. $\bigwedge y \sim\bigvee \sim x(Hx \wedge Gy)$
9. $\bigwedge y(Hy \rightarrow \bigvee xHx)$
10. $\bigwedge x(\bigwedge x(Hx \rightarrow \sim\bigvee y \sim Gy) \vee Fx)$
11. $(\bigvee x) \sim Fx$
12. $\bigwedge x(FGx \rightarrow Gy)$
13. $(FA \rightarrow \sim GK)$
14. $\bigvee x(P \rightarrow \bigwedge x \sim Qx)$
15. $\bigvee x \sim Dx$

2. Bondage and freedom. A variable may occur more than once in a formula. For example, in each of the formulas

(1) $$\bigvee x(Fx \wedge Gx)$$

(2) $$(\bigvee xFx \wedge Gx) \quad ,$$

the first an existential generalization of a conjunction and the second a conjunction of an existential generalization and an atomic formula, there are three occurrences of the variable 'x'. All three occurrences of 'x' are *bound in* (1). Only the first and second occurrences of 'x' are *bound in* (2); the third occurrence of 'x' (that following 'G') is not *bound in* (2) but instead is *free in* (2).

In general, an *occurrence of a variable* α is *bound in* a symbolic formula ϕ just in case it stands within an occurrence in ϕ of a formula

$$\bigwedge\alpha\psi$$

or

$$\bigvee\alpha\psi \quad ,$$

where ψ is a formula. An *occurrence of a variable* is *free in* a symbolic formula ϕ just in case it stands within ϕ but is not bound in ϕ.

The claim that all three occurrences of 'x' are bound in (1) is verified by noticing that each stands within an occurrence in (1) of '$\bigvee x(\mathrm{F}x \wedge \mathrm{G}x)$'. Likewise, the first and second occurrences of 'x' in (2) stand within an occurrence in (2) of '$\bigvee x\mathrm{F}x$'. However, the third occurrence of 'x' in (2) does not stand within an occurrence of any formula beginning with a quantifier phrase; thus the third occurrence of 'x' in (2) is free in (2). In the formula

(3) $$((\mathrm{F}x \wedge \mathrm{G}y) \vee \bigwedge x(\mathrm{F}x \wedge \mathrm{G}y))$$

the second and third occurrences of the variable 'x' are bound, because they stand within an occurrence in (3) of

(4) $$\bigwedge x(\mathrm{F}x \wedge \mathrm{G}y)$$

However, the first occurrence of 'x' and both occurrences of 'y' are free in (3). Although the second occurrence of 'y' in (3) stands within an occurrence of (4), it is still free in (3), because the quantifier phrase with which (4) begins does not contain 'y'.

The previous considerations apply to *occurrences* of a variable. A *variable* itself is *bound in* a symbolic formula ϕ just in case some occurrence of it is bound in ϕ. Similarly, a *variable* is *free in* ϕ just in case some occurrence of it is free in ϕ. For example, the variable 'x' is both bound and free in (3), while 'y' is only free in (3).

By a *symbolic sentence* is understood a symbolic formula in which no variable is free. For example, (1) but not (2) is a symbolic sentence; this fact will be important in connection with exercises 19 and 20 of section 4.

The bound and free occurrences of a variable in a symbolic formula can be identified mechanically by means of a modified grammatical tree for the formula, and this mechanical procedure may be useful to a reader who has trouble, initially, understanding the more abstract characterization of bondage and freedom given above. The modification consists of the following: whenever an expression of either of the forms

$$\bigwedge \alpha \phi$$

or

$$\bigvee \alpha \phi \quad ,$$

where α is a variable and ϕ is a formula, enters into the generation of a tree, attach a link to the occurrence of the variable α in the quantifier phrase and connect it with all occurrences of α in ϕ that are not already in a linkage;

links once entered remain throughout the generation of the remainder of the tree. For example, a tree for the formula (10) of the preceding section,

$$(5) \qquad \bigvee x(\bigvee x(Fx \vee Gy) \rightarrow \bigwedge y(Fx \vee \bigvee zGy)) \quad ,$$

appears as follows with the links included:

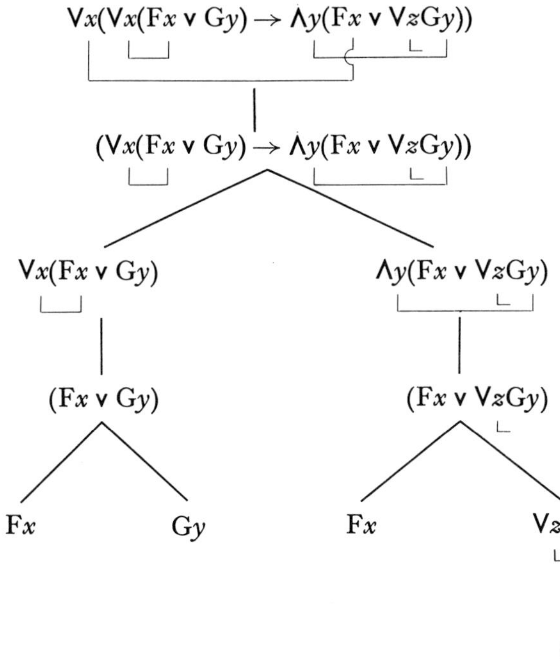

An occurrence of a variable in (5) is bound in (5) if and only if it is linked in the top node of the modified grammatical tree for (5). Thus all occurrences of 'x', the second and third occurrences of 'y' (but not the first), and the only occurrence of 'z' are bound in (5). Generally, an occurrence of a variable in a symbolic formula ϕ is bound in ϕ if and only if it is linked in the top node of a modified grammatical tree for ϕ.

EXERCISES

Consider the formula

$$\bigwedge y((\bigvee x(Fx \vee Hy) \vee Gx) \rightarrow \bigwedge z(Fz \vee (Gy \rightarrow \bigwedge xGz)))$$

16. In this formula identify (perhaps with the aid of a modified grammatical tree) each occurrence of a variable as bound or free.

17. Which variables are bound in the formula? Which variables are free in it?

3. Informal notational conventions. We shall continue to use the conventions of chapter II (pp. 51, 64, and 79) for omitting parentheses and replacing them by brackets. For practical purposes, then, we shall deal with a larger class of symbolic formulas than that given in section 1. It should be emphasized, however, that in theoretical discussions—for instance, in the criteria of bondage and freedom given in the last section and in the rules of derivation that will appear in section 5—the word 'formula' is always to be understood in the official sense characterized in section 1.

4. Translation and symbolization. The English sentence

(1) For each x, x is bald

may be paraphrased in a variety of ways, for instance, as

Everything is bald ,
Each thing is bald ,
All things are bald ,
For all x, x is bald ;

and the English sentence

(2) There is an object x such that x is bald

may be paraphrased as

Something is bald ,
At least one thing is bald ,
There is a bald thing ,
For some x, x is bald .

Using phrases of quantity together with the phrases of connection of chapters I and II, we can develop stylistic variants of a number of English expressions in addition to those just mentioned. For instance,

Nothing is bald

may be paraphrased as either

(3) For each x, it is not the case that x is bald

or

(4) It is not the case that there is an object x such that x is bald

Other examples are afforded by sentences of the familiar Aristotelian forms.

(5) All dogs are canine ,
(6) Some dogs are cats ,
No dogs are canine ,
Some dogs are not cats

are stylistic variants, respectively, of

(7) For each x (if x is a dog, then x is a canine) ,

(8) There is an object x such that (x is a dog and x is a cat) ,

(9) For each x (if x is a dog, then it is not the case that x is a canine) ,

(10) There is an object x such that (x is a dog and it is not the case that x is a cat) .

The supposition that the true sentence (5) has

(11) For each x (x is a dog and x is canine)

as a stylistic variant can be rejected by observing that (11) is false, for it logically implies the falsehood 'for each x, x is a canine'. (See exercise 102, section 11.) Similarly, the supposition that the false sentence (6) has

(12) There is an object x such that (if x is a dog, then x is a cat)

as a stylistic variant can be rejected by observing that (12) is true, for it is implied by the truth 'there is an object x such that x is a cat'. (See exercise 103, section 11.)

Somewhat less obvious examples of stylistic variance are provided by the sentences

Only citizens are voters

and

None but citizens are voters ,

both of which may be paraphrased as

For each x (if x is a voter, then x is a citizen) .

It is impractical to list all the combinations that are expressible in terms of phrases of quantity; however, further examples of stylistic variance will be given when we illustrate the processes of translation and symbolization and also in connection with the exercises for this section.

The processes of translation and symbolization are more interesting here than in the sentential calculus. Some English sentences that previously entered into these processes as unanalyzed units can now have their internal structure represented in the expanded symbolic language. First, we must extend the notion of an abbreviation, for now names of English and formulas of English with one variable as well as sentences of English will require symbolic representation. Accordingly, we presently understand by an *abbreviation* either an ordered pair of which the first member is a sentence letter and the second member is a sentence of English, an ordered pair of which the first member is a name letter and the second member a name of English, or an ordered pair of which the first member is a predicate letter and the second member a formula of English whose only variable is '*a*'. (The adequacy of employing only the variable '*a*' in an abbreviation will become apparent when we characterize the process of translation.) Again, a *scheme of abbreviation* is to be a collection of abbreviations such that no two abbreviations in the collection have the same first member. For example, the following is a scheme of abbreviation:

P : appearances are deceptive
A : Socrates
F : *a* is bald .

On the basis of this scheme of abbreviation, we shall regard the English sentences

Socrates is bald
Either Socrates is bald or appearances are deceptive

as literal translations, respectively, of the symbolic sentences

$$\mathrm{FA}$$
$$\mathrm{FA} \vee \mathrm{P} \quad ;$$

and the latter as symbolizations, respectively, of the former. Also, on the basis of this scheme, we shall regard the English sentences (1)–(4) above as literal translations, respectively, of the symbolic sentences

$$\bigwedge x \mathrm{F}x$$
$$\bigvee x \mathrm{F}x$$
$$\bigwedge x \sim \mathrm{F}x$$
$$\sim \bigvee x \mathrm{F}x \quad .$$

Further, we shall count the latter symbolic sentences as symbolizations not only of their literal translations but also of all the stylistic variants of their literal translations. Thus, for example, '$\bigwedge x\mathrm{F}x$' is a symbolization of 'Everything is bald' as well as of (1) above.

The pairs

F : *a* is a dog
G : *a* is a canine
H : *a* is a cat

are another example of a scheme of abbreviation. On the basis of this scheme we shall consider the English sentences (7)–(10) above literal translations, respectively, of the symbolic sentences

(13) $\bigwedge x(\mathrm{F}x \rightarrow \mathrm{G}x)$
(14) $\bigvee x(\mathrm{F}x \wedge \mathrm{H}x)$
$\bigwedge x(\mathrm{F}x \rightarrow \sim \mathrm{G}x)$
$\bigvee x(\mathrm{F}x \wedge \sim \mathrm{H}x)$.

And we shall count these symbolic sentences as symbolizations not only of their literal translations but also as symbolizations of all stylistic variants of their literal translations. Thus, for example, (13) is a symbolization of both (7) and (5), and (14) is a symbolization of both (8) and (6). With these examples as an introduction, we now turn to a general characterization of the processes of translation and symbolization.

The process of *literal translation into English on the basis of a given scheme of abbreviation* now begins with a symbolic formula and if successful ends with a formula of English. The process consists of the following steps:

(*i*) *Restore any parentheses that may have disappeared as a result of informal conventions.*

(*ii*) *Replace name letters and sentence letters by English names and sentences in accordance with the scheme of abbreviation.*

(*iii*) *Replace each predicate letter by the formula of English with which it is paired in the scheme of abbreviation, flanking the latter with a pair of braces. (The result of this step will contain parts of the form*

$$\{\phi\}\,\zeta \quad ,$$

where ϕ is a formula of English and ζ is either the variable or the name of English that accompanies the predicate letter being replaced.)

(*iv*) *Replace all parts of the form*

$$\{\phi\}\,\zeta \quad ,$$

where ϕ is a formula of English and ζ is either a variable or a name of English, by the result of replacing in ϕ all occurrences of the variable 'a' by ζ.

(*v*) *Eliminate sentential connectives and quantifier phrases in favor of the corresponding phrases of connection and quantity, preserving all parentheses.*

As before, we say that an English formula is a *free translation* (or simply a *translation*) of a symbolic formula ϕ on the basis of a given scheme of abbreviation if it is a stylistic variant of the literal English translation of ϕ based on that scheme.

Consider, for example, the symbolic sentence

(15) $$\bigwedge x(\mathrm{F}x \rightarrow \mathrm{G}x) \rightarrow \mathrm{P} \vee \mathrm{GA} \quad .$$

Let us translate it into English on the basis of the following scheme of abbreviation:

(16)

P : there are exceptions
A : Socrates
F : *a* is a person
G : *a* is mortal .

In step (i) of the process of literal translation into English, (15) becomes

$$(\bigwedge x(Fx \rightarrow Gx) \rightarrow (P \vee GA)) \quad ;$$

in step (ii)

$$(\bigwedge x(Fx \rightarrow Gx) \rightarrow (\text{there are exceptions} \vee \text{G Socrates})) \quad ;$$

in step (iii)

$$(\bigwedge x(\{a \text{ is a person}\}\, x \rightarrow \{a \text{ is mortal}\}\, x) \rightarrow (\text{there are exceptions} \vee \{a \text{ is mortal}\} \text{ Socrates})) \quad ;$$

in step (iv)

$$(\bigwedge x(x \text{ is a person} \rightarrow x \text{ is mortal}) \rightarrow (\text{there are exceptions} \vee \text{Socrates is mortal})) \quad ;$$

and in step (v)

(17) (If for each *x* (if *x* is a person, then *x* is mortal), then (there are exceptions or Socrates is mortal)) .

Thus (17) is a literal translation of (15) into English on the basis of the scheme (16); and the more idiomatic sentence

> If all persons are mortal, then either there are exceptions or Socrates is mortal ,

being a stylistic variant of (17), qualifies as a free translation of (15) on the basis of the same scheme.

The reader should note that the single variable '*a*' of an abbreviation passes into the various variables and name letters of the symbolic formula being translated into English in the passage from step (iii) to step (iv) of the process of translation. Thus the variable '*a*' in an abbreviation serves as a *place holder*. The utility of this service will be emphasized in the exercises that follow.

We say that ϕ is a *symbolization* of a formula ψ of English on the basis of a given scheme of abbreviation just in case ϕ is a symbolic formula which has ψ as a translation on the basis of that scheme.

To find a symbolization of a given formula of English on the basis of a given scheme of abbreviation, it is useful to proceed roughly as follows:

(*1*) *Introduce phrases of quantity and connection, the latter accompanied by parentheses and occurring canonically* (*that is, standing only before or between formulas*), *in place of their stylistic variants.*

(*2*) *Reverse the steps leading from a symbolic formula to a literal English translation.*

For example, consider the sentence

(18) If a woman is married and all married women are wives, then she is a wife ,

together with the scheme of abbreviation

F : *a* is a woman
G : *a* is married
H : *a* is a wife .

Some points should be noted before a symbolization is attempted. First, the indefinite article is often used as a stylistic variant of a phrase of quantity, and this is true of the first occurrence of 'a' in (18). Secondly, despite the fact that (18) begins with 'if', its symbolization should clearly be not a conditional but a universal generalization of a conditional. Thirdly, English pronouns often play a role like that of variables in our symbolic language; this is the case with 'she' in (18). These points suggest that (18) should become in step (1)

For each x (if ((x is a woman and x is married) and for each y (if (y is a woman and y is married), then y is a wife)), then x is a wife) .

Let us now perform step (2) of the process of symbolization. Reversing step (v) of the process of literal translation into English, we obtain

$\bigwedge x(((x$ is a woman $\wedge$ x is married) $\wedge$ $\bigwedge y((y$ is a woman $\wedge$ y is married) $\rightarrow y$ is a wife)) $\rightarrow x$ is a wife) .

When step (iv) is reversed, this becomes

$\bigwedge x(((\{a$ is a woman$\} x \wedge \{a$ is married$\} x) \wedge \bigwedge y((\{a$ is a woman$\} y \wedge \{a$ is married$\} y) \rightarrow \{a$ is a wife$\} y)) \rightarrow \{a$ is a wife$\} x)$.

Reversing step (iii), we obtain

$$\bigwedge x((Fx \wedge Gx) \wedge \bigwedge y((Fy \wedge Gy) \rightarrow Hy) \rightarrow Hx) \quad .$$

Finally, reversing step (i) (for step (ii) is irrelevant), we obtain

(19) $$\bigwedge x(Fx \wedge Gx \wedge \bigwedge y(Fy \wedge Gy \rightarrow Hy) \rightarrow Hx) \quad .$$

(The use of two variables, 'x' and 'y', is not necessary for a symbolization of (18); it could equally well become '$\bigwedge x(Fx \wedge Gx \wedge \bigwedge x(Fx \wedge Gx \rightarrow Hx) \rightarrow Hx)$', which is, however, somewhat less perspicuous than (19).)

EXERCISES, GROUP I

On the basis of the scheme of abbreviation

F : *a* is an even number
G : *a* is a prime number
H : *a* is honest
J : *a* is a person
A : 2
B : the son of Lysimachus ,

translate the following symbolic formulas into idiomatic English. Exercises 18–20 are solved for illustration.

18. $\bigwedge x(Jx \wedge Hx \rightarrow HB)$

In steps (i) and (ii) of the process of literal translation into English, No. 18 becomes

$$\bigwedge x((Jx \wedge Hx) \rightarrow \text{H the son of Lysimachus}) \quad ,$$

in steps (iii) and (iv)

$\bigwedge x((x$ is a person $\wedge$ x is honest) $\rightarrow$ the son of Lysimachus is honest) ,

and in step (v)

(20) For each x (if (x is a person and x is honest), then the son of Lysimachus is honest) .

Thus (20) is the literal English translation of No. 18, and the following stylistic variant of (20) is a translation of that symbolic formula into idiomatic English:

If anyone is honest, then the son of Lysimachus is honest .

19. $GA \rightarrow \bigvee x(Fx \wedge Gx)$

20. $GA \rightarrow \bigvee xFx \wedge Gx$

On the basis of the given scheme, the literal translations into English of Nos. 19 and 20 are, respectively,

(If 2 is a prime number, then there is an object x such that (x is an even number and x is a prime number))

and

(If 2 is a prime number, then (there is an object x such that x is an even number, and x is a prime number)) ;

and the following stylistic variants are respective translations into idiomatic English of the symbolic formulas:

If 2 is a prime number, then there is an even prime number ,
If 2 is a prime number, then there is an even number and x is a prime number .

To account for the fact that No. 19 has a different translation from No. 20, it is sufficient to note that the latter, in contrast with the former, is not a symbolic *sentence*. In the translation of the symbolic formula (20), the variable 'x' is comparable to a third person singular pronoun that lacks an antecedent referent and is a counterpart to the free occurrence of 'x' in (20).

21. $GA \leftrightarrow \bigwedge x(Fx \rightarrow Gx)$
22. $\bigvee x(Fx \wedge Gx) \rightarrow \bigvee xFx \wedge \bigvee xGx$
23. $GA \wedge \bigvee xFx \rightarrow \bigvee x(Fx \wedge Gx)$
24. $\bigwedge x(Fx \wedge Gx \rightarrow GA)$
25. $\bigvee x(Fx \wedge Gx) \rightarrow GA$

EXERCISES, GROUP II

Symbolize each of the following sentences on the basis of the scheme of abbreviation that accompanies it. Exercises 26–29 are solved for illustration.

26. Only citizens are voters. (F : *a* is a citizen; G : *a* is a voter)

To symbolize No. 26, we recall the remarks concerning that sentence given on page 127 and obtain in step (1) of the process of symbolization

For each x (if x is a voter, then x is a citizen) .

In step (2), we first reverse step (v) of the process of literal translation into English to obtain

$\bigwedge x$(x is a voter $\rightarrow$ x is a citizen) ;

and then reverse steps (iv) and (iii) to obtain as a symbolization of No. 26 (for steps (ii) and (i) of the process of literal translation are irrelevant here) the sentence

$$\bigwedge x(Gx \rightarrow Fx) \quad .$$

27. All and only philosophers love wisdom. (F : *a* is a philosopher; G : *a* loves wisdom)

Here we recall first our comments in chapter II concerning canonical stylistic variants (see p. 56) and paraphrase No. 27 by

All philosophers love wisdom and only philosophers love wisdom ,

and then recall our earlier remarks in this section in order to obtain in step (1) of the process of symbolization

(For each x (if x is a philosopher, then x loves wisdom) and for each x (if x loves wisdom, then x is a philosopher)) .

In step (2), we first reverse step (v) of the process of literal translation into English to obtain

$$(\bigwedge x(x \text{ is a philosopher} \rightarrow x \text{ loves wisdom}) \wedge \bigwedge x(x \text{ loves wisdom} \rightarrow x \text{ is a philosopher})) \quad ;$$

next we reverse steps (iv) and (iii) to obtain

$$(\bigwedge x(Fx \rightarrow Gx) \wedge \bigwedge x(Gx \rightarrow Fx)) \quad ;$$

and finally, reversing step (i) (for step (ii) is irrelevant), we obtain as a symbolization of No. 27 the sentence

$$\bigwedge x(Fx \rightarrow Gx) \wedge \bigwedge x(Gx \rightarrow Fx) \quad .$$

28. Among snakes, only copperheads and rattlers are poisonous. (F : *a* is a snake; G : *a* is a copperhead; H : *a* is a rattler; J : *a* is poisonous)

To symbolize No. 28 we must supplement our preceding comment on 'only' (p. 127) with an intuitive observation about English; this intuition suggests that the sentence pass in step (1) of the process of symbolization into either

> For each *x* (if *x* is a snake, then (if *x* is poisonous, then (*x* is a copperhead or *x* is a rattler)))

or

> For each *x* (if (*x* is a snake and *x* is poisonous), then (*x* is a copperhead or *x* is a rattler)) .

Let us now perform step (2) of the process of symbolization, using the first alternative above. Reversing step (v) of the process of literal translation into English, we obtain

$$\bigwedge x(x \text{ is a snake} \rightarrow (x \text{ is poisonous} \rightarrow (x \text{ is a copperhead} \vee x \text{ is a rattler}))) \quad ;$$

reversing steps (iv) and (iii), we obtain

$$\bigwedge x(Fx \rightarrow (Jx \rightarrow (Gx \vee Hx))) \quad ;$$

and finally, reversing step (i) (for step (ii) is irrelevant), we obtain

$$\bigwedge x(Fx \rightarrow [Jx \rightarrow Gx \vee Hx]) \quad .$$

(Idiomatic English often employs the definite article 'the' as a phrase of quantity; for example,

> The only poisonous snakes are copperheads and rattlers

is a stylistic variant of No. 28 and thus has the same symbolization as that sentence.)

29. No one is civilized unless he or she loves classical music. (F : *a* is a person; G : *a* is civilized; H : *a* loves classical music)

Intuition, perhaps aided by some of our earlier and immediately preceding comments on stylistic variance, suggests that No. 29 pass in step (1) of the process of symbolization into

> For each x (if x is a person, then (either it is not the case that x is civilized or x loves classical music)) .

and then in step (2) into

$$\bigwedge x(Fx \rightarrow \sim Gx \vee Hx) \quad .$$

Alternative first steps, based on such paraphrases of No. 29 as

> Only those who love classical music are civilized

> It is not the case that someone is civilized and does not love classical music ,

would yield as symbolizations of No. 29 the symbolic sentences

$$\bigwedge x(Fx \wedge Gx \rightarrow Hx)$$

$$\sim \bigvee x(Fx \wedge Gx \wedge \sim Hx) \quad .$$

It will sometimes be our (admittedly questionable) practice to treat 'no one', 'someone', 'everyone' as stylistic variants of 'nothing', 'something', 'everything'. Adoption of this practice would be indicated, for example, by omitting the pair 'F : *a* is a person' from the scheme of abbreviation that accompanied No. 29 and accepting the sentences

$$\bigwedge x(\sim Gx \vee Hx)$$

$$\bigwedge x(Gx \rightarrow Hx)$$

$$\sim \bigvee x(Gx \wedge \sim Hx)$$

as symbolizations of No. 29.

As a summary of the immediately preceding and earlier examples of symbolization, we give below a list of frequently encountered patterns of idiomatic English, each accompanied by one or more symbolizations (based on a natural scheme of abbreviation). This list should provide a useful but not infallible guide to symbolization in these and subsequent exercises.

Everything is bald.	$\bigwedge xFx$
Nothing is bald.	$\bigwedge x \sim Fx$, $\sim \bigvee xFx$
Something is bald	$\bigvee xFx$
Something is not bald.	$\bigvee x \sim Fx$
All dogs are canine.	$\bigwedge x(Fx \rightarrow Gx)$
Some dogs are canine.	$\bigvee x(Fx \wedge Gx)$
No dogs are canine.	$\bigwedge x(Fx \rightarrow \sim Gx)$, $\sim \bigvee x(Fx \wedge Gx)$
Some dogs are not canine.	$\bigvee x(Fx \wedge \sim Gx)$
Only (none but) citizens are voters.	$\bigwedge x(Gx \rightarrow Fx)$

All and only philosophers love wisdom.	$\bigwedge x(Fx \to Gx) \wedge \bigwedge x(Gx \to Fx)$
Among snakes, only copperheads and rattlers are poisonous.	$\bigwedge x(Fx \to [Jx \to Gx \vee Hx])$
No one is civilized unless he or she loves classical music.	$\bigwedge x(Fx \to \sim Gx \vee Hx)$, $\bigwedge x(Fx \wedge Gx \to Hx)$, $\sim \bigvee x(Fx \wedge Gx \wedge \sim Hx)$

30. Something is round and something is square, but it is not the case that something is a round square. (F : *a* is round; G : *a* is square)

31. If everything is mental, then nothing is physical unless something is both mental and physical. (F : *a* is mental; G : *a* is physical)

32. None but the brave deserve the fair. (F : *a* is brave; G : *a* deserves the fair)

33. Kettles boil quickly only if not watched. (F : *a* is a kettle; G : *a* boils quickly; H : *a* is watched)

34. Kettles boil quickly if not watched. (F : *a* is a kettle; G : *a* boils quickly; H : *a* is watched)

35. Some soldiers love war, but not all who love war are soldiers. (F : *a* is a soldier; G : *a* loves war)

36. If all persons are mortal, then Christ is not a person. (F : *a* is a person; G : *a* is mortal; A : Christ)

37. If Socrates is a philosopher and all philosophers are risible, then he is risible. (F : *a* is a philosopher; G : *a* is risible; A : Socrates)

38. No one under seventeen is admitted unless accompanied by a parent. (F : *a* is under seventeen; G : *a* is admitted; H : *a* is accompanied by a parent)

39. Married persons and only married persons have spouses. (F : *a* is a married person; G : *a* has a spouse)

40. Among equine mammals, all and only zebras have dark stripes on a white or buffy ground. (F : *a* is an equine mammal; G : *a* is a zebra; H : *a* has dark stripes on a white or buffy ground)

41. Democrats and Republicans who put loyalty above legality are detrimental to democracy. (F : *a* is a Democrat; G : *a* is a Republican; H : *a* puts loyalty above legality; J : *a* is detrimental to democracy)

42. Professors are good lecturers if and only if they are both witty and intellectually competent. (F : *a* is a professor; G : *a* is a good lecturer; H : *a* is witty; J : *a* is intellectually competent)

43. If a registered voter has not declared a party and only those who have declared a party can vote in a primary election, then he or she cannot vote in a primary election. (F : *a* is a registered voter; G : *a* has declared a party; H : *a* can vote in a primary election)

44. If only Republicans support the incumbent and no Democrat

supports the candidate, then if anyone is a Democrat, someone supports neither the incumbent nor the candidate. (F : *a* is a Republican; G : *a* supports the incumbent; H : *a* is a Democrat; J : *a* supports the candidate)

45. If those who believe in God have immortal souls, then, given that God exists, they will have eternal bliss. (F : *a* believes in God; G : *a* has an immortal soul; H : *a* will have eternal bliss; P : God exists)

EXERCISES, GROUP III

Symbolize each of the following pairs of sentences on the basis of the scheme of abbreviation that accompanies the pair. Because these sentences exhibit some of the more subtle aspects of the symbolization of idiomatic English, we solve exercises 46–49 for illustration.

46. (i) Nothing that glitters is gold. (ii) All that glitters is not gold. (F : *a* glitters; G : *a* is gold)

The sentence (i), but not (ii), may be paraphrased

(21) For each *x* (if *x* glitters, then it is not the case that *x* is gold) .

The sentence (ii) is not correctly paraphrased by (21), for (21) entails that gold does not glitter—a consequence clearly not intended by the familiar proverb (which might be more accurately worded as 'Not all that glitters is gold'). Intuition suggests that the proverb may instead be paraphrased

(22) It is not the case that for each *x* (if *x* glitters, then *x* is gold).

On the basis of the scheme provided, (21) and (22), and hence (i) and (ii), are respectively symbolized by

$$\bigwedge x(Fx \to \sim Gx)$$

and

$$\sim \bigwedge x(Fx \to Gx) \quad .$$

47. (i) Alfred can solve every puzzle. (ii) Alfred can solve any puzzle. (F : *a* is a puzzle; G : *a* can be solved by Alfred)

The sentences (i) and (ii) are stylistic variants of each other; thus on the given scheme they can both be symbolized by

$$\bigwedge x(Fx \to Gx) \quad .$$

However, consider these English sentences modified with a phrase of negation:

48. (i) Alfred cannot solve every puzzle. (ii) Alfred cannot solve any puzzle. (F : *a* is a puzzle; G : *a* can be solved by Alfred)

Intuition tells us that it would be a mistake to regard (i) and (ii) of this exercise as stylistic variants of each other. Indeed, if Alfred is like most of us, (i) is true but (ii) is not. (i) can be paraphrased

(23) It is not the case that for each x (if x is a puzzle, then x can be solved by Alfred) ;

and (ii) can be paraphrased

(24) For each x (if x is a puzzle, then it is not the case that x can be solved by Alfred) .

On the basis of the scheme provided, (23) and (24), and hence (i) and (ii) of this exercise, pass respectively into

$$\sim \bigwedge x(\mathrm{F}x \rightarrow \mathrm{G}x)$$

and

$$\bigwedge x(\mathrm{F}x \rightarrow \sim \mathrm{G}x) \quad .$$

49. (i) If any witness lied, then he or she committed perjury. (ii) If any witness lied, then all of them committed perjury. (F : *a* is a witness; G : *a* lied; H : *a* committed perjury)

Although (i) appears to be a conditional, it must be interpreted as a universal generalization of a conditional and may be paraphrased by

(25) For each x (if (x is a witness and x lied), then x committed perjury) .

(To see why (i) cannot be interpreted as an existential generalization of a conditional the reader should review the remarks made on page 127.) However, the sentence (ii) may be paraphrased as a conditional. In this case, intuition must be consulted to determine whether 'any' should pass into a universal or an existential quantifier phrase; the latter seems more appropriate. Thus we obtain as a paraphrase of (ii)

(26) (If there is an object x such that (x is a witness and x lied), then for each x (if x is a witness, then x committed perjury)) .

On the basis of the scheme provided, (25) and (26), and hence (i) and (ii) of this exercise, pass respectively into

$$\bigwedge x(\mathrm{F}x \wedge \mathrm{G}x \rightarrow \mathrm{H}x)$$

and

$$\bigvee x(\mathrm{F}x \wedge \mathrm{G}x) \rightarrow \bigwedge x(\mathrm{F}x \rightarrow \mathrm{H}x) \quad .$$

(The sentence (ii) could also be paraphrased as a universal generalization of a conditional, in which case we would obtain first

For each x (if (x is a witness and x lied), then for each x (if x is a witness, then x committed perjury))

and then

$$\bigwedge x[\mathrm{F}x \wedge \mathrm{G}x \rightarrow \bigwedge x(\mathrm{F}x \rightarrow \mathrm{H}x)]$$

as an alternative symbolization of (ii).)

50. (i) Not everyone who talks a great deal has a great deal to say. (ii) No one who talks a great deal has a great deal to say. (F : *a* talks a great deal; G : *a* has a great deal to say)

51. (i) If anyone will spot an error, Alonzo will. (ii) If everyone will spot an error, Alonzo will. (F : *a* will spot an error; A : Alonzo)

52. (i) If something can go wrong, it will go wrong. (ii) If something can go wrong, then everything will go wrong. (F : *a* can go wrong; G : *a* will go wrong)

53. (i) A doctor should uphold the Hippocratic Oath. (ii) A doctor is in the house. (F : *a* is a doctor; G : *a* should uphold the Hippocratic Oath; H : *a* is in the house)

54. (i) Alfred married an intelligent woman, and Rudolf married one too. (ii) Alfred married an intelligent woman, and Rudolf married her too. (F : Alfred married *a*; G : Rudolf married *a*; H : *a* is an intelligent woman)

55. (i) There are diamonds. (ii) There are fake diamonds. (We leave the scheme of abbreviation as well as the symbolization to the reader.)

56. (i) Some students were protesting, but not all of them were arrested. (ii) If some students were protesting, they were arrested. (F : *a* is a student; G : *a* was protesting; H : *a* was arrested)

57. (i) The politician who always promises prosperity is a prevaricator. (ii) Politicians, who always promise prosperity, are prevaricators. (F : *a* is a politician; G : *a* always promises prosperity; H : *a* is a prevaricator)

5. Inference rules. For the logic of quantifiers we shall add three inference rules to our original stock. To facilitate the formulation of these new rules we introduce an auxiliary notion; and for perspicuity in the characterization of this notion we write one Greek letter as a subscript to another. We say that a symbolic formula ϕ_ζ *comes from* a symbolic formula ϕ_α *by proper substitution of a name letter* ζ *for a variable* α if ϕ_ζ is like ϕ_α except for having occurrences of ζ wherever ϕ_α has *free* occurrences of α; and we say that a symbolic formula ϕ_β *comes from* a symbolic formula ϕ_α *by proper substitution of a variable* β *for a variable* α if ϕ_β is like ϕ_α except for having *free* occurrences of β wherever ϕ_α has *free occurrences* of α. Consider for example the formula

(1) $$\bigvee z(Fx \wedge Gy) \rightarrow \bigvee x Hx \vee Gx \quad .$$

The formula

$$\bigvee z(FA \wedge Gy) \rightarrow \bigvee x Hx \vee GA$$

comes from (1) by proper substitution of 'A' for 'x', and

$$\bigvee z(Fy \wedge Gy) \rightarrow \bigvee x Hx \vee Gy$$

comes from (1) by proper substitution of 'y' for 'x'.

The rules of *universal instantiation* and *existential generalization* lead respectively from

$$\bigwedge \alpha \phi_\alpha$$

to

$$\phi_\zeta \quad ,$$

and from

$$\phi_\zeta$$

to

$$\bigvee \alpha \phi_\alpha \quad ,$$

where α is a variable, ζ is a symbolic term, ϕ_α and ϕ_ζ are symbolic formulas, and ϕ_ζ comes from ϕ_α by proper substitution of ζ for α. In both cases α is called the *variable of generalization* and ζ the *instantial term.* Universal instantiation corresponds to the intuitively valid inference from 'Everything is wise' to 'Socrates is wise', that is, more generally, to the intuitive principle that what is true of everything is true of any given thing. Existential generalization corresponds to the intuitively valid inference from 'Socrates is snub-nosed' to 'Something is snub-nosed', that is, more generally, to the intuitive principle that what is true of a given thing is true of something. For example, from the formula '$\bigwedge x \mathrm{F}x$', each of the formulas

$$\mathrm{FA}$$
$$\mathrm{F}x$$
$$\mathrm{F}y$$

follows by universal instantiation; and from each of these formulas, the formula '$\bigvee y \mathrm{F}y$' follows by existential generalization. In both cases, 'A', 'x', and 'y' are instantial terms. In the first case the variable of generalization is 'x'; in the second case it is 'y'.

Now consider the following informal derivation:

(1) Show that if m is even, then $m \cdot n$ is even.
(2) Assume that m is even.
(3) For some k, $m = 2 \cdot k$.
(4) Let k_0 be such a k; thus $m = 2 \cdot k_0$.
(5) Hence $m \cdot n = (2 \cdot k_0) \cdot n = 2 \cdot (k_0 \cdot n)$.
(6) Therefore $m \cdot n$ is even.

The third new inference rule, called the rule of *existential instantiation*, accounts for the intuitive transition from step (3) to step (4), and corresponds to the following principle: what is true of something may be asserted to hold for some particular object. In general, existential instantiation leads from

$$\bigvee \alpha \phi_\alpha$$

to

$$\phi_\beta \quad ,$$

where again α is a variable, β is also a variable, ϕ_α and ϕ_β are symbolic formulas, and ϕ_β comes from ϕ_α by proper substitution of β for α. Note here that, in contrast to the two inference rules previously discussed, β cannot be a name letter. Further, to avoid fallacies, a restriction on the use of existential instantiation is incorporated into clause (5b) of the directions to be given in section 6 for constructing a derivation: the *variable of instantiation* (that is, the variable which replaces α) must be new. (Without such a restriction we would risk an unjustifiable identification of the object of which ϕ is asserted to hold with objects already mentioned in the derivation.)

Diagrammatically, the three new rules appear as follows:

Universal instantiation (UI): $\dfrac{\bigwedge \alpha \phi_\alpha}{\phi_\zeta}$

Existential generalization (EG): $\dfrac{\phi_\zeta}{\bigvee \alpha \phi_\alpha}$

Existential instantiation (EI): $\dfrac{\bigvee \alpha \phi_\alpha}{\phi_\beta}$

Here α and β are to be variables, ζ a symbolic term, ϕ_ζ a symbolic formula that comes from the symbolic formula ϕ_α by proper substitution of ζ for α, and ϕ_β a symbolic formula that comes from the symbolic formula ϕ_α by proper substitution of β for α.

We shall continue to employ the inference rules of the sentential calculus, together with these new rules, in the development of the logic of quantifiers, but they must be reconstrued in such a way as to be applicable to any symbolic *formulas* of appropriate sentential structure (not merely to symbolic *sentences*). For example, the formula 'G*x*' will now be considered to follow by MP from the formulas '(F*x* → G*x*)' and 'F*x*'.

EXERCISES

58. None of the formulas

(i) $\bigvee z(\mathrm{FA} \wedge \mathrm{G}y) \rightarrow \bigvee x\mathrm{H}x \vee \mathrm{G}x$
(ii) $\bigvee z(\mathrm{FA} \wedge \mathrm{G}y) \rightarrow \bigvee x\mathrm{HA} \vee \mathrm{GA}$
(iii) $\bigvee z(\mathrm{F}z \wedge \mathrm{G}y) \rightarrow \bigvee x\mathrm{H}x \vee \mathrm{G}z$

comes from the formula

$$\text{(iv)}\ \bigvee z(Fx \wedge Gy) \rightarrow \bigvee xHx \vee Gx$$

(which is formula (1) of this section) by proper substitution of a term for the variable '*x*'. For each of (i)–(iii), indicate what term has replaced occurrences of '*x*' in (iv) and why that replacement is not a proper substitution. (In doing this exercise, recognize that if ζ is a term, α is a variable, and ϕ_ζ is a symbolic formula that comes from a symbolic formula ϕ_α by proper substitution of ζ for α, then the following must hold:

(a) all free occurrences of α in ϕ_α are replaced by ζ;
(b) only free occurrences of α in ϕ_α are replaced by ζ; and
(c) if ζ is a variable, then all occurrences of ζ in ϕ_ζ that correspond to replaced occurrences of α in ϕ_α are free occurrences.)

59. From the formula

$$\bigwedge x \bigvee y(Fx \leftrightarrow Gy \wedge Hz)$$

which of the formulas

$$\text{(i)}\ \bigvee y(Fx \leftrightarrow Gy \wedge Hx)$$
$$\text{(ii)}\ \bigvee y(Fz \leftrightarrow Gy \wedge Hz)$$
$$\text{(iii)}\ \bigvee y(FA \leftrightarrow Gy \wedge Hz)$$
$$\text{(iv)}\ \bigvee y(FA \leftrightarrow Gy \wedge HA)$$
$$\text{(v)}\ \bigvee y(Fy \leftrightarrow Gy \wedge Hz)$$

follow by UI?

60. From the formula

$$Fx \rightarrow Gx$$

which of the formulas

$$\text{(i)}\ \bigvee y(Fy \rightarrow Gy)$$
$$\text{(ii)}\ \bigvee y(Fy \rightarrow Gx)$$
$$\text{(iii)}\ \bigvee y(Fx \rightarrow Gy)$$
$$\text{(iv)}\ \bigvee y(Fx \rightarrow Gx)$$
$$\text{(v)}\ \bigvee x(Fx \rightarrow Gx)$$
$$\text{(vi)}\ \bigvee xFx \rightarrow Gx$$

follow by EG?

61. From the formula

$$FA \leftrightarrow Gx$$

which of the formulas

$$\text{(i)}\ \bigvee x(Fx \leftrightarrow Gx)$$
$$\text{(ii)}\ \bigvee y(Fy \leftrightarrow Gx)$$
$$\text{(iii)}\ \bigvee x(FA \leftrightarrow Gx)$$
$$\text{(iv)}\ FA \leftrightarrow \bigvee xGx$$

follow by EG?

62. Given the restriction that the variable of instantiation be new, from the formula

$$\bigvee x(Fx \wedge Gy)$$

which of the formulas

(i) $Fz \wedge Gy$
(ii) $Fy \wedge Gy$
(iii) $FA \wedge Gy$

follow by EI?

6. Derivations. In addition to the inference rules UI, EG, and EI, a new form of derivation is needed for the logic of quantifiers. It is known as *universal derivation* and in its simplest form appears as follows:

Show $\bigwedge \alpha\phi$
χ_1
.
.
.
χ_m ,

where ϕ occurs unboxed among χ_1 through χ_m. In a universal derivation one shows that everything has a certain property by showing that an arbitrary thing has that property. To ensure arbitrariness a restriction will be imposed: the variable α, called the *variable of generalization*, must not be free in any antecedent line.

This form of derivation is familiar to every student of plane geometry, wherein one shows, for instance, that every triangle has a certain property by considering an arbitrary triangle and showing that it has the property in question.

It is natural to permit a more inclusive form of universal derivation, in which several variables of generalization occur. Thus *universal derivation* appears in general as follows:

Show $\bigwedge \alpha_1 \ldots \bigwedge \alpha_k \, \phi$
χ_1
.
.
.
χ_m ,

where ϕ occurs unboxed among χ_1 through χ_m. Here one shows that all objects stand in a certain relation to one another by showing that arbitrary objects do so. To insure arbitrariness, the following restriction is imposed in clause (6) below: the *variables of generalization*, α_1 through α_k, may not be free in antecedent lines.

We may call that branch of logic which essentially involves quantifiers as well as sentential connectives the *quantifier calculus*. That part of the quantifier calculus which concerns the rather restricted symbolic language of the present chapter is called the *monadic quantifier calculus*. The directions for constructing a derivation within this discipline (which in the next chapter will be extended only slightly in order to arrive at the full quantifier calculus) transcend in two ways those given for the sentential calculus. On the one hand, the earlier procedures are extended so as to apply not only to symbolic sentences but to arbitrary symbolic formulas; on the other hand, additional provisions are made for the accommodation of quantifiers. The directions for constructing a *derivation* from given symbolic premises become, then, the following.

(1) *If ϕ is any symbolic formula, then*

$$\textit{Show } \phi$$

may occur as a line. (Annotation: 'Assertion'.)

(2) *Any one of the premises may occur as a line. (Annotation: 'Premise'.)*

(3) *If ϕ, ψ are symbolic formulas such that*

$$\textit{Show } (\phi \rightarrow \psi)$$

occurs as a line, then ϕ may occur as the next line. (Annotation: 'Assumption'.)

(4) *If ϕ is a symbolic formula such that*

$$\textit{Show } \phi$$

occurs as a line, then

$$\sim \phi$$

may occur as the next line; if ϕ is a symbolic formula such that

$$\textit{Show } \sim \phi$$

occurs as a line, then ϕ may occur as the next line. (Annotation: 'Assumption'.)

(5a) *A symbolic formula may occur as a line if it follows from antecedent lines by an inference rule of the sentential calculus (that is, MP, MT, DN, R, S, Adj, Add, MTP, BC, or CB), by UI, or by EG.*

(5b) *A symbolic formula may occur as a line if it follows from an antecedent line by EI, provided that the variable of instantiation does not occur in any preceding line. (The annotation for (5a) and (5b) should refer to the inference rule employed and the numbers of the antecedent lines involved.)*

(6) *When the following arrangement of lines has appeared:*

Show ϕ
χ_1
.
.
.
χ_m ,

where none of χ_1 *through* χ_m *contains uncancelled 'Show' and either*
(*i*) ϕ *occurs unboxed among* χ_1 *through* χ_m,
(*ii*) ϕ *is of the form*

$$(\psi_1 \rightarrow \psi_2)$$

and ψ_2 *occurs unboxed among* χ_1 *through* χ_m,
(*iii*) *for some formula* χ, *both* χ *and its negation occur unboxed among* χ_1 *through* χ_m, *or*
(*iv*) ϕ *is of the form*

$$\bigwedge\alpha_1 \ldots \bigwedge\alpha_k \psi \quad ,$$

ψ *occurs unboxed among the lines* χ_1 *through* χ_m, *and the variables* α_1 *through* α_k *are not free in lines antecedent to the displayed occurrence of*

Show ϕ ,

then one may simultaneously cancel the displayed occurrence of 'Show' and box all subsequent lines.

As before, a derivation is *complete* just in case every line either is boxed or contains cancelled '*Show*'. A symbolic formula ϕ is *derivable* (in the quantifier calculus) from given symbolic premises just in case, by using only clauses (1) through (6), a complete derivation from those premises can be constructed in which

~~*Show*~~ ϕ

occurs as an unboxed line. A *proof* is a derivation from an empty class of formulas (that is, a derivation employing no premises), and a *theorem* is a symbolic formula derivable from an empty class of premises.

EXERCISES

63. The formula

(1) $\bigvee x(\mathrm{F}x \rightarrow \bigwedge x\mathrm{F}x)$

is a theorem, but the display

1.	~~*Show*~~ $\bigvee x(Fx \rightarrow \bigwedge xFx)$	
2.	~~*Show*~~ $Fx \rightarrow \bigwedge xFx$	
3.	Fx	
4.	~~*Show*~~ $\bigwedge xFx$	
5.	Fx	3, R
6.	$\bigvee x(Fx \rightarrow \bigwedge xFx)$	2, EG

is not a proof of (1). What is incorrect? (A proof of (1) is given on p. 165.)

64. Intuition, based on an elementary understanding of the two quantifiers, suggests that the formula

$$\bigvee xFx \rightarrow \bigwedge zFz \tag{2}$$

is not a theorem. What is wrong with the following attempt at a proof of (2)?

1.	~~*Show*~~ $\bigvee xFx \rightarrow \bigwedge zFz$	
2.	$\bigvee xFx$	
3.	~~*Show*~~ $\bigwedge yFy$	
4.	Fy	2, EI
5.	~~*Show*~~ $\bigwedge zFz$	
6.	Fz	3, UI

7. Theorems with unabbreviated proofs. We turn now to some theorems and their proofs. For clerical convenience, we assign them numbers beginning with 201.

T201

1.	~~*Show*~~ $\bigwedge x(Fx \rightarrow Gx) \rightarrow (\bigwedge xFx \rightarrow \bigwedge xGx)$	
2.	$\bigwedge x(Fx \rightarrow Gx)$	
3.	~~*Show*~~ $\bigwedge xFx \rightarrow \bigwedge xGx$	
4.	$\bigwedge xFx$	
5.	~~*Show*~~ $\bigwedge xGx$	
6.	Fx	4, UI
7.	$Fx \rightarrow Gx$	2, UI
8.	Gx	6, 7, MP

If, in this derivation, line 6 had preceded line 5, we should not have been able to complete the universal derivation of line 5; for then the variable of generalization, 'x', would have been free in an antecedent line. As a general practice, if a universal derivation is to be employed, it is advisable to begin it before using UI.

In the proof of T201, only one of our new inference rules, UI, was employed; T202 illustrates the application of EI and EG.

T202			
	1.	~~Show~~ $\bigwedge x(Fx \to Gx) \to (\bigvee xFx \to \bigvee xGx)$	
	2.	$\bigwedge x(Fx \to Gx)$	
	3.	~~Show~~ $\bigvee xFx \to \bigvee xGx$	
	4.	$\bigvee xFx$	
	5.	Fy	4, EI
	6.	$Fy \to Gy$	2, UI
	7.	Gy	5, 6, MP
	8.	$\bigvee xGx$	7, EG

In this derivation the order of lines is again important. If line 6 had preceded line 5, we should have been unable to choose 'y' as the variable of instantiation in line 5. As a general practice, it is advisable to use EI before UI.

The intuitive plausibility of theorems can often be seen by translation into English. For example, on the basis of the scheme

F : *a* is a person
G : *a* is mortal ,

the theorems T201 and T202 can be translated, respectively, into

> If all persons are mortal, then if everything is a person, then everything is mortal

and

> If all persons are mortal, then if something is a person, then something is mortal .

Two symbolic formulas ϕ and ψ are said to be *equivalent* if the formula

$$\phi \leftrightarrow \psi$$

is a theorem. T203 – T206 provide equivalent expressions for formulas beginning with various combinations of quantifier phrases and negation signs.

T203

1.	~~*Show*~~ $\sim \bigwedge x Fx \leftrightarrow \bigvee x \sim Fx$	
2.	~~*Show*~~ $\sim \bigwedge x Fx \rightarrow \bigvee x \sim Fx$	
3.	$\sim \bigwedge x Fx$	
4.	~~*Show*~~ $\bigvee x \sim Fx$	
5.	$\sim \bigvee x \sim Fx$	
6.	~~*Show*~~ $\bigwedge x Fx$	
7.	~~*Show*~~ Fx	
8.	$\sim Fx$	
9.	$\bigvee x \sim Fx$	8, EG
10.	$\sim \bigvee x \sim Fx$	5, R
11.	$\sim \bigwedge x Fx$	3, R
12.	~~*Show*~~ $\bigvee x \sim Fx \rightarrow \sim \bigwedge x Fx$	
13.	$\bigvee x \sim Fx$	
14.	~~*Show*~~ $\sim \bigwedge x Fx$	
15.	$\bigwedge x Fx$	
16.	$\sim Fy$	13, EI
17.	Fy	15, UI
18.	$\sim \bigwedge x Fx \leftrightarrow \bigvee x \sim Fx$	2, 12, CB

T204

1.	~~*Show*~~ $\sim \bigvee x Fx \leftrightarrow \bigwedge x \sim Fx$	
2.	~~*Show*~~ $\sim \bigvee x Fx \rightarrow \bigwedge x \sim Fx$	
3.	$\sim \bigvee x Fx$	
4.	~~*Show*~~ $\bigwedge x \sim Fx$	
5.	~~*Show*~~ $\sim Fx$	
6.	Fx	
7.	$\bigvee x Fx$	6, EG
8.	$\sim \bigvee x Fx$	3, R
9.	~~*Show*~~ $\bigwedge x \sim Fx \rightarrow \sim \bigvee x Fx$	
10.	$\bigwedge x \sim Fx$	
11.	~~*Show*~~ $\sim \bigvee x Fx$	
12.	$\bigvee x Fx$	
13.	Fy	12, EI
14.	$\sim Fy$	10, UI
15.	$\sim \bigvee x Fx \leftrightarrow \bigwedge x \sim Fx$	2, 9, CB

T205 $\bigwedge x Fx \leftrightarrow {\sim} \bigvee x {\sim} Fx$

T206 $\bigvee x Fx \leftrightarrow {\sim} \bigwedge x {\sim} Fx$

EXERCISES

65. Annotate each line of the following proof.

1. ~~*Show*~~ $\bigwedge x Fx \wedge \bigvee x Gx \rightarrow \bigvee x(Fx \wedge Gx)$

2.	$\bigwedge x Fx \wedge \bigvee x Gx$
3.	$\bigvee x Gx$
4.	Gy
5.	$\bigwedge x Fx$
6.	Fy
7.	$Fy \wedge Gy$
8.	$\bigvee x(Fx \wedge Gx)$

66. Prove T205 and T206.

The reader will find careful study of the proofs of T203 and T204 useful in solving exercise 66.

8. Abbreviated derivations. It is useful at this point to introduce counterparts to the methods for abbreviating derivations that appeared in chapter II and, in addition, one new method. As before, the methods of abbreviation are obtained by supplementing the directions for constructing derivations. The new clauses, (7)–(9), will satisfy the requirements given on page 71; that is, they will be theoretically dispensable, and there will be an automatic procedure for checking the correctness of an abbreviated derivation (that is, a derivation constructed on the basis of clauses (1)–(9)), at least when membership in the class of premises is automatically decidable and annotations are present.

We must modify slightly the notion of an instance of a sentential theorem, now that formulas as well as sentences are at hand. By an *instance* of a *sentential theorem* ϕ we now understand any symbolic *formula* obtained from ϕ by replacing sentence letters uniformly by symbolic formulas. Thus

$$Q \rightarrow (P \rightarrow Q)$$

has as an instance

$$Fx \rightarrow (Gy \rightarrow Fx) \quad ,$$

even though the latter is not a sentence.

We introduce now the counterpart to clause (7) of chapter II.

(7) *If ϕ is an instance of a theorem of the* sentential *calculus that has already been proved, then ϕ may occur as a line.* (*Annotation as in Chapter II;* *see p. 73.*)

We do not admit at this point instances of theorems of the *quantifier* calculus. The relevant notion of an instance is rather complex and will be reserved for chapter VII.

It is convenient, however, to add to our resources the following derived rule involving quantifiers, whose various forms correspond to T203 and T204.

Quantifier negation (QN), in four forms:

$$\frac{\sim \bigwedge \alpha \phi}{\bigvee \alpha \sim \phi} \qquad \frac{\bigvee \alpha \sim \phi}{\sim \bigwedge \alpha \phi} \qquad \frac{\sim \bigvee \alpha \phi}{\bigwedge \alpha \sim \phi} \qquad \frac{\bigwedge \alpha \sim \phi}{\sim \bigvee \alpha \phi}$$

Here α is to be a variable and ϕ a symbolic formula. QN corresponds to the following intuitive principles: to deny that every object satisfies a given condition is to assert that some object satisfies its negation, and to deny that there is an object satisfying a given condition is to assert that every object satisfies its negation.

For example, each of the following is an application of QN:

$$\frac{\sim \bigwedge x(Fx \to Gx)}{\bigvee x \sim (Fx \to Gx)} \qquad \frac{\bigvee x \sim (Fx \to Gx)}{\sim \bigwedge x(Fx \to Gx)} \qquad \frac{\sim \bigvee x(Fx \land Gx)}{\bigwedge x \sim (Fx \land Gx)}$$

$$\frac{\bigwedge x \sim (Fx \land Gx)}{\sim \bigvee x(Fx \land Gx)}$$

We incorporate QN into our system by adding the following clause to the directions for constructing a derivation.

(8) *A symbolic formula may occur as a line if it follows from an antecedent line by QN.* (*Annotation:* 'QN', *together with the number of the antecedent line involved.*)

In the quantifier calculus, as in the sentential calculus, it is again convenient, when constructing a derivation, to compress several steps into one, omitting some lines which an unabbreviated derivation would require. As in chapter II, such compression will be allowed only in certain cases, specifically, only when the omitted steps can be justified on the basis of clause (2) (premises), (5a) (inference rules other than EI), (7) (instances of previously proved theorems of the sentential calculus), or (8) (quantifier negation). We legitimize such compressions by clause (9)—the counterpart to clause (8) of chapter II.

(9) *A symbolic formula may occur as a line if it is the last in a succession of steps, each step in the succession other than the last step is either an antecedent line or can be justified by one of clauses (2), (5a), (7), or (8), and the last step in the succession can be justified by one of clauses (5a), (5b), or (8). (The annotation should determine unambiguously the succession of steps leading to the line in question. This can be done by indicating, in order of application, the antecedent lines, the premises, the inference rules, and the previously proved theorems employed. Also, in connection with the rules Add, UI, and EG, the added disjunct, the variable of instantiation, and the variable of generalization should respectively be indicated whenever there is a chance of ambiguity; and when an instance of a previously proved theorem is involved, the relevant replacement, if not obvious, should be indicated. The special annotations 'SC' and 'CD', which were introduced on pages 78 and 79 to indicate a certain kind of compression, may again be used.)*

For example, clause (9) provides the justification for line 4 in the following abbreviated derivation:

1.	~~*Show*~~ $\sim \bigvee x Fx \rightarrow \bigwedge x(Fx \rightarrow Gx)$	
2.	$\sim \bigvee x Fx$	
3.	~~*Show*~~ $\bigwedge x(Fx \rightarrow Gx)$	
4.	$Fx \rightarrow Gx$	2, QN, UI, T18, MP

The omitted lines are, in order:

(i)	$\bigwedge x \sim Fx$	2, QN
(ii)	$\sim Fx$	(i), UI
(iii)	$\sim Fx \rightarrow (Fx \rightarrow Gx)$	T18

Line 4 follows from (ii) and (iii) by MP.

Another illustration of the application of clause (9) is provided by the following derivation:

1.	~~*Show*~~ $\sim \bigwedge x Fx \rightarrow \bigvee x(Fx \rightarrow Gx)$	
2.	$\sim \bigwedge x Fx$	
3.	$\sim Fy$	2, QN, EI
4.	$\bigvee x(Fx \rightarrow Gx)$	3, T18, MP, EG

However, clause (9) does not permit the omission of line 3 from the derivation above and thus does not countenance the following display as an abbreviated derivation:

1.	~~*Show*~~ $\sim \bigwedge x Fx \rightarrow \bigvee x(Fx \rightarrow Gx)$	
2.	$\sim \bigwedge x Fx$	
3.	$\bigvee x(Fx \rightarrow Gx)$	2, QN, EI, T18, MP, EG

According to clause (9), only clauses (2), (5a), (7), and (8), not clause (5b), which incorporates EI into the directions for constructing a derivation, can justify an omitted step in an abbreviated derivation. Without this limitation on the justification of omitted steps, the variable of instantiation for an application of EI would not have to occur in an abbreviated derivation; and in those cases in which it did not occur, one could not by inspection of the abbreviated derivation check automatically that the instantial variable is, as required, *new* to the derivation.

Indeed, in an abbreviated derivation, the requirement that the variable of instantiation in an application of EI be *new* must be stated more subtly than it was stated for unabbreviated derivations: not only must the variable of instantiation in an application of EI make its first appearance in an abbreviated derivation in the line that is the conclusion of that application of EI; but it must not have any *occurrences* in that line other than those introduced by that application of EI. For example, the following display is not a correctly constructed abbreviated derivation:

1.	~~*Show*~~ $\bigwedge x \bigvee y(Fx \leftrightarrow \sim Fy) \rightarrow \bigvee y(Fy \leftrightarrow \sim Fy)$	
2.	$\bigwedge x \bigvee y(Fx \leftrightarrow \sim Fy)$	
3.	$Fz \leftrightarrow \sim Fz$	2, UI, incorrect application of EI
4.	$\bigvee y(Fy \leftrightarrow \sim Fy)$	3, EG

For the application of EI in line 3 above to be correct, it is not sufficient that 'z', the variable of instantiation for that application of EI, have no occurrences in preceding lines; in addition, it cannot have any occurrences in line 3 itself other than those introduced by the application of EI. Display of the premise of the application of EI, the formula

$$\bigvee y(Fz \leftrightarrow \sim Fy) \quad ,$$

makes it clear that only the second of the two occurrences of 'z' in line 3 entered that line by the application of EI; thus the variable of instantiation is not *new* to the (supposed) abbreviated derivation. This subtlety in the characterization of *new* could be avoided by requiring that the premise as well as the conclusion of any application of EI always occur in an abbreviated derivation; and whenever any doubt occurs concerning the correctness of an abbreviated derivation, the reader should adhere to this stricter requirement. But we do not believe that this subtlety is beyond the sophistication of most readers, and its adoption considerably enhances the convenience introduced by clause (9).

The reader should recall that abbreviated derivations, unlike unabbreviated derivations, require as an essential part their annotations—at least those given in connection with clause (9). Without an indication of omitted steps, it would be impossible to give an automatic procedure for checking the correctness of an abbreviated derivation. (See the remarks on page 107.)

EXERCISES

67. Insert with annotations the lines that have been omitted in passing from step 3 to step 4 in the following abbreviated derivation.

1. ~~Show~~ $\bigwedge x(Fx \rightarrow Gx \vee Hx) \wedge {\sim}\bigwedge x(Fx \rightarrow Gx) \rightarrow \bigvee x(Fx \wedge Hx)$
2. $\bigwedge x(Fx \rightarrow Gx \vee Hx) \wedge {\sim}\bigwedge x(Fx \rightarrow Gx)$
3. ${\sim}(Fy \rightarrow Gy)$ — 2, S, QN, EI
4. $\bigvee x(Fx \wedge Hx)$ — 3, T21, MP, 3, T22, MP, 2, S, UI, MP, MTP, Adj, EG

(Note that clause (9) would not justify the omission from the above derivation of line 3, that is, the conclusion of an application of EI.)

68. Annotate the following abbreviated derivation.

1. ~~Show~~ ${\sim}\bigvee x(Fx \wedge Gx) \leftrightarrow \bigwedge x(Fx \rightarrow {\sim}Gx)$
2. ~~Show~~ ${\sim}\bigvee x(Fx \wedge Gx) \rightarrow \bigwedge x(Fx \rightarrow {\sim}Gx)$
3. ${\sim}\bigvee x(Fx \wedge Gx)$
4. ~~Show~~ $\bigwedge x(Fx \rightarrow {\sim}Gx)$
5. $Fx \rightarrow {\sim}Gx$
6. ~~Show~~ $\bigwedge x(Fx \rightarrow {\sim}Gx) \rightarrow {\sim}\bigvee x(Fx \wedge Gx)$
7. $\bigwedge x(Fx \rightarrow {\sim}Gx)$
8. ~~Show~~ ${\sim}\bigvee x(Fx \wedge Gx)$
9. $\bigvee x(Fx \wedge Gx)$
10. $Fy \wedge Gy$
11. ${\sim}(Fy \wedge Gy)$
12. ${\sim}\bigvee x(Fx \wedge Gx) \leftrightarrow \bigwedge x(Fx \rightarrow {\sim}Gx)$

The reader should note the order of steps in this derivation, specifically, that a universal derivation is started before UI is employed, and that application of EI precedes that of UI.

9. Fallacies. By an *argument* we now understand a sequence of formulas (perhaps empty), called the premises of the argument, together with another formula, called the conclusion of the argument. A *symbolic argument* or *English argument* is one whose premises and conclusion are respectively symbolic formulas or formulas of English. A *symbolization of an English argument on the basis of a given scheme of abbreviation* is a symbolic argument whose premises and conclusion are respective symbolizations, on the basis of that scheme, of the premises and conclusion of the English argument. A symbolic argument is called simply a *symbolization* of an English argument if there is some scheme of abbreviation on the basis of which it is a symbolization of that argument. As before, we call a symbolic argument *valid* if its conclusion is derivable from its premises and call an English argument *valid* (in the monadic quantifier calculus) if it has a valid symbolization.

In stating rules of inference and directions for constructing derivations, we have again imposed a number of restrictions whose significance is perhaps not immediately obvious. All these restrictions are needed in order to prevent the validation of *false English arguments* (arguments whose premises are true sentences of English and whose conclusions are false sentences of English), that is to say, in order to prevent *fallacies*.

Of the restrictions not pertaining to variables, only one needs to be mentioned here. (For the others, see section 5 of chapter I.) According to clauses (3) and (4) of the directions for constructing a derivation, an assumption may be introduced only in the line immediately following the inception of the derivation to which it is relevant. The following false argument, symbolization, and derivation establish the need for this restriction.

Argument:

2 is a number. ∴ Everything is a number.

Symbolization:

$$\mathrm{FA} \quad \therefore \; \bigwedge x \mathrm{F}x$$

Derivation:

1.	~~*Show*~~ $\bigwedge x\mathrm{F}x$	
2.	~~*Show*~~ $\mathrm{F}x$	
3.	~~*Show*~~ $\bigwedge x \sim \mathrm{F}x$	
4.	$\sim \mathrm{F}x$	Fallacious assumption for indirect derivation
5.	FA	Premise
6.	$\sim$FA	3, UI

In this derivation line 4 is incorrect; if line 2 is to begin an indirect derivation, its assumption must occur as the next line. The reader can easily construct a similar example involving a fallacious assumption for conditional derivation.

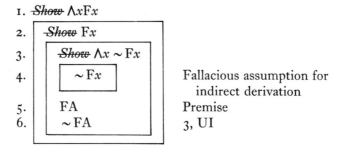

The restriction initially imposed on the variable of instantiation of EI, that it be entirely new to an unabbreviated derivation, is more stringent than necessary. It would be sufficient, but tediously complex, to impose the following three prohibitions: (i) the variable of instantiation may not occur *free* in an antecedent line; (ii) it may not occur *free* in a preceding line containing uncancelled '*Show*'; and (iii) it may not occur *bound* as the variable of generalization in a preceding line containing uncancelled '*Show*'. The following argument, symbolization, and derivation establish the need for (i), and exercises 69 and 70 (at the end of this section) establish the need for (ii) and (iii).

> There is an even number. There is an odd number. ∴ Something is both an even number and an odd number.

Symbolization:

$$\bigvee x Fx \quad . \quad \bigvee x Gx \quad \therefore \bigvee x(Fx \wedge Gx)$$

Derivation:

1. ~~*Show*~~ $\bigvee x(Fx \wedge Gx)$

2.	$\bigvee x Fx$	Premise
3.	Fy	2, EI
4.	$\bigvee x Gx$	Premise
5.	Gy	4, incorrect application of EI
6.	$\bigvee x(Fx \wedge Gx)$	3, 5, Adj, EG

In this derivation line 5 is incorrectly inferred from the second premise. The variable of instantiation, 'y', is free in line 3, which is an antecedent line to line 5.

For abbreviated derivations, in which the premise of an application of EI need not appear as a line, the requirement that the variable of instantiation be new had to be stated somewhat subtly: not only must it satisfy conditions (i), (ii), and (iii) above, but also all its occurrences in the line in which it first appears must have been introduced by the application of EI. This additional requirement guarantees that the variable of instantiation has not already occurred free in the premise of the application of EI, which would have to appear as an antecedent line in an unabbreviated derivation but which could be omitted by clause (9) from an abbreviated derivation. The following argument, symbolization, and derivation show the need for this subtlety.

Argument:

> For each x, there is a y such that x is a number if and only if y is not a number. ∴ Something is such that it is a number if and only if it is not a number.

Symbolization:

$$\bigwedge x \bigvee y(Fx \leftrightarrow \sim Fy) \quad \therefore \bigvee y(Fy \leftrightarrow \sim Fy)$$

Derivation:

1. ~~*Show*~~ $\bigvee y(Fy \leftrightarrow \sim Fy)$

2.	$Fz \leftrightarrow \sim Fz$	Premise, UI, incorrect application of EI
3.	$\bigvee y(Fy \leftrightarrow \sim Fy)$	2, EG

As noted on page 152, line 2 of the above derivation is not correct. The variable of instantiation for the application of EI is not new, for the first occurrence of '*z*' in line 2 was not obtained by the application of EI. This fact can be made more evident by displaying the premise of the application of EI as the top node of a modified grammatical tree:

$$\underbrace{\bigvee y(\mathrm{F}z \leftrightarrow \sim \mathrm{F}y)} \quad .$$

(Any doubt that the reader may have concerning the truth of the premise of the English argument above will be removed by T248 of the next section, which establishes the equivalence of the premise of the symbolic argument and the formula '$\bigvee x\mathrm{F}x \wedge \bigvee x \sim \mathrm{F}x$'; the latter formula passes into the obvious truth 'Something is a number and something is not a number'.)

In addition to being new to the derivation, the instantial term for EI must be a variable; it cannot be either a variable or a name letter, as is the case for UI and EG. The following argument, symbolization, and derivation establish the need for this limitation.

Argument:

> 2 is an even number. Something is an odd number. ∴ Something is both an even number and an odd number.

Symbolization:

$$\mathrm{FA} \quad . \quad \bigvee x\mathrm{G}x \quad \therefore \bigvee x(\mathrm{F}x \wedge \mathrm{G}x)$$

Derivation:

1. ~~*Show*~~ $\bigvee x(\mathrm{F}x \wedge \mathrm{G}x)$

2.	$\bigvee x\mathrm{G}x$	2nd premise
3.	GA	2, incorrect application of EI
4.	FA ∧ GA	1st premise, 2, Adj
5.	$\bigvee x(\mathrm{F}x \wedge \mathrm{G}x)$	4, EG

In this derivation line 3 is incorrect; although 'A' is new to the derivation in line 3, it is not a variable. This example may suggest to the reader that a similar fallacy could be obtained by replacing '2' in the English argument above by a variable, say '*y*'. However, the resulting English argument is not a false English argument: its first premise, '*y* is an even number', being a formula of English that is not a sentence, is neither true nor false. (The role of free variables in premises will be examined in section 11, and further insight on this point will be obtained there.)

The restriction imposed on the variable of generalization in a universal derivation prohibits a free occurrence of that variable in lines antecedent to that derivation. The need for this restriction is shown by the following argument, symbolization, and derivation.

Argument:

There is an odd number. ∴ Everything is an odd number.

Symbolization:

$\bigvee x Fx \quad \therefore \bigwedge x Fx$

Derivation:

1.	~~*Show*~~ $\bigwedge x Fx$	
2.	$\bigvee x Fx$	Premise
3.	Fy	2, EI
4.	~~*Show*~~ $\bigwedge y Fy$	
5.	Fy	3, R
6.	Fx	4, UI

In this derivation the cancellation of '*Show*' in line 4, along with the boxing of line 5, is incorrect. The variable of generalization in the subsidiary universal derivation, '*y*', is free in line 3, which is antecedent to the subsidiary derivation.

The notion of *proper substitution* is involved in the formulation of each of the rules UI, EG, and EI. In order for a symbolic formula $\phi\zeta$ to come from a symbolic formula $\phi\alpha$ by proper substitution of a term ζ for a variable α, two conditions (among others) must be fulfilled: (i) *every* free occurrence of α must be replaced by an occurrence of ζ, and (ii) if ζ is a variable, then each of the occurrences of ζ that replaces an occurrence of α must be *free*. The false argument (1) below shows the need for (i) with respect to UI; exercises 71 and 72 (at the end of this section) show the need for (i) with respect to EG and EI; the false argument (2) below shows the need for (ii) with respect to EG; and exercise 73 (at the end of this section) shows the need for (ii) with respect to UI. (The requirement for EI that the variable of instantiation be new already excludes a legitimate application of that rule in which a free occurrence of α is replaced by a bound occurrence of a variable β.)

Argument:

(1) Every odd number is a number. 3 is an odd number. ∴ Everything is a number.

Symbolization:

$\bigwedge x(Fx \rightarrow Gx) \quad . \quad FA \quad \therefore \bigwedge x Gx$

Derivation:

1.	~~*Show*~~ $\bigwedge x Gx$	
2.	$\bigwedge x(Fx \rightarrow Gx)$	1st premise
3.	$FA \rightarrow Gx$	2, incorrect application of UI
4.	Gx	2nd premise, 3, MP

In this derivation line 3 comes from line 2 incorrectly; not *all* free occurrences of 'x' in '$(Fx \rightarrow Gx)$' have been replaced by 'A'.

Argument:

(2) 2 is a number. ∴ Everything is a number.

Symbolization:

$$FA \quad \therefore \bigwedge x Fx$$

Derivation:

1.	~~*Show*~~ $\bigwedge x Fx$	
2.	~~*Show*~~ $\bigwedge x(Fx \leftrightarrow Fx)$	
3.	$Fx \leftrightarrow Fx$	T91
4.	$\bigvee y \bigwedge x(Fx \leftrightarrow Fy)$	2, incorrect application of EG
5.	$\bigwedge x(Fx \leftrightarrow Fz)$	4, EI
6.	Fz	5, UI, BC, premise, MP
7.	Fx	5, UI, BC, 6, MP

In this derivation line 4 comes from line 2 incorrectly; the occurrence of 'x' that replaces the free occurrence of 'y' in '$\bigwedge x(Fx \leftrightarrow Fy)$' is not *free.*

Incorrect applications of EG often result from an incorrect characterization of that rule. Diagrammatically the rule appears

$$\frac{\phi_\zeta}{\bigvee \alpha \phi_\alpha} \quad .$$

Here α is a variable, ζ is a symbolic term, and ϕ_α and ϕ_ζ are symbolic formulas. Given that ϕ_α occurs in the conclusion of the rule (in contrast to UI, where it occurs in the premise), one might hold that the above diagram represents EG on the condition that ϕ_α comes from ϕ_ζ by proper substitution of α for ζ (in contrast to the correct formulation, which requires that ϕ_ζ come from ϕ_α by proper substitution of ζ for α). That such an incorrect formulation would lead to fallacies is established by the following argument, symbolization, and derivation.

Argument:

2 is an even number. Something is an odd number. ∴ Something is both an even number and an odd number.

Symbolization:

$$\mathrm{FA} \quad . \quad \bigvee x\mathrm{G}x \quad \therefore \bigvee x(\mathrm{F}x \wedge \mathrm{G}x)$$

Derivation:

1.	~~*Show*~~ $\bigvee x(\mathrm{F}x \wedge \mathrm{G}x)$	
2.	$\bigvee x\mathrm{G}x$	2nd premise
3.	$\mathrm{G}y$	2, EI
4.	$\mathrm{FA} \wedge \mathrm{G}y$	1st premise, 3, Adj
5.	$\bigvee y(\mathrm{F}y \wedge \mathrm{G}y)$	4, EG as incorrectly formulated above
6.	$\mathrm{F}z \wedge \mathrm{G}z$	5, EI
7.	$\bigvee x(\mathrm{F}x \wedge \mathrm{G}x)$	6, EG

In this derivation the inference from line 4 to line 5 is an application of the above (incorrect) formulation of EG. For here α is the variable 'y', ζ is the term 'A', ϕ_α is the formula '$(\mathrm{F}y \wedge \mathrm{G}y)$', and ϕ_ζ is the formula '$\mathrm{FA} \wedge \mathrm{G}y$'; hence ϕ_α has come from ϕ_ζ by proper substitution of α for ζ. (Note that ϕ_ζ does not come from ϕ_α by proper substitution of ζ for α, as required by the correct formulation of EG.)

EXERCISES

Each of the following false arguments is accompanied by a symbolization and (alleged) derivation. Indicate the incorrect step in the latter and the fallacy involved.

69. 2 is a number. ∴ Everything is a number.

Symbolization:

$$\mathrm{FA} \quad \therefore \bigwedge x\mathrm{F}x$$

Derivation:

1.	~~*Show*~~ $\bigwedge x\mathrm{F}x$	
2.	~~*Show*~~ $\bigwedge x(\mathrm{F}x \leftrightarrow \mathrm{F}y)$	
3.	$\mathrm{F}x \leftrightarrow \mathrm{F}x$	T91
4.	$\bigvee z(\mathrm{F}x \leftrightarrow \mathrm{F}z)$	3, EG
5.	$\mathrm{F}x \leftrightarrow \mathrm{F}y$	4, EI
6.	$\mathrm{F}y$	2, UI, BC, premise, MP
7.	$\mathrm{F}x$	2, UI, BC, 6, MP

70. Something is a number. ∴ Everything is a number.

Symbolization:

$$\bigvee y\mathrm{F}y \quad \therefore \bigwedge x\mathrm{F}x$$

Derivation:

1.	~~*Show*~~ $\bigwedge x Fx$	
2.	$\bigvee y Fy$	Premise
3.	Fx	2, EI

71. There is an even number. There is an odd number. ∴ Something is both an even number and an odd number.

Symbolization:

$$\bigvee x Fx \quad . \quad \bigvee x Gx \quad \therefore \bigvee x(Fx \wedge Gx)$$

Derivation:

1.	~~*Show*~~ $\bigvee x(Fx \wedge Gx)$	
2.	$\bigvee x Fx$	Premise
3.	Fy	2, EI
4.	$\bigvee x Gx$	Premise
5.	Gz	4, EI
6.	$Fy \wedge Gz$	3, 5, Adj
7.	$\bigvee y(Fy \wedge Gy)$	6, EG
8.	$Fw \wedge Gw$	7, EI
9.	$\bigvee x(Fx \wedge Gx)$	8, EG

72. There is a prime number. ∴ Everything is a number.

Symbolization:

$$\bigvee x(Fx \wedge Gx) \quad \therefore \bigwedge x Gx$$

Derivation:

1.	~~*Show*~~ $\bigwedge x Gx$	
2.	$\bigvee x(Fx \wedge Gx)$	Premise
3.	$Fy \wedge Gx$	2, EI
4.	Gx	3, S

73. For each *x*, there is a *y* such that *x* is a number if and only if *y* is not a number. ∴ Something is such that it is a number if and only if it is not a number.

Symbolization:

$$\bigwedge x \bigvee y(Fx \leftrightarrow \sim Fy) \quad \therefore \bigvee y(Fy \leftrightarrow \sim Fy)$$

Derivation:

1.	~~*Show*~~ $\bigvee y(Fy \leftrightarrow \sim Fy)$	
2.	$\bigwedge x \bigvee y(Fx \leftrightarrow \sim Fy)$	
3.	$\bigvee y(Fy \leftrightarrow \sim Fy)$	2, UI

(Again, in order to remove any doubt concerning the truth of the premise of the English argument above, we call to the reader's attention T248 of the next section.)

74. It is not the case that everything is an even number.
∴ Every even number is an odd number.

Symbolization:

$$\sim \bigwedge x Fx \quad \therefore \bigwedge x(Fx \rightarrow Gx)$$

Derivation:

1.	~~*Show*~~ $\bigwedge x(Fx \rightarrow Gx)$	
2.	~~*Show*~~ $Fx \rightarrow Gx$	
3.	Fx	
4.	$\sim \bigwedge x Fx$	Premise
5.	$\bigwedge x Fx \rightarrow Gx$	4, T18, MP
6.	$Fx \rightarrow Gx$	5, UI
7.	Gx	3, 6, MP

(In connection with this exercise the reader should review the comments on parentheses in section 3, p. 126.)

10. Theorems with abbreviated proofs. T201 and T202 of section 7 (pp. 146–47) are called *distribution laws* for quantifiers; we now state some additional distribution laws.

T207

1.	~~*Show*~~ $\bigvee x(Fx \vee Gx) \leftrightarrow \bigvee x Fx \vee \bigvee x Gx$	
2.	~~*Show*~~ $\bigvee x(Fx \vee Gx) \rightarrow \bigvee x Fx \vee \bigvee x Gx$	
3.	$\bigvee x(Fx \vee Gx)$	
4.	~~*Show*~~ $\sim \bigvee x Fx \rightarrow \bigvee x Gx$	
5.	$\sim \bigvee x Fx$	
6.	$\bigwedge x \sim Fx$	5, QN
7.	$Fy \vee Gy$	3, EI
8.	$\bigvee x Gx$	6, UI, 7, MTP, EG
9.	$\bigvee x Fx \vee \bigvee x Gx$	4, CD
10.	~~*Show*~~ $\bigvee x Fx \rightarrow \bigvee x(Fx \vee Gx)$	
11.	$\bigvee x Fx$	
12.	Fz	11, EI
13.	$\bigvee x(Fx \vee Gx)$	12, Add, EG
14.	~~*Show*~~ $\bigvee x Gx \rightarrow \bigvee x(Fx \vee Gx)$	
15.	$\bigvee x Gx$	
16.	Gw	15, EI
17.	$\bigvee x(Fx \vee Gx)$	16, Add, EG
18.	$\bigvee x Fx \vee \bigvee x Gx \rightarrow \bigvee x(Fx \vee Gx)$	10, 14, SC
19.	$\bigvee x(Fx \vee Gx) \leftrightarrow \bigvee x Fx \vee \bigvee x Gx$	2, 18, CB

It is often convenient to move in an initial negation sign by means of QN, as in the transition from line 5 to line 6 in the proof of T207.

T208 $\bigwedge x(Fx \wedge Gx) \leftrightarrow \bigwedge xFx \wedge \bigwedge xGx$

T209 $\bigvee x(Fx \wedge Gx) \rightarrow \bigvee xFx \wedge \bigvee xGx$

T210 $\bigwedge xFx \vee \bigwedge xGx \rightarrow \bigwedge x(Fx \vee Gx)$

T211 $(\bigvee xFx \rightarrow \bigvee xGx) \rightarrow \bigvee x(Fx \rightarrow Gx)$

T212 $(\bigwedge xFx \rightarrow \bigwedge xGx) \rightarrow \bigvee x(Fx \rightarrow Gx)$

T213 $\bigwedge x(Fx \leftrightarrow Gx) \rightarrow (\bigwedge xFx \leftrightarrow \bigwedge xGx)$

T214 $\bigwedge x(Fx \leftrightarrow Gx) \rightarrow (\bigvee xFx \leftrightarrow \bigvee xGx)$

(None of the biconditionals corresponding to T201, T202, T209 – T214 can be proved; see section 12.)

T215 – T222 are called *confinement laws.* According to these theorems, a generalization of a conjunction, disjunction, or conditional in which only one component contains the relevant variable is equivalent to a formula in which the quantifier phrase is confined to that component. Note that when the relevant component is the antecedent of a conditional (T221 and T222), the quantifier phrase must be changed from universal to existential, or conversely.

T215

1.	~~*Show*~~ $\bigwedge x(P \wedge Fx) \leftrightarrow P \wedge \bigwedge xFx$	
2.	~~*Show*~~ $\bigwedge x(P \wedge Fx) \rightarrow P \wedge \bigwedge xFx$	
3.	$\bigwedge x(P \wedge Fx)$	
4.	~~*Show*~~ $\bigwedge xFx$	
5.	Fx	3, UI, S
6.	$P \wedge \bigwedge xFx$	3, UI, S, 4, Adj
7.	~~*Show*~~ $P \wedge \bigwedge xFx \rightarrow \bigwedge x(P \wedge Fx)$	
8.	$P \wedge \bigwedge xFx$	
9.	~~*Show*~~ $\bigwedge x(P \wedge Fx)$	
10.	$P \wedge Fx$	8, S, S, UI, Adj
11.	$\bigwedge x(P \wedge Fx) \leftrightarrow P \wedge \bigwedge xFx$	2, 7, CB

T216 $\bigvee x(P \wedge Fx) \leftrightarrow P \wedge \bigvee xFx$

T217 $\bigwedge x(P \vee Fx) \leftrightarrow P \vee \bigwedge xFx$

T218 $\bigvee x(P \vee Fx) \leftrightarrow P \vee \bigvee xFx$

T219 $\wedge x(P \rightarrow Fx) \leftrightarrow (P \rightarrow \wedge xFx)$

T220 $\vee x(P \rightarrow Fx) \leftrightarrow (P \rightarrow \vee xFx)$

T221 $\wedge x(Fx \rightarrow P) \leftrightarrow (\vee xFx \rightarrow P)$

T222

1.	~~*Show*~~ $\vee x(Fx \rightarrow P) \leftrightarrow (\wedge xFx \rightarrow P)$	
2.	~~*Show*~~ $\vee x(Fx \rightarrow P) \rightarrow (\wedge xFx \rightarrow P)$	
3.	$\vee x(Fx \rightarrow P)$	
4.	~~*Show*~~ $\wedge xFx \rightarrow P$	
5.	$\wedge xFx$	
6.	$Fy \rightarrow P$	3, EI
7.	P	5, UI, 6, MP
8.	~~*Show*~~ $\sim \wedge xFx \rightarrow \vee x(Fx \rightarrow P)$	
9.	$\sim \wedge xFx$	
10.	$\sim Fz$	9, QN, EI
11.	$\vee x(Fx \rightarrow P)$	10, T18, MP, EG
12.	~~*Show*~~ $P \rightarrow \vee x(Fx \rightarrow P)$	
13.	P	
14.	$\vee x(Fx \rightarrow P)$	13, T2, MP, EG
15.	$(\wedge xFx \rightarrow P) \rightarrow \vee x(Fx \rightarrow P)$	8, 12, Adj, T35, BC, MP
16.	$\vee x(Fx \rightarrow P) \leftrightarrow (\wedge xFx \rightarrow P)$	2, 15, CB

In idiomatic English, counterparts to unconfined quantifier phrases seldom occur. On the basis, however, of a suitable scheme of abbreviation, the two constituents of T221 can be translated into

If anyone is honest, then the son of Lysimachus is honest

and

If someone is honest, then the son of Lysimachus is honest .

There are no simple confinement laws for biconditionals. We can say no more than is expressed in the following four theorems. In no case is the converse also a theorem; this is substantiated in section 12.

T223 $\wedge x(Fx \leftrightarrow P) \rightarrow (\wedge xFx \leftrightarrow P)$

T224 $\wedge x(Fx \leftrightarrow P) \rightarrow (\vee xFx \leftrightarrow P)$

T225 $(\vee xFx \leftrightarrow P) \rightarrow \vee x(Fx \leftrightarrow P)$

T226

1.	~~*Show*~~ $(\bigwedge x Fx \leftrightarrow P) \rightarrow \bigvee x(Fx \leftrightarrow P)$	
2.	~~*Show*~~ $\bigwedge x Fx \wedge P \rightarrow \bigvee x(Fx \leftrightarrow P)$	
3.	$\bigwedge x Fx \wedge P$	
4.	Fx	3, S, UI
5.	$Fx \wedge P$	3, S, 4, Adj
6.	$Fx \leftrightarrow P$	5, T84, MP
7.	$\bigvee x(Fx \leftrightarrow P)$	6, EG
8.	~~*Show*~~ $\sim \bigwedge x Fx \wedge \sim P \rightarrow \bigvee x(Fx \leftrightarrow P)$	
9.	$\sim \bigwedge x Fx \wedge \sim P$	
10.	$\sim Fy$	9, S, QN, EI
11.	$\sim Fy \wedge \sim P$	9, S, 10, Adj
12.	$Fy \leftrightarrow P$	11, T85, MP
13.	$\bigvee x(Fx \leftrightarrow P)$	12, EG
14.	$(\bigwedge x Fx \leftrightarrow P) \rightarrow \bigvee x(Fx \leftrightarrow P)$	2, 8, Adj, T86, BC, MP

T227 and T228 are the laws of *vacuous quantification;* by T227 the seemingly meaningless formula '$\bigwedge x$P' is equivalent to 'P'.

T227

1.	~~*Show*~~ $\bigwedge x P \leftrightarrow P$	
2.	~~*Show*~~ $\bigwedge x P \rightarrow P$	
3.	$\bigwedge x P$	
4.	P	3, UI
5.	~~*Show*~~ $P \rightarrow \bigwedge x P$	
6.	P	
7.	~~*Show*~~ $\bigwedge x P$	
8.	P	6, R
9.	$\bigwedge x P \leftrightarrow P$	2, 5, CB

T228

1.	~~*Show*~~ $\bigvee x P \leftrightarrow P$	
2.	~~*Show*~~ $\bigvee x P \rightarrow P$	
3.	$\bigvee x P$	
4.	P	3, EI
5.	~~*Show*~~ $P \rightarrow \bigvee x P$	
6.	P	
7.	$\bigvee x P$	6, EG
8.	$\bigvee x P \leftrightarrow P$	2, 5, CB

The application of UI, EI, and EG in the proofs of T227 and T228 may seem suspect. For instance, may '$\bigvee x$P' and 'P' be taken as

$$\bigvee \alpha \phi_\alpha$$

and ϕ_ζ in the formulation of EG on page 140? Yes; for examination of this formulation, and specifically of the notion of proper substitution employed in it, will reveal that α need not occur in ϕ_α and that if it does not, ϕ_ζ is ϕ_α. (For further comment on this point, the reader should look at the solution to exercise 60 at the end of this chapter.)

T229 and T230 have a slightly paradoxical character. Their validity depends on the fact that 'x' is not free in '$\bigvee x$Fx' or '$\bigwedge x$Fx', just as the validity of the confinement laws depends on the fact that 'x' is not free in 'P'.

T229	1.	~~Show~~ $\bigvee x(\bigvee x Fx \rightarrow Fx)$	
	2.	$\sim \bigvee x(\bigvee x Fx \rightarrow Fx)$	
	3.	$\sim(\bigvee x Fx \rightarrow Fx)$	2, QN, UI
	4.	Fy	3, T21, MP, EI
	5.	$\sim(\bigvee x Fx \rightarrow Fy)$	2, QN, UI
	6.	$\sim Fy$	5, T22, MP

T230	1.	~~Show~~ $\bigvee x(Fx \rightarrow \bigwedge x Fx)$	
	2.	$\sim \bigvee x(Fx \rightarrow \bigwedge x Fx)$	
	3.	$\sim(Fx \rightarrow \bigwedge x Fx)$	2, QN, UI
	4.	$\sim Fy$	3, T22, MP, QN, EI
	5.	$\sim(Fy \rightarrow \bigwedge x Fx)$	2, QN, UI
	6.	Fy	5, T21, MP

(This proof of T230 should be compared with the display given in exercise 63 at the end of section 6.)

T231 and T232 are called *laws of alphabetic variance* (for bound variables). They reflect the fact that a generalization such as 'Everything is material' may pass, on the basis of a suitable scheme of abbreviation, into either '$\bigwedge x$Fx' or '$\bigwedge y$Fy'; the choice of variable is unimportant. Detailed consideration will be given to these laws in chapter VII.

T231

1.	~~*Show*~~ $\wedge x Fx \leftrightarrow \wedge y Fy$	
2.	~~*Show*~~ $\wedge x Fx \rightarrow \wedge y Fy$	
3.	$\wedge x Fx$	
4.	~~*Show*~~ $\wedge y Fy$	
5.	Fy	3, UI
6.	~~*Show*~~ $\wedge y Fy \rightarrow \wedge x Fx$	
7.	$\wedge y Fy$	
8.	~~*Show*~~ $\wedge x Fx$	
9.	Fx	7, UI
10.	$\wedge x Fx \leftrightarrow \wedge y Fy$	2, 6, CB

T232

1.	~~*Show*~~ $\vee x Fx \leftrightarrow \vee y Fy$	
2.	~~*Show*~~ $\vee x Fx \rightarrow \vee y Fy$	
3.	$\vee x Fx$	
4.	Fz	3, EI
5.	$\vee y Fy$	4, EG
6.	~~*Show*~~ $\vee y Fy \rightarrow \vee x Fx$	
7.	$\vee y Fy$	
8.	Fw	7, EI
9.	$\vee x Fx$	8, EG
10.	$\vee x Fx \leftrightarrow \vee y Fy$	2, 6, CB

Any instance, as well as any universal generalization of an instance, of a theorem of the sentential calculus will clearly be a theorem of the quantifier calculus. Further, certain ways of distributing the universal quantifier through such theorems will again lead to theorems. T233 – T237 are examples. (T235 corresponds to the Aristotelian syllogism in *Barbara*.) Further examples are left to the imagination of the reader.

T233 $(Fx \rightarrow Gx) \wedge (Gx \rightarrow Hx) \rightarrow (Fx \rightarrow Hx)$

T234 $\wedge x[(Fx \rightarrow Gx) \wedge (Gx \rightarrow Hx) \rightarrow (Fx \rightarrow Hx)]$

T235 $\wedge x(Fx \rightarrow Gx) \wedge \wedge x(Gx \rightarrow Hx) \rightarrow \wedge x(Fx \rightarrow Hx)$

T236 $\wedge x(Fx \leftrightarrow Gx) \wedge \wedge x(Gx \leftrightarrow Hx) \rightarrow \wedge x(Fx \leftrightarrow Hx)$

T237 $\wedge x(Fx \rightarrow Gx) \wedge \wedge x(Fx \rightarrow Hx) \leftrightarrow \wedge x(Fx \rightarrow Gx \wedge Hx)$

We list eleven more theorems involving quantifiers.

T238 $\bigwedge x Fx \to \bigvee x Fx$

T239 $\bigwedge x Fx \land \bigvee x Gx \to \bigvee x(Fx \land Gx)$

T240 $\bigwedge x(Fx \to Gx) \land \bigvee x\,(Fx \land Hx) \to \bigvee x(Gx \land Hx)$

T241 $\bigwedge x(Fx \to Gx \lor Hx) \to \bigwedge x(Fx \to Gx) \lor \bigvee x(Fx \land Hx)$

T242 $\sim \bigwedge x(Fx \to Gx) \leftrightarrow \bigvee x(Fx \land \sim Gx)$

T243 $\sim \bigvee x(Fx \land Gx) \leftrightarrow \bigwedge x(Fx \to \sim Gx)$

T244 $\sim \bigvee x Fx \to \bigwedge x(Fx \to Gx)$

T245 $\sim \bigvee x Fx \leftrightarrow \bigwedge x(Fx \to Gx) \land \bigwedge x(Fx \to \sim Gx)$

T246 $\sim \bigvee x Fx \land \sim \bigvee x Gx \to \bigwedge x(Fx \leftrightarrow Gx)$

T247

1.	~~*Show*~~ $\bigvee x(Fx \to Gx) \leftrightarrow \bigvee x \sim Fx \lor \bigvee x Gx$	
2.	~~*Show*~~ $\bigvee x(Fx \to Gx) \to \bigvee x \sim Fx \lor \bigvee x Gx$	
3.	$\bigvee x(Fx \to Gx)$	
4.	$Fa \to Ga$	3, EI
5.	~~*Show*~~ $\sim \bigvee x \sim Fx \to \bigvee x Gx$	
6.	$\sim \bigvee x \sim Fx$	
7.	Fa	6, QN, UI, DN
8.	$\bigvee x Gx$	4, 7, MP, EG
9.	$\bigvee x \sim Fx \lor \bigvee x Gx$	5, CD
10.	~~*Show*~~ $\bigvee x \sim Fx \to \bigvee x(Fx \to Gx)$	
11.	$\bigvee x \sim Fx$	
12.	$\sim Fb$	11, EI
13.	$\bigvee x(Fx \to Gx)$	T18, 12, MP, EG
14.	~~*Show*~~ $\bigvee x Gx \to \bigvee x(Fx \to Gx)$	
15.	$\bigvee x Gx$	
16.	Gc	15, EI
17.	$\bigvee x(Fx \to Gx)$	T2, 16, MP, EG
18.	$\bigvee x \sim Fx \lor \bigvee x Gx \to \bigvee x(Fx \to Gx)$	10, 14, SC
19.	$\bigvee x(Fx \to Gx) \leftrightarrow \bigvee x \sim Fx \lor \bigvee x Gx$	2, 18, CB

T248

1.	~~*Show*~~ $\bigvee x Fx \wedge \bigvee x \sim Fx \leftrightarrow \bigwedge x \bigvee y(Fx \leftrightarrow \sim Fy)$	
2.	~~*Show*~~ $\bigvee x Fx \wedge \bigvee x \sim Fx \rightarrow \bigwedge x \bigvee y(Fx \leftrightarrow \sim Fy)$	
3.	$\bigvee x Fx \wedge \bigvee x \sim Fx$	
4.	~~*Show*~~ $\bigwedge x \bigvee y(Fx \leftrightarrow \sim Fy)$	
5.	~~*Show*~~ $Fx \rightarrow \bigvee y(Fx \leftrightarrow \sim Fy)$	
6.	Fx	
7.	$\sim Fa$	3, S, EI
8.	$\bigvee y(Fx \leftrightarrow \sim Fy)$	6, 7, Adj, T84, MP, EG
9.	~~*Show*~~ $\sim Fx \rightarrow \bigvee y(Fx \leftrightarrow \sim Fy)$	
10.	$\sim Fx$	
11.	Fb	3, S, EI
12.	$\bigvee y(Fx \leftrightarrow \sim Fy)$	11, DN, 10, Adj, T85, MP, EG
13.	$\bigvee y(Fx \leftrightarrow \sim Fy)$	5, 9, SC
14.	~~*Show*~~ $\bigwedge x \bigvee y(Fx \leftrightarrow \sim Fy) \rightarrow \bigvee x Fx \wedge \bigvee x \sim Fx$	
15.	$\bigwedge x \bigvee y(Fx \leftrightarrow \sim Fy)$	
16.	$Fx \leftrightarrow \sim Fc$	15, UI, EI
17.	~~*Show*~~ $\bigvee x Fx$	
18.	$\sim \bigvee x Fx$	
19.	$\bigvee x Fx$	18, QN, UI, 16, BC, MP, EG
20.	~~*Show*~~ $\bigvee x \sim Fx$	
21.	$\sim \bigvee x \sim Fx$	
22.	$\bigvee x \sim Fx$	21, QN, UI, DN, 16, BC, MP, EG
23.	$\bigvee x Fx \wedge \bigvee x \sim Fx$	17, 20, Adj
24.	$\bigvee x Fx \wedge \bigvee x \sim Fx \leftrightarrow \bigwedge x \bigvee y(Fx \leftrightarrow \sim Fy)$	2, 14, CB

EXERCISES

75. Prove T208–T214.
76. Prove T218, T219, T221.
77. Prove T223–T225.
78. Prove T240, T242, T245, T246.

In solving exercises 75–78 (as well as later exercises) the reader will find the following strategic hints helpful (though again not infallible).

(1) *To derive a formula*

$$\phi \vee \psi \rightarrow \chi$$

derive first

$$\phi \rightarrow \chi$$

and

$$\psi \rightarrow \chi \quad ,$$

and then use SC (Form III, p. 78). (See lines 10–18 of the proof of T247, p. 167, for an application of this hint.)

(2) *To derive*

$$(\phi \rightarrow \psi) \rightarrow \chi$$

derive first

$$\sim\phi \rightarrow \chi$$

and

$$\psi \rightarrow \chi \quad ,$$

and then use Adj, T35, BC, MP. (See lines 8–15 of the proof of T222, p. 163, for an application of this hint.)

(3) *To derive*

$$(\phi \leftrightarrow \psi) \rightarrow \chi$$

derive first

$$\phi \wedge \psi \rightarrow \chi$$

and

$$\sim\phi \wedge \sim\psi \rightarrow \chi \quad ,$$

and then use Adj, T86, BC, MP. (See the proof of T226, p. 164, for an application of this hint.)

(4) *To derive*

$$\phi \rightarrow \psi \quad ,$$

where ϕ is neither a disjunction, a conditional, nor a biconditional, use conditional derivation.

(5) *To derive a conjunction, derive first both conjuncts, and then use Adj.*

(6) *To derive*

$$\phi \vee \psi$$

derive first

$$\sim\phi \rightarrow \psi \quad ,$$

and then use CD. (See lines 5–9 of the proof of T247, p. 167, for an application of this hint.)

(7) *To derive a biconditional, derive first the two corresponding conditionals, and then use CB.*

(8) *To derive a formula*

$$\bigwedge\alpha\phi \quad ,$$

use universal derivation if the variable α *does not occur free in an antecedent line, or else use indirect derivation.*

(9) *To derive*

$$\bigvee\alpha\phi_\alpha$$

either derive first ϕ_ζ, *where* ϕ_ζ *comes from* ϕ_α *by proper substitution of the term* ζ *for* α, *and then use EG, or else use indirect derivation. (See lines 8–13 of the proof of T226, p. 164, for an application of the first alternative and the proof of T229, p. 165, for an application of the second.)*

(10) *To derive a formula* χ *when*

$$\phi \vee \psi$$

is an antecedent line, derive first

$$\phi \rightarrow \chi$$

and

$$\psi \rightarrow \chi \quad ,$$

and then use SC (Form II, p. 78).

(11) *To derive anything else, use either indirect derivation or SC (Form I, p. 78).*

(12) *If a disjunction occurs as an antecedent line to which MTP is not applicable, as an alternative to (10) above, derive the negation of one of the disjuncts.*

(13) *If an antecedent line is a negation of a generalization, apply QN; apply EI before UI; and instantiate universal generalizations to variables introduced by EI.*

The reader should also review the remarks accompanying T201 and T202 (section 7), and T207 (section 10).

11. Arguments. Let us pass now to derivations involving premises. Recall that a symbolic argument is *valid* if its conclusion is derivable from its premises and that an English argument is *valid* (in the monadic quanti-fier calculus) if it has a valid symbolization.

Consider, for example, argument (1) from section 1.

All persons are mortal. Socrates is a person. $\therefore$ Socrates is mortal.

Its validity is established by the following symbolization and derivation:

$$\Lambda x(Fx \to Gx) \quad . \qquad FA \quad \therefore \ GA$$

1. ~~Show~~ GA

2. | GA | 1st premise, UI, 2nd premise, MP

The reader who has proved T240 will have no difficulty in establishing the validity of argument (2) from section 1.

EXERCISES, GROUP I

Free variables play various roles in our system of derivation; those relating to existential instantiation and universal derivation have been discussed (see pp. 140 and 143). A few words concerning their role in premises are now in order. It is standard mathematical practice to omit leading universal quantifiers and to express generality by means of free variables. For example, a mathematician will sometimes state a commutative law for addition by writing

$$x + y = y + x \quad ,$$

where it is understood that the formula carries with it implicit universal quantifiers. In our system of derivation, free variables in premises are employed in this way. Consequently, premises have the deductive power of their universal generalizations; however, preserving and utilizing this power often requires some skill in entering premises into a derivation. Exercises 79–82 will require this skill; exercise 79 is solved for illustration.

Demonstrate the validity of each of the following arguments.

79. $Fx \wedge Gy$. Hx $\therefore$ $Gz \wedge \Lambda z Hz$

1. ~~Show~~ $Gz \wedge \Lambda z Hz$

2. | ~~Show~~ $\Lambda y Gy$ |

3. | | $Fx \wedge Gy$ | Premise
4. | | Gy | 3, S

5. | ~~Show~~ $\Lambda x Hx$ |

6. | | Hx | Premise

7. | ~~Show~~ $\Lambda z Hz$ |

8. | | Hz | 5, UI

9. | $Gz \wedge \Lambda z Hz$ | 2, UI, 7, Adj

Note that we did not allow a free occurrence of either 'x' or 'z' to occur in an antecedent line to the subsidiary derivations of "$\bigwedge x\mathrm{H}x$' and '$\bigwedge z\mathrm{H}z$'.

80. $\bigwedge y(\mathrm{F}x \wedge \mathrm{G}y) \quad \therefore\ \mathrm{F}x \wedge \mathrm{G}x$
81. $\mathrm{F}x \wedge \mathrm{G}x \quad \therefore\ \bigwedge y(\mathrm{F}x \wedge \mathrm{G}y)$
82. $\mathrm{F}x \wedge \mathrm{G}y \quad \therefore\ \bigwedge z(\mathrm{F}z \wedge \mathrm{G}z)$

EXERCISES, GROUP II

Demonstrate the validity of each of the following arguments. (Some arguments are accompanied by a suggestion, which the reader may find useful; also use the strategic hints on pp. 169–70.)

83. $\bigwedge x(\mathrm{F}x \rightarrow \mathrm{G}x) \quad . \quad \bigwedge x(\mathrm{G}x \rightarrow \mathrm{H}x) \quad \therefore\ \mathrm{FA} \rightarrow \bigvee x(\mathrm{G}x \wedge \mathrm{H}x)$ [UI to 'A']

84. $\bigwedge x \sim \mathrm{F}x \rightarrow \bigwedge x\mathrm{F}x \quad \therefore\ \bigvee x\mathrm{F}x$ [Use indirect derivation and QN]

85. $\bigwedge x\mathrm{F}x \vee \bigwedge x\mathrm{G}x \quad . \quad \bigwedge x(\mathrm{F}x \rightarrow \sim \mathrm{G}x) \quad \therefore\ \bigvee x\mathrm{F}x \rightarrow \bigwedge x\mathrm{F}x$ [Derive '$\sim \bigwedge x\mathrm{G}x$']

86. $\bigvee x(\mathrm{F}x \vee \mathrm{GA}) \quad . \quad \bigwedge x(\mathrm{F}x \rightarrow \mathrm{G}x) \quad \therefore\ \bigvee x\mathrm{G}x$ [Use EI and then SC (Form II)]

87. $\bigwedge x(\mathrm{F}x \rightarrow \mathrm{G}x) \quad \therefore\ \bigwedge x[\mathrm{F}x \wedge \sim \bigvee y(\mathrm{G}y \wedge \mathrm{H}y) \rightarrow \bigvee x \sim \mathrm{H}x]$

88. $\bigwedge x(\mathrm{F}x \leftrightarrow \mathrm{P}) \quad . \quad \bigvee x\mathrm{F}x \quad \therefore\ \bigwedge x\mathrm{F}x$ [Use EI and then UI twice]

89. $\bigvee y \bigwedge x(\mathrm{F}x \leftrightarrow \mathrm{F}y) \quad . \quad \bigvee x\mathrm{F}x \quad \therefore\ \bigwedge x\mathrm{F}x$

90. $\bigwedge x(\mathrm{F}x \leftrightarrow \mathrm{G}x \vee \mathrm{H}x) \quad . \quad \bigvee x\mathrm{G}x \quad . \quad \bigwedge x(\mathrm{F}x \rightarrow \bigwedge x\mathrm{H}x) \quad \therefore\ \bigwedge x\mathrm{F}x$

91. $\bigwedge x(\mathrm{F}x \rightarrow \bigwedge x\mathrm{G}x) \quad \therefore\ \bigwedge x(\mathrm{F}x \rightarrow \bigwedge x[\mathrm{G}x \vee \mathrm{H}x])$ [Avoid the appearance of a free occurrence of 'x' before commencing a universal derivation]

92. $\bigvee x\mathrm{F}x \rightarrow \bigwedge x\mathrm{G}x \quad . \quad \bigwedge x(\mathrm{G}x \vee \mathrm{H}x) \rightarrow \bigwedge x\mathrm{J}x \quad \therefore\ \bigwedge x(\mathrm{F}x \rightarrow \mathrm{J}x)$

93. $\therefore\ \bigwedge x[\mathrm{F}x \wedge (\sim \bigvee x\mathrm{F}x \vee \bigwedge x\mathrm{G}x) \rightarrow \bigwedge x(\mathrm{F}x \vee \mathrm{G}x)]$

94. $\bigvee x(\mathrm{F}x \rightarrow \mathrm{P}) \quad . \quad \bigvee x(\mathrm{P} \rightarrow \mathrm{F}x) \quad \therefore\ \bigvee x(\mathrm{F}x \leftrightarrow \mathrm{P})$ [Construct cases on 'P' and '$\sim$P', and then use SC (Form I)]

95. $\bigvee x\mathrm{F}x \leftrightarrow \bigvee x\mathrm{G}x \quad \therefore\ \bigvee x \bigvee y(\mathrm{F}x \leftrightarrow \mathrm{G}y)$ [Use T83 and SC (Form II)]

96. $\bigvee x(\mathrm{F}x \leftrightarrow \mathrm{P}) \quad . \quad \bigvee x(\mathrm{G}x \leftrightarrow \mathrm{P}) \quad . \quad \bigwedge x(\mathrm{F}x \leftrightarrow \sim \mathrm{G}x) \quad \therefore\ \bigvee x \bigvee y(\mathrm{F}x \wedge \sim \mathrm{G}x \leftrightarrow \mathrm{G}y \wedge \sim \mathrm{F}y)$

97. $\bigvee x(\mathrm{F}x \wedge \mathrm{H}x) \vee \bigwedge x(\mathrm{J}x \rightarrow \mathrm{G}x) \quad . \quad \bigwedge x(\mathrm{F}x \rightarrow \sim \mathrm{H}x) \quad \therefore\ \bigvee x\mathrm{J}x \rightarrow \bigvee x(\mathrm{G}x \wedge \mathrm{J}x)$ [Derive the negation of one of the disjuncts]

98. $\bigwedge x(\mathrm{F}x \rightarrow \mathrm{G}x) \vee \bigvee x(\mathrm{F}x \wedge \mathrm{H}x) \quad . \quad \bigwedge x(\mathrm{K}x \rightarrow \sim \mathrm{J}x \vee \sim \mathrm{H}x) \quad . \quad \bigwedge x(\mathrm{F}x \rightarrow \mathrm{K}x \wedge \mathrm{J}x) \quad . \quad \bigvee x\mathrm{F}x \quad \therefore\ \bigvee x(\mathrm{G}x \wedge \mathrm{F}x)$

99. $\mathrm{FA} \quad \therefore\ \bigwedge x(\mathrm{F}x \rightarrow \mathrm{G}x) \leftrightarrow \bigwedge x[(\mathrm{F}x \wedge \mathrm{G}x) \vee (\sim \mathrm{F}x \wedge \mathrm{GA})]$

100. $\bigvee x(Fx \wedge \sim Gx)$. $\bigwedge x(Fx \rightarrow Hx)$. $\bigwedge x(Jx \wedge Kx \rightarrow Fx)$. $\bigvee x(Hx \wedge \sim Gx) \rightarrow \bigwedge x(Kx \rightarrow \sim Hx)$ $\therefore$ $\bigwedge x(Jx \rightarrow \sim Kx)$

101. $\bigwedge x(Fx \rightarrow Gx \vee Hx)$. $\bigwedge x(Gx \vee Hx \rightarrow Kx)$. $\sim \bigvee x(Kx \wedge Gx)$. $\sim \bigvee xFx \rightarrow \bigvee xGx$ $\therefore$ $\bigvee x(Fx \wedge Hx)$

EXERCISES, GROUP III

Establish the validity of each of the following English arguments by constructing for it a symbolization and demonstrating the validity of that symbolization. Indicate in each case the scheme of abbreviation used. (Before symbolizing, the reader should review the remarks made in section 4 of chapter I (pp. 33–34). Exercises 102 and 103 substantiate claims made on page 127.)

102. For each *x* (*x* is a dog and *x* is a canine). ∴ For each *x*, *x* is a canine.

103. There is an object *x* such that *x* is a cat. ∴ There is an object *x* such that (if *x* is a dog, then *x* is a cat).

104. A kettle does not boil quickly only if it is watched. ∴ Every kettle either boils quickly or is watched.

105. If the Oracle spoke the truth, then if anyone is wise, Socrates is wise. Only the virtuous are wise, and only those who have knowledge are virtuous. ∴ If Socrates does not have knowledge, then either the Oracle did not speak the truth or no one is wise.

106. There is not a single existentialist who either likes logic or is able to construct derivations correctly. Some impartial seekers of truth are existentialists. Anyone who is not able to construct derivations correctly eschews Philosophy. ∴ Some impartial seekers of truth eschew Philosophy.

107. Everyone who signed the loyalty oath is an honest citizen. If someone signed the loyalty oath and was convicted of perjury, or signed the loyalty oath and is a Communist, then not all who signed the loyalty oath are honest citizens. ∴ No one who signed the loyalty oath is a Communist.

108. If some philatelists are not misers, then all philatelists are philanthropists. Some philatelists are numismatists. ∴ If no philatelists are philanthropists, then some numismatists are misers.

109. All men who have either a sense of humor or the spirit of adventure seek the company of women. Anyone who seeks the company of women and has the spirit of adventure finds life worth living. Whoever examines life has the spirit of adventure. ∴ Every man who examines life finds life worth living.

110. No egghead is a good security risk. Every professor lives in an ivory tower. If there is someone who lives in an ivory tower and is not a good security risk, then no one who is either a professor

or an egghead should be trusted with confidential information. ∴ If some professor is an egghead, then no professor should be trusted with confidential information.

111. No one who is either a skeptic or an atheist hates God. (For can one hate that which one doubts or believes nonexistent?) All those who are atheists only if they will not go to heaven are skeptics and hate God. ∴ Everyone will go to heaven.

12. Invalidity: truth-functional expansions and models. In chapter II truth tables were used to show arguments invalid. The technique employed there can be extended to a method for showing invalidity within the present symbolic language. We shall call the new method that of *truth-functional expansions.*

Suppose we are presented with a symbolic argument whose premises and conclusion are sentences. To obtain a *truth-functional expansion* of such an argument, proceed as follows:

(*1*) *Choose a sequence of distinct variables, say* $\alpha_1, \ldots, \alpha_n$, *that do not occur in the given argument.*

(*2*) *Throughout the argument replace each occurrence of a formula*

$$\bigwedge\alpha\phi_\alpha$$

or

$$\bigvee\alpha\phi_\alpha \quad ,$$

where α *is a variable and* ϕ_α *is a formula, by*

$$\phi_{\alpha_1} \wedge \ldots \wedge \phi_{\alpha_n}$$

or

$$\phi_{\alpha_1} \vee \ldots \vee \phi_{\alpha_n}$$

respectively, where ϕ_{α_1} *comes from* ϕ_α *by proper substitution of* α_1 *for* α, ϕ_{α_2} *comes from* ϕ_α *by proper substitution of* α_2 *for* α, *and so on.*

(*3*) *Throughout the argument replace name letters uniformly by variables of the sequence* $\alpha_1, \ldots, \alpha_n$. (*A replacement is* uniform *just in case all occurrences of a name letter are replaced by the same variable.*) *Different name letters may be replaced by the same variable.*

(*4*) *Throughout the resulting argument replace uniformly formulas of the form*

$$\pi\alpha \quad ,$$

where π *is a predicate letter and* α *is a variable, by sentence letters not occurring in the argument. This replacement must be* biunique; *that is, distinct formulas are to pass into distinct sentence letters.*

For example, consider the argument

(1) $\quad FA \vee FB \rightarrow \bigvee x Gx \quad \therefore \bigwedge x(Fx \rightarrow Gx)$.

In the first step toward obtaining a truth-functional expansion, we may choose the variables '*a*' and '*b*'. In the second step, the argument (1) becomes

$$FA \vee FB \rightarrow Ga \vee Gb \quad \therefore (Fa \rightarrow Ga) \wedge (Fb \rightarrow Gb) \quad ;$$

in the third step it could pass into

$$Fa \vee Fb \rightarrow Ga \vee Gb \quad \therefore (Fa \rightarrow Ga) \wedge (Fb \rightarrow Gb) \quad ;$$

and in the fourth step into

(2) $\quad P \vee Q \rightarrow R \vee S \quad \therefore (P \rightarrow R) \wedge (Q \rightarrow S)$.

Of course, the argument (1) has truth-functional expansions other than (2). The significant differences from (2) would result either from a choice of more or fewer variables in step 1 or from a different replacement of name letters by variables in step 3. For example, in step 3 the argument (1) could have passed into

$$Fb \vee Fb \rightarrow Ga \vee Gb \quad \therefore (Fa \rightarrow Ga) \wedge (Fb \rightarrow Gb) \quad ,$$

and then in the fourth step into

$$Q \vee Q \rightarrow R \vee S \quad \therefore (P \rightarrow R) \wedge (Q \rightarrow S) \quad .$$

It happens that a symbolic argument whose premises and conclusion are sentences is valid if and only if, in each of its truth-functional expansions, the premises tautologically imply the conclusion. Thus to show such an argument invalid it is sufficient to exhibit a truth-functional expansion of it, together with a truth table showing that the premises of that expansion do not tautologically imply its conclusion. In particular, to show that a symbolic sentence is not a theorem, it is sufficient to exhibit a truth-functional expansion of it that is not a tautology.

For instance, the argument (1) is seen to be invalid in view of the truth-functional expansion (2) and the line of a truth table for (2) in which 'P', 'Q', 'R', and 'S' have the respective values *T*, *T*, *F*, *T*.

With different truth-functional expansions of a given argument, the test for tautological implication will, of course, in general lead to different results. It happens, however, that if we obtain tautological implication for *all* truth-functional expansions obtained from a choice of 2^n variables in step 1, where n is the number of different predicate letters appearing in the given argument, then that argument is valid. Thus the method of truth-functional expansions provides not only a means of showing invalidity but also an automatic test of validity for arguments of the kind under consideration.

The method given above is directly applicable only to those symbolic arguments whose premises and conclusions are sentences. We can, however, extend the method to arbitrary symbolic arguments.

We say that a formula ψ is a *closure of formula* ϕ just in case ψ is a sentence and either ψ is ϕ or ψ is a universal generalization of ϕ. For example, the formula '$\bigwedge x \bigwedge y(Fx \vee Gy)$' is a closure of the formula '$Fx \vee Gy$'. We understand by a *closure of an argument* any argument obtained from it by replacing each formula comprised in it by a closure of that formula. For example, the argument

$$Fx \quad \therefore \bigwedge x Fx$$

has as its closure

$$\bigwedge x Fx \quad \therefore \bigwedge x Fx \quad ;$$

and the argument

$$\therefore Fx \rightarrow \bigwedge x Fx$$

has as its closure

$$\therefore \bigwedge x(Fx \rightarrow \bigwedge x Fx) \quad .$$

It happens that a symbolic argument is valid just in case each of its closures is valid, and furthermore that one closure of it is valid if and only if any other is. Thus to test an arbitrary symbolic argument for validity it is sufficient to construct a closure of that argument and to test the closure for validity; and, in particular, to ascertain whether an arbitrary symbolic formula is a theorem it is sufficient to construct a closure of that formula and to ascertain whether that closure is a theorem.

For an illustration, consider the argument

(3) $$\bigvee y(Fx \leftrightarrow \sim Fy) \quad \therefore \bigvee y(Fy \leftrightarrow \sim Fy)$$

and a closure of it

$$\bigwedge x \bigvee y(Fx \leftrightarrow \sim Fy) \quad \therefore \bigvee y(Fy \leftrightarrow \sim Fy) \quad ,$$

which arose in our earlier discussion of the requirement that the variable of instantiation for EI be new (see pp. 152 and 155, and exercise 73, p. 160). An expansion of this closure involving two variables is sufficient to establish the invalidity of (3). Elimination of the two existential quantifiers from the closure leads to

$$\bigwedge x([Fx \leftrightarrow \sim Fa] \vee [Fx \leftrightarrow \sim Fb]) \quad \therefore [Fa \leftrightarrow \sim Fa] \vee [Fb \leftrightarrow \sim Fb] \quad ;$$

and elimination of the universal quantifier from the above leads to

(4) $$([Fa \leftrightarrow \sim Fa] \vee [Fa \leftrightarrow \sim Fb]) \wedge ([Fb \leftrightarrow \sim Fa] \vee [Fb \leftrightarrow \sim Fb])$$
$$\therefore [Fa \leftrightarrow \sim Fa] \vee [Fb \leftrightarrow \sim Fb] \quad .$$

(The reader should note that a different order of elimination of quantifiers, say first removing the universal quantifier from the premise, and then eliminating the existential quantifiers, would also lead to (4).) With the introduction of sentence letters, (4) becomes

(5) $$([P \leftrightarrow \sim P] \vee [P \leftrightarrow \sim Q]) \wedge ([Q \leftrightarrow \sim P] \vee [Q \leftrightarrow \sim Q]) \quad \therefore [P \leftrightarrow \sim P] \vee [Q \leftrightarrow \sim Q] \quad .$$

That the premise of (5) does not tautologically imply its conclusion can be checked easily by considering the row in a truth table for (5) in which 'P' is assigned *T* and 'Q' is assigned *F*. Thus the invalidity of (3) is established, for we have demonstrated by the truth-functional expansion (5) the invalidity of a closure of that argument.

Closely related to a truth-functional expansion is a *model*, which provides a more succinct means than such an expansion for investigating invalidity. A few preliminaries are required for the characterization of a model. A *class* is a collection or totality of objects, such as dogs, cats, prime numbers, these objects being referred to as its *elements*. We countenance among classes an *empty class*, that is, a totality that has no elements, such as the class of even prime numbers greater than 2. A class is *finite but not empty* if the number of its elements is some positive integer. A *subclass* of a given class is any class all of whose elements are also elements of the given class; we include among the subclasses of a given class the empty class and the given class itself. For our present purpose, only finite classes of non-negative integers, the so-called *natural numbers*, will be required; and we shall employ braces and numerals to indicate such a class and its elements. For example, '{0, 1, 2}' designates the class whose elements are the natural numbers zero, one, and two; and we employ '{ }' to designate the empty class.

Now consider an argument without sentence or name letters whose premises and conclusion are sentences. A *model* for such an argument consists of (i) a finite but not empty class of natural numbers, called its *universe* and designated by a boldface '**U**', and (ii) a subclass of that universe corresponding to each predicate letter of the argument, called the *extension* of that predicate letter. The specification of a model for a given argument has an appearance similar to that of a scheme of abbreviation. For example, consider again a closure of argument (3) above:

(6) $$\bigwedge x \bigvee y(Fx \leftrightarrow \sim Fy) \quad \therefore \bigvee y(Fy \leftrightarrow \sim Fy) \quad .$$

A model for this argument is:

(7)

U : {0, 1}
F : {0} .

The model (7) indicates first that the universe **U** consists of just two distinct objects, the numbers 0 and 1. Generally, we take account of no arithmetical properties of numbers other than their distinctness when we employ them as elements of the universe of a model. The model indicates secondly the subclass of **U** that is the extension of the predicate letter 'F'. Generally, a predicate letter is considered *true of* each number in its extension and *false of* each number in the universe of the model but not in its extension. Thus, in (7) the predicate letter 'F' is *true of* the number 0 and *false of* the number 1.

With respect to a model for an argument, quantifiers of that argument are to be understood as asserting generalizations, universal or existential, about the elements of the universe of the model. Thus with respect to the model (7) the quantifiers in the argument (6) are to be understood as asserting generalizations about the elements 0 and 1 of the universe of (7), rather than about all things or at least one arbitrary thing: universal quantification makes an assertion about both 0 and 1, and existential quantification about either 0 or 1.

In order to reveal the intimate relation between expansions and models, let us, when treating invalidity, add numerals to our symbolic language and include in the class of atomic formulas of our symbolic language any predicate letter followed by a numeral. Given this enrichment and the preceding comment about quantification, the premise and conclusion of the argument (6) are *equivalent in* the model (7), respectively, to the premise and conclusion of the new argument of our symbolic language

(8) $([F0 \leftrightarrow \sim F0] \vee [F0 \leftrightarrow \sim F1]) \wedge ([F1 \leftrightarrow \sim F0] \vee [F1 \leftrightarrow \sim F1])$
$\therefore [F0 \leftrightarrow \sim F0] \vee [F1 \leftrightarrow \sim F1]$.

(Comparison of (4) above and (8) makes perspicuous the intimate relation between models and truth-functional expansions.) Further, our assertion above that 'F' is true of 0 and false of 1 in the model (7) can now be expressed by asserting that 'F0' is a sentence *true in* and 'F1' a sentence *false in* the model (7). Given, then, that 'F0' has the value *T* and 'F1' the value *F* in (7), we can establish (by the now familiar process of truth-value analysis) that the premise of (8) has the value *T* in (that is, is *true in*) the model (7) and that the conclusion of (8) has the value *F* in (that is, is *false in*) the model (7). And thus, on the basis of the equivalences in (7) mentioned above, the premise and conclusion of the argument (6) are respectively *true in* and *false in* the model (7).

Now it happens that a symbolic argument whose premises and conclusion are sentences is invalid if there is a model for that argument in which its premises are true and its conclusion false; in particular, it follows that a symbolic sentence is not a theorem if there is a model in which it is false. Thus the model (7) establishes the invalidity of the argument (6).

Clearly, models have a brevity not enjoyed by truth-functional expansions; but it should be just as clear that verification that a model does demonstrate the invalidity of an argument is tantamount to carrying out a truth-functional expansion and testing that expansion by truth-value analysis.

Models can be extended easily to accommodate arguments that contain name and sentence letters as well as predicate letters: a model for such an argument must include for each name letter of the argument an element of its universe as the extension of that name letter, and for each sentence letter of the argument a truth value as the extension of that sentence letter. For example, consider the argument

(9) $\bigwedge x \mathrm{F}x \vee \mathrm{GA} \rightarrow \mathrm{P} \quad \therefore \bigwedge x(\mathrm{F}x \vee \mathrm{GA} \rightarrow \mathrm{P})$.

The following is a model for (9):

(10)
$$\begin{array}{ll} \mathbf{U}: & \{0, 1\} \\ \mathrm{F}: & \{1\} \\ \mathrm{G}: & \{\ \} \\ \mathrm{A}: & 0 \\ \mathrm{P}: & F \ . \end{array}$$

To verify that (9) has a true premise and a false conclusion in the model (10), one eliminates quantifiers from (9) as one does in constructing a truth-functional expansion, employing '0' and '1' rather than variables, and replaces 'A' by '0' to obtain

(11) $(\mathrm{F}0 \wedge \mathrm{F}1) \vee \mathrm{G}0 \rightarrow \mathrm{P} \quad \therefore (\mathrm{F}0 \vee \mathrm{G}0 \rightarrow \mathrm{P}) \wedge (\mathrm{F}1 \vee \mathrm{G}0 \rightarrow \mathrm{P})$.

In the model (10), 'F0' has the value *F*, 'F1' has the value *T*, 'G0' has the value *F*, and 'P' has the value *F*. Therefore, by truth-value analysis, the premise of (11) has the value *T*, and its conclusion the value *F*, in the model (10). Since the premise and conclusion of (9) are equivalent in the model (10), respectively, to the premise and conclusion of (11), the invalidity of the argument (9) is established by the model (10). (The reader should note that not all models for (9) would establish that the argument is invalid; for example, if we replace in (10) the pair

$$\mathrm{G}: \ \{\ \}$$

by the pair

$$\mathrm{G}: \ \{0\} \ ,$$

we obtain a model of (9) in which the premise as well as the conclusion is false.)

Demonstration of invalidity by the method of models is directly applicable only to those symbolic arguments whose premises and conclusion are sentences. But by considering closures, this method, like that of truth-functional expansions, can be extended to arbitrary symbolic arguments.

The invalidity of the arguments we have employed to illustrate the application of our methods of demonstrating invalidity has been established either by a truth-functional expansion involving two variables or a model with a universe of two elements. This fact should not mislead the reader, for it is easy to construct invalid arguments whose invalidity cannot be established by considering only two things. Consider, for example, the clearly invalid argument

$$(12) \qquad \bigvee x(Fx \wedge Gx) \quad . \quad \bigvee x(Fx \wedge \sim Gx) \quad \therefore \bigwedge xFx \quad .$$

This argument passes, in a truth-functional expansion involving two variables, into

$$[(Fa \wedge Ga) \vee (Fb \wedge Gb)] \quad . \quad [(Fa \wedge \sim Ga) \vee (Fb \wedge \sim Gb)] \quad \therefore Fa \wedge Fb \quad ;$$

and then into

$$[(P \wedge Q) \vee (R \wedge S)] \quad . \quad [(P \wedge \sim Q) \vee (R \wedge \sim S)] \quad \therefore P \wedge R \quad .$$

There is no line in a truth table for this sentential argument in which both premises have the value *T* and the conclusion the value *F*. However, the invalidity of (12) can be established by a truth-functional expansion involving three variables, or by a model such as

$$\begin{aligned} \mathbf{U} &: \{0, 1, 2\} \\ F &: \{0, 1\} \\ G &: \{0\} \quad . \end{aligned}$$

Thus we see that the demonstration of invalidity may require that more than two variables be considered when constructing a truth-functional expansion and that more than two elements go into the universe of a model. But the upper bound mentioned earlier holds for models as well as truth-functional expansions. That is, if an argument with n different predicate letters is invalid, then there is some model with at most 2^n elements in its universe in which a closure of that argument has true premises and a false conclusion.

EXERCISES, GROUP I

112. Using either the method of truth-functional expansions or the method of models, demonstrate for each of T201, T202, T209–T214, T223–T226 that its converse is not a theorem. (In no case will the demonstration require more than two variables in the first step of a truth-functional expansion or two elements in the universe of a model.) For illustration we carry out the exercise for T211 and T224.

To find a model in which the converse of T211, that is,

$$\bigvee x(Fx \rightarrow Gx) \rightarrow (\bigvee xFx \rightarrow \bigvee xGx) \quad ,$$

is false, consider first its sentential structure. It is a conditional whose consequent is a conditional; thus it will be false in a model only if

'$\bigvee x(Fx \rightarrow Gx)$' and '$\bigvee xFx$' are true in that model and '$\bigvee xGx$' is false in it. Thus the extension of 'G' in the model must be the empty class; and the extension of 'F' must contain at least one element. Further, there must be at least one element in the universe of the model not in the extension of 'F'; otherwise '$\bigvee x(Fx \rightarrow Gx)$' will be false in the model. Thus the invalidity of the converse of T211 is established by the model:

$$\begin{aligned} \mathbf{U} &: \{0, 1\} \\ F &: \{0\} \\ G &: \{\ \} \quad . \end{aligned}$$

A truth-functional expansion of the converse of T224, that is, of

$$(\bigvee xFx \leftrightarrow P) \rightarrow \bigwedge x(Fx \leftrightarrow P) \quad ,$$

that employs two variables in the first step passes, on the elimination of quantifiers, into

$$(Fa \vee Fb \leftrightarrow P) \rightarrow (Fa \leftrightarrow P) \wedge (Fb \leftrightarrow P) \quad ,$$

and then into

$$(Q \vee R \leftrightarrow P) \rightarrow (Q \leftrightarrow P) \wedge (R \leftrightarrow P) \quad .$$

That the latter sentence is not a tautology can be seen by assigning to 'P' and 'Q' the value *T* and to 'R' the value *F*.

In each of the following exercises, one of the two arguments is valid and the other is invalid. For one of the arguments, demonstrate its validity by means of a derivation; for the other argument, demonstrate its invalidity by one of the two methods now available. (Again, in no case will the demonstration of invalidity require more than two variables or two elements.)

113. $Fx \quad \therefore \bigwedge xFx$
$\therefore Fx \rightarrow \bigwedge xFx$

114. $Fx \rightarrow P \quad \therefore \bigwedge xFx \rightarrow P$
$\bigwedge xFx \rightarrow P \quad \therefore Fx \rightarrow P$

115. $\bigvee x(Fx \rightarrow P) \quad \therefore \bigvee xFx \rightarrow P$
$\bigvee xFx \rightarrow P \quad \therefore \bigvee x(Fx \rightarrow P)$

116. $\therefore \sim[\bigvee x \sim Fx \wedge (FA \wedge FB)]$
$\therefore \sim[(\sim \bigvee xFx \leftrightarrow \bigvee x \sim Fx) \wedge (\sim FA \leftrightarrow FB)]$

117. $\bigvee y \bigwedge x(Fx \leftrightarrow Gy) \quad \therefore \bigwedge x \bigvee y(Fx \leftrightarrow Gy)$
$\bigwedge x \bigvee y(Fx \leftrightarrow Gy) \quad \therefore \bigvee y \bigwedge x(Fx \leftrightarrow Gy)$

We solve exercise 113 for illustration. In order to test for invalidity, we must first pass to closures of the arguments in the exercises. (Recall that premises with free variables have the deductive strength of their closures; see exercises 79–82 at the end of section 11.) Closures of the arguments in exercise 113, as indicated on page 176, are

$$\bigwedge xFx \quad \therefore \bigwedge xFx$$
$$\therefore \bigwedge x(Fx \rightarrow \bigwedge xFx) \quad .$$

Inspection can substitute for a derivation to establish the validity of the first of these arguments; and the model

$$\begin{array}{ll} \mathbf{U}: & \{0, 1\} \\ \mathrm{F}: & \{0\} \end{array}$$

establishes the invalidity of the second. The expansions of the two arguments with respect to the model, that is,

$$\mathrm{F}0 \wedge \mathrm{F}1 \quad \therefore \mathrm{F}0 \wedge \mathrm{F}1$$
$$\therefore (\mathrm{F}0 \rightarrow \mathrm{F}0 \wedge \mathrm{F}1) \wedge (\mathrm{F}1 \rightarrow \mathrm{F}0 \wedge \mathrm{F}1) \quad ,$$

make it clear that only the second is invalidated by the model.

EXERCISES, GROUP II

118. Demonstrate by means of a model the invalidity of each of the following arguments. (In each case a model with a three-element universe is required.)

(i) $\bigvee x(\mathrm{F}x \wedge \sim \mathrm{G}x)$. $\bigvee x(\mathrm{G}x \wedge \sim \mathrm{F}x)$ $\therefore \bigwedge x(\mathrm{F}x \vee \mathrm{G}x)$

(ii) $\bigvee x(\mathrm{F}x \wedge \mathrm{G}x)$. $\bigvee x(\mathrm{F}x \wedge \mathrm{H}x)$. $\sim \bigvee x(\mathrm{G}x \wedge \mathrm{H}x)$ $\therefore \bigwedge x\mathrm{F}x$

(iii) $\bigvee x\mathrm{F}x$. $\bigvee x\mathrm{G}x$. $\bigvee x\mathrm{H}x$. $\bigwedge x[(\mathrm{F}x \wedge \mathrm{G}x) \vee (\mathrm{F}x \wedge \mathrm{H}x) \vee (\mathrm{G}x \wedge \mathrm{H}x) \rightarrow \mathrm{J}x]$ $\therefore \bigvee x\mathrm{J}x$

(iv) $\bigvee x(\mathrm{F}x \wedge \mathrm{J}x)$. $\bigvee x(\mathrm{G}x \wedge \mathrm{H}x)$. $\bigvee x(\sim \mathrm{F}x \wedge \sim \mathrm{G}x)$ $\therefore \bigvee x(\mathrm{H}x \wedge \mathrm{J}x)$

In the monadic quantifier calculus, as we have stated (pp. 175 and 180), our methods of establishing invalidity are also automatic, although tedious, tests for validity. Given an argument with n different predicate letters, if there is no model with 2^n elements in its universe in which a closure of that argument has true premises and a false conclusion, then that argument is valid. It is easy to construct invalid arguments whose invalidity can be established only by using the maximum number of elements that could be required. An example is the argument

(13) $\bigvee x(\mathrm{F}x \wedge \mathrm{G}x)$. $\bigvee x(\mathrm{F}x \wedge \sim \mathrm{G}x)$. $\bigvee x(\sim \mathrm{F}x \wedge \mathrm{G}x)$ $\therefore \bigwedge x(\mathrm{F}x \vee \mathrm{G}x)$

119. Construct a truth-functional expansion for the argument (13) above which employs three variables in the first step, and verify that the premises of this expansion tautologically imply the conclusion.

120. Establish the invalidity of argument (13) above by means of a model. (The preceding exercise shows that no model whose universe contains fewer than $2^2 = 4$ elements will suffice.)

121. Construct an invalid argument analogous to (13) above which contains just the predicate letters 'F', 'G', and 'H' and whose invalidity cannot be established by any model whose universe contains fewer than $2^3 = 8$ elements.

EXERCISES, GROUP III

Give an interesting symbolization of each of the following arguments, and for each symbolization demonstrate either that it is valid or that it is invalid. (In this connection the reader should review the remarks on page 102 that precede exercise 68 of chapter II.)

122. All persons are mortal. ∴ Some persons are mortal.

123. All dogs are animals. All mammals are animals. ∴ All dogs are mammals.

124. Drugs are dangerous if and only if they are habit forming. ∴ If there are drugs, then something is dangerous if and only if something is habit forming.

125. Students are happy if and only if they study logic. ∴ If there is a student, then everything is happy if and only if everything studies logic.

126. If none but the gracious deserve the respect of their compatriots, then Coriolanus deserved his fate. Only the magnanimous deserve the respect of their compatriots. All who are magnanimous are gracious. ∴ Coriolanus deserved his fate.

127. If none but the gracious deserve the respect of their compatriots, then Coriolanus deserved his fate. All who are magnanimous deserve the respect of their compatriots. Only the gracious are magnanimous. ∴ Coriolanus deserved his fate.

EXERCISES, GROUP IV

Exercises 128 through 131, which follow, show that each of the incorrect applications of inference rules in exercises 59 to 62 of section 5 leads to a fallacy; thus the comments in the solutions to exercises 59 to 62 (pp. 189–90) should be reviewed in connection with these exercises.

128. The conditionals

(a) $\bigwedge x \bigvee y(\mathrm{F}x \leftrightarrow \mathrm{G}y \wedge \mathrm{H}z) \rightarrow \bigvee y(\mathrm{F}x \leftrightarrow \mathrm{G}y \wedge \mathrm{H}x)$
(b) $\bigwedge x \bigvee y(\mathrm{F}x \leftrightarrow \mathrm{G}y \wedge \mathrm{H}z) \rightarrow \bigvee y(\mathrm{FA} \leftrightarrow \mathrm{G}y \wedge \mathrm{HA})$
(c) $\bigwedge x \bigvee y(\mathrm{F}x \leftrightarrow \mathrm{G}y \wedge \mathrm{H}z) \rightarrow \bigvee y(\mathrm{F}y \leftrightarrow \mathrm{G}y \wedge \mathrm{H}z)$

have the given formula of exercise 59 (p. 142) as antecedent and, respectively, (i), (iv), and (v) of that exercise as consequents (no one of which followed from the given formula by UI). By means of models, demonstrate that none of these conditionals is a theorem.

For illustration, we carry out the demonstration for (a). That formula is false in a model if an instance of one of its closures is false in a model. Inspection of that formula, together with a little insight, suggests that we consider a model in which 'F' and 'G' have the same extension and 'F' and 'H' have mutually exclusive extensions. Thus, we consider the model

$$\begin{aligned} \mathbf{U} &: \{0, 1\} \\ \mathrm{F} &: \{1\} \\ \mathrm{G} &: \{1\} \\ \mathrm{H} &: \{0\} \end{aligned}$$

and the instance

$$\bigwedge x \bigvee y(\mathrm{F}x \leftrightarrow \mathrm{G}y \wedge \mathrm{H}0) \rightarrow \bigvee y(\mathrm{F}1 \leftrightarrow \mathrm{G}y \wedge \mathrm{H}1) \quad .$$

Without further expansion, we see that the consequent of this instance is false in the model, for 'F1' is true and 'H1' is false in the model. Expansion of the antecedent leads to

$$[(F0 \leftrightarrow G0 \wedge H0) \vee (F0 \leftrightarrow G1 \wedge H0)] \wedge$$
$$[(F1 \leftrightarrow G0 \wedge H0) \vee (F1 \leftrightarrow G1 \wedge H0)] \quad ,$$

whose truth in the model the reader can easily verify.

129. The conditional

$$(Fx \rightarrow Gx) \rightarrow (\bigvee xFx \rightarrow Gx)$$

corresponds to the incorrect application of EG in part (vi) of exercise 60 (at the end of section 5). By means of a truth-functional expansion or a model, demonstrate that this conditional is not a theorem.

130. The conditionals

$$(FA \leftrightarrow Gx) \rightarrow \bigvee x(Fx \leftrightarrow Gx)$$
$$(FA \leftrightarrow Gx) \rightarrow (FA \leftrightarrow \bigvee xGx)$$

correspond to the incorrect applications of EG in exercise 61, parts (i) and (iv), respectively. By means of truth-functional expansions or models, demonstrate that neither of these conditionals is a theorem.

131. The arguments

$$\bigvee x(Fx \wedge Gy) \quad \therefore\ Fy \wedge Gy$$
$$\bigvee x(Fx \wedge Gy) \quad \therefore\ FA \wedge Gy$$

correspond to the incorrect applications of EI in exercise 62, parts (ii) and (iii), respectively. By means of truth-functional expansions or models, demonstrate that neither of these arguments is valid.

132. By means of a model, demonstrate that the following argument is invalid:

$$\bigvee xFx \quad \therefore\ Fy$$

Why is the following *not* a derivation that establishes the validity of this argument?

1.	$\bigvee xFx$	Premise
2.	Fy	1, EI
3.	~~*Show*~~ Fy	
4.	$\boxed{Fy}$	2, R

13. Historical remarks. What we call the quantifier calculus has also been called the functional calculus, the predicate calculus, the first-order functional calculus, the lower predicate calculus, and the restricted predicate calculus.

The essential ideas of the quantifier calculus occur first in Frege [1]. The quantifier calculus was extensively developed, though in a rather informal way, in Whitehead and Russell [1] and received its first completely explicit formulation, containing one error corrected in a later edition and another corrected in Pager [1], in Hilbert and Ackermann [1].

The symbols used here are due to Tarski. The quantificational symbols most frequent in the literature are those of Whitehead and Russell [1]:

$$\text{'}(x)\text{' for '}\bigwedge x\text{'}$$
$$\text{'}(\exists x)\text{' for '}\bigvee x\text{'} \quad .$$

The first automatic test of validity for the monadic quantifier calculus was given in Behmann [1]. The present test is based on a result in Bernays and Schönfinkel [1].

A model is a mathematical counterpart to the philosophical notion of a possible world. The philosophical notion is due to Leibniz; see Mates [3]. A precise definition of truth in a model can be found in Tarski [2]; a comprehensive treatment of models is given in Chang and Keisler [1].

Our formulation of the quantifier calculus admits of one simplification in addition to those indicated in connection with the sentential calculus. The general form of universal derivation may be replaced by the simple form (see p. 143).

14. Appendix: list of theorems of chapter III.

LAWS OF DISTRIBUTION:

T201 $\bigwedge x(Fx \to Gx) \to (\bigwedge xFx \to \bigwedge xGx)$

T202 $\bigwedge x(Fx \to Gx) \to (\bigvee xFx \to \bigvee xGx)$

T207 $\bigvee x(Fx \lor Gx) \leftrightarrow \bigvee xFx \lor \bigvee xGx$

T208 $\bigwedge x(Fx \land Gx) \leftrightarrow \bigwedge xFx \land \bigwedge xGx$

T209 $\bigvee x(Fx \land Gx) \to \bigvee xFx \land \bigvee xGx$

T210 $\bigwedge xFx \lor \bigwedge xGx \to \bigwedge x(Fx \lor Gx)$

T211 $(\bigvee xFx \to \bigvee xGx) \to \bigvee x(Fx \to Gx)$

T212 $(\bigwedge xFx \to \bigwedge xGx) \to \bigvee x(Fx \to Gx)$

T213 $\bigwedge x(Fx \leftrightarrow Gx) \to (\bigwedge xFx \leftrightarrow \bigwedge xGx)$

T214 $\bigwedge x(Fx \leftrightarrow Gx) \to (\bigvee xFx \leftrightarrow \bigvee xGx)$

LAWS OF QUANTIFIER NEGATION:

T203 $\sim \bigwedge xFx \leftrightarrow \bigvee x \sim Fx$

T204 $\sim \bigvee xFx \leftrightarrow \bigwedge x \sim Fx$

T205 $\bigwedge xFx \leftrightarrow \ \sim \bigvee x \sim Fx$

T206 $\bigvee xFx \leftrightarrow \ \sim \bigwedge x \sim Fx$

LAWS OF CONFINEMENT:

T215 $\bigwedge x(P \wedge Fx) \leftrightarrow P \wedge \bigwedge xFx$

T216 $\bigvee x(P \wedge Fx) \leftrightarrow P \wedge \bigvee xFx$

T217 $\bigwedge x(P \vee Fx) \leftrightarrow P \vee \bigwedge xFx$

T218 $\bigvee x(P \vee Fx) \leftrightarrow P \vee \bigvee xFx$

T219 $\bigwedge x(P \rightarrow Fx) \leftrightarrow (P \rightarrow \bigwedge xFx)$

T220 $\bigvee x(P \rightarrow Fx) \leftrightarrow (P \rightarrow \bigvee xFx)$

T221 $\bigwedge x(Fx \rightarrow P) \leftrightarrow (\bigvee xFx \rightarrow P)$

T222 $\bigvee x(Fx \rightarrow P) \leftrightarrow (\bigwedge xFx \rightarrow P)$

T223 $\bigwedge x(Fx \leftrightarrow P) \rightarrow (\bigwedge xFx \leftrightarrow P)$

T224 $\bigwedge x(Fx \leftrightarrow P) \rightarrow (\bigvee xFx \leftrightarrow P)$

T225 $(\bigvee xFx \leftrightarrow P) \rightarrow \bigvee x(Fx \leftrightarrow P)$

T226 $(\bigwedge xFx \leftrightarrow P) \rightarrow \bigvee x(Fx \leftrightarrow P)$

LAWS OF VACUOUS QUANTIFICATION:

T227 $\bigwedge xP \leftrightarrow P$

T228 $\bigvee xP \leftrightarrow P$

T229 $\bigvee x(\bigvee xFx \rightarrow Fx)$

T230 $\bigvee x(Fx \rightarrow \bigwedge xFx)$

LAWS OF ALPHABETIC VARIANCE:

T231 $\bigwedge xFx \leftrightarrow \bigwedge yFy$

T232 $\bigvee xFx \leftrightarrow \bigvee yFy$

T233 $(Fx \rightarrow Gx) \wedge (Gx \rightarrow Hx) \rightarrow (Fx \rightarrow Hx)$

T234 $\bigwedge x[(Fx \rightarrow Gx) \wedge (Gx \rightarrow Hx) \rightarrow (Fx \rightarrow Hx)]$

T235 $\bigwedge x(Fx \rightarrow Gx) \wedge \bigwedge x(Gx \rightarrow Hx) \rightarrow \bigwedge x(Fx \rightarrow Hx)$

T236 $\bigwedge x(Fx \leftrightarrow Gx) \wedge \bigwedge x(Gx \leftrightarrow Hx) \rightarrow \bigwedge x(Fx \leftrightarrow Hx)$

T237 $\bigwedge x(Fx \rightarrow Gx) \wedge \bigwedge x(Fx \rightarrow Hx) \leftrightarrow \bigwedge x(Fx \rightarrow Gx \wedge Hx)$

T238 $\bigwedge xFx \rightarrow \bigvee xFx$

T239 $\bigwedge xFx \wedge \bigvee xGx \rightarrow \bigvee x(Fx \wedge Gx)$

T240	$\bigwedge x(Fx \rightarrow Gx) \wedge \bigvee x(Fx \wedge Hx) \rightarrow \bigvee x(Gx \wedge Hx)$
T241	$\bigwedge x(Fx \rightarrow Gx \vee Hx) \rightarrow \bigwedge x(Fx \rightarrow Gx) \vee \bigvee x(Fx \wedge Hx)$
T242	$\sim \bigwedge x(Fx \rightarrow Gx) \leftrightarrow \bigvee x(Fx \wedge \sim Gx)$
T243	$\sim \bigvee x(Fx \wedge Gx) \leftrightarrow \bigwedge x(Fx \rightarrow \sim Gx)$
T244	$\sim \bigvee xFx \rightarrow \bigwedge x(Fx \rightarrow Gx)$
T245	$\sim \bigvee xFx \leftrightarrow \bigwedge x(Fx \rightarrow Gx) \wedge \bigwedge x(Fx \rightarrow \sim Gx)$
T246	$\sim \bigvee xFx \wedge \sim \bigvee xGx \rightarrow \bigwedge x(Fx \leftrightarrow Gx)$
T247	$\bigvee x(Fx \rightarrow Gx) \leftrightarrow \bigvee x \sim Fx \vee \bigvee xGx$
T248	$\bigvee xFx \wedge \bigvee x \sim Fx \leftrightarrow \bigwedge x \bigvee y(Fx \leftrightarrow \sim Fy)$

15. Appendix: solutions to selected exercises.

Section 1

Nos. 3, 4, 6, 9, and 10 are symbolic formulas. No. 5 is not, for a predicate letter followed by two symbolic terms is not a symbolic formula; Nos. 7 and 8 are not, for a quantifier must be followed immediately by a variable; No. 11 is not, for a quantifier phrase does not bring with it a pair of parentheses; No. 12 is not, for a predicate letter must be followed by a symbolic term not a symbolic formula; No. 13 is not, for 'K' is a predicate letter not a name letter and hence not a symbolic term; No. 14 is not, for 'Q' is a sentence letter not a predicate letter and hence cannot be accompanied by a symbolic term; No. 15 is not, for 'D' is a name letter not a predicate letter and hence cannot combine with a symbolic term to form a symbolic formula.

Section 2

The answers to exercises 16 and 17 can be obtained easily from the top node of the modified grammatical tree of the formula:

$$\bigwedge y((\bigvee x(Fx \vee Hy) \vee Gx) \rightarrow \bigwedge z(Fz \vee (Gy \rightarrow \bigwedge xGz)))$$

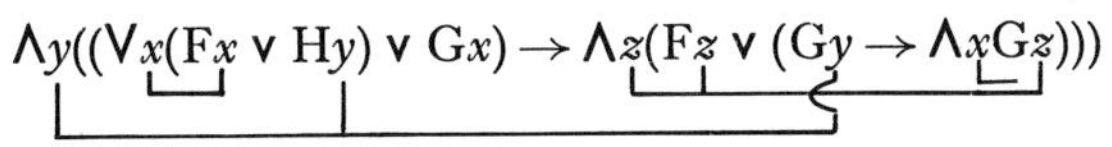

16. As indicated by the links above, all occurrences of variables are bound in the formula except for the third occurrence of 'x'.

17. The variable 'x' is both bound and free in the formula; the variables 'y' and 'z' are bound but not free in the formula.

Section 4, Group I

21. 2 is a prime number if and only if all even numbers are prime numbers.

22. If some even number is a prime, then something is an even number and something is a prime number.

23. If 2 is a prime number and there is an even number, then some even number is a prime.

24. If any even number is a prime, then 2 is a prime number.
25. If some even number is a prime, then 2 is a prime number.

Section 4, Group II

Alternative solutions to exercises in this group are set off by commas; later we will be able to prove the equivalence of these alternative solutions.

30. $(\bigvee x Fx \wedge \bigvee x Gx) \wedge \sim \bigvee x(Fx \wedge Gx)$
31. $\bigwedge x Fx \rightarrow \bigwedge x \sim Gx \vee \bigvee x(Fx \wedge Gx)$, $\bigwedge x Fx \rightarrow \sim \bigvee x Gx \vee \bigvee x(Fx \wedge Gx)$
32. $\bigwedge x(Gx \rightarrow Fx)$
33. $\bigwedge x[Fx \rightarrow (Gx \rightarrow \sim Hx)]$, $\bigwedge x(Fx \wedge Gx \rightarrow \sim Hx)$
34. $\bigwedge x[Fx \rightarrow (\sim Hx \rightarrow Gx)]$, $\bigwedge x(Fx \wedge \sim Hx \rightarrow Gx)$
35. $\bigvee x(Fx \wedge Gx) \wedge \sim \bigwedge x(Gx \rightarrow Fx)$
36. $\bigwedge x(Fx \rightarrow Gx) \rightarrow \sim FA$
37. $FA \wedge \bigwedge x(Fx \rightarrow Gx) \rightarrow GA$
38. $\bigwedge x(Fx \rightarrow \sim Gx \vee Hx)$, $\bigwedge x(Fx \wedge Gx \rightarrow Hx)$, $\sim \bigvee x(Fx \wedge Gx \wedge \sim Hx)$
39. $\bigwedge x(Fx \rightarrow Gx) \wedge \bigwedge x(Gx \rightarrow Fx)$, $\bigwedge x(Fx \leftrightarrow Gx)$

(The latter symbolization is not as literal as the former but is intuitively as adequate.)

40. $\bigwedge x[Fx \rightarrow (Gx \rightarrow Hx)] \wedge \bigwedge x[Fx \rightarrow (Hx \rightarrow Gx)]$, $\bigwedge x(Fx \wedge Gx \rightarrow Hx) \wedge \bigwedge x(Fx \wedge Hx \rightarrow Gx)$, $\bigwedge x[Fx \rightarrow (Gx \leftrightarrow Hx)]$

(The third symbolization is not as literal as the first two but is intuitively as adequate. Definitely incorrect is the symbolization: $\bigwedge x(Fx \wedge Gx \leftrightarrow Hx)$.)

41. $\bigwedge x(Fx \wedge Hx \rightarrow Jx) \wedge \bigwedge x(Gx \wedge Hx \rightarrow Jx)$, $\bigwedge x[(Fx \vee Gx) \wedge Hx \rightarrow Jx]$

(Definitely incorrect is the symbolization: $\bigwedge x[(Fx \wedge Gx) \wedge Hx \rightarrow Jx]$.)

42. $\bigwedge x[Fx \rightarrow (Gx \leftrightarrow Hx \wedge Jx)]$

(Definitely incorrect is the symbolization: $\bigwedge x(Fx \wedge Gx \leftrightarrow Hx \wedge Jx)$.)

43. $\bigwedge x[Fx \wedge \sim Gx \wedge \bigwedge y(Hy \rightarrow Gy) \rightarrow \sim Hx]$
44. $\bigwedge x(Gx \rightarrow Fx) \wedge \bigwedge x(Hx \rightarrow \sim Jx) \rightarrow \bigwedge x[Hx \rightarrow \bigvee y \sim (Gy \vee Jy)]$, $\bigwedge x(Gx \rightarrow Fx) \wedge \sim \bigvee x(Hx \wedge Jx) \rightarrow [\bigvee x Hx \rightarrow \bigvee x(\sim Gx \wedge \sim Jx)]$
45. $\bigwedge x(Fx \rightarrow Gx) \rightarrow [P \rightarrow \bigwedge x(Fx \rightarrow Hx)]$

Section 4, Group III

Alternative solutions to exercises in this group are set off by commas; later we will be able to prove the equivalence of these alternative solutions.

50. (i) $\sim \bigwedge x(Fx \rightarrow Gx)$; (ii) $\bigwedge x(Fx \rightarrow \sim Gx)$, $\sim \bigvee x(Fx \wedge Gx)$
51. (i) $\bigwedge x(Fx \rightarrow FA)$, $\bigvee x Fx \rightarrow FA$; (ii) $\bigwedge x Fx \rightarrow FA$
52. (i) $\bigwedge x(Fx \rightarrow Gx)$; (ii) $\bigvee x Fx \rightarrow \bigwedge x Gx$
53. (i) $\bigwedge x(Fx \rightarrow Gx)$; (ii) $\bigvee x(Fx \wedge Hx)$

(As noted in the symbolization of example (18), the indefinite article 'a' is often used as a stylistic variant of a phrase of quantity; in (i) it is used as a stylistic variant of 'every' and in (ii) as a stylistic variant of 'some'.)

54. (i) $\bigvee x(Hx \wedge Fx) \wedge \bigvee x(Hx \wedge Gx)$; (ii) $\bigvee x(Hx \wedge Fx \wedge Gx)$
55. On the basis of the scheme

F : *a* is a diamond
G : *a* is a fake diamond

we obtain as symbolizations: (i) $\bigvee x Fx$; (ii) $\bigvee x Gx$. (Note that it would be incorrect to let the second pair of the scheme be 'G : *a* is a fake' and the symbolization of (ii) be '$\bigvee x(Gx \wedge Fx)$', for a fake diamond is not a diamond.)

56. (i) $\bigvee x(Fx \wedge Gx) \wedge \sim \bigwedge x(Fx \wedge Gx \rightarrow Hx)$; (ii) $\bigwedge x(Fx \wedge Gx \rightarrow Hx)$
(If in (i) the referent of 'them' is taken to be students rather than protesting students, the second conjunct of its symbolization would be '$\sim \bigwedge x(Fx \rightarrow Hx)$'.)

57. (i) $\bigwedge x(Fx \wedge Gx \rightarrow Hx)$; (ii) $\bigwedge x(Fx \rightarrow Gx \wedge Hx)$
(The difference between (i) and (ii) corresponds roughly to the grammarian's distinction between restrictive and nonrestrictive clauses.)

Section 5

58. In passing from (iv) to (i), the variable '*x*' has been replaced by 'A'; but not all free occurrences of '*x*' have been replaced by 'A', as required for a proper substitution. In passing to (ii), '*x*' has been replaced by 'A'; but here a bound as well as free occurrences of '*x*' have been replaced. In passing to (iii), '*x*' has been replaced by '*z*'; but a free occurrence of '*x*' has passed into a bound occurrence of '*z*'.

59. Each of the formulas (i)–(v) follows from the given formula by UI if and only if it comes from the formula

(1) $$\bigvee y(Fx \leftrightarrow Gy \wedge Hz)$$

by proper substitution of a symbolic term for the variable '*x*'. Thus (i) does not follow, for it is obtained from (1) by replacing '*z*' rather than '*x*'. (ii) and (iii) do follow; the former comes from (1) by proper substitution of '*z*' for '*x*', and the latter by proper substitution of 'A' for '*x*'. (iv) does not follow, for it has been obtained from (1) by replacing '*z*' as well as '*x*' by 'A'. And (v) does not follow, for the occurrence of '*y*' in (v) that replaced the free occurrence of '*x*' in (1) is a bound occurrence. Note with regard to (ii), in contrast to (v), that the occurrence of '*z*' in (1) does not prevent a proper substitution of '*z*' for '*x*'. Do not draw the mistaken conclusion from the contrast of (ii) and (v) that any bound occurrence of a variable in a formula prevents a proper substitution with regard to that variable; for example, the formula '$(Fy \rightarrow \bigvee yGy)$' comes from the formula '$(Fx \rightarrow \bigvee yGy)$' by proper substitution of '*y*' for '*x*', for here a free occurrence of '*x*' passes into a free occurrence of '*y*'.

60. The formula

(1) $$Fx \rightarrow Gx$$

comes from each of the formulas '$Fy \rightarrow Gy$', '$Fy \rightarrow Gx$', and '$Fx \rightarrow Gy$' by proper substitution of '*x*' for '*y*'; thus (i), (ii), and (iii) follow from (1) by EG. (iv) also follows from (1) by EG, for (1) comes from (1) by proper substitution of '*x*' for '*y*'. To see this, note that, in the condition under which a symbolic formula ϕ_ζ comes from a symbolic formula ϕ_α by proper substitution of a symbolic term ζ for the variable α, there is no requirement that α be free, or indeed even that α occur, in ϕ_α. When the variable α is not free in the formula ϕ_α, then for any symbolic term ζ the formula ϕ_ζ is the formula ϕ_α. (The reader should keep this fact in mind when considering in section 10 the proofs of the so-called laws of vacuous quantification.) Less subtle is the recognition that (1) comes from (1) by proper substitution of '*x*' for '*x*'; hence (v) also follows from (1) by EG. However, (vi) does not follow from (1) by EG; indeed, the formula (vi) is a conditional not an existential generalization, as mental restoration of omitted parentheses makes evident.

61. The formula

(1) $\quad \mathrm{FA} \leftrightarrow \mathrm{G}x$

does not come from the formula '$\mathrm{F}x \leftrightarrow \mathrm{G}x$' by proper substitution of 'A' for 'x', for not all free occurrences of 'x' have been replaced by 'A'; thus (i) does not follow from (1) by EG. However, (1) does come from the formula '$\mathrm{F}y \leftrightarrow \mathrm{G}x$' by proper substitution of 'A' for 'y'; thus (ii) follows from (1) by EG. Clearly, (1) comes from (1) by proper substitution of 'x' for 'x'; thus (iii) follows from (1) by EG. Since (iv) is a biconditional rather than an existential generalization, it does not follow from any formula by EG.

62. Each of the formulas (i), (ii), and (iii) follows from '$\bigvee x(\mathrm{F}x \wedge \mathrm{G}y)$' by EI if and only if it comes from the formula

(1) $\quad \mathrm{F}x \wedge \mathrm{G}y$

by proper substitution of some new variable for 'x'. (i) comes from (1) by proper substitution of 'z' for 'x'; hence (i) follows by EI, provided that 'z' is new. (ii) comes from (1) by proper substitution of 'y' for 'x', but 'y' is not new, since it occurs in (1); hence (ii) does not follow by EI. (iii) comes from (1) by proper substitution of 'A' for 'x', but 'A' is not a variable; hence (iii) does not follow by EI.

Section 6

63. The variable of generalization in line 4 is free in an antecedent line, specifically line 3.

64. The variable of instantiation in line 4 is not new; specifically, it occurs in line 3.

Section 8

67. The omitted lines are:

(i)	$\sim(\mathrm{F}y \rightarrow \mathrm{G}y) \rightarrow \mathrm{F}y$	T21
(ii)	$\mathrm{F}y$	3, (i), MP
(iii)	$\sim(\mathrm{F}y \rightarrow \mathrm{G}y) \rightarrow \sim\mathrm{G}y$	T22
(iv)	$\sim\mathrm{G}y$	3, (iii), MP
(v)	$\bigwedge x(\mathrm{F}x \rightarrow \mathrm{G}x \vee \mathrm{H}x)$	2, S
(vi)	$\mathrm{F}y \rightarrow \mathrm{G}y \vee \mathrm{H}y$	(v), UI
(vii)	$\mathrm{G}y \vee \mathrm{H}y$	(ii), (vi), MP
(viii)	$\mathrm{H}y$	(iv), (vii), MTP
(ix)	$\mathrm{F}y \wedge \mathrm{H}y$	(ii), (viii), Adj
(x)	$\bigvee x(\mathrm{F}x \wedge \mathrm{H}x)$	(ix), EG

68. The required annotations are:

Line 5:	3, QN, UI, T39, BC, MP
Line 10:	9, EI
Line 11:	7, UI, T39, BC, MP
Line 12:	2, 6, CB

Section 9

69. Step 5 is incorrect: the variable of instantiation in the application of EI, 'y', occurs *free* in a preceding line containing uncancelled '*Show*'.

70. Step 3 is incorrect: the variable of instantiation in the application of EI, 'x', occurs *bound* as the variable of generalization in a preceding line containing uncancelled '*Show*'.

71. Step 7 is incorrect: '$Fy \wedge Fz$' (line 6), from which '$\bigvee y(Fy \wedge Gy)$' (line 7) is inferred, does not come from '$(Fy \wedge Gy)$' by proper substitution of some term for 'y', for not both occurrences of 'y' have been replaced by the same term; thus line 7 does not follow from line 6 by EG.

72. Step 3 is incorrect: '$Fy \wedge Gx$' (line 3), which is inferred from '$\bigvee x(Fx \wedge Gx)$' (line 2), does not come from '$(Fx \wedge Gx)$' by proper substitution of some term for 'x', for not both occurrences of 'x' have been replaced by the same term; thus line 3 does not follow from line 2 by EI (even though the variable of instantiation 'y' is new).

73. Step 3 is incorrect: '$\bigvee y(Fy \leftrightarrow \sim Fy)$' (line 3), which is inferred from '$\bigwedge x \bigvee y(Fx \leftrightarrow \sim Fy)$' (line 2), does not come from '$\bigvee y(Fx \leftrightarrow \sim Fy)$' by proper substitution of 'y' for 'x', for the occurrence of 'y' that replaces the free occurrence of 'x' in the latter formula is a bound occurrence; thus line 3 does not follow from line 2 by UI.

74. Step 6 is incorrect: the formula '$\bigwedge x Fx \rightarrow Gx$' (line 5) is a conditional, not a universal generalization (as restoration of omitted parentheses makes clear); thus UI is not applicable to line 5, and so line 6 does not follow from line 5 by UI.

Section 10

75. T212

1.	~~*Show*~~ $(\bigwedge x Fx \rightarrow \bigwedge x Gx) \rightarrow \bigvee x(Fx \rightarrow Gx)$	
2.	~~*Show*~~ $\sim \bigwedge x Fx \rightarrow \bigvee x(Fx \rightarrow Gx)$	
3.	$\sim \bigwedge x Fx$	
4.	$\sim Fa$	3, QN, EI
5.	$Fa \rightarrow Ga$	4, T18$\left(\dfrac{P \quad Q}{Fa \quad Ga}\right)$, 4, MP
6.	$\bigvee x(Fx \rightarrow Gx)$	10, EG
7.	~~*Show*~~ $\bigwedge x Gx \rightarrow \bigvee x(Fx \rightarrow Gx)$	
8.	$\bigwedge x Gx$	
9.	$\bigvee x(Fx \rightarrow Gx)$	8, UI, T2$\left(\dfrac{P \quad Q}{Fx \quad Gx}\right)$, EG
10.	$(\bigwedge x Fx \rightarrow \bigwedge x Gx) \rightarrow \bigvee x(Fx \rightarrow Gx)$	2, 7, Adj, T35$\left(\dfrac{P \qquad Q \qquad R}{\bigwedge x Fx \quad \bigwedge x Gx \quad \bigvee x(Fx \rightarrow Gx)}\right)$, BC, MP

76. To obtain a proof of T221, see the proof of T222 (p. 163).

77. To obtain a proof of T225, see the proof of T226 (p. 164).

78. To obtain a proof of T242, see the proof of T243 given in exercise 68 (p. 153); to obtain a proof of T245, T18 should be useful; to obtain a proof of T246, T85 should be useful.

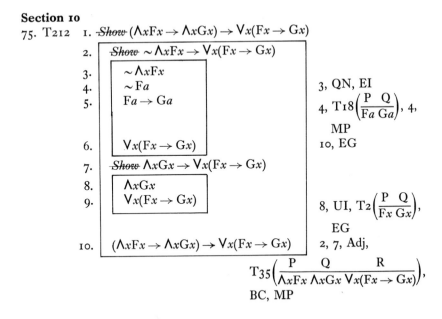

Section 11, Group II

83. $\bigwedge x(Fx \to Gx)$. $\bigwedge x(Gx \to Hx)$ $\therefore$ $FA \to \bigvee x(Gx \land Hx)$

1.	~~Show~~ $FA \to \bigvee x(Gx \land Hx)$	
2.	FA	
3.	$GA \land HA$	1st premise, UI, 2, MP, 2nd premise, UI, MP, Adj
4.	$\bigvee x(Gx \land Hx)$	3, EG

84. $\bigwedge x \sim Fx \to \bigwedge xFx$ $\therefore$ $\bigvee xFx$

1.	~~Show~~ $\bigvee xFx$	
2.	$\sim \bigvee xFx$	
3.	$\bigwedge x \sim Fx \to \bigwedge xFx$	premise
4.	$\bigvee xFx$	2, QN, 3, MP, UI, EG

85. $\bigwedge xFx \lor \bigwedge xGx$. $\bigwedge x(Fx \to \sim Gx)$ $\therefore$ $\bigvee xFx \to \bigwedge xFx$

1.	~~Show~~ $\bigvee xFx \to \bigwedge xFx$	
2.	$\bigvee xFx$	
3.	Fa	2, EI
4.	$\bigvee x \sim Gx$	2nd premise, UI, 3, MP, EG
5.	$\bigwedge xFx$	4, QN, 1st premise, MTP

86. $\bigvee x(Fx \lor GA)$. $\bigwedge x(Fx \to Gx)$ $\therefore$ $\bigvee xGx$

1.	~~Show~~ $\bigvee xGx$	
2.	$\bigvee x(Fx \lor GA)$	1st premise
3.	$Fa \lor GA$	2, EI
4.	~~Show~~ $Fa \to \bigvee xGx$	
5.	Fa	
6.	$\bigvee xGx$	2nd premise, UI, 5, MP, EG
7.	~~Show~~ $GA \to \bigvee xGx$	
8.	GA	
9.	$\bigvee xGx$	8, EG
10.	$\bigvee xGx$	3, 4, 7, SC

87. $\bigwedge x(Fx \to Gx)$ $\therefore$ $\bigwedge x[Fx \land \sim \bigvee y(Gy \land Hy) \to \bigvee x \sim Hx]$

1.	~~Show~~ $\bigwedge x[Fx \land \sim \bigvee y(Gy \land Hy) \to \bigvee x \sim Hx]$	
2.	~~Show~~ $Fx \land \sim \bigvee y(Gy \land Hy) \to \bigvee x \sim Hx]$	
3.	$Fx \land \sim \bigvee y(Gy \land Hy)$	
4.	~~Show~~ $\bigvee x \sim Hx$	
5.	$\sim \bigvee x \sim Hx$	
6.	$\bigwedge x \sim \sim Hx$	5, QN

7. $\bigvee y(Gy \wedge Hy)$ — 3, S, 1st premise, UI, MP, 6, UI, DN, Adj. EG

8. $\sim \bigvee y(Gy \wedge Hy)$ — 3, S

88. $\bigwedge x(Fx \leftrightarrow P)$. $\bigvee xFx$ $\therefore \bigwedge xFx$

1. ~~Show~~ $\bigwedge xFx$
2. Fa — 2nd premise, EI
3. $Fa \leftrightarrow P$ — 1st premise, UI
4. $Fx \leftrightarrow P$ — 1st premise, UI
5. Fx — 3, BC, 2, MP, 4, BC, MP

91. $\bigwedge x(Fx \rightarrow \bigwedge xGx)$ $\therefore \bigwedge x[Fx \rightarrow \bigwedge x(Gx \vee Hx)]$

1. ~~Show~~ $\bigwedge x[Fx \rightarrow \bigwedge x(Gx \vee Hx)]$
2. ~~Show~~ $\bigwedge xGx \rightarrow \bigwedge x(Gx \vee Hx)$
3. $\bigwedge xGx$
4. ~~Show~~ $\bigwedge x(Gx \vee Hx)$
5. $Gx \vee Hx$ — 3, UI, Add
6. ~~Show~~ $Fx \rightarrow \bigwedge x(Gx \vee Hx)$
7. Fx
8. $\bigwedge x(Gx \vee Hx)$ — premise, UI, 7, MP, 2, MP

94. $\bigvee x(Fx \rightarrow P)$. $\bigvee x(P \rightarrow Fx)$ $\therefore \bigvee x(Fx \leftrightarrow P)$

1. ~~Show~~ $\bigvee x(Fx \leftrightarrow P)$
2. ~~Show~~ $P \rightarrow \bigvee x(Fx \leftrightarrow P)$
3. P
4. $P \rightarrow Fa$ — 2nd premise, EI
5. $\bigvee x(Fx \leftrightarrow P)$ — 3, 4, MP, 3, Adj, $T84\left(\frac{P \quad Q}{Fa \quad P}\right)$, MP, EG
6. ~~Show~~ $\sim P \rightarrow \bigvee x(Fx \leftrightarrow P)$
7. $\sim P$
8. $Fb \rightarrow P$ — 1st premise, EI
9. $\bigvee x(Fx \leftrightarrow P)$ — 7, 8, MT, 7, Adj, $T85\left(\frac{P \quad Q}{Fb \quad P}\right)$, MP, EG
10. $\bigvee x(Fx \leftrightarrow P)$ — 2, 6, SC

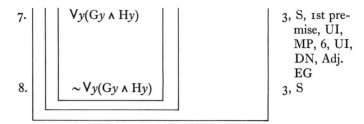

97. $\bigvee x(Fx \wedge Hx) \vee \bigwedge x(Jx \rightarrow Gx)$. $\bigwedge x(Fx \rightarrow \sim Hx)$ $\therefore \bigvee xJx \rightarrow \bigvee x(Gx \wedge Jx)$

1. ~~*Show*~~ $\bigvee xJx \rightarrow \bigvee x(Gx \wedge Jx)$
2. $\bigvee xJx$
3. Ja — 2, EI
4. ~~*Show*~~ $\sim \bigvee x(Fx \wedge Hx)$
5. $\bigvee x(Fx \wedge Hx)$
6. $Fb \wedge Hb$ — 5, EI
7. Hb — 6, S
8. $\sim Hb$ — 6, S, 2nd premise, UI, MP
9. $\bigwedge x(Jx \rightarrow Gx)$ — 1st premise, 4, MTP
10. $\bigvee x(Gx \wedge Jx)$ — 9, UI, 3, MP, 3, Adj, EG

Section 11, Group III

Symbolizations for exercises 104–111 on the basis of natural schemes of abbreviation appear as follows; we leave the derivations to the reader.

104. $\bigwedge x[Fx \rightarrow (\sim Gx \rightarrow Hx)]$ $\therefore \bigwedge x(Fx \rightarrow Gx \vee Hx)$

105. $P \rightarrow \bigwedge x(Fx \rightarrow FA)$. $\bigwedge x(Fx \rightarrow Gx) \wedge \bigwedge x(Gx \rightarrow Hx)$ $\therefore \sim HA \rightarrow \sim P \vee \bigwedge x \sim Fx$

106. $\sim \bigvee x[Fx \wedge (Gx \vee Hx)]$. $\bigvee x(Ix \wedge Fx)$. $\bigwedge x(\sim Hx \rightarrow Jx)$ $\therefore \bigvee x(Ix \wedge Jx)$

107. $\bigwedge x(Fx \rightarrow Gx)$. $\bigvee x[(Fx \wedge Hx) \vee (Fx \wedge Jx)] \rightarrow \sim \bigwedge x(Fx \rightarrow Gx)$ $\therefore \bigwedge x(Fx \rightarrow \sim Jx)$

108. $\bigvee x(Fx \wedge \sim Gx) \rightarrow \bigwedge x(Fx \rightarrow Hx)$. $\bigvee x(Fx \wedge Jx)$ $\therefore \bigwedge x(Fx \rightarrow \sim Hx) \rightarrow \bigvee x(Jx \wedge Gx)$

109. $\bigwedge x[Fx \wedge (Gx \vee Hx) \rightarrow Jx]$. $\bigwedge x(Jx \wedge Hx \rightarrow Kx)$. $\bigwedge x(Lx \rightarrow Hx)$ $\therefore \bigwedge x(Fx \wedge Lx \rightarrow Kx)$

110. $\bigwedge x(Fx \rightarrow \sim Gx)$. $\bigwedge x(Hx \rightarrow Jx)$. $\bigvee x(Jx \wedge \sim Gx) \rightarrow \bigwedge x(Hx \vee Fx \rightarrow \sim Kx)$ $\therefore \bigvee x(Hx \wedge Fx) \rightarrow \bigwedge x(Hx \rightarrow \sim Kx)$

111. $\bigwedge x(Fx \vee Gx \rightarrow \sim Hx)$. $\bigwedge x[(Gx \rightarrow \sim Jx) \rightarrow Fx \wedge Hx]$ $\therefore \bigwedge xJx$

Section 12, Group I

116. The argument

$$\therefore \sim [\bigvee x \sim Fx \wedge (FA \wedge FB)]$$

is invalid. To demonstrate this it is sufficient to consider an expansion based on 2^1 (that is, 2) variables, for the argument contains only one predicate letter. However, it is necessary to consider *all* such expansions. The partial expansion '$\sim [(\sim Fa \vee \sim Fb) \wedge (Fa \wedge Fb)]$' passes into '$\sim [(\sim P \vee \sim Q) \wedge (P \wedge Q)]$', which is a tautology; but the partial expansion '$\sim [(\sim Fa \vee \sim Fb) \wedge (Fa \wedge Fa)]$' passes into '$\sim [(\sim P \vee \sim Q) \wedge (P \wedge P)$', which is not a tautology. We leave to the reader a proof of '$\sim [(\sim \bigvee xFx \leftrightarrow \bigvee x \sim Fx) \wedge (\sim FA \leftrightarrow FB)]$'.

117. The first of the two arguments is valid; we leave the derivation, which is simple, to the reader. To find a model that establishes the invalidity of the second

argument, the reader should note that if 'G' is replaced by 'F' in that argument, the premise of the resulting argument is a theorem. Hence to make the premise true in the model, it is sufficient that 'F' and 'G' have the same extension; and if that extension is neither the universe nor the empty class, the conclusion of the argument is false in the model. Thus the invalidity of the second argument is established by the model

U : {0, 1}
F : {0}
G : {0} .

Section 12, Group II

118. (iv): To make the first premise true, some object must be common to the extensions of 'F' and 'J'; let it be 0. To make the second premise true, some object must be common to the extensions of 'G' and 'H'; if it is 0, then the conclusion is true; so let it be 1. To make the third premise true, there must be an object in the universe that is not in the extension of either 'F' or 'G'; thus this object cannot be either 0 or 1; hence enter 2 into the universe, thereby obtaining the required model:

U : {0, 1, 2}
F : {0}
G : {1}
H : {1}
J : {0} .

120. The invalidity of argument (13) is established by the model

U : {0, 1, 2, 3}; F : {0, 1}; G : {0, 2}

Note that the following sentences are true in this model: 'F0 ∧ G0', 'F1 ∧ ~G1', '~F2 ∧ G2', '~F3 ∧ ~G3'. Note further that adding a fifth element to the universe of this model, say 4, would not add more content to the model for any argument containing just the predicate letters 'F' and 'G'. For exactly one of the following four sentences would be true in the enlarged model: 'F4 ∧ G4', 'F4 ∧ ~G4', '~F4 ∧ G4', '~F4 ∧ ~G4'. If the first of the latter sentences is true, then 4 is indistinguishable (with only 'F' and 'G' available as predicates) from 0; if the second is true, then 4 is indistinguishable from 1; and so on. These observations should give the reader some insight into the claim that an invalid argument with *n* predicate letters will have true premises and a false conclusion in some model whose universe has at most 2^n elements.

121. The argument

⋁*x*(F*x* ∧ G*x* ∧ H*x*) . ⋁*x*(F*x* ∧ G*x* ∧ ~H*x*) .
⋁*x*(F*x* ∧ ~G*x* ∧ H*x*) . ⋁*x*(F*x* ∧ ~G*x* ∧ ~H*x*) .
⋁*x*(~F*x* ∧ G*x* ∧ H*x*) . ⋁*x*(~F*x* ∧ G*x* ∧ ~H*x*) .
⋁*x*(~F*x* ∧ ~G*x* ∧ H*x*) ∴ ⋀*x*(F*x* ∨ G*x* ∨ H*x*)

is invalid, but it can be shown to be invalid only by means of a model with eight elements in its universe. We leave the construction of such a model to the reader. With argument (13) and the above argument as guides, given any finite number

n, it is possible with time and patience to construct an invalid argument whose invalidity can be established only by a model whose universe has no fewer than n elements.

Section 12, Group III

For each of the exercises in this group we provide a symbolization; we leave to the reader the demonstration of validity or invalidity for each of these symbolizations.

122. $\bigwedge x(Fx \to Gx) \quad \therefore \bigvee x(Fx \wedge Gx)$
123. $\bigwedge x(Fx \to Gx) \quad . \quad \bigwedge x(Hx \to Gx) \quad \therefore \bigwedge x(Fx \to Hx)$
124. $\bigwedge x[Fx \to (Gx \leftrightarrow Hx)] \quad \therefore \bigvee xFx \to (\bigvee xGx \leftrightarrow \bigvee xHx)$
125. $\bigwedge x[Fx \to (Gx \leftrightarrow Hx)] \quad \therefore \bigvee xFx \to (\bigwedge xGx \leftrightarrow \bigwedge xHx)$
126. $\bigwedge x(Gx \to Fx) \to HA \quad . \quad \bigwedge x(Gx \to Jx) \quad . \quad \bigwedge x(Jx \to Fx) \quad \therefore HA$
127. $\bigwedge x(Gx \to Fx) \to HA \quad . \quad \bigwedge x(Jx \to Gx) \quad . \quad \bigwedge x(Jx \to Fx) \quad \therefore HA$

Section 12, Group IV

128. A closure of the formula (b) is false in the model

$$\begin{array}{ll} \mathbf{U}: & \{0, 1\} \\ F: & \{1\} \\ G: & \{1\} \\ H: & \{0\} \\ A: & 1\ . \end{array}$$

A closure of the formula (c) is false in the model

$$\begin{array}{ll} \mathbf{U}: & \{0, 1\} \\ F: & \{1\} \\ G: & \{0\} \\ H: & \{0, 1\} \end{array}$$

129. In the model

$$\begin{array}{ll} \mathbf{U}: & \{0, 1\} \\ F: & \{0\} \\ G: & \{\ \} \end{array}$$

the instance '$(F1 \to G1) \to (\bigvee xFx \to G1)$' of a closure of the given conditional is false.

130. A closure of the first of the two conditionals is false in the model

$$\begin{array}{ll} \mathbf{U}: & \{0, 1\} \\ F: & \{0\} \\ G: & \{1\} \\ A: & 0 \end{array}$$

A closure of the second of the two conditionals is false in the model

$$\begin{array}{ll} \mathbf{U}: & \{0, 1\} \\ F: & \{\ \} \\ G: & \{0\} \\ A: & 0 \end{array}$$

131. Closures of the two arguments are

$$\bigwedge y \bigvee x(Fx \wedge Gy) \quad \therefore \bigwedge y(Fy \wedge Gy)$$
$$\bigwedge y \bigvee x(Fx \wedge Gy) \quad \therefore \bigwedge y(FA \wedge Gy)$$

And both of these arguments have a true premise and false conclusion in the model

U : {0, 1}
F : {0}
G : {0, 1}
A : 1

132. The display is a derivation, but not a *complete* derivation, for it contains unboxed lines that do not contain cancelled '*Show*' (see definition of 'complete' on p. 145). The validity of a symbolic argument is defined by means of a *complete* derivation.

16. Appendix: summary of the system of logic developed in chapters I–III.

INFERENCE RULES

PRIMITIVE SENTENTIAL RULES (here ϕ, ψ are symbolic formulas):

$$\frac{\phi \rightarrow \psi \quad \phi}{\psi}$$ *Modus ponens* (MP)

$$\frac{\phi \rightarrow \psi \quad \sim\psi}{\sim\phi}$$ *Modus tollens* (MT)

$$\frac{\phi}{\sim\sim\phi} \qquad \frac{\sim\sim\phi}{\phi}$$ Double negation (DN)

$$\frac{\phi}{\phi}$$ Repetition (R)

$$\frac{\phi \wedge \psi}{\phi} \qquad \frac{\phi \wedge \psi}{\psi}$$ Simplification (S)

$$\frac{\phi \quad \psi}{\phi \wedge \psi}$$ Adjunction (Adj)

$$\frac{\phi}{\phi \vee \psi} \qquad \frac{\psi}{\phi \vee \psi}$$ Addition (Add)

$$\frac{\phi \vee \psi \quad \sim\phi}{\psi} \qquad \frac{\phi \vee \psi \quad \sim\psi}{\phi}$$

Modus tollendo ponens (MTP)

$$\frac{\phi \leftrightarrow \psi}{\phi \rightarrow \psi} \qquad \frac{\phi \leftrightarrow \psi}{\psi \rightarrow \phi}$$

Biconditional-conditional (BC)

$$\frac{\phi \rightarrow \psi \quad \psi \rightarrow \phi}{\phi \leftrightarrow \psi}$$

Conditional-biconditional (CB)

DERIVED SENTENTIAL RULES (here ϕ, ψ, χ are symbolic formulas):

$$\frac{\phi \rightarrow \psi \quad \sim\phi \rightarrow \psi}{\psi} \qquad \frac{\phi \vee \psi \quad \phi \rightarrow \chi \quad \psi \rightarrow \chi}{\chi} \qquad \frac{\phi \rightarrow \chi \quad \psi \rightarrow \chi}{\phi \vee \psi \rightarrow \chi}$$

Separation of cases (SC)

$$\frac{\sim\phi \rightarrow \psi}{\phi \vee \psi}$$

Conditional-disjunction (CD)

PRIMITIVE QUANTIFICATIONAL RULES:

$$\frac{\bigwedge\alpha\phi_\alpha}{\phi_\zeta}$$

Universal instantiation (UI)

$$\frac{\phi_\zeta}{\bigvee\alpha\phi_\alpha}$$

Existential generalization (EG)

$$\frac{\bigvee\alpha\phi_\alpha}{\phi_\beta}$$

Existential instantiation (EI)

where α and β are variables, ζ a symbolic term (that is, a variable or a name letter), ϕ_ζ a symbolic formula that comes from the symbolic formula ϕ_α by proper substitution of ζ for α, and ϕ_β a symbolic formula that comes from the symbolic formula ϕ_α by proper substitution of β for α. (See p. 139 for a definition of 'proper substitution'.)

DERIVED QUANTIFICATIONAL RULES (here ϕ is a symbolic formula and α a variable):

$$\frac{\sim\bigwedge\alpha\phi}{\bigvee\alpha\sim\phi} \qquad \frac{\bigvee\alpha\sim\phi}{\sim\bigwedge\alpha\phi}$$

$$\frac{\sim\bigvee\alpha\phi}{\bigwedge\alpha\sim\phi} \qquad \frac{\bigwedge\alpha\sim\phi}{\sim\bigvee\alpha\phi}$$

Quantifier negation (QN)

DIRECTIONS FOR CONSTRUCTING A DERIVATION FROM A CLASS *K* OF SYMBOLIC FORMULAS

(1) If ϕ is any symbolic formula, then

$$\textit{Show}\ \phi$$

may occur as a line. (Annotation: 'Assertion'.)

(2) Any member of *K* may occur as a line. (Annotation: 'Premise'.)

(3) If ϕ, ψ are symbolic formulas such that

$$\textit{Show}\ (\phi \rightarrow \psi)$$

occurs as a line, then ϕ may occur as the next line. (Annotation: 'Assumption'.)

(4) If ϕ is a symbolic formula such that

$$\textit{Show}\ \phi$$

occurs as a line, then

$$\sim\phi$$

may occur as the next line; if ϕ is a symbolic formula such that

$$\textit{Show}\ \sim\phi$$

occurs as a line, then ϕ may occur as the next line. (Annotation: 'Assumption'.)

(5a) A symbolic formula may occur as a line if it follows from antecedent lines (see p. 24) by a primitive inference rule other than EI.

(5b) A symbolic formula may occur as a line if it follows from an antecedent line by the inference rule EI, provided that the variable of instantiation (see p. 141) does not occur in any preceding line. (The annotation for (5a) and (5b) should refer to the inference rule employed and the numbers of the antecedent lines involved.)

(6) When the following arrangement of lines has appeared:

$$\begin{array}{l} \textit{Show}\ \phi \\ \chi_1 \\ \cdot \\ \cdot \\ \cdot \\ \chi_m\quad , \end{array}$$

where none of χ_1 through χ_m contain uncancelled '*Show*' and either

(i) ϕ occurs unboxed among χ_1 through χ_m;

(ii) ϕ is of the form

$$(\psi_1 \rightarrow \psi_2)$$

and ψ_2 occurs unboxed among χ_1 through χ_m;

(iii) for some formula χ, both χ and its negation occur unboxed among χ_1 through χ_m; or

(iv) ϕ is of the form

$$\wedge\alpha_1 \ldots \wedge\alpha_k\psi \quad ,$$

ψ occurs unboxed among the lines χ_1 through χ_m, and the variables α_1 through α_k are not free in lines antecedent to the displayed occurrence of

$$\mathit{Show}\ \phi \quad ,$$

then one may simultaneously cancel the displayed occurrence of '*Show*' and box all subsequent lines.

The remaining clauses are abbreviatory (in the sense of page 71).

(7) If ϕ is an instance of a theorem of the sentential calculus that has already been proved, then ϕ may occur as a line. (Annotation: the number of the theorem of which ϕ is an instance, sometimes together with a diagrammatic indication of the sequence of substitutions involved.) (For the notion of *instance*, see chapter II, section 5.)

(8) A symbolic formula may occur as a line if it follows from an antecedent line by QN. (Annotation: 'QN', together with the number of the antecedent line involved.)

(9) A symbolic formula may occur as a line if it is the last in a succession of steps, each step in the succession other than the last step either is an antecedent line or can be justified by one of clauses (2), (5a), (7), or (8), and the last step can be justified by one of clauses (5a), (5b), or (8). (The annotation should determine unambiguously the succession of steps leading to the line in question. This can be done by indicating, in order of application, the antecedent lines, the premises, the inference rules, and the previously proved theorems employed. Also, in connection with the rules Add, UI, and EG, the added disjunct, the variable of instantiation, and the variable of generalization should respectively be indicated whenever there is a chance of ambiguity; and when an instance of a previously proved theorem is involved, the relevant replacement, if not obvious, should be indicated.) (The use of derived sentential inference rules is comprehended under this clause.)

DERIVABILITY

A derivation is *complete* just in case every line either is boxed or contains cancelled '*Show*'. A symbolic formula ϕ is *derivable* from a class K of symbolic formulas just in case a complete derivation from K can be constructed in which

~~*Show*~~ ϕ

occurs as an unboxed line.

Chapter IV

'ALL' and 'SOME', *continued*

1. Terms and formulas. There are arguments whose validity depends essentially on phrases of quantity and their stylistic variants but which cannot be reached by the theory of chapter III. For example, the arguments

(1) 3 is a number, and the square of 3 is odd. Therefore the square of some number is odd

(2) All horses are animals. Therefore every head of a horse is a head of an animal ,

though intuitively valid, cannot be validated by the methods of the previous chapter. Before extending the symbolic apparatus of chapter III to cover such cases, we must supplement the grammatical considerations given there.

We have already spoken of *sentences of English*, *formulas of English*, and *names of English* (pp. 117–18). There are expressions that resemble names in the manner in which formulas resemble sentences. For example,

(3) $7 + x$

is related to the names '$7 + 5$' and '$7 + 6$' but is not itself a name of English; it designates neither 12, 13, nor any other object. We shall call expressions such as (3) *terms of English*. As a limiting case, an English name itself will also be regarded as a term of English. Accordingly, a *term of English* is either a name of English or an expression containing occurrences of variables that becomes a name of English when some or all of these occurrences are replaced by names of English. Each of the following, then, is a term of English:

(4) Sir Walter Scott ,

(5) the native state of z ,

(6) the square of x ,

(7) the product of x and y ;

for (4) is a name of English, and on replacement of '*z*' by 'Lincoln', '*x*' by '3', and '*y*' by '2', (5)–(7) become, respectively, the names

the native state of Lincoln ,
the square of 3 ,
the product of 3 and 2 ,

which designate Kentucky, 9, and 6, respectively.

We want now to have in our symbolic language abbreviations not only for names of English but for all terms of English, and these abbreviations will be constructed with the help of operation letters. The symbols

$$A^0 \;,\quad B^0 \;,\quad C^0 \;,\quad D^0 \;,\quad E^0$$

are *0-place operation letters;*

$$A^1 \;, \;\ldots\;, E^1$$

are *1-place operation letters;* and

$$A^2 \;, \;\ldots\;, E^2$$

are *2-place operation letters*. Additional *0-place*, *1-place*, or *2-place operation letters* may be obtained by adding numerical subscripts to the symbols above. For any nonnegative integer *k*, we may characterize *k-place operation letters* in a similar way. Thus an *operation letter* consists of one of the letters 'A' through 'E' accompanied by either a numerical superscript and subscript or only a superscript. The superscript indicates the number of places of the operation letter.

Names of English will be abbreviated by 0-place operation letters, which assume the role formerly played by name letters. Other terms of English will be symbolized by operation letters together with variables. For instance, the expressions

(8) A^0 ,
(9) B^1z ,
(10) C^1x ,
(11) D^2xy

may be construed as symbolizing the respective terms (4) – (7).

As in chapter III, we shall continue to have in our symbolic language abbreviations for sentences of English and formulas of English with one variable, but here we shall also provide means for abbreviating formulas with arbitrarily many variables. To this end, we introduce *predicate letters* of arbitrarily many places in analogy with the operation letters introduced above. The symbols

$$F^0 \ ,$$

$$\vdots$$

$$Z^0 \ ,$$

with or without subscripts, are *0-place predicate letters;*

$$F^1 \ ,$$

$$\vdots$$

$$Z^1 \ ,$$

again with or without subscripts, are *1-place predicate letters;* and so on. Thus a *predicate letter* consists of one of the letters 'F' through 'Z' accompanied by either a superscript and subscript or only a superscript; the number of places of the letter in question is denoted by its superscript.

In this chapter, 0-place predicate letters will assume the role played by sentence letters in earlier chapters, and 1-place predicate letters that of the predicate letters of chapter III. Formulas of English containing k variables may be symbolized by k-place predicate letters accompanied by those variables. For instance, the formulas

$$x \text{ loves } y$$

and

$$x \text{ lies between } y \text{ and } z$$

may be symbolized by

$$F^2xy$$

and

$$G^3xyz$$

respectively.

The *symbolic language* with which we are now concerned contains sentential connectives, parentheses, quantifiers, variables, predicate letters, and operation letters.

As *symbolic terms* we reckon variables and symbolic counterparts to terms of English, the latter consisting of a k-place operation letter followed by k occurrences of symbolic terms. To be more explicit, the class of *symbolic terms* can be exhaustively characterized as follows:

(*i*) *All variables are symbolic terms.*
(*ii*) *If* δ *is a k-place operation letter and* $\zeta_1, \ldots, \zeta_k$ *are symbolic terms, then*

$$\delta\zeta_1 \ldots \zeta_k$$

is a symbolic term. (In particular, a 0-place operation letter is itself a symbolic term.)

As *symbolic formulas* we reckon symbolic counterparts to formulas of English, these consisting of a k-place predicate letter followed by k occurrences of terms, and symbolic expressions constructed correctly from these by means of sentential connectives and quantifier phrases. Again, to be more explicit, the class of *symbolic formulas* can be exhaustively characterized as follows:

(*1*) *If* π *is a k-place predicate letter and* $\zeta_1, \ldots, \zeta_k$ *are symbolic terms, then*

$$\pi\zeta_1 \ldots \zeta_k$$

is a symbolic formula. (In particular, a 0-place predicate letter is itself a symbolic formula.)
(*2*) *If* ϕ *and* ψ *are symbolic formulas, so are*

$$\sim\phi \quad ,$$
$$(\phi \rightarrow \psi) \quad ,$$
$$(\phi \wedge \psi) \quad ,$$
$$(\phi \vee \psi) \quad ,$$
$$(\phi \leftrightarrow \psi) \quad .$$

(*3*) *If* ϕ *is a symbolic formula and* α *a variable, then*

$$\bigwedge\alpha\phi \quad ,$$
$$\bigvee\alpha\phi$$

are symbolic formulas.

The only symbolic terms occurring in the language of chapter III were name letters (presently 0-place operation letters) and variables. We now countenance symbolic terms such as (8)–(11) above as well as more complex terms such as

(12) $$C^1 D^2 xy$$

and

(13) $$D^2 C^1 xy \quad ,$$

which might respectively be regarded as symbolizing

the square of the product of x and y

and

the product of x^2 and y .

To see that (12) is a term, we observe first that 'x' and 'y' are terms (clause (i)) and hence that 'D^2xy' is a term (clause (ii)). Applying clause (ii) again, we see that 'C^1D^2xy' is a term. The analysis of (13) is slightly different; this time we consider the following sequence of terms: 'x', 'C^1x', 'y', and 'D^2C^1xy'.

The class of symbolic formulas also expands. Clause (1) leads not only to formulas such as 'P^0' and 'F^1x' but also to formulas such as

(14) G^2xy ,

(15) F^1A^0 ,

(16) G^2A^0x ,

(17) G^2xB^2xy ;

the latter two might respectively be regarded as symbolizing

zero is less than x

and

x is less than the sum of x and y .

Formulas such as (14)–(17), that is, formulas comprehended under clause (1), constitute the *atomic formulas* of our present symbolic language. Thus here, as before, an *atomic formula* is one in which neither a sentential connective nor a quantifier occurs. Clauses (2) and (3) provide us with compounds constructed from atomic formulas.

In our present symbolic language, terms as well as formulas have grammatical trees. Variables and 0-place operation letters constitute the initial nodes in the grammatical tree for a symbolic term; other nodes are obtained by clause (ii) of the characterization of symbolic terms. As before, atomic formulas constitute the initial nodes in the grammatical tree for a symbolic formula; other nodes are obtained by clauses (2) and (3) in the above characterization of symbolic formulas. For example, the formula

(18) $\bigwedge z(\bigvee xG^3A^1xB^1yz \vee G^2A^1xB^2yz)$

is generated by the following tree:

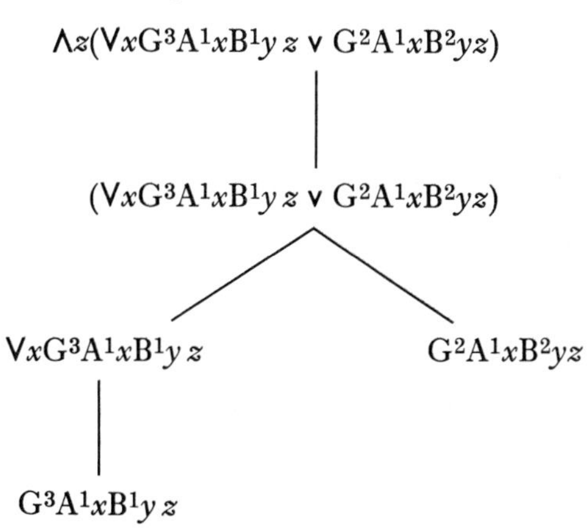

EXERCISES

State whether each of the following expressions is a symbolic term, a symbolic formula, or neither. Exercise 1 is solved for illustration.

1. $(\bigwedge x F^2 x A^0 \rightarrow G^1 A^1 B^1 x)$

This expression is a symbolic formula. We refer to the clauses characterizing terms and formulas (p. 204). 'x' is a symbolic term (clause (i)) and 'A^0' is a symbolic term (clause (ii)); hence '$F^2 x A^0$' is a symbolic formula (clause (1)) and '$B^1 x$' is a symbolic term (clause (ii)). Since '$B^1 x$' is a symbolic term, '$A^1 B^1 x$' is a symbolic term (clause (ii)), and hence '$G^1 A^1 B^1 x$' is a symbolic formula (clause (1)). Since '$F^2 x A^0$' is a symbolic formula, so is '$\bigwedge x F^2 x A^0$' (clause (3)). Finally, since '$\bigwedge x F^2 x A^0$' and '$G^1 A^1 B^1 x$' are symbolic formulas, No. 1 is a symbolic formula (clause (2)).

2. $A^1 F^1 x$
3. $L^2 A^1 x B^1 y$
4. $\bigwedge B^0 (F^1 B^0 \rightarrow G^1 B^0)$
5. $A^1 x B^2 y z$
6. $A^2 A^1 A^0 x$
7. $G^3 C^1 y D^1 x A^1 A^0$
8. $\bigvee x \bigvee y \bigwedge x F^2 x y$
9. $\bigwedge x (A^1 x \rightarrow B^1 x)$
10. $\sim(\bigvee x (\bigwedge y (F^2 y A^0 \rightarrow G^2 x B^0) \rightarrow H^1 A^1 B^3 A^0 x B^0) \leftrightarrow F^1 z)$

2. Bondage and freedom. With the inclusion of terms other than name letters and variables in our symbolic language, we must reconsider the notions of bondage and freedom; they are now to apply not only to variables but to arbitrary symbolic terms.

An *occurrence* of a symbolic term ζ is said to be *bound in* a symbolic formula ϕ if it stands within an occurrence in ϕ of a formula

$$\bigwedge \alpha \psi$$

or

$$\bigvee \alpha \psi \quad ,$$

where ψ is a formula and α is a variable occurring in ζ; an *occurrence* of a symbolic term is *free in* ϕ if and only if it stands within ϕ but is not bound in ϕ. A symbolic *term* is itself *bound* or *free in* ϕ according as there is a bound or free occurrence of it in ϕ.

For example, consider the formula

$$(\bigvee x F^1 A^1 x \vee G^1 A^1 x) \quad .$$

In this formula the first occurrence of the term '$A^1 x$' is bound, the second occurrence is free, and the term itself is both bound and free.

The reader should note that bondage and freedom of occurrences of variables and of variables, as characterized in the preceding chapter, are simply special cases of the present notions, which apply to arbitrary symbolic terms and their occurrences.

As in chapter III, a *symbolic sentence* may be characterized as a symbolic formula in which no variable is free. We can also characterize a *symbolic name* as a symbolic term in which no variable occurs. Thus terms such as 'A^0', 'B^1A^0', '$C^2A^0B^1A^0$', in contrast to terms such as 'B^1x' and '$C^2yB^1A^0$', are symbolic names. The reader should note that any occurrence of a symbolic name is a free occurrence.

Here, as in chapter III, a modified grammatical tree can be employed to identify bound occurrences of a term mechanically. An occurrence of a term in a symbolic formula ϕ is bound in ϕ if and only if in the top node of a modified grammatical tree for ϕ there stands within it a linked occurrence of some variable. (If the term is a variable, this criterion is the same as that given in chapter III, on p. 125, for an occurrence of a variable stands within itself.) For example, a modified grammatical tree for formula (18) of the preceding section,

(1) $$\bigwedge z(\bigvee x G^3A^1xB^1yz \vee G^2A^1xB^2yz) \quad ,$$

appears as follows:

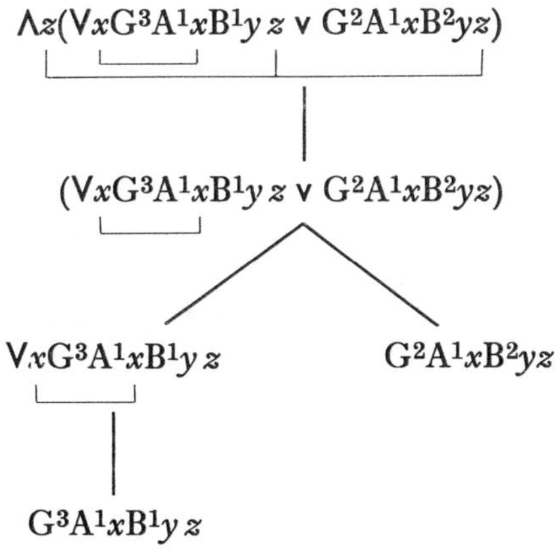

On the basis of the links in the top node of this tree, we see that the first but not the second occurrence of 'A^1x' is bound in (1); the occurrence of 'B^1y' is not bound in (1); and the occurrence of 'B^2yz' is bound in (1).

EXERCISES

Consider the following formula:

$$(\bigwedge y(\bigvee x G^2A^0A^1x \vee G^2B^2yzA^1x) \rightarrow \bigwedge z(G^2B^1yz \vee G^1B^2yz))$$

11. In this formula identify (perhaps with the aid of a modified grammatical tree) each occurrence of a term as bound or free.

12. Which terms are bound in the formula? Which are free in the formula?

3. Informal notational conventions. We shall again employ the conventions of chapter II (pp. 51, 64, and 79) for omitting parentheses and replacing them by brackets.

In addition, it will be our usual practice to omit superscripts from operation letters and predicate letters, inserting parentheses and brackets to avoid ambiguity. In the case of 0-place operation letters, and 0-place and 1-place predicate letters, no parentheses or brackets will be employed. In the case of operation letters of one or more places, and predicate letters of two or more places, we shall enclose the terms accompanying the letter in question in a pair of parentheses or brackets. For instance, the terms (12) and (13) of section 1 (p. 204) may become

$$\mathrm{C}[\mathrm{D}(xy)] \quad ,$$
$$\mathrm{D}[\mathrm{C}(x)y]$$

respectively, and the formulas (14)–(17) on page 205 may become

$$\mathrm{G}(xy) \quad ,$$
$$\mathrm{F\,A} \quad ,$$
$$\mathrm{G}(\mathrm{A}\,x) \quad ,$$
$$\mathrm{G}[x\ \mathrm{B}(xy)]$$

respectively. Restoration of official notation is completely automatic; the superscript of a letter is determined by the sequence of terms following it.

Again, we must emphasize that in theoretical discussions—for instance, the definitions of bondage and freedom and the ensuing characterization of derivability—the words 'term' and 'formula' are always to be understood in the official sense.

EXERCISES

13. For each of the following formulas in unofficial notation, delete the parentheses and brackets inserted, and restore the superscripts and parentheses omitted, in accordance with the informal notational conventions introduced in this section.

(i) $\mathrm{F\,A}(x)$
(ii) $\mathrm{G}(\mathrm{B}\,x)$
(iii) $\mathrm{H}[\mathrm{C}(\mathrm{B\,B})\ \mathrm{A}(\mathrm{B})\ \mathrm{B}]$
(iv) $\bigwedge x \mathrm{F}x \vee \mathrm{P} \rightarrow \mathrm{G}(xy) \wedge \mathrm{H}(xyz)$

4. Translation and symbolization. Many symbolic sentences of our present language cannot be translated into English on the basis of the schemes of abbreviation used in chapter III; an example is

$$(1) \qquad \sim \bigvee x F(xA) \quad .$$

For present purposes we must admit, in addition to the abbreviations of the last chapter, abbreviations involving operation letters of more than zero place as well as predicate letters of more than one place.

It is convenient to establish a standard order of variables; the order we will use is represented by the following list:

$$a, \ldots, z, a_0, \ldots, z_0, a_1, \ldots, z_1, \ldots \quad .$$

Thus the *first variable* will be '*a*', the *second variable* '*b*', the *twenty-sixth variable* '*z*', and so on.

We shall admit abbreviations only of those formulas and terms of English whose variables are the first k variables, for some nonnegative integer k. We shall abbreviate such a formula or term by a k-place predicate letter or operation letter.

Thus an *abbreviation* will now be either (1) an ordered pair whose first member is a k-place predicate letter, for some $k \geqslant 0$, and whose second member is a formula of English containing exactly the first k variables, or (2) an ordered pair whose first member is a k-place operation letter, for some $k \geqslant 0$, and whose second member is a term of English containing exactly the first k variables.

As in earlier chapters, a *scheme of abbreviation* is to be a collection of abbreviations such that no two abbreviations in the collection have the same first member. The following is an example:

(2) A^0 : Adam
F^2 : *a* is father of *b* .

The process of *literal translation into English on the basis of a given scheme of abbreviation* begins, as before, with a symbolic formula and if successful ends with a formula of English. The process consists of the following steps:

(*i*) *Restore official notation by reversing the conventions of the preceding section.*

(*ii*) *Replace 0-place operation letters and 0-place predicate letters by English names and sentences in accordance with the scheme of abbreviation.*

(*iii*) *Replace each operation letter and predicate letter of one or more places by the term or formula of English with which it is paired in the scheme of abbreviation, flanking the latter with a pair of braces. (The result of this step will contain parts of the form*

$$\{\phi\}\zeta_1 \ldots \zeta_k \quad ,$$

where ϕ is a term or formula of English containing exactly the first k variables and $\zeta_1, \ldots, \zeta_k$ are variables or terms of English.)

(*iv*) *Successively replace all parts of the form*

$$\{\phi\}\zeta_1 \ldots \zeta_k \quad ,$$

where ϕ is a term or formula of English containing exactly the first k variables and $\zeta_1, \ldots, \zeta_k$ are variables or terms of English, by the term or formula of English obtained from ϕ by simultaneously replacing all occurrences of 'a' by ζ_1, 'b' by ζ_2, etc., up to the kth variable, which is to be replaced by ζ_k.

(*v*) *Eliminate sentential connectives and quantifier phrases in favor of the corresponding phrases of connection and quantity, preserving all parentheses.*

As before, we say that an English formula is a *free translation* (or simply a *translation*) of a symbolic formula ϕ on the basis of a given scheme of abbreviation if it is a stylistic variant of the literal English translation of ϕ based on that scheme.

Let us, for example, translate the sentence (1) into English on the basis of the scheme (2). In step (i) of the process of literal translation into English, (1) becomes

$$\sim \bigvee x \; F^2 \, x \; A^0 \quad ,$$

in step (ii)

$$\sim \bigvee x \; F^2 \, x \text{ Adam} \quad ,$$

in step (iii)

$$\sim \bigvee x \; \{a \text{ is father of } b\} \; x \text{ Adam} \quad ,$$

in step (iv)

$$\sim \bigvee x \; x \text{ is father of Adam} \quad ,$$

and in step (v)

(3) It is not the case that there is an object x such that x is father of Adam .

Thus (3) is the literal translation of (1) into English on the basis of the scheme (2); and the more idiomatic sentence

Adam has no father ,

being a stylistic variant of (3), qualifies as a free translation of (1) on the basis of the same scheme.

As a slightly more involved illustration, consider the symbolic sentence

(4) $$\bigwedge x \bigwedge y(Fx \wedge Fy \wedge Gy \rightarrow G \; A(xy))$$

and the scheme of abbreviation

(5) F^1 : *a* is a number
G^1 : *a* is even
A^2 : the product of *a* and *b* .

Let us find the literal English translation of (4) based on the scheme (5). Applying step (i), we obtain

$$\wedge x \wedge y(((F^1x \wedge F^1y) \wedge G^1y) \rightarrow G^1\ A^2xy) \quad .$$

Step (ii) is irrelevant. In step (iii) we obtain

$\wedge x \wedge y(((\{a$ is a number$\}\, x \wedge \{a$ is a number$\}\, y) \wedge \{a$ is even$\}\, y) \rightarrow$
$\{a$ is even$\}\{$the product of a and $b\}\, x\, y)$.

Applying step (iv), we obtain first

$\wedge x \wedge y(((\{a$ is a number$\}\, x \wedge \{a$ is a number$\}\, y) \wedge \{a$ is even$\}\, y) \rightarrow$
$\{a$ is even$\}$ the product of x and $y)$,

and then

$\wedge x \wedge y(((x$ is a number $\wedge$ y is a number$) \wedge y$ is even$) \rightarrow$
the product of x and y is even$)$.

Finally, by step (v), we obtain as the literal translation of (4) the English sentence

(6) For each *x*, for each *y* (if ((*x* is a number and *y* is a number) and *y* is even), then the product of *x* and *y* is even) .

Moreover,

The product of any number and any even number is even ,

being a stylistic variant of (6), is a free English translation of (4) on the basis of (5).

As before, ϕ is said to be a *symbolization* of an English formula ψ on the basis of a given scheme of abbreviation just in case ϕ is a symbolic formula that has ψ as a translation on the basis of that scheme.

To find a symbolization of a given formula of English on the basis of a given scheme of abbreviation the reader will again find it useful to proceed roughly as follows:

(1) *Introduce phrases of quantity and connection, the latter accompanied by parentheses and occurring canonically, in place of their stylistic variants.*

(2) *Reverse the steps leading from a symbolic formula to a literal English translation.*

For an example of the process of symbolization, consider the sentence

(7) There is no composer whose contrapuntal ingenuity surpasses that of Bach ,

together with the scheme of abbreviation

F^1 : *a* is a composer
G^2 : *a* surpasses *b*
A^1 : the contrapuntal ingenuity of *a*
B^0 : Bach .

In step (1), with intuition as guide, we transform (7) into

It is not the case that there is an object *x* such that (*x* is a composer and the contrapuntal ingenuity of *x* surpasses the contrapuntal ingenuity of Bach) .

Let us now perform step (2) of the process of symbolization. Reversing step (v) of the process of literal translation into English, we obtain

$\sim \bigvee x$(*x* is a composer $\wedge$ the contrapuntal ingenuity of *x* surpasses the contrapuntal ingenuity of Bach) .

Reversing step (iv), this becomes first

$\sim \bigvee x$({*a* is a composer} *x* $\wedge$ {*a* surpasses *b*} the contrapuntal ingenuity of *x* the contrapuntal ingenuity of Bach) ,

and then

$\sim \bigvee x$({*a* is a composer} *x* $\wedge$ {*a* surpasses *b*} {the contrapuntal ingenuity of *a*} *x* {the contrapuntal ingenuity of *a*} Bach) .

Reversing step (iii), we obtain

$$\sim \bigvee x(F^1x \wedge G^2\ A^1x\ A^1\text{Bach}) \quad ;$$

reversing step (ii),

$$\sim \bigvee x(F^1x \wedge G^2\ A^1x\ A^1B^0) \quad ;$$

and reversing step (i),

$$\sim \bigvee x(Fx \wedge G[A(x)A(B)]) \quad .$$

An example of stylistic variance of rather frequent incidence is the mutual conversion of active and passive voice. Consider, for example, the sentence

If someone is loved by one whom he does not love and by nobody else, then he does not love his lover ,

together with the following scheme of abbreviation:

L^2 : *a* loves *b*
T^2 : *a* differs from *b*
A^1 : the lover of *a* .

In step (1), if we construe '*x* is loved by *y*' as a stylistic variant of '*y* loves *x*' and ignore gender, the sentence above becomes

> For each *x* (if there is an object *y* such that ((*y* loves *x* and it is not the case that *x* loves *y*) and it is not the case that there is an object *z* such that (*z* differs from *y* and *z* loves *x*)), then it is not the case that *x* loves the lover of *x*) ;

and carrying through the successive parts of step (2), we obtain the symbolization

$$\bigwedge x[\bigvee y(L(yx) \wedge {\sim} L(xy) \wedge {\sim}\bigvee z[T(zy) \wedge L(zx)]) \rightarrow {\sim} L(x\, A(x))] \quad .$$

The order of quantifiers in a symbolization is now of particular importance. For example, if we adopt the scheme of abbreviation

$$T^2 : \quad a \text{ differs from } b \quad ,$$

then

$$\bigwedge x \bigvee y \; T(xy)$$

is a symbolization of the true sentence

> Each thing differs from something ,

whereas

$$\bigvee y \bigwedge x \; T(xy)$$

is a symbolization of the false sentence

> Something is such that everything differs from it .

EXERCISES, GROUP I

14. On the basis of the scheme of abbreviation

$$F^1 : \; a \text{ is a person}$$
$$G^2 : \; a \text{ loves } b \quad ,$$

find for each sentence of group A a sentence of group B that is a symbolization of it.

GROUP A

(1) Everyone loves someone.
(2) Someone loves someone.
(3) If anything is a person, then someone loves himself.
(4) Someone loves everyone.
(5) Everyone loves everyone.

GROUP B

(a) $\bigvee x(Fx \wedge \bigwedge y[Fy \rightarrow G(xy)])$
(b) $\bigwedge x(Fx \wedge \bigwedge y[Fy \rightarrow G(xy)])$
(c) $\bigvee y(Fy \wedge \bigvee x[Fx \wedge G(yx)])$
(d) $\bigwedge x(Fx \rightarrow \bigvee x[Fx \wedge G(xx)])$
(e) $\bigwedge y(Fy \rightarrow \bigwedge x[Fx \rightarrow G(yx)])$
(f) $\bigvee x(Fx \rightarrow \bigvee y[Fy \wedge G(xy)])$
(g) $\bigwedge x(Fx \rightarrow \bigvee y[Fy \wedge G(xy)])$

15. On the basis of the scheme of abbreviation

F^1 : *a* is a student
G^1 : *a* is a teacher
H^1 : *a* is a subject
S^3 : *a* studies *b* with *c* ,

find for each sentence of group B a sentence of group A that is a translation of it.

GROUP A

(1) Every student studies every subject with every teacher.
(2) Every student studies some subject with some teacher.
(3) No student studies every subject with a teacher.
(4) Only students study every subject with a teacher.
(5) No subject is such that every student studies it with every teacher.
(6) Every teacher has some subject that some student studies with him or her.
(7) Each subject has some student who studies it with some teacher.
(8) None but teachers are such that all students study all subjects with them.
(9) Anyone who studies any subject with any teacher is a student.
(10) There is a teacher such that every student studies some subject with him or her.
(11) There is a teacher such that some student studies every subject with him or her.
(12) Teachers who study some subject with a teacher are students.
(13) No student who does not study every subject with a teacher is a teacher.
(14) Any student who studies any subject with himself or herself is a teacher.
(15) Some teacher who studies every subject with himself or herself is a student.
(16) There is no teacher with whom any student studies all subjects.

GROUP B

(a) $\bigwedge x(\bigwedge y \bigwedge z[Fy \wedge Hz \rightarrow S(yzx)] \rightarrow Gx)$
(b) $\sim \bigvee x(Gx \wedge \bigvee y[Fy \wedge \bigwedge z(Hz \rightarrow S(yzx))])$
(c) $\bigwedge x(Fx \rightarrow \bigwedge y \bigwedge z[Hy \wedge Gz \rightarrow S(xyz)])$
(d) $\bigwedge x(Hx \rightarrow \bigvee y \bigvee z[Fy \wedge Gz \wedge S(yxz)])$

(e) $\bigwedge x(Fx \rightarrow \bigvee y \bigvee z[Hy \wedge Gz \wedge S(xyz)])$

(f) $\bigwedge x(Fx \wedge \bigvee y[Hy \wedge S(xyx)] \rightarrow Gx)$

(g) $\bigvee x(Gx \wedge \bigwedge y[Fy \rightarrow \bigvee z(Hz \wedge S(yzx))])$

(h) $\bigwedge x \bigwedge y \bigwedge z(Fx \wedge Hy \wedge Gz \rightarrow S(xyz))$

(i) $\sim \bigvee x(Hx \wedge \bigwedge y \bigwedge z[Fy \wedge Gz \rightarrow S(yxz)])$

(j) $\bigwedge x(Fx \rightarrow \sim \bigwedge y[Hy \rightarrow \bigvee z(Gz \wedge S(xyz))])$

(k) $\bigwedge x(Fx \wedge \sim \bigwedge y[Hy \rightarrow \bigvee z(Gz \wedge S(xyz))] \rightarrow \sim Gx)$

(l) $\bigwedge x(Fx \rightarrow \bigwedge y[Hy \rightarrow \bigwedge z(Gz \rightarrow S(xyz))])$

(m) $\bigwedge x(\bigvee y \bigvee z[Hy \wedge Gz \wedge S(xyz)] \rightarrow Fx)$

(n) $\bigvee x(Gx \wedge \bigwedge y[Hy \rightarrow S(xyx)] \wedge Fx)$

(o) $\bigwedge x(Fx \rightarrow \bigvee y\ [Hy \wedge \bigvee z(Gz \wedge S(xyz))])$

(p) $\bigwedge x(\bigwedge y[Hy \rightarrow \bigvee z(Gz \wedge S(xyz))] \rightarrow Fx)$

(q) $\sim \bigvee x(Fx \wedge \bigvee y[Hy \wedge \sim \bigvee z(Gz \wedge S(xyz))] \wedge Gx)$

(r) $\bigvee x \bigvee y(Gx \wedge Fy \wedge \bigwedge z[Hz \rightarrow S(yzx)])$

(s) $\bigwedge x(Gx \rightarrow \bigvee y \bigvee z[Fy \wedge Hz \wedge S(yzx)])$

(t) $\sim \bigvee x(Fx \wedge \bigwedge y[Hy \rightarrow \bigvee z(Gz \wedge S(xyz))])$

(u) $\bigwedge x(Gx \wedge \bigvee y \bigvee z[Hy \wedge Gz \wedge S(xyz)] \rightarrow Fx)$

EXERCISES, GROUP II

Translate each of the following symbolic formulas into idiomatic English on the basis of the scheme of abbreviation that accompanies it. An example is solved for illustration.

$$\bigwedge x \bigwedge y \bigwedge z \bigwedge w[Fx \wedge G(yx) \wedge G(zx) \wedge G(wx) \wedge H(yz) \wedge H(yw) \wedge H(zw) \rightarrow I(A(B[y]\ B[z])\ B[w])]$$

(F^1 : *a* is a triangle; G^2 : *a* is a side of *b*; H^2 : *a* is different from *b*; I^2 : *a* is greater than *b*; A^2 : the sum of *a* and *b*; B^1 : the length of *a*)

In step (i) of the process of literal translation into English, the symbolic formula becomes

$$\bigwedge x \bigwedge y \bigwedge z \bigwedge w(((((((F^1x \wedge G^2yx) \wedge G^2zx) \wedge G^2wx) \wedge H^2yz) \wedge H^2yw) \wedge H^2zw) \rightarrow I^2\ A^2B^1yB^1z\ B^1w) \quad ;$$

in step (iii), for no change occurs in step (ii),

$\bigwedge x \bigwedge y \bigwedge z \bigwedge w$((((((({*a* is a triangle} *x* $\wedge$ {*a* is a side of *b*} *y x*) $\wedge$ {*a* is a side of *b*} *z x*) $\wedge$ {*a* is a side of *b*} *w x*) $\wedge$ {*a* is different from *b*} *y z*) $\wedge$ {*a* is different from *b*} *y w*) $\wedge$ {*a* is different from *b*} *z w*) $\rightarrow$ {*a* is greater than *b*} {the sum of *a* and *b*} {the length of *a*} *y* {the length of *a*} *z* {the length of *a*} *w*) ;

in step (iv), first

$\bigwedge x \bigwedge y \bigwedge z \bigwedge w$(((((((*x* is a triangle $\wedge$ *y* is a side of *x*) $\wedge$ *z* is a side of x) ∧ w is a side of x) ∧ y is different from z) ∧ y is different from w) ∧ z is different from w) → {a is greater than b} {the sum of a and b} the length of y the length of z the length of w) ,

next

⋀x⋀y⋀z⋀w((((((x is a triangle ∧ y is a side of x) ∧ z is a side of x) ∧ w is a side of x) ∧ y is different from z) ∧ y is different from w) ∧ z is different from w) → {a is greater than b} the sum of the length of y and the length of z the length of w) ,

and finally

⋀x⋀y⋀z⋀w((((((x is a triangle ∧ y is a side of x) ∧ z is a side of x) ∧ w is a side of x) ∧ y is different from z) ∧ y is different from w) ∧ z is different from w) → the sum of the length of y and the length of z is greater than the length of w) ;

and in step (v)

For each x, for each y, for each z, for each w (if (x is a triangle and y is a side of x) and z is a side of x) and w is a side of x) and y is different from z) and y is different from w) and z is different from w), then the sum of the length of y and the length of z is greater than the length of w) ,

which is the literal translation of the symbolic formula into English; and the following stylistic variant is a free translation:

The sum of the lengths of any two sides of a triangle is greater than the length of the third side .

16. ⋁x(Fx ∧ ⋀y[Fy → GA(xy)]) → ⋁x(Fx ∧ Gx)

(F^1 : a is a number; G^1 : a is even; A^2 : the product of a and b)

17. ⋀x(Fx → ⋁yG(yx) ∧ ⋁yH(yx)) ∧ ⋁x(Fx ∧ ∼[⋁yG(xy) ∨ ⋁yH(xy)])

(F^1 : a is a person; G^2 : a is father of b; H^2 : a is mother of b)

18. ⋀x(F(x E) → ⋁y[G(y E) ∧ H(xy) ∧ I(y B(C(E)))])

(F^2 : a is a student of b; E^0 : the course; G^2 : a is a workshop of b; H^2 : a attends b; I^2 : a is taught by b; B^1 : the teaching assistant of a; C^1 : the instructor of a)

EXERCISES, GROUP III

Symbolize each of the following formulas on the basis of the scheme of abbreviation that accompanies it. An example is solved for illustration.

A person pays a dollar for the banquet of the club only if he or she belongs to at least one of the club's committees and attends every meeting of that committee. (F^1 : *a* is a person; G^2 : *a* pays a dollar for *b*; H^2 : *a* is a committee of *b*; I^2 : *a* belongs to *b*; J^2 : *a* is a meeting of *b*; K^2 : *a* attends *b*; A^1 : the banquet of *a*; B^0 : the club)

Linguistic insight would suggest that this example become in step (1) of the process of symbolization

> For each *x* (if (*x* is a person and *x* pays a dollar for the banquet of the club), then there is an object *y* such that ((*y* is a committee of the club and *x* belongs to *y*) and for each *z* (if *z* is a meeting of *y*, then *x* attends *z*))) .

By performing the successive stages of step (2), we obtain first

> $\bigwedge x$((*x* is a person $\wedge$ *x* pays a dollar for the banquet of the club) $\rightarrow \bigvee y$((*y* is a committee of the club $\wedge$ *x* belongs to *y*) $\wedge$ $\bigwedge z$(*z* is a meeting of *y* $\rightarrow$ *x* attends *z*))) ,

next

> $\bigwedge x$(({*a* is a person} *x* $\wedge$ {*a* pays a dollar for *b*} *x* {the banquet of *a*} the club) $\rightarrow \bigvee y$(({*a* is a committee of *b*} *y* the club $\wedge$ {*a* belongs to *b*} *x y*) $\wedge$ $\bigwedge z$({*a* is a meeting of *b*} *z y* $\wedge$ {*a* attends *b*} *x z*))) ,

next

> $\bigwedge x((F^1 x \wedge G^2\, x\, A^1$ the club$) \rightarrow \bigvee y((H^2\, y$ the club $\wedge I^2 xy) \wedge \bigwedge z(J^2 zy \rightarrow K^2 xz)))$,

next

> $\bigwedge x((F^1 x \wedge G^2\, x\, A^1 B^0) \rightarrow \bigvee y((H^2 y\, B^0 \wedge I^2 xy) \wedge \bigwedge z(J^2 zy \rightarrow K^2 xz)))$,

and finally

> $\bigwedge x[Fx \wedge G(x\ A(B)) \rightarrow \bigvee y(H(y\ B) \wedge I(xy) \wedge \bigwedge z[J(zy) \rightarrow K(xz)])]$.

19. Every husband and wife has a spouse. (F^1 : *a* is a husband; G^1 : *a* is a wife; H^2 : *a* is a spouse of *b*)
20. No one lacks a father, but not everyone is a father. (F^1 : *a* is a person; G^2 : *a* is father of *b*)
21. Every number has some number as its successor. (F^1 : *a* is a number; G^2 : *a* is a successor of *b*)
22. Some number is a successor of every number. (F^1 : *a* is a number; G^2 : *a* is a successor of *b*)
23. A teacher has no scruples if he or she assigns a problem that has no solution. (F^1 : *a* is a teacher; G^1 : *a* has scruples; H^2 : *a* assigns *b*; J^1 : *a* is a problem; K^2 : *a* is a solution of *b*)

24. The net force acting on a particle is equal to the product of its mass and its acceleration. (F^1 : *a* is a particle; A^1 : the net force acting on *a*; G^2 : *a* is equal to *b*; B^2 : the product of *a* and *b*; C^1 : the mass of *a*; D^1: the acceleration of *a*)

25. No principle is innate unless everyone who hears it assents to it. (F^1 : *a* is a principle; G^1 : *a* is innate; H^1 : *a* is a person; J^2 : *a* hears *b*; K^2 : *a* assents to *b*)

26. The cube of the square of 2 is even. (F^1 : *a* is even; A^1 : the cube of *a*; B^1 : the square of *a*; C^0 : 2)

27. No monk likes every course he takes unless the only courses he takes are theological studies. (F^1 : *a* is a monk; G^1 : *a* is a course; H^1 : *a* is a theological study; J^2 : *a* takes *b*; K^2 : *a* likes *b*)

28. A man who loves himself more than he loves anyone else is not loved by anyone other than himself. (F^1 : *a* is a man; G^1 : *a* is a person; H^2 : *a* loves *b*; J^2 : *a* is different from *b*; L^4 : *a* loves *b* more than *c* loves *d*)

29. If a father has only male children, then he does not have to provide a dowry for any one of them. (F^1 : *a* is a father; G^1 : *a* is male; H^2 : *a* is a child of *b*; J^2 : *a* has to provide a dowry for *b*)

30. The wife of anyone who marries the daughter of the brother of his father marries the son of the brother of the husband of her mother. (F^2 : *a* marries *b*; A^1 : the wife of *a*; B^1 : the daughter of *a*; C^1 : the brother of *a*; D^1 : the father of *a*; E^1 : the son of *a*; A^1_1 : the husband of *a*; B^1_1 : the mother of *a*)

31. If *x* is an integer greater than or equal to zero and every integer is divisible by *x*, then *x* is equal to 1. (F^1 : *a* is an integer; G^2 : *a* is greater than *b*; H^2 : *a* is equal to *b*; I^2 : *a* is divisible by *b*; A^0 : zero; B^0 : 1)

32. The square of the length of the hypotenuse of a right triangle is equal to the sum of the squares of the lengths of the other two sides. (F^1 : *a* is a right triangle; G^2 : *a* is a side of *b*; H^2 : *a* is equal to *b*; A^1 : the square of *a*; B^1 : the hypotenuse of *a*; C^2 : the sum of *a* and *b*; D^1 : the length of *a*)

EXERCISES, GROUP IV

On the basis of the scheme of abbreviation provided, symbolize each of the following sentences. A sentence may be ambiguous, in which case all plausible symbolizations should be provided. Exercise 33 is solved in part for illustration.

33. Someone is hit by a car every day. (F^1 : *a* is a person; G^1 : *a* is a car; H^1: *a* is a day; J^3 : *a* is hit by *b* on *c*)

Two of the four readings for this sentence can be expressed as follows:

> Every day there is some person (or other) who is hit by some car (or other) ,
>
> There is some person (in particular) who is hit every day by some car (or other) .

These sentences, on the basis of the given scheme, are respectively symbolized by

$$\bigwedge z(Hz \rightarrow \bigvee x \bigvee y[Fx \wedge Gy \wedge J(xyz)])$$

and

$$\bigvee x(Fx \wedge \bigwedge z[Hz \rightarrow \bigvee y(Gy \wedge J(xyz))]) \quad .$$

We leave the other two readings of this sentence and their symbolizations to the reader.

34. (i) You can fool some of the people all of the time. (ii) You cannot fool all of the people all of the time. (F^2 : you can fool *a* at *b*; G^1 : *a* is a person; H^1 : *a* is a time)

35. The product of 3 and the square of 6 plus 1 is even. (A^0 : 3; B^0 : 6; C^0 : 1; D^2 : the product of *a* and *b*; E^1 : the square of *a*; A^2_1 : *a* plus *b*; F^1 : *a* is even)

5. Revised inference rules. We must extend the notion of proper substitution for a variable. In chapter III only variables and name letters (presently 0-place operation letters) could be substituted for variables; now we shall admit the substitution of arbitrary symbolic terms for variables. Thus we say that a symbolic formula ϕ_ζ *comes from* a symbolic formula ϕ_α *by proper substitution of a symbolic term* ζ *for a variable* α if ϕ_ζ is like ϕ_α except for having free occurrences of ζ wherever ϕ_α has free occurrences of α.

In chapter III the instantial term for UI and EG had to be either a variable or a name letter. We now reformulate these two rules to permit as the instantial term an arbitrary symbolic term.

Universal instantiation (UI): $$\frac{\bigwedge \alpha \phi_\alpha}{\phi_\zeta}$$

Existential generalization (EG): $$\frac{\phi_\zeta}{\bigvee \alpha \phi_\alpha}$$

In both cases α is to be a variable, ζ is to be *any symbolic term*, and ϕ_ζ is to be a symbolic formula that comes from the symbolic formula ϕ_α by proper substitution of ζ for α.

All previous applications of UI and EG are comprehended under the present formulation; there are additional applications of the following sort. From the sentence '$\bigwedge x Fx$' we can now infer by UI such formulas as

(1) $FB(A)$,

(2) $FB(x)$,

(3) $FC(Ax)$.

Further, from any of (1)–(3) the sentence '$\bigvee x\mathrm{F}x$' follows by EG. From (3) we can also infer by EG the formulas

$$\bigvee y\mathrm{FC}(yx) \quad ,$$
$$\bigvee x\mathrm{FC}(\mathrm{A}x) \quad ,$$
$$\bigvee y\mathrm{FC}(\mathrm{A}y) \quad ;$$

but we cannot infer

$$\bigvee x\mathrm{FC}(xx) \quad ,$$

because (3) does not come from '$\mathrm{FC}(xx)$' by proper substitution of a symbolic term for 'x'.

It should be emphasized that the present extensions concern only UI and EG. The formulation of EI remains exactly as before; that is, from one formula another follows by EI just in case the two formulas have the respective forms

$$\bigvee \alpha \phi_\alpha$$

and

$$\phi_\beta \quad ,$$

where α and also β is a *variable*, and ϕ_β is a symbolic formula that comes from the symbolic formula ϕ_α by proper substitution of β for α.

The directions for constructing an *unabbreviated* and an *abbreviated derivation* remain essentially as in chapter III. For an unabbreviated derivation we adopt clauses (1)–(6) of pages 144–45, with one modification; clause (2) will now read:

(2) *Any one of the premises or any universal generalization of one of the premises may occur as a line.* (*Annotation:* '*Premise*'.)

(The grounds for this liberalization are contained in Group I of the exercises of section 11 of chapter III; see p. 171.) For an abbreviated derivation we supplement clauses (1)–(6) with clauses (7)–(9) of pages 150–51. Throughout all these clauses, however, we must now understand the terms 'formula', 'UI', and 'EG' in the broader sense of the present chapter. We thus arrive at a characterization of a *derivation* in the full (rather than the monadic) quantifier calculus.

The characterizations of a *complete* derivation, *derivability*, a *proof*, a *theorem*, an *argument*, a *symbolic argument*, a *valid symbolic argument*, an *English argument*, a *symbolization* of an English argument, and a *valid English argument* remain exactly as before. (See pp. 145 and 153–54.)

EXERCISES, GROUP I

36. The following argument is invalid:

$$\bigwedge x F[A(x)x] \quad \therefore \bigvee x F[A(x)A(x)] \quad .$$

Identify the incorrect step in each of the following attempts at a derivation of its conclusion from its premise, and state why that step is incorrect.

1.	~~*Show*~~ $\bigvee x F[A(x)A(x)]$	
2.	$\bigwedge x F[A(x)x]$	Premise
3.	$F[A(x)A(x)]$	2, UI
4.	$\bigvee x F[A(x)A(x)]$	3, EG

1.	~~*Show*~~ $\bigvee x F[A(x)A(x)]$	
2.	$\bigwedge x F[A(x)x]$	Premise
3.	$F[A(A(x))A(x)]$	2, UI
4.	$\bigvee x F[A(x)A(x)]$	3, EG

37. Which of the following formulas follow from

$$\bigwedge x \bigvee z F(A(xyx)z)$$

by UI?

(a) $\bigvee z F(zz)$
(b) $\bigvee z F(A(xyx)z)$
(c) $\bigvee z F(A(yyy)z)$
(d) $\bigvee z F(A(xxx)z)$
(e) $\bigvee z F(A(CyB)z)$
(f) $\bigvee z F(A(CyC)z)$
(g) $\bigvee z F(A(ByB)z)$
(h) $\bigvee z F(A(A(xyx)yA(xyx))z)$
(i) $\bigvee z F(A(B(y)yB(y))z)$
(j) $\bigvee z F(A(B(C(z))yB(C(z)))z)$
(k) $\bigvee z F(A(C(B(w))yC(B(w)))z)$

38. Which of the following formulas follow from

$$\bigwedge x F A(xB(y)) \vee G(Cy)$$

by EG?

(a) $\bigvee w[\bigwedge x F A(xB(y)) \vee G(wy)]$
(b) $\bigvee w[\bigwedge x F w \vee G(Cy)]$
(c) $\bigvee w[\bigwedge x F A(xB(w)) \vee G(Cw)]$
(d) $\bigvee w[\bigwedge x F A(xw) \vee G(Cy)]$
(e) $\bigvee x[\bigwedge x F A(xB(y)) \vee G(xy)]$
(f) $\bigvee x[\bigwedge x F A(xB(x)) \vee G(Cx)]$

(g) $\bigvee y[\bigwedge x F A(x B(y)) \vee G(Cy)]$
(h) $\bigvee y[\bigwedge x F A(x B(y)) \vee G(yy)]$
(i) $\bigvee x[\bigwedge x F A(x B(y)) \vee G(Cy)]$
(j) $\bigvee w[\bigwedge x F A(x B(y)) \vee Gw]$

EXERCISES, GROUP II

For each of the following arguments give an unabbreviated derivation of its conclusion from its premise.

39. $\bigwedge x\ F\ A(x\ B)$ $\quad\therefore \bigvee x\ F\ A(xx)$
40. $\bigvee x\ F\ A(xx)$ $\quad\therefore \bigvee x F x$
41. $\bigwedge x \bigwedge y\ F\ A[x\ B(y)\ C]$ $\quad\therefore \bigvee x\ F\ A[B(x)\ B(C)\ x]$
42. $\bigwedge x \bigwedge y\ F\ A[x\ B(y)\ C]$ $\quad\therefore \bigvee x\ F\ A[B(x)\ x\ C]$

EXERCISES, GROUP III

Show the following arguments valid by constructing symbolizations and giving derivations (either abbreviated or unabbreviated) of the conclusions of the symbolizations from their premises. Exercise 43 is discussed for illustration.

43. Argument (2) of page 201.

On the basis of the scheme of abbreviation

F^1 : *a* is a horse
G^1 : *a* is an animal
H^2 : *a* is a head of *b* ,

one obtains the symbolization

$$\bigwedge x(Fx \rightarrow Gx) \quad \therefore \bigwedge x(\bigvee y[H(xy) \wedge Fy] \rightarrow \bigvee y[H(xy) \wedge Gy]) \quad ,$$

whose validity the reader can easily establish.

44. Argument (1) of page 201.
45. The square of 2 is even. ∴ The square of something is even.
46. The square of something is even. ∴ Something is even.
47. The product of numbers is a number. There is a number such that the product of it and any number is even. ∴ There is an even number.

6. Theorems. Symbolic formulas corresponding to those of chapter III are known as *monadic formulas*. More exactly, a *monadic formula* is a symbolic formula that contains no predicate letters of more than one place and no operation letters of more than zero place.

For each of the theorems of chapter III a nonmonadic analogue may be obtained by multiplying variables. For example,

T249 $\quad \bigwedge x \bigwedge y\ F(xy) \rightarrow \bigvee x \bigvee y\ F(xy)$

is a two-variable analogue of T238, and

T250 $\bigwedge x \bigwedge y \bigwedge z\, F(xyz) \leftrightarrow \sim \bigvee x \bigvee y \bigvee z \sim F(xyz)$

is a three-variable analogue of T205. Proofs of these two theorems can be obtained without essential change from the proofs of their earlier counterparts, as the reader can easily confirm; and this applies to all multiple-variable analogues of theorems of chapter III.

There are nonmonadic theorems that cannot be obtained in this way, for example T251 – T253, the laws of *commutation of quantifiers*. According to T251 and T252, a pair of like quantifiers may be commuted. If, however, the quantifiers are unlike, only the conditional, T253, holds.

T251

1.	~~Show~~ $\bigwedge x \bigwedge y F(xy) \leftrightarrow \bigwedge y \bigwedge x F(xy)$	
2.	~~Show~~ $\bigwedge x \bigwedge y F(xy) \rightarrow \bigwedge y \bigwedge x F(xy)$	
3.	$\bigwedge x \bigwedge y F(xy)$	
4.	~~Show~~ $\bigwedge y \bigwedge x F(xy)$	
5.	$\bigwedge y F(xy)$	3, UI
6.	$F(xy)$	5, UI
7.	~~Show~~ $\bigwedge y \bigwedge x F(xy) \rightarrow \bigwedge x \bigwedge y F(xy)$	
8.	$\bigwedge y \bigwedge x F(xy)$	
9.	~~Show~~ $\bigwedge x \bigwedge y F(xy)$	
10.	$\bigwedge x F(xy)$	8, UI
11.	$F(xy)$	10, UI
12.	$\bigwedge x \bigwedge y F(xy) \leftrightarrow \bigwedge y \bigwedge x F(xy)$	2, 7, CB

T252 $\bigvee x \bigvee y F(xy) \leftrightarrow \bigvee y \bigvee x F(xy)$

T253

1.	~~Show~~ $\bigvee x \bigwedge y F(xy) \rightarrow \bigwedge y \bigvee x F(xy)$	
2.	$\bigvee x \bigwedge y F(xy)$	
3.	$\bigwedge y F(wy)$	2, EI
4.	~~Show~~ $\bigwedge y \bigvee x F(xy)$	
5.	$F(wy)$	3, UI
6.	$\bigvee x F(xy)$	5, EG

The reader will find an effort to prove the converse of T253 (which is not a theorem; see page 229) an instructive review of the restrictions on variables that must be observed in constructing a derivation.

We list a few more nonmonadic theorems, whose proofs will constitute exercise 50 of this section.

T254 $\bigvee x \bigvee y F(xy) \leftrightarrow \bigvee x \bigvee y [F(xy) \vee F(yx)]$

T255 $\bigwedge x \bigwedge y F(xy) \rightarrow \bigwedge y \bigwedge x F(yx)$

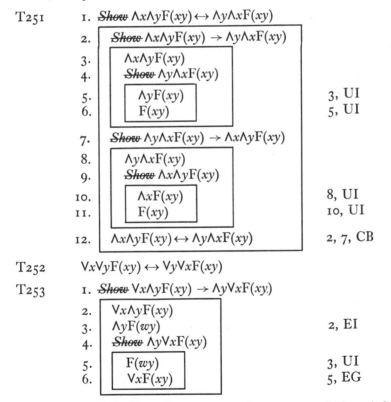

T256 $\bigwedge x \bigvee y[F(xy) \wedge Gy] \rightarrow \bigvee x \bigvee y[F(xy) \wedge Gx]$

T257 $\bigwedge x FA(x) \rightarrow \bigvee x[Fx \wedge FA(x)]$

T258 $F(xA(x)) \leftrightarrow \bigvee y[\bigwedge z[F(zy) \rightarrow F(zA(x))] \wedge F(xy)]$

We consider now some monadic theorems whose intuitive content is less clear than that of the theorems of chapter III. By a *generalization* we understand a formula that is either a universal generalization or an existential generalization, that is, which has the form

$$\bigwedge \alpha \phi$$

or

$$\bigvee \alpha \phi \quad ,$$

where α is a variable and ϕ a formula. A symbolic formula is said to be *without overlay* if it contains no generalization that in turn contains another generalization. T259 and T260 illustrate the following fact: every monadic formula is equivalent to a monadic formula without overlay—indeed, to such a formula with only one variable.

T259

1. ~~Show~~ $\bigwedge x \bigvee z(Fx \rightarrow \bigvee y[Gy \rightarrow Hz]) \leftrightarrow (\bigvee x Fx \wedge \bigwedge x Gx \rightarrow \bigvee x Hx)$
2. ~~Show~~ $\bigwedge x \bigvee z(Fx \rightarrow \bigvee y[Gy \rightarrow Hz]) \rightarrow (\bigvee x Fx \wedge \bigwedge x Gx \rightarrow \bigvee x Hx)$
3. $\bigwedge x \bigvee z(Fx \rightarrow \bigvee y[Gy \rightarrow Hz])$
5. ~~Show~~ $\bigvee x Fx \wedge \bigwedge x Gx \rightarrow \bigvee x Hx$
6. $\bigvee x Fx \wedge \bigwedge x Gx$
7. Fa — 6, S, EI
8. $Fa \rightarrow \bigvee y[Gy \rightarrow Hb]$ — 3, UI, EI
9. $Gc \rightarrow Hb$ — 7, 8, MP, EI
10. $\bigvee x Hx$ — 6, S, UI, 9, MP, EG
11. ~~Show~~ $(\bigvee x Fx \wedge \bigwedge x Gx \rightarrow \bigvee x Hx) \rightarrow \bigwedge x \bigvee z(Fx \rightarrow \bigvee y[Gy \rightarrow Hz])$
12. $\bigvee x Fx \wedge \bigwedge x Gx \rightarrow \bigvee x Hx$
13. ~~Show~~ $\bigwedge x \bigvee z(Fx \rightarrow \bigvee y[Gy \rightarrow Hz])$
14. $\sim \bigwedge x \bigvee z(Fx \rightarrow \bigvee y[Gy \rightarrow Hz])$
15. $\sim \bigvee z(Fd \rightarrow \bigvee y[Gy \rightarrow Hz])$ — 14, QN, EI
16. $\bigvee x Fx$ — 15, QN, UI, T21, MP, EG
17. $\sim \bigvee y(Gy \rightarrow Hz)$ — 15, QN, UI, T22, MP
18. ~~Show~~ $\bigwedge x Gx$
19. Gx — 17, QN, UI, T21, MP
20. He — 16, 18, Adj, 12, MP, EI
21. $\sim He$ — 15, QN, UI, T22, MP, QN, UI, T22, MP

T260 $\bigwedge x(Fx \rightarrow \bigvee y[Gy \wedge (Hy \vee Hx)]) \leftrightarrow$
$\bigvee x(Gx \wedge Hx) \vee \sim \bigvee xFx \vee (\bigvee xGx \wedge \bigwedge x[Fx \rightarrow Hx])$

In T259 and T260 we were interested in 'disentangling' quantifiers. The next theorems, T261 and T262, illustrate the reverse process, that of 'consolidating' quantifiers. More precisely, let us say that a formula is in *prenex normal form* just in case it is a symbolic formula consisting of a string of quantifier phrases followed by a formula without quantifiers. T261 and T262 illustrate the following fact: *every* symbolic formula is equivalent to one in prenex normal form.

T261

1. ~~Show~~ $\bigwedge x[\bigvee yF(xy) \rightarrow \bigvee yG(xy)] \leftrightarrow \bigwedge x\bigwedge y\bigvee z[F(xy) \rightarrow G(xz)]$
2. ~~Show~~ $\bigwedge x[\bigvee yF(xy) \rightarrow \bigvee yG(xy)] \rightarrow \bigwedge x\bigwedge y\bigvee z[F(xy) \rightarrow G(xz)]$
3. $\bigwedge x[\bigvee yF(xy) \rightarrow \bigvee yG(xy)]$
4. ~~Show~~ $\bigwedge x\bigwedge y\bigvee z[F(xy) \rightarrow G(xz)]$
5. ~~Show~~ $\sim \bigvee yF(xy) \rightarrow \bigvee z[F(xy) \rightarrow G(xz)]$
6. $\sim \bigvee yF(xy)$
7. $\bigvee z[F(xy) \rightarrow G(xz)]$ — 6, QN, UI, T18, MP, EG
8. ~~Show~~ $\bigvee yG(xy) \rightarrow \bigvee z[F(xy) \rightarrow G(xz)]$
9. $\bigvee yG(xy)$
10. $G(xa)$ — 9, EI
11. $\bigvee z[F(xy) \rightarrow G(xz)]$ — 10, T2, MP, EG
12. $\bigvee z[F(xy) \rightarrow G(xz)]$ — 5, 8, Adj, T35, BC, MP, 3, UI, MP
13. ~~Show~~ $\bigwedge x\bigwedge y\bigvee z[F(xy) \rightarrow G(xz)] \rightarrow \bigwedge x[\bigvee yF(xy) \rightarrow \bigvee yG(xy)]$
14. $\bigwedge x\bigwedge y\bigvee z[F(xy) \rightarrow G(xz)]$
15. ~~Show~~ $\bigwedge x[\bigvee yF(xy) \rightarrow \bigvee yG(xy)]$
16. ~~Show~~ $\bigvee yF(xy) \rightarrow \bigvee yG(xy)$
17. $\bigvee yF(xy)$
18. $F(xb)$ — 17, EI
19. $F(xb) \rightarrow G(xc)$ — 14, UI, UI, EI
20. $\bigvee yG(xy)$ — 18, 19, MP, EG
21. $\bigwedge x[\bigvee yF(xy) \rightarrow \bigvee yG(xy)] \leftrightarrow \bigwedge x\bigwedge y\bigvee z[F(xy) \rightarrow G(xz)]$ — 2, 13, CB

T262 $\bigvee y[\bigvee xF(xy) \leftrightarrow Gy] \leftrightarrow$
$\bigvee y\bigwedge x\bigvee z([F(xy) \rightarrow Gy] \wedge [Gy \rightarrow F(zy)])$

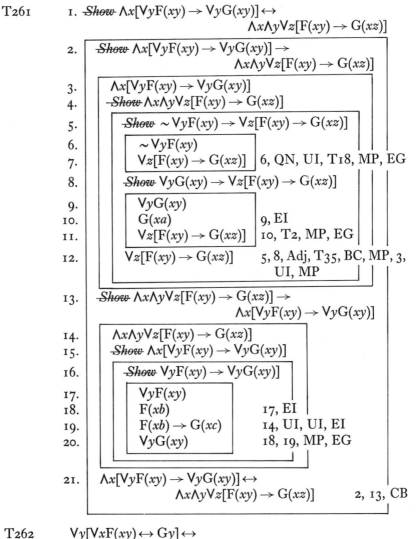

Although proofs of T259–T262 require, within our present system of derivation, some ingenuity, it is possible to characterize derivational procedures that will automatically find for any monadic symbolic formula an equivalent one without overlay and for any symbolic formula an equivalent one in prenex normal form. Such procedures are more sophisticated than those presently available and will not be introduced until chapter VII, but their utility can be suggested now.

The inference rules of instantiation, UI and EI, are applicable only to a quantifier that is the initial symbol of a formula. But since one can automatically find for any symbolic formula an equivalent formula in prenex normal form, this limitation does not prevent, in a derivation, the elimination of all quantifiers from a formula. On the basis of this elimination, infallible but tedious and nonintuitive directions, rather than just helpful strategic hints, can be given for the proof of any formula that is a theorem. Such directions are set forth in chapter IX.

Formulas in prenex normal form, although immediately amenable to instantiation, are not easily translated into idiomatic English. For the latter task, disentangled in contrast to consolidated quantifiers have the advantage. Consider, for example, the following scheme of abbreviation and formula (in prenex normal form):

(1) F^1 : *a* is created by God

(2) $\bigvee x \bigwedge y(Fx \leftrightarrow Fy)$.

A literal translation of (2) on the basis of (1), that is,

(3) There is an object *x* such that for each *y*, *x* is created by God if and only if *y* is created by God ,

is not an infallible guide to an idiomatic translation. But a formula without overlay equivalent to (2), such as

(4) $\sim \bigvee x Fx \vee \bigwedge x Fx$

gives immediately the idiomatic meaning of (3):

(5) Either nothing is created by God or everything is created by God .

Generally, when seeking idiomatic translations of symbolic formulas and symbolizing idiomatic English, seek or approximate (if a formula is not monadic) equivalent formulas without overlay to facilitate the process.

It is seldom the case, where a formula ϕ is not a theorem, that from

$$\bigvee \alpha \phi$$

one can derive

$$\bigwedge \alpha \phi \quad .$$

However, the formula (2) above provides an example of such a case: from (2) one can derive the formula

$$(6) \qquad \bigwedge x \bigwedge y(Fx \leftrightarrow Fy) \quad .$$

Thus (2), (4), and (6) are equivalent, and all three, on the basis of the scheme (1), make the assertion (5). The derivation of (2) from (6) takes one step; the equivalence of (2) and (4) we leave as an exercise (No. 48); the following derivation of (6) from (2) is instructive, for it illustrates the utility of applying UI more than once to an antecedent line that is a universal generalization.

1.	~~*Show*~~ $\bigwedge x \bigwedge y(Fx \leftrightarrow Fy)$	
2.	$\bigvee x \bigwedge y(Fx \leftrightarrow Fy)$	Premise [(2) above]
3.	$\bigwedge y(Fa \leftrightarrow Fy)$	2, EI
4.	$Fa \leftrightarrow Fx$	3, UI
5.	$Fx \leftrightarrow Fa$	T92, BC, 4, MP
6.	$Fa \leftrightarrow Fy$	3, UI
7.	$Fx \leftrightarrow Fy$	5, 6, Adj, T93, MP

A universal and an existential quantifier can in some cases, though not of course in general, be commuted; T263–T266 are illustrations. We prove one of these theorems and leave the proofs of the other three as exercises (No. 52).

T263	1.	~~*Show*~~ $\bigwedge x \bigvee y(Fx \rightarrow Gy) \rightarrow \bigvee y \bigwedge x(Fx \rightarrow Gy)$	
	2.	$\bigwedge x \bigvee y(Fx \rightarrow Gy)$	
	3.	~~*Show*~~ $\bigvee y \bigwedge x(Fx \rightarrow Gy)$	
	4.	$\sim \bigvee y \bigwedge x(Fx \rightarrow Gy)$	
	5.	$\sim(Fa \rightarrow Gy)$	4, QN, UI, QN, EI
	6.	$Fa \rightarrow Gb$	2, UI, EI
	7.	Gb	5, T21, MP, 6, MP
	8.	$\sim(Fc \rightarrow Gb)$	4, QN, UI, QN, EI
	9.	$\sim Gb$	8, T22, MP

T264 $\quad \bigwedge x \bigvee y(Fx \wedge Gy) \rightarrow \bigvee y \bigwedge x(Fx \wedge Gy)$

T265 $\quad \bigwedge x \bigvee y(Fx \vee Gy) \rightarrow \bigvee y \bigwedge x(Fx \vee Gy)$

T266 $\quad \bigwedge x \bigwedge y \bigvee z(Fx \wedge Gy \rightarrow Hz) \rightarrow \bigwedge y \bigvee z \bigwedge x(Fx \wedge Gy \rightarrow Hz)$

The converse of each of T263–T266 is also a theorem. The proof for each converse is trivial; indeed, the steps are to be found in the proof of T253 (p. 223). Thus each of T263–T266 can be strengthened to a biconditional, and they will appear as such in the appendix listing of theorems for this chapter (section 11).

It would be a mistake to conclude on the basis of the immediately preceding theorems that the order of quantifiers in a monadic formula is irrelevant. The formula

$$\bigwedge x \bigvee y(Fx \leftrightarrow Gy) \rightarrow \bigvee y \bigwedge x(Fx \leftrightarrow Gy)$$

is not a theorem, a fact known to those readers who solved exercise 117 in chapter III (see pp. 181 and 194–95).

We conclude this section with some nonmonadic theorems whose proofs make instructive, and sometimes challenging, exercises. The reader who is familiar with Russell's paradox or with axiomatic set theory will perhaps find diversion in proving T269–T272.

T267	$\bigwedge x[Fx \leftrightarrow \sim FA(x)] \rightarrow \bigvee x[Fx \wedge \sim FA(x)]$
T268	$\bigwedge x[F(Ax) \vee \bigwedge yF(xy)] \rightarrow \bigvee x \bigwedge yF(xy)$
T269	$\sim \bigvee y \bigwedge x[F(xy) \leftrightarrow \sim F(xx)]$
T270	$\bigwedge z \bigvee y \bigwedge x[F(xy) \leftrightarrow F(xz) \wedge \sim F(xx)] \rightarrow \sim \bigvee z \bigwedge xF(xz)$
T271	$\sim \bigvee y \bigwedge x(F(xy) \leftrightarrow \sim \bigvee z[F(xz) \wedge F(zx)])$
T272	$\bigvee y \bigwedge x[F(xy) \leftrightarrow F(xx)] \rightarrow \sim \bigwedge x \bigvee y \bigwedge z[F(zy) \leftrightarrow \sim F(zx)]$

EXERCISES

In solving these exercises, the reader will still find the strategic hints listed on pages 169–70 useful.

48. Prove that the formula

$$\bigvee x \bigwedge y(Fx \leftrightarrow Fy) \leftrightarrow \sim \bigvee xFx \vee \bigwedge xFx$$

is a theorem, and thereby verify the claim that formulas (2) and (4) of this section are equivalent.

49. That there are nontrivial cases in which a universal generalization of a formula can be derived from an existential generalization of that formula was illustrated by the derivation of (6) from (2) given on page 227. To establish another case of this kind, prove that the following is a theorem:

$$\bigvee x \bigvee y(Fx \leftrightarrow \sim Fy) \rightarrow \bigwedge x \bigvee y(Fx \leftrightarrow \sim Fy) \quad .$$

(Use indirect derivation, review the derivation of (6) from (2), and recall T90.)

50. Prove T254–T258.

51. Prove T260 and T262.

52. Prove T264–T266 (as listed in this section).

53. Prove T267–T272.

7. Invalidity: truth-functional expansions and models. As Church has shown in [2], there is no automatic test for validity of arguments formulated with the present symbolic language. However, there are several ways of showing symbolic arguments invalid.

In the first place, the method of truth-functional expansions, as described in section 11 of chapter III, remains available. However, it is applicable only to a restricted class of arguments. It can be used only in connection with symbolic arguments whose premises and conclusion contain no terms other than variables and 0-place operation letters, for it does not specify how to eliminate terms of greater complexity. For example, by that method we can verify the claim that the converse of T253,

$$(1) \qquad \bigwedge y \bigvee x F(xy) \rightarrow \bigvee x \bigwedge y F(xy) \quad ,$$

is not a theorem: for it remains a fact in the *full* quantifier calculus that a symbolic argument whose premises and conclusion are sentences is invalid if it has a truth-functional expansion whose premises do not tautologically imply its conclusion, and that a symbolic sentence is not a theorem if it has a truth-functional expansion that is not a tautology.

To obtain the relevant truth-functional expansion of (1), obtain first

$$[F(aa) \vee F(ba)] \wedge [F(ab) \vee F(bb)] \rightarrow [F(aa) \wedge F(ab)] \vee [F(ba) \wedge F(bb)]$$

by eliminating quantifiers from (1), and then pass to

$$[P \vee Q] \wedge [R \vee S] \rightarrow [P \wedge R] \vee [Q \wedge S] \quad ,$$

which is not a tautology, as the reader can verify easily.

Secondly, the models introduced in section 11 of chapter III in connection with truth-functional expansions not only remain available but can be extended to accommodate any argument in the richer language of the present chapter. Recall that a model for a symbolic argument whose premises and conclusion are sentences consisted of a finite but not empty class of natural numbers, referred to as its *universe*, and *extensions* for each of the capital letters of the argument. Specifically, a model for such an argument contained for each name letter (now 0-place operation letter) of the argument an element of its universe as the extension of that name letter, for each sentence letter (now 0-place predicate letter) of the argument a truth value as the extension of that sentence letter, and for each predicate letter (now 1-place predicate letter) of the argument a subclass of its universe as an extension of that predicate letter. To accommodate the richer language of the present chapter, a model for an argument will now have to contain an extension for each n-place predicate letter (where $n > 1$) in the argument and an extension for each n-place operation letter ($n > 0$) in the argument. We shall undertake this accommodation stepwise, considering only 2-place predicate letters and 1-place operation letters at first.

For each 2-place predicate letter in an argument, a model for that argument must contain a class of ordered couples of elements of its universe as the extension of the predicate letter. An *ordered couple* is simply a two-term sequence of objects, one of which is the first term and the other of which is the second term; the same object may be the first and the second term of an ordered couple. We shall employ parentheses to indicate an ordered couple, together with a comma to distinguish numerals. For example, if we have a model whose universe has two elements, which we again indicate by

(2) $$\mathbf{U} : \{0, 1\} \quad ,$$

then the ordered couples of elements of that universe are

$$(0, 0), (0, 1), (1, 0), (1, 1) \quad .$$

(Generally, if a class has *n* elements, the number of ordered couples of elements of that class is n^2.) A class of ordered couples of elements of our given **U** is any class all of whose elements are drawn from the above list of ordered couples. Thus, for example,

$$\{(0, 0), (1, 0), (1, 1)\}$$

and

(3) $$\{(0, 1), (1, 0)\}$$

are classes of ordered couples of elements of our given **U**; and so is the empty class of ordered couples (designated again by '{ }'). We shall indicate the extension in a model of a 2-place predicate letter, say (3) above as the extension of 'F^2', as follows:

(4) $$F^2 : \{(0, 1), (1, 0)\} \quad .$$

In analogy to our treatment of predicate letters in chapter III, we shall consider a 2-place predicate letter *true of* each ordered couple in its extension and *false of* each ordered couple of elements of the universe not in its extension. Thus, in a model composed of (2) and (4), 'F^2' is true of both (0, 1) and (1, 0) and is false of both (0, 0) and (1, 1).

For each 1-place operation letter in an argument, a model for that argument contains as the *extension of* the operation letter a *function* from (all) elements of the universe of the model to elements of the universe of the model, that is, a correlation of each object of its universe with an object of that universe such that no one object is correlated with two different objects (but different objects may be correlated with the same object, and an object may be correlated with itself). For example, a model with the universe indicated by (2) above could contain for a 1-place operation letter, say 'A^1', any one of four functions: the function that correlates both 0 and 1 with 0, the function that correlates 0 with 0 and 1 with 1, the function that correlates 0 with 1 and 1 with 0, or the function that correlates both 0 and 1 with 1. We shall indicate which of these functions (say that which correlates 0 with 1 and 1 with 0) a model contains for 'A^1' as follows:

(5) $$A^1 : A(0) \mapsto 1; A(1) \mapsto 0$$

For later convenience, on the basis of (5), we shall call the numeral '1' the *value* of the expression 'A(0)' and the numeral '0' the value of 'A(1)' (thereby borrowing from but abusing standard mathematical terminology).

Now it happens here in the full quantifier calculus, as in the monadic quantifier calculus of the preceding chapter, that a symbolic argument whose premises and conclusion are sentences is invalid if there is a model (extended in the manner indicated above) in which its premises are true and its conclusion false. In particular, it follows that a symbolic sentence is not a theorem if there is such a model in which it is false. In order to ascertain the *truth* or *falsity in* a model of symbolic sentences, we shall again employ *expansions* analogous to truth-functional expansions. As before, these expansions will contain numerals in place of variables; thus, for the purpose of demonstrating invalidity, we again treat numerals as terms of our symbolic language. Thus we now include in the class of terms of our symbolic language any operation letter followed by the appropriate number of occurrences of terms, which may now be numerals or terms composed with numerals; and thus we now include in the class of formulas of our symbolic language any predicate letter followed by the appropriate number of occurrences of such terms. For example, employing parentheses and brackets in place of superscripts, and commas to prevent ambiguity, we now include expressions such as 'A(0)', 'B(1, 0)', and 'C[2, A(0), 1]' among the *terms* of our symbolic language and expressions such as 'F3', 'G(1, 2)', and 'H[2, 1, A(0)]' among the *atomic formulas* of our symbolic language.

We postpone the general characterization of an *expansion* of a symbolic argument of the full quantifier calculus until we have extended models to accommodate predicate and operation letters of arbitrary degree. But an example of such an expansion and the ascertainment of invalidity by means of it are now in order.

Consider the argument

(6) $\bigwedge x F[A(x)x] \quad \therefore \bigvee x F[A(x)A(x)]$

and the model given by (2), (4), and (5) above:

(7)
$$\begin{array}{lcl} \mathbf{U} & : & \{0, 1\} \\ F^2 & : & \{(0, 1), (1, 0)\} \\ A^1 & : & A(0) \mapsto 1;\ A(1) \mapsto 0 \quad . \end{array}$$

In exercise 36, at the end of section 5, it was pointed out that an application of UI followed by an application of EG would not lead from the premise to the conclusion of (6); indeed, we claimed there that (6) is an invalid argument. Now we confirm that claim by demonstrating, with the aid of an *expansion*, that the premise of (6) is *true in* and the conclusion of (6) is *false in* the model (7). The expansion of (6) begins by eliminating quantifiers, as they are eliminated in a truth-functional expansion (see p. 174), using the numerals '0' and '1' rather than variables. Thus (employing commas for perspicuity) we obtain first

$$(8) \quad F[A(0), 0] \wedge F[A(1), 1] \quad \therefore\ F[A(0), A(0)] \vee F[A(1), A(1)] \quad .$$

Next, and this is new, in (8) we replace 'A(0)' and 'A(1)' uniformly by the *values* they are given in the model (7); thus, the former is replaced by '1' and the latter by '0' to yield

$$(9) \qquad F(1, 0) \wedge F(0, 1) \quad \therefore\ F(1, 1) \vee F(0, 0) \quad ,$$

which is the *expansion of* (6) *with respect to* (7).

In the model (7), 'F^2' is *true of* both (1, 0) and (0, 1) and *false of* both (0, 0) and (1, 1); thus we have both 'F(1, 0)' and 'F(0, 1)' *true in*, and both 'F(0, 0)' and 'F(1, 1)' *false in*, the model (7). Clearly, then, the premise of (9) is *true in*, and the conclusion of (9) *false in*, the model (7).

We understand the premise of (6) to be *equivalent in* (7) to the premise of (9) and the conclusion of (6) to be *equivalent in* (7) to the conclusion of (9). Hence, on the basis of these *equivalences in* the model (7), we have ascertained that the argument (6) has its premise *true in* and its conclusion *false in* the model (7); and this demonstrates the invalidity of the argument (6).

Our next step is to extend models so that they can accommodate predicate letters of degree greater than 2. For each 3-place predicate letter in an argument a model contains as the *extension of* the predicate letter a class of ordered triples of elements of its universe. An ordered triple is simply a three-term sequence of objects. (If a class has n elements, then the number of ordered triples of elements of that class is n^3.) For example,

$$(0, 0, 0), \quad (0, 1, 0), \quad (1, 2, 1), \quad (2, 1, 1), \quad (2, 2, 1), \quad (2, 2, 2)$$

are six of the 27 ordered triples of elements of the class {0, 1, 2}. For each 4-place predicate letter in an argument a model contains as the *extension of* the predicate letter a class of ordered quadruples of elements of its universe. Generally, then, for an n-place predicate letter of an argument, where $1 < n$, a model for that argument contains as the *extension of* the predicate letter a class of ordered n-tuples of elements of the universe of the model.

Consider, for an illustration, the claim that the conclusion of the argument

$$(10) \qquad \bigwedge x \bigwedge y \bigvee z F(xyz) \quad \therefore\ \bigwedge y \bigvee z F(zyz)$$

follows from the premise by UI. The reader, thoroughly familiar with the notion of proper substitution required for a correct application of UI, will reject the claim. Further, we are now able to demonstrate by means of the model

(11) $\quad$ **U** : {0, 1}
$\quad\quad\quad$ F^3 : {(0, 0, 1), (0, 1, 0), (1, 0, 0), (1, 1, 1)}

that the argument is invalid. The premise and conclusion of (10) are equivalent in the model (11), respectively, to

(12) $[F(0, 0, 0) \vee F(0, 0, 1)] \wedge [F(0, 1, 0) \vee F(0, 1, 1)] \wedge$
$\quad\quad$ $[F(1, 0, 0) \vee F(1, 0, 1)] \wedge [F(1, 1, 0) \vee F(1, 1, 1)]$

and

(13) $\quad [F(0, 0, 0) \vee F(1, 0, 1)] \wedge [F(0, 1, 0) \vee F(1, 1, 1)]$.

Since both 'F(0, 0, 0)' and 'F(1, 0, 1)' are false in the model (11), the sentence (13), and hence the conclusion of (10), is false in that model. Since 'F(0, 0, 1)', 'F(0, 1, 0)', 'F(1, 0, 0)', and 'F(1, 1, 1)' are true in the model (11), the sentence (12), and hence the premise of (10), is true in that model. Thus the invalidity of the argument (10) is demonstrated.

Our last step is to extend models so that they can accommodate operation letters of degree greater than 1. For each 2-place operation letter in an argument, a model for that argument contains as the *extension of* the operation letter a function from (all) ordered couples of elements of the universe of the model to elements of the universe of the model. Thus a model with a universe of two elements, say 0 and 1, could contain as an extension for a 2-place operation letter, say 'B^2', functions such as: the function that correlates the couple (0, 0) with 0, the couple (0, 1) with 0, the couple (1, 0) with 0, and the couple (1, 1) with 0; the function that correlates the couple (0, 0) with 0, the couple (0, 1) with 1, the couple (1, 0) with 1, and the couple (1, 1) with 0. We shall indicate which function, say the latter of the two just mentioned, a model contains for 'B^2' as follows:

$$B^2 : \; B(0, 0) \mapsto 0;\; B(0, 1) \mapsto 1;\; B(1, 0) \mapsto 1;\; B(1, 1) \mapsto 0 \quad .$$

(As before, we call the numeral after '$\mapsto$' in an expression such as '$B(0, 0) \mapsto 0$' the *value* of the term that precedes '$\mapsto$'.) For each 3-place operation letter in an argument, a model for that argument contains as the *extension of* the operation letter a function from (all) ordered triples of elements of the universe of the model to elements of the universe of the model. Generally, then, for an *n*-place operation letter of an argument, where $n > 0$, a model for that argument contains as the *extension of* the operation letter a function from (all) *n*-tuples of elements of its universe to elements of its universe.

Again, for illustration, consider the claim that the conclusion of the argument

(14) $\quad\quad \bigwedge x \bigvee y FB(xy) \quad \therefore \bigvee y FB(yy)$

follows from the premise by UI. Not only is the claim incorrect, but the invalidity of the argument is established by means of the following model:

$$(15)\quad \begin{aligned} \mathbf{U} &: \{0, 1\} \\ F^1 &: \{1\} \\ B^2 &: B(0, 0) \mapsto 0;\ B(0, 1) \mapsto 1;\ B(1, 0) \mapsto 1;\ B(1, 1) \mapsto 0 \end{aligned} \quad .$$

On the basis of this model, the argument (14) passes first, upon elimination of quantifiers, into

$$[FB(0, 0) \vee FB(0, 1)] \wedge [FB(1, 0) \vee FB(1, 1)] \quad \therefore\ FB(0, 0) \vee FB(1, 1) \quad ;$$

and then, upon replacing terms by their values, into

$$(16)\qquad [F0 \vee F1] \wedge [F1 \vee F0] \quad \therefore\ F0 \vee F0 \quad .$$

Clearly, the premise of (16) is true in, and the conclusion false in, the model (15). This fact establishes the invalidity of the argument (14).

For a final illustration, consider a slight modification of the preceding example,

$$(17)\qquad \bigwedge x \bigvee y F[xB(A(y))] \quad \therefore\ \bigvee y F[yB(A(y))]$$

and the model

$$(18)\qquad \begin{aligned} \mathbf{U} &: \{0, 1\} \\ F^2 &: \{(0, 0), (1, 1)\} \\ A^1 &: A(0) \mapsto 1;\ A(1) \mapsto 0 \\ B^1 &: B(0) \mapsto 0;\ B(1) \mapsto 1 \end{aligned} \quad .$$

On the basis of this model, the premise of (17), upon elimination of quantifiers, passes into

$$(19)\quad (F[0\,B(A(0))] \vee F[0\,B(A(1))]) \wedge (F[1\,B(A(0))] \vee F[1\,B(A(1))]) \quad .$$

Then, in successive steps, upon replacing terms by their values, (19) passes first into

$$(F[0\,B(1)] \vee F[0\,B(0)]) \wedge (F[1\,B(1)] \vee F[1\,B(0)])$$

and then into

$$[F(0, 1) \vee F(0, 0)] \wedge [F(1, 1) \vee F(1, 0)] \quad ,$$

which is true in the model (18). Similarly, the conclusion of (17) passes first into

$$F[0\,B(A(0))] \vee F[1\,B(A(1))] \quad ,$$

next into

$$F[0\,B(1)] \vee F[1\,B(0)] \quad ,$$

and then into

$$F(0, 1) \vee F(1, 0) \quad ,$$

which is false in the model (18). Thus the invalidity of (17) is established.

In the preceding exposition we have characterized stepwise *models for* symbolic arguments whose premises and conclusion are sentences; and we have indicated by several examples, first how to construct an *expansion of* such an argument *with respect to* a model, and then how to ascertain by means of the expansion the *truth* or *falsity in* the model of the premises and conclusion of such an argument. Now a summary and directions stated generally are in order. (In what follows the language is that of the *full* quantifier calculus and the arguments are composed of symbolic *sentences*.)

A *model for* an argument consists of a *universe* **U**, where **U** is a finite but nonempty class of natural numbers, and *extensions* for capital letters of the argument as follows:

(i) the *extension of* a 0-place operation letter is an element of **U**;
(ii) the *extension of* an n-place operation letter, where $n > 0$, is a function from n-tuples of elements of **U** to elements of **U**;
(iii) the *extension of* a 0-place predicate letter is a truth value (T or F);
(iv) the *extension of* a 1-place predicate letter is a subclass of **U**;
(v) the *extension of* an n-place predicate letter, where $n > 1$, is a class of ordered n-tuples of elements of **U**.

Given a model for an argument, we construct an *expansion of* the argument *with respect to* the model in two steps:

(1) Eliminate from the sentences of the argument quantifiers in the manner of their elimination for a truth-functional expansion (see p. 174), employing numerals rather than variables in this elimination. (Clearly, all elements of the universe of the model for the argument must be accounted for in this step.)

(2) In the result of step (1), replace (perhaps in successive steps) terms by their values on the basis of the extensions assigned by the model to operation letters. (The terms involved here are either 0-place operation letters or expressions constructed correctly by means of n-place operation letters, where $n > 0$, and numerals. Recall that by the *value* of a term we understand the *numeral* that names the element of the universe of the model—that is, the number—designated by the term.)

Given a model for an argument and an expansion of the argument with respect to the model, we ascertain the *truth values in* the model of the premises and conclusion of the expansion in two steps:

(a) On the basis of the extensions assigned by the model to predicate letters, ascertain the truth value of each *atomic formula* in the expansion. (The atomic formulas of the expansion are either 0-place predicate letters or n-place predicate letters, where $n > 0$, followed by n occurrences of numerals. The *truth value in* the model of a formula of the latter kind is determined by the elements of the extension of the predicate letter in the formula: the predicate letter is *true of* each element in its extension and false of each relevant entity not in its extension.)

(b) On the basis of the truth values in the model of the atomic formulas of the expansion, compute (by truth-value analysis) the truth value of each sentence in the expansion.

Given a model for an argument, we understand that argument to have true premises and a false conclusion in the model if it has an expansion with respect to the model whose premises are true in and whose conclusion is false in the model. Thus to demonstrate the invalidity of an argument it is sufficient to construct a model for the argument and an expansion for it with respect to that model whose premises are true in, and whose conclusion is false in, that model; in particular, to demonstrate that a symbolic sentence is not a theorem it is sufficient to construct such a model and expansion for the argument with no premises and that sentence as conclusion.

Our methods for showing invalidity are directly applicable only to symbolic sentences and symbolic arguments whose premises and conclusion are sentences. However, we can extend these methods to arbitrary symbolic formulas and arguments.

As in the monadic quantifier calculus, in the full quantifier calculus it happens that a symbolic argument is valid just in case each of its closures is valid. (For a definition of *closure* see p. 176.) In particular, it follows that a symbolic formula is a theorem just in case each of its closures is a theorem. Thus, in the full quantifier calculus, to establish the invalidity of a symbolic argument it is sufficient to establish by means of either the method of truth-functional expansions or the method of models the invalidity of a closure of the argument, and to establish that a symbolic formula is not a theorem it is sufficient to establish by means of either method that a closure of the formula is not a theorem. However, cases will arise of invalid arguments whose invalidity cannot be established by either of these methods, and such arguments will be considered in the next section.

EXERCISES

For each argument in the following pairs of arguments, demonstrate either its validity or its invalidity. We solve exercise 54 for illustration.

54. (i) $F(xy) \rightarrow \sim F(yx) \quad \therefore \sim F(xx)$
    (ii) $\sim F(xx) \quad \therefore F(xy) \rightarrow \sim F(yx)$

The validity of (i) is established by the derivation

1.	~~*Show*~~ $\sim F(xx)$	
2.	$\bigwedge x \bigwedge y[F(xy) \rightarrow \sim F(yx)]$	Premise
3.	$F(xx) \rightarrow \sim F(xx)$	2, UI, UI
4.	$\sim F(xx)$	3, T20, MP

(Recall the liberalization of clause (2) mentioned on page 220 in connection with the annotation for line 2 in this derivation.) To establish the invalidity of (ii), we consider a closure of the argument,

$$\bigwedge x \sim F(xx) \quad \therefore \bigwedge x \bigwedge y[F(xy) \rightarrow \sim F(yx)] \quad ,$$

and the following model, in which its premise is true and its conclusion false:

$$\mathbf{U}: \{0, 1\}$$
$$F^2: \{(0, 1), (1, 0)\} \quad .$$

55. (i) $F(xy) \wedge F(yz) \rightarrow F(xz) \quad . \quad F(xy) \rightarrow F(yx) \quad \therefore F(xx)$
    (ii) $F(xy) \wedge F(yz) \rightarrow F(xz) \quad . \quad F(xy) \rightarrow F(yx)$
    $\therefore \bigvee y F(xy) \rightarrow F(xx)$
56. (i) $\bigvee y F(yy) \quad \therefore \bigvee x \bigvee y F(xy)$
    (ii) $\bigvee x \bigvee y F(xy) \quad \therefore \bigvee y F(yy)$
57. (i) $\bigwedge x \bigwedge y[F(xy) \vee F(yx)] \quad \therefore \bigwedge x \bigvee y F(xy)$
    (ii) $\bigwedge x \bigvee y[F(xy) \vee F(yx)] \quad \therefore \bigwedge x \bigvee y F(xy)$
58. (i) $\therefore \bigvee y \bigwedge x \bigwedge z[\sim F(zx) \rightarrow F(yx)] \leftrightarrow \bigvee x \bigwedge y F(xy)$
    (ii) $\therefore \bigvee y \bigwedge x \bigwedge z[\sim F(zx) \rightarrow F(yx)] \leftrightarrow \bigwedge x \bigwedge y F(xy)$
59. (i) $\bigvee x \bigwedge y F(xy) \wedge \bigvee x \bigwedge y F(yx) \quad \therefore \bigwedge x \bigwedge y[F(xy) \vee F(yx)]$
    (ii) $\bigwedge x \bigwedge y[F(xy) \vee F(yx)] \quad \therefore \bigvee x \bigwedge y F(xy) \vee \bigvee x \bigwedge y F(yx)$
60. (i) $\bigwedge x F[xA(x)] \quad \therefore \bigvee x F[A(x)x]$
    (ii) $\bigwedge x \bigvee y F(xy) \quad \therefore \bigvee x \bigvee y[F(xy) \wedge F(yx)]$
61. (i) $\bigwedge x \bigvee z[F(xz) \wedge (Gz \rightarrow Gx)]$
    $\therefore \bigwedge x \bigvee z[F(xz) \wedge (Gz \rightarrow \bigwedge x Gx)]$
    (ii) $\bigwedge x \bigvee z[F(xz) \wedge (Gz \rightarrow Gx)]$
    $\therefore \bigvee x \bigvee z[F(xz) \wedge (Gz \rightarrow \bigwedge x Gx)]$
62. (i) $\bigwedge x \bigwedge y \bigvee z F(xyz) \quad . \quad \bigwedge x \bigwedge y \bigwedge z[F(xyz) \rightarrow F(yxz)]$
    $\therefore \bigwedge x \bigwedge y \bigvee z F(zxy)$
    (ii) $\bigwedge x \bigwedge y \bigvee z F(xyz) \quad . \quad \bigwedge x \bigwedge y \bigwedge z[F(xyz) \rightarrow F(yzx)]$
    $\therefore \bigwedge x \bigwedge y \bigvee z F(zxy)$
63. (i) $\bigwedge x \bigvee y F(xy) \quad . \quad \bigvee y \sim \bigvee x F(xy) \quad \therefore \bigvee x \bigvee y[F(xy) \wedge F(yx)]$
    (ii) $\bigvee x[F(Ax) \wedge \sim F(Bx)] \quad . \quad \bigwedge x \bigvee y F(xy) \quad .$
    $\bigwedge x \bigwedge y[F(xy) \rightarrow \sim F(yx)] \quad \therefore \bigvee x[F(xA) \vee F(xB)]$

8. Invalidity: false arithmetical translations. There are invalid arguments in the full quantifier calculus whose invalidity cannot be established by the methods of the preceding section. An example is the argument

(1) $\bigwedge x \bigwedge y \bigwedge z[F(xy) \wedge F(yz) \rightarrow F(xz)]$. $\bigwedge x \bigvee y F(xy)$
$\therefore \bigvee x F(xx)$.

Let us attempt to construct a model for (1) in which its premises are true and its conclusion false. We start with 0 as an element of the universe of the model (for the universe is not empty) and begin the construction of an extension for 'F'. For the second premise of (1) to be true in the model we are constructing, the extension of 'F' must contain an ordered couple whose first term is 0. That couple cannot be (0, 0), for then the conclusion of (1) is true in the model. Thus we enter (0, 1) into the extension of 'F', and thereby 1 into the universe of the model. By the second premise again, the extension of 'F' must contain an ordered couple whose first term is 1. That couple cannot be (1, 1), for then the conclusion of (1) is true in the model; and it cannot be (1, 0), for then, in the absence of (0, 0), the first premise of (1) is false in the model. Thus we enter (1, 2) into the extension of 'F', and thereby 2 into the universe of the model. Now we need an ordered couple in the extension of 'F' whose first term is 2. The preceding considerations indicate that neither (2, 2) nor (2, 1) will serve. And (2, 0) cannot serve either; for if the extension of 'F' contains (2, 0) along with (0, 1) but not (2, 1), then the first premise of (1) is false in the model. Thus we enter (2, 3) into the extension of 'F', and thereby 3 into the universe of the model. Although these remarks are not a formal proof (which remains beyond the techniques now at our disposal), they should suffice to convince the reader that an extension for 'F' such that the premises of (1) are true and the conclusion false in the resulting model cannot be constructed given our requirement that the universe of the model be a finite class of numbers.

One approach to establish the invalidity of the argument (1) is to include among the models for a symbolic argument analogues to our present models that have an infinite rather than a finite class for their universe. (A class is *infinite* if it has at least as many elements as there are natural numbers.) The universe of such an analogue and the extensions in it for operation and predicate letters could not be displayed; they could only be described. For example, the scheme

(2) **U** : the class of all natural numbers
F^2 : the class of all ordered couples of natural numbers such that the first term is less than the second term

could be understood as describing a model. It is intuitively clear that in such a model the premises of (1) are true and the conclusion false. But it is equally clear that no expansion of (1) is available by means of which one could state precisely whether a sentence of (1) is true or false in such a model. (The reader should not find it too difficult to conceive of an infinite class; but it is more than difficult—in fact impossible—to write out an infinite conjunction.)

There is another approach, closely related to the preceding approach, that can be characterized quite precisely, if not simply. We shall call this approach for investigating invalidity the method of *false arithmetical translations*; and to establish the invalidity of arguments such as (1), we shall adopt it rather than introduce models with infinite universes.

By an *arithmetical translation of a symbolic sentence* we understand a translation on the basis of a scheme of abbreviation whose right-hand members are formulas of elementary arithmetic, that is, are formulas of that part of English which might be called the language of the arithmetic of nonnegative integers. (Although a precise characterization of that language is available (see Tarski, Mostowski, Robinson [1]), it is not needed for our present purpose.) And by an *arithmetical translation*, on the basis of a given scheme of abbreviation, *of a symbolic argument* whose premises and conclusion are sentences we understand an English argument whose premises and conclusion are arithmetical translations, on the basis of that scheme, of the respective premises and conclusion of the symbolic argument—in other words, an English argument having the symbolic argument as a symbolization on the basis of the given scheme. As in our earlier discussion of fallacies, where we applied the term 'false' to an English argument as well as to English sentences, we say that an *arithmetical translation* of a symbolic argument *is false* if its premises are true sentences and its conclusion a false sentence in the arithmetic of nonnegative integers.

Now it happens that if a symbolic argument whose premises and conclusion are sentences has an arithmetical translation that is false, then the symbolic argument cannot be valid. In particular, it follows that a symbolic sentence is not a theorem if it has a false arithmetical translation. (This fact will not be proved here; it follows from Montague and Kalish [1].) Thus, for a simple example, the argument

$$\bigvee x \mathrm{F}x \quad . \qquad \bigvee x \mathrm{G}x \quad \therefore \bigvee x(\mathrm{F}x \wedge \mathrm{G}x)$$

is invalid, because it has the following clearly false arithmetical translation:

Something is an odd number. Something is an even number.
∴ Something is both an odd number and an even number .

(Here, and subsequently, when we use the term 'number' we refer to the natural numbers, that is, the nonnegative integers.) But consider again argument (1) above, a more complex example drawn from the symbolic language of the present chapter. It has no obvious false arithmetical translation. At first inspection, the argument

(3) For each x, for each y, for each z, if $x < y$ and $y < z$, then $x < z$. For each x, there is an object y such that $x < y$. ∴ There is an object x such that $x < x$

might present the appearance of a false arithmetical translation of (1). But this is not clear, for the second premise of (3) might reasonably be regarded as false. It does *not* assert that

for every *number* there is a greater ,

which is true, but that

for every *thing* there is a greater ,

which is doubtful. (Though such exceptions as the universe are amusing the doubt attaches to any object that is not a number; the meaning of '$<$' is not clearly determined for such objects.) The difficulty would seem to be resolved if we could in some way restrict the phrases of quantity in (3) so as to apply only to numbers. This is made possible by considering, instead of (1), another argument, called its *relativization.*

If ϕ is a symbolic sentence and π a 1-place predicate letter not occurring in ϕ, then by the *relativization of* ϕ *to* π we understand that sentence which is obtained from ϕ by replacing each part of the form

$$\bigwedge \alpha \psi$$

or

$$\bigvee \alpha \psi \quad ,$$

where α is a variable and ψ a formula, by

$$\bigwedge \alpha(\pi\alpha \rightarrow \psi)$$

or

$$\bigvee \alpha\, (\pi\alpha \wedge \psi)$$

respectively. For example, the relativization of the second premise of (1) to 'G^1' is

$$\bigwedge x(Gx \rightarrow \bigvee y[Gy \wedge F(xy)]) \quad .$$

If δ is a k-place operation letter and π a 1-place predicate letter, then by the *closure axiom* for δ with respect to π we understand the sentence

$$\pi\,\delta$$

if $k = 0$, or the sentence

$$\bigwedge x_1 \ldots \bigwedge x_k[\pi x_1 \wedge \ldots \wedge \pi x_k \rightarrow \pi\delta(x_1 \ldots x_k)]$$

if $k \geqslant 1$. For example, the closure axiom for 'A^0' with respect to 'G^1' is

$$GA \quad ,$$

for 'A^1' with respect to 'G^1' is

$$\bigwedge x_1[Gx_1 \rightarrow GA(x_1)] \quad ,$$

for 'A²' with respect to 'G¹' is

$$\bigwedge x_1 \bigwedge x_2[Gx_1 \wedge Gx_2 \rightarrow GA(x_1x_2)] \quad ,$$

and so forth.

Let A be a symbolic argument whose premises and conclusion are sentences, let π be a 1-place predicate occurring in none of these, and let $\delta_1, \ldots, \delta_n$ be all the operation letters occurring in A. Then a *relativization of A to π* is an argument obtained from A by replacing its premises and conclusion by their relativizations to π and adjoining, as additional premises, the closure axioms for $\delta_1, \ldots, \delta_n$ with respect to π, together with the sentence

$$\bigvee x \pi x \quad ,$$

called the *existence axiom*. For example, a relativization of (1) to 'G¹' is the argument

(4) $\bigwedge x[Gx \rightarrow \bigwedge y(Gy \rightarrow \bigwedge z[Gz \rightarrow (F(xy) \wedge F(yz) \rightarrow F(xz))])]$.
$\bigwedge x(Gx \rightarrow \bigvee y[Gy \wedge F(xy)])$. $\bigvee x Gx$ $\therefore \bigvee x(Gx \wedge F(xx))$.

(Other relativizations to 'G¹' could be obtained by changing the order of the premises.)

If A, B are symbolic arguments whose premises and conclusions are sentences, then A is said to be a *relativization* of B if there is a 1-place predicate letter π not occurring in B such that A is a relativization of B to π.

Now it happens that if an argument whose premises and conclusion are sentences is valid, then so is its relativization to any 1-place predicate letter not occurring in it. Thus to show such an argument invalid it is sufficient to find a false arithmetical translation of one of its relativizations. For example, the invalidity of (1) is established by the following false arithmetical translation of (4):

> For all numbers x, y, z, if $x < y$ and $y < z$, then $x < z$. For each number x, there is a number y such that $x < y$. There is a number. Therefore there is a number x such that $x < x$.

(In connection with this translation, the reader should recall the scheme (2) above.)

As another example consider again argument (6) of the preceding section,

$$\bigwedge x F[A(x)x] \quad \therefore \bigvee x F[A(x)A(x)] \quad ,$$

whose invalidity was established there (p. 231) by means of a model. To establish the invalidity of this argument by means of a false arithmetical translation we consider the relativization

$$\bigwedge x(Gx \rightarrow F[A(x)\,x]) \quad . \quad \bigwedge x_1(Gx_1 \rightarrow GA(x_1)) \quad . \quad \bigvee xGx$$
$$\therefore \bigvee x(Gx \wedge F[A(x)\,A(x)]) \quad ,$$

together with the following false idiomatic arithmetical translation of the latter:

> The successor of a number is greater than that number. The successor of a number is a number. There is a number. Therefore the successor of some number is greater than itself.

The present method for showing invalidity, like the methods of the preceding section, is directly applicable only to symbolic sentences and symbolic arguments whose premises and conclusion are sentences. But, as before, one can extend the method to arbitrary symbolic sentences and arguments by recalling that a symbolic argument is valid just in case each of its closures is valid and that a symbolic formula is a theorem just in case each of its closures is a theorem. Thus to establish that a symbolic argument is invalid it is sufficient to find either a false arithmetical translation of one of its closures or a false arithmetical translation of a relativization of one of its closures; and to establish that a symbolic formula is not a theorem it is sufficient to find either a false arithmetical translation of one of its closures or a false arithmetical translation of a relativization of a closure of the argument having no premises and the formula as its conclusion.

As a matter of fact, for the method of false arithmetical translations, in contrast to the methods of the previous section, we can make a stronger statement: a symbolic argument is invalid (in the full quantifier calculus) *just in case* a relativization of a closure of the argument has a false arithmetical translation. In particular, it follows that a symbolic formula ϕ is not a theorem *just in case* a relativization of a closure of the argument having ϕ as conclusion and no premises has a false arithmetical translation. (This fact will not be proved here; it follows from Montague and Kalish [1] and Hilbert and Bernays [2].) Thus, for any symbolic argument, either a derivation can be supplied or else a false arithmetical translation of a relativization of one of its closures must exist; and for any symbolic formulas, either a proof can be supplied or else there must exist a false arithmetical translation of a relativization of a closure of the argument with no premises and the formula as conclusion. (Yet there is no automatic way of deciding in all cases which alternative holds.)

A few additional remarks about the present techniques for investigating invalidity are in order. First some remarks about the role played by the existence axiom in a relativization.

Consider the clearly valid argument

$$\bigwedge x Fx \quad \therefore \bigvee x Fx \quad .$$

If an existence axiom were not required, the relativization of this argument to the predicate letter 'U^1' would be

$$(5) \qquad \bigwedge x(Ux \rightarrow Fx) \quad \therefore \bigvee x(Ux \wedge Fx) \quad .$$

On the basis of the scheme

U^1 : *a* is odd and *a* is even
F^1 : *a* is odd

the argument (5) has the following clearly false arithmetical translation:

> For each *x*, if *x* is both odd and even, then *x* is odd. ∴ There is an object *x* such that *x* is both odd and even .

Thus our claim that if an argument is valid then so is its relativization would fail if an existence axiom were not incorporated into a relativization. (Note that (5) becomes a valid argument if '$\bigvee xUx$' is entered as an additional premise.) We see also by this example why the universe of a model must be a nonempty class, for the predicate of relativization and the universe of a model play, in their respective methods of invalidity, analogous roles: each restricts the generality of quantification. (Hence our choice here, and subsequently, of 'U^1' as the predicate of relativization to suggest this analogy.) The requirement that the universe of a model be a nonempty class, like that for an existence axiom in a relativization, makes explicit that our system of logic, putatively considered to be *a priori*, is not completely indifferent to empirical facts: it does not countenance the empirical possibility that there are no objects in the (actual) universe. (See, on this point, Quine [3] and Mostowski [1].)

Now some remarks about closure axioms. A class is said to be *closed* under an operation if, whenever that operation is applied to elements of the class, it yields an element of the class. Thus, for example, the class of natural numbers is closed under the operation of addition, for the sum of any two natural numbers is again a natural number; but it is not closed under the operation of subtraction, for the difference between two natural numbers need not be a natural number (it could be a negative number). Closure axioms, as the term suggests, impose upon a relativization of an argument the requirement that the universe to which the quantifiers have been restricted be closed under the operations (operation letters) of the argument. To see the need for this imposition, consider the clearly valid argument

$$(6) \qquad \bigwedge x Fx \quad \therefore FB(A) \quad .$$

If the closure axiom for 'A^0' is omitted, the relativization of this argument to the predicate letter 'U^1' would be

(7) $\bigvee x Ux$. $\bigwedge x[Ux \rightarrow UB(x)]$. $\bigwedge x(Ux \rightarrow Fx)$ $\therefore$ $FB(A)$.

On the basis of the scheme

U^1 : *a* is a positive integer
F^1 : *a* is a positive integer
A^0 : 0
B^1 : the square of *a*

the argument (7) has the following false arithmetical translation (for the square of zero is zero, and zero is not a positive integer):

> Something is a positive integer. The square of a positive integer is a positive integer. Every positive integer is a positive integer. ∴ The square of 0 is a positive integer .

Next consider what would be a relativization of (6) to 'U^1' if the closure axiom for 'B^1' is omitted, that is, the argument

(8) $\bigvee x Ux$. UA . $\bigwedge x(Ux \rightarrow Fx)$ $\therefore$ $FB(A)$.

On the basis of the scheme

U^1 : *a* is an odd number
F^1 : *a* is an odd number
A^0 : 3
B^1 : $2 \cdot a$ (the product of 2 and *a*)

the argument (8) has the following clearly false arithmetical translation:

> There is an odd number. 3 is an odd number. All odd numbers are odd numbers. ∴ $2 \cdot 3$ (that is, 6) is an odd number .

Thus we see, from these two examples, that if a closure axiom is omitted from a relativization, then again our claim—if an argument is valid, so is its relativization—would fail. (The reader should note that the conclusion of the correctly formed relativization of (6) is derivable from its premises and that neither of the above schemes of abbreviation leads to a false arithmetical translation of that argument.) We also see by these examples why the functions within a model, that is, the extensions of operation letters, correlate *n*-tuples of elements of the universe of the model only with elements of the universe of the model, for that universe must be closed under these functions (operations) if incorrect results are to be precluded. The requirement that the universe of a model be closed with respect to the operations involved in an argument, like that for closure axioms in a relativization, makes explicit an important respect in which our symbolic language differs markedly from ordinary discourse. (On this point, see the Preface to the Second Edition.)

We conclude with some deeper remarks about the method of false arithmetical translations itself. As mentioned, the method can be characterized quite precisely. First, the looseness inherent in the notion of stylistic variance can be obviated by employing only literal translations of symbolic sentences, for these can be obtained automatically on the basis of a given scheme of abbreviation. Secondly, not only is a precise characterization of the language of the arithmetic of natural numbers possible, but it is also possible to define precisely the notion of truth (and falsity) for that language; see, for example, Tarski [2]. However, the mathematical methods required for showing truth and falsehood within the arithmetic of natural numbers will in some cases be very deep. Indeed, there are invalid arguments whose invalidity cannot be established with the mathematical system presently used. (This is one version of the incompleteness theorem of Gödel [2].) For such arguments there will be translations into the arithmetic of natural numbers which are in fact false but which we shall be unable to prove false.

EXERCISES, GROUP I

64. The argument

$$(9) \qquad \bigvee x \mathrm{U}x \quad . \quad \bigwedge x(\mathrm{U}x \rightarrow \mathrm{F}x) \quad \therefore \bigvee x[\mathrm{U}x \wedge \mathrm{FB}(x)]$$

omits the closure axiom for 'B^1' from a relativization of the clearly valid argument

$$\bigwedge x \mathrm{F}x \quad \therefore \bigvee x \mathrm{FB}(x) \quad .$$

Establish the invalidity of (9) by means of a false arithmetical translation. (Note that 'B(x)'—in contrast to 'B(A)', which occurs in argument (6) above—is not a name; thus this exercise demonstrates that closure axioms are essential to a relativization whether or not the terms that occur in the argument are names.)

65. The reader who obtained solutions for the exercises of the preceding section knows that each of the following arguments is invalid. Demonstrate this fact by the method of false arithmetical translations. Part (i) is solved for illustration.

(i) $\bigwedge x \bigvee y[\mathrm{F}(xy) \vee \mathrm{F}(yx)] \quad \therefore \bigwedge x \bigvee y \mathrm{F}(xy)$

We construct a relativization of the argument,

$$\bigvee x \mathrm{U}x \quad . \quad \bigwedge x[\mathrm{U}x \rightarrow \bigvee y(\mathrm{U}y \wedge [\mathrm{F}(xy) \vee \mathrm{F}(yx)])]$$
$$\therefore \bigwedge x(\mathrm{U}x \rightarrow \bigvee y[\mathrm{U}y \wedge \mathrm{F}(xy)]) \quad ,$$

and introduce the scheme of abbreviation

U^1 : a is a natural number
F^2 : $a > b$,

on the basis of which the premises of the relativization translate into true sentences of arithmetic and the conclusion into a false sentence of arithmetic. (To see that the conclusion translates into a false sentence of arithmetic, consider the number 0.)

(ii) $\bigvee x \bigwedge y F(xy) \wedge \bigvee x \bigwedge y F(yx) \quad \therefore \bigwedge x \bigwedge y[F(xy) \vee F(yx)]$
(iii) $\bigwedge x \bigwedge y[F(xy) \vee F(yx)] \quad \therefore \bigvee x \bigwedge y F(xy) \vee \bigvee x \bigwedge y F(yx)$
(iv) $\bigwedge x F[xA(x)] \quad \therefore \bigvee x F[A(x)x]$
(v) $\bigwedge x \bigvee y F(xy) \quad \therefore \bigvee x \bigvee y[F(xy) \wedge F(yx)]$
(vi) $\bigwedge x \bigwedge y \bigvee z F(xyz) \quad . \quad \bigwedge x \bigwedge y \bigwedge z[F(xyz) \rightarrow F(yxz)]$
$\therefore \bigwedge x \bigwedge y \bigvee z F(zxy)$
(vii) $\bigvee x[F(Ax) \wedge \sim F(Bx)] \quad . \quad \bigwedge x \bigvee y F(xy) \quad .$
$\bigwedge x \bigwedge y[F(xy) \rightarrow \sim F(yx)] \quad \therefore \bigvee x[F(xA) \vee F(xB)]$

EXERCISES, GROUP II

66. Demonstrate the invalidity of each of the following arguments by the method of false arithmetical translations. (No model with a finite universe is capable of establishing the invalidity of any of these arguments.)

(i) $\bigwedge x \bigvee y(F(xy) \wedge \bigwedge z[F(yz) \rightarrow F(xz)]) \quad \therefore \bigvee x F(xx)$
(ii) $\bigwedge x \bigvee y F(xy) \quad . \quad \bigwedge x \bigwedge y \bigwedge z[F(xy) \wedge F(yz) \rightarrow F(xz)] \quad .$
$\sim \bigvee x F(xx) \quad \therefore \bigwedge x \bigwedge y[Gx \wedge \sim Gy \rightarrow F(xy) \vee F(yx)]$
(iii) $\bigwedge x[\bigvee y F(xy) \wedge \bigvee y F(yx)] \quad . \quad \bigwedge x \bigwedge y \bigwedge z[F(xy) \wedge F(yz) \rightarrow F(xz)]$
$\therefore \bigvee x \bigvee y[F(xy) \wedge F(yx)]$
(iv) $\sim \bigvee x F(xx) \quad . \quad \bigwedge x \bigvee y(F(xy) \wedge \bigwedge z[F(yz) \rightarrow F(xz)])$
$\therefore \bigwedge x \bigwedge y \bigwedge z[F(xy) \wedge F(yz) \rightarrow F(xz)]$

9. Arguments of English. It is often the case that the intuitive validity of an argument of English rests on premises not made explicit in the argument; such an argument has traditionally been called an *enthymeme*. Consider, for example, the simple and intuitively valid argument

Alfred is married. ∴ Alfred is married to someone who is married ,

and the scheme of abbreviation

A^0 : Alfred
F^2 : *a* is married to *b* .

On the basis of this scheme (treating 'someone' as 'something'), the English argument passes into the symbolic argument

(1) $\bigvee x F(Ax) \quad \therefore \bigvee x[F(Ax) \wedge \bigvee y F(xy)]$.

But this symbolic argument is invalid, as the reader can verify (see exercise 67 below). The intuitive validity of the English argument rests on a premise omitted from that argument but implicit in the meaning of the word 'married', specifically, the premise that asserts the symmetry of the marital relation. Thus, to warrant our intuition, we must make this implicit premise explicit by entering its symbolization (on the basis of the scheme above) into our symbolization of the English argument. We then obtain

(2) $\bigwedge x \bigwedge y[F(xy) \rightarrow F(yx)] \quad . \qquad \bigvee x F(Ax) \quad \therefore \bigvee x[F(Ax) \wedge \bigvee y F(xy)]$,

which is valid (see exercise 68 below).

For a more complex example, consider the argument

(3) Students who solve every problem on the final examination also solve every problem on the midterm examination. Some student does not solve the first problem on the midterm examination. ∴ There is a problem on the final examination that some student does not solve ,

and the scheme of abbreviation

F^1	:	*a* is a student
G^2	:	*a* is a problem on *b*
H^2	:	*a* solves *b*
A^1	:	the first problem on *a*
B^0	:	the final examination
C^0	:	the midterm examination .

On the basis of this scheme, the argument passes into

(4) $\bigwedge x(Fx \wedge \bigwedge y[G(yB) \rightarrow H(xy)] \rightarrow \bigwedge y[G(yC) \rightarrow H(xy)])$.
$\bigvee x(Fx \wedge \sim H[xA(C)]) \quad \therefore \bigvee y(G(yB) \wedge \bigvee x[Fx \wedge \sim H(xy)])$,

whose invalidity the reader can demonstrate (see exercise 69 below). But the English argument is intuitively valid. Here the implicit premise is the apodictic assertion that the first problem on the midterm is indeed a problem on the midterm. If the symbolization of this assertion, '$G[A(C)C]$', is added to (4) as an additional premise, one thereby obtains as a symbolization of (3) the argument

(5) $G[A(C)C] \quad . \qquad \bigvee x(Fx \wedge \sim H[xA(C)])$.
$\bigwedge x(Fx \wedge \bigwedge y[G(yB) \rightarrow H(xy)] \rightarrow \bigwedge y[G(yC) \rightarrow H(xy)])$
$\therefore \bigvee y(G(yB) \wedge \bigvee x[Fx \wedge \sim H(xy)])$,

which is valid (see exercise 70 below).

EXERCISES, GROUP I

67. Demonstrate the invalidity of argument (1) of this section.
68. Demonstrate the validity of argument (2) of this section.
69. Demonstrate the invalidity of argument (4) of this section.
70. Demonstrate the validity of argument (5) of this section.

EXERCISES, GROUP II

Establish the validity of each of the following arguments by means of a symbolization and derivation. Exercise 71 is solved for illustration.

71. Alfred shaves all and only those inhabitants of Berkeley who do not shave themselves. Alfred is an inhabitant of Berkeley. Therefore Alfred does not shave himself.

On the basis of the scheme of abbreviation

F^2 : *a* is an inhabitant of *b*
S^2 : *a* shaves *b*
A^0 : Berkeley
B^0 : Alfred ,

the argument becomes

$$\bigwedge x(F(xA) \rightarrow [S(Bx) \leftrightarrow \sim S(xx)]) \quad . \qquad F(BA) \quad \therefore \ \sim S(BB) \quad .$$

Its validity is established by the following derivation:

1.	~~*Show*~~ $\sim S(BB)$	
2.	$S(BB)$	
3.	$F(BA) \rightarrow [S(BB) \leftrightarrow \sim S(BB)]$	1st premise, UI
4.	$\sim S(BB)$	2nd premise, 3 MP, BC, 2, MP

72. Alfred shaves all and only those inhabitants of Berkeley who do not shave themselves. Alfred is an inhabitant of Berkeley. Therefore Alfred shaves himself.

(Exercises 71 and 72 justify the assertions under (2) of page 1.)

73. Every student is able to solve some problems and not able to solve some problems. Some teacher is able to solve all problems. ∴ Some teacher is not a student.

74. No woman likes every course she takes unless she takes no courses but philosophical studies. No mathematical study is a philosophical study. Some woman takes nothing but mathematical studies and likes every course she takes. ∴ Some woman does not take any courses.

75. There are numbers. Every number is less than some even number. ∴ There is an even number less than some number.

76. ∴ If someone is married and anyone to whom someone is married is married to everyone, then everyone is married to everyone.

77. Everything attracts a thing or repels that thing. ∴ Either something attracts everything or everything repels something.

EXERCISES, GROUP III

Symbolize each of the following pairs of arguments on the basis of the scheme of abbreviation that accompanies the pair, and by means of the symbolizations demonstrate for each argument its validity or its invalidity.

78. (i) Alfred is a friend of those who have no friends. ∴ Something is a friend of itself. (ii) Alfred is a friend of those who are not friends of themselves. ∴ Something is a friend of itself. (F^2 : *a* is a friend of *b*; A^0 : Alfred)

79. (i) Alfred envies everyone who does not envy anyone. ∴ Alfred envies someone. (ii) Alfred envies everyone who does not envy anyone. ∴ Alfred envies himself. (F^2 : *a* envies *b*; A^0 : Alfred)

80. (i) Those who love their spouse do not love themselves. ∴ Nothing is such that its spouse loves everything. (ii) Those who love their spouse do not love themselves. ∴ Nothing is such that its spouse loves itself. (F^2 : *a* loves *b*; A^1 : the spouse of *a*)

81. (i) A thing is promiscuous if and only if it is intimate with everything. ∴ Something is intimate with all promiscuous things. (ii) A thing is promiscuous if and only if it is intimate with everything. ∴ Some promiscuous thing is intimate with everything. (F^1 : *a* is promiscuous; G^2 : *a* is intimate with *b*)

82. (i) ∴ If there is something that loves everything, then there is something that everything loves. (ii) ∴ There is something such that if it loves everything, then everything loves it. (F^2 : *a* loves *b*)

EXERCISES, GROUP IV

A literal symbolization, on the basis of an interesting scheme of abbreviation (p. 102), of each of the following arguments of English is invalid. Provide such a scheme and demonstrate its invalidity. But each of the English arguments is intuitively valid. Warrant this intuition by appropriately supplementing your initial symbolization and demonstrating the validity of the supplemented symbolization. (Review pp. 246 and 247 before undertaking these exercises.)

83. No teacher is married to a student. Every teacher is married to a teacher. ∴ No teacher is a student.

84. Alfred likes any woman who laughs at herself but detests any woman who laughs at all her friends. ∴ If any woman laughs at all her friends, then some woman is not a friend of herself.

85. If the product of integers is odd, then the integers are odd. An integer is even if and only if it is not odd. ∴ The product of an even integer with any integer is even.

86. Uncles and aunts of opera lovers are opera lovers. ∴ No nephew of a nonlover of opera is an opera lover.

87. If any number is such that all numbers less than it are interesting, then it is certainly interesting. If there is an uninteresting (that is, not interesting) number, then there is an uninteresting number less than or

equal to all uninteresting numbers (that is, there is a smallest such number). ∴ All numbers are interesting.

88. The distance between A and B is less than the distance between B and C. The distance between B and C is less than the distance between A and C. ∴ The distance between A and B is less than the distance between A and C.

89. For each *x*, for each *y*, for each *z*, the distance between *x* and *y* is less than the distance between *y* and *z*. For each *x*, for each *y*, for each *z*, the distance between *y* and *z* is less than the distance between *x* and *z*. ∴ For each *x*, for each *y*, for each *z*, the distance between *x* and *y* is less than the distance between *x* and *z*.

10. Historical remarks. The observation that every monadic formula is equivalent to one in which no quantifier occurs within the scope of another is found in Behmann [1]. The idea of prenex normal form is due to Peirce (see Peirce [2] and [3]). The process of reduction to prenex normal form is given in Whitehead and Russell [1].

That there is no automatic test for validity in the quantifier calculus was derived in Church [2] from the results in Church [1].

The assertion that a relativization of a closure of an invalid argument of the quantifier calculus always has a false arithmetical translation can be understood as expressing the *completeness*, in a certain sense, of this branch of logic. Completeness, in a somewhat different sense, was demonstrated in Gödel [1] for an axiomatic quantification theory, and the present assertion corresponds to an extension of this result obtained first in Hilbert and Bernays [2] and proved more simply in Kleene [1].

For historical remarks on arguments whose invalidity cannot be demonstrated by a model with a finite universe, see Church [3] and Quine [5].

11. Appendix: list of theorems of chapter IV.

T249	$\bigwedge x \bigwedge y F(xy) \rightarrow \bigvee x \bigvee y F(xy)$
T250	$\bigwedge x \bigwedge y \bigwedge z F(xyz) \leftrightarrow \sim \bigvee x \bigvee y \bigvee z \sim F(xyz)$
T251	$\bigwedge x \bigwedge y F(xy) \leftrightarrow \bigwedge y \bigwedge x F(xy)$
T252	$\bigvee x \bigvee y F(xy) \leftrightarrow \bigvee y \bigvee x F(xy)$
T253	$\bigvee x \bigwedge y F(xy) \rightarrow \bigwedge y \bigvee x F(xy)$
T254	$\bigvee x \bigvee y F(xy) \leftrightarrow \bigvee x \bigvee y [F(xy) \vee F(yx)]$
T255	$\bigwedge x \bigwedge y F(xy) \rightarrow \bigwedge y \bigwedge x F(yx)$
T256	$\bigwedge x \bigvee y [F(xy) \wedge Gy] \rightarrow \bigvee x \bigvee y [F(xy) \wedge Gx]$
T257	$\bigwedge x FA(x) \rightarrow \bigvee x [Fx \wedge FA(x)]$
T258	$F(xA(x)) \leftrightarrow \bigvee y [\bigwedge z [F(zy) \rightarrow F(zA(x))] \wedge F(xy)]$

T259 $\bigwedge x \bigvee z(Fx \to \bigvee y[Gy \to Hz]) \leftrightarrow (\bigvee xFx \wedge \bigwedge xGx \to \bigvee xHx)$

T260 $\bigwedge x(Fx \to \bigvee y[Gy \wedge (Hy \vee Hx)]) \leftrightarrow$
$\bigvee x(Gx \wedge Hx) \vee \sim \bigvee xFx \vee (\bigvee xGx \wedge \bigwedge x[Fx \to Hx])$

T261 $\bigwedge x[\bigvee yF(xy) \to \bigvee yG(xy)] \leftrightarrow \bigwedge x \bigwedge y \bigvee z[F(xy) \to G(xz)]$

T262 $\bigvee y[\bigvee xF(xy) \leftrightarrow Gy] \leftrightarrow$
$\bigvee y \bigwedge x \bigvee z([F(xy) \to Gy] \wedge [Gy \to F(zy)])$

T263 $\bigwedge x \bigvee y(Fx \to Gy) \leftrightarrow \bigvee y \bigwedge x(Fx \to Gy)$

T264 $\bigwedge x \bigvee y(Fx \wedge Gy) \leftrightarrow \bigvee y \bigwedge x(Fx \wedge Gy)$

T265 $\bigwedge x \bigvee y(Fx \vee Gy) \leftrightarrow \bigvee y \bigwedge x(Fx \vee Gy)$

T266 $\bigwedge x \bigwedge y \bigvee z(Fx \wedge Gy \to Hz) \leftrightarrow \bigwedge y \bigvee z \bigwedge x(Fx \wedge Gy \to Hz)$

T267 $\bigwedge x[Fx \leftrightarrow \sim FA(x)] \to \bigvee x[Fx \wedge \sim FA(x)]$

T268 $\bigwedge x[F(Ax) \vee \bigwedge yF(xy)] \to \bigvee x \bigwedge yF(xy)$

T269 $\sim \bigvee y \bigwedge x[F(xy) \leftrightarrow \sim F(xx)]$

T270 $\bigwedge z \bigvee y \bigwedge x[F(xy) \leftrightarrow F(xz) \wedge \sim F(xx)] \to \sim \bigvee z \bigwedge xF(xz)$

T271 $\sim \bigvee y \bigwedge x(F(xy) \leftrightarrow \sim \bigvee z[F(xz) \wedge F(zx)])$

T272 $\bigvee y \bigwedge x[F(xy) \leftrightarrow F(xx)] \to \sim \bigwedge x \bigvee y \bigwedge z[F(zy) \leftrightarrow \sim F(zx)]$

12. Appendix: solutions to selected exercises.

Section 1

2. Neither; an operation letter followed by a formula ('F^1x') is neither a term nor a formula.

3. Symbolic formula; a 2-place predicate letter followed by two symbolic terms ('A^1x' and 'B^1y') is a symbolic formula.

4. Neither; every occurrence of a quantifier must be followed immediately by a variable.

5. Neither; the juxtaposition of two terms ('A^1x' and 'B^2yz') is neither a term nor a formula.

6. Symbolic term; a 2-place operation letter followed by two symbolic terms ('A^1A^0' and 'x') is a symbolic term.

7. Symbolic formula; a 3-place predicate letter followed by three symbolic terms ('C^1y', 'D^1x', and 'A^1A^0') is a symbolic formula.

8. Symbolic formula; a symbolic formula ('F^2xy') prefixed by a string of quantifier phrases is a symbolic formula.

9. Neither; sentential connectives can combine only with symbolic formulas (not symbolic terms 'A^1x' and 'B^1x') to form a symbolic formula.

10. Symbolic formula; it is a negation of a biconditional, of which one constituent is an atomic formula and the other an existential generalization of a conditional whose consequent is an atomic formula (for '$A^1B^3A^0xB^0$' is a term)

and whose antecedent is a universal generalization of a conditional whose antecedent and consequent are atomic formulas. This structure is displayed in the following grammatical tree:

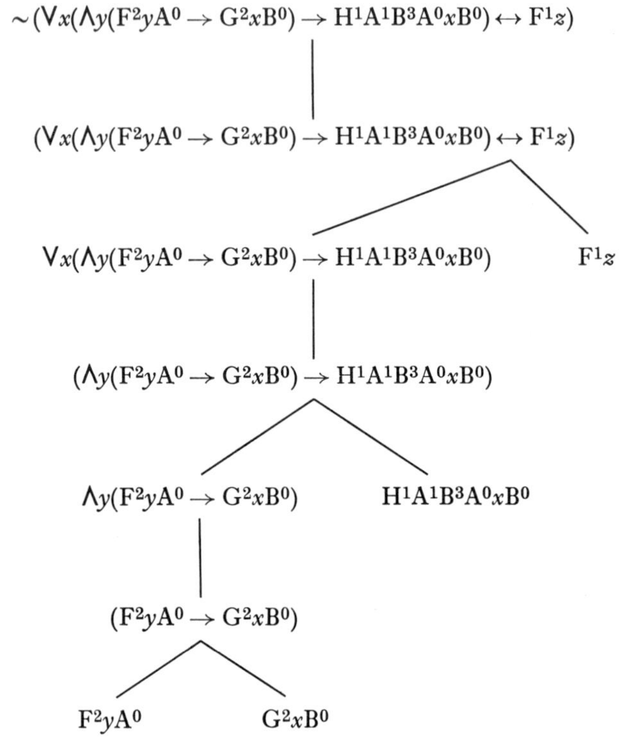

Section 2

11. The linked variables in the top node of a modified grammatical tree of the formula, that is, in

$$(\bigwedge y(\bigvee x G^2A^0A^1x \vee G^2B^2yzA^1x) \rightarrow \bigwedge z(G^2B^1yz \vee G^1B^2yz)) \quad ,$$

are the bound occurrences of variables in the formula; those occurrences of variables not linked in the top node are free occurrences. The occurrence of 'A^0' is free in the formula (indeed, any occurrence of a 0-place operation letter is a free occurrence). The first occurrence of 'A^1x' is bound in the formula, for the occurrence of 'x' in that occurrence is bound; the second occurrence of 'A^1x' is free, for the occurrence of 'x' in that occurrence is not bound. Both occurrences of 'B^2yz) are bound in the formula, the first because the occurrence of 'y' in that occurrence is bound and the second because the occurrence of 'z' in that occurrence is bound. The occurrence of 'B^1y' in the formula is not bound, for the occurrence of 'y' in that occurrence is not bound. (Note that the bound occurrence of 'z' that follows the occurrence of 'B^1y' does not stand within that occurrence of 'B^1y' and hence has no relevance to its bondage or freedom.)

12. 'x', 'y', 'z', and 'A^1x' are both bound and free in the formula; 'A^0' and 'B^1y' are free but not bound in the formula; and 'B^2yz' is bound but not free in the formula.

Section 3

13. (i) F^1A^1x
(ii) G^2B^0x
(iii) $H^3C^2B^0B^0A^1B^0B^0$
(iv) $((\bigwedge xF^1x \vee P^0) \to (G^2xy \wedge H^3xyz))$

Section 4, Group I

14. (1) and (g); (2) and (c); (3) and (d); (4) and (a); (5) and (e)
15. (a) and (8); (b) and (16); (c) and (1); (d) and (7); (e) and (2); (f) and (14); (g) and (10); (h) and (1); (i) and (5); (j) and (3); (k) and (13); (l) and (1); (m) and (9); (n) and (15); (o) and (2); (p) and (4); (q) and (13); (r) and (11); (s) and (6); (t) and (3); (u) and (12)

Section 4, Group II

16. If there is a number such that the product of it and any number is even, then some number is even.
17. Everyone has a father and a mother, but someone is neither a father nor a mother.
18. Every student of the course attends a workshop of the course taught by the teaching assistant of the instructor of the course.

Section 4, Group III

19. $\bigwedge x[Fx \vee Gx \to \bigvee yH(yx)]$
20. $\sim \bigvee x[Fx \wedge \sim \bigvee yG(yx)] \wedge \sim \bigwedge x[Fx \to \bigvee yG(xy)]$
21. $\bigwedge x(Fx \to \bigvee y[Fy \wedge G(yx)])$
22. $\bigvee x(Fx \wedge \bigwedge y[Fy \to G(xy)])$
23. There are two occurrences of the indefinite article 'a' in the sentence

> A teacher has no scruples if he or she assigns a problem that has no solution ,

and linguistic intuition suggests that the first occurrence pass into a universal quantifier phrase and that the second pass into an existential quantifier phrase. To make explicit the former and the internal sentential structure of the sentence we obtain

(i) For each x (if (x is a teacher and x assigns a problem that has no solution), then it is not the case that x has scruples) .

(Note that in passing from No. 23 to (i) we have treated 'no scruples' and 'no solution' differently; this difference was suggested by a glance at the scheme of abbreviation employed.) To make explicit the latter we consider

(ii) x assigns a problem that has no solution ,

and paraphrase it separately. Although one need not always employ a different variable for each phrase of quantity, one cannot be wrong to do so. We can paraphrase (ii) then by

(iii) there is an object y such that ((y is a problem and x assigns y) and it is not the case that there is an object z such that z is a solution of y) .

We now replace (ii) by (iii) in (i) to obtain in step (1) of the process of symbolization

(iv) For each x (if (x is a teacher and there is an object y such that ((y is a problem and x assigns y) and it is not the case that there is an object z such that z is a solution of y)), then it is not the case that x has scruples) .

In step (2) of the process of symbolization, (iv) passes into

$$\bigwedge x(Fx \wedge \bigvee y[Jy \wedge H(xy) \wedge \sim \bigvee z K(zy)] \rightarrow \sim Gx) \quad .$$

24. $\bigwedge x[Fx \rightarrow G(A(x)B[C(x)D(x)])]$
25. $\bigwedge x(Fx \rightarrow \sim Gx \vee \bigwedge y[Hy \wedge J(yx) \rightarrow K(yx)])$
26. $FA[B(C)]$
27. $\bigwedge x(Fx \rightarrow \sim \bigwedge y[Gy \wedge J(xy) \rightarrow K(xy)] \vee \bigwedge z[Gz \wedge J(xz) \rightarrow Hz])$
28. The sentence

    A man who loves himself more than he loves anyone else is not loved by anyone other than himself

contains three phrases of quantity, and we paraphrase the initial one first to obtain

(i) For each x (if (x is a man and x loves x more than x loves anyone else), then x is not loved by anyone other than x) .

Next we paraphrase the clause following 'and' to obtain

for each y (if (y is a person and y is different from x), then x loves x more than x loves y) ;

and then the clause introduced by 'then' to obtain

it is not the case that there is an object y such that ((y is a person and y is different from x) and y loves x) .

We now replace the clauses in (i) by their paraphrases to obtain in step (1) of the process of symbolization

(ii) For each x (if (x is a man and for each y (if (y is a person and y is different from x), then x loves x more than x loves y)), then it is not the case that there is an object y such that ((y is a person and y is different from x) and y loves x)) .

In step (2) of the process of symbolization, (ii) passes into

$$\bigwedge x(Fx \wedge \bigwedge y[Gy \wedge J(yx) \rightarrow L(xxxy)] \rightarrow \sim \bigvee y[Gy \wedge J(yx) \wedge H(yx)]) \quad .$$

29. $\Lambda x(Fx \wedge \Lambda y[H(yx) \rightarrow Gy] \rightarrow \sim V z[H(zx) \wedge Gz \wedge J(xz)])$
30. The sentence

The wife of anyone who marries the daughter of the brother of his father marries the son of the brother of the husband of her mother

contains two complex terms that can be paraphrased:

(i) the daughter of the brother of the father of x
(ii) the son of the brother of the husband of the mother of the wife of x .

Given (i) and (ii), we obtain in step (1) of the process of symbolization

(iii) For each x (if x marries the daughter of the brother of the father of x, then the wife of x marries the son of the brother of the husband of the mother of the wife of x) .

In step (2) of the process of symbolization, (iii) passes into

$$\Lambda x(F[xB(C[D(x)])] \rightarrow F[A(x)E(C[A_1(B_1[A(x)])])]) \quad .$$

31. $Fx \wedge [G(xA) \vee H(xA)] \wedge \Lambda y[Fy \rightarrow I(yx)] \rightarrow H(xB)$

Section 5, Group I

36. In the first derivation, step 3 is incorrect: not all free occurrences of 'x' in '$F[A(x)x]$' have been replaced by '$A(x)$' to obtain a proper application of UI. In the second derivation, step 4 is incorrect: here not all free occurrences of 'x' in '$F[A(x)A(x)]$' have been replaced by '$A(x)$' to obtain a proper application of EG.

37. A formula follows from '$\Lambda x V z F(A(xyx)z)$' by UI if it is obtained from '$V z F(A(xyx)z)$' by proper substitution of a term for 'x'. Thus (a) does not follow, for '$A(xyx)$', not just occurrences of 'x', has been replaced; (d) does not follow, for 'y', not just occurrences of 'x', has been replaced; (e) does not follow, for the replacement of occurrences of 'x' is not uniform—one occurrence is replaced by 'C' and the other by 'B'; and (j) does not follow, for the term '$B(C(z))$' that replaces 'x' uniformly is bound in the formula (j). All the other formulas follow by UI.

38. A formula, which we may represent by

$$V\alpha\phi \quad ,$$

follows from

(4) $$\Lambda x FA(xB(y)) \vee G(Cy)$$

by EG if (4) is obtained from ϕ by proper substitution of some term for α. (b) does not follow; here a free occurrence of α ('w') in ϕ has passed into a bound occurrence of '$A(xB(y))$' in (4). (f) does not follow; here a bound as well as a free occurrence of α ('x') in ϕ has been replaced by 'y' to obtain (4) from ϕ. (h) does not follow; here (4) is not the result of uniform replacement of α ('y') in ϕ by 'C'. (j) does not follow; here to obtain (4) the occurrence of α ('w') in ϕ is replaced by 'Cy', which is not a term. All the other formulas follow by EG.

Section 5, Group II

39.

1.	~~Show~~ $\bigvee x FA(xx)$	
2.	$\bigwedge x FA(xB)$	Premise
3.	$FA(BB)$	2, UI
4.	$\bigvee x FA(xx)$	3, EG

40.

1.	~~Show~~ $\bigvee x Fx$	
2.	$FA(aa)$	Premise, EI
3.	$\bigvee x Fx$	2, EG

41.

1.	~~Show~~ $\bigvee x FA[B(x)B(C)x]$	
2.	$\bigwedge x \bigwedge y FA[xB(y)C]$	Premise
3.	$\bigwedge y FA[B(C)B(y)C]$	2, UI
4.	$FA[B(C)B(C)C]$	3, UI
5.	$\bigvee x FA[B(x)B(C)x]$	4, EG

42.

1.	~~Show~~ $\bigvee x FA[B(x)xC]$	
2.	$\bigwedge x \bigwedge y FA[xB(y)C]$	Premise
3.	$\bigwedge y FA[B(B(x))B(y)C]$	2, UI
4.	$FA[B(B(x))B(x)C]$	3, UI
5.	$\bigvee x FA[B(x)xC]$	4, EG

Section 5, Group III

We symbolize the arguments of exercises 44–47 but provide a derivation only for that of 47.

44. $FA \wedge GB(A) \quad \therefore \bigvee x[Fx \wedge GB(x)]$
45. $FA(B) \quad \therefore \bigvee x FA(x)$
46. $\bigvee x FA(x) \quad \therefore \bigvee x Fx$

47.

1.	~~Show~~ $\bigvee x(Gx \wedge Fx)$	
2.	$\bigwedge x \bigwedge y[Fx \wedge Fy \to FA(xy)]$	Premise
3.	$\bigvee x(Fx \wedge \bigwedge y[Fy \to GA(xy)])$	Premise
4.	$Fa \wedge \bigwedge y[Fy \to GA(ay)]$	3, EI
5.	$Fa \to GA(aa)$	4, S, UI
6.	$Fa \wedge Fa \to FA(aa)$	2, UI, UI
7.	$FA(aa)$	4, S, T41, BC, MP, 6, MP
8.	$\bigvee x(Gx \wedge Fx)$	4, S, 5, MP, 7, Adj, EG

Section 6

48.

1.	~~Show~~ $\bigvee x \bigwedge y(Fx \leftrightarrow Fy) \leftrightarrow \sim \bigvee x Fx \vee \bigwedge x Fx$	
2.	~~Show~~ $\bigvee x \bigwedge y(Fx \leftrightarrow Fy) \to \sim \bigvee x Fx \vee \bigwedge x Fx$	
3.	$\bigvee x \bigwedge y(Fx \leftrightarrow Fy)$	
4.	~~Show~~ $\sim\sim \bigvee x Fx \to \bigwedge x Fx$	
5.	$\sim\sim \bigvee x Fx$	
6.	~~Show~~ $\bigwedge x Fx$	

7. $\bigwedge y(Fa \leftrightarrow Fy)$ — 3, EI
8. Fb — 5, DN, EI
9. Fa — 7, UI, BC, 8, MP
10. Fx — 7, UI, BC, 9, MP
11. $\sim \bigvee xFx \vee \bigwedge xFx$ — 4, CD
12. ~~*Show*~~ $\sim \bigvee xFx \rightarrow \bigvee x \bigwedge y(Fx \leftrightarrow Fy)$
13. $\sim \bigvee xFx$
14. ~~*Show*~~ $\bigwedge y(Fx \leftrightarrow Fy)$
15. $Fx \leftrightarrow Fy$ — 13, QN, UI, UI, Adj, T85, MP
16. $\bigvee x \bigwedge y(Fx \leftrightarrow Fy)$ — 14, EG
17. ~~*Show*~~ $\bigwedge xFx \rightarrow \bigvee x \bigwedge y(Fx \leftrightarrow Fy)$
18. $\bigwedge xFx$
19. ~~*Show*~~ $\bigwedge y(Fx \leftrightarrow Fy)$
20. $Fx \leftrightarrow Fy$ — 18, QN, UI, UI, Adj, T84, MP
21. $\bigvee x \bigwedge y(Fx \leftrightarrow Fy)$ — 19, EG
22. $\sim \bigvee xFx \vee \bigwedge xFx \rightarrow \bigvee x \bigwedge y(Fx \leftrightarrow Fy)$ — 12, 17, SC
23. $\sim \bigvee xFx \vee \bigwedge xFx \leftrightarrow \bigvee x \bigwedge y(Fx \leftrightarrow Fy)$ — 2, 22, BC

50. The proof of T255 requires some ingenuity in the manipulation of variables.

1. ~~*Show*~~ $\bigwedge x \bigwedge yF(xy) \rightarrow \bigwedge y \bigwedge xF(yx)$
2. $\bigwedge x \bigwedge yF(xy)$
3. ~~*Show*~~ $\bigwedge w \bigwedge zF(wz)$
4. $F(wz)$ — 2, UI, UI
5. ~~*Show*~~ $\bigwedge y \bigwedge xF(yx)$
6. $F(yx)$ — 3, UI, UI

For T258, we prove the conditional that has the existential generalization as its consequent. The strategy is that given in hint (9) at the end of section 10 of chapter III: to prove a formula

$$\bigvee \alpha \phi_\alpha$$

we prove $\phi\zeta$ and use EG; here ζ will be the term '$A(x)$'.

1. ~~*Show*~~ $F(xA(x)) \rightarrow \bigvee y[\bigwedge z[F(zy) \rightarrow F(zA(x))] \wedge F(xy)]$
2. $F(xA(x))$
3. ~~*Show*~~ $\bigwedge z[F(zA(x)) \rightarrow F(zA(x))]$
4. $F(zA(x)) \rightarrow F(zA(x))$ — T1
5. $\bigwedge z[F(zA(x)) \rightarrow F(zA(x))] \wedge F(xA(x))$ — 3, 2, Adj
6. $\bigvee y[\bigwedge z[F(zy) \rightarrow F(zA(x))] \wedge F(xy)]$ — 5, EG

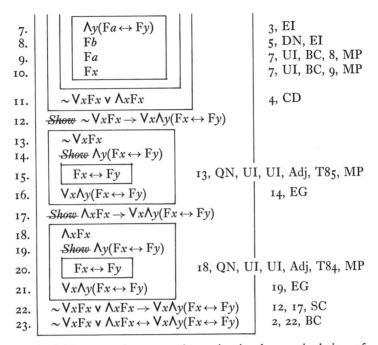

52. We initiate a proof of T264, leaving its completion to the reader.

T264	1.	*Show* $\bigwedge x \bigvee y(Fx \wedge Gy) \rightarrow \bigvee y \bigwedge x(Fx \wedge Gy)$
	2.	$\bigwedge x \bigvee y(Fx \wedge Gy)$
	3.	$Fz \wedge Ga$
	4.	Show $\bigwedge x(Fx \wedge Ga)$

For a proof of T265, see the proof of T263 (p. 227); or, as an alternative to indirect derivation, consider cases in which the antecedents are '$\bigvee x Gx$' and '$\sim \bigvee x Gx$' and then use SC, Form I (p. 78).

53. T267

1.	~~Show~~ $\bigwedge x[Fx \leftrightarrow \sim FA(x)] \rightarrow \bigvee x[Fx \wedge \sim FA(x)]$	
2.	$\bigwedge x[Fx \leftrightarrow \sim FA(x)]$	
3.	$[Fx \wedge \sim FA(x)] \vee [\sim Fx \wedge \sim\sim FA(x)]$	2, UI, T83, BC, MP
4.	~~Show~~ $Fx \wedge \sim FA(x) \rightarrow \bigvee x[Fx \wedge \sim FA(x)]$	
5.	$Fx \wedge \sim FA(x)$	
6.	$\bigvee x[Fx \wedge \sim FA(x)]$	5, EG
7.	~~Show~~ $\sim Fx \wedge \sim\sim FA(x) \rightarrow \bigvee x[Fx \wedge \sim FA(x)]$	
8.	$\sim Fx \wedge \sim\sim FA(x)$	
9.	$FA(x) \leftrightarrow \sim FA(A(x))$	2, UI
10.	$FA(x)$	8, S, DN
11.	$\sim FA(A(x))$	9, BC, 10, MP
12.	$\bigvee x[Fx \wedge \sim FA(x)]$	10, 11, Adj, EG
13.	$\bigvee x[Fx \wedge \sim FA(x)]$	3, 4, 7, SC

T268

1.	~~Show~~ $\bigwedge x[F(Ax) \vee \bigwedge y F(xy)] \rightarrow \bigvee x \bigwedge y F(xy)$	
2.	$\bigwedge x[F(Ax) \vee \bigwedge y F(xy)]$	
3.	~~Show~~ $\bigvee x \bigwedge y F(xy)$	
4.	$\sim \bigvee x \bigwedge y F(xy)$	
5.	$\sim F(Aa)$	4, QN, UI, QN, EI
6.	$\bigvee x \bigwedge y F(xy)$	2, UI, 5, MTP, EG

T270

1.	~~Show~~ $\bigwedge z \bigvee y \bigwedge x[F(xy) \leftrightarrow F(xz) \wedge \sim F(xx)] \rightarrow \sim \bigvee z \bigwedge x F(xz)$	
2.	$\bigwedge z \bigvee y \bigwedge x[F(xy) \leftrightarrow F(xz) \wedge \sim F(xx)]$	
3.	~~Show~~ $\sim \bigvee z \bigwedge x F(xz)$	
4.	$\bigvee z \bigwedge x F(xz)$	
5.	$\bigwedge x F(xa)$	4, EI
6.	$\bigwedge x[F(xb) \leftrightarrow F(xa) \wedge \sim F(xx)]$	2, UI, EI
7.	$F(bb) \leftrightarrow F(ba) \wedge \sim F(bb)$	6, UI
8.	$F(ba)$	5, UI
9.	~~Show~~ $F(bb)$	

10.	~F(*bb*)	
11.	F(*bb*)	8, 10, Adj, 7, BC, MP
12.	~F(*bb*)	7, BC, 9, MP, S

Section 7

55. (i) is invalid; its closure has true premises and a false conclusion in a model in which the extension of 'F' is the empty class. (ii) is valid; by employing closures of the premises one can easily obtain a derivation of the conclusion.

56. (i) is valid; a derivation requires an application of EI to the premise followed by two applications of EG. (ii) is invalid; consider a model in which the extension of 'F' is {(0, 1)}.

57. (i) is valid; UI, sentential logic, and EG should provide the derivation. (ii) is invalid; consider a model in which the extension of 'F' is {(1, 0)}.

58. (i) is valid; little more than sentential logic is required to derive each of the conditionals involved. (ii) is invalid; the validity of (i) suggests that we consider a model in which the extension of 'F' is {(0, 0), (0, 1)}.

59. (i) is invalid; consider a model in which the extension of 'F' is {(0, 0), (0, 1), (1, 0)}. (ii) is also invalid; here we must consider a model with three elements in its universe and let the extension of 'F' be {(0, 0), (0, 1), (1, 1), (1, 2), (2, 0), (2, 2)}

60. (i) is invalid; here too we must consider a model with three elements in its universe, let the extension of 'F' be {(0, 1), (1, 2), (2, 0)}, and let the extension of 'A' be given by: A(0) $\mapsto$ 1; A(1) $\mapsto$ 2; A(2) $\mapsto$ 0. (ii) is also invalid; again we must consider a model with three elements in its universe and let the extension of 'F' be {(0, 1), (1, 2), (2, 0)}.

61. (i) is invalid; consider a model in which the extension of 'F' is {(0, 0), (1, 1)} and that of 'G' is {0}. (ii) is valid; for a derivation, introduce cases whose antecedents are, respectively, '$\bigwedge x$Gx' and '~$\bigwedge x$Gx' and then use SC, Form I (p. 78), or employ an indirect derivation.

62. (i) is invalid; consider a model in which the extension of 'F' is {(0, 0, 1), (0, 1, 1), (1, 0, 1), (1, 1, 1)}. (ii) is valid; standard strategies together with judicious instantiation of the 2nd premise will yield a derivation.

63. (i) is invalid; here we must consider a model with four elements in its universe and let the extension of 'F' be {(0, 1), (1, 2), (2, 3), (3, 1)}. (ii) is also invalid; here we must consider a model with five elements in its universe and let the extension of 'A' be 0, that of 'B' be 1, and that of 'F' be {(0, 2), (1, 3), (2, 3), (3, 4), (4, 2)}.

Section 8, Group I

64. On the basis of the scheme of abbreviation

U^1	:	*a* is an odd number
F^1	:	*a* is an odd number
B^1	:	the product of 2 and *a*

the premises translate into true sentences and the conclusion into a false sentence of arithmetic.

65. We cite for each part an appropriate scheme of abbreviation (omitting superscripts), in which 'U' is the predicate of relativization.

(ii) U : a is a natural number; F : the product of a and b is zero
(iii) U : a is a natural number; F : $(a \leq b \wedge [a \neq 0 \vee b \neq 2]) \vee (a = 2 \wedge b = 0)$
(iv) U : a is a natural number; F : $a < b$; A : $a + 1$
(v) U : a is a natural number; F : $b = a + 1$
(vi) U : a is a natural number; F : $a + b < c$
(vii) U : a is a natural number; A : 0; B : 1; F : $b = a + 2$

Section 8, Group II

66. We cite for each part an appropriate scheme of abbreviation (omitting superscripts), in which 'U' is the predicate of relativization.

(i) U : a is a natural number; F : $a < b$
(ii) U : a is a natural number; F : $a + 1 < b$; G : a is odd
(iii) U : a is a natural number; F : (a is even $\wedge$ b is even $\wedge$ $a < b$) $\vee$ (a is odd $\wedge$ b is odd $\wedge$ $b < a$) $\vee$ (a is odd $\wedge$ b is even)

Section 9, Group I

69. Here the required model is simple despite the complexity of the argument. The simplicity results from letting different symbols have the same extension, a technique that is frequently useful. Thus let the universe have one element; let the extension of 'F' be the universe; and let the extension of 'G' and of 'H' be the empty class. (In a model with a universe of one element, there is only one choice for the extension of any operation letter of an argument.)

Section 9, Group II

We provide symbolizations for exercises 73–77, leaving the derivations to the reader.

73. $\bigwedge x(Fx \rightarrow \bigvee y[Gy \wedge H(xy)] \wedge \bigvee y[Gy \wedge \sim H(xy)])$. $\bigvee x(Jx \wedge \bigwedge y[Gy \rightarrow H(xy)])$ $\therefore \bigvee x(Jx \wedge \sim Fx)$
74. $\bigwedge x(Fx \wedge \bigwedge y[Gy \wedge H(xy) \rightarrow J(xy)] \rightarrow \bigwedge y[Gy \wedge H(xy) \rightarrow Ky])$. $\sim \bigvee y(Ly \wedge Ky)$. $\bigvee x(Fx \wedge \bigwedge y[H(xy) \rightarrow Ly] \wedge \bigwedge y[Gy \wedge H(xy) \rightarrow J(xy)])$ $\therefore \bigvee x(Fx \wedge \sim \bigvee y[Gy \wedge H(xy)])$
75. $\bigvee x Fx$. $\bigwedge x(Fx \rightarrow \bigvee y[Gy \wedge Fy \wedge H(xy)])$ $\therefore \bigvee x(Gx \wedge Fx \wedge \bigvee y[Fy \wedge H(xy)])$
76. $\therefore \bigvee x \bigvee y F(xy) \wedge \bigwedge x[\bigvee y F(yx) \rightarrow \bigwedge y F(xy)] \rightarrow \bigwedge x \bigwedge y F(xy)]$
77. $\bigwedge x \bigwedge y[F(xy) \vee G(xy)]$ $\therefore \bigvee x \bigwedge y F(xy) \vee \bigwedge x \bigvee y G(xy)$

Section 9, Group III

We provide for each argument in this group a symbolization and an indication whether it is valid or invalid; the demonstrations of validity and invalidity are left to the reader.

78. (i) $\bigwedge x[\sim \bigvee y F(yx) \rightarrow F(Ax)]$ $\therefore \bigvee x F(xx)$ (invalid)
(ii) $\bigwedge x[\sim F(xx) \rightarrow F(Ax)]$ $\therefore \bigvee x F(xx)$ (valid)

79. (i) $\bigwedge x[\sim \bigvee y F(xy) \rightarrow F(Ax)] \quad \therefore \bigvee x F(Ax)$ (valid)
(ii) $\bigwedge x[\sim \bigvee y F(xy) \rightarrow F(Ax)] \quad \therefore F(AA)$ (invalid)
80. (i) $\bigwedge x[F(xA(x)) \rightarrow \sim F(xx)] \quad \therefore \sim \bigvee x \bigwedge y F[A(x)y]$ (valid)
(ii) $\bigwedge x[F(xA(x)) \rightarrow \sim F(xx)] \quad \therefore \sim \bigvee x F[A(x)A(x)]$ (invalid)
81. (i) $\bigwedge x[Fx \leftrightarrow \bigwedge y G(xy)] \quad \therefore \bigvee x \bigwedge y[Fy \rightarrow G(xy)]$ (valid)
(ii) $\bigwedge x[Fx \leftrightarrow \bigwedge y G(xy)] \quad \therefore \bigvee x[Fx \wedge \bigwedge y G(xy)]$ (invalid)
82. (i) $\therefore \bigvee x \bigwedge y F(xy) \rightarrow \bigvee x \bigwedge y F(yx)$ (invalid)
(ii) $\therefore \bigvee x[\bigwedge y F(xy) \rightarrow \bigwedge y F(yx)]$ (valid)

Section 9, Group IV

We provide for each argument in this group a literal symbolization and the extra premise required to obtain a valid symbolization. Demonstrations of invalidity for the initial symbolization and of validity for the supplemented symbolization are left to the reader, except in the case of exercise 89; there we provide and discuss the required model.

83. $\sim \bigvee x \bigvee y[Fx \wedge Gy \wedge H(xy)] \quad . \quad \bigwedge x(Fx \rightarrow \bigvee y[Fy \wedge H(xy)])$
$\therefore \sim \bigvee x(Fx \wedge Gx)$
Extra premise: $\bigwedge x \bigwedge y[H(xy) \rightarrow H(yx)]$ (Marriage is a symmetrical relationship.)

84. $\bigwedge x[Fx \wedge G(xx) \rightarrow H(Ax)] \wedge \bigwedge x[Fx \wedge \bigwedge y[J(yx) \rightarrow G(xy)] \rightarrow K(Ax)]$
$\therefore \bigvee x(Fx \wedge \bigwedge y[J(yx) \rightarrow G(xy)]) \rightarrow \bigvee x[Fx \wedge \sim J(xx)]$
Extra premise: $\bigwedge x \bigwedge y[H(xy) \rightarrow \sim K(xy)]$ (To like is not to detest.)

85. $\bigwedge x \bigwedge y[Fx \wedge Fy \wedge GA(xy) \rightarrow Gx \wedge Gy] \quad . \quad \bigwedge x(Fx \rightarrow [Hx \leftrightarrow \sim Gx])$
$\therefore \bigwedge x \bigwedge y[Fx \wedge Fy \wedge Hx \rightarrow HA(xy)]$
Extra premise: $\bigwedge x \bigwedge y[Fx \wedge Fy \rightarrow FA(xy)]$ (The product of integers is an integer.)

86. $\bigwedge x(Fx \rightarrow \bigwedge y[H(yx) \vee J(yx) \rightarrow Fy]) \quad \therefore \bigwedge x(\bigvee y[\sim Fy \wedge G(xy)] \rightarrow \sim Fx)$
Extra premise: $\bigwedge x \bigwedge y[G(xy) \rightarrow H(yx) \vee J(yx)]$ (One is a nephew of an uncle or aunt.)

87. $\bigwedge x(Fx \wedge \bigwedge y[Fy \wedge H(yx) \rightarrow Gy] \rightarrow Gx) \quad .$
$\bigvee x(Fx \wedge \sim Gx) \rightarrow \bigvee x(Fx \wedge \sim Gx \wedge \bigwedge y[Fy \wedge \sim Gy \rightarrow J(xy)]) \quad \therefore \bigwedge x(Fx \rightarrow Gx)$
Extra premise: $\bigwedge x \bigwedge y[Fx \wedge Fy \wedge H(xy) \rightarrow \sim J(yx)]$ (For any numbers n and k, if n is less than k, then k is not less than or equal to n.)

88. $F[D(AB)D(BC)] \quad . \quad F[D(BC)D(AC)] \quad \therefore F[D(AB)D(AC)]$
Extra premise: $\bigwedge x \bigwedge y \bigwedge z[F(xy) \wedge F(yz) \rightarrow F(xz)]$ ('Less than' refers to a transitive relation.)

89. $\bigwedge x \bigwedge y \bigwedge z F[D(xy)D(yz)] \quad . \quad \bigwedge x \bigwedge y \bigwedge z F[D(yz)D(xz)]$
$\therefore \bigwedge x \bigwedge y \bigwedge z F[D(xy)D(xz)]$
Extra premise: $\bigwedge x \bigwedge y \bigwedge z[F(xy) \wedge F(yz) \rightarrow F(xz)]$ ('Less than' refers to a transitive relation.)

To find a model in which the premises of No. 89 are true and the conclusion false, we begin with a universe of two elements, 0 and 1; then we assume the premises to be true and instantiate 'x', 'y', and 'z' to numerals that will make the conclusion false. Given our assumption, the latter cannot be done if 'x' and 'y' are instantiated to the same numeral, for in that case the instance of the conclusion follows from the first premise; similarly, considering the second premise, 'y' and 'z' cannot be instantiated to the same numeral. Thus we instantiate the variables to the numerals '0', '1', and '0', respectively, and construct (in part) our model so that the sentence

(1) $$F[D(0, 1)D(0, 0)]$$

is false (in the model). In order to do so and to maintain the truth of the first premise, the two terms in (1) must have different values. Thus we let

(2) $$D(0, 0) \mapsto 0 \quad ; \qquad D(0, 1) \mapsto 1 \quad ;$$

and we omit the couple (1, 0) from the extension of 'F', thereby making

(3) $$F(1, 0)$$

false (in the model under construction). If the universe of the model contained no elements other than 0 and 1, we must have either

(4) $$D(1, 0) \mapsto 1$$

or

(5) $$D(1, 0) \mapsto 0 \quad .$$

Both of these assignments are precluded by the first premise, for that premise implies both

$$F[D(1, 0)D(0, 0)]$$

and

$$F[D(0, 1)D(1, 0)] \quad ,$$

the first of which is equivalent to the false sentence (3) given (2) and (4), and the second of which is equivalent to the false sentence (3) given (2) and (5). Thus we must enter into the universe of the model (under construction) a third element, say 2, and let the function that is the extension of 'D' correlate 2 with each ordered couple of elements of the universe {0, 1, 2} except the couples (0, 0) and (0, 1). Further, we enter into the extension of 'F' all ordered couples of elements of {0, 1, 2} except the couple (1, 0). Since (1) cannot be reached by any instantiation of either of the premises but can be reached by an instantiation of the conclusion, the premises of No. 89 are true and the conclusion false in the model we have constructed stepwise.

Chapter V

'IS' (in one sense)

1. Terms and formulas. Not all intuitively valid arguments can be reached by the symbolic procedures of chapters I–IV. For example, the argument

(1) Mark Twain is identical with Samuel Clemens. Samuel Clemens wrote *Tom Sawyer*. ∴ Mark Twain wrote *Tom Sawyer* ,

unlike those discussed in the preceding chapters, depends for its validity on the meaning of the phrase 'is identical with'. We understand a sentence of English formed by flanking 'is identical with' by names to be true just in case those names designate the same object. Thus the sentences

Socrates is identical with Socrates
Scott is identical with the author of *Waverley* ,

like the first premise of (1), are true, whereas

Socrates is identical with the author of *Waverley*
Aristotle is the snub-nosed teacher of Plato

are false.

We shall abbreviate 'is identical with' by the familiar sign '=', and refer to that symbol as the *identity sign*. Thus, given the scheme of abbreviation

A^0 : Mark Twain
B^0 : Samuel Clemens ,

the first premise of (1) can be symbolized by

$$A = B \quad .$$

The *symbolic language* with which we shall deal now is that of chapter IV (see pp. 203–4), with '=' added to its symbols. We obtain no new *symbolic terms*; they are just the terms characterized by clauses (i) and (ii) of page 204. But we do enrich the class of *symbolic formulas*, for we now admit as symbolic formulas the result of flanking '=' by symbolic terms; thus expressions such as

$$x = y$$
$$A^0 = B^1x$$

will be counted among the symbolic formulas of our language. To be completely explicit, the class of *symbolic formulas* is exhaustively characterized as follows:

(1) *If* π *is a k-place predicate letter and* $\zeta_1, \ldots, \zeta_k$ *are symbolic terms, then*

$$\pi\zeta_1 \ldots \zeta_k$$

is a symbolic formula. (In particular, a 0-place predicate letter is itself a symbolic formula.)

(2) *If* ϕ *and* ψ *are symbolic formulas, so are*

$$\begin{gathered} \sim\phi \\ (\phi \rightarrow \psi) \quad , \\ (\phi \wedge \psi) \quad , \\ (\phi \vee \psi) \quad , \\ (\phi \leftrightarrow \psi) \quad . \end{gathered}$$

(3) *If* ϕ *is a symbolic formula and* α *a variable, then*

$$\begin{gathered} \bigwedge\alpha\phi \quad , \\ \bigvee\alpha\phi \end{gathered}$$

are symbolic formulas.

(4) *If* ζ *and* η *are symbolic terms, then*

$$\zeta = \eta$$

is a symbolic formula.

Formulas obtained by clause (1) or by clause (4) are *atomic formulas* (for neither a quantifier nor a sentential connective occurs in them); and we shall also refer to formulas obtained by clause (4) as *identity formulas.* We shall continue to use the informal notational conventions introduced in section 3 of chapter IV. In addition we shall adopt the convention of writing the negation of an identity formula

$$\zeta \neq \eta$$

rather than

$$\sim\zeta = \eta \quad .$$

Again we emphasize that official notation must be mentally restored before decisions concerning bondage and freedom and applications of inference rules can be made.

2. Translation and symbolization. An *abbreviation* and a *scheme of abbreviation* are to be understood in the same way as in the preceding chapter (p. 209). And *literal translation into English on the basis of a given* *scheme of abbreviation* is to be handled as in that chapter, section 4, with one modification. In step (v) (p. 210), we replace '=' by 'is identical with', in addition to eliminating sentential connectives and quantifier phrases in favor of the corresponding phrases of connection and quantity.

As before, we say that an English formula ψ is a *free translation* (or simply a *translation*) of a symbolic formula ϕ (or that ϕ is a *symbolization* of ψ) on the basis of a given scheme of abbreviation if ψ is a stylistic variant of the literal English translation of ϕ based on that scheme.

For example, consider the scheme of abbreviation

(1) A^0 : Mark Twain
B^0 : Samuel Clemens

and the symbolic sentence

(2) $A = B$.

The literal English translation of (2) on the basis of the scheme (1) is

(3) Mark Twain is identical with Samuel Clemens ,

and a free translation of (2) would be

(4) Mark Twain is Samuel Clemens .

Thus we regard (4) as a stylistic variant of (3). 'Is' does not, however, always have the sense of *identity*. In some contexts, for example,

(5) Socrates is wise ,

'is' has the sense of *predication*. (5) is true just in case Socrates has the characteristic, possibly common to many individuals, of wisdom; it is not asserted that the words 'Socrates' and 'wise' designate the same object (or even that 'wise' designates any object), as the sense of identity would require.

The logic of predication can best be regarded as part of the theory developed in chapters III and IV. The present chapter concerns the logic of identity.

Sentence (3) has other stylistic variants than (4); for example,

Mark Twain is the same as Samuel Clemens ,
Mark Twain and Samuel Clemens are the same ,
Mark Twain and Samuel Clemens are identical ,
Mark Twain equals Samuel Clemens .

The negation of (2) has free translations other than those suggested by the free translations of (2). For example,

Mark Twain differs from Samuel Clemens ,
Mark Twain is distinct from Samuel Clemens ,

and

Mark Twain is other than Samuel Clemens

are all free translations of

$$A \neq B \quad ,$$

or, in official notation, of

$$\sim A = B \quad ,$$

on the basis of the scheme (1).

To find a symbolization of a given formula of English on the basis of a given scheme of abbreviation, the reader will find it useful to proceed roughly as follows:

(*1*) *Introduce 'is identical with', phrases of quantity, and phrases of connection, the latter accompanied by parentheses and occurring canonically, in the place of their stylistic variants.*

(*2*) *Reverse the steps leading from a symbolic formula to a literal English translation.*

For example, consider the scheme of abbreviation

F^2 : *a* is married to *b*
G^1 : *a* is a monogamous citizen
A^1 : the spouse of *a*

and the sentence

Anyone married to a monogamous citizen is the spouse of such a citizen

In step (1) we obtain

For each *x* (if there is an object *y* such that (*x* is married to *y* and *y* is a monogamous citizen), then there is an object *y* such that (*y* is a monogamous citizen and *x* is identical with the spouse of *y*)) ;

and carrying through the successive parts of step (2), we obtain the symbolization

$$\bigwedge x(\bigvee y[F(xy) \wedge Gy] \rightarrow \bigvee y[Gy \wedge x = A(y)]) \quad .$$

As another example, consider the scheme of abbreviation

F^2 : *a* is a member of *b*
G^2 : *a* has defeated *b*
A^0 : the team
B^1 : the captain of *a*

and the sentence

> The captain of the team has defeated every other member of the team .

The symbolization in this case is

$$F(B(A)A) \wedge \bigwedge x[F(xA) \wedge x \neq B(A) \rightarrow G(B(A)x)] \quad .$$

Closely related to the preceding example is the symbolization of superlatives. On the basis of the scheme of abbreviation

F^2 : *a* is a member of *b*
G^2 : *a* is taller than *b*
A^0 : the team
B^1 : the captain of *a* ,

the sentence

> The captain of the team is the tallest member of the team

is symbolized by

$$F(B(A)A) \wedge \bigwedge x[F(xA) \wedge x \neq B(A) \rightarrow G(B(A)x)] \quad .$$

Frequently in English sentences, the definite article 'the' indicates the identity sense of 'is', which we symbolize by '=', whereas the indefinite article indicates the so-called predication sense of 'is', which we symbolize simply by juxtaposition of predicate letters and symbolic terms. The following sentence is an example.

> If Alice is polyandrous and married to Alfred, then Alfred *is a* husband of Alice but it is not the case that he *is the* only husband of Alice .

On the basis of the scheme of abbreviation

F^1 : *a* is polyandrous
G^2 : *a* is married to *b*
H^2 : *a* is a husband of *b*
A^0 : Alice
B^0 : Alfred

the sentence is symbolized by

$$FA \wedge G(AB) \rightarrow H(BA) \wedge \sim \bigwedge x[H(xA) \rightarrow x = B] \quad .$$

EXERCISES, GROUP I

1. For each sentence of group A, find the sentence of group B that is a symbolization of it.

GROUP A

(1) Something differs from everything except itself.
(2) Everything is identical with something.
(3) Everything is distinct from something.
(4) Everything equal to a thing differs from everything not equal to that thing.
(5) Nothing differs from everything.
(6) Things equal to the same thing are equal to each other.
(7) Nothing differs from itself.

GROUP B

(a) $\sim \bigvee x \bigwedge y \; x \neq y$
(b) $\bigwedge x \bigvee y \; x = y$
(c) $\bigvee x \bigwedge y(y \neq x \rightarrow x \neq y)$
(d) $\bigwedge x \bigwedge y(\bigvee z[x = z \wedge y = z] \rightarrow x = y)$
(e) $\bigwedge x \bigvee y \; y \neq x$
(f) $\sim \bigvee x \; x \neq x$
(g) $\bigwedge x \bigwedge z[x = z \rightarrow \bigwedge y(y \neq z \rightarrow x \neq y)]$

EXERCISES, GROUP II

Symbolize each of the following sentences on the basis of the scheme of abbreviation that accompanies it. Exercises 2 and 3 are solved for illustration.

2. None but Alfred and his teacher are able to solve the problem. (F^2 : *a* is able to solve *b*; A^0 : Alfred; B^0 : the problem; C^1 : the teacher of *a*)

Two interpretations of No. 2 are acceptable. One interpretation would leave open the question whether Alfred and his teacher are able to solve the problem, and the other would answer that question in the affirmative. On the former interpretation, No. 2 passes into

$$\bigwedge x[F(xB) \rightarrow x = A \vee x = C(A)] \quad ;$$

on the latter, it passes into

$$\bigwedge x[F(xB) \leftrightarrow x = A \vee x = C(A)] \quad .$$

3. Alfred attended the conference and arrived at it before everyone else who attended it except Mary. (F^2 : *a* attended *b*; G^3 : *a* arrived at *b* before *c*; A^0 : Alfred; B^0 : the conference; C^0 : Mary)

Here the word 'else' emphasizes our implicit understanding of 'arrives at before', that is, that Alfred did not arrive at the conference before Alfred. And again both a weaker and a stronger interpretation are acceptable; thus No. 3 could pass into either

$$F(AB) \wedge F(CB) \wedge \bigwedge x[F(xB) \wedge x \neq A \wedge x \neq C \rightarrow G(ABx)]$$

or

$$F(AB) \wedge F(CB) \wedge \bigwedge x(F(xB) \rightarrow [x \neq A \wedge x \neq C \leftrightarrow G(ABx)]) \quad .$$

Note that

$$\bigwedge x[\mathrm{F}(x\mathrm{B}) \wedge \mathrm{G}(x\mathrm{BA}) \rightarrow x = \mathrm{C}]$$

could not replace the third conjunct in the symbolization of No. 3. On the given scheme, it symbolizes

> If anyone who attended the conference arrived there before Alfred, it was Mary .

And this last sentence, in contrast to No. 3, would be true if everyone who attended the conference arrived at the same time.

4. Alfred is the only member of the class who can read Greek. (F^2 : *a* is a member of *b*; G^2 : *a* can read *b*; A^0 : Alfred; B^0 : the class; C^0 : Greek)

5. Greensleeves can jump farther than any other frog in Calaveras County. (F^2 : *a* can jump farther than *b*; G^1 : *a* is a frog; H^2 : *a* is in *b*; A^0 : Greensleeves; B^0 : Calaveras County)

6. Pergolesi was the most promising composer of his time. (A^0 : Pergolesi; F^2 : *a* was more promising than *b*; G^1 : *a* is a composer; H^2 : *a* was contemporary with *b*)

7. Anyone whose mother is the wife of a citizen, whose father is married to his or her mother, and whose father has no other children is the child of a citizen. (F^1 : *a* is a citizen; G^2 : *a* is married to *b*; H^2 : *a* is a child of *b*; A^1 : the mother of *a*; B^1 : the wife of *a*; C^1 : the father of *a*; D^1 : the child of *a*)

8. If the sister of Alfred is the wife of the brother-in-law of Alfred, then the father-in-law of Alfred is the father-in-law of the sister of Alfred. (A^0 : Alfred; B^1 : the wife of *a*; C^1 : the sister of *a*; D^1 : the brother-in-law of *a*; E^1 : the father-in-law of *a*)

9. If a sister of Alfred is the wife of a brother-in-law of Alfred, then the father-in-law of Alfred is the father-in-law of a sister of Alfred. (A^0 : Alfred; B^1 : the wife of *a*; C^1 : the father-in-law of *a*; F^2 : *a* is a sister of *b*; G^2 : *a* is a brother-in-law of *b*)

10. If a sister of Alfred is the wife of a brother-in-law of Alfred, then the father-in-law of Alfred is the father-in-law of that sister of Alfred. (A^0 : Alfred; B^1 : the wife of *a*; C^1 : the father-in-law of *a*; F^2 : *a* is a sister of *b*; G^2 : *a* is a brother-in-law of *b*)

11. Brothers and sisters I have none, but that man's father is my father's son. (A^0 : the speaker; B^0 : that man; C^1 : the father of *a*; D^1 : the son of *a*; F^2 : *a* is a brother of *b*; G^2 : *a* is a sister of *b*)

12. The product of distinct positive integers **is** less than their sum if and only if one of them is equal to its square. (A^2 : the product of *a* and *b*; B^2 : the sum of *a* and *b*; C^1 : the square of *a*; F^1 : *a* is a positive integer; G^2 : *a* is less than *b*)

3. Inference rules. Notions of bondage and freedom, as well as the notion of proper substitution of a term for a variable, are to be understood here as in chapter IV (see pp. 206 and 219). For the logic of identity, two inference rules must be added to those already at our disposal. The first of these is essentially Leibniz' principle of the *indiscernibility of identicals* (the converse of his better-known philosophical principle of the identity of indiscernibles). One formulation of the principle is the assertion that if two things are identical, then anything true of one is also true of the other; we understand this principle to assert that if two names designate the same object, then replacement of one by the other in any sentence cannot change the truth value of that sentence. Thus our first new rule leads from two symbolic formulas

$$\zeta = \eta$$
$$\phi_\zeta$$

to a symbolic formula

$$\phi_\eta \quad ,$$

where ζ and η are symbolic terms and ϕ_η is like ϕ_ζ except for having *one or more free* occurrences of η where ϕ_ζ has *free* occurrences of ζ. (Here, as with our sentential inference rules, the order in which the two premise formulas are listed is irrelevant.) Diagrammatically the rule presents the following appearance:

$$\frac{\begin{array}{c}\zeta = \eta \\ \phi_\zeta\end{array}}{\phi_\eta} \quad ,$$

where ζ, η, ϕ_ζ, and ϕ_η are as above. We shall refer to this pattern of inference as *Leibniz' law* and adopt for it the annotation 'LL'.

The rule LL permits the inference from 'A = B' and 'FA' to 'FB', thereby accounting for the intuitive validity of argument (1) of section 1. It also permits an inference from 'A = B' and 'F(AA)' to each of 'F(AB)', 'F(BA)', and 'F(BB)', for it permits replacement of *one or more* occurrences of a term. But it does not permit an inference from 'A(*x*) = B(*x*)' and '⋁*x*FA(*x*)' to '⋁*x*FB(*x*)', for it requires (in order to prevent fallacies) that occurrences of the term replaced and occurrences of the term replacing it be *free* occurrences. (The invalidity of an argument involving such a replacement of bound occurrences is established in section 5.)

Our second rule of inference reflects Aristotle's assertion that each thing is what it is and is nothing else. It differs from our preceding rules in that it has no premise; thus it appears diagrammatically

$$\frac{}{\zeta = \zeta} \quad ,$$

where ζ is any symbolic term. In effect, this rule—the so-called *principle of identity*—permits one to enter the formula

$$\zeta = \zeta \quad ,$$

where ζ is any symbolic term, as a line in a derivation in the same manner in which one enters premises. We shall use 'Id' as an annotation for such a line.

The principle of identity is commonly taken to assert the *reflexivity* of the identity relation. The identity relation is also *symmetric*, that is, where ζ and η are symbolic terms, from the formula

$$\zeta = \eta$$

one can infer the formula

$$\eta = \zeta \quad .$$

A corresponding inference rule can be derived by means of LL and Id, and thus we need not take such a rule as primitive. Given a derivation in which

(7) $$\zeta = \eta$$

occurs as a line, one may add to that derivation by Id the line

(8) $$\zeta = \zeta \quad ;$$

and from (7) and (8) by LL one can infer the line

$$\eta = \zeta \quad .$$

Thus we adopt for the logic of identity a third, but derived, rule of inference, that given diagrammatically by the pattern

$$\frac{\zeta = \eta}{\eta = \zeta} \quad ,$$

where ζ and η are symbolic terms. We shall refer to this pattern of inference as *symmetry* and adopt for it the annotation 'Sm'.

With the aid of a subsidiary indirect derivation, patterns of inference closely related to Sm and LL can be justified. Where again ζ and η are symbolic terms, from the formula

(9) $$\zeta \neq \eta$$

one can obtain the formula

$$\eta \neq \zeta$$

by means of a simple indirect derivation in which Sm is employed. Consider

~~*Show*~~ $\eta \neq \zeta$	
$\eta = \zeta$	Assumption
$\zeta = \eta$	From assumption by Sm
$\zeta \neq \eta$	From (9) by R

Rather than impose this trivial work frequently, we adopt as a further derived rule the pattern

$$\frac{\zeta \neq \eta}{\eta \neq \zeta} \ ,$$

where ζ and η are symbolic terms, and refer to it also by 'Sm'. Thus, for simple illustrations, we can infer 'B = A' from 'A = B', and infer 'B ≠ A' from 'A ≠ B', by Sm.

There are three derived rules of inference corresponding to LL. Let ζ and η be symbolic terms and ϕ_η be a symbolic formula like ϕ_ζ except for having one or more free occurrences of η where ϕ_ζ has free occurrences of ζ. Then the first of these three derived inference rules has the form

$$\frac{\begin{array}{c}\eta = \zeta \\ \phi_\zeta\end{array}}{\phi_\eta} \ .$$

This form is an immediate corollary of LL and Sm. A subsidiary derivation is needed to justify an application of either of the other two forms,

$$\frac{\begin{array}{c}\sim\phi_\zeta \\ \phi_\eta\end{array}}{\zeta \neq \eta} \qquad \frac{\begin{array}{c}\phi_\zeta \\ \sim\phi_\eta\end{array}}{\zeta \neq \eta} \ .$$

We indicate the required steps for one of them. Given as lines of a derivation

(10)	$\sim\phi_\zeta$
(11)	ϕ_η

enter into the derivation the subsidiary derivation

~~*Show*~~ $\zeta \neq \eta$

$\zeta = \eta$	Assumption
$\sim\phi_\eta$	From assumption and (10) by LL
ϕ_η	From (11) by R

We shall employ the annotation 'LL' for each of these derived forms. Examples of inferences that fall under these forms are:

$$\frac{\begin{array}{c}\text{B} = \text{A} \\ \text{FA}\end{array}}{\text{FB}} \qquad \frac{\begin{array}{c}\sim\text{FA} \\ \text{FB}\end{array}}{\text{A} \neq \text{B}} \qquad \frac{\begin{array}{c}\text{FA} \\ \sim\text{FB}\end{array}}{\text{A} \neq \text{B}}$$

The identity relation is also *transitive*; that is, from the two formulas

$$\begin{array}{c}\eta = \zeta \\ \zeta = \theta\end{array} \ ,$$

where ζ, η, and θ are symbolic terms, one can infer the formula

$$\eta = \theta \quad .$$

No special annotation is needed for this familiar inference (things equal to the same thing are equal to each other), for it is simply a special case of the first of the three derived forms of LL above.

One other derived form of identity inference is of historical interest and has some utility; it is known as *Euclid's law*, for it covers such familiar principles as 'equals added to equals are equal'. Diagrammatically, it appears:

$$\frac{\zeta = \eta}{\delta_\zeta = \delta_\eta} \quad .$$

Here ζ and η are symbolic terms and δ_η is a symbolic term like the symbolic term δ_ζ except for having one or more occurrences of η where δ_ζ has occurrences of ζ. Euclid's law, for which the annotation will be 'EL', is an immediate corollary of Id and LL. Let ζ, η, δ_ζ, and δ_η be as above. Then, given the formula

(12) $$\zeta = \eta$$

as a line in a derivation, enter as a line in that derivation by Id the formula

(13) $$\delta_\zeta = \delta_\zeta \quad .$$

The formula

$$\delta_\zeta = \delta_\eta$$

follows from (12) and (13) by LL. For a simple illustration, we can infer 'C(A) = C(B)' from 'A = B' by EL. Note, however, in contrast to the principle of symmetry, where premise and conclusion can be negations as well as affirmations, that we cannot infer 'C(A) ≠ C(B)' from 'A ≠ B' by EL; indeed, the invalidity of such an inference is established in section 5 (see exercise 45).

In summary, then, for the logic of identity we add to our previous stock of rules the following forms of inference.

Principle of Identity (Id):

$$\frac{}{\zeta = \zeta} \quad ,$$

where ζ is a symbolic term.

Principle of symmetry (Sm), in two forms:

$$\frac{\zeta = \eta}{\eta = \zeta} \qquad \frac{\zeta \neq \eta}{\eta \neq \zeta} \quad ,$$

where ζ and η are symbolic terms.

Leibniz' law (LL), in four forms:

$$\frac{\begin{matrix}\zeta = \eta \\ \phi\zeta\end{matrix}}{\phi\eta} \qquad \frac{\begin{matrix}\eta = \zeta \\ \phi\zeta\end{matrix}}{\phi\eta} \qquad \frac{\begin{matrix}\sim\phi\zeta \\ \phi\eta\end{matrix}}{\zeta \neq \eta} \qquad \frac{\begin{matrix}\phi\zeta \\ \sim\phi\eta\end{matrix}}{\zeta \neq \eta}\ ,$$

where ζ and η are symbolic terms and $\phi\eta$ is a symbolic formula like the symbolic formula $\phi\zeta$ except for having one or more free occurrences of η where $\phi\zeta$ has free occurrences of ζ.

Euclid's law (EL):

$$\frac{\zeta = \eta}{\delta\zeta = \delta\eta}\ ,$$

where ζ and η are symbolic terms and $\delta\eta$ is a symbolic term like the symbolic term $\delta\zeta$ except for having one or more occurrences of η where $\delta\zeta$ has occurrences of ζ.

We call that branch of logic which essentially involves the identity sign, as well as quantifiers and sentential connectives, the *identity calculus*. The directions for constructing, within this calculus, a derivation from given symbolic premises continue to be those initially set forth in chapter III (see clauses (1)–(6) on pp. 144–45, the revised form of clause (2) on p. 220, and clauses (7)–(9) on pp. 150–51), with the understanding that Id, Sm, LL, and EL are now to be included among the inference rules of clause (5a). Of course, we now understand by 'UI' and 'EG' the inference rules characterized in chapter IV (see p. 219), and throughout these clauses we give to the term 'formula' its broader sense of the present chapter.

The characterizations of a *complete* derivation, *derivability*, a *proof*, a *theorem*, an *argument*, a *symbolic argument*, a *valid symbolic argument*, an *English argument*, a *symbolization* of an English argument, and a *valid English argument* remain as before (see pp. 145 and 153–54).

EXERCISES

13. Which of the following inference patterns can be justified by LL?

(i) $$\frac{\begin{matrix}\sim \bigvee z G(xzx) \\ \bigvee z G(yzx)\end{matrix}}{x \neq y}$$

(ii) $$\frac{\begin{matrix}\bigvee z G(xzx) \\ y = x\end{matrix}}{\bigvee z G(yzy)}$$

(iii) $$\frac{\begin{matrix}\bigvee x F(xy) \\ y = x\end{matrix}}{\bigvee x F(xx)}$$

(iv) $$\frac{\begin{matrix}\bigvee x F(xy) \\ x = y\end{matrix}}{\bigvee x F(yy)}$$

(v) $$\frac{\begin{matrix}\bigvee z F(zB[A(x)]) \\ \sim \bigvee z F(zB[B(y)])\end{matrix}}{A(x) \neq B(y)}$$

(vi) $$\frac{\begin{matrix}\bigvee y F(yB[A(x)]) \\ A(x) = B(y)\end{matrix}}{\bigvee y F(yB[B(y)])}$$

14. Which of the following inference patterns can be justified by either Sm or EL?

(i) $\dfrac{A(x) = B(y)}{B(y) = A(x)}$ (ii) $\dfrac{A(x) \neq B(y)}{B(y) \neq A(x)}$

(iii) $\dfrac{A(x) = B(y)}{A[A(x)] = A[B(y)]}$ (iv) $\dfrac{A(x) \neq B(x)}{C[A(x)] \neq C[B(x)]}$

(v) $\dfrac{\bigvee x\, A(x) = B(x)}{C[A(x)] = C[B(x)]}$ (vi) $\dfrac{A(x) = B(x)}{C[A(x)B(x)] = C[B(x)B(x)]}$

4. Theorems. We assign to the theorems of the identity calculus numbers beginning with 301. Theorems 301, 302, and 303 are the respective laws of *reflexivity*, *symmetry*, and *transitivity* of identity; they are immediate consequences of our new rules of inference.

T301 $x = x$
T302 $x = y \leftrightarrow y = x$
T303 $x = y \wedge y = z \rightarrow x = z$

Analogues to LL and EL are also immediately forthcoming as theorems:

T304 $x = y \rightarrow (Fx \leftrightarrow Fy)$
T305 $x = y \rightarrow A(x) = A(y)$

If Socrates is wise, then everything identical with him is wise and something identical with him is wise. These platitudes are covered by the following two important theorems.

T306 $Fx \leftrightarrow \bigwedge y(y = x \rightarrow Fy)$
T307 $Fx \leftrightarrow \bigvee y(y = x \wedge Fy)$

T308 and T309 are special cases, and T310 and T311 are two-variable analogues, of T306 and T307, respectively; T312 is a useful sentential corollary of T302; T313 and T314 are useful sentential corollaries of T304.

T308 $x = y \leftrightarrow \bigwedge z(z = x \rightarrow z = y)$
T309 $x = y \leftrightarrow \bigvee z(z = x \wedge z = y)$
T310 $F(xy) \leftrightarrow \bigwedge z \bigwedge w[z = x \wedge w = y \rightarrow F(zw)]$
T311 $F(xy) \leftrightarrow \bigvee z \bigvee w[z = x \wedge w = y \wedge F(zw)]$
T312 $x \neq y \leftrightarrow y \neq x$
T313 $Fx \wedge x = y \leftrightarrow Fy \wedge x = y$
T314 $Fx \vee x \neq y \leftrightarrow Fy \vee x \neq y$

Some English sentences have plausible symbolizations with the identity sign and also without the identity sign. For example, on the basis of the scheme of abbreviation

$$\begin{array}{ll} F^1 : & a \text{ is a citizen} \\ A^1 : & \text{the spouse of } a \quad , \end{array}$$

the sentence 'Anyone who is the spouse of a citizen is also a citizen' passes plausibly into

$$\bigwedge x(\bigvee y[Fy \wedge x = A(y)] \rightarrow Fx)$$

and also into

$$\bigwedge x[Fx \rightarrow FA(x)] \quad .$$

The following theorem establishes the equivalence of these two symbolizations.

T315

1. ~~*Show*~~ $\bigwedge x(\bigvee y[Fy \wedge x = A(y)] \rightarrow Fx) \leftrightarrow \bigwedge x[Fx \rightarrow FA(x)]$
2. ~~*Show*~~ $\bigwedge x(\bigvee y[Fy \wedge x = A(y)] \rightarrow Fx) \rightarrow \bigwedge x[Fx \rightarrow FA(x)]$
3. $\bigwedge x(\bigvee y[Fy \wedge x = A(y)] \rightarrow Fx)$
4. ~~*Show*~~ $\bigwedge x[Fx \rightarrow FA(x)]$
5. ~~*Show*~~ $Fx \rightarrow FA(x)$
6. Fx
7. $A(x) = A(x)$ — Id
8. $\bigvee y[Fy \wedge A(x) = A(y)]$ — 6, 7, Adj, EG
9. $FA(x)$ — 3, UI, 8, MP
10. ~~*Show*~~ $\bigwedge x[Fx \rightarrow FA(x)] \rightarrow \bigwedge x(\bigvee y[Fy \wedge x = A(y)] \rightarrow Fx)$
11. $\bigwedge x[Fx \rightarrow FA(x)]$
12. ~~*Show*~~ $\bigwedge x(\bigvee y[Fy \wedge x = A(y)] \rightarrow Fx)$
13. ~~*Show*~~ $\bigvee y[Fy \wedge x = A(y)] \rightarrow Fx$
14. $\bigvee y[Fy \wedge x = A(y)]$
15. $Fa \wedge x = A(a)$ — 14, EI
16. $FA(a)$ — 11, UI, 15, S, MP
17. Fx — 15, S, 16, LL
18. $\bigwedge x(\bigvee y[Fy \wedge x = A(y)] \rightarrow Fx) \leftrightarrow \bigwedge x[Fx \rightarrow FA(x)]$ — 2, 10, CB

The addition of the identity sign to our symbolism enables us to express numerical conditions symbolically. For example, if we let 'F^1' abbreviate '*a* is god', then

(1) $$\bigvee x Fx$$

asserts that there is at least one god, and

(2) $$\bigwedge x \bigwedge y(Fx \wedge Fy \rightarrow x = y)$$

that there is at most one god; hence the conjunction of (1) and (2) expresses the doctrine of monotheism. The position that there are at least two gods is expressed by

(3) $$\bigvee x \bigvee y(Fx \wedge Fy \wedge x \neq y) \quad ,$$

and that there are no more than two by

(4) $$\bigwedge x \bigwedge y \bigwedge z(Fx \wedge Fy \wedge Fz \rightarrow x = y \vee x = z \vee y = z) \quad .$$

The conjunction of (3) and (4) asserts that there are exactly two gods. In this way we can assert the existence of exactly three gods, exactly four gods, exactly as many gods as we may wish to countenance. And what has been illustrated by reference to gods holds equally well for apostles, apples, Africans—any finite collection the number of whose members we wish to specify.

The fact that exactly one thing satisfies a given condition can be expressed in a variety of ways, some of them, like the right-hand constituents of T316 and T317, shorter than the conjunction of (1) and (2). T318 and T319 provide similar alternatives to the conjunction of (3) and (4).

T316 $$\bigvee x Fx \wedge \bigwedge x \bigwedge y(Fx \wedge Fy \rightarrow x = y) \leftrightarrow \bigvee x(Fx \wedge \bigwedge y[Fy \rightarrow x = y])$$

T317 $$\bigvee x Fx \wedge \bigwedge x \bigwedge y(Fx \wedge Fy \rightarrow x = y) \leftrightarrow \bigvee y \bigwedge x(Fx \leftrightarrow x = y)$$

T318 $$\begin{aligned}&\bigvee x \bigvee y(Fx \wedge Fy \wedge x \neq y) \wedge \\ &\quad \bigwedge x \bigwedge y \bigwedge z(Fx \wedge Fy \wedge Fz \rightarrow x = y \vee x = z \vee y = z) \leftrightarrow \\ &\quad \bigvee x \bigvee y(Fx \wedge Fy \wedge x \neq y \wedge \bigwedge z[Fz \rightarrow x = z \vee y = z])\end{aligned}$$

T319 $$\begin{aligned}&\bigvee x \bigvee y(Fx \wedge Fy \wedge x \neq y) \wedge \\ &\quad \bigwedge x \bigwedge y \bigwedge z(Fx \wedge Fy \wedge Fz \rightarrow x = y \vee x = z \vee y = z) \leftrightarrow \\ &\quad \bigvee x \bigvee y(x \neq y \wedge \bigwedge z[Fz \leftrightarrow x = z \vee y = z])\end{aligned}$$

We have identified above the conjuncts of the left-hand constituent of T319; we now identify its right-hand constituent,

(5) $$\bigvee x \bigvee y(x \neq y \wedge \bigwedge z[Fz \leftrightarrow x = z \vee y = z]) \quad ,$$

and employ identifying numerals in place of formulas in some lines of the following proof of that theorem.

T319

1. ~~*Show*~~ (3) ∧ (4) ↔ (5)
2. ~~*Show*~~ (3) ∧ (4) → (5)
3. (3) ∧ (4)
4. $\bigvee x \bigvee y(Fx \wedge Fy \wedge x \neq y)$ — 3, S
5. $\bigvee y(Fa \wedge Fy \wedge a \neq y)$ — 4, EI
6. $Fa \wedge Fb \wedge a \neq b$ — 5, EI
7. $\bigwedge x \bigwedge y \bigwedge z(Fx \wedge Fy \wedge Fz \rightarrow x = y \vee x = z \vee y = z)$ — 3, S
8. ~~*Show*~~ $\bigwedge z[Fz \leftrightarrow a = z \vee b = z]$
9. ~~*Show*~~ $Fz \rightarrow a = z \vee b = z$
10. Fz
11. $a = b \vee a = z \vee b = z$ — 7, UI, UI, UI, 6, S, 10, Adj, MP
12. $a = z \vee b = z$ — 6, S, 11, T54, BC, MP, MTP
13. ~~*Show*~~ $a = z \rightarrow Fz$
14. $a = z$
15. Fz — 6, S, S, 14, LL
16. ~~*Show*~~ $b = z \rightarrow Fz$
17. $b = z$
18. Fz — 6, S, S, 17, LL
19. $Fz \leftrightarrow a = z \vee b = z$ — 13, 16, SC, 9, CB
20. $\bigvee x \bigvee y(x \neq y \wedge \bigwedge z[Fz \leftrightarrow x = z \vee y = z])$ — 6, S, 8, Adj, EG, EG
21. ~~*Show*~~ (5) → (3) ∧ (4)
22. $\bigvee x \bigvee y(x \neq y \wedge \bigwedge z[Fz \leftrightarrow x = z \vee y = z])$
23. $\bigvee y(c \neq y \wedge \bigwedge z[Fz \leftrightarrow c = z \vee y = z])$ — 22, EI
24. $c \neq d \wedge \bigwedge z[Fz \leftrightarrow c = z \vee d = z]$ — 23, EI
25. $c = c$ — Id
26. Fc — 24, S, UI, BC, 25, Add, MP
27. $d = d$ — Id
28. Fd — 24, S, UI, BC, 27, Add, MP
29. $\bigvee x \bigvee y(Fx \wedge Fy \wedge x \neq y)$ — 26, 28, Adj, 24, S, Adj, EG, EG

30.	~~Show~~ $\bigwedge x \bigwedge y \bigwedge z(Fx \wedge Fy \wedge Fz \rightarrow x = y \vee x = z \vee y = z)$	
31.	~~Show~~ $Fx \wedge Fy \wedge Fz \rightarrow x = y \vee x = z \vee y = z$	
32.	$Fx \wedge Fy \wedge Fz$	
33.	~~Show~~ $\sim(x = y \vee x = z) \rightarrow y = z$	
34.	$\sim(x = y \vee x = z)$	
35.	$x \neq y \wedge x \neq z$	T66, BC, MP, 34, MP
36.	$c = x \vee d = x$	24, S, UI, BC, 32, S, S, MP
37.	$c = y \vee d = y$	24, S, UI, BC, 32, S, S, MP
38.	$c = z \vee d = z$	24, S, UI, BC, 32, S, MP
39.	~~Show~~ $c = x \rightarrow y = z$	
40.	$c = x$	
41.	$c \neq y$	35, S, 40, LL
42.	$c \neq z$	35, S, 40, LL
43.	$d = y$	41, 37, MTP
44.	$d = z$	42, 38, MTP
45.	$y = z$	43, 44, LL
46.	~~Show~~ $d = x \rightarrow y = z$	Similar to derivation of line 39
47.	$y = z$	36, 39, 46, SC
48.	$x = y \vee x = z \vee y = z$	33, CD
49.	$(3) \wedge (4)$	29, 30, Adj
50.	$(3) \wedge (4) \leftrightarrow (5)$	2, 21, CB

To deny that exactly one thing satisfies a given condition is to assert that either nothing or at least two things satisfy that condition; and to deny that exactly two things satisfy a given condition is to assert that either at most one or at least three things satisfy that condition. These facts are expressed, respectively, in T320 and T321.

T320 $\sim \bigvee y \bigwedge x(Fx \leftrightarrow x = y) \leftrightarrow \sim \bigvee x Fx \vee \bigvee x \bigvee y(x \neq y \wedge Fx \wedge Fy)$

T321 $\sim \bigvee x \bigvee y(x \neq y \wedge \bigwedge z[Fz \leftrightarrow z = x \vee z = y]) \leftrightarrow$
$\bigwedge x \bigwedge y(Fx \wedge Fy \rightarrow x = y) \vee$
$\bigvee x \bigvee y \bigvee z(Fx \wedge Fy \wedge Fz \wedge x \neq y \wedge x \neq z \wedge y \neq z)$

Recall the comment (p. 243) that our logic does not countenance the empirical possibility that there are no objects in the actual universe. Thus to assert within our logic that there is at most one object is equivalent to asserting that there is exactly one object; this equivalence is expressed in

T322 $\bigvee x \bigwedge y\, y = x \leftrightarrow \bigwedge x \bigwedge y\, y = x$.

Further, we can assert that there are at least two things by employing either the universal or the existential quantifier, as the next theorem indicates.

T323 $\bigvee x \bigvee y\, x \neq y \leftrightarrow \bigwedge x \bigvee y\, x \neq y$

If it is not the case that there are at least two things, then an existential generalization has the same truth value as a universal generalization:

T324 $\sim \bigvee x \bigvee y\, x \neq y \to (\bigvee x \mathrm{F}x \leftrightarrow \bigwedge x \mathrm{F}x)$.

Just as one can find succinct as well as explicit ways of asserting that a definite number of objects satisfy a given condition, one can find succinct as well as explicit ways of asserting that a definite number of objects exist. T325 gives us two such ways of asserting that at most two objects exist.

T325 $\bigvee x \bigvee y \bigwedge z(z = x \lor z = y) \leftrightarrow$
$\bigvee x \bigwedge y\, y = x \lor \bigvee x \bigvee y(x \neq y \land \bigwedge z[z = x \lor z = y])$

Further, there are intuitive and not so intuitive ways of asserting that a definite number of objects exist. T326 is such an example for the assertion that exactly two objects exist; for it is seldom the case that the replacement of '$\land$' by '$\leftrightarrow$' in a formula yields an equivalent formula.

T326 $\bigvee x \bigvee y \bigwedge z[x \neq y \land (z = x \lor z = y)] \leftrightarrow$
$\bigvee x \bigvee y \bigwedge z[x \neq y \leftrightarrow (z = x \lor z = y)]$

We know that unlike quantifiers cannot, generally, be commuted. Hence, where 'F^1' abbreviates '*a* is a god', it would be a serious mistake to symbolize 'There is exactly one god' by

$$\bigwedge x \bigvee y(\mathrm{F}x \leftrightarrow x = y)$$

rather than by the right-hand constituent of T317, that is, the formula '$\bigvee y \bigwedge x(\mathrm{F}x \leftrightarrow x = y)$'. But the question 'What is asserted about gods by this incorrect symbolization?' is interesting; the answer 'Either there are two things or everything is a god' is a great departure from the doctrine of monotheism, and that it is the answer is established by the following theorem.

T327 $\bigwedge x \bigvee y(\mathrm{F}x \leftrightarrow x = y) \leftrightarrow \bigvee x \bigvee y\, x \neq y \lor \bigwedge x \mathrm{F}x$

It would also be a serious mistake, given the above abbreviation, to symbolize 'There is at most one god' by

$$\bigwedge x \bigwedge y(\mathrm{F}x \land \mathrm{F}y \leftrightarrow x = y)$$

rather than by (2) above. And again the question 'What is asserted about gods by this incorrect symbolization?' is interesting; the answer 'There is exactly one thing and it is a god' clearly overstates the doctrine of unitarianism, and that it is the answer is established by the following theorem.

T328 $\bigwedge x \bigwedge y(Fx \wedge Fy \leftrightarrow x = y) \leftrightarrow \bigvee x(\bigwedge y\, y = x \wedge Fx)$

T329 expresses the fact that each thing is identical with at least one thing (itself); T330, that each thing is identical with exactly one thing.

T329 $\bigvee x\, x = y$

T330 $\bigvee z \bigwedge x(x = y \leftrightarrow x = z)$

T331–T334 are interesting here and will be particularly useful in subsequent chapters.

T331 $\bigvee y[\bigwedge x(Fx \leftrightarrow x = y) \wedge Gy] \leftrightarrow$
$\bigvee y \bigwedge x(Fx \leftrightarrow x = y) \wedge \bigwedge x(Fx \rightarrow Gx)$

T332 $\sim \bigvee y[\bigwedge x(Fx \leftrightarrow x = y) \wedge Gy] \leftrightarrow$
$\sim \bigvee y \bigwedge x(Fx \leftrightarrow x = y) \vee \bigvee y[\bigwedge x(Fx \leftrightarrow x = y) \wedge \sim Gy]$

T333 $\bigvee y \bigwedge x(Fx \leftrightarrow x = y) \rightarrow [\bigwedge x(Fx \rightarrow Gx) \leftrightarrow \bigvee x(Fx \wedge Gx)]$

T334 $\sim \bigvee y \bigwedge x(x \neq x \leftrightarrow x = y)$

If we let 'F^1' again abbreviate '*a* is a god' and 'G^1' abbreviate '*a* is benevolent', then T331 informs us that there is exactly one god and that god is benevolent just in case there is exactly one god and all gods are benevolent; T332 informs us that it is not the case that there is exactly one god and that god is benevolent just in case either there is not exactly one god or there is exactly one god and that god is not benevolent; and T333 informs us that all gods are benevolent just in case some god is benevolent, provided that there is exactly one god. T334 asserts that it is not the case that there is exactly one nonidentical thing.

We conclude with two trivial theorems that will be useful in chapter VII.

T335 $\bigvee y\, y = x \wedge P \leftrightarrow P$

T336 $\sim \bigvee y\, y = x \vee P \leftrightarrow P$

EXERCISES, GROUP I

15. Prove T317 and T320.
16. Prove T330, T334, and T323.
17. Prove T331, T333, and T332.
18. Prove T327 and T328.
19. Prove T325 and T326.

EXERCISES, GROUP II

Symbolize each sentence in exercises 20–25 on the basis of the scheme of abbreviation that accompanies it.

20. There is exactly one even prime number. (F^1 : *a* is even; G^1 : *a* is a prime; H^1 : *a* is a number)

21. There is exactly one even number, and it is a prime. (F^1 : *a* is even; G^1 : *a* is a prime; H^1 : *a* is a number)

22. No monogamous person has more than one spouse. (F^1 : *a* is a monogamous person; G^2 : *a* is a spouse of *b*)

23. An opera is enjoyable if and only if it has exactly two acts. (F^1 : *a* is an opera; G^1 : *a* is enjoyable; H^2 : *a* is an act of *b*)

24. At most one student missed at most one problem. (F^1 : *a* is a student; G^2 : *a* missed *b*; H^1 : *a* is a problem)

25. At least two soldiers shot at least one demonstrator. (F^1 : *a* is a soldier; G^2 : *a* shot *b*; H^1 : *a* is a demonstrator)

26. On the basis of the scheme of abbreviation

F^1 : *a* is a class
G^2 : *a* is a member of *b* ,

symbolize each of the following sentences.

(i) Classes are identical if and only if they have the same members.
(ii) For every class *x*, if every member of *x* has a member and no two members of *x* have any member in common, then there is a class *y* such that every member of *x* has exactly one member in common with *y*.

On the basis of the scheme of abbreviation

F^1 : *a* is an instructor
G^1 : *a* is a course
H^2 : *a* teaches *b* ,

symbolize each sentence in exercises 27–30.

27. Some course is taught by exactly one instructor, and some instructor teaches exactly one course.

28. Exactly one instructor teaches a course, and exactly one course is taught by an instructor.

29. There is exactly one instructor and exactly one course, and that instructor teaches that course.

30. There is exactly one instructor who teaches exactly one course.

31. Given the meager scheme of abbreviation

A^0 : Alfred
F^2 : *a* is a son of *b* ,

find a symbolic sentence whose translation on the basis of this scheme expresses the statement that Alfred has exactly one half-brother.

EXERCISES, GROUP III

32. On the basis of the scheme of abbreviation

$$\begin{aligned} A^0 &: \text{Alfred} \\ F^2 &: a \text{ loves } b \end{aligned}$$

translate each of the following formulas into idiomatic English.

(i) $\bigvee y \bigwedge x[F(xA) \leftrightarrow x = y]$
(ii) $\bigvee y \bigwedge x[F(Ax) \leftrightarrow x = y]$
(iii) $\bigvee y \bigwedge x[F(xy) \leftrightarrow x = y]$
(iv) $\bigvee y \bigwedge x[F(yx) \leftrightarrow x = y]$

33. On the basis of the scheme of abbreviation

$$F^1 : a \text{ is a god}$$

translate each of the following formulas into idiomatic English. (For (i) and (ii), see respectively T317 and T327, together with the discussion that precedes each theorem.)

(i) $\bigvee y \bigwedge x(Fx \leftrightarrow x = y)$
(ii) $\bigwedge x \bigvee y(Fx \leftrightarrow x = y)$
(iii) $\bigwedge x \bigwedge y(Fx \leftrightarrow x = y)$
(iv) $\bigvee x \bigvee y(Fx \leftrightarrow x = y)$
(v) $\bigvee x \bigwedge y(Fx \leftrightarrow x = y)$
(vi) $\bigwedge y \bigvee x(Fx \leftrightarrow x = y)$

34. For each of the following formulas, state how many objects exist if it is true.

(i) $\bigwedge x \bigvee y \bigwedge z(z \neq x \rightarrow z = y)$
(ii) $\bigvee y \bigwedge x \bigwedge z(z \neq x \rightarrow z = y)$

35. Given, again, the scheme of abbreviation

$$F^1 : a \text{ is a god} \quad ,$$

state succinctly and precisely what each of the following formulas asserts about the number of gods that exist.

(i) $\bigvee x[Fx \wedge \bigvee y(Fy \wedge \bigwedge z[Fz \rightarrow x = z \vee y = z])]$
(ii) $\bigwedge x[Fx \rightarrow \bigvee z(Fz \wedge \bigwedge y[Fy \rightarrow (x \neq y \rightarrow y = z)])]$
(iii) $\bigwedge x[Fx \rightarrow \bigvee z(Fz \wedge \bigwedge y[Fy \rightarrow (x \neq y \leftrightarrow y = z)])]$

36. Given the scheme of abbreviation

$$L^2 : a \text{ loves } b \quad ,$$

state in succinct, idiomatic English what is asserted by each of the following formulas.

(i) $\bigwedge x(L(xx) \wedge \bigwedge y[L(xy) \rightarrow x = y] \rightarrow \bigwedge y[L(yx) \rightarrow x = y])$
(ii) $\bigwedge x \bigwedge y(L(xx) \wedge [L(xy) \rightarrow x = y] \rightarrow [L(yx) \rightarrow x = y])$
(iii) $\bigwedge x \bigwedge y([L(xy) \leftrightarrow x = y] \rightarrow [L(yx) \leftrightarrow x = y])$
(iv) $\bigvee z \bigwedge x[\bigvee y L(xy) \leftrightarrow x = z] \wedge \bigvee z \bigwedge y[\bigvee x L(xy) \leftrightarrow y = z]$

(v) $\bigvee z \bigvee w \bigwedge x \bigwedge y[\mathrm{L}(xy) \leftrightarrow x = z \wedge y = w]$
(vi) $\bigvee z \bigwedge x(\bigvee w \bigwedge y[\mathrm{L}(xy) \leftrightarrow y = w] \leftrightarrow x = z)$
(vii) $\bigvee w \bigwedge y(\bigvee z \bigwedge x[\mathrm{L}(xy) \leftrightarrow x = z] \leftrightarrow y = w)$

EXERCISES, GROUP IV

37. Prove that each of the following formulas is a theorem.

(iii) $\bigwedge x \bigwedge y(\mathrm{F}x \leftrightarrow x = y) \leftrightarrow \bigvee x(\bigwedge y\, y = x \wedge \mathrm{F}x)$
(iv) $\bigvee x \bigvee y(\mathrm{F}x \leftrightarrow x = y) \leftrightarrow \bigvee x \bigvee y\, x \neq y \vee \bigwedge x \mathrm{F}x$
(v) $\bigvee x \bigwedge y(\mathrm{F}x \leftrightarrow x = y) \leftrightarrow \bigvee x(\bigwedge y\, y = x \wedge \mathrm{F}x)$
(vi) $\bigwedge y \bigvee x(\mathrm{F}x \leftrightarrow x = y) \leftrightarrow \bigwedge x \mathrm{F}x \vee \bigvee x \bigvee y(x \neq y \wedge \sim \mathrm{F}x \wedge \sim \mathrm{F}y)$

(These theorems are the basis, respectively, for the translations of (iii)–(vi) of exercise 33; see the solutions to selected exercises at the end of this chapter.)

38. Prove that each of the following formulas is a theorem.

(i) $\bigwedge x \bigvee y \bigwedge z(z \neq x \rightarrow z = y) \leftrightarrow \bigvee x \bigvee y \bigwedge z(z = x \vee z = y)$
(ii) $\bigvee y \bigwedge x \bigwedge z(z \neq x \rightarrow z = y) \leftrightarrow \bigvee y \bigwedge x\, x = y$

(These theorems are the basis, respectively, for the translations of (i) and (ii) of exercise 34; see the solutions to selected exercises at the end of this chapter.)

39. Prove that each of the following formulas is a theorem.

(i) $\bigvee x[\mathrm{F}x \wedge \bigvee y(\mathrm{F}y \wedge \bigwedge z[\mathrm{F}z \rightarrow x = z \vee y = z])] \leftrightarrow$
$\bigvee x \mathrm{F}x \wedge \bigwedge x \bigwedge y \bigwedge z(\mathrm{F}x \wedge \mathrm{F}y \wedge \mathrm{F}z \rightarrow x = y \vee x = z \vee y = z)$
(ii) $\bigwedge x[\mathrm{F}x \rightarrow \bigvee z(\mathrm{F}z \wedge \bigwedge y[\mathrm{F}y \rightarrow (x \neq y \rightarrow y = z)])] \leftrightarrow$
$\bigwedge x \bigwedge y \bigwedge z(\mathrm{F}x \wedge \mathrm{F}y \wedge \mathrm{F}z \rightarrow x = y \vee x = z \vee y = z)$
(iii) $\bigwedge x[\mathrm{F}x \rightarrow \bigvee z(\mathrm{F}z \wedge \bigwedge y[\mathrm{F}y \rightarrow (x \neq y \leftrightarrow y = z)])] \leftrightarrow$
$\sim \bigvee x \mathrm{F}x \vee \bigvee x \bigvee y[x \neq y \wedge \bigwedge z(\mathrm{F}z \leftrightarrow z = x \vee z = y)]$

(These theorems are the basis, respectively, for the translations of (i)–(iii) of exercise 35; see the solutions to selected exercises at the end of this chapter.)

40. Prove that the following formulas are theorems.

(ii) $\bigwedge x \bigwedge y(\mathrm{L}(xx) \wedge [\mathrm{L}(xy) \rightarrow x = y] \rightarrow [\mathrm{L}(yx) \rightarrow x = y]) \leftrightarrow$
$\bigwedge x(\mathrm{L}(xx) \rightarrow \bigwedge y[\mathrm{L}(yx) \rightarrow \mathrm{L}(xy)])$
(iii) $\bigwedge x \bigwedge y([\mathrm{L}(xy) \leftrightarrow x = y] \rightarrow [\mathrm{L}(yx) \leftrightarrow x = y]) \leftrightarrow$
$\bigwedge x \bigwedge y[\mathrm{L}(yx) \rightarrow \mathrm{L}(xy)]$

(These theorems are the basis, respectively, for the translations of (ii) and (iii) of exercise 36; see the solutions to selected exercises at the end of this chapter.)

41. Prove the equivalence of (iv) and (v) of exercise 36. (This equivalence is the basis for translating the two formulas into the same sentence of English; see the solutions to selected exercises at the end of this chapter.)

42. Derive both (vi) and (vii) of exercise 36 from (v) of that exercise.

(That the latter cannot be derived from either of the former will be established in exercise 70 of the next section.)

43. Given the formula

$$\bigvee x \bigvee y[x \neq y \wedge \bigwedge z(z = x \vee z = y)]$$

as a premise, show that each of (vi) and (vii) of exercise 36 can be derived from the other. (That neither can be derived from the other without some premise will be established in exercise 71 in the next section.)

44. Show that the following argument is valid.

$$\bigwedge y \bigvee z \bigwedge x[\mathrm{F}(xz) \leftrightarrow x = y]$$
$$\therefore \sim\bigvee w \bigwedge x(\mathrm{F}(xw) \leftrightarrow \bigwedge u[\mathrm{F}(xu) \rightarrow \bigvee y(\mathrm{F}(yu) \wedge \sim\bigvee z[\mathrm{F}(zu) \wedge \mathrm{F}(zy)])])$$

(Exercise 44 corresponds to the *paradox of grounded classes* as described in Montague [1].)

5. Invalidity. Here, as in the quantifier calculus, it is impossible to devise an automatic test for validity. We can, however, establish invalidity by use of the various methods introduced in earlier chapters.

Least interesting is the method of truth-functional expansions, first introduced in chapter III. As characterized there, the method will no longer yield correct results, even in connection with symbolic arguments containing no operation letters of degree greater than zero. The reader will perhaps be interested in showing this and in adapting the method to the identity calculus.

The method of models will continue to play here the prominent role in demonstrating invalidity of symbolic arguments that it played in chapter IV (although it remains the case that there are invalid arguments in the identity calculus whose invalidity cannot be demonstrated by this method). That is, here, as in the quantifier calculus, to demonstrate the invalidity of a symbolic argument it is sufficient to find a model in which a closure of the argument has true premises and a false conclusion, and to demonstrate that a symbolic formula is not a theorem it is sufficient to find a model in which a closure of the formula is false. As before, we shall determine the *truth in* or the *falsity in* a model of the sentences of a symbolic argument by means of an *expansion of* the argument *with respect to* the model. Thus, for this purpose we again incorporate numerals into our symbolic language (see p. 231). Within the expansion of a symbolic argument with respect to a model, each part of the form

$$\zeta = \eta \quad ,$$

where ζ and η are numerals, is true in that model if and only if ζ and η are the same numeral. (Recall that we take account of no arithmetical properties of numbers other than their distinctness when we employ them as elements of the universe of a model and that an identity sentence is true just in case its terms designate the same object.) Truth or falsity of other atomic components of an expansion is determined as before by the extensions in the model of the predicate letters.

For an illustration, consider the argument

(1) $\bigvee x \mathrm{FA}(x) \quad \therefore \mathrm{A}(x) = \mathrm{B}(x) \rightarrow \bigvee x \mathrm{FB}(x)$.

To demonstrate its invalidity, we first form a closure of it,

(2) $\bigvee x \mathrm{FA}(x) \quad \therefore \bigwedge x[\mathrm{A}(x) = \mathrm{B}(x) \rightarrow \bigvee x \mathrm{FB}(x)]$,

and then introduce a model:

$$\begin{array}{lll} \mathbf{U} & : & \{0, 1\} \\ \mathrm{F}^1 & : & \{0\} \\ \mathrm{A}^1 & : & \mathrm{A}(0) \mapsto 0;\ \mathrm{A}(1) \mapsto 1 \\ \mathrm{B}^1 & : & \mathrm{B}(0) \mapsto 1;\ \mathrm{B}(1) \mapsto 1 \ . \end{array}$$

In forming an expansion of (2) with respect to this model, we obtain first, by eliminating quantifiers,

$$\mathrm{FA}(0) \vee \mathrm{FA}(1) \quad \therefore [\mathrm{A}(0) = \mathrm{B}(0) \rightarrow \mathrm{FB}(0) \vee \mathrm{FB}(1)] \wedge [\mathrm{A}(1) = \mathrm{B}(1) \rightarrow \mathrm{FB}(0) \vee \mathrm{FB}(1)] \ ;$$

and then, by introducing values for terms,

(3) $\mathrm{F}0 \vee \mathrm{F}1 \quad \therefore [0 = 1 \rightarrow \mathrm{F}1 \vee \mathrm{F}1] \wedge [1 = 1 \rightarrow \mathrm{F}1 \vee \mathrm{F}1]$.

Given the truth condition for identity sentences stated above and the fact that 'F0' is true and 'F1' false in the model, truth-value analysis reveals that (3) has a true premise and a false conclusion in the model. Thus we have established the invalidity of the argument (1). (Recall in connection with this illustration the comment made on p. 270 concerning replacement of only *free* occurrences of terms in the formulation of LL.)

Here, as in the quantifier calculus, it is sometimes the case that interesting symbolizations of intuitively valid arguments of English are not valid symbolic arguments. For example, consider the following argument, scheme of abbreviation, and symbolization.

Argument: Alfred is the tallest person. ∴ No one is taller than Alfred and no one different from Alfred is the same height as Alfred.

Scheme:

A^0 : Alfred
F^2 : *a* is taller than *b*
G^2 : *a* is the same height as *b*

Symbolization: $\bigwedge x[x \neq \mathrm{A} \rightarrow \mathrm{F}(\mathrm{A}x)]$
$\therefore \sim \bigvee x \mathrm{F}(x\mathrm{A}) \wedge \sim \bigvee x[x \neq \mathrm{A} \wedge \mathrm{G}(x\mathrm{A})]$

The symbolic argument is invalid; it has a true premise and a false conclusion in the model

$$\begin{array}{lcl} \mathbf{U} & : & \{0, 1\} \\ A^0 & : & 0 \\ F^2 & : & \{(0, 1), (1, 0)\} \\ G^2 & : & \{(1, 0)\} \quad . \end{array}$$

The intuitive validity of the English argument rests on our acceptance of the sentences 'For each x, for each y, if x is taller than y, then y is not taller than x' and 'For each x, for each y, if x is the same height as y, then x is not taller than y and y is not taller than x' as true on the basis of the meaning of 'taller than' and that of 'same height as'. If we symbolize these two sentences on the basis of the above scheme of abbreviation and add their symbolizations to the premises of the above symbolic argument, we obtain the argument

$$\bigwedge x \bigwedge y[F(xy) \rightarrow \sim F(yx)] \quad . \quad \bigwedge x \bigwedge y[G(xy) \rightarrow \sim F(xy) \wedge \sim F(yx)] \quad .$$
$$\bigwedge x[x \neq A \rightarrow F(Ax)] \quad \therefore \sim \bigvee x F(xA) \wedge \sim \bigvee x[x \neq A \wedge G(xA)] \quad ,$$

whose validity we leave for the reader to establish. (Note that both additional premises are false in the model above.)

Similar to premises implicit in the meanings of words of ordinary English are the basic principles of a formal discipline, such as arithmetic. For example, within arithmetic the inference from

For each x, there is an object y such that $x + y$ is even

to

For each x, there is an object y such that $y + x$ is even

is considered valid, for addition is understood to be a commutative operation. But a symbolization of this pattern of inference, such as

$$(4) \qquad \bigwedge x \bigvee y F B(xy) \quad \therefore \bigwedge x \bigvee y F B(yx) \quad ,$$

is invalid; its premise is true and its conclusion false in the model

$$\begin{array}{lcl} \mathbf{U} & : & \{0, 1\} \\ F^1 & : & \{0\} \\ B^2 & : & B(0, 0) \mapsto 0; B(0, 1) \mapsto 1; B(1, 0) \mapsto 0; B(1, 1) \mapsto 1 \quad . \end{array}$$

But if we supplement argument (4) with an additional premise that imposes commutativity on the extension of 'B', we obtain the valid argument

$$\bigwedge x \bigwedge y\, B(xy) = B(yx) \quad . \quad \bigwedge x \bigvee y F B(xy) \quad \therefore \bigwedge x \bigvee y F B(yx) \quad .$$

Interesting exercises can be obtained by supplementing (4) with an assertion that some terms commute, such as

(5) $\bigvee x \bigwedge y\, B(xy) = B(yx)$. $\bigwedge x \bigvee y FB(xy)$ $\therefore$ $\bigwedge x \bigvee y FB(yx)$
(6) $\bigvee x \bigvee y(x \neq y \wedge \bigwedge z[B(xz) = B(zx) \wedge B(yz) = B(zy)])$.
$\bigwedge x \bigvee y FB(xy)$ $\therefore$ $\bigwedge x \bigvee y FB(yx)$.

Neither (5) nor (6) is valid. But to demonstrate invalidity, we must pass, in each case, to a model whose universe contains more than two elements; indeed, the size of the universe required is proportional to the number of terms that commute. For example, (5) can be transformed into a valid argument by adding to its premises a symbolization of the assertion that there are at most two things; and (6) can be transformed into a valid argument by adding to its premises a symbolization of the assertion that there are at most three things. These claims can be verified by the reader who works exercises 63–66 at the end of this section.

The method of false arithmetical translations of section 8 of the preceding chapter can be adopted without modification. Thus we employ again the notions introduced in that section of a *relativization* of a symbolic argument and of an *arithmetical translation* of a symbolic argument, for here (as in the quantifier calculus) an argument is invalid if a closure of that argument or a relativization of a closure of that argument has a false arithmetical translation.

For an illustration, consider the following argument, relativization, scheme of abbreviation, and arithmetical translation.

(7) Argument: $\bigwedge x \bigwedge y[x \neq y \rightarrow A(x) \neq A(y)]$ $\therefore$ $\bigwedge x \bigvee y\, x = A(y)$

Relativization: $\bigwedge x[Ux \rightarrow \bigwedge y(Uy \rightarrow [x \neq y \rightarrow A(x) \neq A(y)])]$.
$\bigvee x Ux$. $\bigwedge x[Ux \rightarrow UA(x)]$
$\therefore$ $\bigwedge x(Ux \rightarrow \bigvee y[Uy \wedge x = A(y)])$

Scheme U^1 : *a* is a natural number
A^1 : the successor of *a* (that is, *a* + 1)

(8) Translation: If natural numbers differ, then so do their successors. There is a natural number. The successor of a natural number is a natural number. ∴ Every natural number is the successor of some natural number.

The conclusion of (8) is false, for 0 is a natural number but not the successor of any natural number. And it is evident to anyone familiar with the basic principles of the arithmetic of natural numbers that the premises of (8) are true; indeed, we have here essentially four of Peano's five postulates for the arithmetic of natural numbers. (The reader who has forgotten this arithmetic will enjoy chapter X, wherein the relevant principles are stated precisely and proofs provided or left as exercises; see, specifically, pp. 468–70.) Thus the invalidity of (7) is established.

What is not so evident, but is important to recognize, is the fact that the invalidity of argument (7) cannot be established by any model with a finite universe. Thus to establish the invalidity of some arguments essentially involving the identity sign '=' we must employ the method of false arithmetical translations. (As mentioned in section 8 of chapter IV, an alternative to the method of false arithmetical translations is to employ models with an infinite class for their universe—an alternative we did not and do not adopt, for the expansions by means of which we characterized truth in a model are not available for such models.)

Some insight into the fact that the invalidity of (7) cannot be established by a model with a finite universe can be obtained by supplementing argument (7) with *any* premise whose truth requires the universe to be finite, such as

$$\text{(9)} \qquad \bigvee x \bigvee y[x \neq y \wedge \bigwedge z(z = x \vee z = y)] \quad ,$$

which asserts that there are exactly two things; for the argument obtained by adding (9), or any comparable assertion (e.g., there are three things, there are four things), to the premises of (7) is a valid argument, as the reader who works exercise 73 at the end of this section will verify for the assertion (9). (The sentence 'there are finitely many things', in contrast to specification of a definite finite number of things, cannot be symbolized in the language of the identity calculus. This follows from the so-called *compactness theorem*; see Chang and Keisler [1].) A mathematical proof that the invalidity of (7) cannot be established by a model with a finite universe rests on a principle known to every child (see Fraenkel [1]): the elements of a finite class cannot be put into one-to-one correspondence with a proper part of that class. That is to say, if such a correspondence is imposed upon the elements of a finite class, then every element of that class must be a value of the biunique function that imposes the correspondence. Now note that if the premise of (7) is true in a model, then the function that is the extension of 'A' in that model imposes a one-to-one correspondence on the elements of the universe of that model. If the conclusion of (7) is false in that model, then some element of the universe of the model is not a value of that function. But then it follows, by the principle just mentioned, that the universe of that model is not finite.

It is the case here, as in the quantifier calculus, that a symbolic argument is invalid *just in case* a relativization of a closure of that argument has a false arithmetical translation; and, in particular, that a symbolic formula ϕ is not a theorem *just in case* a relativization of a closure of the argument having ϕ as conclusion and no premises has a false arithmetical translation. Thus, as before, for any symbolic argument, either a derivation may be supplied or else a false arithmetical translation of a relativization of one of its closures will exist; and for any symbolic formula, either a proof may be supplied or else there will exist a false arithmetical translation of a relativization of a closure of the argument with no premises and the formula as conclusion. (Again, there is no automatic way of deciding in all cases which alternative holds.) Of course, to establish that an argument is invalid or that a formula is not a theorem, it remains sufficient to exhibit a false arithmetical translation of a closure, without passing to a relativization.

EXERCISES, GROUP I

45. Demonstrate by means of a model the invalidity of the following argument:

$$A \neq B \quad \therefore\ C(A) \neq C(B) \quad .$$

(This exercise confirms the remark (p. 273) that EL, in contrast to Sm, cannot have the negation of an identity formula for its premise.)

46. Neither (iii) nor (iv) of exercise 13 (p. 274) is a pattern of inference comprehended under LL (see the solutions to selected exercises at the end of this chapter); if either pattern of inference were comprehended under LL, the arguments

(iii) $\bigwedge y \bigvee x F(xy) \quad \therefore\ \bigwedge x \bigwedge y[y = x \rightarrow \bigvee x F(xx)]$
(iv) $\bigwedge y \bigvee x F(xy) \quad \therefore\ \bigwedge x \bigwedge y[x = y \rightarrow \bigvee x F(yy)]$,

which correspond respectively to (iii) and (iv) of exercise 13, would be valid. For each of these arguments, demonstrate its invalidity by means of a model. (This exercise confirms the remark (p. 270) that LL would lead to fallacies without the restriction that only free occurrences of a term can be replaced and that those occurrences must be replaced by free occurrences of a term.)

EXERCISES, GROUP II

For each argument in the following pairs of arguments, demonstrate its validity or its invalidity.

47. (i) $\bigvee x Fx \wedge \bigvee x \sim Fx \quad \therefore\ \bigvee x \bigvee y\, x \neq y$
(ii) $\bigvee x \bigvee y\, x \neq y \quad \therefore\ \bigvee x Fx \wedge \bigvee x \sim Fx$

48. (i) $\bigvee x Fx \quad \therefore\ \bigwedge x \bigvee y(Fx \leftrightarrow x = y)$
(ii) $\sim \bigvee x Fx \quad \therefore\ \bigwedge x \bigvee y(Fx \leftrightarrow x = y)$

49. (i) $\bigwedge x(Fx \leftrightarrow Gx \vee Hx) \quad . \quad \bigvee y \bigwedge x(Gx \leftrightarrow x = y) \quad .$
$\bigvee y \bigwedge x(Hx \leftrightarrow x = y) \quad \therefore\ \bigvee x \bigvee y(x \neq y \wedge Fx \wedge Fy)$
(ii) $\bigwedge x(Fx \leftrightarrow Gx \vee Hx) \quad . \quad \bigvee y \bigwedge x(Gx \leftrightarrow x = y) \quad .$
$\bigvee y \bigwedge x(Hx \leftrightarrow x = y) \quad \therefore\ \bigvee x \bigvee y \bigwedge z(Fz \rightarrow z = x \vee z = y)$

50. (i) $\bigvee x \bigvee y\, x \neq y \quad \therefore\ \bigvee x \bigvee y[x \neq y \leftrightarrow \bigwedge z(z = x \vee z = y)]$
(ii) $\bigvee x \bigvee y[x \neq y \leftrightarrow \bigwedge z(z = x \vee z = y)]$
$\therefore\ \bigvee x \bigvee y[x \neq y \wedge \bigwedge z(z = x \vee z = y)]$
(In connection with this exercise, see T326 on p. 280.)

51\. (i) $\bigvee x \bigwedge y(Fx \leftrightarrow x = y) \quad \therefore \bigwedge x \bigwedge y(Fx \leftrightarrow x = y)$
(ii) $\bigvee x \bigvee y(Fx \leftrightarrow x = y) \quad \therefore \bigwedge x \bigvee y(Fx \leftrightarrow x = y)$

52\. (i) $\bigvee x Fx \wedge \bigvee x \bigvee y\, x \neq y \quad \therefore \bigvee x \bigvee y(Fx \wedge x \neq y)$
(ii) $\bigwedge y[Fy \vee \bigvee x(x \neq y \wedge \sim Fx)] \quad \therefore \bigwedge y Fy \vee \bigwedge y \bigvee x(x \neq y \wedge \sim Fx)$

EXERCISES, GROUP III

For each of the following pairs of arguments, provide a scheme of abbreviation, symbolize the two arguments on the basis of that scheme, and by means of the symbolizations demonstrate for each argument its validity or invalidity.

53\. (i) ∴ It is not the case that there is a student who admires all and only those students who do not admire themselves.

(ii) ∴ It is not the case that there is a student who admires all and only those other students who do not admire themselves.

54\. (i) There are at most two things. ∴ Either everything is a god, all gods are benevolent, or no god is benevolent.

(ii) There are at least two things. ∴ Either everything is a god, all gods are benevolent, or no god is benevolent.

55\. (i) Everything differs from at most one thing. ∴ There are exactly two things.

(ii) There are exactly two things. ∴ Everything differs from exactly one thing.

EXERCISES, GROUP IV

Symbolize each of the following arguments on the basis of an interesting scheme of abbreviation, and by means of that symbolization ascertain the validity or invalidity of the argument. For each argument that is invalid, supplement the premises of the argument with a sentence that is true on the basis of the meanings of the words in the argument and add the symbolization of that sentence to the symbolization of the argument; and then by means of the supplemented symbolization demonstrate the validity of the supplemented argument. (See the example on pp. 286–87 for an illustration.)

56\. No one is taller than Alfred, and no one different from Alfred is the same height as Alfred. ∴ Alfred is the tallest person.

57\. There is at most one god. Every person is created by some god. ∴ No god is a person.

58\. There are at least two men but at most one woman. Each man is married to some woman. ∴ Some woman is married to more than one man.

59\. According to an old riddle (due to the 19th-century logician Augustus De Morgan), a woman was asked about her relationship to a certain young man who was understood to be a relative of hers. There were reasons why she was embarrassed about the true relationship. But not wishing either to refuse an answer or to be untruthful, she replied by saying 'His mother was my mother's only child'. Her questioner, with insight, concluded that the woman was the young man's mother. Demonstrate that her statement alone is not sufficient to support this insight, but that it can be justified with the aid of a supplementary premise implicit in her statement.

60. 'The boxed sentence is not true' is true if and only if the boxed sentence is not true. The boxed sentence is 'the boxed sentence is not true'. ∴ The boxed sentence is neither true nor not true. (The reference is to the boxed sentence on page 1; this is the *paradox of the liar* as formulated in Tarski [2].)

EXERCISES, GROUP V

61. Demonstrate by means of a model that argument (5) on page 288 is invalid.

62. Add to the premises of argument (5) on page 288 a symbolization of the assertion that there are at most two things, and demonstrate the validity of the resulting argument.

63. Demonstrate by means of a model that argument (6) on page 288 is invalid.

64. Add to the premises of argument (6) on page 288 a symbolization of the assertion that there are at most three things, and demonstrate the validity of the resulting argument.

65. Demonstrate by means of a model the invalidity of the following argument, and by means of a proof that the model you construct is such that no model with a smaller universe could establish the invalidity of the argument.

$$\bigwedge x[F(xA) \vee x = A \rightarrow GB(x)] \quad . \qquad \bigwedge x \bigwedge z F[xB(z)] \quad \therefore \bigwedge x GB(x)$$

In the preceding chapter each of the arguments

(i) $\bigwedge x F[xA(x)] \quad \therefore \bigvee x F[A(x)x]$

(ii) $\bigwedge x \bigvee y F(xy) \quad \therefore \bigvee x \bigvee y[F(xy) \wedge F(yx)]$

was shown to be invalid by means of a model whose universe contained three elements; the argument

(iii) $\bigwedge x \bigvee y F(xy) \quad . \qquad \bigvee y \sim \bigvee x F(xy) \quad \therefore \bigvee x \bigvee y[F(xy) \wedge F(yx)]$

was shown to be invalid by means of a model whose universe contained four elements; and the argument

(iv) $\bigvee x[F(Ax) \wedge \sim F(Bx)] \quad . \qquad \bigwedge x \bigvee y F(xy) \quad .$
$\bigwedge x \bigwedge y[F(xy) \rightarrow \sim F(yx)] \quad \therefore \bigvee x[F(xA) \vee F(xB)]$

was shown to be invalid by means of a model whose universe contained five elements. (See solutions to exercises 60 and 63 of chapter IV, p. 259.)

66. Add to the premise of (i) above a symbolization of the assertion that there are at most two things, and demonstrate the validity of the resulting argument.

67. Add to the premise of (ii) above a symbolization of the assertion that there are at most two things, and demonstrate the validity of the resulting argument.

68. Add to the premises of (iii) above a symbolization of the assertion that there are at most three things, and demonstrate the validity of the resulting argument.

69. Add to the premises of (iv) above a symbolization of the assertion that there are at most four things, and demonstrate the validity of the resulting argument.

70. Demonstrate by means of models that the formula

$$\text{(v)} \quad \bigvee z \bigvee w \bigwedge x \bigwedge y[\mathrm{L}(xy) \leftrightarrow x = z \wedge y = w]$$

cannot be derived from either of the formulas

$$\text{(vi)} \quad \bigvee z \bigwedge x(\bigvee w \bigwedge y[\mathrm{L}(xy) \leftrightarrow y = w] \leftrightarrow x = z)$$
$$\text{(vii)} \quad \bigvee w \bigwedge y(\bigvee z \bigwedge x[\mathrm{L}(xy) \leftrightarrow x = z] \leftrightarrow y = w) \quad ,$$

and thereby verify the claim made in exercise 42 of the preceding section. (For translations into English of (v), (vi), and (vii), see the solutions for exercise 36 of the preceding section.)

71. Demonstrate by means of models that neither of the formulas (vi) or (vii) above can be derived from the other, and thereby verify the claim made in exercise 43 of the preceding section.

72. Demonstrate by means of a model that the conclusion of the argument in exercise 44,

$$\sim \bigvee w \bigwedge x(\mathrm{F}(xw) \leftrightarrow \bigwedge u[\mathrm{F}(xu) \rightarrow \bigvee y(\mathrm{F}(yu) \wedge \sim \bigvee z[\mathrm{F}(zu) \wedge \mathrm{F}(zy)])]) \quad ,$$

is not a theorem.

EXERCISES, GROUP VI

73. Demonstrate the validity of the following argument.

$$\bigvee x \bigvee y[x \neq y \wedge \bigwedge z(z = x \vee z = y)] \quad .$$
$$\bigwedge x \bigwedge y[x \neq y \rightarrow \mathrm{A}(x) \neq \mathrm{A}(y)] \quad \therefore \bigwedge x \bigvee y\, x = \mathrm{A}(y)$$

(This demonstration verifies a comment made on p. 289 concerning argument (7).)

74. Demonstrate by means of a relativization and false arithmetical translation the invalidity of the following argument.

$$\bigwedge x \bigwedge y \bigwedge z[\mathrm{F}(yx) \wedge \mathrm{F}(zx) \rightarrow y = z] \quad . \qquad \bigwedge x \bigvee y \mathrm{F}(xy) \quad \therefore \bigwedge y \bigvee x \mathrm{F}(xy)$$

75. As a step toward an insight that the invalidity of the argument in

the preceding exercise could not be established by a model with a finite universe, demonstrate the validity of the following argument.

$$\bigvee x \bigvee y \bigwedge z(z = x \vee z = y) \quad . \quad \bigwedge x \bigwedge y \bigwedge z[F(yx) \wedge F(zx) \rightarrow y = z] \quad . \quad \bigwedge x \bigvee y F(xy) \quad \therefore \bigwedge y \bigvee x F(xy)$$

76. Demonstrate by means of a relativization and false arithmetical translation the invalidity of the following argument.

$$\bigwedge x \bigwedge y[x \neq y \rightarrow A(x) \neq A(y)] \quad . \quad \bigwedge x[Fx \rightarrow GA(x)] \quad . \quad \bigvee x(Fx \wedge \sim Gx) \quad \therefore \bigvee x \sim Fx$$

77. Again, as a step toward an insight that the invalidity of the argument in the preceding exercise could not be established by a model with a finite universe, demonstrate the validity of the following argument.

$$\bigvee x \bigvee y[x \neq y \wedge \bigwedge z(z = x \vee z = y)] \quad . \quad \bigwedge x \bigwedge y[x \neq y \rightarrow A(x) \neq A(y)] \quad . \quad \bigwedge x[Fx \rightarrow GA(x)] \quad . \quad \bigvee x(Fx \wedge \sim Gx) \quad \therefore \bigvee x \sim Fx$$

EXERCISES, GROUP VII

In these exercises, operation letters but no predicate letters occur; they provide an opportunity to employ Euclid's law (EL).

78. Consider a self-centered universe in which the lover of a person is that person. Prove that in such a universe the lover of any person is the lover of the lover of the lover of that person; that is, where 'A^1' abbreviates 'the lover of *a*', show that the following argument is valid.

$$\bigwedge x\, A(x) = x \quad \therefore \bigwedge x\, A(x) = A(A[A(x)])$$

79. Suppose the lover of the lover of a person is the lover of that person; then anyone who is the lover of someone is the lover of himself or herself. Verify this fact by demonstrating the validity of the following argument.

$$\bigwedge x\, A[A(x)] = A(x) \quad \therefore \bigwedge x[\bigvee y\, x = A(y) \rightarrow x = A(x)]$$

In exercises 80–82, as an aid to intuition, understand the operation letter 'A^2' as an abbreviation for '$a + b$', that is, for the arithmetical operation of addition, and 'E^0'as an abbreviation for 'o'; and recall that not only a premise but any universal generalization of a premise may occur as a line in a derivation.

80. Demonstrate the validity of the following argument.

$$A[xA(yz)] = A[A(xy)z] \quad \therefore A(xA[yA(zw)]) = A(A[A(xy)z]w)$$

(Recognize that the premise of this argument, given the abbreviations mentioned above, symbolizes the associative law of addition.)

81. Given as premises the formulas

(1) $A[A(xy)z] = A[xA(yz)]$ (associativity)
(2) $A(Ex) = x$ (left identity)
(3) $\bigvee y A(yx) = E$ (left inverses)

derive from these premises the following two formulas

(4) $A(xy) = A(xz) \rightarrow y = z$ (left cancellation)
(5) $A(yx) = E \rightarrow A(xy) = E$ (left inverses are also right inverses)

(The premises (1)–(3) are symbolizations, on the basis of the abbreviations mentioned above, of the axioms for a mathematical structure known as a *group*.)

82. By means of a model, demonstrate that the formula

(6) $A(xy) = A(yx)$ (commutativity)

cannot be derived from the premises (1)–(3) of the preceding exercise. (Thus, although all of the formulas (1)–(6) symbolize, on the basis of the abbreviations mentioned above, familiar truths of the arithmetic of integers (positive and negative), only some such truths are logical consequences of (1)–(3).)

For the next exercise, another guide to intuition than that suggested for exercises 80–82 is required. In this exercise, understand 'A^2' as an abbreviation for 'or' in the exclusive sense and 'E^0' as an abbreviation for 'falsehood' (the name of one of the two truth values).

83. From the formulas (1) and (2) of exercise 81 above and the formula

(7) $A(xx) = E$,

derive the formula (6) of exercise 82 above. (The reader can verify that under the interpretation suggested for this exercise, with variables treated as sentence letters, all the formulas involved symbolize tautologies.)

6. Historical remarks. The identity calculus is often called the first-order predicate calculus with identity. It has been discussed extensively in Whitehead and Russell [1], Hilbert and Bernays [1], and Scholz [1], and it occurs in Frege [1].

The claim that if no closure of a symbolic argument has a relativization with a false arithmetical translation, then the argument is valid in the identity calculus, corresponds to an extension of Gödel's completeness theorem for this calculus (see Gödel [1], Hilbert and Bernays [2], and Kleene [1]).

The principle of the indiscernibility of identicals is first to be found in Leibniz [1].

7. Appendix: list of theorems of chapter V.

T301 $x = x$

T302 $x = y \leftrightarrow y = x$

T303 $x = y \wedge y = z \rightarrow x = z$

T304 $x = y \rightarrow (\mathrm{F}x \leftrightarrow \mathrm{F}y)$

T305 $x = y \rightarrow \mathrm{A}(x) = \mathrm{A}(y)$

T306 $\mathrm{F}x \leftrightarrow \bigwedge y(y = x \rightarrow \mathrm{F}y)$

T307 $\mathrm{F}x \leftrightarrow \bigvee y(y = x \wedge \mathrm{F}y)$

T308 $x = y \leftrightarrow \bigwedge z(z = x \rightarrow z = y)$

T309 $x = y \leftrightarrow \bigvee z(z = x \wedge z = y)$

T310 $\mathrm{F}(xy) \leftrightarrow \bigwedge z \bigwedge w(z = x \wedge w = y \rightarrow \mathrm{F}(zw)]$

T311 $\mathrm{F}(xy) \leftrightarrow \bigvee z \bigvee w(z = x \wedge w = y \wedge \mathrm{F}(zw)]$

T312 $x \neq y \leftrightarrow y \neq x$

T313 $\mathrm{F}x \wedge x = y \leftrightarrow \mathrm{F}y \wedge x = y$

T314 $\mathrm{F}x \vee x \neq y \leftrightarrow \mathrm{F}y \vee x \neq y$

T315 $\bigwedge x[\bigvee y[\mathrm{F}y \wedge x = \mathrm{A}(y)] \rightarrow \mathrm{F}x) \leftrightarrow \bigwedge x[\mathrm{F}x \rightarrow \mathrm{FA}(x)]$

T316 $\bigvee x\mathrm{F}x \wedge \bigwedge x \bigwedge y(\mathrm{F}x \wedge \mathrm{F}y \rightarrow x = y) \leftrightarrow \bigvee x(\mathrm{F}x \wedge \bigwedge y[\mathrm{F}y \rightarrow x = y])$

T317 $\bigvee x\mathrm{F}x \wedge \bigwedge x \bigwedge y(\mathrm{F}x \wedge \mathrm{F}y \rightarrow x = y) \leftrightarrow \bigvee y \bigwedge x(\mathrm{F}x \leftrightarrow x = y)$

T318 $\bigvee x \bigvee y(\mathrm{F}x \wedge \mathrm{F}y \wedge x \neq y) \wedge$
$\bigwedge x \bigwedge y \bigwedge z(\mathrm{F}x \wedge \mathrm{F}y \wedge \mathrm{F}z \rightarrow x = y \vee x = z \vee y = z) \leftrightarrow$
$\bigvee x \bigvee y(\mathrm{F}x \wedge \mathrm{F}y \wedge x \neq y \wedge \bigwedge z[\mathrm{F}z \rightarrow x = z \vee y = z])$

T319 $\bigvee x \bigvee y(\mathrm{F}x \wedge \mathrm{F}y \wedge x \neq y) \wedge$
$\bigwedge x \bigwedge y \bigwedge z(\mathrm{F}x \wedge \mathrm{F}y \wedge \mathrm{F}z \rightarrow x = y \vee x = z \vee y = z) \leftrightarrow$
$\bigvee x \bigvee y(x \neq y \wedge \bigwedge z[\mathrm{F}z \leftrightarrow x = z \vee y = z])$

T320 $\sim \bigvee y \bigwedge x(\mathrm{F}x \leftrightarrow x = y) \leftrightarrow \sim \bigvee x\mathrm{F}x \vee \bigvee x \bigvee y(x \neq y \wedge \mathrm{F}x \wedge \mathrm{F}y)$

T321 $\sim \bigvee x \bigvee y(x \neq y \wedge \bigwedge z[\mathrm{F}z \leftrightarrow z = x \vee z = y]) \leftrightarrow$
$\bigwedge x \bigwedge y(\mathrm{F}x \wedge \mathrm{F}y \rightarrow x = y) \vee$
$\bigvee x \bigvee y \bigvee z(\mathrm{F}x \wedge \mathrm{F}y \wedge \mathrm{F}z \wedge x \neq y \wedge x \neq z \wedge y \neq z)$

T322 $\bigvee x \bigwedge y\, y = x \leftrightarrow \bigwedge x \bigwedge y\, y = x$

T323 $\bigvee x \bigvee y\, x \neq y \leftrightarrow \bigwedge x \bigvee y\, x \neq y$

T324 $\sim \bigvee x \bigvee y\, x \neq y \rightarrow (\bigvee x\mathrm{F}x \leftrightarrow \bigwedge x\mathrm{F}x)$

T325 $\bigvee x \bigvee y \bigwedge z(z = x \vee z = y) \leftrightarrow$
$\bigvee x \bigwedge y\, y = x \vee \bigvee x \bigvee y(x \neq y \wedge \bigwedge z[z = x \vee z = y])$

T326 $\bigvee x \bigvee y \bigwedge z[x \neq y \wedge (z = x \vee z = y)] \leftrightarrow$
$\bigvee x \bigvee y \bigwedge z[x \neq y \leftrightarrow (z = x \vee z = y)]$

T327 $\bigwedge x \bigvee y(Fx \leftrightarrow x = y) \leftrightarrow \bigvee x \bigvee y\, x \neq y \vee \bigwedge x Fx$

T328 $\bigwedge x \bigwedge y(Fx \wedge Fy \leftrightarrow x = y) \leftrightarrow \bigvee x(\bigwedge y\, y = x \wedge Fx)$

T329 $\bigvee x\, x = y$

T330 $\bigvee z \bigwedge x(x = y \leftrightarrow x = z)$

T331 $\bigvee y[\bigwedge x(Fx \leftrightarrow x = y) \wedge Gy] \leftrightarrow$
$\bigvee y \bigwedge x(Fx \leftrightarrow x = y) \wedge \bigwedge x(Fx \rightarrow Gx)$

T332 $\sim \bigvee y[\bigwedge x(Fx \leftrightarrow x = y) \wedge Gy] \leftrightarrow$
$\sim \bigvee y \bigwedge x(Fx \leftrightarrow x = y) \vee \bigvee y[\bigwedge x(Fx \leftrightarrow x = y) \wedge \sim Gy]$

T333 $\bigvee y \bigwedge x(Fx \leftrightarrow x = y) \rightarrow [\bigwedge x(Fx \rightarrow Gx) \leftrightarrow \bigvee x(Fx \wedge Gx)]$

T334 $\sim \bigvee y \bigwedge x(x \neq x \leftrightarrow x = y)$

T335 $\bigvee y\, y = x \wedge P \leftrightarrow P$

T336 $\sim \bigvee y\, y = x \vee P \leftrightarrow P$

8. Appendix: solutions to selected exercises.

Section 2, Group I

1. (1) and (c), (2) and (b), (3) and (e), (4) and (g), (5) and (a), (6) and (d), (7) and (f).

Section 2, Group II

4. $F(AB) \wedge G(AC) \wedge \bigwedge x[F(xB) \wedge G(xC) \rightarrow x = A]$;
$\bigwedge x[F(xB) \wedge G(xC) \leftrightarrow x = A]$

(These two alternatives are equivalent, as the reader will soon be able to establish.)

5. $GA \wedge H(AB) \wedge \bigwedge x[Gx \wedge H(xB) \wedge x \neq A \rightarrow F(Ax)]$
6. $GA \wedge \bigwedge x[Gx \wedge H(xA) \wedge x \neq A \rightarrow F(Ax)]$
7. $\bigwedge x(\bigvee y[Fy \wedge A(x) = B(y)] \wedge G[C(x)A(x)] \wedge \sim \bigvee y(y \neq x \wedge H[yC(x)]) \rightarrow$
$\bigvee y[Fy \wedge x = D(y)])$
8. $C(A) = B[D(A)] \rightarrow E(A) = E[C(A)]$
9. $\bigvee x(F(xA) \wedge \bigvee y[G(yA) \wedge x = B(y)]) \rightarrow \bigvee x[F(xA) \wedge C(A) = C(x)]$
10. $\bigwedge x[F(xA) \wedge \bigvee y[G(yA) \wedge x = B(y)] \rightarrow C(A) = C(x)]$
11. $\sim \bigvee x F(xA) \wedge \sim \bigvee x G(xA) \wedge C(B) = D[C(A)]$
12. $\bigwedge x \bigwedge y(Fx \wedge Fy \wedge x \neq y \rightarrow [G(A[xy]B[xy]) \leftrightarrow x = C(x) \vee y = C(y)])$

Section 3

13. Each of (i), (ii), and (v) follows by LL. None of (iii), (iv), or (vi) follows by LL, for that rule permits only replacement of *free* occurrences of a term by *free* occurrences of a term: in (iii) a free occurrence of 'y' has been replaced by a bound occurrence of 'x'; in (iv) a bound occurrence of 'x' has been replaced by a free occurrence of 'y'; and in (vi) a free occurrence of '$A(x)$' has been replaced by a bound occurrence of '$B(y)$'.

14. Both (i) and (ii) follow by Sm. Both (iii) and (vi) follow by EL. Clearly, neither (iv) nor (v) follows by Sm; and neither (iv) nor (v) follows by EL, for the premise of (iv) is the negation of an identity formula and that of (v) an existential generalization of an identity formula rather than, as required by EL, an identity formula.

Section 4, Group I

In the suggestions for proofs of theorems that follow (and subsequently) we employ a new notation. Let

$$\text{T320} \qquad \phi \leftrightarrow \psi$$

be the theorem in question. By 'T320→' we understand the conditional

$$\phi \rightarrow \psi \quad ;$$

and by 'T320←' we understand the conditional

$$\psi \rightarrow \phi \quad .$$

15. The reader who has followed the proof of T319 on pages 278–79 should have no difficulty with the similar but much simpler proof of T317. To prove T320→, one obtains as assumptions by the strategies of earlier chapters '$\sim \bigvee y \bigwedge x(Fx \leftrightarrow x = y)$' and '$\sim \sim \bigvee x Fx$', from which one can obtain first 'Fa' and then '$Fb \leftrightarrow b \neq a$'. Next, by a subsidiary indirect derivation, show '$b \neq a$'. Then '$\bigvee x \bigvee y(x \neq y \wedge Fx \wedge Fy)$' can be obtained by sentential logic and EG. To prove T320←, use cases (Form III), with a subsidiary indirect derivation in each case.

16. To prove T330, show '$\bigwedge x(x = y \leftrightarrow x = y)$', and use EG. We leave the proof of T334 to the reader. The proof of T323← is trivial; for a proof of T323→, obtain '$a \neq b$', enter '*Show* $\bigwedge x \bigvee y\, x \neq y$', and then consider the cases '$x = a$' and '$x \neq a$' (that is, show each of '$x = a \rightarrow \bigvee y\, x \neq y$' and '$x \neq a \rightarrow \bigvee y\, x \neq y$').

17. Proofs for T331 and T333 are straightforward. To prove T332←, use cases (Form III), with a subsidiary indirect derivation in each case; in the second case, one obtains '$\bigwedge x(Fx \leftrightarrow x = a) \wedge \sim Ga$' and '$\bigwedge x(Fx \leftrightarrow x = b) \wedge Gb$', after which by a subsidiary indirect derivation show '$b = a$' and then use LL. For a proof of T332→, by employing standard strategies one can obtain '$\bigwedge x(Fx \leftrightarrow x = c)$' and '$\sim [\bigwedge x(Fx \leftrightarrow x = c) \wedge Gc]$'; '$\bigvee y[\bigwedge x(Fx \leftrightarrow x = y) \wedge \sim Gy]$' follows from those two formulas by sentential logic and EG.

18. To prove T327→, obtain (by standard strategies) as antecedent lines '$\bigwedge x \bigvee y(Fx \leftrightarrow x = y)$' and '$\sim \bigvee x \bigvee y\, x \neq y$'; next enter '*Show* $\bigwedge x Fx$'; then obtain from the former of the two antecedent lines '$Fx \leftrightarrow x = a$' and from the latter '$x = a$', from which lines 'Fx' follows immediately. To prove T327←, use cases

(Form III). For one case, it is sufficient to recognize that from 'Fx' and '$x = x$', '$\bigvee y(Fx \leftrightarrow x = y)$' follows by sentential logic and EG. For the other case, the following is an outline of a derivation:

$$
\begin{array}{ll}
\textit{Show } \bigwedge x \bigvee y(Fx \leftrightarrow x = y) & \\
\quad b \neq c & \text{(from case assumption)} \\
\quad \textit{Show } Fx \rightarrow \bigvee y(Fx \leftrightarrow x = y) & \\
\quad \textit{Show } {\sim} Fx \rightarrow \bigvee y(Fx \leftrightarrow x = y) & \\
\quad\quad \textit{Show } x = b \rightarrow \bigvee y(Fx \leftrightarrow x = y) & \\
\quad\quad \textit{Show } x \neq b \rightarrow \bigvee y(Fx \leftrightarrow x = y) &
\end{array}
$$

For a proof of T328→, Id and familiar principles of sentential and quantifier logic are sufficient; for a proof of T328←, LL and such familiar principles are sufficient (recall that by T84 a biconditional can be derived from a conjunction).

19. To prove T325→, obtain as antecedent lines '$\bigvee x \bigvee y \bigwedge z(z = x \vee z = y)$' and '${\sim}\bigvee x \bigwedge y\, y = x$'; from the former obtain '$\bigwedge z(z = a \vee z = b)$', and then show '$a \neq b$' by assuming otherwise and contradicting '${\sim}\bigvee x \bigwedge y\, y = x$'. The proof of T325← is by cases (Form III), both of which are simple. The proof of T326 is simple; T84 plays a key role in the derivation of one conditional, and Id in the other.

Section 4, Group II

20. $\bigvee y \bigwedge x(Fx \wedge Gx \wedge Hx \leftrightarrow x = y)$
21. $\bigvee y[\bigwedge x(Fx \wedge Hx \leftrightarrow x = y) \wedge Gy]$
22. $\bigwedge x(Fx \rightarrow \bigwedge y \bigwedge z[G(yx) \wedge G(zx) \rightarrow y = z])$;
    ${\sim}\bigvee x(Fx \wedge \bigvee y \bigvee z[G(yx) \wedge G(zx) \wedge y \neq z])$
23. $\bigwedge x(Fx \rightarrow [Gx \leftrightarrow \bigvee y \bigvee z(y \neq z \wedge \bigwedge w[H(wx) \leftrightarrow w = y \vee w = z])])$
24. $\bigwedge x \bigwedge y(Fx \wedge \bigwedge z \bigwedge w[Hz \wedge Hw \wedge G(xz) \wedge G(xw) \rightarrow z = w] \wedge$
    $Fy \wedge \bigwedge z \bigwedge w[Hz \wedge Hw \wedge G(yz) \wedge G(yw) \rightarrow z = w] \rightarrow x = y)$
25. $\bigvee x \bigvee y(x \neq y \wedge Fx \wedge Fy \wedge \bigvee z[Hz \wedge G(xz)] \wedge \bigvee z[Hz \wedge G(yz)])$

(Note that both

$$\bigvee x \bigvee y(x \neq y \wedge Fx \wedge Fy \wedge \bigvee z[Hz \wedge G(xz) \wedge G(yz)])$$

and

$$\bigvee x \bigvee y(x \neq y \wedge Fx \wedge Fy \wedge \bigvee z \bigvee w[Hz \wedge Hw \wedge z \neq w \wedge G(xz) \wedge G(yw)])$$

are too definitive; for the former states that at least two soldiers shot the same demonstrator, and the latter that at least two soldiers shot different demonstrators.)

26. (i) $\bigwedge x \bigwedge y[Fx \wedge Fy \rightarrow (x = y \leftrightarrow \bigwedge z[G(zx) \leftrightarrow G(zy)])]$
    (ii) $\bigwedge x(Fx \wedge \bigwedge y[G(yx) \rightarrow \bigvee z G(zy)]$
    $\wedge \bigwedge y \bigwedge z(G(yx) \wedge G(zx) \wedge y \neq z \rightarrow {\sim}\bigvee w[G(wy) \wedge G(wz)]) \rightarrow$
    $\bigvee y[Fy \wedge \bigwedge z(G(zx) \rightarrow \bigvee w \bigwedge u[G(uz) \wedge G(uy) \leftrightarrow u = w])])$

(The reader familiar with set theory will recognize (i) as a formulation of the principle of extensionality for classes and (ii) as one of the formulations of the so-called Axiom of Choice.)

27. $\bigvee x[Gx \wedge \bigvee z \bigwedge y(Fy \wedge H(yx) \leftrightarrow y = z)] \wedge$
    $\bigvee y[Fy \wedge \bigvee z \bigwedge x(Gx \wedge H(yx) \leftrightarrow x = z)]$

28. $\bigvee z \bigwedge y(Fy \wedge \bigvee x[Gx \wedge H(yx)] \leftrightarrow y = z) \wedge$
$\bigvee z \bigwedge x(Gx \wedge \bigvee y[Fy \wedge H(yx)] \leftrightarrow x = z)$

29. $\bigvee z \bigvee w[\bigwedge y(Fy \leftrightarrow y = z) \wedge \bigwedge x(Gx \leftrightarrow x = w) \wedge H(zw)]$

30. $\bigvee z \bigwedge y(Fy \wedge \bigvee w \bigwedge x[Gx \wedge H(yx) \leftrightarrow x = w] \leftrightarrow y = z)$

31. Alternative solutions are:

$$\bigvee x \bigvee y[F(Ax) \wedge F(Ay) \wedge \bigvee w \bigwedge z([F(zx) \vee F(zy)] \wedge \sim [F(zx) \wedge F(zy)] \leftrightarrow z = w)]$$

$$\bigvee x \bigwedge y(\bigvee w \bigwedge z[F(yz) \wedge F(Az) \leftrightarrow z = w] \leftrightarrow y = x)$$

Section 4, Group III

32. (i) Exactly one thing loves Alfred.
(ii) Alfred loves exactly one thing.
(iii) Something is such that it is loved by nothing but itself.
(iv) Something loves itself and nothing else.

(The translations of (iii) and (iv) given here are based on the theorems

$$\bigvee y \bigwedge x[F(xy) \leftrightarrow x = y] \leftrightarrow \bigvee y(F(yy) \wedge \sim \bigvee x[x \neq y \wedge F(xy)])$$
$$\bigvee y \bigwedge x[F(yx) \leftrightarrow x = y] \leftrightarrow \bigvee y(F(yy) \wedge \sim \bigvee x[x \neq y \wedge F(yx)])$$

which the reader can prove easily.)

33. (iii) There is exactly one thing, and it is a god.
(iv) Either there are at least two things or everything is a god.
(v) There is exactly one thing, and it is a god.
(vi) Either everything is a god or there are at least two things that are not gods.

(See exercise 37 for the justification of the above translations.)

34. (i) At most two things exist.
(ii) Exactly one thing exists.

(See exercise 38 for the justification of the above translations.)

35. (i) There is at least one god but at most two gods.
(ii) There are at most two gods.
(iii) Either there are no gods or there are exactly two gods.

(See exercise 39 for the justification of the above translations.)

36. (i) Anything that loves itself and loves only itself is loved by only itself.
(ii) A self-lover loves everything who loves it.
(iii) Love is mutual (that is, for each x, for each y, if y loves x, then x loves y).

(See exercise 40 for the justification of translations (ii) and (iii).)

(iv) Exactly one thing loves something and exactly one thing is loved by something (or, more idiomatically, there is exactly one lover and exactly one beloved).
(v) There is exactly one lover and exactly one beloved.

(See exercise 41 for the justification of translation (v).)

(vi) Exactly one thing loves exactly one thing.
(vii) Exactly one thing is loved by exactly one thing.

(See exercises 43 and 44 for the logical relations that hold among (v), (vi), and (vii).)

Section 5, Group I

45. The argument has a true premise and false conclusion in the model

$$\begin{array}{ll} \mathbf{U} : & \{0, 1\} \\ A^0 : & 0 \\ B^0 : & 1 \\ C^1 : & C(0) \mapsto 0;\ C(1) \mapsto 0 \quad . \end{array}$$

46. Both arguments have a true premise and a false conclusion in the model

$$\begin{array}{ll} \mathbf{U} : & \{0, 1\} \\ F^2 : & \{(0, 1), (1, 0)\} \quad . \end{array}$$

Section 5, Group II

47. Argument (i) is valid and (ii) invalid; we leave the demonstrations, which are simple, to the reader.

48. Argument (i) is valid; for a derivation, after the standard steps consider the cases 'Fx' and '$\sim$Fx'. Argument (ii) is invalid; consider a model whose universe has one element and in which the extension of 'F' is the empty class.

49. Argument (i) is invalid; consider a model whose universe has one element and in which the extension of 'F', 'G', and 'H' is the universe. Argument (ii) is valid; for a derivation, obtain '$\bigwedge x(\mathrm{G}x \leftrightarrow x = a)$' and '$\bigwedge x(\mathrm{H}x \leftrightarrow x = b)$' from the premises, and show '$\bigwedge z(\mathrm{F}z \to z = a \vee z = b)$', which can be done by showing '$\mathrm{G}z \to z = a \vee z = b$' and '$\mathrm{H}z \to z = a \vee z = b$)' and then employing SC (Form II).

50. Argument (i) is valid; for a derivation, obtain '$a \neq b$' from the premise, show '$\sim \bigwedge z(z = a \vee z = a)$', and then obtain the conclusion with the aid of Id, sentential logic, and EG. Argument (ii) is invalid; the conclusion is false in any model with more than two elements in its universe, and the validity of (i) shows that the premise is true in such a model.

51. Contrary to appearances (for it is seldom the case that a universal generalization of a formula follows from an existential generalization of that formula), both (i) and (ii) are valid. For a derivation of (i), obtain '$\bigwedge y(\mathrm{F}a \leftrightarrow a = y)$' from the premise and show '$\bigwedge x \bigwedge y(\mathrm{F}x \leftrightarrow x = y)$'; to do so, derive '$\mathrm{F}x \leftrightarrow x = y$' with the aid of Id, LL, UI, and sentential logic. A derivation of (ii) is more complex: obtain '$\mathrm{F}a \leftrightarrow a = b$' from the premise and show '$\bigwedge x \bigvee y(\mathrm{F}x \leftrightarrow x = y)$'; to do so, show each of '$\mathrm{F}x \to \bigvee y(\mathrm{F}x \leftrightarrow x = y)$' and '$\sim \mathrm{F}x \to \bigvee y(\mathrm{F}x \leftrightarrow x = y)$'; to do the latter, consider as cases '$x = a$' and '$x \neq a$'.

52. Again, contrary to appearances (for it is seldom that an existential quantifier distributes over '$\wedge$' and that a universal quantifier distributes over '$\vee$'), both (i) and (ii) are valid. For a derivation of (i), obtain from the premise '$\mathrm{F}a$' and '$\bigvee y\, b \neq y$', and then consider the cases '$a = b$' and '$a \neq b$'. For a derivation of (ii), employ the CD strategy; from the assumption of that strategy obtain '$\sim \mathrm{F}a$'; and to show '$\bigwedge y \bigvee x(x \neq y \wedge \sim \mathrm{F}x)$' consider the cases '$y = a$' and '$y \neq a$'.

Section 5, Group III

53. (i) $\therefore\ \sim \bigvee x[\mathrm{F}x \wedge \bigwedge y(\mathrm{F}y \to [\mathrm{G}(xy) \leftrightarrow \sim \mathrm{G}(yy)])]$

(ii) $\therefore\ \sim \bigvee x[\mathrm{F}x \wedge \bigwedge y(\mathrm{F}y \wedge y \neq x \to [\mathrm{G}(xy) \leftrightarrow \sim \mathrm{G}(yy)])]$

Argument (i) is valid; the reader encountered essentially that argument in exercises 71 and 72 of chapter IV. Argument (ii) is invalid; consider a model with one element in its universe and in which the extension of 'F' is the universe.

54. (i) $\bigvee x \bigvee y \bigwedge z(z = x \vee z = y) \quad \therefore \bigwedge x Fx \vee \bigwedge x(Fx \rightarrow Gx) \vee \bigwedge x(Fx \rightarrow \sim Gx)$
(ii) $\bigvee x \bigvee y\, x \neq y \quad \therefore \bigwedge x Fx \vee \bigwedge x(Fx \rightarrow Gx) \vee \bigwedge x(Fx \rightarrow \sim Gx)$

Argument (i) is valid. For a derivation employ the CD strategy: from the premise and assumptions obtain '$\bigwedge z(z = a \vee z = b)$', '$\sim Fc$', '$Fd \wedge \sim Gd$', and '$Fx$'; then obtain the disjunctions '$x = a \vee x = b$', '$c = a \vee c = b$', and '$d = a \vee d = b$'; and then consider the cases '$x = a$' and '$x = b$' and employ SC (Form II). Argument (ii) is invalid; (i) informs us that the required model, whose construction we leave to the reader, must have at least three elements in its universe.

55. (i) $\bigwedge x \bigwedge y \bigwedge z(x \neq y \wedge x \neq z \rightarrow y = z) \quad \therefore \bigvee x \bigvee y[x \neq y \wedge \bigwedge z(z = x \vee z = y)]$
(ii) $\bigvee x \bigvee y[x \neq y \wedge \bigwedge z(z = x \vee z = y)] \quad \therefore \bigwedge x \bigvee z \bigwedge y(x \neq y \leftrightarrow y = z)$

Argument (i) is invalid; consider a model whose universe contains only one element. Argument (ii) is valid. Do a universal derivation: obtain '$a \neq b$' and '$x = a \vee x = b$' from the premise; then show each of '$x = a \rightarrow \bigvee z \bigwedge y(x \neq y \leftrightarrow y = z)$' and '$x = b \rightarrow \bigvee z \bigwedge y(x \neq y \leftrightarrow y = z)$', and employ SC (Form II); for the former, assume the antecedent, show '$\bigwedge y(x \neq y \leftrightarrow y = b)$', and employ EG; for the latter, do the same with 'a' for 'b'.

Section 5, Group IV

56. The argument is invalid; a valid argument is obtained by the addition of 'For each *x*, for each *y*, either *x* is the same height as *y*, *x* is taller than *y*, or *y* is taller than *x*'.

57. The argument is invalid; a valid argument is obtained by the addition of 'Nothing creates itself'.

58. The argument is invalid; a valid argument is obtained by the addition of 'For each *x*, for each *y*, if *x* is married to *y*, then *y* is married to *x*'.

59. On the basis of the scheme of abbreviation

A^0 : the woman answering the question
B^0 : the young man about whom she is speaking
F^2 : *a* is a mother of *b*
G^2 : *a* is a child of *b* ,

one obtains from a symbolization of the woman's answer and the insightful conclusion the argument

$$\bigvee x(F(xB) \wedge \bigvee y[F(yA) \wedge \bigwedge z(G(zy) \rightarrow z = x)]) \quad \therefore F(AB) \quad .$$

This argument is invalid; but if we add to its premise a symbolization, on the basis of the above scheme, of the sentence 'For each *x*, for each *y*, if *x* is a mother of *y*, then *y* is a child of *x*', we obtain a valid symbolic argument. We leave to the reader the construction of the model to verify the former claim and the derivation to verify the latter.

60. The argument is valid; on the basis of the scheme of abbreviation

A^0 : 'The boxed sentence is not true'
B^0 : the boxed sentence
F^1 : a is true ,

the argument passes into

$$FA \leftrightarrow \sim FB \quad . \quad B = A \quad \therefore \sim(FB \vee \sim FB) \quad ,$$

whose validity the reader can verify easily.

Section 5, Group V

61. The premises of the argument are true and the conclusion false in the model

U : {0, 1, 2}
F^1 : {1}
B^2 : B(0, 0) ↦ 1; B(1, 1) ↦ 1; B(2, 1) ↦ 1; otherwise 0 .

62. For a derivation, let the additional premise take the following form '$\wedge x \wedge y \wedge z(x = y \vee x = z \vee y = z)$'; then obtain from the premises of the supplemented argument '$\wedge y\, B(ay) = B(ya)$', '$FB(xb)$', '$x = a \vee x = b \vee a = b$', and consider the three cases suggested by the last of these formulas.

66. For a derivation, let the additional premise take the following form '$\vee x \vee y \wedge z(z = x \vee z = y)$' and obtain from it '$\wedge z(z = a \vee z = b)$' and then from this latter formula '$A(a) = a \vee A(a) = b$' and '$A(b) = a \vee A(b) = b$'; then consider as two cases '$A(a) \neq a \wedge A(b) \neq b$' and '$\sim[A(a) \neq a \wedge A(b) \neq b]$', and in the latter case, after a sentential step, consider the cases '$A(a) = a$' and '$A(b) = b$'.

72. A model with a universe of two elements is sufficient to demonstrate that the conclusion of the argument in exercise 44 is not a theorem; we leave to the reader construction of the model.

Section 5, Group VI

73. For a derivation, obtain from the first premise '$a \neq b \wedge \wedge z(z = a \vee z = b)$'; from the first conjunct of this formula and the second premise obtain '$A(a) \neq A(b)$'; from the second conjunct of the former formula obtain the disjunctions '$x = a \vee x = b$', '$A(a) = a \vee A(a) = b$', '$A(b) = a \vee A(b) = b$'; then consider the cases '$A(a) = a$' and '$A(a) = b$'.

Section 5, Group VII

80.

1.	~~*Show*~~ $A(xA[yA(zw)]) = A(A[A(xy)z]w)$	
2.	$\wedge z \wedge y \wedge x\, A[xA(yz)] = A[A(xy)z]$	Premise
3.	$A[yA(zw)] = A[A(yz)w]$	2, UI, UI, UI
4.	$A(xA[yA(zw)]) = A(xA[A(yz)w])$	3, EL
5.	$A(xA[A(yz)w]) = A(A[xA(yz)]w)$	2, UI, UI, UI
6.	$A(xA[yA(zw)]) = A(A[xA(yz)]w)$	4, 5, LL
7.	$A[xA(yz)] = A[A(xy)z]$	2, UI, UI, UI
8.	$A(xA[yA(zw)]) = A(A[A(xy)z]w)$	6, 7, LL

82. A model in which closures of the formulas (1), (2), and (3) are true and a closure of the formula (6) is false has for its universe the class {0, 1, 2, 3, 4, 5} and for the extension of 'E' the number 0. We indicate the extension for 'A' in this model by means of the following table:

	0	1	2	3	4	5
0	0	1	2	3	4	5
1	1	2	0	4	5	3
2	2	0	1	5	3	4
3	3	5	4	0	2	1
4	4	3	5	1	0	2
5	5	4	3	2	1	0

To find from this table the value of any relevant term, say 'A(3, 5)', we consider the row indexed by '3' and the column indexed by '5' and select the numeral at their intersection (in this case, the numeral '1').

Row 1 of the table establishes that a closure of formula (2) is true in the model. The fact that '0' occurs in every row of the table establishes that a closure of formula (3) is true in the model; for example, to see that '$\bigvee y \mathrm{A}(y1) = \mathrm{E}$' is true, we consider the row indexed by '2'. Verification of the truth in the model of a closure of formula (1) is tedious; however, it should be convincing to check some of the instances to be considered, such as

$$\mathrm{A}(\mathrm{A}(4, 2), 1) = \mathrm{A}(4, \mathrm{A}(2, 1)) \quad ,$$

which passes into

$$\mathrm{A}(5, 1) = \mathrm{A}(4, 0)$$

and then into the truth

$$4 = 4 \quad .$$

That a closure of formula (6) is false in the model is established by the instance

$$\mathrm{A}(3, 2) = \mathrm{A}(2, 3)$$

which, on the basis of the table, passes into the falsehood

$$4 = 5 \quad .$$

This model was discovered by employing several well-known mathematical facts, which the reader with some mathematical background may find interesting. Consider a class K with three distinct elements and construct the class U of all biunique functions definable on K, that is, functions that correlate no two elements of K with the same element of K. U will have six functions as elements: for a biunique function definable on K could correlate a first element of K with any one of the three elements of K; a second element of K with any one of the remaining two, and finally a third element of K with the remaining element of K; thus there are $3 \times 2 \times 1$ biunique functions. Now take as the extension of 'E' the identity function, that is, the function that correlates each element of K with that element of K, and take as the extension of 'A' the composition of functions.

We thereby obtain a model (in the broader mathematical sense of 'model' than that which we have defined) in which the formulas (1), (2), and (3) are true and the formula (6) is false, for

(i) the identity function is an identity element for the composition of biunique functions,
(ii) the inverse of a biunique function is a biunique function,
(iii) composition of biunique functions is associative,
(iv) composition of biunique functions is not generally commutative and indeed fails to be so in the above model.

We obtain a model, in our sense, from the above considerations by substituting the numbers 0 through 5 for the six functions and then constructing the table above from the comparable table for the composition of the six functions.

Chapter VI
'THE'

1. Descriptive phrases, terms, formulas. There are arguments whose intuitive validity depends on the meaning of 'the' in its use as the singular definite article. For example, the argument

(1) Exactly one student failed. Alfred is the student who failed. Anyone who failed is illogical. ∴ Alfred is illogical

is intuitively valid, yet a natural symbolization in the identity calculus,

$$\bigvee y \bigwedge x(\mathrm{F}x \wedge \mathrm{G}x \leftrightarrow x = y) \quad . \quad \mathrm{A} = \mathrm{B} \quad . \quad \bigwedge x(\mathrm{G}x \rightarrow \mathrm{H}x)$$
$$\therefore \mathrm{HA} \quad ,$$

is not sufficient to establish its validity.

The word 'the', in its use as the singular definite article, may be replaced by 'the object x such that'. For instance, the second premise of (1) may be paraphrased as

(2) Alfred is identical with the object x such that x is a student and x failed ,

and 'the composer of *Don Giovanni*' as

(3) the object x such that x composed *Don Giovanni* .

We shall abbreviate 'the object . . . such that' by '$\imath$'. Given the scheme

F^1 : *a* is a student
G^1 : *a* failed
H^2 : *a* composed *b*
A^0 : Alfred
B^0 : *Don Giovanni* ,

(2) and (3) can be symbolized by

$$\mathrm{A} = \imath x(\mathrm{F}x \wedge \mathrm{G}x)$$

and

$$\imath x\mathrm{H}(x\mathrm{B})$$

respectively. 'ι' is known as the *descriptive operator* and may be written before any variable to form a *descriptive phrase*; thus 'ιx' and 'ιy' are descriptive phrases.

The reader will recall that an *English name* is an expression of English that purports to designate (at least within a given context) a single object, an *English sentence* is an expression of English that is either true or false, a *term of English* is either an English name or an expression containing occurrences of variables that becomes an English name when some or all of these occurrences are replaced by English names, and a *formula of English* is either an English sentence or an expression containing occurrences of variables that becomes an English sentence when some or all of these occurrences are replaced by English names.

We shall regard expressions of the form

the object α such that ,

where α is a variable, as belonging to English; such expressions will be called *phrases of description*. Accordingly, (2) will be construed as an English sentence, and (3) as an English name.

An expression of the form

the object α such that ϕ ,

where α is a variable and ϕ a formula of English whose only variable is α, will be called a *definite description*. Examples are (3) above,

(4) the object x such that x is presently king of France ,

and

(5) the object x such that x wrote *Iolanthe* .

English usage is not always clear as to the designation of definite descriptions. Some clarification is therefore in order. A definite description

(6) the object α such that ϕ

is said to be *proper* if exactly one object satisfies ϕ; in this case, following ordinary usage, we understand (6) as designating that object. In the case of *improper* definite descriptions, that is, expressions of the form (6) for which either no object or more than one object satisfy ϕ, ordinary usage provides no guidance; it therefore falls to us to make some decision concerning their designation. Our decision is based on the observation in Frege [2] that

> it is a defect of languages that expressions are possible within them, which, in their grammatical form, seemingly determined to designate an object, nevertheless do not fulfill this condition in special cases .

Frege points out that

> it is customary in logic texts to warn against the ambiguity of expressions as a source of fallacies

and deems

> it at least as appropriate to issue a warning against apparent names that have no designation ;

indeed, he demands

> that in a logically perfect language (logical symbolism) every expression constructed as a name in a grammatically correct manner out of already introduced symbols, in fact designate an object .

Thus we shall specify a designation for every improper definite description. It is convenient to select a common designation for all improper definite descriptions. What object we choose for this purpose is unimportant until we consider invalidity again; but for the sake of definiteness let us initially choose the number 0. Thus expressions of the form (6), if improper, will presently be understood as designating 0.

It follows that (4) and (5), as well as (3), are English names that designate; (3)–(5) respectively designate Mozart, 0, and 0. (4) and (5) are improper because nothing is presently king of France and there are two things (Gilbert and Sullivan) that wrote *Iolanthe*.

It also follows from our Fregean convention regarding the designation of definite descriptions that the sentences

The object x such that x is presently king of France is married

and

The object x such that x is presently king of France is less than 1

are respectively false and true.

More generally, we now understand every expression of the form

the object α such that ϕ ,

where α is a variable and ϕ an arbitrary formula of English, to be a term of English. Thus

(7) the x such that x is presently king of y ,

as well as (3)–(5) above, is a term of English; (7) is a *description* rather than a *definite description*, for it contains a variable other than that accompanying the descriptive operator. If 'y' is replaced in (7) by 'France', we obtain a definite description that designates 0; if 'y' is replaced in (7) by 'Sweden', we obtain a definite description that designates Carl Gustaf Folke Hubertus.

For the treatment of descriptions we now consider a symbolic language obtained from that of chapter V (see pp. 263–64) by adding the descriptive operator '$\imath$' to its symbols.

The characterization of *symbolic terms* and *symbolic formulas* must be somewhat more involved than before, for the following reason. The grammatical function of descriptive phrases (as of their English counterparts) is to produce symbolic terms from symbolic formulas. Consequently, not only may symbolic terms occur within symbolic formulas, but also symbolic formulas within symbolic terms. The best way of introducing the present notions of symbolic term and symbolic formula is, it seems, to characterize them simultaneously. Like earlier characterizations, the one below is to be regarded as exhaustive; that is, nothing is to be regarded as a symbolic term or symbolic formula unless it can be reached by successive applications of the following clauses.

(1) *All variables are symbolic terms.*

(2) *If* δ *is a k-place operation letter and* $\zeta_1, \ldots, \zeta_k$ *are symbolic terms, then*

$$\delta\zeta_1 \ldots \zeta_k$$

is a symbolic term. (In particular, a 0-place operation letter is itself a symbolic term.)

(3) *If* π *is a k-place predicate letter and* $\zeta_1, \ldots, \zeta_k$ *are symbolic terms, then*

$$\pi\zeta_1 \ldots \zeta_k$$

is a symbolic formula. (In particular, a 0-place predicate letter is itself a symbolic formula.)

(4) *If* ζ, η *are symbolic terms, then*

$$\zeta = \eta$$

is a symbolic formula.

(5) *If* ϕ, ψ *are symbolic formulas, then so are*

$$\sim\phi \quad ,$$
$$(\phi \rightarrow \psi) \quad ,$$
$$(\phi \vee \psi) \quad ,$$
$$(\phi \wedge \psi) \quad ,$$
$$(\phi \leftrightarrow \psi) \quad .$$

(6) *If* ϕ *is a symbolic formula and* α *a variable, then*

$$\bigwedge\alpha\phi \quad ,$$
$$\bigvee\alpha\phi$$

are symbolic formulas.

(7) *If* ϕ *is a symbolic formula and* α *is a variable, then*

$$\imath\alpha\phi$$

is a symbolic term.

Symbolic terms produced by clause (7) are called *descriptive terms*. Thus, for example,

$$\imath x F^1 x$$
$$\imath x G^2 x A^0$$
$$\imath y \bigwedge x(x = y \leftrightarrow H^2 xy)$$
$$\imath x G^2 xy$$
$$\imath z\, z = \imath x H^2 xy$$

are descriptive terms. Clause (7) also leads to seemingly meaningless combinations such as

$$\iota x F^0 \quad .$$

As with vacuous quantification, it would be artificial to exclude these possibilities; their interpretation will be explained in due course.

As before, generation of a term or formula can be made perspicuous by means of a grammatical tree; but in our present language a tree takes on a new complexity, because the notions of symbolic term and symbolic formula have been characterized simultaneously. The initial nodes of a grammatical tree for either a symbolic term or a symbolic formula are variables, 0-place operation letters, or 0-place predicate letters; every other node, which may be either a symbolic term or a symbolic formula, is generated in accordance with one of clauses (2)–(7) above (inserting '$k > 0$' in clauses (2) and (3)). For example, a grammatical tree for the formula

(8) $$\bigvee x\, \iota x F^2 x A^0 = \iota z(P^0 \vee F^2 xz)$$

appears as follows:

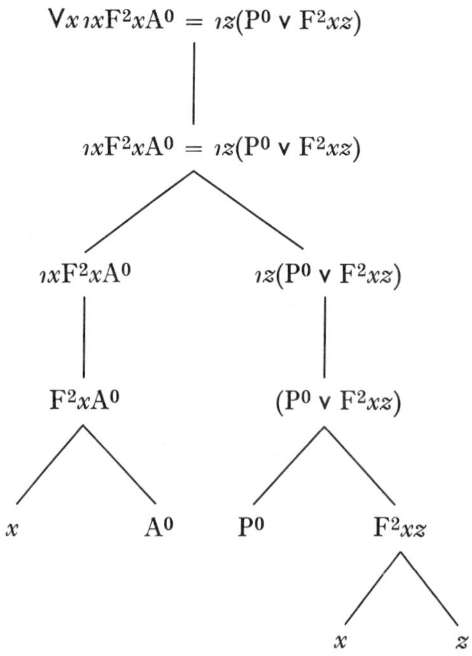

EXERCISES

1. For each of the following expressions state whether it is a symbolic term, a symbolic formula, or neither.

(a) $\iota x \mathrm{F}^0$
(b) $\iota x \mathrm{F}^1 x$
(c) $\iota x \mathrm{F}^1 y$
(d) $\iota x(x = y)$
(e) $\iota x(\mathrm{F}^1 x \wedge \mathrm{G}^1 x)$
(f) $\iota x \mathrm{A}^1 x$
(g) $\mathrm{A}^1 \iota x \mathrm{F}^1 x$
(h) $\mathrm{F}^1 \iota x \mathrm{G}^1 x$
(i) $\mathrm{F}^2 \iota x \mathrm{G}^1 x y$
(j) $\mathrm{A}^1 \iota x \mathrm{A}^1 x = x$
(k) $\iota x x = \iota x x = x$
(l) $\mathrm{F}^2 \mathrm{A}^0 \iota x \mathrm{F}^2 x \mathrm{A}^0$

2. Bondage and freedom. The descriptive operator, like the quantifiers, binds variables. For example, in the formula

$$\mathrm{G}^1 \iota x \mathrm{F}^1 x$$

we shall say that both occurrences of 'x' are bound. Further, we shall speak of *bondage in a term* as well as bondage in a formula. For example, we shall say that 'x' is bound in the term

$$\iota x \mathrm{F}^1 x \quad .$$

Revisions are thus necessitated in our characterizations of bondage and freedom. It is convenient to treat bondage and freedom for variables separately before considering the case of arbitrary symbolic terms.

An *occurrence* of a *variable* α is now said to be *bound in* a symbolic term or formula ϕ just in case it stands within an occurrence in ϕ of an expression

$$\wedge \alpha \psi \quad ,$$
$$\vee \alpha \psi \quad ,$$

or

$$\iota \alpha \psi \quad ,$$

where ψ is a symbolic formula. An *occurrence* of a *variable* is *free in* a symbolic term or formula ϕ just in case it stands within ϕ but is not bound in ϕ. A *variable* itself is *bound* or *free in* a symbolic term or formula ϕ according as there is a bound or free occurrence of it in ϕ.

For example, in the formula

$$\mathrm{G}^2 \iota x \mathrm{F}^1 x x \quad ,$$

the first and second occurrences of 'x' are bound, but the third occurrence is free, and 'x' itself is both bound and free.

An *occurrence* of an arbitrary symbolic *term* ζ is said to be *bound in* a symbolic term or formula ϕ if it stands within an occurrence in ϕ of some expression

$$\bigwedge \alpha \psi \quad ,$$
$$\bigvee \alpha \psi \quad ,$$

or

$$\imath \alpha \psi \quad ,$$

where ψ is a symbolic formula and α a variable which is free in ζ. An *occurrence* of a symbolic *term* is *free in* ϕ if and only if it stands within ϕ but is not bound in ϕ. A symbolic *term* is itself *bound* or *free in* ϕ according as there is a bound or free occurrence of it in ϕ.

For example, in the formula

(1) $$(\bigvee y F^1 \imath x H^2 xy \vee G^1 \imath x H^2 xy) \quad ,$$

the first occurrence of the term

(2) $$\imath x H^2 xy$$

is bound, and the second free. Thus (2) is both bound and free in (1).

Observe that bondage and freedom as applied to variables (and as characterized above) are special cases of bondage and freedom as applied to arbitrary symbolic terms.

A *symbolic sentence* can be characterized as a symbolic formula in which no variable is free, and a *symbolic name* as a symbolic term in which no variable is free. Descriptive terms that are names will be referred to as *descriptive names*. (Thus, among the examples of descriptive terms on p. 309, the first three but not the last two are descriptive names.)

The characterization of *proper substitution of a symbolic term for a variable* remains as before, even though our language now includes descriptive terms. Thus we again say that a symbolic formula ϕ_ζ *comes from* a symbolic formula ϕ_α *by proper substitution of the symbolic term* ζ *for the variable* α if ϕ_ζ is like ϕ_α except for having free occurrences of ζ wherever ϕ_α has free occurrences of α.

Once again a modified grammatical tree can be employed to identify bound occurrences of a term mechanically. Here, in constructing a modified grammatical tree, the descriptive operator as well as a quantifier introduces a link. The criterion for bondage of an occurrence of a term other than a descriptive term remains as in chapter IV (p. 207), but here it applies to bondage in a term as well as in a formula. Thus, an occurrence of such a term in a symbolic term or formula ϕ is bound in ϕ if and only if in the top node of a modified grammatical tree for ϕ there stands within it a linked occurrence of some variable. The criterion for bondage of an occurrence of a descriptive term is a little more complex: an occurrence of a descriptive term in a term or formula ϕ is bound in ϕ if and only if in the top node of a modified grammatical tree for ϕ there stands within it an occurrence of some variable that is linked to an occurrence of a variable that does not stand within it. For example, a modified grammatical tree for formula (8) of the preceding section, that is, for

(3) $$\bigvee x\, \text{℩}x F^2 x A^0 = \text{℩}z(P^0 \vee F^2 xz) \quad ,$$

appears as follows:

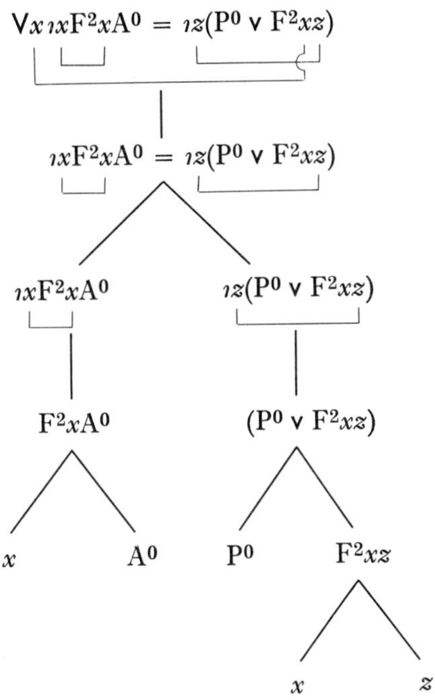

On the basis of the links in the top node of this tree, we see that in (3) the occurrence of '$\text{℩}z(P^0 \vee F^2 xz)$' is bound, for the occurrence of 'x' that stands within it is linked to the initial occurrence of 'x' and the latter does not stand within it; and we see that in (3) the occurrence of '$\text{℩}x F^2 x A^0$' is not bound, for no occurrence of a variable that stands within it (even though both such occurrences are linked) is linked to an occurrence of a variable that does not stand within it.

EXERCISES

Consider the formula

$$\bigvee x\, \text{℩}x\, x = B^1 y = \text{℩}z(\bigwedge y\, A^1 x = B^1 y \vee H^2 B^1 y A^1 z) \quad .$$

2. In this formula identify (perhaps with the aid of a modified grammatical tree) each occurrence of a term that is not a variable as bound or free.

3. Which terms (including variables) are bound in the formula?

4. Which terms (including variables) are free in the formula?

3. Informal notational conventions. Once again we shall employ the conventions of chapter II for omitting parentheses and replacing some of them by brackets.

As in chapters IV and V, we shall usually omit superscripts from operation and predicate letters and employ the convention of inserting parentheses and brackets to avoid ambiguity. In the present context, however, the fact that our convention does not require parentheses or brackets to accompany a 1-place predicate letter could lead to ambiguity. For example, given our previous convention, the expression

$$\text{(1)} \qquad A(\imath x F x)$$

could have as its official counterpart either

$$\text{(2)} \qquad A^1 \imath x F^1 x$$

or

$$\text{(3)} \qquad A^2 \imath x F^0 x \quad .$$

To avoid such an ambiguity, without the cumbersome requirement that 1-place predicate letters be accompanied by parentheses or brackets, we shall never omit a superscript from a 0-place predicate letter and shall always understand expressions like (1) to have expressions like (2) as their official counterpart. Thus the best we can obtain as an informal counterpart to (3) is the expression

$$A(\imath x F^0 x) \quad .$$

We shall also continue the convention of writing, where ζ and η are symbolic terms,

$$\zeta \neq \eta$$

for

$$\sim \zeta = \eta \quad .$$

In formulating inference rules and criteria of bondage and freedom, we always have in mind official notation.

EXERCISES

5. For each term or formula (in unofficial notation) below, delete inserted parentheses and brackets and restore omitted superscripts in accordance with the conventions of this section.

(a) $F[A \imath x F(xA)]$
(b) $A[\imath x A(xy) = x]$
(c) $G \imath x G(Ax)$
(d) $A(\imath x F^0 x A)$
(e) $A(\imath x F x A)$

4. Translation and symbolization. An *abbreviation* is to be understood in the same way as in chapter IV (p. 209). The process of *literal translation into English on the basis of a given scheme of abbreviation* may now begin with either a symbolic term or a symbolic formula, and if successful will end with a term or formula of English. The process consists of the steps given in chapter IV (pp. 209–10), with one modification. Step (v) should now read as follows:

(*v*) *Eliminate sentential connectives, quantifier phrases,* '=', *and descriptive phrases in favor of the corresponding phrases of English, preserving all parentheses.*

An English term or formula ψ is said to be a *free translation* (or simply a *translation*) of a symbolic term or formula ϕ (and ϕ is said to be a *symbolization* of ψ) on the basis of a given scheme of abbreviation if ψ is a stylistic variant of the literal English translation of ϕ based on that scheme.

For example, on the basis of the scheme

F^1	:	*a* is a doctor
G^2	:	*a* is father of *b*
H^2	:	*a* loves *b*
J^2	:	*a* wrote *b*
K^2	:	*a* is larger than *b*
A^0	:	Socrates
B^0	:	*Waverley* ,

the descriptive names

(1) $\imath x Fx$,
(2) $\imath x G(xA)$,
(3) $\imath y \bigwedge x H(xy)$,
(4) $\imath z\, z = \imath y J(yB)$,
(5) $\imath x \bigwedge y [y \neq x \rightarrow K(xy)]$

have the following respective literal English translations:

the object *x* such that *x* is a doctor ,
the object *x* such that *x* is father of Socrates ,
the object *y* such that, for each *x*, *x* loves *y* ,
the object *z* such that *z* is identical with the object *y* such that *y* wrote *Waverley* ,
the object *x* such that for each *y* (if it is not the case that *y* is identical with *x*, then *x* is larger than *y*) .

On the basis of the same scheme, the following terms of English are free translations of (1)–(5):

(6) the doctor ,

(7) the father of Socrates ,
what everyone loves ,
he who is identical with the one who wrote *Waverley* ,
(8) the largest thing .

Thus we regard 'the', 'what', 'he who', and 'the one who', in some of their uses, as stylistic variants of 'the object . . . such that'.

It should not be supposed that every occurrence of 'the' can be supplanted by a phrase of description. Consider, for example, the sentences

(9) The whale is a mammal ,
(10) The members of the club are Republicans ,
(11) The trespassers were prosecuted .

(9) asserts that every whale is a mammal, not that the object x such that x is a whale is a mammal; and attempts to express (10) and (11) with the help of phrases of description would lead to ungrammatical results. In (6) – (8), 'the' generates a name, but this is not the case in (9) – (11); even 'the whale' cannot reasonably be construed as designating in (9) a single object.

To find a symbolization of a given term or formula of English on the basis of a given scheme of abbreviation the reader will find it useful to proceed roughly as follows:

(*1*) *Introduce 'is identical with', phrases of description, phrases of quantity, and phrases of connection, the latter accompanied by parentheses and occurring canonically, in place of their stylistic variants.*

(*2*) *Reverse the steps leading from a symbolic term or formula to a literal English translation.*

For example, consider the scheme of abbreviation

F^2 : *a* is wife of *b*
G^2 : *a* is more salacious than *b*
H^1 : *a* is a woman
J^2 : *a* is mentioned by *b*
A^0 : Justinian
B^0 : Gibbon

and the sentence

The wife of Justinian is the most salacious woman mentioned by Gibbon .

In step (1) we might obtain

The object x such that x is wife of Justinian is identical with the object x such that ((x is a woman and x is mentioned by Gibbon) and for each y (if ((y is a woman and y is mentioned by Gibbon) and it is not the case that y is identical with x), then x is more salacious than y)) ,

and carrying through the successive parts of step (2) we obtain the symbolization

$$\imath x F(xA) = \imath x(Hx \wedge J(xB) \wedge \bigwedge y[Hy \wedge J(yB) \wedge y \neq x \rightarrow G(xy)]) \quad .$$

EXERCISES

6. Provide a literal and a free translation into English of the term

$$\imath x F[x \, \imath y F(yx)]$$

on the basis of the scheme

$$F^2 : \quad a \text{ loves } b \quad .$$

Symbolize each of the following sentences on the basis of the scheme of abbreviation that accompanies it. Exercise 7 is solved for illustration.

7. The man who lives at the North Pole does not live there.

On the basis of the scheme of abbreviation

F^1 : *a* is man
G^2 : *a* lives at *b*
A^0 : the North Pole ,

No. 7 becomes

$$\sim G(\imath x[Fx \wedge G(xA)]A) \quad .$$

8. The positive square root of 2 is a positive even prime. (F^1 : *a* is positive; G^2 : *a* is a square root of *b*; H^1 : *a* is even; J^1 : *a* is prime; A^0 : 2)

9. Mary loves the one who loves Mary. (F^2 : *a* loves *b*; A^0 : Mary)

10. If he who murdered Desdemona was murdered by Desdemona's murderer, then he committed suicide. (F^2 : *a* murdered *b*; G^1 : *a* committed suicide; A^0 : Desdemona)

11. The hardest problem on the examination was solved by no one. (F^1 : *a* is a problem on the examination; G^2 : *a* is harder than *b*; H^2 : *a* was solved by *b*)

12. If the author of *Waverley* is the author of *Ivanhoe*, then the author of *Ivanhoe* is an author of *Waverley*. (F^2 : *a* is an author of *b*; A^0 : *Waverley*; B^0 : *Ivanhoe*)

13. God is that than which nothing greater can be conceived. (A^0 : God; G^2 : *a* is greater than *b*; F^1 : *a* can be conceived)

14. The positive square root of the square of the even prime is irrational. (F^1 : *a* is positive; G^2 : *a* is a square root of *b*; H^1 : *a* is even; I^1 : *a* is prime; J^1 : *a* is irrational; A^1 : the square of *a*)

15. The smallest positive integer is that positive integer which

when multiplied by itself equals itself. (F^2 : a is less than b; G^1 : a is positive; H^1 : a is an integer; A^2 : the product of a and b)

16. There is no greatest positive integer. (F^2 : a is greater than b; G^1 : a is positive; H^1 : a is an integer)

5. Inference rules. For the logic of the descriptive operator we must adopt two new inference rules, the first of which is the following:

$$\text{Proper descriptions (PD):} \quad \frac{\bigvee\beta\bigwedge\alpha(\phi_\alpha \leftrightarrow \alpha = \beta)}{\phi\,\mathrm{\imath}\alpha\phi}$$

Here α and β are variables, ϕ_α is a symbolic formula in which β is not free, and

$$\phi\,\mathrm{\imath}\alpha\phi$$

comes from ϕ_α by proper substitution of the term

$$\mathrm{\imath}\alpha\phi$$

for α. PD corresponds to the principle that if a given condition is satisfied by one and only one object, then the object satisfying that condition satisfies it. PD leads, for example, from the sentence

$$\bigvee y\bigwedge x(Fx \leftrightarrow x = y)$$

(which could be translated as the assertion that exactly one thing wrote *Waverley*) to the sentence

$$F\mathrm{\imath}xFx$$

(which would then assert that the author of *Waverley* wrote *Waverley*). A somewhat more complex application of PD is the inference from the formula

$$\bigvee y\bigwedge x(Fx \wedge G(xzw) \leftrightarrow x = y)$$

(which could be taken as asserting that there is exactly one integer between z and w) to the formula

$$F\mathrm{\imath}x[Fx \wedge G(xzw)] \wedge G(\mathrm{\imath}x[Fx \wedge G(xzw)]\,z\,w)$$

(which would then assert that the integer between z and w is an integer between z and w).

Upon first consideration of such examples, one might believe that any English sentence that is a translation of a conclusion of PD is true. But consideration of further examples would quickly dispel this belief. The sentence

> The man who lives at the center of the earth is a man living at the center of the earth

is false, for it implies the falsehood that some man lives at the center of the earth. The assumption of propriety that constitutes the premise of PD is, however, sufficient to exclude such examples.

Because we seldom have occasion to use improper descriptive names (that is, symbolic terms corresponding to improper definite descriptions), we could develop a significant part of the logic of the descriptive operator on the basis of the single rule PD. There is, however, a strong reason for introducing along with PD a rule pertaining to improper descriptive terms. Without further rules we could not justify inferences that are intuitively plausible whether the descriptive terms are proper or not, such as that from '$F\imath xGx$' to either '$F\imath yGy$' or '$F\imath x \sim\sim Gx$'. There are other reasons for adding a rule concerned with improper descriptions, and these will appear in sections 6 and 7 of this chapter.

The relevant new rule has the following form:

Improper descriptions (ID): $$\frac{\sim \bigvee\beta \bigwedge\alpha(\phi_\alpha \leftrightarrow \alpha = \beta)}{\imath\alpha\phi = \imath\gamma\, \gamma \neq \gamma} \quad .$$

Here α, β, and γ are variables and ϕ_α is a symbolic formula in which β is not free.

The rule ID has no intuitive counterpart, simply because ordinary language shuns improper definite descriptions. The rule corresponds, however, to the resolution that every improper definite description is to designate the same object as the particular improper definite description

the object x such that x differs from x ,

and this resolution accords with the Fregean decision made on page 308.

ID leads, for example, from the sentence

(1) $$\sim \bigvee y \bigwedge x(Fx \leftrightarrow x = y)$$

(which could be translated as the assertion that not exactly one object is presently king of France), to the sentence

(2) $$\imath xFx = \imath x\, x \neq x$$

(which would then assert that the present king of France is the object x such that x differs from x; or, less paradoxically, that the descriptive names 'the present king of France' and 'the object x such that x differs from x' designate the same object).

The descriptive name '$\imath x\, x \neq x$' that occurs in (2) could be read idiomatically 'the nonidentical thing'. Given this reading, it is essential to distinguish carefully between linguistic expressions and nonlinguistic objects. Clearly there is no unique nonidentical thing (see T334, p. 281), and it is just that necessary fact that enables the linguistic expression 'the nonidentical thing' to play its intended role in (2), that is, in the conclusion of ID. Since it is impossible for the descriptive name '$\imath x\, x \neq x$' to designate an object, no ambiguity can occur if some arbitrary object is chosen as its designation. And (2) then asserts, given (1), that the improper description

'$\iota x \mathrm{F}x$' also designates this arbitrarily chosen object. It would be a gross confusion to understand (2) as asserting that '$\iota x \mathrm{F}x$' designated the non-identical thing.

We may call that branch of logic which essentially involves the description operator, as well as the identity sign, quantifiers, and sentential connectives, the *description calculus.* The directions for constructing a *derivation* within this calculus, again, continue to be those set forth in clauses (1)–(9) of chapter III (see pp. 199–200, and p. 220 for a modification of clause (2)), with the understanding that our new rules PD and ID, as well as the identity rules, are now to be included among the inference rules of clause (5a). Three of the identity rules, Id, Sm, and LL, can be adopted as formulated in section 3 of chapter V. But now that terms can have bound occurrences in terms, a slight reformulation of EL is required.

Euclid's Law (EL): $$\frac{\zeta = \eta}{\delta_\zeta = \delta_\eta},$$

where ζ and η are symbolic terms, and δ_η is a symbolic term like the symbolic term δ_ζ except for having one or more *free* occurrences of η where δ_ζ has *free* occurrences of ζ. Of course, throughout clauses (1)–(9), and in the formulations of the various inference rules mentioned therein and above, the words 'term' and 'formula' are now to assume the broader sense of the present chapter.

The characterizations of a *complete* derivation, *derivability*, a *proof*, a *theorem*, an *argument*, a *symbolic argument*, a *valid symbolic argument*, an *English argument*, a *symbolization of* an English argument, and a *valid English argument* remain as before (see pp. 145 and 153–54).

EXERCISES

17. For each of the following, state whether or not it is a proof; if it is not, give a reason why not.

(i)

1. ~~*Show*~~ $\mathrm{A}(x) = \mathrm{B}(x) \rightarrow \iota x\, \mathrm{A}(x) = y = \iota x\, \mathrm{B}(x) = y$
2. $\mathrm{A}(x) = \mathrm{B}(x)$
3. $\iota x\, \mathrm{A}(x) = y = \iota x\, \mathrm{B}(x) = y$ — 2, EL

(ii)

1. ~~*Show*~~ $\mathrm{G}\iota x \mathrm{F}[x\mathrm{A}(x)] \rightarrow \bigvee y \mathrm{G}\iota x \mathrm{F}[xy]$
2. $\mathrm{G}\iota x \mathrm{F}[x\mathrm{A}(x)]$
3. $\bigvee y \mathrm{G}\iota x \mathrm{F}[xy]$ — 2, EG

(iii)

1. ~~*Show*~~ $\bigvee y\, y = \iota x \mathrm{F}(xy)$
2. $\iota x \mathrm{F}(xy) = \iota x \mathrm{F}(xy)$ — Id
3. $\bigvee y\, y = \iota x \mathrm{F}(xy)$ — 2, EG

18. For each of the following pairs of formulas, state whether the second follows from the first by PD, by ID, or does not follow by

either one of these rules; and if the latter, state why it does not follow by one of these rules.

(a) $\bigvee y \bigwedge x(\mathrm{F}x \wedge x = z \leftrightarrow x = y)$
$\mathrm{F}\iota x(\mathrm{F}x \wedge x = z) \wedge \iota x(\mathrm{F}x \wedge x = z) = z$

(b) $\sim \bigvee y \bigwedge x(\mathrm{H}z \leftrightarrow x = y)$
$\iota z\mathrm{H}z = \iota x\, x \neq x$

(c) $\bigvee y \bigwedge x[\mathrm{F}(xy) \leftrightarrow x = y]$
$\mathrm{F}[\iota x\mathrm{F}(xy)y]$

(d) $\bigvee y \bigwedge x(z = \iota z\, z = x \leftrightarrow x = y)$
$z = \iota z\, z = \iota x\, z = \iota z\, z = x$

(e) $\sim \bigvee y \bigwedge x[\bigvee y\mathrm{F}(xy) \leftrightarrow x = y]$
$\iota x \bigvee y\mathrm{F}(xy) = \iota x\, x \neq x$

(f) $\bigvee y \bigwedge x(\bigvee x\mathrm{F}x \leftrightarrow x = y)$
$\bigvee x\mathrm{F}x$

(g) $\sim \bigvee y \bigwedge x[\mathrm{F}(xy) \leftrightarrow x = y]$
$\iota x\mathrm{F}(xy) = \iota x\, x \neq x$

(h) $\bigvee y \bigwedge x(\bigvee x\mathrm{F}x \wedge \mathrm{G}x \leftrightarrow x = y)$
$\bigvee x\mathrm{F}\iota x(\bigvee x\mathrm{F}x \wedge \mathrm{G}x) \wedge \mathrm{G}\iota x(\bigvee x\mathrm{F}x \wedge \mathrm{G}x)$

(i) $\bigvee y \bigwedge x[\mathrm{F}(xx) \leftrightarrow x = y]$
$\mathrm{F}(\iota x\mathrm{F}(xx)x)$

6. Theorems. Theorems of the description calculus will be given numbers beginning with 401.

T401 1. ~~*Show*~~ $\bigwedge x(\mathrm{F}x \leftrightarrow x = y) \to \iota x\mathrm{F}x = y$

2.	$\bigwedge x(\mathrm{F}x \leftrightarrow x = y)$	
3.	$\bigvee y \bigwedge x(\mathrm{F}x \leftrightarrow x = y)$	2, EG
4.	$\mathrm{F}\iota x\mathrm{F}x$	3, PD
5.	$\mathrm{F}\iota x\mathrm{F}x \leftrightarrow \iota x\mathrm{F}x = y$	2, UI
6.	$\iota x\mathrm{F}x = y$	5, BC, 4, MP

Under the scheme

F^1 : a is an author of *Waverley*

T401 asserts:

If y and only y is an author of *Waverley*, then the author of *Waverley* is (identical with) y .

The next two theorems are immediate consequences of our new rules of inference.

T402 $\bigvee y \bigwedge x(\mathrm{F}x \leftrightarrow x = y) \to \mathrm{F}\iota x\mathrm{F}x$

T403 $\sim \bigvee y \bigwedge x(\mathrm{F}x \leftrightarrow x = y) \to \iota x\mathrm{F}x = \iota x\, x \neq x$

Descriptive names will designate the same object if they are formed by prefixing the descriptive operator to coextensive formulas. This fact is exemplified by the next theorem, which is the analogue for the descriptive operator to the quantifier laws of distribution exemplified by T213 and T214 of chapter III.

T404 $\bigwedge x(Fx \leftrightarrow Gx) \rightarrow \iota x Fx = \iota x Gx$

A proof of T404, which we give first informally, requires cases. If 'F' is true of exactly one object, then, by the antecedent of T404, 'G' is true of just that object. But then, clearly, both '$\iota x Fx$' and '$\iota x Gx$' designate that object, and hence the consequent of T404 holds. If 'F' is not true of exactly one object, then, again by the antecedent of T404, the same holds for 'G'. But then the consequent of T404 holds on the basis of ID and LL.

T404

1.	~~*Show*~~ $\bigwedge x(Fx \leftrightarrow Gx) \rightarrow \iota x Fx = \iota x Gx$	
2.	$\bigwedge x(Fx \leftrightarrow Gx)$	
3.	~~*Show*~~ $\bigvee z \bigwedge x(Fx \leftrightarrow x = z) \rightarrow \iota x Fx = \iota x Gx$	
4.	$\bigvee z \bigwedge x(Fx \leftrightarrow x = z)$	
5.	$\bigwedge x(Fx \leftrightarrow x = a)$	4, EI
6.	~~*Show*~~ $\bigwedge x(Gx \leftrightarrow x = a)$	
7.	$Gx \leftrightarrow Fx$	2, UI, T92, BC, MP
8.	$Gx \leftrightarrow x = a$	5, UI, 7, Adj, T93, MP
9.	$F\iota x Fx \rightarrow \iota x Fx = a$	5, UI, BC
10.	$F\iota x Fx$	4, PD
11.	$\iota x Fx = a$	9, 10, MP
12.	$G\iota x Gx \rightarrow \iota x Gx = a$	6, UI, BC
13.	$\iota x Gx = a$	6, EG, PD, 12, MP
14.	$\iota x Fx = \iota x Gx$	11, 13, LL
15.	~~*Show*~~ $\sim \bigvee z \bigwedge x(Fx \leftrightarrow x = z) \rightarrow \iota x Fx = \iota x Gx$	
16.	$\sim \bigvee z \bigwedge x(Fx \leftrightarrow x = z)$	
17.	~~*Show*~~ $\sim \bigvee z \bigwedge x(Gx \leftrightarrow x = z)$	
18.	$\bigvee z \bigwedge x(Gx \leftrightarrow x = z)$	
19.	$\bigwedge x(Gx \leftrightarrow x = b)$	18, EI
20.	~~*Show*~~ $\bigwedge x(Fx \leftrightarrow x = b)$	
21.	$Fx \leftrightarrow x = b$	2, UI, 19, UI, Adj, T93, MP
22.	$\bigvee z \bigwedge x(Fx \leftrightarrow x = z)$	20, EG
23.	$\sim \bigvee z \bigwedge x(Fx \leftrightarrow x = z)$	16, R
24.	$\iota x Fx = \iota w\, w \neq w$	16, ID
25.	$\iota x Gx = \iota w\, w \neq w$	17, ID
26.	$\iota x Fx = \iota x Gx$	24, 25, LL
27.	$\iota x Fx = \iota x Gx$	3, 15, SC

In chapter III we introduced the relation of *equivalence* between *formulas*. Two symbolic *formulas* ϕ and ψ are said to be *equivalent* just in case the biconditional

$$\phi \leftrightarrow \psi$$

is a theorem. This notion can be extended naturally so as to apply as well to terms. The symbolic *terms* ζ and η are said to be *equivalent* just in case the identity formula

$$\zeta = \eta$$

is a theorem.

Descriptive terms differing only in their initial bound variables, like generalizations differing only in this manner, are equivalent. This fact is exemplified by our next theorem, which is the analogue for the descriptive operator to the quantifier laws of alphabetic variance exemplified by T231 and T232 of chapter III.

T405 $\quad \iota x\mathrm{F}x = \iota y\mathrm{F}y$

The proof of T405 is similar to that of T404; indeed, it involves the same cases as those employed in the proof of T404. In order to carry out the details, it is necessary to recognize that one can derive '$\bigvee z \bigwedge y(\mathrm{F}y \leftrightarrow y = z)$' from '$\bigvee z \bigwedge x(\mathrm{F}x \leftrightarrow x = z)$' and '$\sim \bigvee z \bigwedge y(\mathrm{F}y \leftrightarrow y = z)$' from '$\sim \bigvee z \bigwedge x(\mathrm{F}x \leftrightarrow x = z)$'. (The former and the latter pairs of formulas are more subtle examples of alphabetic variance than the pairs of formulas in T231 and T232.) We leave the details to the reader, in exercise 19 below.

T404 and T405, like their quantificational analogues, are essential for the justification of supplementary derivational techniques to be introduced in the next chapter. Neither of these two theorems of the description calculus could be proved without the rule ID.

If there is exactly one even prime, then any object is *an* even prime if and only if it is *the* even prime. This loss of distinction between the indefinite and the definite article under the propriety hypothesis is expressed in the following theorem.

T406

1.	~~*Show*~~ $\bigvee y \bigwedge x(\mathrm{F}x \leftrightarrow x = y) \rightarrow \bigwedge x(\mathrm{F}x \leftrightarrow x = \iota x\mathrm{F}x)$	
2.	$\bigvee y \bigwedge x(\mathrm{F}x \leftrightarrow x = y)$	
3.	$\bigwedge x(\mathrm{F}x \leftrightarrow x = a)$	2, EI
4.	$\mathrm{F}\iota x\mathrm{F}x \rightarrow \iota x\mathrm{F}x = a$	3, UI, BC
5.	$\iota x\mathrm{F}x = a$	2, PD, 4, MP
6.	$\bigwedge x(\mathrm{F}x \leftrightarrow x = \iota x\mathrm{F}x)$	5, 3, LL

The converse of T406,

T407 $\quad \bigwedge x(\mathrm{F}x \leftrightarrow x = \iota x\mathrm{F}x) \rightarrow \bigvee y \bigwedge x(\mathrm{F}x \leftrightarrow x = y)$,

is also a theorem; EG is sufficient to provide a proof. Thus the consequent of T406 is both a necessary and sufficient condition for a descriptive term to be proper.

To obtain the converse of T404, we must assume that the descriptive terms involved are proper.

T408 $\quad \bigvee y \bigwedge x(Fx \leftrightarrow x = y) \wedge \bigvee y \bigwedge x(Gx \leftrightarrow x = y) \rightarrow [\iota xFx = \iota xGx \rightarrow \bigwedge x(Fx \leftrightarrow Gx)]$

As we have seen (pp. 318–19), not all assertions such as

The author of *Waverley* is an author of *Waverley*
The fountain of youth is a fountain of youth

are true. T409 gives a necessary and sufficient condition for the truth of such sentences.

T409

1. ~~*Show*~~ $F\iota xFx \leftrightarrow \bigvee y \bigwedge x(Fx \leftrightarrow x = y) \vee F\iota x\, x \neq x$
2. ~~*Show*~~ $F\iota xFx \rightarrow \bigvee y \bigwedge x(Fx \leftrightarrow x = y) \vee F\iota x\, x \neq x$
3. $F\iota xFx$
4. ~~*Show*~~ $\sim \bigvee y \bigwedge x(Fx \leftrightarrow x = y) \rightarrow F\iota x\, x \neq x$
5. $\sim \bigvee y \bigwedge x(Fx \leftrightarrow x = y)$
6. $F\iota x\, x \neq x$ — 5, ID, 3, LL
7. $\bigvee y \bigwedge x(Fx \leftrightarrow x = y) \vee F\iota x\, x \neq x$ — 4, CD
8. ~~*Show*~~ $\bigvee y \bigwedge x(Fx \leftrightarrow x = y) \rightarrow F\iota xFx$
9. $\bigvee y \bigwedge x(Fx \leftrightarrow x = y)$
10. $F\iota xFx$ — 9, PD
11. ~~*Show*~~ $F\iota x\, x \neq x \rightarrow F\iota xFx$
12. $F\iota x\, x \neq x$
13. ~~*Show*~~ $F\iota xFx$
14. $\sim F\iota xFx$
15. $F\iota xFx$ — 14, 8, MT, ID, 12, LL
16. $F\iota xFx \leftrightarrow \bigvee y \bigwedge x(Fx \leftrightarrow x = y) \vee F\iota x\, x \neq x$ — 8, 11, SC, 2, CB

The converse of T401, like that of T404, requires a hypothesis of propriety.

T410 $\quad \bigvee y \bigwedge x(Fx \leftrightarrow x = y) \rightarrow [\iota xFx = y \rightarrow \bigwedge x(Fx \leftrightarrow x = y)]$

Given as facts that there are no horses with wings and that the monumental logical treatise *Principia Mathematica* had two authors (Whitehead and Russell), we have seen (p. 308) that it follows from our Fregean convention regarding the designation of definite descriptions that the sentence 'The winged horse is identical with the author of *Principia Mathematica*' is true. (Although the convention has such nonintuitive consequences, it does not have the false consequence that some horse was involved in the writing of *Principia Mathematica*.) The counterpart, within the description calculus, to this convention (that is, that any two improper descriptive names designate the same object) can be shown easily with the aid of ID and LL.

T411 $\sim \bigvee y \bigwedge x(Fx \leftrightarrow x = y) \wedge \sim \bigvee y \bigwedge x(Gx \leftrightarrow x = y) \rightarrow \iota xFx = \iota xGx$

What might be called the *essence of Frege* is expressed in the next theorem, for it indicates the necessary and sufficient condition for the truth of a sentence symbolized by '$G\iota xFx$'. For example, the sentence 'The author of *Waverley* is a poet' is true if and only if either exactly one object wrote *Waverley* and that object is a poet or it is not the case that exactly one object wrote *Waverley* and the object chosen as the designation of 'the nonidentical thing' is a poet.

T412

1. ~~*Show*~~ $G\iota xFx \leftrightarrow \bigvee y[\bigwedge x(Fx \leftrightarrow x = y) \wedge Gy] \vee [\sim \bigvee y \bigwedge x(Fx \leftrightarrow x = y) \wedge G\iota x\, x \neq x]$
2. ~~*Show*~~ $G\iota xFx \rightarrow \bigvee y[\bigwedge x(Fx \leftrightarrow x = y) \wedge Gy] \vee [\sim \bigvee y \bigwedge x(Fx \leftrightarrow x = y) \wedge G\iota x\, x \neq x]$
3. $G\iota xFx$
4. ~~*Show*~~ $\sim \bigvee y[\bigwedge x(Fx \leftrightarrow x = y) \wedge Gy] \rightarrow \sim \bigvee y \bigwedge x(Fx \leftrightarrow x = y) \wedge G\iota x\, x \neq x$
5. $\sim \bigvee y[\bigwedge x(Fx \leftrightarrow x = y) \wedge Gy]$
6. ~~*Show*~~ $\sim \bigvee y \bigwedge x(Fx \leftrightarrow x = y)$
7. $\bigvee y \bigwedge x(Fx \leftrightarrow x = y)$
8. $\bigwedge x(Fx \leftrightarrow x = a)$ — 7, EI
9. $\iota xFx = a$ — 7, PD, 8, UI, BC, MP
10. $\bigwedge x(Fx \leftrightarrow x = \iota xFx)$ — 8, 9, LL
11. $\sim [\bigwedge x(Fx \leftrightarrow x = \iota xFx) \wedge G\iota xFx]$ — 5, QN, UI
12. $\bigwedge x(Fx \leftrightarrow x = \iota xFx) \wedge G\iota xFx$ — 10, 3, Adj
13. $\iota xFx = \iota x\, x \neq x$ — 6, ID
14. $\sim \bigvee y \bigwedge x(Fx \leftrightarrow x = y) \wedge G\iota x\, x \neq x$ — 13, 3, LL, 6, Adj
15. $\bigvee y[\bigwedge x(Fx \leftrightarrow x = y) \wedge Gy] \vee [\sim \bigvee y \bigwedge x(Fx \leftrightarrow x = y) \wedge G\iota x\, x \neq x]$ — 4, CD

16.	~~*Show*~~ $\bigvee y[\bigwedge x(Fx \leftrightarrow x = y) \wedge Gy] \rightarrow G\iota xFx$	
17.	$\bigvee y[\bigwedge x(Fx \leftrightarrow x = y) \wedge Gy]$	
18.	$\bigwedge x(Fx \leftrightarrow x = b) \wedge Gb$	17, EI
19.	$F\iota xFx \rightarrow \iota xFx = b$	18, S, UI, BC
20.	$\iota xFx = b$	18, S, EG, PD, 19, MP
21.	$G\iota xFx$	18, S, 20, LL
22.	~~*Show*~~ $\sim \bigvee y \bigwedge x(Fx \leftrightarrow x = y) \wedge G\iota x\, x \neq x \rightarrow G\iota xFx$	
23.	$\sim \bigvee y \bigwedge x(Fx \leftrightarrow x = y) \wedge G\iota x\, x \neq x$	
24.	$G\iota xFx$	23, S, ID, 23, S, LL
25.	$G\iota xFx \leftrightarrow \bigvee y[\bigwedge x(Fx \leftrightarrow x = y) \wedge Gy] \vee [\sim \bigvee y \bigwedge x(Fx \leftrightarrow x \rightarrow y) \wedge G\iota x\, x \neq x]$	16, 22, SC, 2, CB

The thing identical with an object is that object; for instance, the thing identical with Socrates is Socrates. This quite intuitive claim is expressed, generally, in

T413 $\quad \iota x\, x = y = y$.

Counterintuitive is the claim that the self-identical thing and the nonidentical thing are the same, which is one reading of our next theorem.

T414 $\quad \iota x\, x = x = \iota x\, x \neq x$

Another and preferable reading of T414, that the terms 'the identical thing' and 'the nonidentical thing' are equivalent and hence designate the same object, can be made intuitive. If there is exactly one thing, then '$\iota x\, x = x$' and '$\iota x\, x \neq x$' must designate that object, and hence they must designate the same object; if it is not the case that there is exactly one thing, then '$\iota x\, x = x$' is an improper descriptive name, and hence (by ID) '$\iota x\, x = x$' and '$\iota x\, x \neq x$' again designate the same object.

Vacuous application of the descriptive operator is comprehended under clause (7) of the simultaneous characterization of formulas and terms (see p. 310). The designation to be assigned to *vacuous* descriptive terms is indicated by

T415 $\quad \iota xF^0 = \iota x\, x \neq x$.

Cases involving the propriety and impropriety of 'ιxF^0' will lead to a proof of T415 and thereby again emphasize the role of ID as well as PD in the description calculus.

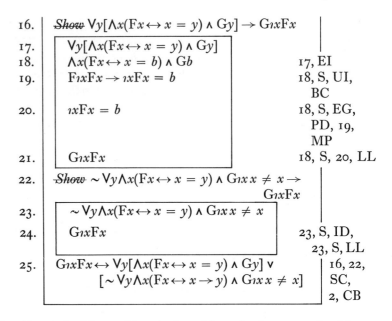

Our last theorem,

T416 $\text{F}\imath x\text{F}x \vee \sim \text{F}\imath x \sim \text{F}x$,

is aesthetically appealing but not immediately intuitive. We outline a proof by cases but leave the details for exercise 19.

1. *Show* $\text{F}\imath x\text{F}x \vee \sim \text{F}\imath x \sim \text{F}x$
2. *Show* $\bigvee y \bigwedge x(\text{F}x \leftrightarrow x = y) \rightarrow \text{F}\imath x\text{F}x \vee \sim \text{F}\imath x \sim \text{F}x$
3. *Show* $\bigvee y \bigwedge x(\sim \text{F}x \leftrightarrow x = y) \rightarrow \text{F}\imath x\text{F}x \vee \sim \text{F}\imath x \sim \text{F}x$
4. *Show* $\sim [\bigvee y \bigwedge x(\text{F}x \leftrightarrow x = y) \vee \bigvee y \bigwedge x(\sim \text{F}x \leftrightarrow x = y)]$
$\rightarrow \text{F}\imath x\text{F}x \vee \sim \text{F}\imath x \sim \text{F}x$

T416 follows from lines 2, 3, and 4 above by two applications of SC; specifically, first apply Form III of SC (see p. 78) to lines 2 and 3 and then apply Form I of SC to the result of the former application and line 4.

EXERCISES

19. Prove the following theorems: T405, T408, T410, T414, T415, T416.

7. Invalidity. We consider first the method of false arithmetical translations and then the method of models; the method of truth-functional expansions cannot easily accommodate the descriptive operator and thus will be ignored here.

The notions of an *arithmetical translation* of a symbolic argument and of a *closure axiom* are to be characterized as before (see chapter IV, section 8), but the notions of a *relativization of a symbolic sentence* and *of a symbolic argument* must be modified as follows.

If ϕ is a symbolic sentence and π a 1-place predicate letter not occurring in ϕ, then by the *relativization of* ϕ *to* π we now understand that sentence which is obtained from ϕ by replacing each part of the form

$$\bigwedge \alpha \psi \quad ,$$
$$\bigvee \alpha \psi \quad ,$$

or

$$\imath \alpha \psi \quad ,$$

where α is a variable and ψ a symbolic formula, by

$$\bigwedge \alpha(\pi\alpha \rightarrow \psi) \quad ,$$
$$\bigvee \alpha(\pi\alpha \wedge \psi) \quad ,$$

or

$$\imath \alpha (\pi\alpha \wedge \psi)$$

respectively. For example, the relativization of the formula

$$\bigwedge x\text{F}[\imath y\text{G}(xy)]$$

to the predicate letter 'U^1' is

$$\Lambda x(Ux \rightarrow F\imath y[Uy \wedge G(xy)]) \quad .$$

Let A be a symbolic argument whose premises and conclusion are sentences, let π be a 1-place predicate occurring in none of these, and let $\delta_1, \ldots, \delta_n$ be all the operation letters occurring in A. Then a *relativization of A* to π is an argument obtained from A by replacing its premises and conclusion by their relativizations to π and adjoining, as additional premises, the closure axioms for $\delta_1, \ldots, \delta_n$ with respect to π, together with the sentence

(1) $$\pi \imath x\, x \neq x \quad .$$

(An existence axiom is no longer required in a relativization, for it follows from (1) by EG.)

Consider, for example, the argument

(2) $$\Lambda x[x = A(x) \rightarrow Fx] \quad . \qquad \mathrm{V}x A(x) = \imath x Fx \quad \therefore\ F\imath x Fx$$

A relativization of (2) to 'U^1' is the argument

(3) $$\Lambda x(Ux \rightarrow [x = A(x) \rightarrow Fx]) \quad . \qquad \mathrm{V}x[Ux \wedge A(x) = \imath x(Ux \wedge Fx)] \,.$$
$$\Lambda x[Ux \rightarrow UA(x)] \quad . \qquad U\imath x\, x \neq x \quad \therefore\ F\imath x(Ux \wedge Fx)$$

Generally, if A and B are symbolic arguments whose premises and conclusion are sentences, then A is said to be a *relativization* of B if there is a 1-place predicate letter π not occurring in B such that A is a relativization of B to π.

In order to ascertain the truth value of the translation into English (or more specifically, for our present purpose, into arithmetical English) of a symbolic sentence in which the descriptive operator occurs, it is necessary to supplement the scheme of abbreviation on which the translation is based. The supplementation required is an additional pair that is not strictly an abbreviation but that indicates the designation of the descriptive name '$\imath x\, x \neq x$' that now occurs in a relativization. Thus, for example, the collection of pairs

(4)

U^1	:	a is a natural number
F^1	:	$a < 2$
A^1	:	a^2
$\imath x\, x \neq x$	:	9

is an appropriate scheme for the argument (3).

In the description calculus, as in the quantifier calculus and in the identity calculus, it happens that a symbolic argument is invalid *just in case* a relativization of one of its closures has (on the basis of an appropriately supplemented scheme of abbreviation) a false arithmetical translation. (This assertion would not hold in the absence of the rule ID.) In particular, it follows that a symbolic formula ϕ is not a theorem *just in case* a relativization of a closure of the argument having ϕ as conclusion and no premises has a false arithmetical translation. Thus here in the description calculus, as in the quantifier calculus and in the identity calculus, given a symbolic argument or a symbolic formula, either a derivation or proof may be supplied or else a false arithmetical translation of a relativization of a closure of the relevant argument exists. (Of course, it remains the case that there is no automatic way of deciding in all cases which alternative holds.) As before, to establish that an argument is invalid or that a formula is not a theorem, it remains sufficient to exhibit a false translation of a closure, without passing to a relativization.

To illustrate application of the method of false arithmetical translations within the description calculus, consider the translation, on the basis of the scheme (4), of the relativization (3) of the argument (2):

(5) Any natural number equal to its square is less than 2. The square of some natural number equals the natural number less than 2. The square of a natural number is a natural number. 9 is a natural number. ∴ The natural number less than 2 is less than 2 .

There is no question, for those familiar with the arithmetic of natural numbers, concerning the truth of the first, third, and fourth premise of (5). However, in order to ascertain the truth value of the second premise and that of the conclusion of (5), an auxiliary notion is required.

We say that an *arithmetical sentence* of English *is derivable from* other *arithmetical sentences* just in case there is a valid English argument with the latter as premises and the former as conclusion. If an arithmetical sentence ϕ is derivable from true arithmetical sentences, then ϕ will be regarded as true; and if a false arithmetical sentence is derivable from ϕ, then ϕ will be regarded as false.

Now note that, on the basis of ID, the arithmetical sentence

(6) The natural number less than 2 is the nonidentical thing

is derivable from

> It is not the case that there is exactly one natural number less than 2 ,

and that the latter sentence is true (for both 0 and 1 are less than 2); thus (6) is true. On the basis of the scheme (4), the sentence (6) asserts that the natural number less than 2 is the number 9. Thus the second premise of (5) makes the true assertion that the square of some natural number equals 9 (for the square of 3 is 9); and the conclusion of (5) makes the patently false assertion that 9 is less than 2.

Thus we have established the invalidity of the argument (2), for we have ascertained that (5) is a false arithmetical translation of a relativization of that argument.

Further illustration is perhaps in order. There are, in contrast to the preceding example, invalid arguments containing the descriptive operator whose descriptive names must translate into proper definition descriptions in order to establish invalidity. For example, the argument

$$(7) \qquad \bigvee y \bigwedge x(Fx \leftrightarrow x = y) \quad \therefore \, \imath xFx \neq \imath x\, x \neq x \quad ,$$

which amounts to the converse of T402, is shown to be invalid by means of the scheme

$$F^1 : \ a \text{ is an even prime number}$$
$$\imath x\, x \neq x : \ 2$$

and the translation

> There is exactly one even prime number. ∴ The even prime number differs from 2

based on it (for 2 is the only even prime number). Clearly, no scheme on the basis of which '$\imath xFx$' passes into an improper definite description would yield a true translation of the premise of (7). And there are arguments and formulas whose invalidity can be established regardless of the choice of designation for '$\imath x\, x \neq x$'. For example, consider a closure of the converse of T401,

$$(8) \qquad \bigwedge y[\imath xFx = y \rightarrow \bigwedge x(Fx \leftrightarrow x = y)] \quad ,$$

and recall the comment that preceded T410 (p. 324). From (8) one can derive

$$(9) \qquad \imath xFx = \imath x\, x \neq x \rightarrow (F\imath xFx \leftrightarrow \imath xFx = \imath x\, x \neq x) \quad .$$

On the basis of the unsupplemented scheme

$$F^1 : \ a \neq a$$

the symbolic sentence (9) passes into the arithmetical sentence

> If the nonidentical thing equals the nonidentical thing, then the nonidentical thing differs from the nonidentical thing if and only if the nonidentical thing equals the nonidentical thing ,

whose falsity is a matter of logic alone.

Models, like schemes of abbreviation, must be supplemented to accommodate the descriptive operator. A model as characterized in chapter IV consisted of a universe and extensions for operation and predicate letters. In the description calculus a model, in addition, must contain an extension for the descriptive name '$\imath x\, x \neq x$', which is simply an element of the universe of the model. This supplementation specifies the element of the universe of the model that is the designation of any improper descriptive name. For example, a model for the argument

(10) $\bigvee x(Fx \wedge Gx)$. $F\imath xFx$. $G\imath xGx$ $\therefore \imath xFx = \imath xGx$

is given by

(11)
$$\begin{aligned} \mathbf{U} &: \{0, 1\} \\ F^1 &: \{0\} \\ G^1 &: \{0, 1\} \\ \imath x\, x \neq x &: 1 \ . \end{aligned}$$

Models supplemented as indicated are sufficient for the demonstration of invalidity; that is, to demonstrate in the description calculus the invalidity of a symbolic argument it is sufficient to find such a model in which a closure of the argument has true premises and a false conclusion, and to demonstrate that a symbolic formula is not a theorem it is sufficient to find such a model in which a closure of the formula is false.

As before, we shall determine the *truth in* or *falsity in* a model of the sentences in a symbolic argument by means of an *expansion of* the argument *with respect to* the model. Thus, for this purpose, we once again incorporate numerals into our symbolic language. We thereby obtain not only additional terms and formulas such as those employed in demonstrating invalidity in the quantifier and identity calculus but also terms such as '$\imath x\, x = 1$' and '$\imath xF(x2)$' and formulas containing such terms. In the description calculus, as in the quantifier calculus, construction of an expansion consists of the elimination of quantifiers and then the replacement of names by their respective *values* (see (1) and (2) on p. 235). The value of a descriptive name, like that of other names, will be a numeral (continuing our practice to use but abuse standard mathematical terminology); however, except for '$\imath x\, x \neq x$', the value of a descriptive name is not given directly by a model. Thus here, in order to carry out the replacement of names by their respective values, we must provide directions for ascertaining the value of a descriptive name. But first let us consider some examples.

We take argument (10) and model (11), above, as our first example. We begin the construction of an expansion of (10) with respect to (11) by eliminating quantifiers from (10), in a manner now familiar. This step leads to

(12) $(F0 \wedge G0) \vee (F1 \wedge G1)$. $F\imath xFx$. $G\imath xGx$
$\therefore \imath xFx = \imath xGx$.

Next we replace the descriptive names in (12) by their respective values. To ascertain the value of '$\imath xFx$' in (11), we look at the sentences

$$\bigwedge x(Fx \leftrightarrow x = 0)$$
$$\bigwedge x(Fx \leftrightarrow x = 1) \ .$$

If one of these sentences is true in (11), then the value of '$\imath x Fx$' in (11) is the numeral in that formula; if neither of these sentences is true in (11), then the value of '$\imath x Fx$' is the value of '$\imath x\, x \neq x$' in (11). (Note that it cannot be the case that both sentences are true.) Similarly, to ascertain the value of '$\imath x Gx$' in (11), we look at the sentences

$$\bigwedge x(Gx \leftrightarrow x = 0)$$
$$\bigwedge x(Gx \leftrightarrow x = 1) \quad .$$

Neither of the latter pair of sentences is true in (11); this can be determined by constructing expansions if inspection is not sufficient. Thus the value of '$\imath x Gx$' in (11) is the same as that of '$\imath x\, x \neq x$' in (11), that is, the numeral '1'. The sentence '$\bigwedge x(Fx \leftrightarrow x = 0)$' is true in (11); hence the value of '$\imath x Fx$' in (11) is the numeral '0'. With these values at our disposal, we obtain from (12), as an expansion of (10) with respect to (11), the argument

$$(F0 \wedge G0) \vee (F1 \wedge G1) \quad . \qquad F0 \quad . \qquad G1 \quad \therefore 0 = 1 \quad .$$

This argument has true premises and a false conclusion in the model (11); and this demonstrates the invalidity of the argument (10). (These claims are based on considerations no different from those set forth in earlier chapters; see (a), (b), and the paragraph following (b) on pp. 235–36, and also p. 285).

A few remarks about this example are in order, before we look at another. With respect to a model, descriptive names, like definite descriptions of ordinary language, are *proper* or *improper*; thus the reader should review our comments concerning definite descriptions (pp. 307–8) and those that accompany the introduction of our inference rules PD and ID (section 5 of this chapter). The truth values (in the model) of the sentences in the pairs of sentences considered above determine the propriety or impropriety of the descriptive names in (10) and thereby their designations in the model. (Clearly, the number of such sentences to be considered in determining the propriety or impropriety of a descriptive name is not, generally, two but the number of elements in the universe of the model.) Thus in our example, '$\imath x Fx$' is a proper and '$\imath x Gx$' an improper descriptive name. In order to demonstrate the invalidity of (10), it is essential that the model have as the common designation for improper descriptive names (specified by the extension assigned to '$\imath x\, x \neq x$') an element of its universe different from that designated by '$\imath x Fx$'. Indeed, it should be recognized that one of the descriptive names in (10) must be proper and the other improper in any model capable of demonstrating the invalidity of that argument: for if both are improper in a model, then the conclusion of (10) is true in that model (see T411 on p. 325); and if both are proper in a model, then either the conclusion of (10) is true in that model or its first premise is false in that model (see exercise 20, at the end of this section).

For a second example, consider the sentence

(13) $$\bigvee y\, A(y) = A(\imath x F[xy])$$

and the model

(14)
$$\begin{aligned} \mathbf{U} &: \{0, 1\} \\ F^2 &: \{(0, 1), (1, 0)\} \\ A^1 &: A(0) \mapsto 0;\ A(1) \mapsto 1 \\ \imath x\, x \neq x &: 0 \quad , \end{aligned}$$

by means of which we will demonstrate that (13) is not a theorem. The descriptive term in (13), that is, '$\imath x F[xy]$', is not a name, for it contains a free variable. Thus we do not deal with it directly, for only names have values. We begin the construction of an expansion (for the argument with no premises and (13) as conclusion) by eliminating the quantifiers from (13); by this first step we obtain

$$A(0) = A(\imath x F[x0]) \vee A(1) = A(\imath x F[x1]) \quad .$$

Next we consider terms that neither are nor contain descriptive terms and in the result of the first step replace them by their respective values, for these values can be obtained directly from the model. Thus we obtain by this second step

(15) $$0 = A(\imath x F[x0]) \vee 1 = A(\imath x F[x1]) \quad .$$

Our third step is to replace the descriptive names in (15) by their respective values. In order to take this step, we must ascertain the value of each. Thus we consider the pair of sentences

$$\begin{aligned} &\bigwedge x(F[x0] \leftrightarrow x = 0) \\ &\bigwedge x(F[x0] \leftrightarrow x = 1) \end{aligned}$$

and the pair

$$\begin{aligned} &\bigwedge x(F[x1] \leftrightarrow x = 0) \\ &\bigwedge x(F[x1] \leftrightarrow x = 1) \quad . \end{aligned}$$

The second sentence of the former pair and the first sentence of the latter pair are true in (14); thus in (14) the value of '$\imath x F[x0]$' is '1' and the value of '$\imath x F[x1]$' is '0'. With these values at our disposal, (15) passes in the third step into the sentence

$$0 = A(1) \vee 1 = A(0) \quad .$$

Our fourth, and last, step is to replace in this sentence composite names by their respective values, which are again given directly by the model. We thus obtain by this fourth step the sentence

$$0 = 1 \vee 1 = 0 \quad ,$$

which is the expansion of (13) with respect to (14). Since this expansion is clearly false (in any model), we have demonstrated that (13) is not a theorem.

Again, a few remarks are in order. Here the specification in the model of the common designation for *improper* descriptive names is irrelevant, for no such name occurs in (13) or the steps that lead to its expansion. To aid the intuition, let 'A^1' designate the identity function, that is, the function that correlates each thing with itself, and let 'F^2' abbreviate '*a* is a spouse of *b*'. Then the model (14) is a miniature world—in which everyone is monogamous. In such a world, any name formed from the term (of English) 'the object *x* such that *x* is a spouse of *y*' is a proper definite description; and since no one in this world is his or her own spouse, the sentence (13), under the interpretation indicated, is false in this miniature world.

For a third example, consider the sentence

$$(16) \qquad \imath x[\imath x Gx = \imath z F(zx)] = \imath z F(z\,\imath x Gx)$$

and the model

$$(17) \qquad \begin{array}{rcl} \mathbf{U} & : & \{0, 1\} \\ G^1 & : & \{1\} \\ F^2 & : & \{(0, 0), (0, 1)\} \\ \imath x\, x \neq x & : & 1 \quad . \end{array}$$

Since there are neither quantifiers nor operation letters in (16), we turn our attention immediately to descriptive terms. (16) has a complexity that did not appear in our preceding examples: descriptive terms stand within descriptive terms. But this complexity presents no problem. We ignore initially the terms within terms, that is, '$\imath z F(xz)$' and '$\imath x Gx$', even though one of them is a descriptive name and therefore has a value. For each of the terms not standing within a term, that is,

$$(18) \qquad \imath x[\imath x Gx = \imath z F(zx)]$$

and

$$(19) \qquad \imath z F(z\,\imath x Gx) \quad ,$$

we ascertain its value; and by replacing in (16) each by the value it has in the model (17), we obtain an expansion of (16) with respect to that model. To ascertain the value of (18), we consider the sentences

$$\bigwedge x[\imath x Gx = \imath z F(zx) \leftrightarrow x = 0]$$
$$\bigwedge x[\imath x Gx = \imath z F(zx) \leftrightarrow x = 1]$$

and determine the truth value of each (in the model (17)) by means of an expansion. Upon elimination of quantifiers we obtain

$$[\imath x Gx = \imath z F(z0) \leftrightarrow 0 = 0] \wedge [\imath x Gx = \imath z F(z1) \leftrightarrow 1 = 0]$$
$$[\imath x Gx = \imath z F(z0) \leftrightarrow 0 = 1] \wedge [\imath x Gx = \imath z F(z1) \leftrightarrow 1 = 1] \quad .$$

Next we replace in these sentences descriptive names by their respective values; these values can be ascertained by considering relevant pairs of sentences, or simply by inspection of the model (17). We thus obtain

$$[1 = 0 \leftrightarrow 0 = 0] \wedge [1 = 0 \leftrightarrow 1 = 0]$$
$$[1 = 0 \leftrightarrow 0 = 1] \wedge [1 = 0 \leftrightarrow 1 = 1] \quad ,$$

neither of which is true in any model. And we thereby establish that (18) is an improper descriptive name in the model (17) and thus has in that model the value of '$\imath x\, x \neq x$', that is, the numeral '1'. To ascertain the value of (19), we consider the sentences

$$\bigwedge z(\mathrm{F}[z\, \imath x \mathrm{G}x] \leftrightarrow z = 0)$$
$$\bigwedge z(\mathrm{F}[z\, \imath x \mathrm{G}x] \leftrightarrow z = 1) \quad ,$$

and then pass to their expansions

$$[\mathrm{F}(0, 1) \leftrightarrow 0 = 0] \wedge [\mathrm{F}(1, 1) \leftrightarrow 1 = 0]$$
$$[\mathrm{F}(0, 1) \leftrightarrow 0 = 1] \wedge [\mathrm{F}(1, 1) \leftrightarrow 1 = 1] \quad .$$

The first sentence of the latter pair is true in the model (17), and thus the value of (19) in that model is the numeral '0'. We now replace in (16) the descriptive names (18) and (19) by their respective values to obtain

$$1 = 0 \quad ,$$

which is the expansion of (16) with respect to the model (17) and which is patently false in that, indeed any, model. We have thereby demonstrated that (16) is false in the model (17) and therefore is not a theorem.

This third example, by its complexity (which perhaps inhibits intuition), should reassure the reader that for any symbolic argument of the description calculus there exists, with respect to a model for a closure of that argument, an expansion whose sentences are either atomic formulas composed of 0-place predicate letters, n-place ($n > 0$) predicate letters and numerals, or the identity sign and numerals, or sentential compounds composed from such atomic formulas.

A summary is now in order. A *model* in the description calculus for a closure of a symbolic argument consists, as before (see chapter IV, section 7), of a *universe* and of *extensions for the operation and predicate letters* of the argument, and in addition, of an *extension for* '$\imath x\, x \neq x$', which may be any element of the universe of the model.

Given such a model for a closure of a symbolic argument, we construct an expansion of that closure with respect to the model as follows:

(1) *Eliminate quantifiers from the sentences of the closure in the manner now familiar.*

(2) *In the result of step* (1), *replace by their respective values* (*in a manner*

now familiar) terms that are operation letters or are composed solely of operation letters and numerals. (Thus no descriptive term or term containing a descriptive term is replaced in this step.)

(3) *In the result of step (2), replace by their respective values (occurrences of) descriptive names not standing within a descriptive name.*

(4) *In the result of step (3), replace by their respective values terms composed solely of operation letters and numerals. (Such terms may be introduced by step (3), for some operation letters may not have been removed in step (2); see our second example above, pp. 333–34.)*

Given a model for a closure of a symbolic argument, we again understand that closure to have true premises and a false conclusion in the model if it has an expansion with respect to the model whose premises are true in and whose conclusion is false in the model, the latter truth values being determined as before (see (a) and (b) of p. 235). Thus in the description calculus, to demonstrate the invalidity of an argument it is again sufficient to construct a model for a closure of the argument and an expansion with respect to the model of the closure whose premises are true in and whose conclusion false in that model; in particular, to demonstrate that a symbolic formula is not a theorem it is sufficient to construct such a model and expansion for a closure of the argument with no premises and that formula as conclusion.

What remains, to complete this summary, is a statement of directions for ascertaining the value in a model of a descriptive name.

(5) *Given a closure of a symbolic argument, a model for that closure, and a descriptive name that occurs in the argument, that is, a term*

$$\text{(20)} \qquad \imath\alpha\phi_\alpha \quad ,$$

where α is a variable and ϕ_α is a formula with no free variables other than α, we ascertain the value of (20) in the given model as follows. Consider, for each element n of the universe of the model, the sentence

$$\bigwedge\alpha(\phi_\alpha \leftrightarrow \alpha = \bar{n}) \quad ,$$

where $\bar{n}$ is the numeral that designates the number n. By steps (1)–(4) above, obtain an expansion with respect to the model of each such sentence and, in the familiar manner, determine by means of that expansion the truth value in the model of that sentence. If there is an element n of the universe of the model such that for that element the sentence

$$\bigwedge\alpha(\phi_\alpha \leftrightarrow \alpha = \bar{n}) \quad ,$$

where again $\bar{n}$ is the numeral that designates the number n, is true in the model, then the value in the model of the descriptive name (20) is the numeral $\bar{n}$;

otherwise, the value of (20) *in the model is the same as the value of* '$\imath x\, x \neq x$' *in the model.*

The invalidity of (2), (7), and (8), established earlier in this section by the method of false arithmetical translations, can also be demonstrated by the method of models. However, the method of false arithmetical translations remains essential for arguments containing the descriptive operator. One has only to formulate with that operator argument (7) on page 288, that is, to replace in it '$A(x)$' by '$\imath z F(zx)$' and '$A(y)$' by '$\imath z F(zy)$', to obtain an argument whose invalidity cannot be established by any model with a finite universe.

EXERCISES

20. We have mentioned that argument (10) cannot be refuted by a model in which both descriptive names of the argument are proper. Verify this claim by demonstrating the validity of the following argument.

$$\bigvee y \bigwedge x(Fx \leftrightarrow x = y) \quad . \quad \bigvee y \bigwedge x(Gx \leftrightarrow x = y) \quad .$$
$$\bigvee x(Fx \wedge Gx) \quad \therefore\ \imath x Fx = \imath x Gx$$

21. The converses of T401–T404 are not theorems. For T401 and T403 this fact has been established; see, respectively, (8) and (7), and the accompanying remarks. By means of models or false arithmetical translations, demonstrate this fact for T402 and T404.

22. In exercise 17 (section 5) each of the formulas

(a) $A(x) = B(x) \rightarrow \imath x\, A(x) = y = \imath x\, B(x) = y$
(b) $G \imath x F[xA(x)] \rightarrow \bigvee y G \imath x F[xy]$
(c) $\bigvee y\, y = \imath x F(xy)$

occurred in the assertion line of a fallacious proof. Demonstrate now (by means of models or false arithmetical translations) that none of these formulas is a theorem. (Review the comments on exercise 17 in the solutions to selected exercises before undertaking this exercise.) Part (a) is worked for illustration.

We attempt a demonstration of invalidity by means of a model with a two-element universe; thus, we let

$$\mathbf{U} : \ \{0, 1\} \quad .$$

We now select, arbitrarily or by insight, a conjunct of the partial expansion of a closure of the formula in part (a), say

$$(21) \quad A(0) = B(0) \rightarrow \imath x\, A(x) = 1 = \imath x\, B(x) = 1 \quad ,$$

and construct, if possible, a model with universe **U** above in which this conjunct is false; for that is sufficient to demonstrate the falsity in the model of the formula in part (a). To make the antecedent of (21) true in the model (under construction), the functions assigned as extensions to

'A^1' and 'B^1' must have the same value for the element 0; to make the consequent false in the model, it is sufficient to make one of the descriptive names proper and the other improper (and then assign an appropriate extension to '$\imath x\, x \neq x$'). Thus we try

$$\begin{array}{ll} A^1 : & A(0) \mapsto 0;\ A(1) \mapsto 1 \\ B^1 : & B(0) \mapsto 0;\ B(1) \mapsto 0 \quad . \end{array}$$

The reader can verify that '$\bigwedge x[A(x) = 1 \leftrightarrow x = 1]$' is true in the model and that both '$\bigwedge x[B(x) = 1 \leftrightarrow x = 0]$' and '$\bigwedge x[B(x) = 1 \leftrightarrow x = 1]$' are false in the model. These facts inform us, according to the directions set forth in clause (5) above, that '$\imath x\, A(x) = 1$' has the value '1' and '$\imath x\, B(x) = 1$' has the same value as '$\imath x\, x \neq x$'. We now choose the appropriate designation for improper descriptive names by assigning an extension to '$\imath x\, x \neq x$', specifically

$$\imath x\, x \neq x \ :\ 0 \quad ,$$

to complete our model. With respect to this completed model, (21) above passes into the clearly false sentence '$0 = 0 \rightarrow 1 = 0$'. (This exercise demonstrates that EL as formulated in section 3 of chapter V, rather than as reformulated in section 5 of this chapter, would lead to fallacies in the description calculus.)

23. In exercise 18 (at the end of section 5) the second formula does not follow by either PD or ID from the first in each of the pairs of formulas (b), (c), (d), (g), (h), and (i). For each of these pairs of formulas, find a model in which a closure of the first formula is true and a closure of the second formula is false. (Review the comments on exercise 18 in the solutions to selected exercises before undertaking this exercise, which establishes that the restrictions on variables that occur in the formulations of PD and ID are necessary to prevent fallacies.) Part (d) is solved for illustration.

Our task is to find a model in which

$$\bigwedge z \bigvee y \bigwedge x(z = \imath z\, z = x \leftrightarrow x = y) \tag{22}$$

is true and in which

$$\bigwedge z\, z = \imath z\, z = \imath x\, z = \imath z\, z = x \tag{23}$$

is false. (Note that we have passed to closures of the formulas in (d) of exercise 18.) Often the task of finding such a model is facilitated by making informal logical transformations on the formulas involved, and such is the case here. The formula (22) is equivalent to the formula

$$\bigwedge z \bigvee y \bigwedge x(x = y \leftrightarrow x = z) \quad ,$$

which is a closure of a variant of T330; thus the formula (22) is a theorem, and hence true in every model. The formula (23) is equivalent to

$$\bigwedge z\, z = \imath z\, z = z \quad . \tag{24}$$

Thus to find a model in which (22) is true and (23) false it is sufficient to find a model in which (24) is false; and this is simple, for any model with a universe of two elements suffices. (The skeptical reader can verify this claim by constructing expansions for (22) and (23). Formal proofs of the equivalences cited here would involve nothing more than analogues of the theorem '$\imath x\, x = y = y$' (T413, p. 326). In the next chapter, wherein the notion of an *instance* of a theorem, now available only for formulas of the sentential calculus, will be extended to all formulas, such proofs will be easy to construct.)

8. Arguments of English. In section 9 of chapter IV we encountered intuitively plausible arguments of English, especially those containing relation words, whose literal symbolizations in the quantifier calculus are invalid. Valid symbolizations were obtained by making explicit premises implicit in ordinary usage. Arguments containing definite descriptions often manifest this phenomenon, for the propriety of definite descriptions often rests on implicit premises. An example is the following argument.

(1) Some problem on Examination I is harder than any other problem on that examination. Students who solve every problem on Examination II also solve every problem on Examination I. Alfred, a student, does not solve the hardest problem on Examination I. ∴ There is a problem on Examination II that not every student solves .

On the basis of the interesting scheme of abbreviation

F^1 : *a* is a problem on Examination I
G^2 : *a* is harder than *b*
H^1 : *a* is a student
J^1 : *a* is a problem on Examination II
K^2 : *a* solves *b*
A^0 : Alfred ,

the intuitively plausible English argument (1) passes into

(2)
$$\bigvee x(Fx \wedge \bigwedge y[Fy \wedge y \neq x \rightarrow G(xy)]) \;.$$
$$\bigwedge x(Hx \wedge \bigwedge y[Jy \rightarrow K(xy)] \rightarrow \bigwedge y[Fy \rightarrow K(xy)]) \;.$$
$$HA \wedge \sim K[A\, \imath x(Fx \wedge \bigwedge y[Fy \wedge y \neq x \rightarrow G(xy)])]$$
$$\therefore \bigvee y(Jy \wedge \sim \bigwedge x[Hx \rightarrow K(xy)])$$

The argument (2) is invalid, as the reader is asked to verify in exercise 24 at the end of this section. To capture the intuitive plausibility of (1) we must assert explicitly the asymmetry of the relation *harder than*, which is implicit in the ordinary use of a comparative such as 'harder'. Thus if we supplement (2) with the additional premise

(3)
$$\bigwedge x \bigwedge y[G(xy) \rightarrow \sim G(yx)] \;,$$

which asserts on the basis of the above scheme of abbreviation the asymmetry of the relation *harder than*, we obtain a valid symbolic argument (as the reader can demonstrate by solving exercise 25 below) and thereby warrant our initial intuition.

EXERCISES, GROUP I

24. Demonstrate the invalidity of the symbolic argument (2) above.

25. Add to the symbolic argument (2) above the symbolic sentence (3) above as another premise, and then demonstrate that the resulting symbolic argument is valid. (Suggestion: derive from the first premise of (2) and the sentence (3) the sentence '$\bigvee z \bigwedge x(Fx \wedge \bigwedge y[Fy \wedge y \neq x \rightarrow G(xy)] \leftrightarrow x = z)$' and then employ PD to obtain '$F\iota x(Fx \wedge \bigwedge y[Fy \wedge y \neq x \rightarrow G(xy)])$', which asserts, on the basis of the scheme of abbreviation above, that the hardest problem on Examination I is a problem on Examination I. With the latter symbolic sentence at one's disposal the derivation of the conclusion of argument (2) is straightforward.)

EXERCISES, GROUP II

Provide a literal symbolization for each of the following arguments on the basis of the scheme of abbreviation that accompanies it or of an interesting scheme of abbreviation if none accompanies it, and then demonstrate either that the symbolization is valid or that it is invalid. If the English argument is intuitively plausible but your symbolization of it is invalid, then warrant this intuition by appropriately supplementing your initial symbolization and then demonstrating the validity of the supplemented symbolization.

26. Argument (1) on page 306.

27. Exactly one thing differs from Alfred. ∴ Everything is Alfred or the thing that differs from Alfred.

28. Alfred loves exactly one thing. Alfred loves the thing that loves him. ∴ The lover of Alfred is the thing Alfred loves.

29. Everything has exactly one spouse. The spouse of Alfred is Betty. ∴ The spouse of Betty is Alfred. (F^2 : *a* is a spouse of *b*; A^0 : Alfred; B^0 : Betty)

30. There is a perfect being. The perfect being is benevolent. ∴ There is a perfect being who is benevolent. (F^1 : *a* is a perfect being; G^1 : *a* is benevolent)

31. There is exactly one perfect being. There are some gods. The perfect being is the god. All gods are benevolent. ∴ The perfect being is benevolent. (F^1 : *a* is a perfect being; G^1 : *a* is a god; H^1 : *a* is benevolent)

32. The god is not the nonidentical thing. The god is the perfect being. ∴ There is exactly one god, and it is a perfect being. (F^1 : *a* is a perfect being; G^1 : *a* is a god)

33. Either the nonidentical thing is a perfect being or God is not the nonidentical thing. God is the perfect being. ∴ God and only God is a perfect being. (F^1 : *a* is a perfect being; A^0 : God)

34. God can be conceived and is that than which nothing greater can be conceived. If a nonexistent object can be conceived, then something greater can also be conceived. ∴ God exists. (F^1 : *a* exists; G^2 : *a* is greater than *b*; H^1 : *a* can be conceived; A^0 : God) (This English argument is, essentially, St. Anselm's ontological argument; compare p. 2.)

35. ∴ If the object *z* such that *z* is a square of *x* equals the object *z* such that *z* is a cube of *x*, then the object *x* such that *x* equals the object *z* such that *z* is a square of *x* equals the object *x* such that *x* equals the object *z* such that *z* is a cube of *x*.

36. Tully is the man who denounced Catiline. Cicero is a man. Cicero preferred Pompey to Caesar. Everyone who preferred Pompey to Caesar denounced Catiline. There is exactly one man who denounced Catiline. ∴ Tully and Cicero are identical.

37. There is exactly one man whom Mary loves. There is exactly one man who loves Alice. The man whom Mary loves is the man whom Alice loves. Alfred is the man whom Alice loves. Mary loves the man who loves Alice. ∴ The man who loves Alice is Alfred.

38. 2 is the even prime. The positive square root of 4 is an even prime. There is exactly one even prime. ∴ 2 equals the positive square root of 4.

39. There is exactly one sophist who teaches without remuneration, and he is Socrates. Socrates argues better than any other sophist. Plato argues better than some sophist who teaches without remuneration. ∴ Plato is not a sophist.

40. Any fish is faster than any smaller one. For each *x* and *y*, if *x* is faster than *y*, then *y* is not faster than *x*. For each *x* and *y*, if *x* is neither smaller than *y* nor the same size as *y*, then *y* is smaller than *x*. ∴ If there is a largest fish, then the largest fish is the fastest fish. (F^1 : *a* is a fish; G^2 : *a* is faster than *b*; H^2 : *a* is smaller than *b*; J^2 : *a* is the same size as *b*; K^2 : *a* is larger than *b*)

41. (i) There is no greatest positive integer. ∴ For any positive integer there is a greater one.

(ii) For any positive integer there is a greater one. ∴ There is no greatest positive integer.

9. Historical remarks. The earliest theories of descriptions are those of Frege (summarized in Carnap [2]) and Russell [1] (summarized in Quine [3]). In both treatments, descriptive terms were regarded as defined expressions. Frege's theory has the disadvantage of requiring, in any language to which it is applied, the presence of at least one name that is not a descriptive term. Russell's theory, which does not specify a designation for improper definite descriptions and thus countenances nondenoting descriptive terms, has more serious drawbacks. In the first-place, the rules of the quantifier calculus must be significantly curtailed when applied to formulas containing descriptive terms. In addition, a descriptive term must always be accompanied by a *scope* indicator, and formulas differing only in the scope of their descriptive terms will not always be equivalent. (See in this context chapter VIII, pp. 404 and 405.) In Rosser [1] and Scott [1] the descriptive operator, '$\imath$', is treated as a primitive symbol. Rosser's system, however, is not *complete* in the sense that a symbolic argument is valid if none of its closures has a relativization with a false arithmetical translation; Scott's system is complete. The present treatment is like that of Rosser's and Scott's in that '$\imath$' is taken as primitive, but in other respects it resembles Frege's theory. (Specifically, it resembles Method IIIb of Carnap [2]; T412 corresponds to the Fregean contextual definition of descriptive terms for that method.) Complete systems in the Russellian tradition can be found in van Fraassen and Lambert [1] and Burge [1], the latter conforming more closely to that tradition than the former.

The completeness of the calculus of this chapter is proved in Montague and Kalish [1].

10. Appendix: list of theorems of chapter VI.

T401 $\bigwedge x(Fx \leftrightarrow x = y) \rightarrow \imath xFx = y$

T402 $\bigvee y \bigwedge x(Fx \leftrightarrow x = y) \rightarrow F\imath xFx$

T403 $\sim \bigvee y \bigwedge x(Fx \leftrightarrow x = y) \rightarrow \imath xFx = \imath x\, x \neq x$

T404 $\bigwedge x(Fx \leftrightarrow Gx) \rightarrow \imath xFx = \imath xGx$

T405 $\imath xFx = \imath yFy$

T406 $\bigvee y \bigwedge x(Fx \leftrightarrow x = y) \rightarrow \bigwedge x(Fx \leftrightarrow x = \imath xFx)$

T407 $\bigwedge x(Fx \leftrightarrow x = \imath xFx) \rightarrow \bigvee y \bigwedge x(Fx \leftrightarrow x = y)$

T408 $\bigvee y \bigwedge x(Fx \leftrightarrow x = y) \wedge \bigvee y \bigwedge x(Gx \leftrightarrow x = y) \rightarrow [\imath xFx = \imath xGx \rightarrow \bigwedge x(Fx \leftrightarrow Gx)]$

T409 $F\imath xFx \leftrightarrow \bigvee y \bigwedge x(Fx \leftrightarrow x = y) \vee F\imath x\, x \neq x$

T410 $\bigvee y \bigwedge x(Fx \leftrightarrow x = y) \rightarrow [\imath xFx = y \rightarrow \bigwedge x(Fx \leftrightarrow x = y)]$

T411 $\sim \bigvee y \bigwedge x(Fx \leftrightarrow x = y) \wedge \sim \bigvee y \bigwedge x(Gx \leftrightarrow x = y) \rightarrow \imath xFx = \imath xGx$

T412 $G\imath xFx \leftrightarrow \bigvee y[\bigwedge x(Fx \leftrightarrow x = y) \wedge Gy] \vee [\sim \bigvee y \bigwedge x(Fx \leftrightarrow x = y) \wedge G\imath x\, x \neq x]$

T413 $\imath x\, x = y = y$

T414 $\imath x\, x = x = \imath x\, x \neq x$

T415	$\iota x F^0 = \iota x\, x \neq x$
T416	$F \iota x Fx \vee \sim F \iota x \sim Fx$

11. Appendix: solutions to selected exercises.

Section 1

1. (a), (b), (c), (e), (g), (j), and (k) are symbolic terms; (h), (i), and (l) are symbolic formulas; and (d) and (f) are neither.

Section 2

2. The linkage in the top node of a modified grammatical tree of the formula, that is, in

$$\bigvee x \iota x\, x = B^1 y = \iota z(\bigwedge y\, A^1 x = B^1 y \vee H^2 B^1 y A^1 z) \quad ,$$

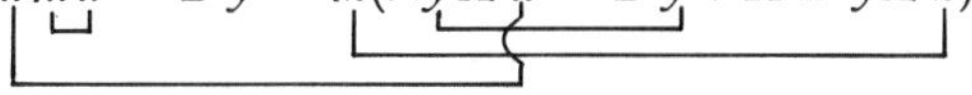

indicates that the occurrence of '$A^1 x$', the second occurrence of '$B^1 y$', the occurrence of '$A^1 z$', and the occurrence of '$\iota z(\bigwedge y\, A^1 x = B^1 y \vee H^2 B^1 y A^1 z)$' are bound in the formula, and that the first and the third occurrence of '$B^1 y$' and the occurrence of '$\iota x\, x = B^1 y$' are free in the formula. (Note that no linked occurrence of a variable that stands within the occurrence of '$\iota x\, x = B^1 y$' is linked to an occurrence of a variable that does not stand within it.)

3. 'x', 'y', 'z', '$A^1 x$', '$B^1 y$', '$A^1 z$', and '$\iota z(\bigwedge y\, A^1 x = B^1 y \vee H^2 B^1 y A^1 z)$' are bound in the formula.

4. 'y', '$B^1 y$', and '$\iota x\, x = B^1 y$' are free in the formula.

Section 3

5. (a) $F^2 A^0 \iota x F^2 x A^0$; (b) $A^1 \iota x\, A^2 xy = x$; (c) $G^1 \iota x G^2 A^0 x$; (d) $A^3 \iota x F^0 x A^0$; (e) $A^2 \iota x F^1 x A^0$.

Section 4

6. the object x such that x loves the object y such that y loves x; that which loves its lover

9. $F[A \iota x F(xA)]$

10. $F[\iota x F(xA) \iota x F(xA)] \rightarrow G \iota x F(xA)$

12. $\iota x F(xA) = \iota x F(xB) \rightarrow F[\iota x F(xB) A]$

(This exercise illustrates the difference between the 'is' of identity and the 'is' of predication.)

16. $\sim \bigvee x(Gx \wedge Hx \wedge \bigwedge y[Gy \wedge Hy \wedge y \neq x \rightarrow F(xy)])$

(Note that it would be incorrect to symbolize No. 16 by

$$\sim \bigvee x[x = \iota x(Gx \wedge Hx \wedge \bigwedge y[Gy \wedge Hy \wedge y \neq x \rightarrow F(xy)])] \quad ;$$

indeed, given the description calculus (see section 5), it is trivial to prove that this incorrect symbolization is the negation of a theorem rather than the symbolization of a true sentence. The reader who solves exercise 41 in section 8 will see that

$$\bigwedge x(Gx \wedge Hx \rightarrow \bigvee y[Gy \wedge Hy \wedge F(yx)])$$

is also incorrect.)

Section 5

17. (i) is not a proof; line 3 does not follow from line 2 by EL, for EL permits only replacement of free occurrences by free occurrences (see formulation in section 5) and the occurrences of '$A(x)$' and '$B(x)$' in line 3 are bound. (ii) is not a proof; line 3 does not follow from line 2 by EG, for the free occurrence of 'y' in '$G\iota xF[xy]$' has passed into a bound occurrence of '$A(x)$' in '$G\iota xF[xA(x)]$'. (iii) is not a proof; line 3 does not follow from line 2 by EG, for line 2 does not come from '$y = \iota xF(xy)$' by replacing both occurrences of 'y' by '$\iota xF(xy)$'.

18. (a) Follows by PD.

(b) Does not follow by either. In an application of ID, for the conclusion to be formed correctly the variable that accompanies the first occurrence of the descriptive operator must be the variable that accompanies the universal quantifier in the premise; thus for a correct application of ID to the first formula in part (b), the second formula should be '$\iota xHz = \iota x\, x \neq x$'.

(c) Does not follow by either. The condition 'β is to be a variable not free in ϕ_α' in the formulation of PD (see section 5) is not satisfied, for 'y' is free in '$F(xy)$'.

(d) Does not follow by either. The proper substitution condition in the formulation of PD is not satisfied, for '$\iota x\, z = \iota z\, z = x$' is bound in the second formula of part (d).

(e) Follows by ID.

(f) Follows by PD.

(g) Does not follow by either. The condition 'β is not free in ϕ_α' in the formulation of ID (see section 5) is not satisfied, for 'y' is free in '$F(xy)$'.

(h) Does not follow by either. PD does not countenance the replacement of bound (as well as free) occurrences of the relevant variable.

(i) Does not follow by either. The proper substitution condition in the formulation of PD (see section 5) is not satisfied, for the second formula of part (i) has been obtained from '$F(xx)$' by replacing only one occurrence, not both occurrences, of 'x' by '$\iota xF(xx)$'.

Section 8, Group II

For each exercise of this group we provide an interesting symbolization and state whether or not that symbolization is valid. For those cases in which the English argument is intuitively plausible but our symbolization invalid, we indicate the appropriate additional premise required to obtain a valid symbolization. We leave the demonstrations of validity and invalidity to the reader.

26. $\bigvee y \bigwedge x(Fx \wedge Gx \leftrightarrow x = y)$. $A = \iota x(Fx \wedge Gx)$. $\bigwedge x(Gx \rightarrow Hx)$ $\therefore HA$ (valid)

27. $\bigvee y \bigwedge x(x \neq A \leftrightarrow x = y)$ $\therefore \bigwedge x(x = A \vee x = \iota x\, x \neq A)$ (valid)

28. $\bigvee y \bigwedge x[F(Ax) \leftrightarrow x = y]$. $F[A\iota xF(xA)]$ $\therefore \iota xF(xA) = \iota xF(Ax)$ (valid)

29. $\bigwedge x \bigvee y \bigwedge z[F(zx) \leftrightarrow z = y]$. $\iota xF(xA) = B$ $\therefore \iota xF(xB) = A$ (invalid)

Extra premise: $\bigwedge x \bigwedge y[(F(xy) \rightarrow F(yx)]$ (*spouse of* is a symmetrical relation)

30. $\bigvee xFx$. $G\iota xFx$ $\therefore \bigvee x(Fx \wedge Gx)$ (invalid)

31. $\bigvee y \bigwedge x(Fx \leftrightarrow x = y)$. $\bigvee x Gx$. $\imath x Fx = \imath x Gx$. $\bigwedge x(Gx \rightarrow Hx)$ $\therefore$ $H\imath x Fx$ (invalid)

32. $\imath x Gx \neq \imath x\, x \neq x$. $\imath x Gx = \imath x Fx$ $\therefore$ $\bigvee y[\bigwedge x(Gx \leftrightarrow x = y) \wedge Fy]$ (valid)

33. $F\imath x\, x \neq x \vee A \neq \imath x\, x \neq x$. $A = \imath x Fx$ $\therefore$ $\bigwedge x(x = A \leftrightarrow Fx)$ (invalid)

34. $HA \wedge A = \imath x \sim \bigvee y[G(yx) \wedge Hy]$. $\bigwedge x(\sim Fx \wedge Hx \rightarrow \bigvee y[G(yx) \wedge Hy])$ $\therefore$ FA (invalid)
(If one supplements the symbolization with an additional premise of propriety, that is, '$\bigvee z \bigwedge x(\sim \bigvee y[G(yx) \wedge Hy] \leftrightarrow x = z)$', then one obtains a valid symbolic argument. But one has not thereby proved the existence of God; indeed, one has simply begged the question.)

35. $\therefore$ $\imath z F(zx) = \imath z G(zx) \rightarrow \imath x\, x = \imath z F(zx) = \imath x\, x = \imath z G(zx)$ (invalid)

36. $A = \imath x[Fx \wedge G(xB)]$. FC . H(CDE) . $\bigwedge x[H(xDE) \rightarrow G(xB)]$. $\bigvee y \bigwedge x[Fx \wedge G(xB) \leftrightarrow x = y]$ $\therefore$ A = C (valid)

37. $\bigvee y \bigwedge x[Fx \wedge G(Ax) \leftrightarrow x = y]$. $\bigvee y \bigwedge x[Fx \wedge G(xB) \leftrightarrow x = y]$. $\imath x[Fx \wedge G(Ax)] = \imath x[Fx \wedge G(Bx)]$. $C = \imath x[Fx \wedge G(Bx)]$. $G(A\imath x[Fx \wedge G(xB)])$ $\therefore$ $\imath x[Fx \wedge G(xB)] = C$ (valid)

38. $A = \imath x Fx$. F[C(B)] . $\bigvee y \bigwedge x(Fx \leftrightarrow x = y)$ $\therefore$ A = C(B) (valid)

39. $\bigvee y[\bigwedge x(Fx \wedge Gx \leftrightarrow x = y) \wedge y = A]$. $\bigwedge x[Fx \wedge x \neq A \rightarrow H(Ax)]$. $\bigvee x[Fx \wedge Gx \wedge H(Bx)]$ $\therefore$ $\sim$FB (invalid) Extra premise: $\bigwedge x \bigwedge y[H(xy) \rightarrow \sim H(yx)]$ (asymmetry of the relation *argues better than*)

40. $\bigwedge x \bigwedge y[Fx \wedge Fy \wedge H(yx) \rightarrow G(xy)]$. $\bigwedge x \bigwedge y[G(xy) \rightarrow \sim G(yx)]$. $\bigwedge x \bigwedge y[\sim H(xy) \wedge \sim J(xy) \rightarrow H(yx)]$ $\therefore$ $\bigvee x(Fx \wedge \bigwedge y(Fy \wedge y \neq x \rightarrow K(xy)]) \rightarrow \imath x(Fx \wedge \bigwedge y[Fy \wedge y \neq x \rightarrow K(xy)]) = \imath x(Fx \wedge \bigwedge y[Fy \wedge y \neq x \rightarrow G(xy)])$ (invalid) Extra premise: $\bigwedge x \bigwedge y[H(xy) \vee J(xy) \rightarrow \sim K(xy)]$ (For each x and y, if either x is smaller than y or x is the same size as y, then x is not larger than y.)

41. For symbolizations see the solution to exercise 16. Both (i) and (ii) are invalid. Extra premise for (i): $\bigwedge y \bigwedge x[y \neq x \rightarrow F(yx) \vee F(xy)]$ (comparability of the relation *greater than*). Extra premise for (ii): $\bigwedge x \bigwedge y[F(xy) \rightarrow \sim F(yx)]$ (asymmetry of the relation *greater than*).

Chapter VII
Additional derivational procedures

IN the preceding chapters we have developed four systems of logic: the sentential calculus, the quantifier calculus, the identity calculus, and the description calculus. Our development of each of these systems is *complete*. That is to say, for any symbolic argument of one of these systems, it is possible either to derive its conclusion from its premises or to demonstrate its invalidity (but not both). Thus the derivational procedures of the preceding chapters cannot be strengthened without introducing fallacies (that is, without making possible the demonstration of both the validity and the invalidity of a symbolic argument). However, they can be simplified and made more sophisticated, and these simplifications and sophistications are the subject matter of the present chapter.

1. Alphabetic variance. In chapter III the equivalence of two generalizations differing only in their initial bound variables was observed (see pp. 165–66); and a similar observation was made in chapter VI concerning descriptive terms differing only in this manner (see p. 323). We may refer to symbolic formulas or terms related in this way as *immediate alphabetic variants* of one another. Symbolic formulas differing only in immediate alphabetic variants are also equivalent and may be called *alphabetic variants*.

More precisely, we say that the pair of symbolic formulas

$$\bigwedge \alpha \phi_{\alpha}$$
$$\bigwedge \beta \phi_{\beta} \quad ,$$

the pair of symbolic formulas

$$\bigvee \alpha \phi_{\alpha}$$
$$\bigvee \beta \phi_{\beta} \quad ,$$

and the pair of symbolic terms

$$\iota \alpha \phi_{\alpha}$$
$$\iota \beta \phi_{\beta}$$

are *immediate alphabetic variants*. Here α and β are variables and ϕ_α and ϕ_β are symbolic formulas such that (i) ϕ_β comes from ϕ_α by proper substitution of β for α and (ii) ϕ_α comes from ϕ_β by proper substitution of α for β.

We say that a symbolic formula ψ is an *alphabetic variant* of a symbolic formula ϕ if there is a finite sequence of symbolic formulas beginning with ϕ and ending with ψ such that each formula of the sequence (except the first) is obtained from its predecessor by replacing an occurrence of a term or formula by an immediate alphabetic variant of that term or formula.

The definition of alphabetic variant makes a symbolic formula ϕ an alphabetic variant of itself (consider the 1-term sequence that begins and ends with ϕ); it makes the symbolic formula ϕ an alphabetic variant of the symbolic formula ψ if ψ is an alphabetic variant of ϕ; and it makes the symbolic formula χ an alphabetic variant of the symbolic formula ϕ if χ is an alphabetic variant of some symbolic formula ψ that is an alphabetic variant of ϕ. Further, immediate alphabetic variants, such as

$$\begin{gathered} \bigwedge x \bigvee y \mathrm{F}(xy) \\ \bigwedge z \bigvee y \mathrm{F}(zy) \quad , \end{gathered}$$

are alphabetic variants, for our understanding of the word 'occurrence' is such that each formula occurs in itself. And clearly formulas that differ only in immediate alphabetic variants, such as

$$\begin{gathered} \bigwedge y\, y = \imath x\, x = y \\ \bigwedge y\, y = \imath z\, z = y \quad , \end{gathered}$$

are alphabetic variants. Also formulas such as

$$\begin{gathered} \bigvee y \bigwedge x \mathrm{F}(xy) \\ \bigvee x \bigwedge y \mathrm{F}(yx) \quad , \end{gathered}$$

which are not immediate alphabetic variants and do not differ only in immediate alphabetic variants, are alphabetic variants. Their status as alphabetic variants is established by the following sequence:

$$\begin{gathered} \bigvee y \bigwedge x \mathrm{F}(xy) \\ \bigvee z \bigwedge x \mathrm{F}(xz) \\ \bigvee z \bigwedge y \mathrm{F}(yz) \\ \bigvee x \bigwedge y \mathrm{F}(yx) \quad . \end{gathered}$$

The identification of alphabetic variants, as well as an insight into their equivalence, can be facilitated by inspecting the top nodes of modified grammatical trees. For two formulas are alphabetic variants just in case the top nodes in their modified grammatical trees differ only in the lettering of bound variables; in particular, the linkage in each of these nodes is identical.

To illustrate, we display such nodes for each of the pairs of alphabetic variants considered above.

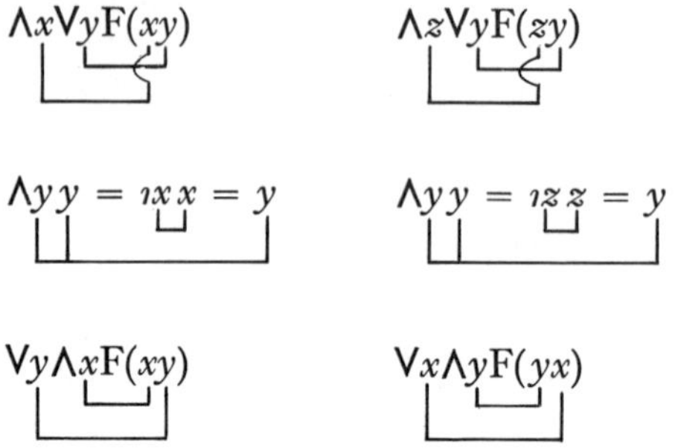

Alphabetic variance will play an important role in section 3, in connection with abbreviatory clauses to be introduced there.

EXERCISES

For each of the following pairs of formulas, indicate (perhaps with the aid of top nodes of modified grammatical trees) whether they are alphabetic variants. Exercise 1 is solved for illustration.

1. $\bigwedge x \bigvee y G(xy)$
   $\bigwedge x \bigvee x G(xx)$

These formulas are not alphabetic variants; although '$G(xx)$' comes from '$G(xy)$' by proper substitution of 'x' for 'y'. '$G(xy)$' does not come from '$G(xx)$' by proper substitution of 'y' for 'x'. This fact is made conspicuous by inspection of the following nodes:

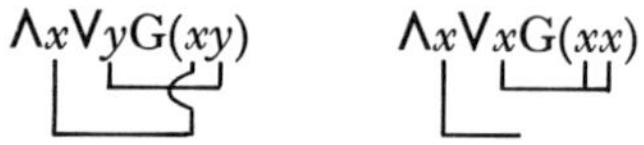

2. $\bigwedge x(Fx \rightarrow \bigvee x Gx \wedge Hy)$
   $\bigwedge x(Fx \rightarrow \bigvee y Gy \wedge Hy)$
3. $\bigwedge x(Fx \rightarrow \bigvee x[Gx \wedge Hy])$
   $\bigwedge x(Fx \rightarrow \bigvee y[Gy \wedge Hy])$
4. $\bigvee z(\bigvee x Hx \wedge Gz)$
   $\bigvee z(\bigvee z Hz \wedge Gz)$
5. $\bigvee y\, y = \iota x F(xy)$
   $\bigvee x\, x = \iota y F(yx)$
6. $\bigvee z G[\iota x F(xz)\, z]$
   $\bigvee x G[\iota x F(xx)\, x]$
7. $\bigvee x\, \iota x F(xy) = x$
   $\bigvee y\, \iota x F(xy) = y$
8. $G(\iota x Fx\, \iota x Fx\, y)$
   $G(\iota x Fx\, \iota y Fy\, y)$

2. Substitution. Present abbreviations make available, as lines of a derivation, instances of *sentential* theorems that have previously been proved. The reader may already have considered the possibility of extending this practice to *all* theorems previously proved, that is, the possibility of using instances of theorems of the quantifier, identity, and description calculus as well as the sentential calculus in constructing derivations. Such an extension is indeed possible, but it has been deferred to the present point because the relevant notion of an *instance* exhibits complexities that did not arise in connection with sentential theorems.

Let us take as an example the theorem

$$(1) \qquad \wedge x Fx \rightarrow FA(z) \quad .$$

(For perspicuity we employ here and in other illustrations the informal notation permitted by our conventions on superscripts and parentheses; in general formulations, however, the words 'term' and 'formula' are always to be understood in the official sense.) In forming instances of (1), we must make replacements that do not change its logical structure, that is, replacements of components other than sentential connectives, quantifiers, the identity sign, the descriptive operator, and parentheses. The replaceable components fall then into three categories: predicate letters, operation letters, and variables.

Let us first consider the replacement of predicate letters. We wish to say that the formula

$$(2) \qquad \wedge x \sim G(xy) \rightarrow \sim G(A(z)\,y)$$

comes from (1) by *substitution* for the *predicate letter* 'F'. We may think of (2) as obtained from (1) in two steps.

We first consider the formula

$$(3) \qquad \sim G(ay)$$

(which may be called the *substituend*, and in which, the reader will note, the variable '*a*' is free), and in (1) replace all occurrences of 'F' by (3) enclosed in braces. Thus we obtain

$$(4) \qquad \wedge x\,\{\sim G(ay)\}\,x \rightarrow \{\sim G(ay)\}\,A(z)$$

(which is not a formula).

Next we replace each part

$$\{\sim G(ay)\}\zeta$$

of (4), where ζ is a term, by

$$\sim G(\zeta y) \quad ,$$

that is, the result of replacing in (3) all free occurrence of '*a*' by ζ. Thus we obtain the formula (2).

We consider now the general situation. Let δ be a k-place predicate letter occurring in a symbolic formula ϕ. Let χ be a symbolic formula that is to be substituted for δ. (In the example above, δ is 'F', ϕ is (1), and χ is (3).) The *substitution* takes place in two steps, as follows:

I. Throughout ϕ, replace δ by χ enclosed in braces.

II. In the expression resulting from I (which will in general not be a formula), successively consider each part of the form

$$\{\chi\}\zeta_1 \ldots \zeta_k \quad ,$$

where $\zeta_1, \ldots, \zeta_k$ are terms. Replace each such part by a certain formula—in fact, by the formula obtained from χ by replacing all free occurrences of 'a' by ζ_1, 'b' by ζ_2, etc., up to the kth variable (in the standard ordering of variables), whose free occurrences are to be replaced by ζ_k.

Certain restrictions are necessary in connection with substitution. Otherwise we could obtain nontheorems by substitution on theorems.

For example, let ϕ, the formula in which the substitution is to take place, be

(5) $$\bigwedge x \mathrm{F}x \rightarrow \bigwedge x \mathrm{FB} \quad .$$

((5) is obviously a theorem.) By substituting 'G(xa)' for 'F', we secure first

$$\bigwedge x\{\mathrm{G}(xa)\}\, x \rightarrow \bigwedge x\{\mathrm{G}(xa)\}\, \mathrm{B} \quad ,$$

and then

(6) $$\bigwedge x \mathrm{G}(xx) \rightarrow \bigwedge x \mathrm{G}(x\mathrm{B}) \quad .$$

But this formula is not a theorem, as the reader can demonstrate easily by means of a model.

As a second example, consider the theorem

$$\bigwedge x \mathrm{F}x \rightarrow \mathrm{F}y \quad ,$$

and substitute for 'F' the formula

$$\bigvee y \mathrm{G}(ay) \quad .$$

We obtain first

$$\bigwedge x\{\bigvee y \mathrm{G}(ay)\}\, x \rightarrow \{\bigvee y \mathrm{G}(ay)\}\, y \quad ,$$

and then

(7) $$\bigwedge x \bigvee y \mathrm{G}(xy) \rightarrow \bigvee y \mathrm{G}(yy) \quad .$$

But this formula too is not a theorem, as the reader can again verify by means of a model.

The difficulties uncovered by these two examples result from a clash of variables and can be avoided by requiring that the substituend and the formula in which the substitution is to take place contain no variable in common. But for formulas containing the descriptive operator this requirement is not sufficient to prevent obtaining nontheorems by substitution on theorems, as the next example reveals.

Consider T402 of the preceding chapter,

$$(6) \qquad \bigvee y \bigwedge x(\mathrm{F}x \leftrightarrow x = y) \rightarrow \mathrm{F}\imath x\mathrm{F}x \quad ,$$

and substitute for 'F' in (6) the formula

$$(7) \qquad [\bigvee z\mathrm{G}(za) \wedge \mathrm{H}z] \quad ,$$

no variable of which occurs in (6). We obtain first

$$\bigvee y \bigwedge x(\{[\bigvee z\mathrm{G}(za) \wedge \mathrm{H}z]\}x \leftrightarrow x = y) \rightarrow \{[\bigvee z\mathrm{G}(za) \wedge \mathrm{H}z]\}\imath x\{[\bigvee z\mathrm{G}(za) \wedge \mathrm{H}z]\}x \quad ,$$

and then, in successive steps,

$$\bigvee y \bigwedge x(\bigvee z\mathrm{G}(zx) \wedge \mathrm{H}z \leftrightarrow x = y) \rightarrow \{[\bigvee z\mathrm{G}(za) \wedge \mathrm{H}z]\}\imath x[\bigvee z\mathrm{G}(zx) \wedge \mathrm{H}z]$$

and

$$\bigvee y \bigwedge x(\bigvee z\mathrm{G}(zx) \wedge \mathrm{H}z \leftrightarrow x = y) \rightarrow \bigvee z\mathrm{G}(z\,\imath x[\bigvee z\mathrm{G}(zx) \wedge \mathrm{H}z]) \wedge \mathrm{H}z \quad .$$

But this last formula is not a theorem. (Here we display the relevant model,

$$\begin{array}{rcl} \mathbf{U} & : & \{0, 1\} \\ \mathrm{H}^1 & : & \{0\} \\ \mathrm{G}^2 & : & \{(1, 0)\} \\ \imath x\, x \neq x & : & 1 \quad ; \end{array}$$

to verify that this last formula is false in this model, note that the occurrence of 'z' that accompanies the second occurrence of 'H' is bound rather than free.) In this example, the clash of variables results from the fact that (7), although it contains no variable in common with (6), contains both a bound and a free occurrence of the variable 'z'. Thus in making substitutions we must require that no variable occurs both bound and free in the substituend.

No other restrictions than those to which we were led by the preceding examples are required to guarantee that only theorems will be obtained from theorems by substitution on predicate letters. Accordingly, we say that a symbolic formula ψ comes from a symbolic formula ϕ by *proper substitution of* a symbolic formula χ *for* a k-place *predicate letter* δ just in case ψ can be obtained from ϕ by steps I and II above, and in addition

(i) no variable occurs in both ϕ and χ; and
(ii) no variable occurs both bound and free in χ.

We turn now to substitution on operation letters. We wish to say that the formula

(8) $$\land x Fx \rightarrow FB(zy)$$

comes from (1) by *substitution for* the *operation letter* 'A'. As in the case of (2), we may think of (8) as obtained from (1) in two steps.

We consider a certain term, the *substituend*,

(9) $$B(ay) \quad ,$$

and in (1) replace all occurrences of 'A' by (9) enclosed in braces, obtaining

(10) $$\land x Fx \rightarrow F\{B(ay)\}z$$

(which is not a formula).

Next we replace each part

$$\{B(ay)\}\zeta$$

of (10), where ζ is a term, by

$$B(\zeta y) \quad ,$$

that is, the result of replacing in (9) all occurrences of 'a' by ζ. Thus we obtain the formula (8).

Again we may ascend to the general situation. Let δ be a k-place operation letter occurring in a symbolic formula ϕ, and let η be a symbolic term that is to be substituted for δ. (In the example, δ is 'A', ϕ is again (1), and η is (9).) The *substitution* takes place in two steps, exactly analogous to those involved in substitution on predicate letters.

I. Throughout ϕ, replace δ by η enclosed in braces.

II. In the expression resulting from I, successively consider each part of the form

$$\{\eta\}\, \zeta_1 \ldots \zeta_k \quad ,$$

where $\zeta_1, \ldots, \zeta_k$ are terms. Replace each such part by a certain term—in fact, by the term obtained from η by replacing all occurrences of 'a' by ζ_1, 'b' by ζ_2, etc., up to the kth variable, whose occurrences are to be replaced by ζ_k.

If substitution is to lead from theorems only to theorems, restrictions are again necessary, as the reader who solves exercises 9, 10, and 11 will verify. Accordingly, we say that a symbolic formula ψ comes from a symbolic formula ϕ by *proper substitution of* a symbolic term η *for* a k-place *operation letter* δ just in case ψ can be obtained from ϕ by steps I and II above, and in addition

(i) no variable occurs in both ϕ and η, and
(ii) no variable occurs both bound and free in η.

Let us now consider substitution on variables. For free occurrences of variables the relevant notion has already been introduced on page 219; the notion is that of ***proper substitution of a term for a variable.*** For bound occurrences of variables no notion of substitution is required, for the role it would play can be handled by alphabetic variance.

Thus we have three kinds of proper substitution—for predicate letters, for operation letters, and for (free) variables. An *instance* of a symbolic formula is obtained by iterated proper substitution; also, we shall consider each symbolic formula as an instance of itself. Thus a symbolic formula ψ is said to be an *instance* of a symbolic formula ϕ just in case ψ is ϕ or is obtainable from ϕ by one or more operations of proper substitution; that is to say, in the case in which ψ is not ϕ, there is a finite sequence of formulas beginning with ϕ and ending with ψ such that each formula of the sequence (except the first) is obtained from its predecessor by a proper substitution.

For example, the theorem

$$(11) \qquad \bigwedge x \mathrm{F}x \rightarrow \mathrm{F}y$$

has as an instance

$$\bigwedge x(\mathrm{F}x \vee \mathrm{G}x) \rightarrow (\mathrm{FA} \vee \mathrm{GA}) \quad .$$

In this case we have made two proper substitutions; for 'F' we have substituted '(Fa v Ga)' and for 'y' we have substituted 'A'. We may indicate this sequence of substitutions diagrammatically as follows:

$$\frac{\mathrm{F} \qquad\qquad y}{(\mathrm{F}a \vee \mathrm{G}a) \qquad \mathrm{A}} \quad .$$

Here the order in which the substitutions are made is unimportant, but this is not always true. For example,

$$\bigwedge x(\bigvee y\mathrm{F}y \vee \mathrm{G}x) \rightarrow (\bigvee y\mathrm{F}y \vee \mathrm{GA})$$

is also an instance of (11), in view of the sequence of substitutions

$$\frac{y \qquad\qquad \mathrm{F}}{\mathrm{A} \qquad (\bigvee y\mathrm{F}y \vee \mathrm{G}a)} \quad .$$

The reverse sequence,

$$\frac{\mathrm{F} \qquad\qquad y}{(\bigvee y\mathrm{F}y \vee \mathrm{G}a) \qquad \mathrm{A}} \quad ,$$

would lead, however, to an improper substitution on 'F'.

That the former sequence of substitutions is proper and the latter improper can be seen easily by considering the sequences of formulas involved in addition to the sequences of substitutions. In the former case one first passes from (11) to

(12) $$\bigwedge x \mathrm{F}x \rightarrow \mathrm{FA}$$

by the substitution of 'A' for 'y' and then passes from (12) to the instance by the substitution of '($\bigvee y \mathrm{F}y \vee \mathrm{G}a$)' for 'F'. Both steps satisfy the restrictions (i) and (ii). In the latter case one first passes from (11) to

(13) $$\bigwedge x(\bigvee y \mathrm{F}y \vee \mathrm{G}x) \rightarrow (\bigvee y \mathrm{F}y \vee \mathrm{G}y)$$

by the substitution of '($\bigvee y \mathrm{F}y \vee \mathrm{G}a$)' for 'F' and then passes from (13) to the instance by the substitution of 'A' for the free occurrence of 'y'. But here the first step violates restriction (i), for the variable 'y' occurs in both the substituend and the formula in which the substitution takes place.

Often, because of restrictions (i) and (ii), more than one substitution must take place to obtain properly what is intuitively an immediate instance of a theorem. For example, to obtain

(14) $$\mathrm{G}[x\mathrm{A}(x)] \rightarrow \bigvee y \mathrm{G}[y\mathrm{A}(x)]$$

as an instance of the obvious theorem

(15) $$\mathrm{F}x \rightarrow \bigvee y \mathrm{F}y$$

one cannot substitute for 'F' the formula

(16) $$\mathrm{G}[a\mathrm{A}(x)] \quad .$$

Such a substitution into (15), although it yields (14), is improper; the variable 'x' occurs in both (15) and (16), in violation of restriction (i) on proper substitution for predicate letters. Instead, one could substitute first 'G[az]' for 'F', thereby obtaining

(17) $$\mathrm{G}[xz] \rightarrow \bigvee y \mathrm{G}[yz] \quad ;$$

and then substitute 'A(x)' for 'z' in (17) to obtain (14). The substitution of 'A(x)' for 'z' in (17) is proper, even though the variable 'x' occurs in both that term and the formula (17), for neither of the restrictions (i) nor (ii) imposed on proper substitution for predicate and operation letters is imposed on proper substitution for free variables; the only requirement to prevent clash of variables for the latter is that free occurrences be replaced by free occurrences, and this condition is satisfied by the substitution of 'A(x)' for 'z' in (17). (The reader should note that the sequence of substitutions

$$\frac{\mathrm{F}}{\mathrm{G}[a\mathrm{A}(z)]} \qquad \frac{z}{x}$$

would also lead properly from (15) to (14); but the substitution of

'$G[aA(a)]$' for 'F', although proper, would yield '$G[xA(x)] \to \bigvee y G[yA(y)]$' rather than (14).)

Although our new notion of an instance is characterized by means of iterated (sequential) rather than simultaneous substitutions on different letters, it nevertheless subsumes the earlier notion of an instance of a sentential theorem. To see this, it is sufficient to consider substitution on 0-place predicate letters and to recognize that with no upper bound on the number of these letters one can always obtain by sequential substitutions that which can be obtained by simultaneous substitutions. For example, by the process of substitution characterized in chapter II one can obtain from

T2 $$Q \to (P \to Q)$$

the instance

(18) $$P \to (Q \to P)$$

by the simultaneous substitution of 'P' for 'Q' and 'Q' for 'P'. By our present notion of instance, (18) can be obtained from T2 by the sequence of substitutions

$$\frac{Q \quad P \quad R}{R \quad Q \quad P} \quad .$$

EXERCISES

9. The formula

(19) $$\bigwedge y[Fy \to GA(y)] \to \bigwedge z[Fz \to GA(z)]$$

is clearly a theorem, for its consequent is simply an alphabetic variant of its antecedent. Substitution of '$B(ya)$' for 'A' in (19) leads first to

$$\bigwedge y[Fy \to G\{B(ya)\}(y)] \to \bigwedge z[Fz \to G\{B(ya)\}(z)]$$

and then to

(20) $$\bigwedge y[Fy \to GB(yy)] \to \bigwedge z[Fz \to GB(yz)] \quad .$$

Demonstrate by means of a model that (20) is not a theorem, and thereby verify the need for restriction (i) in the formulation of proper substitution on operation letters. (In this exercise a free occurrence of a variable in the substituend becomes a bound occurrence in the formula obtained by the substitution.)

10. The formula

(21) $$FA(x) \to \bigvee y FA(y)$$

is clearly a theorem. Substitution of '$\imath x G(xa)$' for 'A' in (21) leads first to

$$F\{\imath x G(xa)\}(x) \to \bigvee y F\{\imath x G(xa)\}(y)$$

and then to

$$(22) \qquad \mathrm{F}\imath x\mathrm{G}(xx) \rightarrow \bigvee y\mathrm{F}\imath x\mathrm{G}(xy) \quad .$$

Demonstrate by means of a model that (22) is not a theorem, and thereby verify again the need for restriction (i) in the formulation of proper substitution on operation letters. (In this exercise a free occurrence of a variable in (21) becomes a bound occurrence in the formula obtained by the substitution.)

11. The formula

$$(23) \qquad \bigvee y\bigwedge x[\mathrm{FA}(x) \leftrightarrow x = y] \rightarrow \mathrm{FA}[\imath x\mathrm{FA}(x)]$$

is a theorem; it is an instance of T402 obtained by substituting 'FA(a)' for 'F'. Substitution of '$\imath w(\mathrm{H}z \vee \bigwedge z\, w = a)$' for 'A' in (23) leads first to

$$\bigvee y\bigwedge x[\mathrm{F}\{\imath w(\mathrm{H}z \vee \bigwedge z\, w = a)\}(x) \leftrightarrow x = y] \rightarrow \mathrm{F}\{\imath w(\mathrm{H}z \vee \bigwedge z\, w = a)\}[\imath x\mathrm{F}\{\imath w(\mathrm{H}z \vee \bigwedge z\, w = a)\}(x)] \quad ,$$

and then (in successive steps) to

$$\bigvee y\bigwedge x[\mathrm{F}\imath w(\mathrm{H}z \vee \bigwedge z\, w = x) \leftrightarrow x = y] \rightarrow \mathrm{F}\{\imath w(\mathrm{H}z \vee \bigwedge z\, w = a)\}(\imath x\mathrm{F}\imath w(\mathrm{H}z \vee \bigwedge z\, w = x))$$

and

$$(24) \qquad \bigvee y\bigwedge x[\mathrm{F}\imath w(\mathrm{H}z \vee \bigwedge z\, w = x) \leftrightarrow x = y] \rightarrow \mathrm{F}\imath w[\mathrm{H}z \vee \bigwedge z\, w = \imath x\mathrm{F}\imath w(\mathrm{H}z \vee \bigwedge z\, w = x)] \quad .$$

Demonstrate by means of a model that (24) is not a theorem, and thereby verify the need for restriction (ii) in the formulation of proper substitution on operation letters. (Note that the variable 'z' is both bound and free in the substituend of this exercise.)

12. Substitute (according to steps I and II) each of the formulas (i)–(iii) below for 'F' in the theorem

$$\mathrm{F}(\mathrm{A}(x)y) \rightarrow \bigvee z\mathrm{F}(zy) \quad .$$

In which cases is the substitution proper? This exercise is solved for illustration.

(i) G(bba)

Step I leads to

$$\{\mathrm{G}(bba)\}(\mathrm{A}(x)y) \rightarrow \bigvee z\{\mathrm{G}(bba)\}(zy) \quad .$$

In step II the place holders 'a' and 'b' are considered in their alphabetic order and the terms that accompany 'F' in the theorem are considered in their sequential order from left to right: all free occurrences of the first letter of the alphabet are replaced by occurrences of the first (leftmost) term in the sequence, and so forth. Thus '$\{\mathrm{G}(bba)\}(\mathrm{A}(x)y)$' passes into '$\mathrm{G}(yy\mathrm{A}(x))$' and '$\bigvee z\{\mathrm{G}(bba)\}(zy)$' into '$\bigvee z\mathrm{G}(yyz)$', yielding

$$\mathrm{G}(yy\mathrm{A}(x)) \rightarrow \bigvee z\mathrm{G}(yyz)$$

as the result of the substitution; and this substitution is proper, for no variable in (i) occurs in the theorem and no variable occurs both bound and free in (i).

(ii) Gb

Step I leads to

$$\{Gb\}(A(x)y) \rightarrow \bigvee z\{Gb\}(zy) \quad ;$$

step II to

$$Gy \rightarrow \bigvee zGy \quad ;$$

and the substitution is proper. (Thus, if the *n*th letter of the alphabet does not occur in the substituend, then the *n*th term in the sequence of terms that accompanied the predicate letter is ignored in step II.)

(iii) G(acz)

Step I leads to

$$\{G(acz)\}(A(x)y) \rightarrow \bigvee z\{G(acz)\}(zy) \quad ;$$

step II to

$$G(A(x)cz) \rightarrow \bigvee zG(zcz) \quad ;$$

and the substitution is improper, for the variable 'z' occurs in both (iii) and the theorem. (Note that 'y' does not replace 'c', for the latter is the third letter of the alphabet and 'y' the second term in the sequence of terms accompanying 'F'.)

The reader should note in connection with this exercise and those immediately following that proper substitution preserves logical structure. Thus, for each of the two formulas obtained here by proper substitution, the consequent follows from the antecedent by EG, as is the case for the theorem of the exercise; but the consequent of the formula obtained in part (iii), which resulted from an improper substitution, does not follow from the antecedent of that formula by EG.

13. Substitute (according to steps I and II) each of the formulas (i) – (x) for 'F' in the theorem

$$F(xy) \rightarrow \bigvee zF(zy) \quad .$$

In which cases is the substitution proper?

(i) G(bba)
(ii) G(bxa)
(iii) G(baa)
(iv) $\bigvee w$G(awb)
(v) $\bigvee y$Gy
(vi) $\bigvee w$Gw
(vii) G(abc)
(viii) G(bw)
(ix) G(azb)
(x) Ga

14. For each of the formulas (i) – (x) below, state whether it comes from the theorem

(25) $$Fx \rightarrow \bigvee y Fy$$

by proper substitution of a formula for 'F'; if so, indicate the relevant substituend. Parts (i) and (ii) are solved for illustration.

(i) $\sim G(xz) \rightarrow \bigvee y \sim G(yz)$

(The formula (i) comes from (25) by proper substitution of

$$\sim G(az)$$

for 'F'.)

(ii) $\sim G(xy) \rightarrow \bigvee y \sim G(yy)$

(The formula (ii) does not come from (25) by proper substitution on 'F'. As the reader can verify, '$\sim G(ay)$' is the only substituend that will permit the passage from (25) to (ii); but a clash of variables makes this substitution improper.)

(iii) $G(xx) \rightarrow \bigvee y G(yy)$
(iv) $G(xx) \rightarrow \bigvee y G(xy)$
(v) $G(xx) \rightarrow \bigvee y G(yx)$
(vi) $\bigwedge w G(wx) \rightarrow \bigvee y \bigwedge w G(wy)$
(vii) $\bigwedge w G(ww) \rightarrow \bigvee y \bigwedge w G(wy)$
(viii) $\bigwedge w G(ww) \rightarrow \bigvee y \bigwedge w G(ww)$
(ix) $G(xx) \rightarrow \bigvee y G(yz)$
(x) $P \rightarrow \bigvee y P$

15. Substitute each of the terms (i) – (x) below for 'A' in the theorem

$$\bigwedge x F A(xz) \rightarrow \bigvee y F A(yz) \quad .$$

In which cases is the substitution proper?

(i) $B(C(b)\ a)$
(ii) $B(ayb)$
(iii) $B(a)$
(iv) $B(b)$
(v) B
(vi) $B(acb)$
(vii) $B(C(a))$
(viii) w
(ix) a
(x) $B(A(bw)\ C(a))$

16. For each of the formulas (i) – (v) below, state whether it comes from the theorem

$$F(A(zy)\ y) \rightarrow \bigvee x\ F(A(xy)\ y)$$

by proper substitution of a term for 'A'; if so, indicate the relevant substituend.

(i) $F(B[C(z)]\,y) \rightarrow \bigvee x F(B[C(x)]\,y)$
(ii) $F\ B(zyy) \rightarrow \bigvee x FB(xyy)$
(iii) $F(A(yz)\,y) \rightarrow \bigvee x F(A(yx)\,y)$
(iv) $F(zy) \rightarrow \bigvee x F(xy)$
(v) $F(yy) \rightarrow \bigvee x F(yy)$

17. For each of the following pairs of formulas state whether the second is an instance of the first obtainable by the indicated sequence of substitutions. Cases (i) and (ii) are solved for illustration.

(i) $Fx \rightarrow \bigvee y Fy$; $G(xx) \rightarrow \bigvee y G(xy)$

$$\begin{array}{cc} F & z \\ \hline G(za) & x \end{array}$$

The second formula is an instance of the first obtainable by the indicated sequence of substitutions. (The reader should compare this case with part (iv) of exercise 14.)

(ii) $F(xy) \rightarrow \bigvee y F(xy)$; $[\bigvee x Hx \vee G(yz)] \rightarrow \bigvee y[\bigvee x Hx \vee G(yz)]$

$$\begin{array}{c} F \\ \hline [\bigvee x Hx \vee G(bz)] \end{array}$$

Here the second formula is not an instance of the first obtained by the indicated substitution. (The second can, however, be obtained as an instance of the first by the following sequence of substitutions:

$$\begin{array}{cc} x & F \\ \hline z & [\bigvee x Hx \vee G(ba)] \end{array} .)$$

(iii) $\bigwedge x(Fx \rightarrow P) \leftrightarrow (\bigvee x Fx \rightarrow P)$; $\bigwedge x[F(xy) \rightarrow \bigwedge z G(yz)] \leftrightarrow [\bigvee x F(xy) \rightarrow \bigwedge z G(yz)]$

$$\begin{array}{ccc} P & F & w \\ \hline \bigwedge z G(yz) & F(aw) & y \end{array}$$

(iv) $\sim \bigvee x Fx \rightarrow \bigwedge x(Fx \rightarrow Gx)$; $\sim \bigvee x \bigvee y F(xy) \rightarrow \bigwedge x[\bigvee y F(xy) \rightarrow \bigwedge z G(A(x)\ z\ B(x))]$

$$\begin{array}{cc} F & G \\ \hline \bigvee y F(ay) & \bigwedge z G(A(a)\ z\ B(a)) \end{array}$$

(v) $\bigwedge x FA(x\ B) \rightarrow \bigvee x FA(xx)$; $\bigwedge x FD(B(xz)) \rightarrow \bigvee x FD(B(xx))$

$$\begin{array}{cc} B & A \\ \hline z & D(B(ab)) \end{array}$$

(vi) $Fy \rightarrow \bigvee x Fx$; $F(xy) \rightarrow \bigvee x F(xx)$

$$\frac{\mathrm{F} \qquad z}{\mathrm{F}(za) \qquad x}$$

18. For each of the terms (i) – (v) below indicate the instance, if any, that can be obtained from the theorem

$$\bigwedge x\, y = A(x) \rightarrow \bigvee x\, y = A(x)$$

by proper substitution of that term for ‘A’.

(i) $\imath z\; z = a$
(ii) $\imath a\; a = a$
(iii) $\imath z\; x = a$
(iv) $\imath z[\bigvee a F(az) \vee G(a)]$
(v) $\imath w\; a = a$

19. The second of each of the following pairs of formulas is an instance of the first; indicate in each case a sequence of substitutions by which the instance can be obtained.

(i) $\bigvee y\; A(x) = y$; $\bigvee y\; \imath x\; z = x = y$
(ii) $\bigvee y\; A(x) = y$; $\bigvee y\; \imath x\; x = x = y$
(iii) $\bigvee y\; A(x) = y$; $\bigvee y\; \imath z\; x = z = y$
(iv) $Fx \leftrightarrow \bigwedge y(y = x \rightarrow Fy)$; $Fx \leftrightarrow \bigwedge y(y = x \rightarrow Fx)$

20. Is the second of each of the following pairs of formulas an instance of the first? If so, indicate the proper substitution or sequence of such substitutions that yields the instance; if not, state why not.

(i) $\bigwedge x[Fx \leftrightarrow x = y] \rightarrow \imath x Fx = y$
$\bigwedge x[F(xy) \leftrightarrow x = y] \rightarrow \imath x F(xy) = y$
(ii) $\bigvee y \bigwedge x[Fx \leftrightarrow x = y] \rightarrow F\imath x Fx$
$\bigvee y \bigwedge x[F(xy) \leftrightarrow x = y] \rightarrow F[\imath x F(xy) y]$
(iii) $\bigwedge x[Fx \leftrightarrow x = y] \rightarrow \imath x Fx = y$
$\bigwedge x[Fz \wedge \bigvee z G(xz) \leftrightarrow x = y] \rightarrow \imath x[Fz \wedge \bigvee z G(xz)] = y$
(iv) $\bigvee y \bigwedge x[Fx \leftrightarrow x = y] \rightarrow F\imath x Fx$
$\bigvee y \bigwedge x[Fz \wedge \bigvee z G(xz) \leftrightarrow x = y] \rightarrow Fz \wedge \bigvee z G(\imath x[Fz \wedge \bigvee z G(xz)]z)$

(In this exercise the first formula in (i) and (iii) is T401, and the first formula in (ii) and (iv) is T402, of chapter VI.)

3. Abbreviated derivations reconsidered; biconditional derivations. Using the notions of the last two sections, we can now introduce more sweeping methods of abbreviating derivations than those employed in chapters III–VI, that is, those characterized by clauses (7)–(9) on pages 150–51. To begin with, we can drop from clause (7) the restriction to sentential theorems, since the general notion of an instance is now available.

Thus we replace (7) as formulated in chapters II and III by the following:

(7) *If ϕ is an instance of an alphabetic variant of a theorem that has already been proved, then ϕ may occur as a line. (Annotation: the number of the theorem in question, sometimes together with a diagrammatic indication of the sequence of substitutions involved.)*

As an illustration of the utility of our new clause (7), consider again T413 of the description calculus. We purposely omitted a proof of this theorem in the preceding chapter, for it is an immediate consequence of a theorem of the identity calculus.

T413	1.	~~*Show*~~ $\imath x\, x = y = y$	
	2.	$\bigvee z \bigwedge x(x = y \leftrightarrow x = z)$	T330
	3.	$\imath x\, x = y = y$	2, PD

Line 2 in this derivation is an instance of a previously proved theorem, for our definition of *instance* (see section 2) makes every formula an instance of itself.

Our new clause (7) permits us to enter instances of alphabetic variants of theorems as well as instances of theorems as lines in a derivation. The convenience of this permission is illustrated by the following example.

In chapter V we stated that

T308 $\quad x = y \leftrightarrow \bigwedge z(z = x \rightarrow z = y)$

is a special case of

T306 $\quad Fx \leftrightarrow \bigwedge y(y = x \rightarrow Fy)$;

indeed, T308 can be obtained from

$$Fx \leftrightarrow \bigwedge z(z = x \rightarrow Fz) \quad ,$$

which is an alphabetic variant of T306, by substituting in that formula '$a = y$' for 'F'. Thus T308 is an instance of an alphabetic variant of T306, but it is not an instance of T306 itself.

Clause (8) of chapter III is no longer needed; any application of QN can be obtained by the revised clause (7) (applied to T203 or T204), together with one or two sentential steps. We replace the old clause (8) by a new clause involving the notion of alphabetic variance:

(8) *A symbolic formula may occur as a line if it is an alphabetic variant of an antecedent line. (Annotation: 'AV' and the number of the antecedent line.)*

The utility of clause (8) as an auxiliary to the employment of instances in obtaining succinct proofs is illustrated by our next example.

In chapter III (p. 165) we gave a rather complex indirect proof of T229. Now, with the aid of AV and an instance of

T220 $\quad \bigvee x(P \rightarrow Fx) \leftrightarrow (P \rightarrow \bigvee xFx)$,

we are able to give a simple, direct proof of that theorem.

T229

1.	~~Show~~ $\bigvee x(\bigvee xFx \rightarrow Fx)$	
2.	$\bigvee x(\bigvee zFz \rightarrow Fx) \leftrightarrow (\bigvee zFz \rightarrow \bigvee xFx)$	T220$\left(\frac{P}{\bigvee zFz}\right)$
3.	$\bigvee x(\bigvee xFx \rightarrow Fx) \leftrightarrow (\bigvee xFx \rightarrow \bigvee xFx)$	2, AV
4.	$\bigvee xFx \rightarrow \bigvee xFx$	T1$\left(\frac{P}{\bigvee xFx}\right)$
5.	$\bigvee x(\bigvee xFx \rightarrow Fx)$	3, BC, 4, MP

(Note that the formula in line 3 of this derivation is not an instance of T220, for the substitution of '$\bigvee xFx$' for 'P' in T220 is improper.)

AV is useful even when instances are not involved. Consider the obviously valid argument

$$\bigwedge x\bigwedge yF(xy) \quad \therefore F(yx) \quad .$$

The conclusion of this argument cannot be derived from the premise by two applications of UI; indeed, without AV a tedious subsidiary derivation is needed. (See the proof of T255 given on p. 257.) But with AV the validity of the argument can be established by the following derivation.

1.	~~Show~~ $F(yx)$	
2.	$\bigwedge x\bigwedge yF(xy)$	Premise
3.	$\bigwedge x\bigwedge zF(xz)$	2, AV
4.	$\bigwedge zF(yz)$	3, UI
5.	$F(yx)$	4, UI

Symbolic formulas differing only in equivalent parts are themselves equivalent, and this fact provides us with another useful device for abbreviating derivations. To incorporate this device into our system we first introduce a new inference rule and then replace the former clause (9) (which we have employed in some of the illustrations above and which will reappear as clause (10)) by a new clause that accommodates this rule.

If ϕ and ψ are symbolic formulas such that either of

$$\phi \leftrightarrow \psi$$
$$\psi \leftrightarrow \phi$$

is an alphabetic variant of an instance of an alphabetic variant of a previously proven theorem, and χ_ϕ and χ_ψ are symbolic formulas such that χ_ψ

is like χ_ϕ except for having one or more occurrences of ψ where χ_ϕ has occurrences of ϕ, then we say that χ_ψ *follows from* χ_ϕ *by interchange of equivalents*.

For example, each of the following is an application of our new rule based on obvious instances of

T110 $\quad P \leftrightarrow \sim\sim P$.

$$\frac{P \vee Q}{P \vee \sim\sim Q} \qquad \frac{\bigvee x Fx}{\bigvee x \sim\sim Fx} \qquad \frac{F\mathrm{\iota}xGx}{F\mathrm{\iota}x \sim\sim Gx}$$

The inference

$$\frac{\bigvee xFx \vee \bigvee xGx}{\bigvee x(Fx \vee Gx)}$$

is comprehended under the new rule on the basis of T207, for (as we mentioned in section 1) our understanding of the word 'occurrence' is such that each formula occurs in itself. Note, however, that an inference such as

$$\frac{\bigwedge xFx \vee \bigwedge xGx}{\bigwedge x(Fx \vee Gx)} \quad ,$$

although valid, is not comprehended by our new rule on the basis of T210, for that theorem (in contrast to T207) is not a biconditional.

A more complex illustration of our new rule in which alphabetic variance is involved is the inference

$$\frac{\bigwedge x(Fx \vee \bigvee xGx)}{\bigwedge x\bigvee y(Fx \vee Gy)} \quad .$$

Here the formulas interchanged are '$(Fx \vee \bigvee xGx)$' and '$\bigvee y(Fx \vee Gy)$'. Thus to show that this inference is a correct application of interchange of equivalents, it is sufficient to show that the formula

$$(1) \qquad \bigvee y(Fx \vee Gy) \leftrightarrow (Fx \vee \bigvee xGx)$$

is an alphabetic variant of an instance of an alphabetic variant of some theorem. And this we do as follows: we consider T218, that is,

$$\bigvee x(P \vee Fx) \leftrightarrow (P \vee \bigvee xFx) \quad ,$$

and form an alphabetic variant of that theorem, specifically the formula

$$\bigvee y(P \vee Fy) \leftrightarrow (P \vee \bigvee yFy) \quad ;$$

next we make the sequence of substitutions

$$\frac{F \qquad P}{Ga \qquad Fx}$$

into this alphabetic variant of T218 to obtain

$$\bigvee y(Fx \vee Gy) \leftrightarrow (Fx \vee \bigvee yGy) \quad ;$$

and lastly we form an alphabetic variant of this instance of an alphabetic variant of T218 to obtain (1) above.

We now incorporate interchange of equivalents into our system of derivation.

(9) *A symbolic formula may occur as a line if it follows from an antecedent line by interchange of equivalents.* [*Annotation: 'IE', the number of the biconditional theorem on which the interchange is based (sometimes accompanied by a diagrammatic indication of the sequence of substitutions involved), and the number of the antecedent line.*]

We immediately reintroduce the permission to compress steps for the convenience it provides and then consider some applications of our new clause (9).

(*10*) *A symbolic formula may occur as a line if it is the last in a succession of steps, each step in the succession other than the last step is either an antecedent line or can be justified by one of clauses (2), (5a), (7), (8), or (9), and the last step can be justified by one of clauses (5a), (5b), (8), or (9). (The annotation should determine the succession of steps by indicating, in the order of application, the antecedent lines, the premises, the inference rules, and the previously proved theorems employed. It should also contain such indication of terms and formulas involved in the intermediate steps as may be required to dispel remaining ambiguity.)*

(In the statement of clause (10), we include in clause (5a) all inference rules, primitive and derived, employed in chapters I–VI.)

The proof of T229 given above is an improvement on that given in chapter III; but clause (9) provides us with an even more succinct proof of that theorem.

T229	1.	~~*Show*~~ $\bigvee x(\bigvee xFx \rightarrow Fx)$	
	2.	$\bigvee xFx \rightarrow \bigvee xFx$	T1
	3.	$\bigvee x(\bigvee xFx \rightarrow Fx)$	2, T220, IE

The formula in line 3 of the proof of T229 given on page 362 is the alphabetic variant of an instance of T220 on which the passage from line 2 to line 3 of the present proof is based.

Consider again the proof of T247 presented on page 167. Given the strategic hints pertaining to the sentential rules CD and SC, that proof is relatively simple; but it is also relatively tedious. Clause (9) allows us to bypass relatively tedious application of now familiar rules, as the following proof illustrates.

T247

1.	~~*Show*~~ $\bigvee x(Fx \rightarrow Gx) \leftrightarrow \bigvee x \sim Fx \vee \bigvee xGx$	
2.	~~*Show*~~ $\bigvee x(Fx \rightarrow Gx) \rightarrow \bigvee x \sim Fx \vee \bigvee xGx$	
3.	$\bigvee x(Fx \rightarrow Gx)$	
4.	$\bigvee x(\sim Fx \vee Gx)$	3, T46, IE
5.	$\bigvee x \sim Fx \vee \bigvee xGx$	4, T207, IE
6.	~~*Show*~~ $\bigvee x \sim Fx \vee \bigvee xGx \rightarrow \bigvee x(Fx \rightarrow Gx)$	
7.	$\bigvee x \sim Fx \vee \bigvee xGx$	
8.	$\bigvee x(\sim Fx \vee Gx)$	7, T207, IE
9.	$\bigvee x(Fx \rightarrow Gx)$	8, T46, IE
10.	$\bigvee x(Fx \rightarrow Gx) \leftrightarrow \bigvee x \sim Fx \vee \bigvee xGx$	2, 6, CB

But the above proof is also tedious, for we have merely reversed the steps of the first subsidiary derivation in the second subsidiary derivation. This fact recommends a new form of derivation: *biconditional derivation.*

If the following arrangement of lines occurs

Show $\phi \leftrightarrow \psi$

χ_1

.

.

.

χ_m ,

where χ_1 is the symbolic formula ϕ, χ_m is the symbolic formula ψ, and for each i, $1 \leq i < m$, the formula χ_{i+1} follows from the formula χ_i by IE or AV, then one may box the lines $\chi_1, \ldots, \chi_m$ and cancel the displayed occurrence of '*Show*'. (The formula χ_1, that is, ϕ, is called *the assumption for biconditional derivation*; every line other than χ_1 must be accompanied by an annotation indicating the preceding line, which of the rules AV or IE is employed, and in the case of IE the previously proved theorem involved.)

With biconditional derivation at our disposal, the ten-line proof of T247 above can be dispensed with in favor of the following four-line proof.

T247

1.	~~*Show*~~ $\bigvee x(Fx \rightarrow Gx) \leftrightarrow \bigvee x \sim Fx \vee \bigvee xGx$	
2.	$\bigvee x(Fx \rightarrow Gx)$	Assumption (Biconditional derivation)
3.	$\bigvee x(\sim Fx \vee Gx)$	2, T46, IE
4.	$\bigvee x \sim Fx \vee \bigvee xGx$	3, T207, IE

Another illustration of the economy achieved by biconditional proofs is obtained by comparing the following proof of T243 with that given in exercise 68 at the end of section 8 of chapter III.

T243	1.	~~*Show*~~ $\sim \bigvee x(Fx \wedge Gx) \leftrightarrow \bigwedge x(Fx \rightarrow \sim Gx)$	
	2.	$\sim \bigvee x(Fx \wedge Gx)$	Assumption
	3.	$\bigwedge x \sim (Fx \wedge Gx)$	2, T204, IE
	4.	$\bigwedge x(Fx \rightarrow \sim Gx)$	3, T39, IE

Our familiar rule QN could account for the passage above from line 2 to line 3 (although not within the context of a biconditional derivation), but it could not account for the passage from line 3 to line 4 in the following derivation.

1.	~~*Show*~~ $\bigwedge x \bigwedge y F(xy) \leftrightarrow \sim \bigvee x \bigvee y \sim F(xy)$	
2.	$\bigwedge x \bigwedge y F(xy)$	
3.	$\sim \bigvee x \sim \bigwedge y F(xy)$	2, T205, IE
4.	$\sim \bigvee x \bigvee y \sim F(xy)$	3, T203, IE

In the latter derivation, the passage from line 2 to line 3 was based on an instance of T205 obtained by substituting '$\bigwedge y F(ay)$' for 'F', and the passage from line 3 to line 4 on an instance of an alphabetic variant ('y' for 'x') of T203 obtained by substituting 'F(xa)' for 'F'.

As a final illustration within the quantifier calculus of the economy achieved by biconditional derivations, compare the following proof of T263 with that given for one of the conditionals involved on page 227.

T263	1.	~~*Show*~~ $\bigwedge x \bigvee y(Fx \rightarrow Gy) \leftrightarrow \bigvee y \bigwedge x(Fx \rightarrow Gy)$	
	2.	$\bigwedge x \bigvee y(Fx \rightarrow Gy)$	
	3.	$\bigwedge x(Fx \rightarrow \bigvee y Gy)$	2, T220, IE
	4.	$\bigvee x Fx \rightarrow \bigvee y Gy$	3, T221, IE
	5.	$\bigvee y(\bigvee x Fx \rightarrow Gy)$	4, T220, IE
	6.	$\bigvee y \bigwedge x(Fx \rightarrow Gy)$	5, T221, IE

Instances of an alphabetic variant of T220, specifically,

(2) $$\bigvee y(P \rightarrow Fy) \leftrightarrow (P \rightarrow \bigvee y Fy) \quad ,$$

are the basis for the passage in the derivation above from line 2 to line 3 and that from line 4 to line 5. The sequence of substitutions into (2) for the former is

$$\frac{F \quad P}{Ga \quad Fx} \; ;$$

and the sequence of substitutions into (2) for the latter is

$$\frac{\mathrm{F} \qquad \mathrm{P}}{\mathrm{G}a \qquad \bigvee x\mathrm{F}x} \quad .$$

T221 itself, that is,

$$\bigwedge x(\mathrm{F}x \rightarrow \mathrm{P}) \leftrightarrow (\bigvee x\mathrm{F}x \rightarrow \mathrm{P}) \quad ,$$

is the basis for the passage from line 3 to line 4 and that from line 5 to line 6. The substitution into T221 for the former is '$\bigvee y\mathrm{G}y$' for 'P', and the substitution into T221 for the latter is '$\mathrm{G}y$' for 'P'.

This last illustration suggests a strategy that is sometimes useful when employing biconditional derivations—that of confining and then unconfining quantifiers on the bases of the laws of confinement of chapter III. Generally, however, the sophistication gained by employing succinct biconditional proofs of theorems is obtained at a price: one must rely on insight rather than strategic hints to identify the previously proved theorems to be employed.

Our new derivational procedures are useful in the identity calculus, as comparison of the following proof of T315 with that given on page 276 illustrates.

T315 1. ~~Show~~ $\bigwedge x(\bigvee y[\mathrm{F}y \wedge x = \mathrm{A}(y)] \rightarrow \mathrm{F}x) \leftrightarrow \bigwedge x[\mathrm{F}x \rightarrow \mathrm{FA}(x)]$

2.	$\bigwedge x(\bigvee y[\mathrm{F}y \wedge x = \mathrm{A}(y)] \rightarrow \mathrm{F}x)$	
3.	$\bigwedge x\bigwedge y(\mathrm{F}y \wedge x = \mathrm{A}(y) \rightarrow \mathrm{F}x)$	2, T221, IE
4.	$\bigwedge y\bigwedge x(\mathrm{F}y \wedge x = \mathrm{A}(y) \rightarrow \mathrm{F}x)$	3, T251, IE
5.	$\bigwedge y\bigwedge x(x = \mathrm{A}(y) \wedge \mathrm{F}y \rightarrow \mathrm{F}x)$	4, T24, IE
6.	$\bigwedge y\bigwedge x(x = \mathrm{A}(y) \rightarrow [\mathrm{F}y \rightarrow \mathrm{F}x])$	5, T27, IE
7.	$\bigwedge y[\mathrm{F}y \rightarrow \mathrm{FA}(y)]$	6, T306, IE
8.	$\bigwedge x[\mathrm{F}x \rightarrow \mathrm{FA}(x)]$	7, AV

In passing from line 6 to line 7 in this derivation, we first replaced the variable 'y' in T306 by a new variable, say 'z', to obtain the alphabetic variant

$$\mathrm{F}x \leftrightarrow \bigwedge z(z = x \rightarrow \mathrm{F}z)$$

of that theorem. Next we made the sequence of substitutions

$$\frac{\mathrm{F} \qquad x}{[\mathrm{F}y \rightarrow \mathrm{F}a] \qquad \mathrm{A}(y)}$$

into that alphabetic variant of T306, obtaining first

$$[\mathrm{F}y \rightarrow \mathrm{F}x] \leftrightarrow \bigwedge z(z = x \rightarrow [\mathrm{F}y \rightarrow \mathrm{F}z]) \quad ,$$

and then

$$[\mathrm{F}y \rightarrow \mathrm{FA}(y)] \leftrightarrow \bigwedge z(z = \mathrm{A}(y) \rightarrow [\mathrm{F}y \rightarrow \mathrm{F}z]) \quad .$$

From the latter formula, replacing 'z' by 'x', we obtained the formula

$$[Fy \rightarrow FA(y)] \leftrightarrow \bigwedge x(x = A(y) \rightarrow [Fy \rightarrow Fx]) \quad ,$$

and then passed from line 6 to line 7 by IE on the basis of this alphabetic variant of an instance of an alphabetic variant of T306.

Biconditional derivations are not as useful in the description calculus as they are in the quantifier and the identity calculus; but economical proofs of some interesting theorems containing the descriptive operator can be obtained by employing instances of previously proved theorems and sometimes IE. The proof of T413 given at the beginning of this section is an example; the reader will encounter others in the next chapter.

Variants of the confinement laws, which will be useful in forthcoming exercises, subsequent sections of this chapter, and the next chapter, can now be obtained without the tedious proofs they would have required in chapter III.

T273

1.	~~*Show*~~ $\bigwedge x(Fx \wedge P) \leftrightarrow \bigwedge xFx \wedge P$	
2.	$\bigwedge x(P \wedge Fx) \leftrightarrow P \wedge \bigwedge xFx$	T215
3.	$\bigwedge x(Fx \wedge P) \leftrightarrow P \wedge \bigwedge xFx$	2, T24, IE
4.	$\bigwedge x(Fx \wedge P) \leftrightarrow \bigwedge xFx \wedge P$	3, T24, IE

T274 $\bigvee x(Fx \wedge P) \leftrightarrow \bigvee xFx \wedge P$

T275 $\bigwedge x(Fx \vee P) \leftrightarrow \bigwedge xFx \vee P$

T276 $\bigvee x(Fx \vee P) \leftrightarrow \bigvee xFx \vee P$

Also useful in forthcoming exercises and subsequent sections are the following simple theorems.

T277 $(\bigvee xFx \vee \bigvee x \sim Fx) \wedge P \leftrightarrow P$

T278 $(\sim \bigvee xFx \wedge \bigwedge xFx) \vee P \leftrightarrow P$

T279 $\bigwedge xFx \wedge \bigvee xFx \leftrightarrow \bigwedge xFx$

T280 $\bigwedge xFx \vee \bigvee xFx \leftrightarrow \bigvee xFx$

(T277 and T278 are quantificational analogues, respectively, of the sentential theorems T119 and T120; T279 is an immediate corollary of T238 and T72; T280 is an immediate corollary of T238 and T73.)

EXERCISES

21. Provide annotations for the following conditional derivation.

1.	~~*Show*~~ $\bigwedge x(Fx \leftrightarrow P) \rightarrow (\bigwedge xFx \leftrightarrow P)$
2.	$\bigwedge x(Fx \leftrightarrow P)$
3.	$\bigwedge xFx \leftrightarrow \bigwedge xP$
4.	$\bigwedge xFx \leftrightarrow P$

Why would it be incorrect to consider this derivation a biconditional derivation and thereby a proof of '$\bigwedge x(Fx \leftrightarrow P) \leftrightarrow (\bigwedge xFx \leftrightarrow P)$'? (The reader can demonstrate easily by means of a model that the latter formula is not a theorem.)

22. By means of a three-line derivation prove the following theorem.

T230 $\quad \bigvee x(Fx \rightarrow \bigwedge xFx)$

(See the proof of T229 given in this section for an analogue. Compare the proof you give here with that given on p. 165.)

23. By means of a four-line biconditional derivation prove the following theorem.

T242 $\quad \sim\bigwedge x(Fx \rightarrow Gx) \leftrightarrow \bigvee x(Fx \wedge \sim Gx)$

(See the proof of T243 given in this section for an analogue.)

24. By means of an indirect derivation in which the only inference rules employed are IE, BC, and MP, demonstrate the validity of the following argument.

$$\bigvee y\bigwedge x(Fx \leftrightarrow x = y) \quad . \quad \bigwedge x[Fx \wedge \sim Gx \rightarrow \bigvee x(Fx \wedge Gx)] \quad \therefore \bigwedge x(Fx \rightarrow Gx)$$

25. The formula

(3) $\qquad \bigwedge y(Fx \rightarrow Gy) \leftrightarrow (Fx \rightarrow \bigwedge xGx)$

is an alphabetic variant of an instance of an alphabetic variant of a law of confinement. Identify the law by number, indicate the relevant alphabetic variant of that theorem, and then indicate the instance of that variant (together with the sequence of substitutions by which it was obtained) that has (3) as an alphabetic variant.

26. Provide annotations for the following biconditional derivation.

1. ~~*Show*~~ $\bigvee x\bigvee y[F(xy) \rightarrow Gy] \leftrightarrow \bigvee y[\bigwedge xF(xy) \rightarrow \bigvee xGx]$
2. $\bigvee x\bigvee y[F(xy) \rightarrow Gy]$
3. $\bigvee x\bigvee y[\sim F(xy) \vee Gy]$
4. $\bigvee x[\bigvee y\sim F(xy) \vee \bigvee xGx]$
5. $\bigvee x[\sim\bigwedge yF(xy) \vee \bigvee xGx]$
6. $\bigvee x[\bigwedge yF(xy) \rightarrow \bigvee xGx]$
7. $\bigwedge x\bigwedge yF(xy) \rightarrow \bigvee xGx$
8. $\bigwedge y\bigwedge xF(xy) \rightarrow \bigvee xGx$
9. $\bigvee y[\bigwedge xF(xy) \rightarrow \bigvee xGx]$

27. By means of biconditional derivations, prove that each of the following formulas is a theorem.

(i) $\bigvee x(Fx \rightarrow \bigvee xGx) \leftrightarrow \bigvee x(Fx \rightarrow Gx)$
(ii) $\bigwedge x\bigwedge y\bigvee z(Fx \wedge Gy \rightarrow Hz) \leftrightarrow \bigwedge y\bigvee z\bigwedge x(Fx \wedge Gy \rightarrow Hz)$ [T266]
(iii) $\bigvee x\bigvee y[y = x \wedge (Fy \vee Fx)] \leftrightarrow \bigvee xFx$
(iv) $\bigwedge x\bigvee y[y = x \wedge (Gy \rightarrow \bigwedge xGx)] \leftrightarrow (\bigvee xGx \rightarrow \bigwedge xGx)$
(v) $\bigwedge x\bigwedge y[F(xy) \rightarrow y \neq x] \leftrightarrow \sim\bigvee xF(xx)$

(vi) $\bigvee z \bigwedge x \bigwedge y(x = z \vee y = z) \leftrightarrow \bigvee z \bigwedge x\, x = z$
(vii) $\bigvee x \bigvee y[x \neq y \wedge (Fx \vee Fy)] \leftrightarrow \bigvee x \bigvee y(x \neq y \wedge Fx)$

(Hints: T46 and quantifier distribution and confinement are useful in a proof of (i). Only quantifier confinement is needed for (ii); see the proof of T263 given in this section. T47 and T307 should be useful in (iii), T307 and quantifier confinement in (iv), T112, T306, and T204 in (v), and quantifier confinement and distribution, AV, and T47 in (vi). Sentential and quantifier distribution, AV, T312, T252, and T47 are useful in (vii).)

28. Generally, unlike quantifiers cannot be commuted; however, we found some exceptions among monadic formulas (see p. 227). The following theorem, which is not monadic, provides another exception.

$$\bigvee y \bigwedge z[\bigwedge x(Fx \leftrightarrow x = y) \wedge G(yz)] \leftrightarrow \bigwedge z \bigvee y[\bigwedge x(Fx \leftrightarrow x = y) \wedge G(yz)]$$

Prove this theorem by means of a biconditional derivation. (Here T331, together with confinement and commutation of quantifiers, is useful.)

29. Exercises 33 and 37 at the end of section 4 of chapter V made us familiar with formulas such as

(i) $\bigwedge x \bigvee y(Fx \leftrightarrow x = y) \leftrightarrow \bigvee x Fx \vee \bigwedge x \bigvee y\, x \neq y$
(ii) $\bigwedge x \bigwedge y(Fx \leftrightarrow x = y) \leftrightarrow \bigwedge x Fx \wedge \bigwedge x \bigwedge y\, x = y$
(iii) $\bigvee x \bigvee y(Fx \leftrightarrow x = y) \leftrightarrow \bigvee x Fx \vee \bigvee x \bigvee y\, x \neq y$
(iv) $\bigvee x \bigwedge y(Fx \leftrightarrow x = y) \leftrightarrow \bigwedge x Fx \wedge \bigvee x \bigwedge y\, x = y$
(v) $\bigwedge x Fx \vee \bigvee x \bigvee y({\sim} Fx \wedge {\sim} Fy \wedge x \neq y) \leftrightarrow \bigwedge y \bigvee x(Fx \leftrightarrow x = y)$

Now, as an exercise in ingenuity rather than economy, prove by means of a biconditional derivation that each of (i)–(v) is a theorem. We carry out the exercise for part (i); in doing so we adopt a new style of annotation for biconditional derivations, about which we will comment after we set forth the derivation.

1. ~~*Show*~~ $\bigwedge x \bigvee y(Fx \leftrightarrow x = y) \leftrightarrow \bigvee x Fx \vee \bigwedge x \bigvee y\, x \neq y$

2.	$\bigwedge x \bigvee y(Fx \leftrightarrow x = y)$	
3.	$\bigwedge x \bigvee y[(x = y \wedge Fx) \vee ({\sim} Fx \wedge x \neq y)]$	TE
4.	$\bigwedge x[\bigvee y(x = y \wedge Fx) \vee \bigvee y({\sim} Fx \wedge x \neq y)]$	Dist-Q
5.	$\bigwedge x[\bigvee y(y = x \wedge Fx) \vee \bigvee y({\sim} Fx \wedge x \neq y)]$	T302
6.	$\bigwedge x[(\bigvee y\, y = x \wedge Fx) \vee \bigvee y({\sim} Fx \wedge x \neq y)]$	Conf-Q
7.	$\bigwedge x[Fx \vee \bigvee y({\sim} Fx \wedge x \neq y)]$	T335
8.	$\bigwedge x \bigvee y[Fx \vee ({\sim} Fx \wedge x \neq y)]$	Conf-Q
9.	$\bigwedge x \bigvee y(Fx \vee x \neq y)$	TE
10.	$\bigwedge x \bigvee y(Fy \vee x \neq y)$	T314
11.	$\bigwedge x(\bigvee y Fy \vee \bigvee y\, x \neq y)$	Dist-Q
12.	$\bigvee y Fy \vee \bigwedge x \bigvee y\, x \neq y$	Conf-Q
13.	$\bigvee x Fx \vee \bigwedge x \bigvee y\, x \neq y$	AV

In a biconditional derivation each line must follow from the immediately preceding line and by either AV or IE; thus in the annotations above we have omitted reference to lines, specified AV, and understood IE for all lines with no specification of an inference rule. For each line that follows by IE, we have indicated specifically (lines 5, 7, and 10) or generically (lines 3, 4, 6, 8, 9, 11, and 12) the theorems involved and have taken the liberty of making more than one interchange in steps involving only sentential theorems. By 'TE', for 'tautological equivalence' (see the preamble to exercise 55 at the end of section 8 of chapter II), we have indicated the use of one or more biconditional sentential theorems; in step 3, T83 and T24 were employed, and in step 9, T62 and T119. By 'Dist-Q', for 'distribution of quantifiers', we have indicated the use of one of the biconditional laws of distribution for quantifiers; in steps 4 and 11, T207 was employed. By 'Conf-Q', for 'confinement of quantifiers', we have indicated the use of one of the biconditional laws of confinement for quantifiers; in step 6, T274 was employed, in step 8, T218, and in step 12, T217. We recommend generic annotations (those employed here and others that may be invented) to the sophisticated reader more interested in principles than in numbers.

4. Formulas without overlay and prenex normal form, again. In section 6 of chapter IV we mentioned and illustrated two facts: (1) that every monadic formula is equivalent to a monadic formula with one variable and without overlay of quantification, and (2) that every symbolic formula is equivalent to one in prenex normal form. Proofs of such equivalences by means of biconditional derivations are much simpler than those available in chapter IV, as comparison of the derivations given there with those in the following illustrations reveals. Indeed, biconditional derivations make available infallible directions for finding and proving such equivalences. In section 6 of chapter IX, we will set forth an automatic procedure for conversion of an arbitrary symbolic formula into an equivalent formula in prenex normal form. Here, to anticipate that section and to provide further exercise with biconditional derivations, we convert some monadic formulas in prenex normal form into formulas with one variable and without overlay.

Consider first some generalizations of the conditional '$\mathrm{F}x \rightarrow \mathrm{G}y$', that is,

$$\begin{array}{l} \bigwedge x \bigwedge y(\mathrm{F}x \rightarrow \mathrm{G}y) \\ \bigwedge x \bigvee y(\mathrm{F}x \rightarrow \mathrm{G}y) \\ \bigvee x \bigwedge y(\mathrm{F}x \rightarrow \mathrm{G}y) \\ \bigvee x \bigvee y(\mathrm{F}x \rightarrow \mathrm{G}y) \quad . \end{array}$$

To convert any one of these formulas into an equivalent formula with one variable and without overlay, we begin a biconditional derivation with the given formula and then simply 'move in' the quantifiers on the basis of the laws of confinement. For example, to convert '$\bigwedge x \bigwedge y(\mathrm{F}x \rightarrow \mathrm{G}y)$', we treat it as the assumption for a biconditional derivation and take the following steps:

2. $\bigwedge x \bigwedge y(Fx \rightarrow Gy)$
3. $\bigwedge x(Fx \rightarrow \bigwedge y Gy)$ Conf-Q (T219)
4. $\bigvee x Fx \rightarrow \bigwedge x Gx$ Conf-Q (T221)

We have now found (in line 4 above) the required equivalent; and by supplementing lines 2–4 with the appropriate assertion line, that is, with

1. *Show* $\bigwedge x \bigwedge y(Fx \rightarrow Gy) \leftrightarrow (\bigvee x Fx \rightarrow \bigwedge x Gx)$,

we have a biconditional proof of the equivalence. We leave as an exercise (No. 30) conversion of the other three formulas above.

Consider next some generalizations of the biconditional '$Fx \leftrightarrow Gy$', that is,

$$\bigwedge x \bigwedge y(Fx \leftrightarrow Gy)$$
$$\bigwedge x \bigvee y(Fx \leftrightarrow Gy)$$
$$\bigvee x \bigvee y(Fx \leftrightarrow Gy)$$
$$\bigvee y \bigwedge x(Fx \leftrightarrow Gy) \quad .$$

To convert any one of these formulas into an equivalent formula with one variable and without overlay we cannot simply 'move in' the quantifiers, for the laws of confinement for '$\leftrightarrow$' are not biconditionals (see T223–T226). Thus we must first eliminate '$\leftrightarrow$' in favor of '$\wedge$' or '$\vee$', and this can be accomplished with the aid of T81 or T83. We employ the former elimination in order to move in a universal quantifier, for T208 of the laws of distribution permits the distribution of that quantifier over a conjunction; and we employ the latter elimination in order to move in an existential quantifier, for T207 of the laws of distribution permits the distribution of that quantifier over a disjunction. For conversion of one of the above formulas with a pair of like quantifiers no further instructions are necessary, as the following column illustrates.

2. $\bigwedge x \bigwedge y(Fx \leftrightarrow Gy)$
3. $\bigwedge x \bigwedge y[(Fx \rightarrow Gy) \wedge (Gy \rightarrow Fx)]$ TE (T81)
4. $\bigwedge x[\bigwedge y(Fx \rightarrow Gy) \wedge \bigwedge y(Gy \rightarrow Fx)]$ Dist-Q (T208)
5. $\bigwedge x[(Fx \rightarrow \bigwedge x Gx) \wedge \bigwedge y(Gy \rightarrow Fx)]$ Conf-Q (T219)
6. $\bigwedge x[(Fx \rightarrow \bigwedge x Gx) \wedge (\bigvee x Gx \rightarrow Fx)]$ Conf-Q (T221)
7. $\bigwedge x(Fx \rightarrow \bigwedge x Gx) \wedge \bigwedge x(\bigvee x Gx \rightarrow Fx)$ Dist-Q (T208)
8. $(\bigvee x Fx \rightarrow \bigwedge x Gx) \wedge \bigwedge x(\bigvee x Gx \rightarrow Fx)$ Conf-Q (T221)
9. $(\bigvee x Fx \rightarrow \bigwedge x Gx) \wedge (\bigvee x Gx \rightarrow \bigwedge x Fx)$ Conf-Q (T219)

The formula in line 9 above contains only one variable, is without overlay, and is equivalent to the formula in line 2; and a biconditional proof of the theorem displaying that equivalence, that is, of

T281 $\bigwedge x \bigwedge y(Fx \leftrightarrow Gy) \leftrightarrow (\bigvee x Fx \rightarrow \bigwedge x Gx) \wedge (\bigvee x Gx \rightarrow \bigwedge x Fx)$, is obtained by supplementing the above column with the appropriate assertion line.

For conversion of one of the above formulas with a pair of unlike quantifiers, some transformations in addition to those taken above are required. After we have moved in the right-hand quantifier of the pair, we must employ a principle of sentential distribution (T116–T118) to permit the distribution of the other quantifier. Further, although not essential, contradictory disjuncts and valid conjuncts that appear in the process of conversion can be eliminated on the basis of T119 or T120, or on the basis of T277 or T278. Such elimination simplifies both the process of conversion and the resulting formula without overlay. The following column is an illustration.

2.	$\bigwedge x \bigvee y(Fx \leftrightarrow Gy)$	
3.	$\bigwedge x \bigvee y[(Fx \wedge Gy) \vee (\sim Fx \wedge \sim Gy)]$	TE (T83)
4.	$\bigwedge x[\bigvee y(Fx \wedge Gy) \vee \bigvee y(\sim Fx \wedge \sim Gy)]$	Dist-Q (T207)
5.	$\bigwedge x[(Fx \wedge \bigvee xGx) \vee \bigvee y(\sim Fx \wedge \sim Gy)]$	Conf-Q (T216)
6.	$\bigwedge x[(Fx \wedge \bigvee xGx) \vee (\sim Fx \wedge \bigvee x \sim Gx)]$	Conf-Q (T216)
7.	$\bigwedge x[(Fx \vee \sim Fx) \wedge (Fx \vee \bigvee x \sim Gx) \wedge$ $(\bigvee xGx \vee \sim Fx) \wedge (\bigvee xGx \vee \bigvee x \sim Gx)]$	TE (T116)
8.	$\bigwedge x[(Fx \vee \bigvee x \sim Gx) \wedge (\bigvee xGx \vee \sim Fx) \wedge$ $(\bigvee xGx \vee \bigvee x \sim Gx)]$	TE (T119)
9.	$\bigwedge x[(Fx \vee \bigvee x \sim Gx) \wedge (\bigvee xGx \vee \sim Fx)]$	T277
10.	$\bigwedge x(Fx \vee \bigvee x \sim Gx) \wedge \bigwedge x(\bigvee xGx \vee \sim Fx)$	Dist-Q (T208)
11.	$(\bigwedge xFx \vee \bigvee x \sim Gx) \wedge \bigwedge x(\bigvee xGx \vee \sim Fx)$	Conf-Q (T273)
12.	$(\bigwedge xFx \vee \bigvee x \sim Gx) \wedge (\bigvee xGx \vee \bigwedge x \sim Fx)$	Conf-Q (T217)

Here the formula in line 12 contains only one variable, is without overlay, and is equivalent to the formula in line 2; and a biconditional proof of the theorem displaying this equivalence, that is, of

T282 $\bigwedge x \bigvee y(Fx \leftrightarrow Gy) \leftrightarrow (\bigwedge xFx \vee \bigvee x \sim Gx) \wedge (\bigvee xGx \vee \bigwedge x \sim Fx)$,

is obtained, as in the preceding illustration, by supplementing the column above with the appropriate assertion line.

EXERCISES

30. Convert each of the following formulas in prenex normal form into an equivalent formula with one variable and without overlay.

(i) $\bigwedge x \bigvee y(Fx \rightarrow Gy)$
(ii) $\bigvee x \bigwedge y(Fx \rightarrow Gy)$
(iii) $\bigvee x \bigvee y(Fx \rightarrow Gy)$

31. With the aid of instances of T281 and T282 (stated in this section), find for each of the following formulas in prenex normal form an

equivalent sentence that is without overlay, has just one variable, has no redundant conjunct or disjunct, and has no conjunct or disjunct equivalent to a shorter formula.

(i) $\bigwedge x \bigwedge y(Fx \leftrightarrow Fy)$
(ii) $\bigwedge x \bigwedge y(Fx \leftrightarrow \sim Fy)$
(iii) $\bigwedge x \bigvee y(Fx \leftrightarrow Fy)$
(iv) $\bigwedge x \bigvee y(Fx \leftrightarrow \sim Fy)$

Part (iv) is solved for illustration. By an instance of T282, the formula of part (iv) is equivalent to

$$(\bigwedge xFx \vee \bigvee x\sim \sim Fx) \wedge (\bigvee x\sim Fx \vee \bigwedge x\sim Fx) \quad .$$

On the basis of familiar sentential theorems and T280 (stated in section 3), each conjunct of this formula can be replaced by a shorter equivalent formula; thus we obtain as the solution to part (iv) the formula

$$\bigvee xFx \wedge \bigvee x\sim Fx \quad .$$

(The reader should compare the proof obtained here that the formulas '$\bigwedge x \bigvee y(Fx \leftrightarrow \sim Fy)$' and '$\bigvee xFx \wedge \bigvee x\sim Fx$' are equivalent with that given for T248 in section 10 of chapter III.)

32. Convert each of the following formulas in prenex normal form into an equivalent formula with one variable and without overlay, indicating the steps by means of which the conversion is carried out and the theorem thereby obtained.

(i) $\bigvee x \bigvee y(Fx \leftrightarrow Gy)$
(ii) $\bigvee y \bigwedge x(Fx \leftrightarrow Gy)$

33. With the aid of the theorems obtained in the preceding exercise (see the solution to exercise 32, at the end of this chapter), find for each of the following sentences in prenex normal form an equivalent formula that is without overlay, has just one variable, has no redundant conjunct or disjunct, and has no conjunct or disjunct equivalent to a shorter formula.

(i) $\bigvee x \bigvee y(Fx \leftrightarrow Fy)$
(ii) $\bigvee x \bigvee y(Fx \leftrightarrow \sim Fy)$
(iii) $\bigvee x \bigwedge y(Fx \leftrightarrow Fy)$
(iv) $\bigvee x \bigwedge y(Fx \leftrightarrow \sim Fy)$

34. By means of biconditional derivations, prove each of T259–T262 (stated in chapter IV). Compare these derivations with those given for T259 and T261 in section 6 of chapter IV and with those obtained in working exercise 51 of that chapter. We give a biconditional derivation of T260 for illustration, employing the annotations introduced in exercise 29 at the end of section 3.

1. ~~*Show*~~ $\bigwedge x(Fx \rightarrow \bigvee y[Gy \wedge (Hy \vee Hx)]) \leftrightarrow$
$\bigvee x(Gx \wedge Hx) \vee \sim \bigvee xFx \vee (\bigvee xGx \wedge \bigwedge x[Fx \rightarrow Hx])$

2.	$\bigwedge x(Fx \rightarrow \bigvee y[Gy \wedge (Hy \vee Hx)])$	
3.	$\bigwedge x(Fx \rightarrow \bigvee y[(Gy \wedge Hy) \vee (Gy \wedge Hx)])$	TE
4.	$\bigwedge x[Fx \rightarrow \bigvee x(Gx \wedge Hx) \vee \bigvee y(Gy \wedge Hx)]$	Dist-Q
5.	$\bigwedge x[Fx \rightarrow \bigvee x(Gx \wedge Hx) \vee (\bigvee xGx \wedge Hx)]$	Conf-Q
6.	$\bigwedge x(\bigvee x(Gx \wedge Hx) \vee [(Fx \rightarrow \bigvee xGx) \wedge (Fx \rightarrow Hx)])$	TE
7.	$\bigvee x(Gx \wedge Hx) \vee \bigwedge x[(Fx \rightarrow \bigvee xGx) \wedge (Fx \rightarrow Hx)]$	Conf-Q
8.	$\bigvee x(Gx \wedge Hx) \vee [\bigwedge x(Fx \rightarrow \bigvee xGx) \wedge \bigwedge x(Fx \rightarrow Hx)]$	Dist-Q
9.	$\bigvee x(Gx \wedge Hx) \vee [(\bigvee xFx \rightarrow \bigvee xGx) \wedge \bigwedge x(Fx \rightarrow Hx)]$	Conf-Q
10.	$\bigvee x(Gx \wedge Hx) \vee (\sim \bigvee xFx \wedge \bigwedge x[Fx \rightarrow Hx]) \vee$ $(\bigvee xGx \wedge \bigwedge x[Fx \rightarrow Hx])$	TE
11.	$\bigvee x(Gx \wedge Hx) \vee (\bigwedge x \sim Fx \wedge \bigwedge x[Fx \rightarrow Hx]) \vee$ $(\bigvee xGx \wedge \bigwedge x[Fx \rightarrow Hx])$	T204
12.	$\bigvee x(Gx \wedge Hx) \vee \bigwedge x(\sim Fx \wedge [Fx \rightarrow Hx]) \vee$ $(\bigvee xGx \wedge \bigwedge x[Fx \rightarrow Hx])$	Dist-Q
13.	$\bigvee x(Gx \wedge Hx) \vee \bigwedge x \sim Fx \vee (\bigvee xGx \wedge \bigwedge x[Fx \rightarrow Hx])$	TE
14.	$\bigvee x(Gx \wedge Hx) \vee \sim \bigvee xFx \vee (\bigvee xGx \wedge \bigwedge x[Fx \rightarrow Hx])$	T204

5. Abbreviated derivations justified; generalized principles of interchange. Clauses (7)–(10) introduced in section 3 of this chapter, like clauses (7)–(9) of earlier chapters, satisfy the requirements given in section 5 of chapter II; that is, they are theoretically dispensable, and derivations constructed on their basis can be automatically checked for correctness (at least when membership in the class of premises is automatically decidable and annotations are present). It should be mentioned that an exact demonstration of the theoretical dispensability of clauses (7)–(10) would be more involved than in the case of previous abbreviations. Such a demonstration will not be attempted here, for it is beyond the scope of this book; however, a few relevant remarks are appropriate, for they lead to more general principles of inference than those introduced in section 3.

To obtain a proof of an instance of a theorem of the quantifier, identity, or description calculus from the proof of the theorem itself it is not sufficient, as is the case in the sentential calculus, simply to make throughout the proof of the theorem the substitutions that generated the instance: the restrictions imposed on variables by our basic clauses and by the requirement of proper substitution in the formulation of inference rules necessitate some systematic changes before the substitutions are made. For example, consider the following proof.

1. ~~*Show*~~ $\bigvee x(Fx \wedge P) \rightarrow \bigvee xFx \wedge P$

2.	$\bigvee x(Fx \wedge P)$	
3.	$Fy \wedge P$	2, EI
4.	$\bigvee xFx \wedge P$	3, S, EG, 3, S, Adj

We cannot obtain a proof of the formula '$\bigvee x(Fx \wedge Gy) \rightarrow \bigvee xFx \wedge Gy$', which is an instance of the assertion line in this proof, by substituting 'Gy' for 'P' in each of lines 1 through 4; for then the passage from line 2 to line 3 is not in accordance with the restriction that the variable of instantiation for EI be new. But a simple modification of the above proof, say replacement of 'y' by 'z', yields a proof of its assertion line that is amenable to the substitution of 'Gy' for 'P'.

The modification often necessitated by the restriction on the variable of generalization in a universal derivation is not as simple as that imposed by the restriction on EI, as the following trivial theorem and proof illustrate.

(1) $$P \wedge Gz \rightarrow \bigwedge x(Fx \vee Gz)$$

1. ~~Show~~ $P \wedge Gz \rightarrow \bigwedge x(Fx \vee Gz)$
2. $P \wedge Gz$
3. ~~Show~~ $\bigwedge x(Fx \vee Gz)$
4. $Fx \vee Gz$ — 2, S, Add

The formula

(2) $$Hx \wedge Gz \rightarrow \bigwedge x(Fx \vee Gz)$$

is an instance of (1) obtained by the following sequence of substitutions:

P	w
Hw	x

But we cannot obtain a proof of (2) by making this sequence of substitutions in each line of the above proof of (1); for then the cancellation of '*Show*' in line 3 is not in accordance with the restriction that the variable of generalization not occur free in an antecedent line. However, we can obtain from the proof of (1) a proof of a universal generalization from which (2) follows by UI:

1. ~~Show~~ $Hx \wedge Gz \rightarrow \bigwedge x(Fx \vee Gz)$
2. ~~Show~~ $\bigwedge w[Hw \wedge Gz \rightarrow \bigwedge x(Fx \vee Gz)]$
3. ~~Show~~ $Hw \wedge Gz \rightarrow \bigwedge x(Fx \vee Gz)$
4. $Hw \wedge Gz$
5. ~~Show~~ $\bigwedge x(Fx \vee Gz)$
6. $Fx \vee Gz$ — 4, S, Add
7. $Hx \wedge Gz \rightarrow \bigwedge x(Fx \vee Gz)$ — 2, UI

Lines 3 through 6 of this proof are obtained from the original proof of (1) by substituting throughout the latter 'Hw' for 'P', and the cancellation of

'*Show*' in line 5 is in accordance with the restriction that the variable of generalization not occur free in an antecedent line.

We shall let the preceding illustrations, together with exercises 1 and 2 below, rather than the formulation of precise instructions, warrant the claim that a proof of an instance of a theorem of the quantifier, identity, or description calculus can be obtained automatically, if not always simply, from a proof of the theorem of which it is an instance.

The rules IE and AV raise a special problem. IE and AV (except in those applications of the latter in which one formula is an immediate alphabetic variant of the other) cannot be regarded as abbreviations of the same kind as QN, SC, and CD, for there is no one theorem, for either IE or AV, to whose instances all applications of the rule correspond. For example, to eliminate from a derivation an application of IE that leads from either one of the formulas '$F\imath xGx$' or '$F\imath x \sim\sim Gx$' to the other, we would introduce into the derivation the following lines.

~~*Show*~~ $\bigwedge x(Gx \leftrightarrow \sim\sim Gx)$	
$\boxed{Gx \leftrightarrow \sim\sim Gx}$	T110
$\bigwedge x(Gx \leftrightarrow \sim\sim Gx) \rightarrow \imath xGx = \imath x \sim\sim Gx$	T404
$\imath xGx = \imath x \sim\sim Gx \rightarrow [F\imath xGx \leftrightarrow F\imath x \sim\sim Gx]$	T304

With these lines available, either one of '$F\imath xGx$' or '$F\imath x \sim\sim Gx$' can be inferred from the other by familiar sentential rules. The various theorems useful in eliminating applications of IE, and AV in some of its applications, are the same as those required to warrant more general principles of interchange of which IE, and some applications of AV, are special cases. Thus we now introduce these more general principles and then make our few remarks relevant to the dispensability of clauses (8) and (9).

The more general forms of interchange now contemplated have the following forms:

Form (1) $$\frac{\bigwedge\alpha_1 \ldots \bigwedge\alpha_n(\phi \leftrightarrow \psi)}{\chi_\phi \leftrightarrow \chi_\psi},$$

where ϕ and ψ are symbolic formulas, χ_ψ is a symbolic formula like the symbolic formula χ_ϕ except for having one or more occurrences of ψ where χ_ϕ has occurrences of ϕ, and $\alpha_1, \ldots, \alpha_n$ include all the variables bound in χ_ϕ.

Form (2) $$\frac{\bigwedge\alpha_1 \ldots \bigwedge\alpha_n(\phi \leftrightarrow \psi)}{\delta_\phi = \delta_\psi},$$

where ϕ and ψ are symbolic formulas, δ_ψ is a symbolic term like the symbolic term δ_ϕ except for having one or more occurrences of ψ where δ_ϕ has occurrences of ϕ, and $\alpha_1, \ldots, \alpha_n$ include all the variables bound in δ_ϕ.

Form (3) $$\frac{\bigwedge\alpha_1 \ldots \bigwedge\alpha_n\, \zeta = \eta}{\phi_\zeta \leftrightarrow \phi_\eta},$$

where ζ and η are symbolic terms, ϕ_η is a symbolic formula like the symbolic formula ϕ_ζ except for having one or more occurrences of η where ϕ_ζ has occurrences of ζ, and $\alpha_1, \ldots, \alpha_n$ include all the variables bound in ϕ.

Form (4) $$\frac{\bigwedge\alpha_1 \ldots \bigwedge\alpha_n\, \zeta = \eta}{\delta_\zeta = \delta_\eta},$$

where ζ and η are symbolic terms, δ_η is a symbolic term like the symbolic term δ_ζ except for having one or more occurrences of η where δ_ζ has occurrences of ζ, and $\alpha_1, \ldots, \alpha_n$ include all the variables bound in δ_ζ.

We shall refer to each of these four forms by the single name 'Interchange' (abbreviated 'Int'), specifying a particular form by its number whenever the context so requires.

To see that IE is comprehended under form (1) of Int it is sufficient to recognize that a formula is a theorem just in case all of its universal generalizations are theorems. Interchange of immediate alphabetic variants that are formulas is itself just a special case of IE; and interchange of immediate alphabetic variants that are terms is comprehended under Form (3) of Int (employing, when required, a universal generalization of an instance of T405 to obtain the premise). Form (3) closely resembles the rule LL, and Form (4) the rule EL; but note that Int, because of the stronger premise, does not contain the restriction imposed on LL and EL that only *free* occurrences of terms can be interchanged.

The four forms of Int are respectively illustrated by the following inferences:

(Form (1)) $$\frac{\bigwedge x \bigwedge y[F(xy) \leftrightarrow G(xy)]}{\bigwedge x[Hx \vee \bigvee y F(xy)] \leftrightarrow \bigwedge x[Hx \vee \bigvee y G(xy)]}$$

(Form (2)) $$\frac{\bigwedge z \bigwedge x[F(xy) \leftrightarrow G(xy)]}{\imath z\, z = \imath x F(xy) = \imath z\, z = \imath x G(xy)}$$

(Form (3)) $$\frac{\bigwedge x\, A(x) = B(x)}{\bigvee x FA(x) \leftrightarrow \bigvee x FB(x)}$$

(Form (4)) $$\frac{\bigwedge x\, A(x) = B(x)}{C(\imath x\, A(x) = x) = C(\imath x\, B(x) = x)}$$

Theorems particularly useful in eliminating from a derivation an inference by Int, and hence an inference justified by clause (8) or clause (9), are:

T96 $(P \leftrightarrow Q) \rightarrow (\sim P \leftrightarrow \sim Q)$

T101 $(Q \leftrightarrow S) \rightarrow [(P \rightarrow Q) \leftrightarrow (P \rightarrow S)]$

T101 $(Q \leftrightarrow S) \rightarrow [(Q \rightarrow P) \leftrightarrow (S \rightarrow P)]$

T102 $(Q \leftrightarrow S) \rightarrow [P \wedge Q \leftrightarrow P \wedge S]$
$(Q \leftrightarrow S) \rightarrow [Q \wedge P \leftrightarrow S \wedge P]$

T103 $(Q \leftrightarrow S) \rightarrow [P \vee Q \leftrightarrow P \vee S]$
$(Q \leftrightarrow S) \rightarrow [Q \vee P \leftrightarrow S \vee P]$

T104 $(Q \leftrightarrow S) \rightarrow [(P \leftrightarrow Q) \leftrightarrow (P \leftrightarrow S)]$
$(Q \leftrightarrow S) \rightarrow [(Q \leftrightarrow P) \leftrightarrow (S \leftrightarrow P)]$

T201 $\bigwedge x(Fx \rightarrow Gx) \rightarrow (\bigwedge xFx \rightarrow \bigwedge xGx)$

T213 $\bigwedge x(Fx \leftrightarrow Gx) \rightarrow (\bigwedge xFx \leftrightarrow \bigwedge xGx)$

T214 $\bigwedge x(Fx \leftrightarrow Gx) \rightarrow (\bigvee xFx \leftrightarrow \bigvee xGx)$

T227 $\bigwedge xP \leftrightarrow P$

T304 $x = y \rightarrow (Fx \leftrightarrow Fy)$

T305 $x = y \rightarrow A(x) = A(y)$

T404 $\bigwedge x(Fx \leftrightarrow Gx) \rightarrow \iota xFx = \iota xGx$

(Exercise 37 below will illustrate the role played by these theorems.)

The four forms of Int are more significant in applications of our systems of logic than in their development. That is, Int will not enable us to improve significantly on the proofs of theorems that can be constructed by our primitive procedures and the abbreviations introduced in section 3 of this chapter. But in the development of formal theories, the subject matter of chapters X and XI, Int is indispensable. Thus here its role is more theoretical than practical. Its four forms not only comprehend some of our earlier principles but also characterize our systems of logic as *extensional*, that is, as systems in which the designation of a complex expression is determined solely by the designations of its components.

EXERCISES

35. The formula

(3) $$\bigwedge x[F(xy) \leftrightarrow x = y] \rightarrow \iota xF(xy) = y$$

is an instance of T401 obtained by the following sequence of substitutions:

$$\frac{F \quad\quad w}{F(aw) \quad\quad y}\ .$$

Indicate why a proof of (3) cannot be obtained from the proof of T401 given on page 321 by making the above sequence of substitutions throughout that proof. Then indicate a modification of that proof from which a proof of (3) can be obtained by making the appropriate substitutions throughout. (The comments on the solutions to parts (i) and (ii) of exercise 20, given at the end of this chapter, are relevant to this exercise.)

36. The formula

$$(4)\qquad \bigwedge x[Fz \wedge \bigvee zG(xz) \leftrightarrow x = y] \rightarrow \imath x[Fz \wedge \bigvee zG(xz)] = y$$

is an instance of T401 obtained by the following sequence of substitutions:

$$\frac{F \qquad\qquad w}{Fw \wedge \bigvee zG(az) \qquad z}\ .$$

Indicate why a proof of (4) cannot be obtained from the proof of T401 given on page 321 by making the above sequence of substitutions throughout that proof. Then obtain from that proof a proof of a universal generalization from which (4) follows by UI. (See, in connection with this exercise, the proof of (2) of this section; also review the remarks on the solutions to parts (iii) and (iv) of exercise 20 given at the end of this chapter.)

37. Inferences illustrating the four forms of Int were displayed on page 378. With the aid of theorems listed after those illustrations, indicate for each of these inferences the lines that should be introduced into a derivation in order to eliminate that application of Int.

The inference comprehended under Form (1) of Int is handled for illustration. We assume that

$$(5)\qquad \bigwedge x\bigwedge y[F(xy) \leftrightarrow G(xy)]$$

is an antecedent line in a derivation; we want to obtain

$$(6)\qquad \bigwedge x[Hx \vee \bigvee yF(xy)] \leftrightarrow \bigwedge x[Hx \vee \bigvee yG(xy)]$$

as a line in a systematic way. (That is, the point of this exercise is not to obtain (6) from (5) in just any manner, but in a sequence of steps that has generality of application.) We introduce into the derivation the following lines:

(i)	~~*Show*~~ $\bigwedge x(\bigwedge y[F(xy) \leftrightarrow G(xy)] \rightarrow$ $[\bigvee yF(xy) \leftrightarrow \bigvee yG(xy)])$	By T214
(ii)	$\bigwedge x\bigwedge y[F(xy) \leftrightarrow G(xy)] \rightarrow$ $\bigwedge x[\bigvee yF(xy) \leftrightarrow \bigvee yG(xy)]$	(i), T201, MP
(iii)	~~*Show*~~ $\bigwedge x([\bigvee yF(xy) \leftrightarrow \bigvee yG(xy)] \rightarrow$ $[Hx \vee \bigvee yF(xy) \leftrightarrow Hx \vee \bigvee yG(xy)])$	By T103
(iv)	$\bigwedge x[\bigvee yG(xy) \leftrightarrow \bigvee yG(xy)] \rightarrow$ $\bigwedge x[Hx \vee \bigvee yF(xy) \leftrightarrow Hx \vee \bigvee yG(xy)]$	(iii), T201, MP
(v)	$\bigwedge x[Hx \vee \bigvee yF(xy) \leftrightarrow Hx \vee \bigvee yG(xy)] \rightarrow$ $(\bigwedge x[Hx \vee \bigvee yF(xy)] \leftrightarrow \bigwedge x[Hx \vee \bigvee yG(xy)])$	T213

Now (6) follows from (5) and lines (ii), (iv), and (v) by several applications of MP.

38. With the aid of Int, demonstrate by means of short derivations the validity of the following arguments.

(i) $\bigvee y \bigwedge x\ A(x) = y \quad \therefore\ A[\imath x\ x = A(x)] = \imath x\ x = A(x)$
(ii) $\bigwedge x\ A(x) = \imath x F(xy) \quad \therefore\ \bigvee y F[yA(y)] \leftrightarrow \bigvee y F[y \imath x F(xy)]$

6. Historical remarks. The notion of an *instance* of a theorem of the quantifier calculus has appeared in many forms. Inadequate versions occur in Hilbert and Ackermann [1], Carnap [1], and Quine [1]. Correct, though highly complex, forms are to be found in Hilbert and Bernays [1], Hilbert and Ackermann [2] and [3], and Church [3]. Our formulation is the result of simplifying and extending the version of Quine [3] and profits from a suggestion in Pager [1].

The rule IE was demonstrated for the sentential calculus in Post [1] and for the quantifier calculus in Hilbert and Ackermann [1].

The principle of interchange, in its full generality, is justified in Quine [2].

7. Appendix: list of theorems of chapter VII.

T273	$\bigwedge x(Fx \wedge P) \leftrightarrow \bigwedge xFx \wedge P$
T274	$\bigvee x(Fx \wedge P) \leftrightarrow \bigvee xFx \wedge P$
T275	$\bigwedge x(Fx \vee P) \leftrightarrow \bigwedge xFx \vee P$
T276	$\bigvee x(Fx \vee P) \leftrightarrow \bigvee xFx \vee P$
T277	$(\bigvee xFx \vee \bigvee x \sim Fx) \wedge P \leftrightarrow P$
T278	$(\sim \bigvee xFx \wedge \bigwedge xFx) \vee P \leftrightarrow P$
T279	$\bigwedge xFx \wedge \bigvee xFx \leftrightarrow \bigwedge xFx$
T280	$\bigwedge xFx \vee \bigvee xFx \leftrightarrow \bigvee xFx$
T281	$\bigwedge x \bigwedge y(Fx \leftrightarrow Gy) \leftrightarrow (\bigvee xFx \rightarrow \bigwedge xGx) \wedge (\bigvee xGx \rightarrow \bigwedge xFx)$
T282	$\bigwedge x \bigvee y(Fx \leftrightarrow Gy) \leftrightarrow (\bigwedge xFx \vee \bigvee x \sim Gx) \wedge (\bigvee xGx \vee \bigwedge x \sim Fx)$
T283	$\bigvee x \bigvee y(Fx \leftrightarrow Gy) \leftrightarrow (\bigvee xFx \wedge \bigvee xGx) \vee (\bigvee x \sim Fx \wedge \bigvee x \sim Gx)$
T284	$\bigvee y \bigwedge x(Fx \leftrightarrow Gy) \leftrightarrow (\sim \bigvee xFx \wedge \bigvee x \sim Gx) \vee (\bigvee xGx \wedge \bigwedge xFx)$

8. Appendix: solutions to selected exercises.

Section 1

Nos. 2, 4, 5, and 8 each contain pairs of formulas which are alphabetic variants; Nos. 3, 6, and 7 do not.

Section 2

9. The invalidity of (20) is established by the model

$$\begin{array}{lcl} \mathbf{U} & : & \{0, 1\} \\ F^1 & : & \{0\} \\ G^1 & : & \{0\} \\ B^2 & : & B(0,0) \mapsto 0;\ B(0,1) \mapsto 0;\ B(1,0) \mapsto 1;\ B(1,1) \mapsto 0 \end{array} \quad ,$$

in which the following instance of a closure of (20) is false.

$$\Lambda y[Fy \rightarrow GB(yy)] \rightarrow \Lambda z[Fz \rightarrow GB(1z)]$$

10. The invalidity of (22) is established by the model

$$\begin{array}{rcl} \mathbf{U} & : & \{0, 1\} \\ F^1 & : & \{0\} \\ G^2 & : & \{(1, 0), (0, 0)\} \\ \imath x\, x \neq x & : & 1 \quad . \end{array}$$

11. The invalidity of (24) is established by the model

$$\begin{array}{rcl} \mathbf{U} & : & \{0, 1\} \\ F^1 & : & \{0\} \\ H^1 & : & \{1\} \\ \imath x\, x \neq x & : & 1 \quad , \end{array}$$

in which the following instance of a closure of (24) is false.

$$\begin{array}{l} \mathrm{V}y\Lambda x[F\imath w[H0 \vee \Lambda z\, w = x] \leftrightarrow x = y] \rightarrow \\ \quad F\imath w[H0 \vee \Lambda z\, w = \imath x F\imath w(Hz \vee \Lambda z\, w = x)] \end{array}$$

The link attached to this instance indicates how the free occurrence of 'z' in the term '$\imath w[Hz \vee \Lambda z\, w = a]$' (the substituend in which 'z' is both free and bound) becomes bound at one of its occurrences in (24) and thus is not replaced by '0' in forming this instance. On the basis of the principle of vacuous quantification (T227), the theorem '$\imath w\, w = x = x$' (an alphabetic variant of T413), and the fact that 'H0' is false in the model, this instance of (24) is equivalent in the model to

$$\mathrm{V}y\Lambda x(Fx \leftrightarrow x = y) \rightarrow F\imath w(\Lambda z\, w = \imath x F\imath w[Hz \vee w = x]) \quad .$$

Inspection of the model is sufficient to verify the truth in the model of the antecedent of this formula. Application to the descriptive term that occurs in the consequent of this formula of the procedure set forth in clause (5) in section 7 of chapter VI will reveal that the term is improper and thus has the value '1' in the model; hence the consequent of this formula is false in the model, for 'F1' is false in the model.

13. The resulting substitutions are

(i)	$G(yyx) \rightarrow \mathrm{V}zG(yyz)$
(ii)	$G(yxx) \rightarrow \mathrm{V}zG(yxz)$
(iii)	$G(yxx) \rightarrow \mathrm{V}zG(yzz)$
(iv)	$\mathrm{V}wG(xwy) \rightarrow \mathrm{V}z\mathrm{V}wG(zwy)$

(v)	$\bigvee y Gy \rightarrow \bigvee z \bigvee y Gy$
(vi)	$\bigvee w Gw \rightarrow \bigvee z \bigvee w Gw$
(vii)	$G(xyc) \rightarrow \bigvee z G(zyc)$
(viii)	$G(yw) \rightarrow \bigvee z G(yw)$
(ix)	$G(xzy) \rightarrow \bigvee z G(zzy)$
(x)	$Gx \rightarrow \bigvee z Gz$

Each of the formulas (ii), (v), and (ix) contains a variable that occurs in the given theorem; hence the substitution of each of these formulas is improper. The other substitutions are proper.

14. Formulas (iii), (vi), (viii), and (x) can be obtained from (25) by proper substitution of a formula for 'F'. Formulas (iv) and (v) cannot be obtained from (25) by a proper substitution of a formula for 'F' but can be obtained by a sequence of substitutions. Formulas (vii) and (ix) are not theorems and thus cannot be obtained from (25) by any proper substitution of a formula for 'F' or by any sequence of proper substitutions. The relevant substitutions are:

(iii)	by substitution of '$G(aa)$' for 'F'.
(iv)	by substitution of '$G(za)$' for 'F' and then 'x' for 'z'; substitution of '$G(xa)$' for 'F' is improper.
(v)	by substitution of '$G(az)$' for 'F' and then 'x' for 'z'; substitution of '$G(ax)$' for 'F' is improper.
(vi)	by substitution of '$\bigwedge w G(wa)$' for 'F'.
(viii)	by substitution of '$\bigwedge w G(ww)$' for 'F'.
(x)	by substitution of 'P' for 'F'.

15. Only the substitution of (ii) for 'A' in the given theorem is improper (for 'y' occurs in both (ii) and the given theorem); the resulting substitutions are as follows.

(i)	$\bigwedge x FB(C(z)x) \rightarrow \bigvee y FB(C(z)y)$
(ii)	$\bigwedge x FB(xyz) \rightarrow \bigvee y FB(yyz)$
(iii)	$\bigwedge x FB(x) \rightarrow \bigvee y FB(y)$
(iv)	$\bigwedge x FB(z) \rightarrow \bigvee y FB(z)$
(v)	$\bigwedge x FB \rightarrow \bigvee y FB$
(vi)	$\bigwedge x FB(xcz) \rightarrow \bigvee y FB(ycz)$
(vii)	$\bigwedge x FB(C(x)) \rightarrow \bigvee y FB(C(y))$
(viii)	$\bigwedge x Fw \rightarrow \bigvee y Fw$
(ix)	$\bigwedge x Fx \rightarrow \bigvee y Fy$
(x)	$\bigwedge x FB(A(zw)C(x)) \rightarrow \bigvee y FB(A(zw)C(y))$

16. The formula (ii) cannot be obtained from the given theorem by proper substitution for 'A'; the result is not a symbolic formula if 'F' is a 2-place predicate letter. The proper substitutions that lead to the other formulas are '$B[C(a)]$' to obtain (i), '$A(ba)$' to obtain (iii), 'a' to obtain (iv), and 'b' to obtain (v).

17. In parts (iii), (iv), and (v) the second formula is an instance of the first obtained by the indicated sequence of substitutions. In part (vi) the second formula is not an instance of the first: the substitution of '$F(za)$' for 'F' is proper and yields '$F(zy) \rightarrow \bigvee x F(zx)$'; but the substitution of 'x' for 'z' in this latter

formula is improper, for the free occurrence of 'z' in the consequent passes into a bound occurrence of 'x'.

18. The substitution of (iii) is improper, for 'x' occurs in that term and the given theorem; and the substitution of (iv) is improper, for the variable 'a' occurs both bound and free in that term. The other substitutions are proper, and the formulas obtained are:

(i) $\bigwedge x\, y = \iota z\, z = x \rightarrow \bigvee x\, y = \iota z\, z = x$
(ii) $\bigwedge x\, y = \iota a\, a = a \rightarrow \bigvee x\, y = \iota a\, a = a$
(v) $\bigwedge x\, y = \iota w\, x = x \rightarrow \bigvee x\, y = \iota w\, x = x$

19. The second formula can be obtained as an instance of the first in

(i) by substituting first 'w' for 'x' and then '$\iota x\, z = x$' for 'A';
(ii) by substituting first 'w' for 'x' and then '$\iota x\, x = x$' for 'A';
(iii) by substituting '$\iota z\, a = z$' for 'A';
(iv) by substituting first 'z' for 'x', then 'Fx' for 'F', and then 'x' for 'z'.

20. (i) Yes. The second formula is obtained as an instance of the first by substituting 'F(az)' for 'F' and then substituting 'y' for 'z'.

(ii) No. The substitution of 'F(ay)' for 'F' in the first formula is improper (for 'y' occurs in both). The substitution of 'F(az)' for 'F' in the first formula leads to

$$\bigvee y \bigwedge x[\mathrm{F}(xz) \leftrightarrow x = y] \rightarrow \mathrm{F}[\iota x \mathrm{F}(xz)z] \quad ;$$

but the second formula cannot be obtained from this formula by proper substitution of 'y' for 'z', for the first free occurrence of 'z' passes into a bound occurrence of 'y'.

(iii). Yes. The second formula is obtained as an instance of the first by substituting 'Fw ∧ ⋁zG(az)' for 'F' and then substituting 'z' for 'w'.

(iv) No. The substitution of 'Fz ∧ ⋁zG(az)' for 'F' in the first formula is improper, for 'z' occurs both bound and free in the former formula. The substitution of 'Fw ∧ ⋁zG(az)' for 'F' in the first formula leads to

$$\bigvee y \bigwedge x[\mathrm{F}w \wedge \bigvee z \mathrm{G}(xz) \leftrightarrow x = y] \rightarrow \mathrm{F}w \wedge \bigvee z \mathrm{G}(\iota x[\mathrm{F}w \wedge \bigvee x \mathrm{G}(xz)]z) \quad ;$$

but the second formula cannot be obtained from this formula by proper substitution of 'z' for 'w', for the third free occurrence of 'w' passes into a bound occurrence of 'z'.

Section 3

24.

1.	~~*Show*~~ $\bigwedge x(\mathrm{F}x \rightarrow \mathrm{G}x)$	
2.	$\sim \bigwedge x(\mathrm{F}x \rightarrow \mathrm{G}x)$	
3.	$\bigvee x(\mathrm{F}x \wedge \sim \mathrm{G}x)$	2, T242, IE
4.	$\bigvee x(\mathrm{F}x \wedge \sim \mathrm{G}x) \rightarrow \bigvee x(\mathrm{F}x \wedge \mathrm{G}x)$	2nd premise, T221, IE
5.	$\bigwedge x(\mathrm{F}x \rightarrow \mathrm{G}x) \leftrightarrow \bigvee x(\mathrm{F}x \wedge \mathrm{G}x)$	1st premise, T333, MP
6.	$\bigwedge x(\mathrm{F}x \rightarrow \mathrm{G}x)$	3, 4, MP, 5, BC, MP

25. T219 is the theorem, of which '$\bigwedge y(\mathrm{P} \rightarrow \mathrm{F}y) \leftrightarrow (\mathrm{P} \rightarrow \bigwedge y \mathrm{F}y)$' is an alphabetic variant, and from which '$\bigwedge y(\mathrm{F}x \rightarrow \mathrm{G}y) \leftrightarrow (\mathrm{F}x \rightarrow \bigwedge y \mathrm{G}y)$' is obtained

by substitution of 'G*a*' for 'F' and 'F*x*' for 'P', and of which (3) is an alphabetic variant.

26. The required annotations for lines 2–9 are, respectively:
assumption; 2, T46, IE; 3, T207, IE; 4, T203, IE;
5, T46, IE; 6, T222, IE; 7, T251, IE; 8, T222, IE.

Section 4

30. (i) $\bigvee x Fx \rightarrow \bigvee x Gx$; (ii) $\bigwedge x Fx \rightarrow \bigwedge x Gx$; (iii) $\bigwedge x Fx \rightarrow \bigvee x Gx$

31. (i) $\bigvee x Fx \rightarrow \bigwedge x Fx$; (ii) $\bigwedge x(Fx \wedge \sim Fx)$; (iii) $\bigvee x(Fx \vee \sim Fx)$

32. For (i) we display just the theorem; for (ii) we display both theorem and proof.

(i) T283 $\bigvee x \bigvee y(Fx \leftrightarrow Gy) \leftrightarrow (\bigvee x Fx \wedge \bigvee x Gx) \vee (\bigvee x \sim Fx \wedge \bigvee x \sim Gx)$

(ii) T284 $\bigvee y \bigwedge x(Fx \leftrightarrow Gy) \leftrightarrow (\sim \bigvee x Fx \wedge \bigvee x \sim Gx) \vee (\bigvee x Gx \wedge \bigwedge x Fx)$

1. ~~Show~~ $\bigvee y \bigwedge x(Fx \leftrightarrow Gy) \leftrightarrow$
$(\sim \bigvee x Fx \wedge \bigvee x \sim Gx) \vee (\bigvee x Gx \wedge \bigwedge x Fx)$

2.	$\bigvee y \bigwedge x(Fx \leftrightarrow Gy)$	
3.	$\bigvee y \bigwedge x[(Fx \rightarrow Gy) \wedge (Gy \rightarrow Fx)]$	2, T81, IE
4.	$\bigvee y[\bigwedge x(Fx \rightarrow Gy) \wedge \bigwedge x(Gy \rightarrow Fx)]$	3, T208, IE
5.	$\bigvee y[(\bigvee x Fx \rightarrow Gy) \wedge \bigwedge x(Gy \rightarrow Fx)]$	4, T221, IE
6.	$\bigvee y[(\bigvee x Fx \rightarrow Gy) \wedge (Gy \rightarrow \bigwedge x Fx)]$	5, T219, IE
7.	$\bigvee y[(\sim \bigvee x Fx \wedge \sim Gy) \vee (\sim \bigvee x Fx \wedge \bigwedge x Fx) \vee (Gy \wedge \sim Gy) \vee (Gy \wedge \bigwedge x Fx)]$	6, T118, IE
8.	$\bigvee y[(\sim \bigvee x Fx \wedge \sim Gy) \vee (\sim \bigvee x Fx \wedge \bigwedge x Fx) \vee (Gy \wedge \bigwedge x Fx)]$	7, T120, IE
9.	$\bigvee y[(\sim \bigvee x Fx \wedge \sim Gy) \vee (Gy \wedge \bigwedge x Fx)]$	8, T278, IE
10.	$\bigvee y(\sim \bigvee x Fx \wedge \sim Gy) \vee \bigvee y(Gy \wedge \bigwedge x Fx)$	9, T207, IE
11.	$(\sim \bigvee x Fx \wedge \bigvee x \sim Gx) \vee \bigvee y(Gy \wedge \bigwedge x Fx)$	10, T216, IE
12.	$(\sim \bigvee x Fx \wedge \bigvee x \sim Gx) \vee (\bigvee x Gx \wedge \bigwedge x Fx)$	11, T274, IE

33. (i) $\bigvee x(Fx \vee \sim Fx)$; (ii) $\bigvee x Fx \wedge \bigvee x \sim Fx$; (iii) $\bigvee x Fx \rightarrow \bigwedge x Fx$; (iv) $\bigvee x(Fx \wedge \sim Fx)$

Section 5

38. (i) 1. ~~Show~~ $A[\iota x\, x = A(x)] = \iota x\, x = A(x)$

2.	$\bigvee y \bigwedge x\, A(x) = y$	Premise
3.	$\bigwedge x\, A(x) = a$	2, EI
4.	$\iota x\, x = a = a$	T413
5.	$A[\iota x\, x = A(x)] = a$	3, UI
6.	$\iota x\, x = A(x) = \iota x\, x = a$	3, Int (Form (4))
7.	$A[\iota x\, x = A(x)] = \iota x\, x = A(x)$	4, 5, LL, 6, LL

(ii) 1. ~~Show~~ $\bigvee y F[y A(y)] \leftrightarrow \bigvee y F[y\, \iota x F(xy)]$

2.	~~Show~~ $\bigwedge y\, A(y) = \iota x F(xy)$	
3.	$A(y) = \iota x F(xy)$	Premise, UI
4.	$\bigvee y F[y\, A(y)] \leftrightarrow \bigvee y F[y\, \iota x F(xy)]$	2, Int (Form (2))

9. Appendix: summary of the system of logic developed in chapters I–VII.

INFERENCE RULES

PRIMITIVE SENTENTIAL RULES (ϕ, ψ, χ symbolic formulas):

$$\begin{array}{l} \phi \rightarrow \psi \\ \phi \\ \hline \psi \end{array}$$

Modus ponens (MP)

$$\begin{array}{l} \phi \rightarrow \psi \\ \sim\psi \\ \hline \sim\phi \end{array}$$

Modus tollens (MT)

$$\begin{array}{c} \sim\sim\phi \\ \hline \phi \end{array} \qquad \begin{array}{c} \phi \\ \hline \sim\sim\phi \end{array}$$

Double negation (DN)

$$\begin{array}{c} \phi \\ \hline \phi \end{array}$$

Repetition (R)

$$\begin{array}{c} \phi \wedge \psi \\ \hline \phi \end{array} \qquad \begin{array}{c} \phi \wedge \psi \\ \hline \psi \end{array}$$

Simplification (S)

$$\begin{array}{l} \phi \\ \psi \\ \hline \phi \wedge \psi \end{array}$$

Adjunction (Adj)

$$\begin{array}{c} \phi \\ \hline \phi \vee \psi \end{array} \qquad \begin{array}{c} \psi \\ \hline \phi \vee \psi \end{array}$$

Addition (Add)

$$\begin{array}{c} \phi \vee \psi \\ \sim\phi \\ \hline \psi \end{array} \qquad \begin{array}{c} \phi \vee \psi \\ \sim\psi \\ \hline \phi \end{array}$$

Modus tollendo ponens (MTP)

$$\begin{array}{c} \phi \leftrightarrow \psi \\ \hline \phi \rightarrow \psi \end{array} \qquad \begin{array}{c} \phi \leftrightarrow \psi \\ \hline \psi \rightarrow \phi \end{array}$$

Biconditional-conditional (BC)

$$\begin{array}{l} \phi \rightarrow \psi \\ \psi \rightarrow \phi \\ \hline \phi \leftrightarrow \psi \end{array}$$

Conditional-biconditional (CB)

DERIVED SENTENTIAL RULES (ϕ, ψ, χ symbolic formulas):

$$\begin{array}{c} \phi \rightarrow \psi \\ \sim\phi \rightarrow \psi \\ \hline \psi \end{array} \qquad \begin{array}{c} \phi \vee \psi \\ \phi \rightarrow \chi \\ \psi \rightarrow \chi \\ \hline \chi \end{array} \qquad \begin{array}{c} \phi \rightarrow \chi \\ \psi \rightarrow \chi \\ \hline \phi \vee \psi \rightarrow \chi \end{array}$$

Separation of cases (SC)

$$\frac{\sim\phi \rightarrow \psi}{\phi \vee \psi}$$ Conditional-disjunction (CD)

PRIMITIVE QUANTIFICATIONAL RULES:

$$\frac{\bigwedge\alpha\phi_\alpha}{\phi_\zeta},$$ Universal instantiation (UI)

$$\frac{\phi_\zeta}{\bigvee\alpha\phi_\alpha},$$ Existential generalization (EG)

$$\frac{\bigvee\alpha\phi_\alpha}{\phi_\zeta},$$ Existential instantiation (EI)

where α and β are variables, ζ a symbolic term, ϕ_ζ a symbolic formula that comes from the symbolic formula ϕ_α by proper substitution of ζ for α, and ϕ_β a symbolic formula that comes from the symbolic formula ϕ_α by proper substitution of β for α. (See p. 219 for a definition of 'proper substitution'.)

DERIVED QUANTIFICATIONAL RULES (α a variable and ϕ a symbolic formula):

$$\frac{\sim\bigwedge\alpha\phi}{\bigvee\alpha\sim\phi} \qquad \frac{\bigvee\alpha\sim\phi}{\sim\bigwedge\alpha\phi}$$ Quantifier negation (QN)

$$\frac{\sim\bigvee\alpha\phi}{\bigwedge\alpha\sim\phi} \qquad \frac{\bigwedge\alpha\sim\phi}{\sim\bigvee\alpha\phi}$$

PRIMITIVE IDENTITY RULES:

Identity (Id)

$$\frac{}{\zeta = \zeta},$$

where ζ is a symbolic term.

$$\frac{\begin{array}{c}\zeta = \eta\\ \phi_\zeta\end{array}}{\phi_\eta},$$ Leibniz' law (LL)

where ζ and η are symbolic terms and ϕ_η is a symbolic formula like the symbolic formula ϕ_ζ except for having one or more free occurrences of η where ϕ_ζ has free occurrences of ζ.

DERIVED IDENTITY RULES:

$$\frac{\begin{array}{c}\eta = \zeta\\ \phi_\zeta\end{array}}{\phi_\eta}, \quad \frac{\begin{array}{c}\sim\phi_\zeta\\ \phi_\eta\end{array}}{\zeta \neq \eta}, \quad \frac{\begin{array}{c}\phi_\zeta\\ \sim\phi_\eta\end{array}}{\zeta \neq \eta},$$ Leibniz' law (LL)

where ζ and η are symbolic terms, and ϕ_η is a symbolic formula like the symbolic formula ϕ_ζ except for having one or more free occurrence of η where ϕ_ζ has free occurrences of ζ.

$$\frac{\zeta = \eta}{\eta = \zeta}\ ,\quad \frac{\zeta \neq \eta}{\eta \neq \zeta}\ ,$$ Symmetry (Sm)

where ζ and η are symbolic terms.

$$\frac{\zeta = \eta}{\delta_\zeta = \delta_\eta}\ ,$$ Euclid's law (EL)

where ζ and η are symbolic terms and δ_η is a symbolic term like the symbolic term δ_ζ except for having one or more free occurrences of η where δ_ζ has free occurrences of ζ.

PRIMITIVE RULES OF DESCRIPTION:

$$\frac{\bigvee\beta\bigwedge\alpha(\phi_\alpha \leftrightarrow \alpha = \beta)}{\phi_{\imath\alpha\phi}}\ ,$$ Proper descriptions (PD)

where α and β are variables, ϕ_α is a symbolic formula in which β is not free, and

$$\phi_{\imath\alpha\phi}$$

comes from ϕ_α by proper substitution of

$$\imath\alpha\phi$$

for α.

$$\frac{\sim\bigvee\beta\bigwedge\alpha(\phi_\alpha \leftrightarrow \alpha = \beta)}{\imath\alpha\phi = \imath\gamma\,\gamma \neq \gamma}\ ,$$ Improper descriptions (ID)

where α, β, and γ are variables and ϕ_α is a symbolic formula in which β is not free.

INTERCHANGE OF EQUIVALENTS (IE)

If ϕ and ψ are symbolic formulas such that either of

$$\phi \leftrightarrow \psi$$
$$\psi \leftrightarrow \phi$$

is an alphabetic variant of an instance of an alphabetic variant of a previously proved theorem, and χ_ϕ and χ_ψ are symbolic formulas such that χ_ψ is like χ_ϕ except for having one or more occurrences of ψ where χ_ϕ has occurrences of ϕ, then χ_ψ follows from χ_ϕ by interchange of equivalents.

INTERCHANGE (Int)

Form (1)

$$\frac{\bigwedge\alpha_1 \ldots \bigwedge\alpha_n(\phi \leftrightarrow \psi)}{\chi_\phi \leftrightarrow \chi_\psi},$$

where ϕ and ψ are symbolic formulas, χ_ψ is a symbolic formula like the symbolic formula χ_ϕ except for having one or more occurrences of ψ where χ_ϕ has occurrences of ϕ, and $\alpha_1, \ldots, \alpha_n$ include all the variables bound in χ_ϕ.

Form (2)

$$\frac{\bigwedge\alpha_1 \ldots \bigwedge\alpha_n(\phi \leftrightarrow \psi)}{\delta_\phi = \delta_\psi},$$

where ϕ and ψ are symbolic formulas, δ_ψ is a symbolic term like the symbolic term δ_ϕ except for having one or more occurrences of ψ where δ_ϕ has occurrences of ϕ, and $\alpha_1, \ldots, \alpha_n$ include all the variables bound in δ_ϕ.

Form (3)

$$\frac{\bigwedge\alpha_1 \ldots \bigwedge\alpha_n\, \zeta = \eta}{\phi_\zeta \leftrightarrow \phi_\eta},$$

where ζ and η are symbolic terms, ϕ_η is a symbolic formula like the symbolic formula ϕ_ζ except for having one or more occurrences of η where ϕ_ζ has occurrences of ζ, and $\alpha_1, \ldots, \alpha_n$ include all the variables bound in ϕ.

Form (4)

$$\frac{\bigwedge\alpha_1 \ldots \bigwedge\alpha_n\, \zeta = \eta}{\delta_\zeta = \delta_\eta},$$

where ζ and η are symbolic terms, δ_η is a symbolic term like the symbolic term δ_ζ except for having one or more occurrences of η where δ_ζ has occurrences of ζ, and $\alpha_1, \ldots, \alpha_n$ include all the variables bound in δ_ζ.

DIRECTIONS FOR CONSTRUCTING A DERIVATION FROM A CLASS *K* OF SYMBOLIC FORMULAS

(1) If ϕ is any symbolic formula, then

Show ϕ

may occur as a line. (Annotation: 'Assertion'.)

(2) Any member of *K*, or any universal generalization of a member of *K*, may occur as a line. (Annotation: 'Premise'.)

(3) If ϕ, ψ are symbolic formulas such that

Show $(\phi \rightarrow \psi)$

occurs as a line, then ϕ may occur as the next line. (Annotation: 'Assumption'.)

(4) If ϕ is a symbolic formula such that

$$\textit{Show } \phi$$

occurs as a line, then

$$\sim \phi$$

may occur as the next line; if ϕ is a symbolic formula such that

$$\textit{Show } \sim \phi$$

occurs as a line, then ϕ may occur as the next line. (Annotation: 'Assumption'.)

(5a) A symbolic formula may occur as a line if it follows from antecedent lines (see p. 24) by a primitive inference rule other than EI.

(5b) A symbolic formula may occur as a line if it follows from an antecedent line by the inference rule EI, provided that the variable of instantiation (see p. 141) does not occur in any preceding line. (The annotation for (5a) and (5b) should refer to the inference rule employed and the numbers of the antecedent lines involved.)

(6) When the following arrangement of lines has appeared:

$$\begin{array}{l} \textit{Show } \phi \\ \chi_1 \\ \cdot \\ \cdot \\ \cdot \\ \chi_m \quad , \end{array}$$

where none of χ_1 through χ_m contains uncancelled '*Show*' and either

(i) ϕ occurs unboxed among χ_1 through χ_m;

(ii) ϕ is of the form

$$(\psi_1 \rightarrow \psi_2)$$

and ψ_2 occurs unboxed among χ_1 through χ_m;

(iii) for some formula χ, both χ and its negation occur unboxed among χ_1 through χ_m; or

(iv) ϕ is of the form

$$\land \alpha_1 \ldots \land \alpha_k \, \psi \quad ,$$

ψ occurs unboxed among the lines χ_1 through χ_m, and the variables α_1 through α_k are not free in lines antecedent to the displayed occurrence of

$$\textit{Show } \phi \quad ;$$

or

(v) ϕ is of the form

$$\psi \leftrightarrow \theta \quad ,$$

where χ_1 is ψ, χ_m is θ, and for each i, $1 \leq i < m$, χ_{i+1} follows from χ_i by IE or AV,

then one may simultaneously cancel the displayed occurrence of '*Show*' and box all subsequent lines.

The remaining clauses are abbreviatory (in the sense of page 71):

(7) If ϕ is an instance of an alphabetic variant of a theorem that has already been proved, then ϕ may occur as a line. (Annotation: the number of the theorem in question, sometimes together with a diagrammatic indication of the sequence of substitutions involved.) (For the notion of *instance* see chapter VII, p. 353.)

(8) A symbolic formula may occur as a line if it is an alphabetic variant of an antecedent line. (Annotation: 'AV' and the number of the antecedent line.) (For the notion of *alphabetic variance* see chapter VII, p. 347.)

(9a) A symbolic formula may occur as a line if it follows from an antecedent line by interchange of equivalents. (Annotation: 'IE', the number of the theorem involved, and the number of the antecedent line.)

(9b) A symbolic formula may occur as a line if it follows from an antecedent line by interchange. (Annotation 'Int' and the number of the antecedent line.)

(10) A symbolic formula may occur as a line if it is the last in a succession of steps, each step in the succession other than the last step is either an antecedent line or can be justified by one of clauses (2), (5a), (7), (8), (9a), or (9b), and the last step can be justified by one of clauses (5a), (5b), (8), (9a), or (9b). (The annotation should determine the succession of steps by indicating, in the order of application, the antecedent lines, the premises, the inference rules, and the previously proved theorems employed. It should also contain such indication of terms and formulas involved in the intermediate steps as may be required to dispel remaining ambiguity.)

DERIVABILITY

A derivation is *complete* just in case every line either is boxed or contains cancelled '*Show*'. A symbolic formula ϕ is *derivable* from a class K of symbolic formulas just in case one can construct a complete derivation from K in which

~~*Show*~~ ϕ

occurs as an unboxed line.

Chapter VIII

'THE' again: A Russellian theory of descriptions

1. The Fregean theory of chapter VI reconsidered. Some interesting theorems of the description calculus were omitted from chapter VI, for they are corollaries of theorems listed there and hence have simple proofs now that any instance of any theorem already proved can be employed in a derivation. For example,

T417 $\quad x = \imath x Fx \wedge (x \neq \imath x\, x \neq x \vee F\imath x\, x \neq x) \rightarrow Fx$

is a corollary of T409; it gives alternative conditions under which the inference from '$x = \imath x Fx$' to 'Fx' is valid. Our next theorem,

T418 $\quad A = \imath x Fx \leftrightarrow$
$$\bigwedge x(Fx \leftrightarrow x = A) \vee [\sim \bigvee y \bigwedge x(Fx \leftrightarrow x = y) \wedge A = \imath x\, x \neq x] \quad ,$$

is essentially an instance of 'the essence of Frege' (T412); interchange of equivalents based on T302, T24, and T307 are also useful in its proof. T418 informs us, for example, that the sentence 'Scott is the author of *Waverley*' is true just in case either Scott and only Scott wrote *Waverley* or not exactly one thing wrote *Waverley* and Scott is the object chosen as the common designation of improper definite descriptions. This example of the information provided by T418 brings out clearly that our Fregean treatment of definite descriptions gives to sentences containing such terms truth conditions that differ from those suggested by ordinary usage. Let us look at some other examples.

Consider the sentences

(1) Betty is Alfred's only spouse
(2) Betty is the spouse of Alfred

Ordinary usage suggests that these sentences, if not synonymous, are at least equivalent, that is, must have the same truth value. But if Alfred is unmarried and Betty is the object chosen as the common designation of improper definite descriptions, then (1) is false but (2) is true. (By means of a model the reader can easily show that their respective symbolizations,

(3) $\bigwedge x[F(xA) \leftrightarrow x = B]$

(4) $B = \imath x F(xA)$,

are not equivalent.)

For another illustration, consider the sentence

(5) The father of the father of Alfred is a grandfather of Alfred but is not the (only) grandfather of Alfred .

A symbolization of this sentence containing the descriptive operator,

(6) $G(BA) \wedge B \neq \imath x G(xA)$,

is not equivalent to a symbolization that lacks that symbol, such as

(7) $G(BA) \wedge \sim \bigwedge x[G(xA) \rightarrow x = B]$.

The symbolic sentence (7) can be derived easily from the symbolic sentence (6) with the aid of T418 above. But (6) cannot be derived from (7); however, (6) can easily be derived (again with the aid of T418) from (7) and the sentence

(8) $B \neq \imath x\, x \neq x$.

Given a treatment of phrases of description in which improper definite descriptions have no designation (a treatment which does not heed Frege's 'warning concerning apparent names that have no designation' (see section 1 of chapter VI) but which perhaps conforms more closely to ordinary usage than the Fregean treatment), we would want symbolic formulas such as

(9) $\bigwedge x[F(xA) \leftrightarrow x = B] \leftrightarrow B = \imath x F(xA)$

and

(10) $G(BA) \rightarrow [\sim \bigwedge x(G(xA) \rightarrow x = B) \leftrightarrow B \neq \imath x G(xA)]$

to be theorems of a description calculus based on such a treatment. Thus, in such a description calculus, the respective symbolizations (3) and (4) of the intuitively equivalent English sentences (1) and (2) above will be equivalent; and the two symbolizations (6) and (7) of the English sentence (5) above will be equivalent. This conformity to ordinary usage by such a calculus recommends at least an outline of its development and then a more detailed comparison of this development with our Fregean logic of chapter VI; and we shall provide such an outline and comparison after we have listed, with comments, a few more theorems of our Fregean logic.

The following theorems, some quite aesthetic in appearance and some somewhat implausible, are listed here rather than in chapter VI because the proof of each can be significantly simplified by employing in the derivation previously proved theorems. (We understand any theorem with a lower number than that of a theorem under consideration to be, for the theorem under consideration, a previously proved theorem.) To illustrate we prove

T419 1. ~~*Show*~~ $\bigvee y[\bigwedge x(Fx \leftrightarrow x = y) \wedge (Gy \wedge Hy)] \rightarrow \imath x(Fx \wedge Gx) = \imath x(Fx \wedge Hx)$

2. $\bigvee y[\bigwedge x(Fx \leftrightarrow x = y) \wedge (Gy \wedge Hy)]$

3. $\bigwedge x(Fx \rightarrow Gx \wedge Hx)$ — T331, BC, 2, MP, S

4. ~~*Show*~~ $\bigwedge x(Fx \wedge Gx \leftrightarrow Fx \wedge Hx)$

5. $Fx \wedge Gx \leftrightarrow Fx \wedge Hx$ — 3, UI, T125, MP

6. $\imath x(Fx \wedge Gx) = \imath x(Fx \wedge Hx)$ — 4, T404, MP

T420 $F\imath x x = x \rightarrow \bigvee y F\imath x x = y$

T421 $\imath x Fx = \imath x x \neq x \vee \imath x \sim Fx = \imath x x \neq x$

T422 $G\imath x Fx \wedge G\imath x \sim Fx \rightarrow G\imath x Gx$

T423 $G\imath x Fx \wedge F\imath x Gx \rightarrow \imath x Fx = \imath x Gx$

T424 $\imath x Fx = \imath x \bigwedge y(Fy \leftrightarrow y = x)$

(Cases, together with T404, are useful in a proof of T424.)

T425 $\bigwedge x \bigwedge y[F(xy) \rightarrow \sim F(yx)] \wedge \bigwedge x \bigvee y F(xy) \rightarrow \imath x \bigvee y F(xy) = \imath x \bigwedge y[x \neq y \rightarrow F(yx)]$

(For a proof of T425, show that both descriptive names are improper and use T411.)

EXERCISES

1. Prove T417 and T418.
2. Derive (7) from (6).
3. Find a model in which (6) is false and (7) is true.
4. Derive (6) from (7) and (8).
5. With the aid of T331 and T333, find a shorter proof of 'the essence of Frege' (T412) than that given in chapter VI.
6. With the aid of theorems proved in chapter VI, find a shorter proof of T416 than that outlined in chapter VI.
7. Prove T420–T425.

2. A Russellian theory of descriptions. A subject–predicate sentence of ordinary language is said, roughly speaking, to be true if the object designated by the subject term has the characteristic referred to by the predicate term and to be false otherwise. Given the *Fregean* treatment of descriptive phrases, this rough characterization can be accepted even for the case in which the subject term of a subject–predicate sentence is an improper definite description; for given the Fregean treatment one chooses arbitrarily (but often judiciously) from the objects of the universe a designation for such a subject term. By a *Russellian*, in contrast to a Fregean, theory of descriptions we mean a treatment of descriptive phrases that does not artificially provide (from the universe of objects) a designation for improper definite descriptions but instead considers false any subject–predicate sentence whose subject term is an improper definite description. (See Russell [1].)

In order to facilitate a formal comparison of our Fregean with a Russellian theory of descriptions, we drop from the language of chapter VI all operation letters of degree greater than zero; this is no loss of expressiveness, for whatever could be symbolized by a k-place ($k > 0$) operation letter can be symbolized equally well by the descriptive operator and a ($k + 1$)-place predicate letter. Thus the terms of the language we shall employ here are variables, name letters (to be interpreted always as designating an object), numerals (which we reserve for the purposes of expansion with respect to a model), and descriptive terms (which may be proper or improper).

We shall refer to the models of chapter VI as *Fregean models*, and we now characterize *Russellian models*. A *Russellian model* for a symbolic argument differs from a Fregean model in only one respect: the extension of '$\iota x\, x \neq x$' in the model is to be some number *not* in the universe of the model. In a Russellian model for a symbolic argument we determine the value of a descriptive name that occurs in the argument as before; see clause (5) on page 336. Thus all improper descriptive names of an argument will designate the same number; and since that number is *not* in the universe of the model, it cannot be the extension of a name letter, an element in the extension of a 1-place predicate letter, or a term in any k-tuple that is an element of the extension of a k-place ($k > 1$) predicate letter. Except for identity sentences, the truth or falsity in a Russellian model of a symbolic sentence is to be determined as before; see (a) and (b) on pages 235–36. For identity sentences we modified the truth condition set forth in chapter V (p. 285): within the expansion of a symbolic argument with respect to a Russellian model, each part of the form

$$\zeta = \eta \quad ,$$

where ζ and η are numerals, is true in that model if and only if ζ and η are the same numeral and that numeral is the name of a number in the universe of the model. By this characterization of a model and of truth or falsity in such a model, we achieve the Russellian intuition that any atomic sentence that contains an improper descriptive name is false (in the model). To achieve Russellian terminology, we ascribe to a descriptive name a *denotation* in a model if and only if the number designated by that name is an element of the universe of the model. (See Russell [1].)

For our present purpose, that of comparing a Fregean and Russellian theory of descriptions, we shall limit our attention to theorems. Recall that in our Fregean logic, to show that a symbolic formula is not a theorem, it is sufficient to find a (Fregean) model in which a closure of that formula is false; likewise, in a Russellian logic, to show that a symbolic formula is not a theorem, it is sufficient to find a (Russellian) model in which a closure of that formula is false. Thus, as a preliminary to the construction of a logic for our Russellian theory, let us ascertain some of the theorems of our Fregean logic that cannot be theorems of a Russellian logic.

We consider first some aspects of the identity calculus for a Russellian logic. The principle of identity itself (the rule Id) fails to hold for descriptive terms, although it continues to hold for variables and name letters. We have only to consider the sentence

(1) $$\imath x\mathrm{F}x = \imath x\mathrm{F}x$$

and the model

(2) $$\begin{aligned} \mathbf{U} &: \ \{0\} \\ \mathrm{F} &: \ \{\ \} \\ \imath x\, x \neq x &: \ 1 \ . \end{aligned}$$

The expansion of (1) with respect to (2) is '1 = 1', and that sentence is false in (2), for the number 1 is not an element of the universe of (2). Euclid's law also fails to hold; we have only to consider the sentence

(3) $$x = y \rightarrow \imath z\mathrm{F}(xz) = \imath z\mathrm{F}(yz) \quad ,$$

the model (2), and the instance (with respect to (2))

$$0 = 0 \rightarrow \imath z\mathrm{F}(0z) = \imath z\mathrm{F}(0z)$$

of a closure of (3). This instance, on completing the expansion, passes into

$$0 = 0 \rightarrow 1 = 1 \quad ,$$

which has a true antecedent and false consequent in (2), for 0 is, and 1 is not, an element of the universe of (2).

Leibniz' law and the symmetry of identity will hold in our Russellian logic; that is, sentences such as

$$\imath x\mathrm{F}x = \imath x\mathrm{G}x \rightarrow (\mathrm{H}\imath x\mathrm{F}x \leftrightarrow \mathrm{H}\imath x\mathrm{G}x)$$
$$\imath x\mathrm{F}x = \imath x\mathrm{G}x \rightarrow \imath x\mathrm{G}x = \imath x\mathrm{F}x$$

should appear as theorems, for if either descriptive term in one of these sentences is improper in a model, then the antecedent of that sentence will be false in that model and hence the sentence true in that model.

Now let us look at some aspects of the description calculus itself. AV in the form of T405 fails for descriptive terms in a Russellian logic; that is,

$$[\text{T405}] \qquad \mathrm{\iota} x \mathrm{F} x = \mathrm{\iota} y \mathrm{F} y$$

cannot be a theorem. To see this it is again sufficient to consider the model (2) above. The Fregean principle that descriptive terms formed from coextensive formulas designate the same object, as exemplified by the sentence

$$[\text{T404}] \qquad \bigwedge x(\mathrm{F}x \leftrightarrow \mathrm{G}x) \rightarrow \mathrm{\iota} x \mathrm{F} x = \mathrm{\iota} x \mathrm{G} x \quad ,$$

fails to hold in a Russellian logic. To see this, it is sufficient to add

$$\mathrm{G} : \{ \ \}$$

to the model (2) above. (Although T404 cannot be a Russellian theorem, its converse will be a Russellian theorem; recall that the converse of T404 is not a Fregean theorem.)

PD will continue to hold in a Russellian logic; and its antecedent can take a simpler form. The Fregean theorem

$$(4) \qquad \bigvee y\, y = \mathrm{\iota} x \mathrm{F} x$$

cannot be a Russellian theorem; again the model (2) is sufficient to establish this fact. Indeed, in a Russellian logic, (4) asserts the propriety of the descriptive term '$\mathrm{\iota} x \mathrm{F} x$'; thus we should have forthcoming as a Russellian theorem the sentence

$$\bigvee y\, y = \mathrm{\iota} x \mathrm{F} x \leftrightarrow \bigvee y \bigwedge x(\mathrm{F}x \leftrightarrow x = y) \quad .$$

And then T402 can take in a Russellian logic the simpler form

$$\bigvee y\, y = \mathrm{\iota} x \mathrm{F} x \rightarrow \mathrm{F} \mathrm{\iota} x \mathrm{F} x \quad ;$$

indeed, the basic Russellian intuition guarantees that this theorem can be strengthened to a biconditional.

ID fails to hold in a Russellian system; in fact, such a principle is irrelevant. However, the Fregean principle that improper definite descriptions designate the same object (see T411) will have a Russellian analogue; specifically, the instance of T246 (chapter III)

$$\sim \bigvee y\, y = \mathrm{\iota} x \mathrm{F} x \wedge \sim \bigvee y\, y = \mathrm{\iota} x \mathrm{G} x \rightarrow \bigwedge y(y = \mathrm{\iota} x \mathrm{F} x \leftrightarrow y = \mathrm{\iota} x \mathrm{G} x)$$

will be a Russellian theorem.

For most aspects of quantification theory, the logic of our Russellian theory will not differ from that of our Fregean theory. Thus universal derivation, EI, and the principles of distribution, confinement, commutation, and vacuous quantification will hold in a Russellian logic. But in a Russellian logic, in contrast to a Fregean logic, UI and EG cannot be applied without qualification to descriptive terms. When descriptive terms are involved, each of these principles must be supplemented with an additional premise that asserts the propriety of the instantial descriptive term. That is, sentences such as

$$\bigwedge x Gx \rightarrow G\imath x Fx$$
$$\sim G\imath x Fx \rightarrow \bigvee x \sim Gx$$

cannot be Russellian theorems; to see this it is sufficient to supplement the model (2) above with

$$G : \{0\} \quad .$$

Instead, the sentences

$$\bigvee y\, y = \imath x Fx \wedge \bigwedge x Gx \rightarrow G\imath x Fx$$
$$\bigvee y\, y = \imath x Fx \wedge \sim G\imath x Fx \rightarrow \bigvee x \sim Gx$$

will be Russellian theorems. However, the supplemented principles of instantiation and generalization of which the latter sentences are exemplifications need not be adopted as primitive rules of inference, for such rules can be derived easily given quantificational rules restricted to variables and Leibniz' law.

As we have seen, in some cases a Russellian treatment of descriptive terms assigns to a subject-predicate sentence (or an identity sentence) a truth value different from that assigned to the sentence by a Fregean treatment. But the Russellian treatment, like the Fregean treatment, always assigns to each such sentence exactly one of our two truth values *T* or *F*. Further, a Russellian treatment assigns truth values to negations, conditionals, conjunctions, disjunctions, and biconditionals on the basis of the truth values assigned to their component sentences in the same manner as a Fregean treatment (see summary of rules (1)–(6) on p. 89). Thus the sentential logic of a Russellian treatment of descriptive terms is the same as that of a Fregean treatment.

These preliminary remarks are sufficient to indicate the depth of insight that motivated Frege's demand that 'every expression constructed as a name in a grammatically correct manner...designate an object'. (This depth was not fully fathomed in Russell [1].) That insight extends also to the Fregean principle expressed in clause (7) of section 3 of the preceding chapter, that is, that any instance of any Fregean theorem is again a Fregean theorem, for that principle does not hold for Russellian theorems. To illustrate, consider the sentence

(5) $$G\imath x Fx \leftrightarrow \bigvee y[\bigwedge x(Fx \leftrightarrow x = y) \wedge Gy] \quad ,$$

which is the Russellian analogue of the 'essence of Frege' (T412). (A slight modification of Russell's example in Whitehead and Russell [1] of a translation of (5) into English is the sentence 'The author of *Waverley* was a poet if and only if exactly one object wrote *Waverley* and that object was a poet'.) The sentence (5) must be a theorem of the theory of descriptions we are developing if the label 'Russellian' is to be applied to that theory; and it will be. But one of the simplest instances of (5) (other than just a change of letters), that is,

$$(6) \qquad \sim G\imath x Fx \leftrightarrow \bigvee y[\bigwedge x(Fx \leftrightarrow x = y) \wedge \sim Gy] \quad ,$$

cannot be a theorem of the theory. To see this it is again sufficient to consider the model (2) above, for the sentence (6) is false (in a model) if the extension of 'F' is the empty class regardless of the extension assigned to 'G'. This contrast between a Fregean and Russellian theory of descriptions, and in particular the sentence (6), will be considered again after we construct a Russellian logic—the task to which we turn now.

For our Russellian logic we can adopt clause (1)–(9) of chapter III, with the limitation that the instantial term for UI or EG must be (as in chapter III) a variable or a name letter. We thus obtain for our Russellian logic all the theorems of chapters I–IV, except those that contain operation letters of degree greater than 0 (for we have discarded such letters for our present purpose). Indeed, we can extend clause (7) to cover instances obtained by proper substitution on predicate letters (but not proper substitution on free variables or name letters) of alphabetic variants of the quantifier theorems of chapters III and IV, as well as any instance of a sentential theorem of chapters I and II. (As mentioned above, however, we cannot accept generally for our Russellian logic the principle that an instance of a theorem is again a theorem.)

To extend this sentential and quantificational base to the identity calculus we add to clause (5a) the identity rules LL and Sm in their full generality and the identity rule Id for variables and name letters (but, as mentioned above, not for descriptive terms). Also, as mentioned above, we omit Euclid's law.

Now we consider the principles of universal instantiation and existential generalization for descriptive terms; the rules appear as follows:

UI for descriptions (UID):

$$\frac{\bigvee\gamma\, \gamma = \imath\alpha\phi \qquad \bigwedge\beta\psi_\beta}{\psi_{\imath\alpha\phi}}$$

EG for descriptions (EGD):

$$\frac{\bigvee\gamma\, \gamma = \imath\alpha\phi \qquad \psi_{\imath\alpha\phi}}{\bigvee\beta\psi_\beta}$$

Here α, β, and γ are variables, ϕ is a symbolic formula in which γ is not free, and

$$\psi_{\imath\alpha\phi}$$

is a symbolic formula that comes from the symbolic formula ψ_β by proper substitution of

$$\imath\alpha\phi$$

for β. As mentioned above, these rules need not be adopted as primitive rules of inference for our Russellian logic, for all applications of them can be derived easily with the aid of UI and EG restricted to variables and name letters, EI, and LL. Indeed, these rules, although characteristic of a Russellian logic, will play no role in our proofs of Russellian theorems.

Next we consider the counterpart to our rule PD (as mentioned, ID has no counterpart in a Russellian logic). Here we adopt an inference rule that shares with Id the characteristic that it has no premise; it is a generalization of T401 strengthened to a biconditional, that is, a generalization of the sentence

$$y = \imath x \mathrm{F}x \leftrightarrow \bigwedge x(\mathrm{F}x \leftrightarrow x = y) \quad .$$

The rule appears as follows:

Russellian descriptions (RD): $\overline{\bigwedge\beta[\beta = \imath\alpha\phi \leftrightarrow \bigwedge\alpha(\phi \leftrightarrow \alpha = \beta)]}$

Here α and β are *different* variables and ϕ a symbolic formula.

To complete our Russellian logic we need two rules that embody the initial Russellian intuition that subject–predicate sentences are false if the subject term lacks a denotation. Within our symbolic language this principle is reflected by sentences such as

$$\mathrm{G}\imath x\mathrm{F}x \rightarrow \bigvee y\, y = \imath x\mathrm{F}x$$
$$\imath x\mathrm{F}x = \imath x\mathrm{G}x \rightarrow \bigvee y\, y = \imath x\mathrm{F}x \quad ,$$

which are not false in any Russellian model (with finite or infinite universe). The rules appear as follows:

Denotation principle (DP-1) $\dfrac{\pi\zeta_1 \ldots \zeta_k}{\bigvee\alpha\, \alpha = \zeta_1 \wedge \ldots \wedge \bigvee\alpha\, \alpha = \zeta_k}$

Here π is a *k*-place predicate letter, $\zeta_1, \ldots, \zeta_k$ are (any) terms, and α is a variable not free in any of $\zeta_1, \ldots, \zeta_k$.

Denotation principle (DP-2) $\dfrac{\zeta = \eta}{\bigvee\alpha\, \alpha = \zeta}$

Here ζ and η are (any) terms and α is a variable not free in ζ.

Now let us prove some Russellian theorems; we begin with 500.

We prove first that (4) above does indeed assert the propriety of a descriptive term.

T500

1.	~~Show~~ $\bigvee y\, y = \iota x Fx \leftrightarrow \bigvee y \bigwedge x(Fx \leftrightarrow x = y)$	
2.	$\bigwedge y[y = \iota x Fx \leftrightarrow \bigwedge x(Fx \leftrightarrow x = y)]$	RD
3.	$\bigvee y\, y = \iota x Fx \leftrightarrow \bigvee y \bigwedge x(Fx \leftrightarrow x = y)$	2, T214, MP

The principle of identity does hold for proper (that is, denoting) descriptive terms; indeed, it is equivalent to the assertion of propriety. This fact is exemplified by our next theorem.

T501

1.	~~Show~~ $\bigvee y\, y = \iota x Fx \leftrightarrow \iota x Fx = \iota x Fx$	
2.	~~Show~~ $\bigvee y\, y = \iota x Fx \rightarrow \iota x Fx = \iota x Fx$	
3.	$\bigvee y\, y = \iota x Fx$	
4.	$a = \iota x Fx$	3, EI
5.	$a = a$	Id
6.	$\iota x Fx = \iota x Fx$	4, 5, LL
7.	~~Show~~ $\iota x Fx = \iota x Fx \rightarrow \bigvee y\, y = \iota x Fx$	
8.	$\iota x Fx = \iota x Fx$	
9.	$\bigvee y\, y = \iota x Fx$	8, DP-2
10.	$\bigvee y\, y = \iota x Fx \leftrightarrow \iota x Fx = \iota x Fx$	2, 7, CB

(Recall that in our Russellian logic, Id holds for variables and name letters and LL holds for arbitrary terms; see p. 399.)

We now consider in order each of the theorems of chapter VI and seek its analogue, if any, in our Russellian logic.

T401 is an immediate consequence of RD; hence we do not list it here.

T402, which exemplifies PD, can be strengthened to a biconditional in our Russellian logic. Given T500, we shorten the formulation of its analogue.

T502

1.	~~Show~~ $\bigvee y\, y = \iota x Fx \leftrightarrow F\iota x Fx$	
2.	~~Show~~ $F\iota x Fx \rightarrow \bigvee y\, y = \iota x Fx$	
3.	$F\iota x Fx$	
4.	$\bigvee y\, y = \iota x Fx$	3, DP-1
5.	~~Show~~ $\bigvee y\, y = \iota x Fx \rightarrow F\iota x Fx$	
6.	$\bigvee y\, y = \iota x Fx$	
7.	$a = \iota x Fx$	6, EI
8.	$\bigwedge x(Fx \leftrightarrow x = a)$	RD, UI, BC, 7, MP
9.	Fa	8, UI, BC, Id, MP
10.	$F\iota x Fx$	7, 9, LL
11.	$\bigvee y\, y = \iota x Fx \leftrightarrow F\iota x Fx$	2, 5, CB

T403 does not hold in our Russellian logic; but it has an analogue that is an immediate corollary of

T503a	1.	~~*Show*~~ $\sim \bigvee y\, y = \imath x\, x \neq x$	
	2.	$\bigvee y\, y = \imath x\, x \neq x$	
	3.	$a = \imath x\, x \neq x$	2, EI
	4.	$\bigwedge x(x \neq x \leftrightarrow x = a)$	RD, UI, BC, 3, MP
	5.	$a = a$	Id
	6.	$a \neq a$	4, UI, BC, 5, MP

T503b	1.	~~*Show*~~ $\sim \bigvee y\, y = \imath x\mathrm{F}x \rightarrow \bigwedge y(y = \imath x\mathrm{F}x \leftrightarrow y = \imath x\, x \neq x)$	
	2.	$\sim \bigvee y\, y = \imath x\mathrm{F}x$	
	3.	$\bigwedge y(y = \imath x\mathrm{F}x \leftrightarrow y = \imath x\, x \neq x)$	2, T503a, Adj, T246, MP

Given our Russellian use of 'denotation', T503b may be understood to assert that the denotation of an improper descriptive term is not different from that of 'the nonidentical thing', for terms that lack denotation cannot have different denotations. Generally, within a Russellian theory, a symbolic formula

$$\bigwedge \alpha(\alpha = \zeta \leftrightarrow \alpha = \eta) \quad ,$$

where the variable α is not free in either of the symbolic terms ζ or η, may be read: ζ and η do not differ in denotation. Within a Fregean theory, such a formula is equivalent to the symbolic formula

$$\zeta = \eta \quad ;$$

thus, within a Fregean theory, to assert that terms do not differ in denotation is simply to assert that they have the same denotation. That 'do not differ in denotation' and 'have the same denotation' make different assertions within a Russellian theory is established by the model

U	:	{0}
F	:	{ }
G	:	{ }

in which the sentence

$$\bigwedge y(y = \imath x\mathrm{F}x \leftrightarrow y = \imath x\mathrm{G}x) \rightarrow \imath x\mathrm{F}x = \imath x\mathrm{G}x$$

is false.

As we have seen (p. 397), neither T404 nor T405 holds in our Russellian logic; but we obtain analogues by introducing a hypothesis of propriety.

T504	1.	~~*Show*~~ $\bigvee y\, y = \imath x\mathrm{F}x \wedge \bigwedge x(\mathrm{F}x \leftrightarrow \mathrm{G}x) \rightarrow \imath x\mathrm{F}x = \imath x\mathrm{G}x$	
	2.	$\bigvee y\, y = \imath x\mathrm{F}x \wedge \bigwedge x(\mathrm{F}x \leftrightarrow \mathrm{G}x)$	
	3.	$a = \imath x\mathrm{F}x$	2, S, EI
	4.	$\bigwedge x(\mathrm{F}x \leftrightarrow x = a)$	RD, UI, BC, 3, MP
	5.	~~*Show*~~ $\bigwedge x(\mathrm{G}x \leftrightarrow x = a)$	
	6.	$\mathrm{G}x \leftrightarrow x = a$	2, S, UI, T92, BC, MP, 4, UI, Adj, T93, MP

7.	$a = \iota x Gx$	RD, UI, BC, 5, MP
8.	$\iota x Fx = \iota x Gx$	3, 7, LL

T505 $\quad \bigvee y\, y = \iota x Fx \rightarrow \iota x Fx = \iota y Fy$

(Other analogues of T404 and T405 appear in exercise 19.)

T406, but not its converse T407, holds in our Russellian logic. We list the analogue to the former and leave it to the reader to find a Russellian model in which the latter is false.

T506 $\quad \bigvee y\, y = \iota x Fx \rightarrow \bigwedge x(Fx \leftrightarrow x = \iota x Fx)$

T408 holds in our Russellian logic without propriety hypotheses; thus we have

T508 $\quad \iota x Fx = \iota x Gx \rightarrow \bigwedge x(Fx \leftrightarrow Gx)$

Given T500, the analogue to T409 is T502 above. T410, like T408, holds in our Russellian logic without a hypothesis of propriety; indeed, as mentioned above, it holds as a biconditional and follows immediately by RD, sentential logic, and Sm.

T510 $\quad \bigwedge x(Fx \leftrightarrow x = y) \leftrightarrow \iota x Fx = y$

T411 does not hold in our Russellian logic; but it has an analogue like that for T403.

T511 $\quad \sim \bigvee y\, y = \iota x Fx \wedge \sim \bigvee y\, y = \iota x Gx \rightarrow \bigwedge y(y = \iota x Fx \leftrightarrow y = \iota x Gx)$

Thus, under the reading mentioned above, T511 informs us that improper descriptive terms do not have different denotations.

We come now to the analogue of 'the essence of Frege' (T412); thus it must be 'the essence of Russell'.

T512

1.	~~*Show*~~ $G\iota x Fx \leftrightarrow \bigvee y[\bigwedge x(Fx \leftrightarrow x = y) \wedge Gy]$	
2.	~~*Show*~~ $G\iota x Fx \rightarrow \bigvee y[\bigwedge x(Fx \leftrightarrow x = y) \wedge Gy]$	
3.	$G\iota x Fx$	
4.	$\bigvee y\, y = \iota x Fx$	3, DP-1
5.	$a = \iota x Fx$	4, EI
6.	$\bigwedge x(Fx \leftrightarrow x = a)$	RD, UI, BC, 5, MP
7.	Ga	5, 3, LL
8.	$\bigwedge x(Fx \leftrightarrow x = a) \wedge Ga$	6, 7, Adj
9.	$\bigvee y[\bigwedge x(Fx \leftrightarrow x = y) \wedge Gy]$	8, EG
10.	~~*Show*~~ $\bigvee y[\bigwedge x(Fx \leftrightarrow x = y) \wedge Gy] \rightarrow G\iota x Fx$	
11.	$\bigvee y[\bigwedge x(Fx \leftrightarrow x = y) \wedge Gy]$	
12.	$\bigwedge x(Fx \leftrightarrow x = b) \wedge Gb$	11, EI
13.	$b = \iota x Fx$	RD, UI, BC, 12, S, MP
14.	$G\iota x Fx$	12, S, 13, LL
15.	$G\iota x Fx \leftrightarrow \bigvee y[\bigwedge x(Fx \leftrightarrow x = y) \wedge Gy]$	2, 10, CB

This theorem informs us that the sentence 'The author of *Waverley* is a poet' is true if and only if exactly one object wrote *Waverley* and that object is a poet; thus for Russell, in contrast to Frege, there is no condition under which the sentence is true if it is not the case that exactly one object wrote *Waverley*. (See our remarks in section 1, which led us to consider a Russellian theory of descriptions.)

T413 holds in our Russellian logic, because its free term is a variable; but an instance with the variable replaced by a descriptive term requires within our Russellian logic a hypothesis of propriety.

T513 $\bigvee y\, y = \imath x Fx \rightarrow \imath x\, x = \imath x Fx = \imath x Fx$

The negation of T414 holds in our Russellian logic.

T514 $\imath x\, x = x \neq \imath x\, x \neq x$

We also have the negation of T415 as a Russellian theorem, but that theorem does not give us any interesting information about vacuous application of the descriptive operator. The interesting information is given by the following theorem, which informs us that the vacuous application of the descriptive operator forms a proper descriptive term if and only if there is only one object in the universe and the operator is applied to a truth.

T515 $\bigvee y\, y = \imath x F^0 \leftrightarrow F^0 \wedge \bigvee y \bigwedge x\, x = y$

We let the reader conclude this search for analogues of the theorems of chapter VI by either proving that T416 is a Russellian theorem or demonstrating that it is not a Russellian theorem (exercise 15).

We cannot claim for our Russellian logic, as we could for our Fregean logic, that an instance of *any* theorem is again a theorem. If a Russellian theorem can be proved without employing either DP-1 or DP-2, then an instance of that theorem is again a theorem; but some theorems that cannot be proved without employing one of DP-1 or DP-2 have instances that are not theorems. As mentioned earlier, 'the essence of Russell' is an example of the latter: we do not obtain a Russellian theorem by the substitution of '$\sim Ga$' for 'G' in T512. But the basic Russellian intuition indicates the truth conditions for sentences symbolized by '$\sim G\imath x Fx$', and they are expressed by our next theorem.

T517 $\sim G\imath x Fx \leftrightarrow \bigvee y[\bigwedge x(Fx \leftrightarrow x = y) \wedge \sim Gy] \vee \sim \bigvee y\, y = \imath x Fx$

Here our Russellian theory differs in detail from Russell's theory as set forth in Whitehead and Russell [1]. For Russell the descriptive operator was not a primitive symbol of his language but was introduced by a *contextual* definition that was tantamount to T512. This definitional treatment of the descriptive operator makes the symbolization of sentences such as

(7) The present king of France is not bald

by '$\sim G\imath x Fx$' ambiguous. (Here we have borrowed another example from Whitehead and Russell [1].) From a Russellian point of view, (7) could be understood to assert that presently there is exactly one king who is not bald, in symbols

(8) $$\bigvee y[\bigwedge x(Fx \leftrightarrow x = y) \wedge \sim Gy] \quad ;$$

or it could be understood to assert that it is not the case that presently there is exactly one king who is bald, in symbols

(9) $$\sim \bigvee y[\bigwedge x(Fx \leftrightarrow x = y) \wedge Gy] \quad .$$

Given T512 as a contextual definition of the symbol '$\imath$', the symbolic sentence (8) is obtained by taking the *scope* of '$\imath x Fx$' in '$\sim G\imath x Fx$' to be '$\sim G$'; and the symbolic sentence (9) is obtained by taking the *scope* of '$\imath x Fx$' in '$\sim G\imath x Fx$' to be 'G'. The sentences (8) and (9) are not equivalent, as the reader can easily verify by means of a model (exercise 13). (For formulas without descriptive terms, there is no difference between Fregean and Russellian models.) In contrast, from a Fregean point of view, the alternative readings of (7) have the following respective symbolizations:

(10) $$\bigvee y[\bigwedge x(Fx \leftrightarrow x = y) \wedge \sim Gy] \vee \\ [\sim \bigvee y \bigwedge x(Fx \leftrightarrow x = y) \wedge \sim G\imath x\, x \neq x]$$

(11) $$\sim (\bigvee y[\bigwedge x(Fx \leftrightarrow x = y) \wedge Gy] \vee \\ [\sim \bigvee y \bigwedge x(Fx \leftrightarrow x = y) \wedge G\imath x\, x \neq x]) \quad .$$

The symbolic sentences (10) and (11) are equivalent (exercise 14); a very short proof of their equivalence can be obtained with the aid of 'the essence of Frege' (T412), T96, and an instance of 'the essence of Frege'. Thus, within a Fregean treatment, even if the descriptive operator is introduced by a contextual definition (T412 being taken as that definition), no notion of *scope* for the descriptive operator is required. However, again the Russellian treatment is perhaps closer to ordinary usage.

T412 and T512 are the basis for yet another way of contrasting our two theories of descriptions. Within our Russellian theory, every formula that contains descriptive terms is equivalent to a formula in which no descriptive term occurs, and T512 is the guide to be employed in finding such a formula. Within our Fregean theory, no complete elimination of descriptive terms can be achieved; however, within that theory every formula that contains descriptive terms is equivalent to a formula in which no descriptive term other than '$\imath x\, x \neq x$' occurs, and T412 is the guide to be employed in finding such a formula. Further, given a formula with descriptive terms, the Russellian equivalent with no descriptive term will be simpler than the Fregean equivalent with no descriptive term other than the descriptive term '$\imath x\, x \neq x$'. Consider, for example, the formula

(12) $$H(\imath x Fx\, \imath x Gx) \quad .$$

On the basis of the proof of T512, we can claim as Russellian theorems

$$\mathrm{H}(\imath x \mathrm{F}x\, \imath x \mathrm{G}x) \leftrightarrow \bigvee y[\bigwedge x(\mathrm{F}x \leftrightarrow x = y) \wedge \mathrm{H}(y\, \imath x \mathrm{G}x)]$$
$$\mathrm{H}(y\, \imath x \mathrm{G}x) \leftrightarrow \bigvee z[\bigwedge x(\mathrm{G}x \leftrightarrow x = z) \wedge \mathrm{H}(yz)] \quad .$$

Given these two theorems, the principle of interchange of equivalents (which holds for our Russellian logic), and a familiar law of confinement, we obtain as a Russellian theorem

T526 $$\mathrm{H}(\imath x \mathrm{F}x\, \imath x \mathrm{G}x) \leftrightarrow \bigvee y \bigvee z[\bigwedge x(\mathrm{F}x \leftrightarrow x = y) \wedge \bigwedge x(\mathrm{G}x \leftrightarrow x = z) \wedge \mathrm{H}(yz)] \quad ,$$

and thereby obtain within our Russellian logic a formula equivalent to (12) in which no descriptive term occurs. (A straightforward proof of T526, not involving interchange of equivalents, is available, but it is not illustrative of Russell's use of contextual definitions.) With the aid of instances of T412, AV, and IE based on now familiar sentential and quantificational theorems, we obtain as a Fregean theorem

T426 $$\begin{aligned} &\mathrm{H}(\imath x \mathrm{F}x\, \imath x \mathrm{G}x) \leftrightarrow \\ &\bigvee y \bigvee z[\bigwedge x(\mathrm{F}x \leftrightarrow x = y) \wedge \bigwedge x(\mathrm{G}x \leftrightarrow x = z) \wedge \mathrm{H}(yz)] \vee \\ &(\sim \bigvee z \bigwedge x(\mathrm{G}x \leftrightarrow x = z) \wedge \bigvee y[\bigwedge x(\mathrm{F}x \leftrightarrow x = y) \wedge \mathrm{H}(y\, \imath x\, x \neq x)]) \vee \\ &(\sim \bigvee y \bigwedge x(\mathrm{F}x \leftrightarrow x = y) \wedge \bigvee z[\bigwedge x(\mathrm{G}x \leftrightarrow x = z) \wedge \mathrm{H}(\imath x\, x \neq x\, z)]) \vee \\ &[\sim \bigvee y \bigwedge x(\mathrm{F}x \leftrightarrow x = y) \wedge \sim \bigvee z \bigwedge x(\mathrm{G}x \leftrightarrow x = z) \wedge \mathrm{H}(\imath x\, x \neq x\, \imath x\, x \neq x)] \end{aligned}$$

and thereby obtain within our Fregean logic a formula equivalent to (12) in which no descriptive term other than '$\imath x\, x \neq x$' occurs. The reader who solves exercise 17 will discover for the formula

(13) $$\mathrm{H} \imath x \sim \mathrm{G}(x\, \imath x \mathrm{F}x)$$

a Russellian equivalent in which no descriptive term occurs and a Fregean equivalent in which no descriptive term other than '$\imath x\, x \neq x$' occurs.

We conclude this comparison of two treatments of descriptive terms by formulating a Russellian analogue to Euclid's law and listing a theorem that is an instance of this analogue; we leave to the reader a proof of the theorem (exercise 18).

Russellian Euclid's law (REL):

$$\frac{\begin{array}{l} \bigwedge \alpha(\alpha = \zeta \leftrightarrow \alpha = \eta) \\ \bigvee \alpha\, \alpha = \delta_\zeta \end{array}}{\delta_\zeta = \delta_\eta}$$

Here α is a variable not free in any of the symbolic terms ζ, η, or δ_ζ and δ_η is like δ_ζ except for having one or more free occurrences of η where δ_ζ has free occurrences of ζ.

T518 $$\bigwedge x(x = \imath x \mathrm{G}x \leftrightarrow x = \imath x \mathrm{H}x) \wedge \bigvee x\, x = \imath x \sim \mathrm{F}(x\, \imath x \mathrm{G}x) \rightarrow \imath x \sim \mathrm{F}(x\, \imath x \mathrm{G}x) = \imath x \sim \mathrm{F}(x\, \imath x \mathrm{H}x)$$

EXERCISES

8. Prove that (9) and (10) of the preceding section are Russellian theorems.

9. Prove T505, T506, T508, T511, T513, and T515.

10. Prove that T407 of chapter VI is not a Russellian theorem.

11. Prove that the sentence '$\bigwedge x[x = \imath x Fx \leftrightarrow \bigwedge x(Fx \leftrightarrow x = x)]$' is not a Russellian theorem, and thereby establish the need for distinct variables in the formulation of RD.

12. Prove that the formula '$\imath x F(xy) = A \rightarrow \bigvee y\, y = \imath x F(xy)$' is not a Russellian theorem, and thereby establish the necessity for the stipulation in the formulation of DP-2 that the variable of quantification not be free in the term.

13. Find a model in which one of (8) and (9) of this section is true and the other is false.

14. Prove within the Fregean logic that (10) and (11) of this section are equivalent.

15. Determine whether or not T416 of chapter VI is a Russellian theorem.

16. For each of T421–T423 of the preceding section, determine whether or not it is a Russellian theorem.

17. Find for (13) of this section (i) a Russellian equivalent in which no descriptive term occurs and (ii) a Fregean equivalent in which no descriptive term other than '$\imath x\, x \neq x$' occurs.

18. Prove T517 and prove T518 without employing REL.

19. Prove without employing the rules of UI and EG for descriptions that are formulated on page 399 that the following exemplifications of these rules are Russellian theorems

$$\bigvee y\, y = \imath x Fx \wedge \bigwedge x Gx \rightarrow G\imath x Fx$$
$$\bigvee y\, y = \imath x Fx \wedge \sim G\imath x Fx \rightarrow \bigvee x \sim Gx \quad ;$$

and prove that the following analogues of T404 and T405 are Russellian theorems

$$\bigwedge x(Fx \leftrightarrow Gx) \rightarrow (H\imath x Fx \leftrightarrow H\imath x Gx)$$
$$\bigwedge x(Fx \leftrightarrow Gx) \rightarrow \bigwedge y(y = \imath x Fx \leftrightarrow y = \imath x Gx)$$
$$H\imath x Fx \leftrightarrow H\imath y Fy$$
$$\bigwedge z(z = \imath x Fx \leftrightarrow z = \imath y Fy) \quad .$$

3. Historical remarks. Russell's theory of descriptions is set forth informally in Russell [1] and Russell [3], and formally in Whitehead and Russell [1]. In Scott [1] the common designation of improper descriptions is an object outside the universe of a model, but the theory of descriptions developed there is not Russellian. The Russellian theory outlined and developed in this chapter is a modification of that in Burge [1]. Other comparisons of Frege and Russell are in Carnap [2] and Kaplan [1].

4. Appendix: list of theorems of chapter VIII.

Fregean theorems

T417 $x = \imath x Fx \wedge (x \neq \imath x\, x \neq x \vee F\imath x\, x \neq x) \rightarrow Fx$

T418 $A = \imath x Fx \leftrightarrow$
$\bigwedge x(Fx \leftrightarrow x = A) \vee [\sim \bigvee y \bigwedge x(Fx \leftrightarrow x = y) \wedge A = \imath x\, x \neq x]$

T419 $\bigvee y[\bigwedge x(Fx \leftrightarrow x = y) \wedge (Gy \wedge Hy)] \rightarrow$
$\imath x(Fx \wedge Gx) = \imath x(Fx \wedge Hx)$

T420 $F\imath x\, x = x \rightarrow \bigvee y F\imath x\, x = y$

T421 $\imath x Fx = \imath x\, x \neq x \vee \imath x \sim Fx = \imath x\, x \neq x$

T422 $G\imath x Fx \wedge G\imath x \sim Fx \rightarrow G\imath x Gx$

T423 $G\imath x Fx \wedge F\imath x Gx \rightarrow \imath x Fx = \imath x Gx$

T424 $\imath x Fx = \imath x \bigwedge y(Fy \leftrightarrow y = x)$

T425 $\bigwedge x \bigwedge y[F(xy) \rightarrow \sim F(yx)] \wedge \bigwedge x \bigvee y F(xy) \rightarrow$
$\imath x \bigvee y F(xy) = \imath x \bigwedge y[x \neq y \rightarrow F(yx)]$

T426 $H(\imath x Fx\, \imath x Gx) \leftrightarrow$
$\bigvee y \bigvee z[\bigwedge x(Fx \leftrightarrow x = y) \wedge \bigwedge x(Gx \leftrightarrow x = z) \wedge H(yz)] \vee$
$(\sim \bigvee z \bigwedge x(Gx \leftrightarrow x = z) \wedge \bigvee y[\bigwedge x(Fx \leftrightarrow x = y) \wedge H(y\, \imath x\, x \neq x)]) \vee$
$(\sim \bigvee y \bigwedge x(Fx \leftrightarrow x = y) \wedge \bigvee z[\bigwedge x(Gx \leftrightarrow x = z) \wedge H(\imath x\, x \neq x\, z)]) \vee$
$[\sim \bigvee y \bigwedge x(Fx \leftrightarrow x = y) \wedge \sim \bigvee z \bigwedge x(Gx \leftrightarrow x = z) \wedge H(\imath x\, x \neq x\, \imath x\, x \neq x)]$

Russellian theorems

T500 $\bigvee y\, y = \imath x Fx \leftrightarrow \bigvee y \bigwedge x(Fx \leftrightarrow x = y)$

T501 $\bigvee y\, y = \imath x Fx \leftrightarrow \imath x Fx = \imath x Fx$

T502 $\bigvee y\, y = \imath x Fx \leftrightarrow F\imath x Fx$

T503a $\sim \bigvee y\, y = \imath x\, x \neq x$

T503b $\sim \bigvee y\, y = \imath x Fx \rightarrow \bigwedge y(y = \imath x Fx \leftrightarrow y = \imath x\, x \neq x)$

T504 $\bigvee y\, y = \imath x Fx \wedge \bigwedge x(Fx \leftrightarrow Gx) \rightarrow \imath x Fx = \imath x Gx$

T505 $\bigvee y\, y = \imath x Fx \rightarrow \imath x Fx = \imath y Fy$

T506 $\bigvee y\, y = \imath x Fx \rightarrow \bigwedge x(Fx \leftrightarrow x = \imath x Fx)$

T508 $\imath x Fx = \imath x Gx \rightarrow \bigwedge x(Fx \leftrightarrow Gx)$

T510 $\bigwedge x(Fx \leftrightarrow x = y) \leftrightarrow \imath x Fx = y$

T511 $\sim \bigvee y\, y = \imath x Fx \wedge \sim \bigvee y\, y = \imath x Gx \rightarrow \bigwedge y(y = \imath x Fx \leftrightarrow y = \imath x Gx)$

T512 $G\imath x Fx \leftrightarrow \bigvee y[\bigwedge x(Fx \leftrightarrow x = y) \wedge Gy]$

T513 $\bigvee y\, y = \imath x Fx \rightarrow \imath x\, x = \imath x Fx = \imath x Fx$

T514 $\imath x\, x = x \neq \imath x\, x \neq x$

T515 $\bigvee y\, y = \imath x F^0 \leftrightarrow F^0 \wedge \bigvee y \bigwedge x\, x = y$

T516 $\sim F\imath x \sim Fx$

T517 $\sim G\imath x Fx \leftrightarrow \bigvee y[\bigwedge x(Fx \leftrightarrow x = y) \wedge \sim Gy] \vee \sim \bigvee y\, y = \imath x Fx$

T518 $\bigwedge x(x = \imath x Gx \leftrightarrow x = \imath x Hx) \wedge \bigvee x\, x = \imath x \sim F(x\,\imath x Gx) \rightarrow \imath x \sim F(x\,\imath x Gx) = \imath x \sim F(x\,\imath x Hx)$

T522 $G\imath x Fx \wedge G\imath x \sim Fx \rightarrow \sim G\imath x Gx$

T523 $G\imath x Fx \wedge F\imath x Gx \rightarrow \imath x Fx = \imath x Gx$

T525 $G(BA) \rightarrow [\sim \bigwedge x(G(xA) \rightarrow x = B) \leftrightarrow B \neq \imath x G(xA)]$

T526 $H(\imath x Fx\, \imath x Gx) \leftrightarrow \bigvee y \bigvee z[\bigwedge x(Fx \leftrightarrow x = y) \wedge \bigwedge x(Gx \leftrightarrow x = z) \wedge H(yz)]$

T527 $\bigvee y\, y = \imath x Fx \wedge \bigwedge x Gx \rightarrow G\imath x Fx$

T528 $\bigvee y\, y = \imath x Fx \wedge \sim G\imath x Fx \rightarrow \bigvee x \sim Gx$

5. Appendix: solutions to selected exercises.

Section 2

15. T416 is a Russellian theorem; indeed, the second disjunct (that is, '$\sim F\imath x \sim Fx$') is a Russellian theorem and hence is the appropriate analogue of T416.

16. Neither T421 nor T422 is a Russellian theorem; T423 is a Russellian theorem. An analogue for T422 is: T522 $G\imath x Fx \wedge G\imath x \sim Fx \rightarrow \sim G\imath x Gx$.

17. To find a Russellian equivalent to (13) in which no descriptive term occurs, we obtain '$G(x\,\imath x Fx) \leftrightarrow \bigvee y[\bigwedge x(Fx \leftrightarrow x = y) \wedge G(xy)]$' as a theorem, using T512 as a guide; then by interchange of equivalents we obtain '$H\imath x \sim \bigvee y[\bigwedge x(Fx \leftrightarrow x = y) \wedge G(xy)]$' as equivalent to (13); and then, again with T512 as a guide, we obtain

$$\bigvee y[\bigwedge x(\sim \bigvee y[\bigwedge x(Fx \leftrightarrow x = y) \wedge G(xy)] \leftrightarrow x = y) \wedge Hy]$$

as an equivalent to (13) in which no descriptive term occurs. To find a Fregean equivalent to (13) in which no descriptive term other than '$\imath x\, x \neq x$' occurs, we obtain first by means of an instance of T412

$$\bigvee y[\bigwedge x(\sim G(x\,\imath x Fx) \leftrightarrow x = y) \wedge Hy] \vee [\sim \bigvee y \bigwedge x(\sim G(x\,\imath x Fx) \leftrightarrow x = y) \wedge H\imath x\, x \neq x] \quad ;$$

then, as an instance of T412, we obtain

$$\sim G(x\,\imath x Fx) \leftrightarrow$$
$$\bigvee y[\bigwedge x(Fx \leftrightarrow x = y) \wedge \sim G(xy)] \vee [\sim \bigvee y \bigwedge x(Fx \leftrightarrow x = y) \wedge \sim G(x\,\imath x\, x \neq x)] \quad ;$$

and then, by IE, we replace both occurrences of '$\sim G(x\,\imath x Fx)$' in the former formula by the right-hand constituent of the latter formula to obtain an equivalent to (13) in which no descriptive term other than '$\imath x\, x \neq x$' occurs.

18. To obtain a proof of T518, separate cases on the basis of '$\bigvee y\, y = \imath x Gx \vee \bigvee y\, y = \imath x Hx$' and '$\sim(\bigvee y\, y = \imath x Gx \vee \bigvee y\, y = \imath x Hx)$'. The derivation of the consequent of the theorem is straightforward in the former case. In the latter case, derive first '$\sim \bigvee x F(x\,\imath x Gx)$' and '$\sim \bigvee x F(x\,\imath x Hx)$', from which

$$\bigwedge x[\sim F(x\,\imath x Gx) \leftrightarrow \sim F(x\,\imath x Hx)]$$

follows by now familiar steps; then follow the steps in the proof of T504 to derive the consequent of the theorem.

6. Appendix: summary of the Russellian system of logic developed in chapter VIII. In section 2, to expedite the comparison of the Fregean and Russellian theories of descriptions, we embedded the Russellian system into the Fregean system and thereby obtained immediately the theory of quantification of the latter within the former. Here we give an independent characterization of the Russellian system, employing reference to our Fregean systems to simplify the exposition.

The language of the Russellian system is the language of chapter VI, except that no operation letter of degree greater than zero occurs in the Russellian language.

An *unabbreviated Russellian proof* (we leave derivations from one or more premises and abbreviated proofs to the reader) is characterized by clauses (1) and (3)–(6) of chapter III, with the modification that the inference rules included in clause (5a) are the following:

(i) the sentential rules of chapters I and II;
(ii) the quantificational rules UI and EG restricted to variables and name letters, and the quantificational rule EI;
(iii) the identity rule Id restricted to variables and name letters, and the identity rule LL;
(iv) the description rule RD (see p. 400);
(v) the denotation rules DP-1 and DP-2 (see p. 400).

A Russellian proof is *complete* just in case every line either is boxed or contains cancelled '*Show*'; and a symbolic formula ϕ is a Russellian theorem just in case there exists a complete Russellian proof in which

~~*Show*~~ ϕ

occurs as an unboxed line.

Chapter IX
Automatic procedures

1. Introduction. In earlier chapters we have given informal suggestions concerning the construction of derivations. For instance, the reader was advised on page 84 to derive each conjunct of a conjunction before attempting to derive the conjunction, and to derive a disjunction by first deriving a corresponding conditional. It was emphasized on several occasions that these suggestions are not infallible—that they will not lead to a derivation in every case in which one is possible.

The main purpose of this chapter is to present some infallible procedures of derivation. The new procedures, like the old suggestions, will consist of directions that can be followed automatically, without the exercise of ingenuity. They will differ from the earlier suggestions in two respects. The new procedures will lead to a derivation whenever one is possible; they are, however, less intuitive than the suggestions previously offered, and in some cases lead to much lengthier derivations.

Before presenting these automatic procedures, we must add three abbreviatory clauses to the directions for constructing a derivation. The new clauses, which will occupy the two following sections, are intended for use only in the present chapter.

2. Tautologies reconsidered. The tautologies of chapter II are always symbolic sentences, but the notion of a tautology can easily be extended so as to apply to arbitrary symbolic formulas. Accordingly, we define first a *molecular* formula as one that has the form

$$\sim \psi \ ,$$
$$(\psi \rightarrow \chi) \ ,$$
$$(\psi \wedge \chi) \ ,$$
$$(\psi \vee \chi) \ ,$$

or

$$(\psi \leftrightarrow \chi) \ ,$$

for some symbolic formulas ψ and χ. An *assignment* now correlates with each nonmolecular symbolic *formula* one of the truth values T or F. The *truth value* of an arbitrary symbolic formula, on the basis of a given assignment, can be computed just as in chapter II (pp. 88–89). A *tautology* is a symbolic formula whose truth value is T with respect to every possible assignment. A symbolic argument is *tautologically valid* if the truth value of its conclusion is T under every assignment for which all its premises have the value T; under the same conditions, the premises of the argument are said to *imply tautologically* the conclusion. Just as before, we may use *truth tables* to check whether a symbolic formula is a tautology or whether a symbolic argument with finitely many premises is tautologically valid.

A *subformula* of a formula ϕ is any formula that occurs within ϕ.

In the present section we shall add the following abbreviatory clause to the directions for constructing a derivation:

(11) *Any tautology may occur as a line.*

The theoretical superfluity of clause (11) depends on the fact that every tautology is a theorem; this was asserted in chapter II and will be substantiated here. We shall, in fact, give directions on the basis of which we can construct a proof of any given tautology.

Suppose that we are confronted with a tautology, for example,

(1) $$(P \to Q) \to (P \land Q \leftrightarrow P) \quad .$$

We must first construct a truth table whose last column is headed by the tautology in question. The last column, then, will not contain 'F'. In connection with (1) we have

P	Q	P → Q	P ∧ Q	P ∧ Q ↔ P	(P → Q) → (P ∧ Q ↔ P)
T	*T*	*T*	*T*	*T*	*T*
T	*F*	*F*	*F*	*F*	*T*
F	*T*	*T*	*F*	*T*	*T*
F	*F*	*T*	*F*	*T*	*T*

On the basis of the truth table, now, we construct a proof of the tautology; intuitively, the proof can be regarded as a separation of cases, which correspond to the rows of the truth table. For simplicity, we give the construction only in connection with (1); the reader will observe, however, that the procedure is quite general.

If χ is the formula (1), then the proof of χ will have the following over-all structure:

1.	~~*Show*~~ χ	
2.	~~*Show*~~ $P \rightarrow \chi$	
3.	P	
4.	~~*Show*~~ $Q \rightarrow \chi$	
10.	~~*Show*~~ $\sim Q \rightarrow \chi$	
16.	χ	4, 10, SC
17.	~~*Show*~~ $\sim P \rightarrow \chi$	
18.	$\sim P$	
19.	~~*Show*~~ $Q \rightarrow \chi$	
25.	~~*Show*~~ $\sim Q \rightarrow \chi$	
31.	χ	19, 25, SC
32.	χ	2, 17, SC

The argument by which line 4 will be established (in which 'P' and 'Q' serve as assumptions) will correspond to the first row of the truth table. The argument for line 10 (under the assumptions 'P' and '$\sim$Q') will correspond to the second row. Similarly, the arguments for lines 19 and 25 will correspond to the third and fourth rows respectively.

In greater detail, the general directions for proving (1) are as follows. We begin the proof by indicating that the tautology is to be shown:

1. *Show* $(P \rightarrow Q) \rightarrow (P \wedge Q \leftrightarrow P)$

We indicate next that the tautology holds when its first nonmolecular part is true:

1. *Show* $(P \rightarrow Q) \rightarrow (P \wedge Q \leftrightarrow P)$
2. *Show* $P \rightarrow [(P \rightarrow Q) \rightarrow (P \wedge Q \leftrightarrow P)]$

We assume the antecedent of line 2:

1. *Show* $(P \rightarrow Q) \rightarrow (P \wedge Q \leftrightarrow P)$
2. *Show* $P \rightarrow [(P \rightarrow Q) \rightarrow (P \wedge Q \leftrightarrow P)]$
3. P

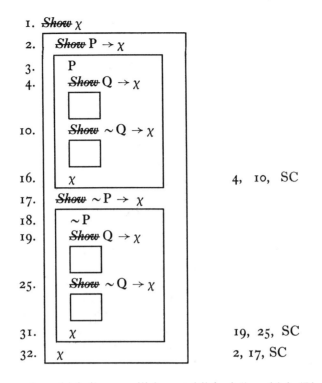

We indicate now that the tautology holds when its second nonmolecular part is true:

1. *Show* $(P \rightarrow Q) \rightarrow (P \wedge Q \leftrightarrow P)$
2. *Show* $P \rightarrow [(P \rightarrow Q) \rightarrow (P \wedge Q \leftrightarrow P)]$
3. P
4. *Show* $Q \rightarrow [(P \rightarrow Q) \rightarrow (P \wedge Q \leftrightarrow P)]$

Again we assume the antecedent:

1. *Show* $(P \rightarrow Q) \rightarrow (P \wedge Q \leftrightarrow P)$
2. *Show* $P \rightarrow [(P \rightarrow Q) \rightarrow (P \wedge Q \leftrightarrow P)]$
3. P
4. *Show* $Q \rightarrow [(P \rightarrow Q) \rightarrow (P \wedge Q \leftrightarrow P)]$
5. Q

We have now, in lines 3 and 5, the assumptions corresponding to the first row of the truth table. On the basis of these assumptions, we proceed to 'compute' the values of the molecular subformulas of (1). That is, we treat the molecular subformulas of (1) in the order in which they appear at the head of our truth table, and for each subformula ϕ we derive either ϕ or its negation, according as '*T*' or '*F*' appears below ϕ in the first row of the truth table. (This can always be done because we have at our disposal the theorems

T18	$\sim P \rightarrow (P \rightarrow Q)$,
T2	$Q \rightarrow (P \rightarrow Q)$,
T42	$P \wedge \sim Q \rightarrow \sim(P \rightarrow Q)$,
T43	$\sim P \rightarrow \sim(P \wedge Q)$,
T44	$\sim Q \rightarrow \sim(P \wedge Q)$,
T67	$\sim P \wedge \sim Q \rightarrow \sim(P \vee Q)$,
T84	$P \wedge Q \rightarrow (P \leftrightarrow Q)$,
T85	$\sim P \wedge \sim Q \rightarrow (P \leftrightarrow Q)$,
T88	$P \wedge \sim Q \rightarrow \sim(P \leftrightarrow Q)$,
T89	$\sim P \wedge Q \rightarrow \sim(P \leftrightarrow Q)$,

which, together with the inference rules DN, Adj, and Add, correspond completely to the rules for assigning truth values.) In the truth table for (1), '*F*' does not appear in the first row; thus we obtain

1. *Show* $(P \rightarrow Q) \rightarrow (P \wedge Q \leftrightarrow P)$
2. *Show* $P \rightarrow [(P \rightarrow Q) \rightarrow (P \wedge Q \leftrightarrow P)]$

3.	P	
4.	*Show* $Q \to [(P \to Q) \to (P \wedge Q \leftrightarrow P)]$	
5.	Q	
6.	$P \to Q$	5, T2, MP
7.	$P \wedge Q$	3, 5, Adj
8.	$P \wedge Q \leftrightarrow P$	3, 7, Adj, T84, MP
9.	$(P \to Q) \to (P \wedge Q \leftrightarrow P)$	8, T2, MP

The conditional proof of line 4 is complete. We box and cancel, and pass to the case in which 'Q' is false.

1.	*Show* $(P \to Q) \to (P \wedge Q \leftrightarrow P)$	
2.	*Show* $P \to [(P \to Q) \to (P \wedge Q \leftrightarrow P)]$	
3.	P	
4.	~~*Show*~~ $Q \to [(P \to Q) \to (P \wedge Q \leftrightarrow P)]$	
5.	Q (boxed)	
6.	$P \to Q$ (boxed)	
7.	$P \wedge Q$ (boxed)	
8.	$P \wedge Q \leftrightarrow P$ (boxed)	
9.	$(P \to Q) \to (P \wedge Q \leftrightarrow P)$ (boxed)	
10.	*Show* $\sim Q \to [(P \to Q) \to (P \wedge Q \leftrightarrow P)]$	
11.	$\sim Q$	

Again we derive 'computed' values, this time in accordance with the second row of the truth table:

1.	*Show* $(P \to Q) \to (P \wedge Q \leftrightarrow P)$	
2.	*Show* $P \to [(P \to Q) \to (P \wedge Q \leftrightarrow P)]$	
3.	P	
4.	~~*Show*~~ $Q \to [(P \to Q) \to (P \wedge Q \leftrightarrow P)]$	
5.	Q (boxed)	
6.	$P \to Q$ (boxed)	
7.	$P \wedge Q$ (boxed)	
8.	$P \wedge Q \leftrightarrow P$ (boxed)	
9.	$(P \to Q) \to (P \wedge Q \leftrightarrow P)$ (boxed)	
10.	*Show* $\sim Q \to [(P \to Q) \to (P \wedge Q \leftrightarrow P)]$	
11.	$\sim Q$	
12.	$\sim (P \to Q)$	3, 11, Adj, T42, MP
13.	$\sim (P \wedge Q)$	11, T44, MP
14.	$\sim (P \wedge Q \leftrightarrow P)$	3, 13, Adj, T89, MP
15.	$(P \to Q) \to (P \wedge Q \leftrightarrow P)$	12, T18, MP

The conditional proof of line 10 is complete. Again, we box and cancel:

1. *Show* $(P \rightarrow Q) \rightarrow (P \wedge Q \leftrightarrow P)$
2. *Show* $P \rightarrow [(P \rightarrow Q) \rightarrow (P \wedge Q \leftrightarrow P)]$
3. P
4. ~~*Show*~~ $Q \rightarrow [(P \rightarrow Q) \rightarrow (P \wedge Q \leftrightarrow P)]$
5. Q
6. $P \rightarrow Q$
7. $P \wedge Q$
8. $P \wedge Q \leftrightarrow P$
9. $(P \rightarrow Q) \rightarrow (P \wedge Q \leftrightarrow P)$
10. ~~*Show*~~ $\sim Q \rightarrow [(P \rightarrow Q) \rightarrow (P \wedge Q \leftrightarrow P)]$
11. $\sim Q$
12. $\sim (P \rightarrow Q)$
13. $\sim (P \wedge Q)$
14. $\sim (P \wedge Q \leftrightarrow P)$
15. $(P \rightarrow Q) \rightarrow (P \wedge Q \leftrightarrow P)$

But the tautology in question now follows from lines 4 and 10 by separation of cases; thus we can complete the conditional proof of line 2:

1. *Show* $(P \rightarrow Q) \rightarrow (P \wedge Q \leftrightarrow P)$
2. ~~*Show*~~ $P \rightarrow [(P \rightarrow Q) \rightarrow (P \wedge Q \leftrightarrow P)]$
3. P
4. ~~*Show*~~ $Q \rightarrow [(P \rightarrow Q) \rightarrow (P \wedge Q \leftrightarrow P)]$
5. Q
6. $P \rightarrow Q$
7. $P \wedge Q$
8. $P \wedge Q \leftrightarrow P$
9. $(P \rightarrow Q) \rightarrow (P \wedge Q \leftrightarrow P)$
10. ~~*Show*~~ $\sim Q \rightarrow [(P \rightarrow Q) \rightarrow (P \wedge Q \leftrightarrow P)]$
11. $\sim Q$
12. $\sim (P \rightarrow Q)$
13. $\sim (P \wedge Q)$
14. $\sim (P \wedge Q \leftrightarrow P)$
15. $(P \rightarrow Q) \rightarrow (P \wedge Q \leftrightarrow P)$
16. $(P \rightarrow Q) \rightarrow (P \wedge Q \leftrightarrow P)$ 4, 10, SC

We continue in the same way, constructing 'cases' for the remaining rows of the truth table and 'computing' corresponding values, until finally all possibilities are exhausted:

1.	~~*Show*~~ $(P \rightarrow Q) \rightarrow (P \wedge Q \leftrightarrow P)$	
2.	~~*Show*~~ $P \rightarrow [(P \rightarrow Q) \rightarrow (P \wedge Q \leftrightarrow P)]$	
3.	P	
4.	~~*Show*~~ $Q \rightarrow [(P \rightarrow Q) \rightarrow (P \wedge Q \leftrightarrow P)]$	
5.	Q	
6.	$P \rightarrow Q$	5, T2, MP
7.	$P \wedge Q$	3, 5, Adj
8.	$P \wedge Q \leftrightarrow P$	3, 7, Adj, T84, MP
9.	$(P \rightarrow Q) \rightarrow (P \wedge Q \leftrightarrow P)$	8, T2, MP
10.	~~*Show*~~ $\sim Q \rightarrow [(P \rightarrow Q) \rightarrow (P \wedge Q \leftrightarrow P)]$	
11.	$\sim Q$	
12.	$\sim(P \rightarrow Q)$	3, 11, Adj, T42, MP
13.	$\sim(P \wedge Q)$	11,T44,MP
14.	$\sim(P \wedge Q \leftrightarrow P)$	3, 13, Adj, T89, MP
15.	$(P \rightarrow Q) \rightarrow (P \wedge Q \leftrightarrow P)$	12,T18,MP
16.	$(P \rightarrow Q) \rightarrow (P \wedge Q \leftrightarrow P)$	4, 10, SC
17.	~~*Show*~~ $\sim P \rightarrow [(P \rightarrow Q) \rightarrow (P \wedge Q \leftrightarrow P)]$	
18.	$\sim P$	
19.	~~*Show*~~ $Q \rightarrow [(P \rightarrow Q) \rightarrow (P \wedge Q \leftrightarrow P)]$	
20.	Q	
21.	$P \rightarrow Q$	20, T2, MP
22.	$\sim(P \wedge Q)$	18,T43,MP
23.	$P \wedge Q \leftrightarrow P$	18, 22, Adj, T85, MP
24.	$(P \rightarrow Q) \rightarrow (P \wedge Q \leftrightarrow P)$	23, T2, MP
25.	~~*Show*~~ $\sim Q \rightarrow [(P \rightarrow Q) \rightarrow (P \wedge Q \leftrightarrow P)]$	
26.	$\sim Q$	
27.	$P \rightarrow Q$	18,T18,MP
28.	$\sim(P \wedge Q)$	26,T44,MP
29.	$P \wedge Q \leftrightarrow P$	18, 28, Adj, T85, MP
30.	$(P \rightarrow Q) \rightarrow (P \wedge Q \leftrightarrow P)$	29, T2, MP
31.	$(P \rightarrow Q) \rightarrow (P \wedge Q \leftrightarrow P)$	19, 25, SC
32.	$(P \rightarrow Q) \rightarrow (P \wedge Q \leftrightarrow P)$	2, 17, SC

Thus we secure a complete proof of (1)—overly long, to be sure, but obtained by a simple general method.

EXERCISES

Prove the following tautologies by the procedure of this section.

1. $(P \leftrightarrow [P \rightarrow Q]) \rightarrow Q$
2. $(Q \leftrightarrow P \wedge \sim P) \leftrightarrow \sim Q$
3. $([P \rightarrow Q] \rightarrow P) \rightarrow P$
4. $([P \rightarrow Q] \rightarrow Q) \leftrightarrow ([Q \rightarrow P] \rightarrow P)$

3. Tautological implication; generalized indirect derivation. The preceding discussion suggests two additional methods of abbreviating derivations, which, like clause (11), will be used only in the present chapter. The first of these consists in employing the following clause in the construction of derivations:

(12) A symbolic formula may occur as a line if it is tautologically implied by antecedent lines. (Annotation: 'TI', together with the numbers of the antecedent lines involved.)

The second of the new abbreviations concerns indirect derivation. In order to complete such a derivation, we must, according to earlier instructions, derive an *explicit contradiction*, that is, a pair of formulas of which one is the negation of the other. Our next abbreviation liberalizes these instructions: to complete an indirect derivation, we shall henceforth need only to derive a *truth-functional contradiction*, that is, a combination of formulas that cannot all simultaneously receive the truth value *T*. To be explicit, we say that the symbolic formulas $\phi_1 \ldots, \phi_n$ are *truth-functionally incompatible* just in case there is no assignment of truth values to nonmolecular symbolic formulas under which all of $\phi_1, \ldots, \phi_n$ receive the value *T*. Then the following clause introduces a new form of derivation, which we shall call *generalized indirect derivation.*

(13) When the following arrangement of lines has appeared:

$$\begin{array}{l} \textit{Show } \phi \\ \chi_1 \\ \cdot \\ \cdot \\ \cdot \\ \chi_k \quad , \end{array}$$

where none of χ_1 through χ_k contains uncancelled 'Show', and among χ_1 through χ_k there occur unboxed truth-functionally incompatible lines, then one may simultaneously cancel the displayed occurrence of 'Show', and box all subsequent lines.

Thus, for example, in the derivation

1.	~~*Show*~~ $\bigvee x(\mathrm{F}x \wedge \bigvee y\mathrm{G}y)$	
2.	$\sim \bigvee x(\mathrm{F}x \wedge \bigvee y\mathrm{G}y)$	
3.	$\sim \bigwedge x(\mathrm{F}x \rightarrow \mathrm{H}x)$	Premise
4.	$\sim(\mathrm{F}z \rightarrow \mathrm{H}z)$	3, QN, EI
5.	$\bigwedge x(\bigvee y\mathrm{G}y \leftrightarrow \mathrm{F}x)$	Premise
6.	$\bigvee y\mathrm{G}y \leftrightarrow \mathrm{F}z$	5, UI
7.	$\sim(\mathrm{F}z \wedge \bigvee y\mathrm{G}y)$	2, QN, UI

the cancellation of '*Show*' and boxing of lines 2 through 7 are legitimized by clause (13); for, as the reader can verify by means of a truth table, lines 4, 6, and 7 are truth-functionally incompatible.

Clauses (12) and (13) are reducible to (11), and hence theoretically superfluous.

4. A proof procedure for prenex formulas. By a *prenex formula* we shall understand a formula in prenex normal form or, equivalently, a symbolic formula in which no quantifier occurs to the right of a parenthesis or negation sign. (This criterion is equivalent to the one on page 225 for formulas in official notation.) We are now in a position to describe an automatic procedure, applicable to any prenex formula, which will lead to a proof of that formula, if indeed the formula is a theorem. We shall content ourselves with presenting the procedure, without attempting to justify the claim made for it. (See, however, the historical remarks accompanying this chapter.) The reader will notice that the proofs generated by the procedure have a particularly simple structure. Only one form of derivation is employed—generalized indirect derivation—and no subsidiary derivations appear; further, only three inference rules are used—IE (used in connection with the laws of quantifier negation), UI, and EI.

Suppose that χ is a prenex formula. We begin an indirect derivation, as follows:

Show χ

$\sim \chi$ (Assumption)

We now convert

$\sim \chi$

into prenex normal form by successive applications of IE, used in connection with the theorems

$\sim \bigwedge x\mathrm{F}x \leftrightarrow \bigvee x \sim \mathrm{F}x$, (T203)

$\sim \bigvee x\mathrm{F}x \leftrightarrow \bigwedge x \sim \mathrm{F}x$. (T204)

Thus we obtain

$$\begin{array}{l} \textit{Show } \chi \\ \sim \chi \\ \cdot \\ \cdot \\ \cdot \\ \psi \quad , \end{array}$$

where ψ is obtained from

$$\sim \chi$$

by 'moving in' the negation sign.

The remainder of the derivation, starting with ψ, constitutes an *elimination column*, constructed roughly as follows. We drop initial quantifiers one at a time by means of UI and EI. In the process we make sure that if the column contains a universal generalization

$$\Lambda\alpha\phi$$

and a free occurrence, in one of its lines, of a term ζ, then it will also contain the formula that comes from ϕ by proper substitution of ζ for α.

To be more explicit, we begin by examining ψ. If ψ has the form

$$\Lambda\alpha\phi$$

and $\zeta_1, \ldots, \zeta_n$ are all the terms that are free in ψ, then we add to the column all the formulas that come from ϕ by proper substitution of one of $\zeta_1, \ldots, \zeta_n$ for α; if there are no terms free in ψ, we add a formula that comes from ϕ by proper substitution for α of some variable not bound in any line of the derivation. If ψ has the form

$$\mathrm{V}\alpha\phi \quad ,$$

we add to the column a formula that comes from ϕ by proper substitution for α of some variable new to the derivation. These additions are legitimate; they follow from ψ by either UI or EI. If ψ is *quantifier-free* (that is, contains no quantifiers), we make no additions; the elimination column then consists of ψ alone.

We now examine the second line of the elimination column (if a second line has been obtained) and add lines to the column as follows.

(1) If the second line has the form

$$\Lambda\alpha\phi$$

and $\zeta_1, \ldots, \zeta_n$ are all the terms that are free in the first two lines of the elimination column, then we extend the column by subjoining all formulas that come from ϕ by proper substitution of one of $\zeta_1, \ldots, \zeta_n$ for α. (The addition is justified by UI.)

(2) If the second line has the form

$$\bigvee\alpha\phi \quad ,$$

then we subjoin to the column a formula that comes from ϕ by proper substitution for α of some variable new to the derivation. (The addition is justified by EI.)

(3) Whatever the form of the second line, we determine whether any terms are free in it that were not already free in the first line. If so, and if the first line is a universal generalization

$$\bigwedge\alpha\phi \quad ,$$

then we subjoin to the column all formulas that come from ϕ by proper substitution of one of these terms for α. (The addition is justified by UI.)

We pass now to the third line (if indeed a third line has been obtained) and subject it to the same sort of treatment as the second line; and so on, for all following lines. In general, when we examine any line of the elimination column other than the first, we add lines at the bottom of the column in accordance with the following instructions. (It is clear that each addition is justified by either UI or EI.)

(1) If the line in question has the form

$$\bigwedge\alpha\phi$$

and $\zeta_1, \ldots, \zeta_n$ are all the terms that are free in lines of the elimination column up to and including this line, then we add as lines all formulas that come from ϕ by proper substitution of one of $\zeta_1, \ldots, \zeta_n$ for α.

(2) If the line in question has the form

$$\bigvee\alpha\phi \quad ,$$

then we add as a line a formula that comes from ϕ by proper substitution for α of some variable new to the derivation.

(3) Whatever the form of the line in question, we determine whether any terms are free in it that were not already free in the preceding lines. If so, let these terms be $\zeta_1, \ldots, \zeta_n$. For each universal generalization

$$\bigwedge\alpha\phi$$

that precedes the line in question in the elimination column, we add as lines all formulas that come from ϕ by proper substitution of one of $\zeta_1, \ldots, \zeta_n$ for α.

Now if the original formula χ is a theorem, this procedure will eventually lead to a truth-functional contradiction. It may be convenient, at various stages of the derivation, to test by a truth table the truth-functional compatibility of the formulas so far obtained; in fact, it will be sufficient to test the quantifier-free formulas of the elimination column, for among these the truth-functional contradiction, if there is one, must always appear. When we obtain a truth-functional contradiction, we may box and cancel in accordance with generalized indirect derivation. We shall then have a complete proof of χ.

Let us prove, by means of the general procedure, the symbolic formula '$\bigwedge y \bigvee x(\mathrm{F}x \rightarrow \mathrm{F}y)$'. We begin an indirect derivation:

1. *Show* $\bigwedge y \bigvee x(\mathrm{F}x \rightarrow \mathrm{F}y)$
2. $\sim \bigwedge y \bigvee x(\mathrm{F}x \rightarrow \mathrm{F}y)$

Next we 'move in' the negation sign:

3.	$\bigvee y \sim \bigvee x(\mathrm{F}x \rightarrow \mathrm{F}y)$	2, T203
4.	$\bigvee y \bigwedge x \sim (\mathrm{F}x \rightarrow \mathrm{F}y)$	3, IE(T204)

Now we are to construct an elimination column, beginning with line 4. We notice that line 4 is an existential generalization and that the variable 'a' has not yet occurred. Thus we add a fifth line, as follows:

5.	$\bigwedge x \sim (\mathrm{F}x \rightarrow \mathrm{F}a)$	4, EI

We now examine the fifth line of the derivation (the second of the elimination column), and observe that it is a universal generalization and that 'a' is the only term free in this line or the preceding. Thus instruction (1) for adding lines leads us to

6.	$\sim(\mathrm{F}a \rightarrow \mathrm{F}a)$	5, UI

Instruction (2) is not applicable to line 5, because line 5 is not an existential generalization; nor is instruction (3), because the preceding line is not a universal generalization. Thus we pass to line 6. But none of the instructions is applicable here. Hence the procedure for extending the column has come to an end. But we easily see that line 6, the only quantifier-free line, forms by itself a truth-functional contradiction; that is, its truth value is *F* under any assignment of truth values to nonmolecular formulas. Thus, by generalized indirect derivation, we box and cancel, obtaining

1.	~~*Show*~~ $\bigwedge y \bigvee x(\mathrm{F}x \rightarrow \mathrm{F}y)$	
2.	$\sim \bigwedge y \bigvee x(\mathrm{F}x \rightarrow \mathrm{F}y)$	
3.	$\bigvee y \sim \bigvee x(\mathrm{F}x \rightarrow \mathrm{F}y)$	2, T203
4.	$\bigvee y \bigwedge x \sim (\mathrm{F}x \rightarrow \mathrm{F}y)$	3, IE(T204)
5.	$\bigwedge x \sim (\mathrm{F}x \rightarrow \mathrm{F}a)$	4, EI
6.	$\sim(\mathrm{F}a \rightarrow \mathrm{F}a)$	5, UI

In the example just considered, the general procedure for extending the elimination column comes to an end. This is not always the case. For example, let us apply the procedure to the formula

$$\bigvee x \bigvee y \bigwedge z([\mathrm{F}x \rightarrow \mathrm{G}x] \rightarrow [\mathrm{F}y \rightarrow \mathrm{G}z]) \quad .$$

We begin as before:

1.	*Show* $\bigvee x \bigvee y \bigwedge z([Fx \rightarrow Gx] \rightarrow [Fy \rightarrow Gz])$	
2.	$\sim \bigvee x \bigvee y \bigwedge z([Fx \rightarrow Gx] \rightarrow [Fy \rightarrow Gz])$	
3.	$\bigwedge x \sim \bigvee y \bigwedge z([Fx \rightarrow Gx] \rightarrow [Fy \rightarrow Gz])$	2, T204
4.	$\bigwedge x \bigwedge y \sim \bigwedge z([Fx \rightarrow Gx] \rightarrow [Fy \rightarrow Gz])$	3, IE(T204)
5.	$\bigwedge x \bigwedge y \bigvee z \sim ([Fx \rightarrow Gx] \rightarrow [Fy \rightarrow Gz])$	4, IE(T203)

Since no terms are free in the first line of the elimination column (line 5), we choose a variable so far not bound, say '*a*', and add a corresponding sixth line:

6.	$\bigwedge y \bigvee z \sim ([Fa \rightarrow Ga] \rightarrow [Fy \rightarrow Gz])$	5, UI

We turn to line 6, find it to be a universal generalization, and observe that '*a*' is the only term that is free so far. Thus, following instruction (1) of page 421, we add a seventh line:

7.	$\bigvee z \sim (Fa \rightarrow Ga] \rightarrow [Fa \rightarrow Gz])$	6, UI

Instruction (3) is also applicable to line 6, for that line contains freely for the first time the variable '*a*', and the preceding line is a universal generalization. Thus instruction (3) would lead us to add

$$\bigwedge y \bigvee z \sim ([Fa \rightarrow Ga] \rightarrow [Fy \rightarrow Gz]) \quad .$$

We do not, however, make this addition, for it would amount only to repeating line 6. (In general, we shall not add lines that repeat earlier lines.) We now consider line 7. (2) is the only applicable instruction. We obtain

8.	$\sim ([Fa \rightarrow Ga] \rightarrow [Fa \rightarrow Gb])$	7, EI

Instruction (3) is applicable to line 8; it contains freely for the first time the variable '*b*', and there are two earlier universal generalizations (lines 5 and 6). Thus we obtain

9.	$\bigwedge y \bigvee z \sim ([Fb \rightarrow Gb] \rightarrow [Fy \rightarrow Gz])$	5, UI
10.	$\bigvee z \sim ([Fa \rightarrow Ga] \rightarrow [Fb \rightarrow Gz])$	6, UI

To line 9, only instruction (1) is applicable. There are two terms free up to this point, '*a*' and '*b*'; thus we obtain

11.	$\bigvee z \sim ([Fb \rightarrow Gb] \rightarrow [Fa \rightarrow Gz])$	9, UI
12.	$\bigvee z \sim ([Fb \rightarrow Gb] \rightarrow [Fb \rightarrow Gz])$	9, UI

Only instruction (2) is applicable to line 10. We obtain

13.	$\sim ([Fa \rightarrow Ga] \rightarrow [Fb \rightarrow Gc])$	10, EI

Again, in connection with line 11, only instruction (2) is applicable.

We obtain

14.	$\sim([Fb \rightarrow Gb] \rightarrow [Fa \rightarrow Gd)]$	11, EI

But now we observe that lines 8, 13, and 14 form a truth-functional contradiction; the reader may check this fact by constructing a truth table. Thus we may box and cancel, to obtain the complete (abbreviated) proof

1.	~~*Show*~~ $\bigvee x \bigvee y \bigwedge z([Fx \rightarrow Gx] \rightarrow [Fy \rightarrow Gz])$	
2.	$\sim \bigvee x \bigvee y \bigwedge z([Fx \rightarrow Gx] \rightarrow [Fy \rightarrow Gz])$	
3.	$\bigwedge x \sim \bigvee y \bigwedge z([Fx \rightarrow Gx] \rightarrow [Fy \rightarrow Gz])$	2, T204
4.	$\bigwedge x \bigwedge y \sim \bigwedge z([Fx \rightarrow Gx] \rightarrow [Fy \rightarrow Gz])$	3, IE(T204)
5.	$\bigwedge x \bigwedge y \bigvee z \sim ([Fx \rightarrow Gx] \rightarrow [Fy \rightarrow Gz])$	4, IE(T203)
6.	$\bigwedge y \bigvee z \sim ([Fa \rightarrow Ga] \rightarrow [Fy \rightarrow Gz])$	5, UI
7.	$\bigvee z \sim ([Fa \rightarrow Ga] \rightarrow [Fa \rightarrow Gz])$	6, UI
8.	$\sim([Fa \rightarrow Ga] \rightarrow [Fa \rightarrow Gb])$	7, EI
9.	$\bigwedge y \bigvee z \sim ([Fb \rightarrow Gb] \rightarrow [Fy \rightarrow Gz])$	5, UI
10.	$\bigvee z \sim ([Fa \rightarrow Ga] \rightarrow [Fb \rightarrow Gz])$	6, UI
11.	$\bigvee z \sim ([Fb \rightarrow Gb] \rightarrow [Fa \rightarrow Gz])$	9, UI
12.	$\bigvee z \sim ([Fb \rightarrow Gb] \rightarrow [Fb \rightarrow Gz])$	9, UI
13.	$\sim([Fa \rightarrow Ga] \rightarrow [Fb \rightarrow Gc])$	10, EI
14.	$\sim([Fb \rightarrow Gb] \rightarrow [Fa \rightarrow Gd])$	11, EI

Instead of boxing and cancelling, we might well have added lines to the column. Consideration of lines 12, 13, and 14 would have led to new lines, and these to further lines. Indeed, the general procedure would never, in this case, terminate naturally. It is of course pointless to continue adding lines after a contradiction has been obtained; there is, however, no general method for computing when, if ever, this stage will be reached.

EXERCISES

Apply the general procedure just described to obtain proofs of the following theorems. Exercise 5 is solved for illustration.

5. $\bigvee x \bigvee y[FA(xB) \rightarrow Fy]$

1.	~~*Show*~~ $\bigvee x \bigvee y[FA(xB) \rightarrow Fy]$	
2.	$\sim \bigvee x \bigvee y[FA(xB) \rightarrow Fy]$	
3.	$\bigwedge x \sim \bigvee y[FA(xB) \rightarrow Fy]$	2, T204
4.	$\bigwedge x \bigwedge y \sim [FA(xB) \rightarrow Fy]$	3, IE(T204)
5.	$\bigwedge y \sim [FA(BB) \rightarrow Fy]$	4, UI
6.	$\sim[FA(BB) \rightarrow FB]$	5, UI
7.	$\sim[FA(BB) \rightarrow FA(BB)]$	5, UI

6. $\bigvee x \bigvee y[FA(xB) \rightarrow FA(yy)]$
7. $\bigvee x \bigwedge y(Fx \vee [Fy \rightarrow Gy])$
8. $\bigwedge y \bigvee x \bigwedge z \bigvee w[F(xy) \rightarrow F(zw)]$
9. $\bigwedge x \bigwedge y \bigwedge z \bigvee w(Fx \wedge \sim Fz \leftrightarrow [Fw \leftrightarrow \sim Fy])$

5. A derivation procedure for prenex arguments. The procedure just described in connection with individual prenex formulas can be extended quite naturally so as to apply to arguments. In particular, we must consider symbolic arguments with finitely many premises, all of whose formulas are prenex, and whose premises are sentences.

Suppose that such an argument has $\phi_1, \ldots, \phi_n$ as its premises and ψ as its conclusion. Then the following general procedure will lead, if the argument is valid, to a complete derivation of ψ from $\phi_1, \ldots, \phi_n$.

We begin an indirect proof of ψ:

Show ψ
$\sim \psi$

As before, we convert

$\sim \psi$

into prenex normal form, obtaining

Show ψ
$\sim \psi$
.
.
.
χ ,

where χ is inferred from

$\sim \psi$

by 'moving in' the negation sign. Now we add the premises of the argument:

Show ψ
$\sim \psi$
.
.
.
χ
ϕ_1
.
.
.
ϕ_n .

The elimination column is again regarded as beginning with χ. Lines are added in accordance with the instructions given on pages 420–21. If the argument is valid, a truth-functional contradiction will be obtained, and the generalized indirect proof may be completed.

To illustrate the present procedure, let us construct a derivation corresponding to the argument

$$\bigwedge x \bigwedge y[Fx \wedge Gy \rightarrow H(xy)] \quad . \quad \bigvee x \bigwedge y(Fx \wedge [Jy \rightarrow \sim H(xy)])$$
$$\therefore \bigwedge x(Gx \rightarrow \sim Jx)$$

Derivation:

1.	~~*Show*~~ $\bigwedge x(Gx \rightarrow \sim Jx)$	
2.	$\sim \bigwedge x(Gx \rightarrow \sim Jx)$	
3.	$\bigvee x \sim (Gx \rightarrow \sim Jx)$	
4.	$\bigwedge x \bigwedge y[Fx \wedge Gy \rightarrow H(xy)]$	Premise
5.	$\bigvee x \bigwedge y(Fx \wedge [Jy \rightarrow \sim H(xy)])$	Premise
6.	$\sim (Ga \rightarrow \sim Ja)$	3, EI
7.	$\bigwedge y(Fb \wedge [Jy \rightarrow \sim H(by)])$	5, EI
8.	$\bigwedge y[Fa \wedge Gy \rightarrow H(ay)]$	4, UI
9.	$Fb \wedge [Ja \rightarrow \sim H(ba)]$	7, UI
10.	$Fb \wedge [Jb \rightarrow \sim H(bb)]$	7, UI
11.	$\bigwedge y[Fb \wedge Gy \rightarrow H(by)]$	4, UI
12.	$Fa \wedge Ga \rightarrow H(aa)$	8, UI
13.	$Fa \wedge Gb \rightarrow H(ab)$	8, UI
14.	$Fb \wedge Ga \rightarrow H(ba)$	11, UI
15.	$Fb \wedge Gb \rightarrow H(bb)$	11, UI

The reader can easily verify that lines 6, 9, and 14 are truth-functionally incompatible.

Here and in subsequent sections we consider only arguments with finitely many premises. The restriction is not essential. A slight modification of the procedures of this chapter would provide derivation procedures for arguments with infinitely many premises, provided only that the set of premises be *recursively enumerable*. (Loosely speaking, a set of expressions is *recursively enumerable* just in case there is an enumeration of the members of the set according to which one can find automatically, for each number *n*, the *n*th expression in the enumeration. For an exact definition, see, for instance, Kleene [1].)

EXERCISES

Establish the validity of the following arguments by the derivation procedure just described.

10. $\bigwedge y \bigvee x([Fy \rightarrow Gy] \vee [Fx \wedge Hx]) \quad . \quad \bigwedge x(Fx \rightarrow \sim Hx) \quad .$
$\bigvee x Fx \quad \therefore \bigvee x(Fx \wedge Gx)$

11. $\bigwedge x \bigwedge y \bigwedge z[F(xy) \wedge F(yz) \rightarrow F(xz)]$. $\bigwedge x \bigwedge y[F(xy) \rightarrow F(yx)]$
$\therefore \bigwedge x \bigwedge y[F(xy) \rightarrow F(xx)]$

12. $\bigwedge x \bigwedge y(Fx \wedge Fy \rightarrow FA(xy))$. $\bigvee x \bigwedge y(Fx \wedge [Fy \rightarrow GA(xy)])$
$\therefore \bigvee x(Fx \wedge Gx)$

6. Conversion to prenex form. In the foregoing sections we considered only those arguments whose formulas are prenex. Before extending our considerations further, we must attend to the task of *converting a formula into prenex form.* It was mentioned in chapter IV that every symbolic formula is equivalent to a formula in prenex normal form. This assertion can be strengthened. Every symbolic formula ϕ is equivalent to a prenex formula with the same free variables as ϕ; such a formula is called a *prenex form* of ϕ. We must now give directions for finding a prenex form of an arbitrary formula ϕ and for proving its equivalence with ϕ. Biconditional derivation makes the task simple.

Suppose we are given a symbolic formula ϕ that is not yet in prenex normal form. First we eliminate '$\leftrightarrow$'; that is, we replace, one at a time, each subformula

$$\psi \leftrightarrow \chi$$

by an equivalent formula, on the basis of T81:

$$(P \leftrightarrow Q) \leftrightarrow (P \rightarrow Q) \wedge (Q \rightarrow P) \quad .$$

This transformation requires several applications of IE, corresponding to the occurrences of '$\leftrightarrow$'. Let the formulas produced by these steps, which lead from ϕ to a formula without '$\leftrightarrow$', be, in order, $\phi_1, \ldots, \phi_n$.

The formula ϕ_n, like the original formula ϕ, is not yet in prenex normal form. Thus ϕ_n contains at least one *noninitial* occurrence of a quantifier phrase, that is, an occurrence standing to the right of a parenthesis or negation sign. (We have in mind our official notation, so that in

$$\bigvee x Fx \rightarrow \bigvee x Gx$$

both occurrences of '$\bigvee x$' are regarded as noninitial.)

We fix our attention on the first such occurrence, and convert it to an initial occurrence. The occurrence will begin a subformula of ϕ_n of the form

(1) $$\bigwedge \alpha \psi$$

or

(2) $$\bigvee \alpha \psi \quad ,$$

where α is a variable and ψ a formula. Now we move the occurrence of

$$\bigwedge \alpha$$

or

$$\vee\alpha$$

to the left of all parentheses and negation signs, proceeding step by step by means of alphabetic variants of instances of alphabetic variants of the laws of quantifier negation and confinement, that is, the following laws:

T203	$\sim \wedge x Fx \leftrightarrow \vee x \sim Fx$
T204	$\sim \vee x Fx \leftrightarrow \wedge x \sim Fx$
T219	$\wedge x(P \rightarrow Fx) \leftrightarrow (P \rightarrow \wedge x Fx)$
T220	$\vee x(P \rightarrow Fx) \leftrightarrow (P \rightarrow \vee x Fx)$
T221	$\wedge x(Fx \rightarrow P) \leftrightarrow (\vee x Fx \rightarrow P)$
T222	$\vee x(Fx \rightarrow P) \leftrightarrow (\wedge x Fx \rightarrow P)$
T215	$\wedge x(P \wedge Fx) \leftrightarrow P \wedge \wedge x Fx$
T273	$\wedge x(Fx \wedge P) \leftrightarrow \wedge x Fx \wedge P$
T216	$\vee x(P \wedge Fx) \leftrightarrow P \wedge \vee x Fx$
T274	$\vee x(Fx \wedge P) \leftrightarrow \vee x Fx \wedge P$
T217	$\wedge x(P \vee Fx) \leftrightarrow P \vee \wedge x Fx$
T275	$\wedge x(Fx \vee P) \leftrightarrow \wedge x Fx \vee P$
T218	$\vee x(P \vee Fx) \leftrightarrow P \vee \vee x Fx$
T276	$\vee x(Fx \vee P) \leftrightarrow \vee x Fx \vee P$

(The variable α may pass into a new variable, and either quantifier into the other, in these steps.)

Let the formulas corresponding to the various steps in this transformation be $\phi_{n+1}, \ldots, \phi_{n+k}$. We now consider the first noninitial occurrence of a quantifier phrase in ϕ_{n+k} and transform this into an initial occurrence just as before. We repeat the process until all noninitial occurrences of quantifier phrases have been removed. Thus, when we combine all stages of the process, we obtain a sequence of formulas $\phi, \phi_1, \ldots, \phi_j, \psi$, in which each formula is equivalent to the preceding by IE (applied in connection with the theorems just listed or T81), and such that the final formula ψ has no noninitial occurrences of quantifier phrases.

The formula ψ is the prenex form that was sought: it is in prenex normal form, it contains the same free variables as ϕ, and it is equivalent to ϕ on the basis of the following biconditional derivation:

1.	~~*Show*~~ $\phi \leftrightarrow \psi$	
2.	ϕ	
3.	ϕ_1	2, T81, IE
	.	.
	.	.
	.	.
$j + 2$.	ϕ_j	$j + 1$, T***, IE
$j + 3$.	ψ	$j + 2$, T***, IE

For example, the formula in line 13 of the following biconditional derivation is a prenex form (with the same free variable) of the formula in line 2; lines 2 through 13 constitute the process of conversion; and the biconditional derivation itself is a proof of the equivalence of the two formulas in question.

1.	~~*Show*~~ $\bigwedge x Fx \leftrightarrow Hx \vee \bigvee x Gx$	
2.	$\bigwedge x Fx \leftrightarrow Hx \vee \bigvee x Gx$	
3.	$(\bigwedge x Fx \rightarrow Hx \vee \bigvee x Gx) \wedge$ $(Hx \vee \bigvee x Gx \rightarrow \bigwedge x Fx)$	2, T81, IE
4.	$\bigvee y(Fy \rightarrow Hx \vee \bigvee x Gx) \wedge$ $(Hx \vee \bigvee x Gx \rightarrow \bigwedge x Fx)$	3, T222, IE
5.	$\bigvee y[(Fy \rightarrow Hx \vee \bigvee x Gx) \wedge$ $(Hx \vee \bigvee x Gx \rightarrow \bigwedge x Fx)]$	4, T274, IE
6.	$\bigvee y[(Fy \rightarrow \bigvee z[Hx \vee Gz]) \wedge$ $(Hx \vee \bigvee x Gx \rightarrow \bigwedge x Fx)]$	5, T218, IE
7.	$\bigvee y[\bigvee z(Fy \rightarrow Hx \vee Gz) \wedge$ $(Hx \vee \bigvee x Gx \rightarrow \bigwedge x Fx)]$	6, T220, IE
8.	$\bigvee y \bigvee z[(Fy \rightarrow Hx \vee Gz) \wedge$ $(Hx \vee \bigvee x Gx \rightarrow \bigwedge x Fx)]$	7, T274, IE
9.	$\bigvee y \bigvee z[(Fy \rightarrow Hx \vee Gz) \wedge$ $(\bigvee w[Hx \vee Gw] \rightarrow \bigwedge x Fx)]$	8, T218, IE
10.	$\bigvee y \bigvee z[(Fy \rightarrow Hx \vee Gz) \wedge$ $\bigwedge w(Hx \vee Gw \rightarrow \bigwedge x Fx)]$	9, T222, IE
11.	$\bigvee y \bigvee z \bigwedge w[(Fy \rightarrow Hx \vee Gz) \wedge$ $(Hx \vee Gw \rightarrow \bigwedge x Fx)]$	10, T215, IE
12.	$\bigvee y \bigvee z \bigwedge w[(Fy \rightarrow Hx \vee Gz) \wedge$ $\bigwedge u(Hx \vee Gw \rightarrow Fu)]$	11, T219, IE
13.	$\bigvee y \bigvee z \bigwedge w \bigwedge u[(Fy \rightarrow Hx \vee Gz) \wedge$ $(Hx \vee Gw \rightarrow Fu)]$	12, T215, IE

EXERCISES

Convert each of the following formulas into prenex form and then prefix an assertion line to the process of conversion to obtain a proof of the equivalence of the formula and its prenex form.

13. $\bigwedge x\mathrm{F}x \leftrightarrow \bigwedge x\mathrm{G}x$
14. $\bigvee x\mathrm{F}x \leftrightarrow \bigvee x\mathrm{G}x$
15. $\bigvee y\bigwedge x\mathrm{F}(xy) \rightarrow \bigvee y\bigwedge x\mathrm{F}(xy)$
16. $\bigwedge x\bigwedge y\mathrm{F}(xy) \leftrightarrow \bigwedge y\bigwedge x\mathrm{F}(xy)$

7. A derivation procedure for arbitrary symbolic arguments. We consider now an arbitrary symbolic argument with finitely many premises. Let these premises be $\phi_1, \ldots, \phi_n$, and let the conclusion be ψ. The derivation procedure is roughly this. We first derive for a closure of each premise and for the conclusion an equivalent prenex formula, and then apply the derivation procedure of section 5 of this chapter.

In greater detail, the derivation procedure is the following. Let

$$(1) \qquad \bigwedge\alpha_1 \ldots \bigwedge\alpha_k\phi_1$$

be a closure of ϕ_1, the first premise. By the procedure described in section 6 of this chapter, we find a prenex sentence ψ_1 that is equivalent to (1) and, in addition, a proof of its equivalence. We begin the derivation with this proof.

~~Show~~ $\bigwedge\alpha_1 \ldots \bigwedge\alpha_k\phi_1 \leftrightarrow \psi_1$

We repeat the procedure for each of the other premises, obtaining

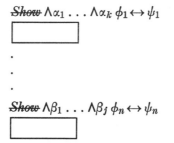

~~Show~~ $\bigwedge\alpha_1 \ldots \bigwedge\alpha_k\, \phi_1 \leftrightarrow \psi_1$

.
.
.

~~Show~~ $\bigwedge\beta_1 \ldots \bigwedge\beta_j\, \phi_n \leftrightarrow \psi_n$

where $\beta_1, \ldots, \beta_j$ are the free variables of ϕ_n. Again by the procedure of section 6, we find a prenex form χ of the conclusion ψ, together with a proof of the equivalence. This proof we add to the derivation:

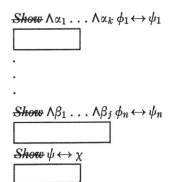

~~*Show*~~ $\bigwedge\alpha_1 \ldots \bigwedge\alpha_k\ \phi_1 \leftrightarrow \psi_1$

.
.
.

~~*Show*~~ $\bigwedge\beta_1 \ldots \bigwedge\beta_j\ \phi_n \leftrightarrow \psi_n$

~~*Show*~~ $\psi \leftrightarrow \chi$

At this point we begin an indirect proof of ψ, and from the assumption

$$\sim\psi\ ,$$

together with an equivalence occurring earlier in the derivation, we infer

$$\sim\chi\ .$$

Next we 'move in' the negation sign, obtaining a prenex counterpart χ' of

$$\sim\chi\ .$$

Thus the derivation becomes:

~~*Show*~~ $\bigwedge\alpha_1 \ldots \bigwedge\alpha_k\ \phi_1 \leftrightarrow \psi_1$

.
.
.

~~*Show*~~ $\bigwedge\beta_1 \ldots \bigwedge\beta_j\ \phi_n \leftrightarrow \psi_n$

~~*Show*~~ $\psi \leftrightarrow \chi$

Show ψ
$\sim\psi$
$\sim\chi$
.
.
.
χ'

Next we enter into the derivation the appropriate closure of each of the premises (see revised clause (2), p. 220), and then infer the formulas ψ_1 through ψ_n, obtaining

~~*Show*~~ $\bigwedge\alpha_1 \ldots \bigwedge\alpha_k\ \phi_1 \leftrightarrow \psi_1$

.
.
.

~~*Show*~~ $\bigwedge\beta_1 \ldots \bigwedge\beta_j\ \phi_n \leftrightarrow \psi_n$

~~*Show*~~ $\psi \leftrightarrow \chi$

Show ψ
$\sim\psi$
$\sim\chi$
.
.
.
χ'
ψ_1
.
.
.
ψ_n

We now proceed as in section 5, regarding the elimination column as beginning with the line χ'. A truth-functional contradiction will ensue just in case the conclusion ψ is derivable from the premises ϕ_1 through ϕ_n.

The present method, besides serving as a derivation procedure for symbolic arguments, provides also a proof procedure for arbitrary symbolic formulas. To apply the method to a formula ϕ, we consider the argument without premises whose conclusion is ϕ.

EXERCISES

Establish the validity of each of the following arguments by the derivation procedure described in this section. Exercise 17 is solved for illustration.

17. $Fx \rightarrow \bigwedge x Gx$. $\bigvee x(Fx \wedge \sim\bigwedge x Hx)$ $\therefore \sim\bigwedge x(Gx \rightarrow Hx)$

1. ~~*Show*~~ $\bigwedge x(Fx \rightarrow \bigwedge x Gx) \leftrightarrow \bigwedge x \bigwedge y(Fx \rightarrow Gy)$
2. $\bigwedge x(Fx \rightarrow \bigwedge x Gx)$
3. $\bigwedge x \bigwedge y(Fx \rightarrow Gy)$ — 2, T219, IE

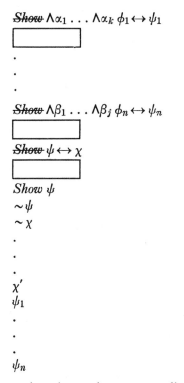

4.	~~Show~~ $\bigvee x(Fx \wedge \sim\bigwedge xHx) \leftrightarrow \bigvee x\bigvee y(Fx \wedge \sim Hy)$	
5.	$\bigvee x(Fx \wedge \sim\bigwedge xHx)$	
6.	$\bigvee x(Fx \wedge \bigvee x\sim Hx)$	5, T203, IE
7.	$\bigvee x\bigvee y(Fx \wedge \sim Hy)$	6, T216, IE
8.	~~Show~~ $\sim\bigwedge x(Gx \to Hx) \leftrightarrow \bigvee x\sim(Gx \to Hx)$	
9.	$\sim\bigwedge x(Gx \to Hx)$	
10.	$\bigvee x\sim(Gx \to Hx)$	9, T203, IE
11.	~~Show~~ $\sim\bigwedge x(Gx \to Hx)$	
12.	$\bigwedge x(Gx \to Hx)$	
13.	$\sim\bigvee x\sim(Gx \to Hx)$	8, 12, TI
14.	$\bigwedge x\sim\sim(Gx \to Hx)$	13, T204, IE
15.	$\bigwedge x\bigwedge y(Fx \to Gy)$	Premise, 1, TI
16.	$\bigvee x\bigvee y(Fx \wedge \sim Hy)$	Premise, 4, TI
17.	$\sim\sim(Ga \to Ha)$	14, UI
18.	$\bigvee y(Fb \wedge \sim Hy)$	16, EI
19.	$\bigwedge y(Fa \to Gy)$	15, UI
20.	$Fb \wedge \sim Hc$	18, EI
21.	$\sim\sim(Gb \to Hb)$	14, UI
22.	$\bigwedge y(Fb \to Gy)$	15, UI
23.	$Fa \to Ga$	19, UI
24.	$Fa \to Gb$	19, UI
25.	$\sim\sim(Gc \to Hc)$	14, UI
26.	$\bigwedge y(Fc \to Gy)$	15, UI
27.	$Fa \to Gc$	19, UI
28.	$Fb \to Ga$	22, UI
29.	$Fb \to Gb$	22, UI
30.	$Fb \to Gc$	22, UI

In each of lines 1, 4, and 8, a closure of a formula of the argument is shown to be equivalent to a prenex form of that formula. Line 11 begins the derivation of the conclusion of the argument, and the elimination column of this derivation begins with line 14. The reader can verify that lines 20, 25, and 30 are truth-functionally incompatible.

18. $Fx \to \bigvee y[Gy \wedge H(xy)] \wedge \bigvee y[Gy \wedge \sim H(xy)]$.
$\bigvee x(Tx \wedge \bigwedge y[Gy \to H(xy)]) \quad \therefore \bigvee x(Tx \wedge \sim Fx)$

19. $\bigvee y(\bigwedge z[F(zy) \to F(z\ A(x))] \wedge F(xy)) \quad \therefore \bigwedge xF(x\ A(x))$

8. A decision procedure for certain prenex formulas. A subsidiary purpose of this chapter is to present *decision procedures* for certain kinds of formulas and arguments. A *decision procedure* for a class of *formulas* is an automatic method for determining of each formula in the class whether or not it is a theorem. A *decision procedure* for a class of *arguments* is an automatic method for determining of each argument in the class whether or not it is valid.

We have observed earlier (p. 228) that for the class of all symbolic formulas (of the full quantifier calculus) and for the class of all symbolic arguments (of this calculus) no decision procedures are available. For some special classes, however, decision procedures may be found. Indeed, in some cases the automatic derivation procedures described earlier in this chapter lead quite simply to decision procedures.

The cases we wish to consider depend upon the following fact (which will not be proved here): for formulas and arguments of certain structures, the elimination column of our automatic derivation procedure will come to an end, and in such cases we may test for provability or validity by generating a complete elimination column and performing a truth-table check of the truth-functional compatibility of the quantifier-free formulas in it. It should be mentioned that we exclude from our considerations formulas containing operation letters.

The first case is that of prenex formulas without operation letters in which no universal quantifier follows an existential quantifier. To determine whether such a formula is a theorem we need only attempt to prove it by means of the derivation procedure described in section 4. The elimination column so obtained will come to an end. Thus it is possible to test the quantifier-free formulas of the elimination column for truth-functional compatibility by constructing a truth table. We shall obtain truth-functional incompatibility just in case the original formula is a theorem.

For instance, the formula

(1) $\bigwedge y \bigvee x(\mathrm{F}x \rightarrow \mathrm{F}y)$

has the required form. Its elimination column, constructed on page 422, was seen to terminate, and a truth-table check would have disclosed that (1) is a theorem.

As another example, consider the formula

(2) $\bigwedge x \bigwedge y \bigvee z[\mathrm{F}(xz) \vee \mathrm{G}(yz) \rightarrow \mathrm{F}(xy)]$.

The automatic derivation procedure leads us to the following:

Show $\bigwedge x \bigwedge y \bigvee z[\mathrm{F}(xz) \vee \mathrm{G}(yz) \rightarrow \mathrm{F}(xy)]$
$\sim \bigwedge x \bigwedge y \bigvee z[\mathrm{F}(xz) \vee \mathrm{G}(yz) \rightarrow \mathrm{F}(xy)]$
$\bigvee x \sim \bigwedge y \bigvee z[\mathrm{F}(xz) \vee \mathrm{G}(yz) \rightarrow \mathrm{F}(xy)]$
$\bigvee x \bigvee y \sim \bigvee z[\mathrm{F}(xz) \vee \mathrm{G}(yz) \rightarrow \mathrm{F}(xy)]$
$\bigvee x \bigvee y \bigwedge z \sim [\mathrm{F}(xz) \vee \mathrm{G}(yz) \rightarrow \mathrm{F}(xy)]$
$\bigvee y \bigwedge z \sim [\mathrm{F}(az) \vee \mathrm{G}(yz) \rightarrow \mathrm{F}(ay)]$
$\bigwedge z \sim [\mathrm{F}(az) \vee \mathrm{G}(bz) \rightarrow \mathrm{F}(ab)]$
$\sim [\mathrm{F}(aa) \vee \mathrm{G}(ba) \rightarrow \mathrm{F}(ab)]$
$\sim [\mathrm{F}(ab) \vee \mathrm{G}(bb) \rightarrow \mathrm{F}(ab)]$

The quantifier-free formulas to be considered are

$$\sim[\mathrm{F}(aa) \vee \mathrm{G}(ba) \rightarrow \mathrm{F}(ab)] \quad ,$$
$$\sim[\mathrm{F}(ab) \vee \mathrm{G}(bb) \rightarrow \mathrm{F}(ab)] \quad .$$

A truth-table check reveals that these formulas are truth-functionally compatible. Thus, according to our decision procedure, the formula (2) is not a theorem.

EXERCISES

Using the decision procedure just described, determine which of Nos. 20 – 28 are theorems.

20. $\bigwedge x \bigwedge y \bigvee z \bigvee w[\mathrm{F}(xy) \vee \mathrm{F}(yx) \rightarrow \mathrm{F}(zw)]$
21. $\bigvee x \bigvee y \bigvee z([\mathrm{F}x \rightarrow \mathrm{G}x] \rightarrow [\mathrm{F}y \rightarrow \mathrm{G}z])$
22. $\bigwedge x \bigwedge y \bigwedge z \bigvee w([\mathrm{F}x \leftrightarrow \mathrm{F}w] \rightarrow \sim \mathrm{F}y \vee \mathrm{F}z)$
23. $\bigwedge z \bigwedge y \bigwedge x \bigwedge u \bigwedge v([\mathrm{F}(xy) \leftrightarrow \mathrm{F}(xz) \wedge \sim \mathrm{F}(xx)] \rightarrow \sim \mathrm{F}(uv))$
24. $\bigwedge x \bigwedge y \bigvee z \bigvee w([\mathrm{F}w \rightarrow \mathrm{G}w] \rightarrow [\mathrm{F}y \wedge \mathrm{H}(xy) \rightarrow \mathrm{G}z \wedge \mathrm{H}(xz)])$
25. $\bigwedge z \bigwedge x \bigwedge w \bigwedge u \bigvee v \bigvee y(\mathrm{F}(xz) \rightarrow [\mathrm{F}(yw) \leftrightarrow (\mathrm{F}(uv) \rightarrow \mathrm{F}(yy))])$
26. $\bigwedge x \bigwedge y \bigwedge z \bigwedge w([\mathrm{F}(xz) \rightarrow \mathrm{G}(yw)] \rightarrow \mathrm{G}(yw))$
27. $\bigwedge z \bigwedge y \bigvee w \bigvee u \bigvee x([\mathrm{F}(xu) \rightarrow \mathrm{G}(xu) \vee \mathrm{H}(xu)] \rightarrow$
    $[\mathrm{F}(yz) \rightarrow \mathrm{G}(yz)] \wedge [\mathrm{F}(wz) \wedge \mathrm{H}(wz)])$
28. $\bigvee y \bigvee x \bigvee z[\mathrm{F}(xyz) \leftrightarrow \mathrm{F}(xzx)]$

29. Give a decision procedure for symbolic formulas without operation letters and *without overlay* (see p. 224), that is, an automatic procedure whereby one can determine whether such a formula is a theorem. In view of the decision procedure just described, it is sufficient to give an automatic procedure for transforming any formula of the kind in question into an equivalent prenex formula, also without operation letters, in which no universal quantifier follows an existential quantifier. (One such procedure can be obtained with the aid of the normal forms mentioned on page 95; see exercises 55 – 58 of chapter II.) Notice that the solution of this problem, combined with the conversion procedure outlined in section 4 of chapter VII, will give a decision procedure for all monadic formulas. (An alternative decision procedure for monadic formulas was given in section 12 of chapter III.)

9. A decision procedure for certain prenex arguments. The second decision procedure we consider is a natural extension of the first. In particular, we treat here arguments (again without operation letters) whose premises, finite in number, are prenex *sentences* in which no existential quantifier follows a universal, and whose conclusion is a prenex formula in which no universal quantifier follows an existential. To determine whether such an argument is valid we apply to the argument the derivation procedure of section 5. Again the elimination column will come to an end, and we may test its quantifier-free formulas for truth-functional compatibility. We shall obtain truth-functional incompatibility just in case the argument is valid.

For example, the argument

$$\bigwedge x \bigwedge y[Fx \wedge Gy \rightarrow H(xy)] \quad . \qquad \bigvee x \bigwedge y(Fx \wedge [Jy \rightarrow H(xy)])$$
$$\therefore \bigwedge x(Gx \rightarrow \sim Jx)$$

has the required form. Its elimination column, constructed on page 426, was seen to terminate and to contain a truth-functional contradiction.

Consider also the argument

$$(1) \quad \bigvee y \bigwedge x(Fx \rightarrow Gy) \quad . \qquad \bigvee y \bigvee z(Gy \rightarrow Hz) \quad \therefore \bigwedge x \bigvee z(Fx \rightarrow Hz)$$

Our derivation procedure leads us to the following:

Show $\bigwedge x \bigvee z(Fx \rightarrow Hz)$
$\sim \bigwedge x \bigvee z(Fx \rightarrow Hz)$
$\bigvee x \sim \bigvee z(Fx \rightarrow Hz)$
$\bigvee x \bigwedge z \sim (Fx \rightarrow Hz)$
$\bigvee y \bigwedge x(Fx \rightarrow Gy)$
$\bigvee y \bigvee z(Gy \rightarrow Hz)$
$\bigwedge z \sim (Fa \rightarrow Hz)$
$\bigwedge x(Fx \rightarrow Gb)$
$\bigvee z(Gc \rightarrow Hz)$
$\sim (Fa \rightarrow Ha)$
$Fa \rightarrow Gb$
$Fb \rightarrow Gb$
$\sim (Fa \rightarrow Hb)$
$Gc \rightarrow Hd$
$\sim (Fa \rightarrow Hc)$
$Fc \rightarrow Gb$
$\sim (Fa \rightarrow Hd)$
$Fd \rightarrow Fb$

A truth-table check of the quantifier-free formulas in this derivation would reveal that these formulas are truth-functionally compatible. Thus, according to our decision procedure, the argument (1) is invalid.

EXERCISES

Using the decision procedure just described, determine which of the following arguments are valid.

30. $\bigwedge x \bigwedge y[Fx \wedge Gy \rightarrow H(xy)])$. $\quad \bigvee x \bigvee y[Fx \wedge Jy \wedge \sim H(xy)]$
$\therefore \bigvee x(Jx \wedge \sim Gx)$

31. $\bigvee y \bigwedge x \bigwedge z(Fx \wedge [Gy \rightarrow H(xy)] \rightarrow [Gz \rightarrow H(xz)])$.
$\bigvee y \bigvee x[Fx \wedge \sim H(xy)] \quad \therefore \bigvee x \bigvee y[Fx \wedge Gy \wedge \sim H(xy)]$

32. $\bigvee x \bigvee y \bigwedge z[Fz \rightarrow Gx \wedge H(zx) \wedge Gy \wedge \sim H(zy)]$.
$\bigvee x \bigwedge y(Jx \wedge [Gy \rightarrow H(xy)]) \quad \therefore \bigvee x(Jx \wedge \sim Fx)$

33. $\bigvee y \bigvee z \bigwedge x(F(xy) \leftrightarrow F(xz) \wedge Gx) \quad \therefore \bigwedge z \bigwedge x \bigvee y(F(xy) \leftrightarrow F(xz) \wedge Gx)$

10. Historical remarks. The task of giving a derivation procedure, if no special conditions are imposed, is trivial. We need only settle upon an ordering of our inference rules and forms of derivation and give directions, based on that ordering, which will ensure that all possible inferences are drawn. If we are presented with a theorem, we may automatically obtain a proof for it by carrying out these directions until they lead us to one. The derivation procedures given in this chapter, however, lead to derivations of a particularly simple structure. For example, we obtain by the procedure of section 4 (our basic procedure for the quantifier calculus) derivations whose lines are always subformulas of the formula to be proved or else come from such subformulas by proper substitution on variables.

The procedure of section 2 (used to show the superfluity of clause (11)) is essentially Kalmár's proof of the completeness of the sentential calculus (see Kalmár [1]). The proof procedure of section 4 is closely related to a procedure given in Herbrand [2]. The claim made on page 419, that our procedure will always lead to a derivation if one is possible, follows from a theorem (known as the *Herbrand Theorem*) proved in Herbrand [2] or, alternatively, from Gentzen's *Extended Hauptsatz*, which is proved in Gentzen [1]. Here we must use the fact that our development of the quantifier calculus is equivalent to those of Herbrand and Gentzen; this follows from Montague and Kalish [1].

A decision procedure (differing considerably from ours) for prenex formulas in which no operation letters occur and no universal quantifier follows an existential quantifier was first given in Bernays and Schönfinkel [1]; a procedure quite similar to ours was given first in Quine [4] and is employed in Quine [5]. For a survey of other cases for which decision procedures have been found, see Church [3], pp. 245 – 94, and the comprehensive treatment in Ackermann [1].

Chapter X

Definitions; formal theories

1. The vocabulary of formal languages. In previous chapters we have considered formulas of English as well as symbolic formulas. At this point we renounce English and limit ourselves to purely symbolic languages. It is in connection with such languages that the notion of a *definition* can most conveniently be treated.

In symbolic languages, as in earlier developments, we distinguish two kinds of meaningful expressions, *terms* and *formulas*. Reverting to our informal characterization of these expressions, we may say that a term is an expression that becomes a name once its free variables are replaced by names, and a formula is an expression that becomes a sentence once its free variables are replaced by names. Before giving a precise characterization of terms and formulas, we must consider the basic symbols from which symbolic languages will be constructed. One category of such symbols is that of *variables*, which are as before lower-case Latin letters with or without numerical subscripts. It is clear that by the allowance for subscripts there are infinitely many variables. We retain the standard order established earlier, in fact, the order

$$a, b, \ldots, z, a_0, b_0, \ldots, z_0, a_1, \ldots \quad .$$

We may thus speak of the *first variable* (which is 'a'), the *second variable* (which is 'b'), and so on.

Variables are the simplest terms. Formulas, together with more complicated terms, are formed with the aid of *constants*, which fall into two classes, *formula-makers* and *term-makers*, according to the kind of expression that they generate. Each constant may be used in combination with a certain number of variables and previously generated terms and formulas to construct a new term or formula. To make this procedure precise, we shall associate with every constant a fixed *degree*, which will be a quadruple $\langle i, m, n, p \rangle$ of nonnegative integers, in which i is either 0 or 1. Here i is 0 or 1 according as the constant in question is a term-maker or a formula-maker, and m, n, and p are respectively the number of variables, the number of terms, and the number of formulas that the constant demands.

Our *terms* and *formulas* can then be exhaustively characterized as follows.

(*1*) *Every variable is a term.*

(*2*) *If* δ *is a constant of degree* $\langle 0, m, n, p \rangle$, $\alpha_1, \ldots, \alpha_m$ *are distinct variables,* $\zeta_1, \ldots, \zeta_n$ *are terms, and* $\phi_1, \ldots, \phi_p$ *are formulas, then the expression*

$$\delta\alpha_1 \ldots \alpha_m \, \zeta_1 \ldots \zeta_n \, \phi_1 \ldots \phi_p$$

is a term.

(*3*) *If* δ *is a constant of degree* $\langle 1, m, n, p \rangle$, $\alpha_1, \ldots, \alpha_m$ *are distinct variables,* $\zeta_1, \ldots, \zeta_n$ *are terms, and* $\phi_1, \ldots, \phi_p$ *are formulas, then the expression*

$$\delta\alpha_1 \ldots \alpha_m \, \zeta_1 \ldots \zeta_n \, \phi_1 \ldots \phi_p$$

is a formula.

(Each of m, n, p may take on the value zero, in which case one of the strings $\alpha_1 \ldots \alpha_m$, $\zeta_1 \ldots \zeta_n$, or $\phi_1 \ldots \phi_p$ will disappear. Thus, for example, if $m = p = 0$, the expression

$$\delta\alpha_1 \ldots \alpha_m \, \zeta_1 \ldots \zeta_n \, \phi_1 \ldots \phi_p$$

will become simply

$$\delta\zeta_1 \ldots \zeta_n \quad .)$$

The preceding characterization employs the notion of a *constant of degree* $\langle i, m, n, p \rangle$ and, before becoming completely intelligible, would have to be supplemented by a characterization of this notion. The most appropriate way of providing the required characterization is by giving a list of symbols that are to be regarded as constants, together with the specification of a degree for each. Such a list, sufficient for the purposes of this and the following chapter, is to be found in an appendix to chapter XI. The list has an arbitrary character, stemming from the accidental features of Chapter XI and the later sections of the present chapter. If the developments there had been more extensive, the list would have been longer. Indeed, for some purposes it would be convenient to have an infinite list of constants. (Such a list could be given, here as in the case of variables, by a general characterization of the structure of the symbols comprised in it.)

At this point, however, we shall not give a complete list of the constants that will be used in the formal languages of later sections; for many constants will be introduced by definition, and it is in connection with their definitions that their meaning can most conveniently be elucidated. We wish to include among our constants all the special symbols introduced in the preceding chapters: '$\sim$', '$\rightarrow$', '$\wedge$', '$\vee$', '$\leftrightarrow$', '$\bigwedge$', '$\bigvee$', '$=$', 'ι'. These symbols are called *logical constants* and are all formula-makers except for 'ι'. The identity sign '$=$' is of degree $\langle 1, 0, 2, 0\rangle$; that is, it is a formula-maker that demands two terms to produce a formula. Thus, for example, '$= x\,y$' is a formula. (The reader will note that the order of symbols, both here and in the case of the sentential connectives other than '$\sim$', differs from that which has become familiar.) The negation sign '$\sim$' is of degree $\langle 1, 0, 0, 1\rangle$, and '$\rightarrow$', '$\wedge$', '$\vee$', and '$\leftrightarrow$' are of degree $\langle 1, 0, 0, 2\rangle$; that is, the negation sign is a formula-maker requiring one formula to produce a new formula, and the other sentential connectives are formula-makers demanding two formulas to produce a new formula. Thus, for example, '$\sim\ = x\,y$' is a formula (the *negation* of '$= x\,y$') and '$\wedge = x\,y = y\,z$' is a formula (the *conjunction* of '$= x\,y$' and '$= y\,z$'). The quantifiers are symbols of degree $\langle 1, 1, 0, 1\rangle$; that is, they are formula-makers that demand one variable and one formula to produce a new formula. Thus, for example, '$\bigwedge x = x\,x$' is a formula. The descriptive operator 'ι' is a symbol of degree $\langle 0, 1, 0, 1\rangle$; that is, it is a term-maker that demands one variable and one formula to produce a new term. Thus, for example, '$\iota x = x\,x$' is a term. Constants other than '$\sim$', '$\rightarrow$', '$\wedge$', '$\vee$', '$\leftrightarrow$', '$\bigwedge$', '$\bigvee$', '$=$', and 'ι' are called *nonlogical*.

We wish also to include among our constants the *operation letters* and *predicate letters* of previous chapters, that is, the symbols

$$A^0, \ldots, E^0, A^1, \ldots, E^1, \ldots, F^0, \ldots, Z^0, F^1, \ldots, Z^1, \ldots,$$

together with their subscripted variants. Each n-place operation letter is of degree $\langle 0, 0, n, 0\rangle$, and each n-place predicate letter of degree $\langle 1, 0, n, 0\rangle$.

As additional examples of nonlogical constants we list the following:

$+$	(degree: $\langle 0, 0, 2, 0\rangle$)
$\sqrt[3]{}$	(degree: $\langle 0, 0, 1, 0\rangle$)
ϵ	(degree: $\langle 1, 0, 2, 0\rangle$)
I	(degree: $\langle 1, 0, 1, 0\rangle$)
$\overset{1}{\bigvee}$	(degree: $\langle 1, 1, 0, 1\rangle$)
E	(degree: $\langle 0, 1, 0, 1\rangle$)
lim	(degree: $\langle 0, 1, 1, 0\rangle$)

'$+$' and '$\sqrt[3]{}$' are to be understood in their familiar mathematical senses, as signs for addition and cube root, and

$$\epsilon\, x\, y\ ,$$
$$\mathrm{I}\, x\ ,$$
$$\overset{1}{\bigvee} x\ F^1 x\ ,$$
$$\mathrm{E} x\ F^1 x\ ,$$
$$\lim\ n\ A^1 n$$

are to be read respectively

x is a member of the set y ,
x is an integer ,
there is exactly one x such that F^1x ,
the set of objects x such that F^1x ,
the limit of A^1n as n approaches infinity .

It will be convenient to provide a terminology for certain kinds of constants. Those constants which must be followed immediately by one or more variables (that is, which have degree $\langle i, m, n, p \rangle$ with $m > 0$) will be called *operators;* these variables will turn out, in the light of section 2, to be *bound*. Among the logical constants, '$\bigwedge$', '$\bigvee$', and 'ι' are the only operators; '$\overset{1}{\forall}$', 'E', and 'lim' are also operators. The identity sign is not an operator; for even though it *may* be followed immediately by variables, as in '$= x\ y$', these variables will be free. Further, it is not required that the identity sign be followed immediately by variables, as the formula '$= \iota\ x = x\ x\ y$' indicates. Operators will sometimes for emphasis be called *variable-binding operators.*

A constant of degree $\langle 1, 0, n, 0 \rangle$ is called an *n-place predicate;* that is, an n-place predicate is a formula-maker requiring exactly n terms to produce a formula. The identity symbol, then, is a 2-place predicate; predicate letters are predicates; 'ϵ' and 'I' are predicates. A constant of degree $\langle 0, 0, n, 0 \rangle$ is called an *n-place operation symbol;* that is, an n-place operation symbol is a term-maker requiring exactly n terms to produce a new term. Operation letters are operation symbols, and so are '+' and '$\sqrt[3]{}$'. Finally, we shall call a 0-place operation symbol an *individual constant,* and a constant of degree $\langle 1, 0, 0, p \rangle$ with $p > 0$ a *sentential connective.*

2. Bondage and freedom; proper substitution; alphabetic variance. Variables may now be bound not only by quantifiers and 'ι' but by arbitrary operators. For example, if δ is an operator of degree $\langle 0, 1, 0, 1 \rangle$, then each occurrence of the variable α in the term

$$\delta\ \alpha = \alpha\ \beta$$

is bound. Thus we must give a more general characterization of bondage and freedom than the earlier treatment provides.

An *occurrence* of a *variable* α is said to be *bound in* a term or formula ϕ just in case it stands within an occurrence in ϕ of some expression

$$\delta\alpha_1 \ldots \alpha_m\ \zeta_1 \ldots \zeta_n\ \phi_1 \ldots \phi_p \quad ,$$

where δ is a constant of degree $\langle 0, m, n, p \rangle$ or $\langle 1, m, n, p \rangle$, $\alpha_1, \ldots, \alpha_m$ are distinct variables, $\zeta_1, \ldots, \zeta_n$ are terms, $\phi_1, \ldots, \phi_p$ are formulas, and α is one of $\alpha_1, \ldots, \alpha_m$. An *occurrence* of a *variable* is *free in* ϕ just in case it stands within ϕ but is not bound in ϕ. A *variable* is *bound* or *free in* ϕ according as it has a bound or free occurrence in ϕ. Thus, in

$$\overset{1}{\forall} x\ F^2 x\ y \quad ,$$

both occurrences of 'x' are bound, the only occurrence of 'y' is free, the variable 'x' is bound but not free, and the variable 'y' is free but not bound.

We now consider freedom and bondage of arbitrary terms. If ϕ is a formula or term, then an *occurrence* of a *term* ζ is *bound in* ϕ just in case it stands within an occurrence in ϕ of some expression

$$\delta\alpha_1 \ldots \alpha_m \, \zeta_1 \ldots \zeta_n \, \phi_1 \ldots \phi_p \quad ,$$

where δ is a constant of degree $\langle 0, m, n, p \rangle$ or $\langle 1, m, n, p \rangle$, $\alpha_1, \ldots, \alpha_m$ are distinct variables, $\zeta_1, \ldots, \zeta_n$ are terms, $\phi_1, \ldots, \phi_p$ are formulas, and at least one of the variables $\alpha_1, \ldots, \alpha_m$ is free in ζ. An *occurrence* of a *term* is said to be *free in* ϕ if it stands within ϕ but is not bound in ϕ. A *term* is *bound* or *free in* ϕ according as it has a bound or free occurrence in ϕ. For example, in

(1) $$\Lambda x \, F^1 \, EyG^2xy \quad ,$$

the occurrence of 'EyG^2xy' is bound, but in

(2) $$\Lambda x \, F^1 \, EyG^2zy \quad ,$$

the occurrence of 'EyG^2zy' is free. Observe that the characterization of bondage and freedom for the special case of variables and their occurrences is subsumed under the more general characterization just given. Thus in (1) and (2) both 'x' and 'y' are bound, and 'z' is free in (2), no matter whether we apply the definitions pertaining only to variables or the more general definitions pertaining to arbitrary terms.

A *sentence* is as before a formula in which no variable is free, and a *name* is a term in which no variable is free.

Proper substitution will be useful in this chapter, and in chapter XI will acquire additional importance in connection with definitions. The following characterization of this notion is essentially identical with the earlier treatment.

If α is a variable, ζ a term, and ϕ, ψ formulas, then ψ is said to *come from* ϕ *by proper substitution of* ζ *for* α just in case ψ is like ϕ except for containing free occurrences of ζ wherever ϕ contains free occurrences of α. For example, if ϕ is the formula

$$\Lambda x \in x \, y \quad ,$$

then

$$\Lambda x \in x \, EzG^2wz$$

comes from ϕ by proper substitution of 'EzG^2wz' for 'y'.

If δ is an n-place operation symbol or predicate, χ is correspondingly a term or a formula, and ϕ, ψ are formulas, then ψ is said to *come from* ϕ by *proper substitution of* χ *for* δ just in case ψ can be obtained from ϕ by

(I) replacing, throughout ϕ, the constant δ by

$$\{\chi\} \quad ,$$

and,

(II) in the expression resulting from (I), successively replacing each part of the form

$$\{\chi\}\, \zeta_1 \ldots \zeta_n \quad ,$$

where $\zeta_1, \ldots, \zeta_n$ are terms, by the expression obtained from χ by replacing all free occurrences of 'a' by ζ_1, 'b' by ζ_2, etc., up to the nth variable, whose free occurrences are to be replaced by ζ_n;

we require in addition that χ and ϕ have no variables in common, and that no variable occurs both bound and free in χ. For example, consider the formula

(3) $$\Lambda x\, G^2 xy \quad .$$

The formula

$$\Lambda x = \text{E}z = yz\, x$$

comes from (3) by proper substitution of

(4) $$= \text{E}z = bz\, a$$

for the 2-place predicate 'G^2'. In performing the substitution we obtain in the first step

$$\Lambda x \{ = \text{E}z = bz\, a \}\, xy \quad ,$$

and in the second step

$$\Lambda x = \text{E}z = yz\ x \quad ;$$

we observe, moreover, that (3) and (4) have no variables in common and that no variable occurs both bound and free in (4).

If K is a class consisting of variables, operation symbols, and predicates, then a formula ψ is said to *come from* a formula ϕ *by iterated proper substitution on members of* K just in case ψ is ϕ or there is a finite sequence of formulas beginning with ϕ and ending with ψ and each formula in the sequence except ϕ is obtained from the preceding formula of the sequence by the proper substitution of either (1) a term for a variable belonging to K, (2) a term for an operation symbol belonging to K, or (3) a formula for a predicate belonging to K. A formula ψ is an *instance* of a formula ϕ if and only if ψ comes from ϕ by iterated proper substitution on members of some class consisting of variables, operation symbols, and predicates.

The notion of alphabetic variance must also be extended. Let δ be an operator of degree $\langle 0, m, n, p \rangle$ or $\langle 1, m, n, p \rangle$, let $i \leq m$, and let ϕ, ψ be expressions of the respective forms

$$\delta\alpha_1 \ldots \alpha_m\, \phi_1 \ldots \phi_n\, \phi_{n+1} \ldots \phi_{n+p} \quad ,$$
$$\delta\beta_1 \ldots \beta_m\, \psi_1 \ldots \psi_n\, \psi_{n+1} \ldots \psi_{n+p} \quad ,$$

where $\alpha_1, \ldots, \alpha_m$ are distinct variables, $\beta_1, \ldots, \beta_m$ are also distinct variables which, except for β_i, are identical with $\alpha_1, \ldots, \alpha_m$ respectively, $\phi_1, \ldots, \phi_n, \psi_1, \ldots, \psi_n$ are terms, and $\phi_{n+1}, \ldots, \phi_{n+p}, \psi_{n+1}, \ldots, \psi_{n+p}$ are formulas. (Thus ϕ, ψ are both either terms or formulas.) We say that ϕ, ψ are *immediate alphabetic variants* if, for each $j \leqslant n+p$, ψ_j comes from ϕ_j by proper substitution of β_i for α_i and, conversely, ϕ_j comes from ψ_j by proper substitution of α_i for β_i.

This definition is the natural extension to arbitrary operators of the notion of immediate alphabetic variance considered in chapter VII.

More generally, a term or formula ψ is said to be an *alphabetic variant* of a term or formula ϕ if there is a finite sequence of expressions beginning with ϕ and ending with ψ, and such that each expression of the sequence (except the first) is obtained from its predecessor by replacing an occurrence of a term or formula by an immediate alphabetic variant of that term or formula.

For example,

$$= \mathrm{E}x\mathrm{F}^1 x\imath y \Lambda x \mathrm{G}^2 xy$$

is an alphabetic variant of

$$= \mathrm{E}y\mathrm{F}^1 y\imath x \Lambda z \mathrm{G}^2 zx$$

by virtue of the sequence

$$\begin{aligned} &= \mathrm{E}y\mathrm{F}^1 y\imath x \Lambda z \mathrm{G}^2 zx \quad , \\ &= \mathrm{E}x\mathrm{F}^1 x\imath x \Lambda z \mathrm{G}^2 zx \quad , \\ &= \mathrm{E}x\mathrm{F}^1 x\imath y \Lambda z \mathrm{G}^2 zy \quad , \\ &= \mathrm{E}x\mathrm{F}^1 x\imath y \Lambda x \mathrm{G}^2 xy \quad , \end{aligned}$$

3. Informal notational conventions. The official characterization in section 1 of *term* and *formula* introduces a notation that, though highly convenient for the formulation of the general definitions of the last two sections, leads to virtual unreadability when we consider specific formulas of any length. This remark applies even to the formula (4) of the previous section, which according to a more customary notational style would assume the following perspicuous form:

$$\mathrm{E}z[b = z] = a \quad .$$

A more compelling example can be provided by considering the associative law for the addition of integers. According to the style of section 1 this law has the following awkward appearance:

$$\Lambda x \Lambda y \Lambda z \rightarrow \wedge \wedge \mathrm{I}x\mathrm{I}y\mathrm{I}z = + + x\, y\, z + x + y\, z \quad ,$$

rather than the more customary:

$$\Lambda x \Lambda y \Lambda z\, [\mathrm{I}x \wedge \mathrm{I}y \wedge \mathrm{I}z \rightarrow (x + y) + z = x + (y + z)] \quad .$$

To simplify the appearance of formulas and to bring them into closer accord with customary usage, we shall adopt some informal notational conventions.

Although official notation requires that a constant always stand *before* the variables, terms, and formulas to which it applies, we shall often depart from this order. For example, sentential connectives of degree $\langle 1, 0, 0, 2 \rangle$ will be written between their attendant formulas, as in chapters I – IX, and operation symbols and predicates of some mathematical currency will be transposed to the position that mathematical usage prescribes. Parentheses and brackets, unnecessary in official notation, must now be introduced to avoid ambiguity and, along with other symbols of punctuation, will sometimes also be used purely for perspicuity. The number of parentheses required to avoid ambiguity will be somewhat reduced by adoption of the conventions given in earlier chapters for their omission. For instance, '$\rightarrow$' and '$\leftrightarrow$' will be regarded as marking a greater break than '$\wedge$' and '$\vee$', and in an iterated conjunction or disjunction without parentheses the components are to be understood as associated to the left.

As in earlier chapters, operation letters and predicate letters will be relieved of their superscripts provided no ambiguity ensues. However, we do not adopt now the convention of writing, where ζ and η are terms,

$$\zeta \neq \eta$$

for

$$\sim \zeta = \eta \quad ;$$

that convenience will not be introduced until we encounter definitions in section 7 of this chapter.

4. Derivability. We must now specify the circumstances under which a formula will be considered *derivable* from a class of formulas. The characterization will follow the lines of the earlier development. Indeed, clauses (1)–(10) of section 9 of chapter VII are taken as the directions for constructing a *derivation from a class K of formulas.* Of course, we must now understand 'symbolic term' and 'symbolic formula' in the sense of 'term' and 'formula' given in the present chapter. The *primitive inference rules,* to which reference is made in clause (5a), are to be just those of chapter VII, and *interchange* (clause (9b)) is to be defined as before; throughout the characterizations, however, 'symbolic formula' and 'symbolic term' are to be replaced by 'formula' and 'term' respectively. *Alphabetic variance* (clause (8)) is to be understood in the sense of the present chapter.

It should be pointed out that clauses (8) and (9b) can no longer be regarded as theoretically dispensable (in the sense of section 5 of chapter II). The passage from

$$\forall x\, Fx$$

to

$$\overset{1}{\forall} y \, Fy$$

and the passage from

$$\bigwedge x(Fx \leftrightarrow Gx)$$

to

$$ExFx = ExGx$$

are justified by AV and Int respectively; but neither of these inferences can be reduced to applications of clauses (1) – (6). Thus we must regard the directions for constructing an unabbreviated derivation as consisting of clauses (1)–(6), (8), and (9b). The remaining clauses will then be theoretically dispensable. (Clause (9a), though not reducible to (1)–(6), can be eliminated once (9b) is available.) In practice, however, we shall draw no distinction between an abbreviated and an unabbreviated derivation.

As before, a derivation is said to be *complete* if every line either is boxed or contains cancelled '*Show*', and a formula ϕ is *derivable* from a class K of formulas if one can construct a complete derivation from K in which

~~*Show*~~ ϕ

occurs as an unboxed line.

5. Formal theories; the theory of commutative ordered fields. A *theory* consists of two things: (1) a class L of *constants*, which may be any class of nonlogical constants, and (2) a class of *axioms*, which may be any class of formulas containing no nonlogical constants beyond those in L.

As an example, we consider the *theory of commutative ordered fields*, which has the following constants:

$+$	(2-place operation symbol)
$-$	(1-place operation symbol)
0	(individual constant)
$\cdot$	(2-place operation symbol)
$^{-1}$	(1-place operation symbol)
1	(individual constant)
$\leqslant$	(2-place predicate)

(In characterizing a theory, it is unnecessary to specify any interpretation. To facilitate comprehension, however, a few remarks concerning what may be regarded as the standard interpretation of this theory will be useful. The domain of discourse, or the class of objects to which the variables of the theory are construed as referring, is to consist either of the rational numbers (that is, numbers expressible as the quotient of two integers) or of the real numbers (that is, the numbers ordinarily considered in elementary algebra; in particular, beyond the rationals, such numbers as π and $\sqrt{2}$ are included, but complex numbers, built up with the aid of $\sqrt{-1}$, are not); and the constants listed above are to have their usual mathematical meaning. The symbol '$-$', which is often used in two ways, as both a 1-place operation symbol (as in '-2') and a 2-place operation symbol (as in '$3 - 2$'), is here restricted to the first usage; thus we read '$-x$' as 'the negative of x'. The symbol '${}^{-1}$' occurs as a superscript, as in 'x^{-1}', which is read 'the reciprocal of x', and designates the number $\frac{1}{x}$. The term '0^{-1}', to which no meaning is ordinarily assigned, may be interpreted as designating any fixed number; the axioms below place no restriction on the choice of that number.)

The axioms of the theory of commutative ordered fields are the following formulas, $A1 - A15$:

$A1$	$x + (y + z) = (x + y) + z$
$A2$	$x + y = y + x$
$A3$	$x + 0 = x$
$A4$	$x + -x = 0$
$A5$	$x \cdot (y \cdot z) = (x \cdot y) \cdot z$
$A6$	$x \cdot y = y \cdot x$
$A7$	$x \cdot 1 = x$
$A8$	$\sim x = 0 \rightarrow x \cdot x^{-1} = 1$
$A9$	$x \cdot (y + z) = (x \cdot y) + (x \cdot z)$
$A10$	$\sim 0 = 1$
$A11$	$0 \leqslant x \vee 0 \leqslant -x$
$A12$	$\sim x = 0 \rightarrow \sim 0 \leqslant x \vee \sim 0 \leqslant -x$
$A13$	$0 \leqslant x \wedge 0 \leqslant y \rightarrow 0 \leqslant x + y$
$A14$	$0 \leqslant x \wedge 0 \leqslant y \rightarrow 0 \leqslant x \cdot y$
$A15$	$x \leqslant y \leftrightarrow 0 \leqslant y + -x$

Now if T is an arbitrary theory, then a *term*, *formula*, or *sentence of* T is respectively a term, formula, or sentence that contains no nonlogical constants beyond the constants of T, and a *theorem of* T is a formula of T that is derivable from the axioms of T. (In clause (7) of the directions for constructing a derivation, which permits the use of previously proved theorems, a *theorem* is, as always, to be understood as a *theorem of logic*—that is, a formula derivable from the empty class of premises—and not as a theorem of a theory. A limited use of previously proved theorems of a theory will be introduced below, after *T*1.)

For example, let us return to the theory of commutative ordered fields and derive a few theorems. Theorems 1 and 2 are *cancellation laws for addition*, and 3 and 4 *cancellation laws for multiplication*. (Theorems of the present theory and its extensions will be numbered *T*1, *T*2, and so on; we italicize "T" here to prevent confusion with the numbering system of the theorems of chapters I–VIII.)

*T*1   1. ~~*Show*~~ $x + z = y + z \rightarrow x = y$

2.	$x + z = y + z$	
3.	$\bigwedge x \bigwedge y \bigwedge z\; x + (y + z) = (x + y) + z$	$A1$ (closure of)
4.	$\bigwedge x\; x + -x = 0$	$A4$ (closure of)
5.	$\bigwedge x\; x + 0 = x$	$A3$ (closure of)
6.	$(x + z) + -z = (y + z) + -z$	2, EL
7.	$x + (z + -z) = y + (z + -z)$	3, AV, UI, UI, UI, 3, AV, UI, UI, UI, 6, LL, LL
8.	$x + 0 = y + 0$	4, UI, 7, LL
9.	$x = y$	5, UI, 5, UI, 8, LL, LL

The proof of *T*1 is made unduly long by the introduction of closures of axioms. For example, line 3 is required to obtain

(1) $$(x + z) + -z = x + (z + -z) \quad ,$$

which in turn is required to infer line 7 from line 6. Now (1) comes from *A*1 by iterated substitution on variables but is not itself an axiom. We shall in the future dispense with lines such as 3, 4, and 5, and, when showing a formula to be a theorem of a theory *T*, permit as a line of a derivation any formula that comes by iterated substitution on variables from an alphabetic variant of an axiom of *T* or a previously proved theorem of *T*. For annotation we shall simply refer to the axiom or theorem involved.

Using this informal abbreviation, we may simplify as follows the derivation of *T*1:

1. ~~*Show*~~ $x + z = y + z \rightarrow x = y$

2.	$x + z = y + z$	
3.	$(x + z) + -z = (y + z) + -z$	2, EL
4.	$x + (z + -z) = y + (z + -z)$	$A1$, $A1$, 3, LL, LL
5.	$x + 0 = y + 0$	$A4$, 4, LL
6.	$x = y$	$A3$, $A3$, 5, LL, LL

*T*2 $z + x = z + y \rightarrow x = y$

*T*3 $\sim z = 0 \wedge x \cdot z = y \cdot z \rightarrow x = y$

*T*4 $\sim z = 0 \wedge z \cdot x = z \cdot y \rightarrow x = y$

*T*5

1.	~~*Show*~~ $-0 = 0$	
2.	$0 + -0 = 0$	*A*4
3.	$0 + 0 = 0$	*A*3
4.	$-0 = 0$	2, 3, LL, *T*2, MP

*T*6

1.	~~*Show*~~ $x \cdot 0 = 0$	
2.	$(x \cdot 1) + (x \cdot 0) = x \cdot (1 + 0)$	*A*9, Sm
3.	$(x \cdot 1) + (x \cdot 0) = x \cdot 1$	*A*3, 2, LL
4.	$(x \cdot 1) + 0 = x \cdot 1$	*A*3
5.	$x \cdot 0 = 0$	3, 4, LL, *T*2, MP

*T*7 $x + -y = 0 \leftrightarrow x = y$

*T*8 $x = -y \leftrightarrow y = -x$

*T*9 $x = 0 \leftrightarrow -x = 0$

The next group of theorems, *T*10 – *T*14, are laws of *signs*.

*T*10 $--x = x$

*T*11

1.	~~*Show*~~ $-(x + y) = -x + -y$	
2.	$(x + y) + (-x + -y) = (x + -x) + (y + -y)$	*A*1, *A*2, LL
3.	$(x + y) + (-x + -y) = 0$	*A*4, 2, LL, *A*3, LL
4.	$(x + y) + -(x + y) = 0$	*A*4
5.	$-(x + y) = (-x + -y)$	4, 3, LL, *T*2, MP

(To obtain line 2 above, several applications of *A*1, *A*2, and LL are required. But here and henceforth we shall for the most part omit repetitions in annotations.)

*T*12 $(-x) \cdot y = -(x \cdot y)$

*T*13 $x \cdot (-y) = -(x \cdot y)$

*T*14

1.	~~*Show*~~ $(-x) \cdot (-y) = x \cdot y$	
2.	$(-x) \cdot (-y) = -(x \cdot -(y))$	*T*12
3.	$= --(x \cdot y)$	2, *T*13, LL
4.	$= x \cdot y$	3, *T*10, LL

(In the derivation above, the left side of line 2 is imagined to be repeated in the blanks of lines 3 and 4.)

*T*15

1.	~~*Show*~~ $\sim x = 0 \rightarrow (-x)^{-1} = -(x^{-1})$	
2.	$\sim x = 0$	
3.	$x \cdot (x^{-1}) = 1$	2, *A*8, MP
4.	$(-x) \cdot -(x^{-1}) = 1$	3, *T*14, LL
5.	$\sim -x = 0$	2, *T*9, BC, MT
6.	$(-x) \cdot (-x)^{-1} = 1$	5, *A*8, MP
7.	$(-x)^{-1} = -(x^{-1})$	4, 6, T, 5, Adj, *T*4, MP

We state next two basic principles of multiplication.

*T*16 $x \cdot y = 0 \leftrightarrow x = 0 \vee y = 0$

*T*17 $\sim x \cdot y = 0 \rightarrow (x \cdot y)^{-1} = x^{-1} \cdot y^{-1}$

We turn now to theorems on order. *T*18 – *T*21 assert that $\leqslant$ is respectively *reflexive*, *antisymmetric*, *transitive*, and *connected*, and hence is a *simple ordering*.

*T*18

1.	~~*Show*~~ $x \leqslant x$	
2.	~~*Show*~~ $0 \leqslant 0$	
3.	$\sim 0 \leqslant 0$	
4.	$0 \leqslant -0$	3, *A*11
5.	$0 \leqslant 0$	4, *T*5, LL
6.	$0 \leqslant x + -x$	2, *A*4, LL
7.	$x \leqslant x$	6, *A*15

In the annotation for lines 4 and 7 above, reference to theorems and inference rules of the sentential calculus has been omitted; this practice will be adopted henceforth.

*T*19

1.	~~*Show*~~ $x \leqslant y \wedge y \leqslant x \rightarrow x = y$	
2.	$x \leqslant y \wedge y \leqslant x$	
3.	$0 \leqslant y + -x \wedge 0 \leqslant x + -y$	2, *A*15
4.	$0 \leqslant -(x + -y) \wedge 0 \leqslant x + -y$	3, *T*10, *T*11, *A*2, LL
5.	$x + -y = 0$	4, *A*12
6.	$x = y$	5, *T*7

*T*20

1.	~~*Show*~~ $x \leqslant y \wedge y \leqslant z \rightarrow x \leqslant z$	
2.	$x \leqslant y \wedge y \leqslant z$	
3.	$0 \leqslant y + -x \wedge 0 \leqslant z + -y$	2, *A*15
4.	$0 \leqslant (y + -x) + (z + -y)$	3, *A*13
5.	$0 \leqslant z + -x$	4, *A*1, *A*2, *A*3, *A*4, LL
6.	$x \leqslant z$	5, *A*15

*T*21

1.	~~*Show*~~ $x \leq y \vee y \leq x$	
2.	$0 \leq y + -x \vee 0 \leq -(y + -x)$	*A*11
3.	$0 \leq y + -x \vee 0 \leq x + -y$	2, *T*11, *T*10, *A*2, LL
4.	$x \leq y \vee y \leq x$	3, *A*15

*T*22 asserts that squares are always nonnegative; hence (*T*23) 1 is nonnegative.

*T*22

1.	~~*Show*~~ $0 \leq x \cdot x$	
2.	~~*Show*~~ $0 \leq x \rightarrow 0 \leq x \cdot x$	
3.	$0 \leq x$	
4.	$0 \leq x \cdot x$	3, *A*14
5.	~~*Show*~~ $0 \leq -x \rightarrow 0 \leq x \cdot x$	
6.	$0 \leq -x$	
7.	$0 \leq (-x) \cdot (-x)$	6, *A*14
8.	$0 \leq x \cdot x$	7, *T*14, LL
9.	$0 \leq x \cdot x$	2, 5, *A*11

*T*23 $\quad 0 \leq 1$

The remaining theorems of this section are familiar laws of *inequality*.

*T*24

1.	~~*Show*~~ $x \leq y \rightarrow x + z \leq y + z$	
2.	$x \leq y$	
3.	$0 \leq y + -x$	2, *A*15
4.	$(y + z) + -(x + z)$	
	$= (y + z) + (-x + -z)$	*T*11, EL
5.	$= y + -x$	4, *A*1, *A*2, *A*3, *A*4, LL
6.	$0 \leq (y + z) + -(x + z)$	3, 5, LL
7.	$x + z \leq y + z$	6, *A*15

*T*25 $\quad x + z \leq y + z \rightarrow x \leq y$

*T*26 $\quad x \leq y \wedge z \leq w \rightarrow x + z \leq y + w$

*T*27 $\quad \sim y + 1 \leq y$

*T*28 $\quad \sim y \leq y + -1$

*T*29 $\quad x \leq y \rightarrow -y \leq -x$

*T*30 $\quad -y \leq -x \rightarrow x \leq y$

*T*31 $\quad x \leq 0 \leftrightarrow 0 \leq -x$

*T*32 $0 \leqslant x \wedge y \leqslant 0 \rightarrow x \cdot y \leqslant 0$

*T*33

1.	~~*Show*~~ $x \leqslant y \wedge 0 \leqslant z \rightarrow x \cdot z \leqslant y \cdot z$	
2.	$x \leqslant y \wedge 0 \leqslant z$	
3.	$0 \leqslant y + -x \wedge 0 \leqslant z$	2, *A*15
4.	$0 \leqslant (y + -x) \cdot z$	3, *A*14
5.	$0 \leqslant (y \cdot z) + -(x \cdot z)$	4, *A*6, *A*9, *T*13, *A*6, LL
6.	$x \cdot z \leqslant y \cdot z$	5, *A*15

*T*34

1.	~~*Show*~~ $x \leqslant y \wedge z \leqslant 0 \rightarrow y \cdot z \leqslant x \cdot z$	
2.	$x \leqslant y \wedge z \leqslant 0$	
3.	$0 \leqslant -z$	2, *T*31
4.	$x \cdot (-z) \leqslant y \cdot (-z)$	2, 3, *T*33
5.	$-(x \cdot z) \leqslant -(y \cdot z)$	4, *T*13, LL
6.	$y \cdot z \leqslant x \cdot z$	5, *T*30

*T*35

1.	~~*Show*~~ $0 \leqslant z \wedge \sim z = 0 \rightarrow 0 \leqslant z^{-1}$	
2.	$0 \leqslant z \wedge \sim z = 0$	
3.	~~*Show*~~ $0 \leqslant z^{-1}$	
4.	$\sim 0 \leqslant z^{-1}$	
5.	$0 \leqslant -(z^{-1})$	4, *A*11
6.	$0 \leqslant z \cdot -(z^{-1})$	2, 5, *A*14
7.	$0 \leqslant -(z \cdot z^{-1})$	6, *T*13, LL
8.	$0 \leqslant -1$	7, 2, *A*8, LL
9.	$\sim 0 \leqslant -1$	*T*23, *A*10, *A*12

*T*36

1.	~~*Show*~~ $x \cdot z \leqslant y \cdot z \wedge 0 \leqslant z \wedge \sim z = 0 \rightarrow x \leqslant y$	
2.	$x \cdot z \leqslant y \cdot z \wedge 0 \leqslant z \wedge \sim z = 0$	
3.	$(x \cdot z) \cdot z^{-1} \leqslant (y \cdot z) \cdot z^{-1}$	2, *T*35, *T*33
4.	$x \leqslant y$	3, *A*5, 2, *A*8, *A*7, LL

*T*37 $y \cdot z \leqslant x \cdot z \wedge z \leqslant 0 \wedge \sim z = 0 \rightarrow x \leqslant y$

*T*38 $x = y \rightarrow x \leqslant y$

6. Extensions of theories; the theory of real numbers. If *T* is a theory and ϕ an arbitrary formula (whether of *T* or not), then by an *instance of* ϕ *within T* is understood any formula of *T* that comes from ϕ by iterated proper substitution on some class of symbols that contains no constant of *T*.

If *T* and *U* are theories, then *U* is said to be an *extension of T* if all constants of *T* are constants of *U* and all axioms of *T* are axioms of *U*. For example, the theory of commutative ordered fields has as an extension the *theory of real numbers*, which can be characterized as follows: the *constants of the theory of real numbers* are those of the theory of commutative ordered fields together with the 1-place predicate 'I', which is read 'is an integer'. The *axioms of the theory of real numbers* are $A1 - A15$ above, together with

$A16$ $\quad \mathrm{I}(0)$,

$A17$ $\quad \mathrm{I}(x) \rightarrow \mathrm{I}(x + 1) \wedge \mathrm{I}(x + -1)$,

$A18$ $\quad \mathrm{I}(x) \wedge \mathrm{I}(y) \wedge x \leqslant y \wedge y \leqslant x + 1 \rightarrow y = x \vee y = x + 1$,

and all instances within the present theory of the formula

$$AS19 \qquad \bigvee x \mathrm{F}(x) \wedge \bigvee y \bigwedge x(\mathrm{F}(x) \rightarrow x \leqslant y) \rightarrow \bigvee z[\bigwedge x(\mathrm{F}(x) \rightarrow x \leqslant z) \wedge \bigwedge y(\bigwedge x[\mathrm{F}(x) \rightarrow x \leqslant y] \rightarrow z \leqslant y)] \ .$$

Axioms 16 through 18 assert that 0 is an integer, that the successor and the predecessor of an integer are again integers, and that between an integer and its successor there is no other integer. Note that the formula called $AS19$ is not a formula of the theory of real numbers because it contains the constant 'F' and hence is not itself an axiom of this theory. It enables us, however, to describe easily an infinity of axioms of the theory, that is, all its instances within the theory. Thus, in view of $AS19$, the following formula is an axiom of the theory of real numbers:

$$(1) \quad \bigvee x\, x \cdot x \leqslant 1 + 1 \wedge \bigvee y \bigwedge x(x \cdot x \leqslant 1 + 1 \rightarrow x \leqslant y) \rightarrow \bigvee z[\bigwedge x(x \cdot x \leqslant 1 + 1 \rightarrow x \leqslant z) \wedge \bigwedge y(\bigwedge x[x \cdot x \leqslant 1 + 1 \rightarrow x \leqslant y] \rightarrow z \leqslant y)]$$

We may refer to $AS19$ itself as an *axiom schema;* this accounts for the designation '$AS19$'.

$AS19$ is often called the *Continuity Schema* and has the following intuitive content: every nonempty set of numbers that is bounded above has a least upper bound. For example, the instance (1) asserts that on the hypothesis that some number is such that its square is at most 2 and there is a number greater than all numbers fulfilling this condition, there is a least upper bound of the set of numbers whose square is at most 2. (Such a least upper bound indeed exists; it is the square root of 2.)

It should be observed that all of $A1 - A18$ are true in the domain of rational numbers as well as in the domain of real numbers. It is the Continuity Schema that distinguishes between these two domains; it has, for example, the consequence that every positive number is a square ($T129$). On the other hand, the positive rational number 2 has no square root among the rationals ($T128$). Accordingly, we must henceforth regard our variables as referring to the real numbers.

Theorems of the theory of real numbers:

*T*39

1. ~~Show~~ $\mathrm{I}(y) \wedge 0 \leqslant y \wedge \sim y = 0 \rightarrow 1 \leqslant y$
2. $\mathrm{I}(y) \wedge 0 \leqslant y \wedge \sim y = 0$
3. ~~Show~~ $1 \leqslant y$
4. $\sim 1 \leqslant y$
5. $y \leqslant 0 + 1$ — 4, *T*21, *A*3, *A*2, LL
6. $y = 0 + 1$ — *A*18, *A*16, 2, 5
7. $1 \leqslant y$ — *T*18, 6, *A*2, *A*3, LL

Since the theory of real numbers is an extension of the theory of commutative ordered fields, all theorems of the latter are theorems of the former; this accounts for the use of *T*21 and *T*18 in the derivation above.

*T*40 $\quad \mathrm{I}(y) \wedge y \leqslant 0 \wedge \sim y = 0 \rightarrow y \leqslant -1$

It will frequently be convenient to consider theorem schemata as well as axiom schemata. By a *theorem schema* of a theory *T* we understand a formula containing, besides constants of *T*, some additional predicates or operation symbols, and such that all of its instances within *T* are theorems of *T*. For example, *TS*41 – *TS*45 below are theorem schemata of the theory of real numbers.

The derivation of theorem schemata of a theory *T* is simplified by considering a theory *U* that is an extension of *T* and that satisfies the following two conditions: (i) every constant of *U* that is not a constant of *T* is either a predicate or an operation symbol; (ii) every instance within *T* of an axiom of *U* is a theorem of *T*. Then any theorem of *U* that is not a formula of *T* will be a theorem schema of *T*. (This remark requires a justification, which will not, however, be given here.)

In connection with the theory of real numbers we consider a theory *U* whose constants are those of the theory of real numbers together with the 1-place predicate letter 'F', and whose axioms are *A*1 – *A*18 and all instances within *U* of the formula *AS*19. Thus *AS*19 is itself an axiom of *U*, and so is the formula

$$\bigvee x\mathrm{F}(-x) \wedge \bigvee y \bigwedge x(\mathrm{F}(-x) \rightarrow x \leqslant y) \rightarrow$$
$$\bigvee z[\bigwedge x(\mathrm{F}(-x) \rightarrow x \leqslant z) \wedge \bigwedge y(\bigwedge x[\mathrm{F}(-x) \rightarrow x \leqslant y] \rightarrow z \leqslant y)]$$

Clearly, *U* is an extension of the theory of real numbers that satisfies conditions (i) and (ii) above.

*TS*41 provides a simple illustration of these points. It is a theorem of *U*, as the proof below indicates, and hence, by the observations above, a theorem schema of the theory of real numbers.

TS41

1.	~~Show~~ $\bigvee x F(x) \rightarrow \bigvee x F(-x)$	
2.	$\bigvee x F(x)$	
3.	$F(y)$	2, EI
4.	$F(--y)$	3, *T*10, LL
5.	$\bigvee x F(-x)$	4, EG

TS42 is the dual of *AS*19; it asserts, roughly speaking, that every nonempty set of numbers that is bounded below has a greatest lower bound.

TS42

1.	~~Show~~ $\bigvee x F(x) \wedge \bigvee y \bigwedge x(F(x) \rightarrow y \leqslant x) \rightarrow \bigvee z[\bigwedge x(F(x) \rightarrow z \leqslant x) \wedge \bigwedge y(\bigwedge x[F(x) \rightarrow y \leqslant x] \rightarrow y \leqslant z)]$	
2.	$\bigvee x F(x) \wedge \bigvee y \bigwedge x(F(x) \rightarrow y \leqslant x)$	
3.	$\bigwedge x(F(x) \rightarrow u \leqslant x)$	2, EI
4.	~~Show~~ $\bigwedge x(F(-x) \rightarrow x \leqslant -u)$	
5.	$F(-x) \rightarrow x \leqslant -u$	3, UI, *T*10, LL, *T*30
6.	$\bigvee y \bigwedge x(F(-x) \rightarrow x \leqslant y)$	4, EG
7.	$\bigvee z[\bigwedge x(F(-x) \rightarrow x \leqslant z) \wedge \bigwedge y(\bigwedge x[F(-x) \rightarrow x \leqslant y] \rightarrow z \leqslant y)]$	2, *TS*41, 6, *AS*19
8.	$\bigwedge x(F(-x) \rightarrow x \leqslant w) \wedge \bigwedge y(\bigwedge x[F(-x) \rightarrow x \leqslant y] \rightarrow w \leqslant y)$	7, EI
9.	~~Show~~ $\bigwedge x(F(x) \rightarrow -w \leqslant x)$	
10.	$F(x) \rightarrow -w \leqslant x$	8, UI, *T*10, LL, *T*30
11.	~~Show~~ $\bigwedge y(\bigwedge x[F(x) \rightarrow y \leqslant x] \rightarrow y \leqslant -w)$	
12.	$\bigwedge x[F(x) \rightarrow y \leqslant x]$	
13.	~~Show~~ $\bigwedge x(F(-x) \rightarrow x \leqslant -y)$	
14.	$F(-x) \rightarrow x \leqslant -y$	12, UI, *T*10, LL, *T*30
15.	$y \leqslant -w$	8, UI, 13, *T*10, LL, *T*30
16.	$\bigvee z[\bigwedge x(F(x) \rightarrow z \leqslant x) \wedge \bigwedge y(\bigwedge x[F(x) \rightarrow y \leqslant x] \rightarrow y \leqslant z)]$	9, 11, EG

In the preceding derivation a new informal abbreviation was introduced. The subsidiary derivation of line 11 has the following form:

~~*Show*~~ $\wedge\alpha(\phi \rightarrow \psi)$

ϕ
.
.
.
ψ

,

rather than the explicit form:

~~*Show*~~ $\wedge\alpha(\phi \rightarrow \psi)$

> ~~*Show*~~ $\phi \rightarrow \psi$
>
> | ϕ |
> |---|
> | . |
> | . |
> | . |
> | ψ |

This sort of abbreviation corresponds to mathematical practice and will be used frequently in the sequel.

The following theorem schema, whose proof involves a new abbreviation that will be discussed below, makes approximately the following assertion: a greatest lower bound of a class of integers belongs to that class. *TS*44 makes the dual assertion concerning least upper bounds. These assertions, it should be observed, do not hold for arbitrary classes of real numbers. Consider, for example, the class of real numbers greater than 0. It is easily seen that 0 is the greatest lower bound of this class but not a member of it.

*TS*43

1. ~~*Show*~~ $\wedge x[F(x) \rightarrow I(x)] \wedge \wedge x(F(x) \rightarrow y \leqslant x) \wedge \wedge z(\wedge x[F(x) \rightarrow z \leqslant x] \rightarrow z \leqslant y) \rightarrow F(y)$

2.	$\wedge x[F(x) \rightarrow I(x)] \wedge \wedge x(F(x) \rightarrow y \leqslant x) \wedge \wedge z(\wedge x[F(x) \rightarrow z \leqslant x] \rightarrow z \leqslant y)$	
3.	~~*Show*~~ $F(y)$	
4.	$\sim F(y)$	
5.	~~*Show*~~ $\wedge x(F(x) \rightarrow y + 1 \leqslant x)$	
6.	$F(x) \wedge \sim y + 1 \leqslant x$	
7.	~~*Show*~~ $\wedge z(F(z) \rightarrow x \leqslant z)$	
8.	$F(z) \wedge \sim x \leqslant z$	
9.	$y \leqslant z$	2, UI, 8
10.	$y + 1 \leqslant z + 1$	9, *T*24

11.	$x \leqslant y + 1$	6, $T21$
12.	$x \leqslant z + 1$	10, 11, $T20$
13.	$z \leqslant x$	8, $T21$
14.	$I(x) \wedge I(z)$	6, 2, UI, 8, 2, UI
15.	$x = z \vee x = z + 1$	14, 13, 12, $A18$
16.	$\sim x = z$	8, $T38$
17.	$\sim x = z + 1$	6, 10, LL
18.	$x = z + 1$	15, 16
19.	$x \leqslant y$	7, 2, AV, UI
20.	$y \leqslant x$	6, 2, UI
21.	$x = y$	19, 20, $T19$
22.	$\sim F(x)$	4, 21, LL
23.	$F(x)$	6
24.	$y + 1 \leqslant y$	5, 2, UI
25.	$\sim y + 1 \leqslant y$	$T27$

In the preceding derivation we permit the following variant of indirect derivation:

~~*Show*~~ $\wedge\alpha\,(\phi \rightarrow \psi)$

$\phi \wedge \sim \psi$
.
.
.
χ
$\sim\chi$

which, executed in full detail, would read:

~~*Show*~~ $\wedge\alpha(\phi \rightarrow \psi)$
~~*Show*~~ $\phi \rightarrow \psi$
ϕ
~~*Show*~~ ψ
$\sim\psi$
.
.
.
χ
$\sim\chi$

(An analogous variant of indirect derivation, in which the formula derived is not

$$\wedge\alpha(\phi \rightarrow \psi)$$

but simply

$$\phi \rightarrow \psi$$

is also occasionally useful and is in fact employed in the derivations of *T*53 and *T*55 below.) The new abbreviation is employed in the subsidiary derivations of lines 5 and 7 above.

*TS*44 $\bigwedge x[F(x) \rightarrow I(x)] \wedge \bigwedge x(F(x) \rightarrow x \leqslant y) \wedge \bigwedge z(\bigwedge x[F(x) \rightarrow x \leqslant z] \rightarrow y \leqslant z) \rightarrow F(y)$

The next two theorem schemata are the natural principles of *mathematical induction* over all integers. *TS*45 is a simple consequence of the Continuity Schema, together with *TS*43 and *TS*44. The stronger principle *TS*49 can be obtained in a simple way from *TS*45; we leave the derivation to the reader. *T*46 – *T*48 are applications of the induction principle *TS*45; the proofs of *T*47 and *T*48 are left to the reader. Henceforth we shall for the most part omit annotative reference to principles of logic, that is, principles of chapters I – VII.

*TS*45

1. ~~Show~~ $F(0) \wedge \bigwedge x[I(x) \wedge F(x) \rightarrow F(x + 1) \wedge F(x + -1)] \rightarrow \bigwedge x[I(x) \rightarrow F(x)]$
2. $F(0) \wedge \bigwedge x[I(x) \wedge F(x) \rightarrow F(x + 1) \wedge F(x + -1)] \wedge \sim \bigwedge x[I(x) \rightarrow F(x)]$
3. $I(u) \wedge \sim F(u)$ — 2, QN, EI
4. ~~Show~~ $\sim 0 \leqslant u$
5. $0 \leqslant u$
6. ~~Show~~ $\bigwedge x(0 \leqslant x \wedge I(x) \wedge \sim F(x) \rightarrow 0 \leqslant x)$
7. $0 \leqslant x \wedge I(x) \wedge \sim F(x) \rightarrow 0 \leqslant x$
8. $\bigvee x[0 \leqslant x \wedge I(x) \wedge \sim F(x)] \wedge \bigvee y \bigwedge x[0 \leqslant x \wedge I(x) \wedge \sim F(x) \rightarrow y \leqslant x]$ — 3, 5, EG, 6, EG
9. $\bigwedge x(0 \leqslant x \wedge I(x) \wedge \sim F(x) \rightarrow w \leqslant x) \wedge \bigwedge y(\bigwedge x[0 \leqslant x \wedge I(x) \wedge \sim F(x) \rightarrow y \leqslant x] \rightarrow y \leqslant w)$ — 8, *TS*42, EI
10. ~~Show~~ $\bigwedge x[0 \leqslant x \wedge I(x) \wedge \sim F(x) \rightarrow I(x)]$
11. $0 \leqslant x \wedge I(x) \wedge \sim F(x) \rightarrow I(x)$
12. $0 \leqslant w \wedge I(w) \wedge \sim F(w)$ — 10, 9, *TS*43

13.	$\sim 0 = w$	2, 12, LL
14.	$I(w + -1)$	12, *A*17
15.	$0 \leqslant w + -1$	12, 13, *T*39, *T*24, *A*4, LL
16.	~~Show~~ $F(w + -1)$	
17.	$\sim F(w + -1)$	
18.	$w \leqslant w + -1$	9, UI, 15, 14, 17
19.	$\sim w \leqslant w + -1$	*T*28
20.	$F((w + -1) + 1)$	2, UI, 14, 16
21.	$F(w)$	20, *A*1, *A*2, *A*4, *A*3, LL
22.	$\sim F(w)$	12
23.	~~Show~~ $\sim u \leqslant 0$	
	Derivation similar to that of line 4, using *AS*19 and *TS*44 in place of *TS*42 and *TS*43.	
24.	$0 \leqslant u$	23, *T*21

*T*46

1.	~~Show~~ $I(x) \rightarrow I(-x)$	
2.	$I(-0)$	*A*16, *T*5
3.	~~Show~~ $\wedge x[I(x) \wedge I(-x) \rightarrow I(-(x + 1)) \wedge I(-(x + -1))]$	
4.	$I(x) \wedge I(-x)$	
5.	$-(x + 1) = -x + -1$	*T*11
6.	$I(-(x + 1))$	4, *A*17, 5
7.	$-(x + -1) = -x + 1$	*T*11, *T*10
8.	$I(-(x + -1))$	4, *A*17, 7
9.	$I(x) \rightarrow I(-x)$	2, 3, *TS*45

*T*47 $I(x) \wedge I(y) \rightarrow I(x + y)$

*T*48 $I(x) \wedge I(y) \rightarrow I(x \cdot y)$

*TS*49 $\vee x[I(x) \wedge F(x)] \wedge \wedge x[I(x) \wedge F(x) \rightarrow F(x + 1) \wedge F(x + -1)] \rightarrow \wedge x[I(x) \rightarrow F(x)]$

The inductive proofs of the next two theorems, which are included only for use in proving *T*52, are left to the reader. According to *T*52, an integer is always either odd or even but never both. (Here and henceforth parentheses within an iterated sum or product will be dropped.)

*T*50 $I(x) \rightarrow \vee y(I(y) \wedge x = y + y) \vee \vee y(I(y) \wedge x = y + y + 1)$

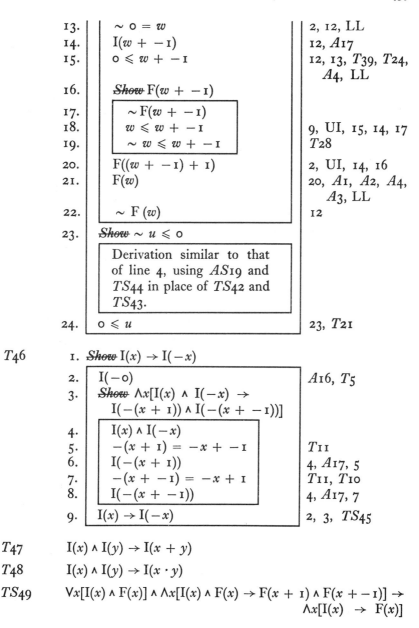

*T*51 $\quad I(x) \rightarrow \sim \bigvee y(I(y) \wedge x + x = y + y + 1)$

*T*52 $\quad I(x) \rightarrow [\bigvee y(I(y) \wedge x = y + y) \leftrightarrow \sim \bigvee y(I(y) \wedge x = y + y + 1)]$

We conclude this section on the Continuity Schema with a proof of the *Principle of Archimedes*, which asserts the following: if y is any number, and x any number other than 0, then y can be exceeded by an integral multiple of x. This assertion is *T*54; it is convenient to prove first the special case in which x is assumed to be positive.

*T*53

1.	~~*Show*~~ $0 \leqslant x \wedge \sim x = 0 \rightarrow \bigvee n(I(n) \wedge y \leqslant n \cdot x)$	
2.	$0 \leqslant x \wedge \sim x = 0 \wedge \sim \bigvee n(I(n) \wedge y \leqslant n \cdot x)$	
3.	~~*Show*~~ $\bigwedge n(I(n) \rightarrow n \leqslant y \cdot x^{-1})$	
4.	$I(n)$	
5.	$\sim y \leqslant n \cdot x$	2, 4
6.	$n \cdot x \leqslant y$	5, *T*80, *T*81
7.	$0 \leqslant x^{-1}$	2, *T*35
8.	$n \cdot x \cdot x^{-1} \leqslant y \cdot x^{-1}$	6, 7, *T*33
9.	$x \cdot x^{-1} = 1$	2, *A*8
10.	$n \leqslant y \cdot x^{-1}$	8, 9, *A*7
11.	$\bigvee z \bigwedge n(I(n) \rightarrow n \leqslant z)$	3, EG
12.	$\bigvee n\, I(n)$	*A*16, EG
13.	$\bigwedge n(I(n) \rightarrow n \leqslant u) \wedge \bigwedge z(\bigwedge n[I(n) \rightarrow n \leqslant z] \rightarrow u \leqslant z)$	11, 12, *AS*19, EI
14.	~~*Show*~~ $\bigwedge n(I(n) \rightarrow I(n))$	
15.	$I(n) \rightarrow I(n)$	
16.	$I(u)$	13, 14, *TS*44
17.	$I(u + 1)$	16, *A*17
18.	$\sim I(u + 1)$	13, 17, *T*27

*T*54

1.	~~*Show*~~ $\sim x = 0 \rightarrow \bigvee n(I(n) \wedge y \leqslant n \cdot x)$	
2.	$\sim x = 0$	
3.	$0 \leqslant x \rightarrow \bigvee n(I(n) \wedge y \leqslant n \cdot x)$	2, *T*53
4.	~~*Show*~~ $x \leqslant 0 \rightarrow \bigvee n(I(n) \wedge y \leqslant n \cdot x)$	
5.	$x \leqslant 0$	
6.	$0 \leqslant -x$	5, *T*31
7.	$\sim -x = 0$	2, *T*9
8.	$I(n_0) \wedge y \leqslant n_0 \cdot (-x)$	6, 7, *T*53, EI
9.	$y \leqslant (-n_0) \cdot x$	8, *T*13, *T*12
10.	$I(-n_0)$	8, *T*46
11.	$\bigvee n(I(n) \wedge y \leqslant n \cdot x)$	10, 9
12.	$\bigvee n(I(n) \wedge y \leqslant n \cdot x)$	3, 4, *T*21

7. Definitions. Of considerable importance, both from the intuitive point of view and for later purposes, is the notion of a *definition* of one constant in terms of others. Loosely speaking, a definition is a formula, more specifically, a biconditional or an identity, which elucidates the meaning of the constant it defines. We shall exclude from consideration, both here and in the next chapter, definitions of logical constants. These symbols will be regarded as completely understood, and accordingly will be used freely in the formulation of definitions. In this chapter we shall further restrict ourselves to definitions of predicates and operation symbols. Definitions of variable-binding operators present special difficulties whose consideration we prefer to postpone till the next chapter.

Thus in the following δ is assumed to be a nonlogical constant and either a predicate or an operation symbol; that is, δ is to be either an operation symbol or a predicate other than '='.

If δ is an n-place predicate (other than '=') and L any class of nonlogical constants not containing δ, then a *possible definition of* δ *in terms of L* is a formula of the form

$$\delta\alpha_1 \ldots \alpha_n \leftrightarrow \phi \quad ,$$

where $\alpha_1, \ldots, \alpha_n$ are distinct variables, and ϕ is a formula all of whose nonlogical constants are members of L and which contains no free variables beyond $\alpha_1, \ldots, \alpha_n$.

For example, let L be the class consisting of the symbols '+', '·', and '0'. Then a possible definition of the 2-place predicate '<' in terms of L is the biconditional

$$x < y \leftrightarrow \bigvee z(\sim z = 0 \land x + (z \cdot z) = y) \quad .$$

Definitions of *operation symbols* will assume the form of identities rather than biconditionals. Thus, if δ is an n-place operation symbol and L any class of nonlogical constants not containing δ, then a *possible definition of* δ *in terms of L* is a formula of the form

$$\delta\alpha_1 \ldots \alpha_n = \zeta \quad ,$$

where $\alpha_1, \ldots, \alpha_n$ are distinct variables, and ζ is a term all of whose nonlogical constants are members of L and which contains no free variables beyond $\alpha_1, \ldots, \alpha_n$.

For example, let L be the class whose only member is the symbol '·'. Then a possible definition of the 1-place operation symbol '$\sqrt[3]{}$' in terms of L is the formula

$$\sqrt[3]{x} = \iota y[(y \cdot y) \cdot y = x] \quad .$$

Generally speaking, the right side of a possible definition is regarded as elucidating the meaning of the constant occurring on the left side; hence the requirement that the latter constant not occur on the right side of the definition.

It is often useful to introduce new constants into a theory T by definition. This consists in passing to an extension of T obtained from T by adding possible definitions of the new constants in terms of the constants of T. More exactly, we say that a theory U is a *definitional extension* of a theory T just in case (i) U is an extension of T, (ii) every constant of U that is not a constant of T is either a predicate or an operation symbol, (iii) for each constant δ of U that is not a constant of T, there occurs among the axioms of U exactly one possible definition of δ in terms of the constants of T, and (iv) every axiom of U that is not an axiom of T is a possible definition, in terms of the constants of T, of some nonlogical constant that is not a constant of T.

The distinctive properties of definitions stem from the following three facts, which concern definitional extensions and do not hold for arbitrary extensions.

(1) If ϕ is a formula of a definitional extension U of a theory T, then there is a formula ψ of T such that

$$\phi \leftrightarrow \psi$$

is a theorem of U. Thus the power of expression of a theory is not essentially increased by the addition of defined symbols.

(2) If ϕ is a theorem of a definitional extension of a theory T and at the same time a formula of T, then ϕ is already a theorem of T. Thus the deductive power of a theory is not essentially enhanced by the addition of definitions.

(3) The assertion (2) has as an immediate consequence the fact that the addition of definitions can never introduce a contradiction into a theory. Accordingly, let us call a theory T *consistent* if there is no sentence ϕ such that both ϕ and its negation are theorems of T. Then a definitional extension of a consistent theory is always consistent.

We should also call attention to the fact that (4) if V is a definitional extension of U and U is a definitional extension of T, then V is equivalent to a definitional extension of T. (Two theories are said to be *equivalent* if they have the same constants and the same theorems.)

The theory of real numbers has as a definitional extension the theory T_1, characterized as follows. The *constants of* T_1 are those of the theory of real numbers, together with:

$\neq$	(2-place predicate)
$<$	(2-place predicate)
2	(individual constant)
^{2}	(1-place operation symbol)
$\mid\ \mid$	(1-place operation symbol)

— (2-place operation symbol)
− (2-place operation symbol) .

The *axioms of* T_1 are those of the theory of real numbers, together with:

*D*1 $x \neq y \leftrightarrow \sim x = y$

*D*2 $x < y \leftrightarrow x \leqslant y \wedge \sim x = y$

*D*3 $2 = 1 + 1$

*D*4 $x^2 = x \cdot x$

*D*5 $|x| = \iota z[(0 \leqslant x \wedge z = x) \vee (\sim 0 \leqslant x \wedge z = -x)]$

*D*6 $x - y = x + -y$

*D*7 $\frac{x}{y} = x \cdot y^{-1}$

The intended reading of the new constants should be clear from the possible definitions *D*1 – *D*7. For example, the operation symbol introduced by *D*5 is read 'the absolute value of *x*'. *D*7 has as a consequence

$$\frac{x}{0} = x \cdot 0^{-1} .$$

Thus division by zero, like the expression '0^{-1}', is regarded as meaningful. Our axioms, however, do not determine the value of '$\frac{x}{0}$' because of the antecedent of *A*8. In deference to mathematical custom, we depart further than usual from our official notation and use '−' both as a 1-place and as a 2-place operation symbol. *D*6 defines binary '−' in terms of singulary '−' and addition. The context will always determine which of the two senses is intended.

We list a number of theorems of T_1, proving a few and leaving the others (which can be easily obtained from preceding theorems and definitions) to the reader.

*T*55

1.	~~*Show*~~ $\mathrm{I}(n) \wedge \mathrm{I}(m) \wedge n < m \rightarrow n + 1 \leqslant m$	
2.	$\mathrm{I}(n) \wedge \mathrm{I}(m) \wedge n < m \wedge \sim n + 1 \leqslant m$	
3.	$n \leqslant m$	2, *D*2
4.	$m \leqslant n + 1$	2, *T*21
5.	$m = n \vee m = n + 1$	3, 4, *A*18
6.	$\sim m = n$	2, *D*2
7.	$n + 1 \leqslant m$	5, 6, *T*38
8.	$\sim n + 1 \leqslant m$	2

*T*56 $x - x = 0$

*T*57 $-(x - y) = y - x$

*T*58 $x - y = (z - y) - (z - x)$

*T*59 $(x - y) + (z - w) = (x + z) - (y + w)$

*T*60 $(x + y)^2 = x^2 + 2xy + y^2$

In *T*60, as in later statements, we adopt the mathematical practices of omitting the multiplication sign and of regarding addition and subtraction as marking greater breaks than multiplication.

*T*61 $1^2 = 1$

*T*62 $(x - y)^2 = x^2 - 2xy + y^2$

*T*63 $(x \cdot y)^2 = x^2 \cdot y^2$

*T*64 $y \neq 0 \rightarrow \left(\frac{x}{y}\right)^2 = \frac{x^2}{y^2}$

*T*65 $\frac{x}{2} + \frac{x}{2} = x$

*T*66 $\frac{0}{x} = 0$

*T*67 $\frac{x+y}{z} = \frac{x}{z} + \frac{y}{z}$

*T*68 $xz \neq 0 \rightarrow \frac{xy}{xz} = \frac{y}{z}$

*T*69 $y \neq 0 \rightarrow -\left(\frac{x}{y}\right) = \frac{-x}{y} \wedge -\left(\frac{x}{y}\right) = \frac{x}{-y}$

*T*70 $0 \leqslant x \wedge x \leqslant 1 \rightarrow x^2 \leqslant x$

*T*71 $0 \leqslant x^2$

*T*72 $x \neq 0 \rightarrow 0 < x^2$

*T*73 $x \leqslant x + y^2$

*T*74 $0 < 1$

*T*75 $1 < 2$

*T*76 $\sim x < x$

*T*77 $x < y \wedge y < z \rightarrow x < z$

*T*78 $x \leqslant y \wedge y < z \rightarrow x < z$

*T*79 $x < y \wedge y \leqslant z \rightarrow x < z$

*T*80 $x \leqslant y \leftrightarrow \sim y < x$

*T*81 $x \leqslant y \leftrightarrow x < y \vee x = y$

*T*82 $x < y \leftrightarrow x + z < y + z$

*T*83 $x < y \wedge z < w \rightarrow x + z < y + w$

*T*84 $0 < x \rightarrow x < 2x$

*T*85 $x < y \leftrightarrow -y < -x$

*T*86 $x < 0 \leftrightarrow 0 < -x$

*T*87 $0 < x \rightarrow 0 < x^{-1}$

*T*88 $x < 0 \rightarrow x^{-1} < 0$

*T*89 $0 < z \rightarrow [x < y \leftrightarrow xz < yz]$

*T*90 $z < 0 \rightarrow [x < y \leftrightarrow yz < xz]$

*T*91 $0 < x \wedge 0 < y \rightarrow [x \leqslant y \leftrightarrow y^{-1} \leqslant x^{-1}]$

*T*92 $x < 0 \wedge y < 0 \rightarrow [x \leqslant y \leftrightarrow y^{-1} \leqslant x^{-1}]$

*T*93 $0 < x \wedge 0 < y \rightarrow [x < y \leftrightarrow y^{-1} < x^{-1}]$

*T*94 $x < 0 \wedge y < 0 \rightarrow [x < y \leftrightarrow y^{-1} < x^{-1}]$

*T*95 $0 < x \wedge x \leqslant y \wedge 0 \leqslant z \rightarrow \frac{z}{y} \leqslant \frac{z}{x}$

*T*96 $0 < x \wedge x < y \wedge 0 < z \rightarrow \frac{z}{y} < \frac{z}{x}$

*T*97 $x \leqslant y \wedge 0 < z \rightarrow \frac{x}{z} \leqslant \frac{y}{z}$

*T*98 $x < y \wedge 0 < z \rightarrow \frac{x}{z} < \frac{y}{z}$

*T*99 $0 < x \wedge x < y \rightarrow 0 < \frac{x}{y} \wedge \frac{x}{y} < 1$

*T*100 1. ~~*Show*~~ $0 \leqslant y \wedge x^2 \leqslant y^2 \rightarrow x \leqslant y$

2. $0 \leqslant y \wedge x^2 \leqslant y^2$

3. ~~*Show*~~ $0 < x \wedge 0 < y \rightarrow x \leqslant y$

4. $0 < x \wedge 0 < y \wedge \sim x \leqslant y$

5. $y < x$ — 4, *T*80

6. $y \cdot y < y \cdot x$ — 4, 5, *T*89

7. $y \cdot x < x \cdot x$ — 4, 5, *T*89

8. $y^2 < x^2$ — 6, 7, *T*77, *D*4

9. $\sim y^2 < x^2$ — 2, *T*80

10. ~~*Show*~~ $x \leqslant 0 \rightarrow x \leqslant y$

11. $x \leqslant 0$

12. $x \leqslant y$ — 11, 2, *T*20

13. ~~*Show*~~ $y = 0 \rightarrow x \leqslant y$

14. $y = 0$

15. $x^2 \leqslant 0$ — 2, 14, *D*4, *T*6

16. $x^2 = 0$ — 15, *T*71, *T*19

17. $x = 0$ — 16, *D*4, *T*16

18. $x \leqslant y$ — 17, 14, *T*18

19. $(0 < x \wedge 0 < y) \vee x \leqslant 0 \vee y = 0$ — 2, *T*81, *T*80

20. $x \leqslant y$ — 3, 10, 13, 19

*T*101 $0 \leqslant x \wedge 0 < y \rightarrow 0 \leqslant \dfrac{x}{y}$

*T*102 $0 < x \wedge 0 < y \rightarrow 0 < \dfrac{x}{y}$

*T*103 $\bigvee t \bigwedge z[(0 \leqslant x \wedge z = x) \vee (\sim 0 \leqslant x \wedge z = -x) \leftrightarrow z = t]$

By the last theorem, the descriptive phrase in *D*5 is proper; with this fact, it is easy to obtain the following two theorems.

*T*104 $0 \leqslant x \rightarrow |x| = x$

*T*105 $x < 0 \rightarrow |x| = -x$

Now that we have obtained *T*104 and *T*105, it will no longer be necessary to refer to *D*5, which has a rather cumbersome form.

*T*106 1. ~~*Show*~~ $0 \leqslant |x|$

2. ~~*Show*~~ $0 \leqslant x \rightarrow 0 \leqslant |x|$

3.	$0 \leqslant x$	
4.	$\lvert x\rvert = x$	3, *T*104
5.	$0 \leqslant \lvert x\rvert$	3, 4
6.	~~*Show*~~ $x < 0 \rightarrow 0 \leqslant \lvert x\rvert$	
7.	$x < 0$	
8.	$\lvert x\rvert = -x$	7, *T*105
9.	$0 < -x$	7, *T*86
10.	$0 \leqslant \lvert x\rvert$	8, 9, *D*2
11.	$0 \leqslant \lvert x\rvert$	2, 6, *T*80

*T*107 $\lvert x\rvert = 0 \leftrightarrow x = 0$

*T*108 $x \leqslant \lvert x\rvert$

*T*109 $-x \leqslant \lvert x\rvert$

*T*110 $\lvert -x\rvert = \lvert x\rvert$

*T*111 $\lvert x\rvert \leqslant y \leftrightarrow x \leqslant y \wedge -x \leqslant y$

*T*112

1.	~~*Show*~~ $\lvert x + y\rvert \leqslant \lvert x\rvert + \lvert y\rvert$	
2.	$x \leqslant \lvert x\rvert$	*T*108
3.	$y \leqslant \lvert y\rvert$	*T*108
4.	$x + y \leqslant \lvert x\rvert + \lvert y\rvert$	2, 3, *T*26
5.	$-x \leqslant \lvert x\rvert$	*T*109
6.	$-y \leqslant \lvert y\rvert$	*T*109
7.	$-x + -y \leqslant \lvert x\rvert + \lvert y\rvert$	5, 6, *T*26
8.	$-(x + y) \leqslant \lvert x\rvert + \lvert y\rvert$	7, *T*11
9.	$\lvert x + y\rvert \leqslant \lvert x\rvert + \lvert y\rvert$	4, 8, *T*111

*T*113, which is an immediate consequence of *T*112, is the familiar *triangular inequality*.

*T*113 $\lvert x - y\rvert \leqslant \lvert x - z\rvert + \lvert z - y\rvert$

*T*114 $\lvert x - y\rvert \leqslant \lvert x\rvert + \lvert y\rvert$

*T*115 $\lvert x - y\rvert = \lvert y - x\rvert$

*T*116 $\lvert x \cdot y\rvert = \lvert x\rvert \cdot \lvert y\rvert$

*T*117 $y \neq 0 \rightarrow \left\lvert \frac{x}{y} \right\rvert = \frac{\lvert x\rvert}{\lvert y\rvert}$

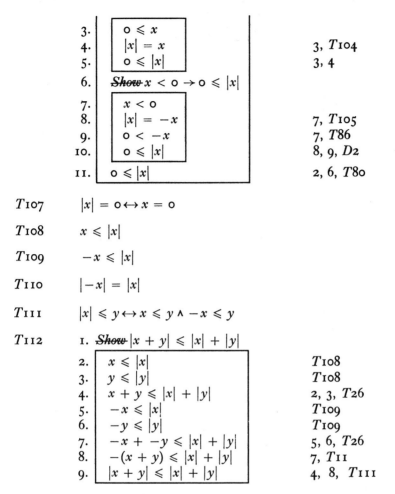

*T*118

1. ~~*Show*~~ $|x - y| < z \leftrightarrow x - z < y \wedge y < x + z$
2. ~~*Show*~~ $x - z < y \wedge y < x + z \rightarrow |x - y| < z$
3. $x - z < y \wedge y < x + z$
4. $-(y - x) < z$ — 3, *T*82, *D*6, *A*2, *A*1, *A*4, *A*3, *T*85, *T*10
5. $y - x < z$ — 3, *T*82, *D*6, *A*2, *A*1, *A*4, *A*3
6. $|y - x| = y - x \vee |y - x| = -(y - x)$ — *T*104, *T*105, *T*80
7. $|x - y| < z$ — 4, 5, 6
8. ~~*Show*~~ $|x - y| < z \rightarrow x - z < y \wedge y < x + z$
9. $|x - y| < z$
10. $x - y < z$ — 9, *T*108, *T*78
11. $x - z < y$ — 10, *T*82, *D*6, *A*2, *A*1, *A*4, *A*3
12. $y - x < z$ — 9, *T*115, *T*108, *T*78
13. $y < x + z$ — 12, *T*82, *D*6, *A*2, *A*1, *A*4, *A*3
14. $x - z < y \wedge y < x + z$ — 11, 13

We pass now to a definitional extension T_2 of T_1, obtained by adjoining the 1-place predicates 'N' and 'R' to the constants of T_1, and the following possible definitions to the axioms of T_1:

*D*8 $\mathrm{N}(x) \leftrightarrow \mathrm{I}(x) \wedge 0 \leqslant x$

*D*9 $\mathrm{R}(x) \leftrightarrow \bigvee y \bigvee z[\mathrm{I}(y) \wedge \mathrm{I}(z) \wedge 0 < z \wedge x = \frac{y}{z}]$

*D*8 introduces the notion of a *natural number*, *D*9 that of a *rational number*. By remark (4) on page 462, T_2 is equivalent to a definitional extension of the theory of real numbers.

The following theorem schema (of T_2) is the *minimum principle* for natural numbers: every nonempty set of natural numbers has a least member.

*TS*119

1. ~~*Show*~~ $\bigvee x \mathrm{F}(x) \wedge \bigwedge x[\mathrm{F}(x) \rightarrow \mathrm{N}(x)] \rightarrow \bigvee x(\mathrm{F}(x) \wedge \bigwedge y\,[\mathrm{F}(y) \rightarrow x \leqslant y])$
2. $\bigvee x \mathrm{F}(x) \wedge \bigwedge x[\mathrm{F}(x) \rightarrow \mathrm{N}(x)]$
3. ~~*Show*~~ $\bigwedge x[\mathrm{F}(x) \rightarrow 0 \leqslant x]$

4.	$F(x)$	
5.	$0 \leqslant x$	2, 4, *D*8
6.	$\bigwedge x[F(x) \rightarrow z_0 \leqslant x] \wedge \bigwedge y(\bigwedge x[F(x) \rightarrow y \leqslant x] \rightarrow y \leqslant z_0)$	2, 3, *TS*42, EI
7.	~~Show~~ $\bigwedge x[F(x) \rightarrow I(x)]$	
8.	$F(x)$	
9.	$I(x)$	2, 8, *D*8
10.	$F(z_0)$	7, 6, *TS*43
11.	$\bigvee x(F(x) \wedge \bigwedge y[F(y) \rightarrow x \leqslant y])$	10, 6 (1st conjunct),AV,EG

We now state two induction principles for natural numbers, both of which are immediate consequences of the minimum principle. *TS*120, whose proof is left to the reader, is the principle of *strong induction;* it asserts that every natural number has the property F, on the assumption that an arbitrary natural number has F if every smaller natural number has F. *TS*121 is the more familiar principle of *weak induction;* if 0 has the property F, and whenever a natural number x has F, so does $x + 1$, then every natural number has F.

*TS*120 $\bigwedge x(N(x) \wedge \bigwedge y[N(y) \wedge y < x \rightarrow F(y)] \rightarrow F(x)) \rightarrow \bigwedge x[N(x) \rightarrow F(x)]$

*TS*121 1. ~~Show~~ $F(0) \wedge \bigwedge x[N(x) \wedge F(x) \rightarrow F(x + 1)] \rightarrow \bigwedge x[N(x) \rightarrow F(x)]$

2.	$F(0) \wedge \bigwedge x[N(x) \wedge F(x) \rightarrow F(x + 1)] \wedge \sim \bigwedge x[N(x) \rightarrow F(x)]$	
3.	$\bigvee x[N(x) \wedge \sim F(x)]$	2 (3rd conjunct.)
4.	$\bigwedge x[N(x) \wedge \sim F(x) \rightarrow N(x)]$	
5.	$N(x_0) \wedge \sim F(x_0) \wedge \bigwedge x(N(x) \wedge \sim F(x) \rightarrow x_0 \leqslant x)$	3, 4, *TS*119, EI
6.	$x_0 \neq 0$	2, 5
7.	$N(x_0 - 1)$	5, *D*8, *A*17, *D*6, 6, *T*39
8.	$F(x_0 - 1)$	5, 7, *T*28, *D*6
9.	$F(x_0)$	2, 7, 8
10.	$\sim F(x_0)$	5

In the annotations of lines 7 and 9 above, we have omitted reference to certain arithmetical principles that are by now completely familiar; this practice will be pursued in the sequel. Also, obvious theorems of logic, such as line 4 above, will sometimes be used even if not listed in chapters I–VII.

The theory of natural numbers was axiomatized for the first time in Peano [1]. Peano's axioms consist of *TS*121, together with *T*122 – *T*125 below. *T*126 expresses the fact that the set of natural numbers is closed under addition and multiplication.

*T*122 $\quad N(0)$

*T*123 $\quad N(x) \rightarrow N(x + 1)$

*T*124 $\quad N(x) \wedge N(y) \wedge x + 1 = y + 1 \rightarrow x = y$

*T*125 $\quad N(x) \rightarrow x + 1 \neq 0$

*T*126 $\quad N(x) \wedge N(y) \rightarrow N(x + y) \wedge N(x \cdot y)$

The next theorem, which is a lemma for *T*128, asserts that if x^2 is an even integer, then so is x. *T*128, whose proof is due to Pythagoras and appears in Euclid [1], states that 2 has no rational square root.

*T*127

1. ~~*Show*~~ $I(x) \wedge \bigvee y(I(y) \wedge x^2 = 2y) \rightarrow \bigvee y(I(y) \wedge x = 2y)$

2.	$I(x) \wedge \bigvee y(I(y) \wedge x^2 = 2y) \wedge \sim\bigvee y(I(y) \wedge x = 2y)$	
3.	$I(y_0) \wedge x = 2y_0 + 1$	2, *T*52
4.	$x^2 = (2y_0)^2 + 2 \cdot 2 \cdot y_0 + 1$	3, *T*60, *T*61
5.	$= 2 \cdot 2 \cdot y_0^2 + 2 \cdot 2 \cdot y_0 + 1$	4, *T*63
6.	$= 2 \cdot (2 \cdot y_0^2 + 2 \cdot y_0) + 1$	5, *A*9
7.	$I(2 \cdot y_0^2 + 2 \cdot y_0)$	3, *T*48, *A*16, *A*17, *T*47
8.	$\bigvee y(I(y) \wedge x^2 = 2 \cdot y + 1)$	7, 6, EG
9.	$\sim\bigvee y(I(y) \wedge x^2 = 2 \cdot y + 1)$	2, *T*48, *T*52

*T*128

1. ~~*Show*~~ $R(x) \rightarrow x^2 \neq 2$

2.	$R(x) \wedge x^2 = 2$	
3.	$\bigvee z \bigvee y[I(y) \wedge I(z) \wedge 0 < z \wedge x = \frac{y}{z}]$	2, *D*9
4.	~~*Show*~~ $\bigwedge z(\bigvee y[I(y) \wedge I(z) \wedge 0 < z \wedge x = \frac{y}{z}] \rightarrow N(z))$ Elementary	
5.	$\bigvee y[I(y) \wedge I(z_0) \wedge 0 < z_0 \wedge x = \frac{y}{z_0}] \wedge \bigwedge z(\bigvee y[I(y) \wedge I(z) \wedge 0 < z \wedge x = \frac{y}{z}] \rightarrow z_0 \leqslant z)$	3, 4, *TS*119, EI

6.	$I(y_0) \wedge I(z_0) \wedge 0 < z_0 \wedge x = \frac{y_0}{z_0}$	5 (1st conjunct), EI
7.	$\frac{y_0^2}{z_0^2} = 2$	6, 2, *T*64
8.	$y_0^2 = 2 \cdot z_0^2$	7, 6, *T*16
9.	$\bigvee v(I(v) \wedge y_0^2 = 2 \cdot v)$	6, *T*48, 8, EG
10.	$I(w_0) \wedge y_0 = 2 \cdot w_0$	6, 9, *T*127, EI
11.	$2 \cdot 2 \cdot w_0^2 = 2 \cdot z_0^2$	8, 10, *T*63
12.	$2 \cdot w_0^2 = z_0^2$	11
13.	$\bigvee n(I(n) \wedge z_0^2 = 2 \cdot n)$	10, *T*48, 12, EG
14.	$I(m_0) \wedge z_0 = 2 \cdot m_0$	6, 13, *T*127, EI
15.	$x = \frac{2 \cdot w_0}{2 \cdot m_0}$	6, 10, 14
16.	$x = \frac{w_0}{m_0}$	14, 6, 15, *T*68
17.	~~*Show*~~ $0 < m_0$	
18.	$\sim 0 < m_0$	
19.	$2 \cdot m_0 \leqslant 0$	18, *T*80, *T*33
20.	$z_0 \leqslant 0$	14, 19
21.	$\sim z_0 \leqslant 0$	6, *T*80
22.	$z_0 \leqslant m_0$	10, 14, 17, 16, EG, 5 (2nd conjunct)
23.	$m_0 < m_0 + m_0$	17
24.	$m_0 < z_0$	23, 14
25.	$\sim z_0 \leqslant m_0$	24, *T*80

While many positive numbers resemble 2 in having no square root among the rationals, it is a consequence of the Continuity Schema that every positive number does have a square root:

*T*129

1.	~~*Show*~~ $0 < x \rightarrow \bigvee y\, x = y^2$	
2.	$0 < x$	
3.	$0^2 < x$	2
4.	$\bigvee y\, y^2 \leqslant x$	3
5.	~~*Show*~~ $\bigwedge y(y^2 \leqslant x \rightarrow y \leqslant 1 \vee y \leqslant x)$	
6.	$y^2 \leqslant x \wedge \sim(y \leqslant 1 \vee y \leqslant x)$	
7.	$1 \leqslant y$	6
8.	$y \cdot 1 \leqslant y^2$	7
9.	$y \leqslant x$	8, 6
10.	$\sim y \leqslant x$	6

11.	~~Show~~ $1 \leqslant x \rightarrow \bigvee z \bigwedge y(y^2 \leqslant x \rightarrow y \leqslant z)$	
12.	$1 \leqslant x$	
13.	~~Show~~ $\bigwedge y(y^2 \leqslant x \rightarrow y \leqslant x)$	
	Elementary, from 5 and 12	
14.	$\bigvee z \bigwedge y(y^2 \leqslant x \rightarrow y \leqslant z)$	13
15.	~~Show~~ $x \leqslant 1 \rightarrow \bigvee z \bigwedge y(y^2 \leqslant x \rightarrow y \leqslant z)$	
	Similar to proof of 11	
16.	$\bigvee z \bigwedge y(y^2 \leqslant x \rightarrow y \leqslant z)$	11, 15, *T*21
17.	$\bigwedge y(y^2 \leqslant x \rightarrow y \leqslant z_0) \wedge \bigwedge u[\bigwedge y(y^2 \leqslant x \rightarrow y \leqslant u) \rightarrow z_0 \leqslant u]$	4, 16, *AS*19, EI
18.	~~Show~~ $1 \leqslant x \rightarrow 0 < z_0$	
19.	$1 \leqslant x$	
20.	$1^2 \leqslant x$	19
21.	$1 \leqslant z_0$	17(1st conjunct), 20
22.	$0 < z_0$	21
23.	~~Show~~ $x \leqslant 1 \rightarrow 0 < z_0$	
24.	$x \leqslant 1$	
25.	$x^2 \leqslant x$	24, 2
26.	$x \leqslant z_0$	17(1st conjunct), 25
27.	$0 < z_0$	2, 26
28.	$0 < z_0$	18, 23, *T*21
29.	~~Show~~ $x \leqslant {z_0}^2$	
30.	$\sim x \leqslant {z_0}^2$	
31.	${z_0}^2 < x$	30
32.	$\bigvee h\, h = \frac{1}{2} \cdot \left(1 - \frac{{z_0}^2}{x}\right)$	T329 of ch. V
33.	$h_0 = \frac{1}{2} \cdot \left(1 - \frac{{z_0}^2}{x}\right)$	32, EI
34.	~~Show~~ $0 < h_0 \wedge h_0 < 1$	
35.	$0 < \frac{{z_0}^2}{x} \wedge \frac{{z_0}^2}{x} < 1$	28, *T*72, 31, *T*99
36.	$-1 < -\frac{{z_0}^2}{x} \wedge -\frac{{z_0}^2}{x} < 0$	35, *T*85

37.	$0 < 1 - \frac{z_0^2}{x} \wedge 1 - \frac{z_0^2}{x} < 1$	36
38.	$0 < h_0 \wedge h_0 < \frac{1}{2}$	37, 33
39.	$0 < h_0 \wedge h_0 < 1$	38, *T*74, *T*75, *T*96
40.	~~*Show*~~ $\left(\frac{z_0}{1 - h_0}\right)^2 \leqslant x$	
41.	$\frac{z_0^2}{x} = 1 - \left(1 - \frac{z_0^2}{x}\right)$	
42.	$= 1 - 2h_0$	41, 33
43.	$1 - 2h_0 \leqslant 1 - 2h_0 + h_0^2$	*T*73
44.	$1 - 2h_0 \leqslant (1 - h_0)^2$	43, *T*62
45.	$\frac{z_0^2}{x} \leqslant (1 - h_0)^2$	42, 44
46.	$z_0^2 \leqslant x \cdot (1 - h_0)^2$	45, 2
47.	$0 < 1 - h_0$	34
48.	$0 < (1 - h_0)^2$	47, *T*72
49.	$\frac{z_0^2}{(1 - h_0)^2} \leqslant x$	46, 48, *T*97
50.	$\left(\frac{z_0}{1 - h_0}\right)^2 \leqslant x$	49, 47, *T*64
51.	$\frac{z_0}{1 - h_0} \leqslant z_0$	17(1st conjunct), 40
52.	$-h_0 < 0$	34
53.	$1 - h_0 < 1$	52
54.	$0 < 1 - h_0$	34
55.	$z_0 < \frac{z_0}{1 - h_0}$	54, 53, 28, *T*96
56.	$\sim z_0 < \frac{z_0}{1 - h_0}$	51
57.	~~*Show*~~ $z_0^2 \leqslant x$	
58.	$\sim z_0^2 \leqslant x$	
59.	$x < z_0^2$	58
60.	$h_1 = \frac{1}{2} \cdot \left(1 - \frac{x}{z_0^2}\right)$	T329 of ch. V, EI

61.	~~Show~~ $0 < h_1 \wedge h_1 < 1$	
62.	$0 < \frac{x}{z_0^2} \wedge \frac{x}{z_0^2} < 1$	2, 59, *T*99
63.	$-1 < -\frac{x}{z_0^2} \wedge -\frac{x}{z_0^2} < 0$	62, *T*85
64.	$0 < 1 - \frac{x}{z_0^2} \wedge 1 - \frac{x}{z_0^2} < 1$	63
65.	$0 < h_1 \wedge h_1 < \frac{1}{2}$	64, 60
66.	$0 < h_1 \wedge h_1 < 1$	65
67.	~~Show~~ $\bigwedge y(y^2 \leqslant x \to y \leqslant z_0 \cdot (1 - h_1))$	
68.	$y^2 \leqslant x$	
69.	$x = z_0^2 \cdot \frac{x}{z_0^2}$	28, *T*72
70.	$= z_0^2 \cdot \left(1 - \left(1 - \frac{x}{z_0^2}\right)\right)$	69
71.	$= z_0^2 \cdot (1 - 2h_1)$	70, 60
72.	$1 - 2h_1 \leqslant (1 - h_1)^2$	*T*73, *T*62
73.	$x \leqslant z_0^2 \cdot (1 - h_1)^2$	72, *T*71, 71
74.	$x \leqslant (z_0 \cdot (1 - h_1))^2$	73, *T*63
75.	$y^2 \leqslant (z_0 \cdot (1 - h_1))^2$	68, 74
76.	$0 < 1 - h_1$	61
77.	$0 \leqslant z_0 \cdot (1 - h_1)$	28, 76, *A*14
78.	$y \leqslant z_0 \cdot (1 - h_1)$	75, 77, *T*100
79.	$z_0 \leqslant z_0 \cdot (1 - h_1)$	17(2nd conjunct), 67
80.	$-h_1 < 0$	61
81.	$1 - h_1 < 1$	80
82.	$z_0 \cdot (1 - h_1) < z_0$	81, 28
83.	$\sim z_0 \cdot (1 - h_1) < z_0$	79
84.	$x = z_0^2$	29, 57, *T*19
85.	$\bigvee y\ x = y^2$	84

It is a simple consequence of *T*22 and *T*129 that a number is non-negative just in case it is a square:

*T*130 $0 \leqslant x \leftrightarrow \bigvee y\ x = y^2$

The following theorem, which follows immediately from *T*130, shows how '$\leqslant$' might have been defined in terms of '+' and '·'.

*T*131 $x \leqslant y \leftrightarrow \bigvee z\ x + z^2 = y$

For historical remarks pertaining to this chapter, see section 4 of chapter XI.

Chapter XI
Variable-binding operators

1. Definitions reconsidered. We turn now to the treatment, deferred from chapter X, of definitions of variable-binding operators. Roughly speaking, in order to define a nonlogical constant δ of degree $\langle i, m, n, p \rangle$, we must provide for each term or formula

$$\delta\alpha_1 \ldots \alpha_m \, \zeta_1 \ldots \zeta_n \, \phi_1 \ldots \phi_p$$

(where $\alpha_1, \ldots, \alpha_m$ are distinct variables, $\zeta_1, \ldots, \zeta_n$ are terms, and $\phi_1, \ldots, \phi_p$ are formulas) a synonymous term or formula not containing δ. To do this precisely, we shall make use of operation and predicate letters and *definitional schemata.*

For simplicity, consider for a moment the special case of constants of degree $\langle 1, 1, 0, 1 \rangle$. Let δ be a nonlogical constant of this kind, and L a class of nonlogical constants not containing δ. Then a *possible definitional schema* for δ *in terms of* L will be a formula of the form

$$\delta\alpha\pi\alpha \leftrightarrow \phi \quad ,$$

where α is a variable, π is a 1-place predicate letter not in L, and ϕ is a formula containing no free variables and no nonlogical constants beyond π and those in L.

More generally, consider an arbitrary nonlogical constant δ, and again let L be a class of nonlogical constants not containing δ.

If δ is a nonlogical constant of degree $\langle 0, m, n, p \rangle$, then a *possible definitional schema for* δ *in terms of* L will take the form

$$\delta\alpha_1 \ldots \alpha_m \, \zeta_1\alpha_1 \ldots \alpha_m \, \ldots \, \zeta_n\alpha_1 \ldots \alpha_m \, \pi_1\alpha_1 \ldots \alpha_m \, \ldots \, \pi_p\alpha_1 \ldots \alpha_m = \eta \quad .$$

Here $\alpha_1, \ldots, \alpha_m$ are to be distinct variables, $\zeta_1, \ldots, \zeta_n$ are to be distinct m-place operation letters, $\pi_1, \ldots, \pi_p$ are to be distinct m-place predicate letters, and η is to be a term containing no free variables, and no nonlogical constants beyond $\zeta_1, \ldots, \zeta_n, \pi_1, \ldots, \pi_p$, and those in L; we assume in addition that $\zeta_1, \ldots, \zeta_n, \pi_1, \ldots, \pi_p$ are not in L, and are distinct from δ.

If, on the other hand, δ is a nonlogical constant of degree $\langle 1, m, n, p \rangle$, then a *possible definitional schema for* δ *in terms of* L will be a formula

$$\delta\alpha_1 \ldots \alpha_m\, \zeta_1\alpha_1 \ldots \alpha_m\ \ldots\ \zeta_n\alpha_1 \ldots \alpha_m\, \pi_1\alpha_1 \ldots \alpha_m\ \ldots\ \pi_p\alpha_1 \ldots \alpha_m \leftrightarrow \phi \quad .$$

As before, $\alpha_1, \ldots, \alpha_m$ are to be distinct variables, $\zeta_1, \ldots, \zeta_n$ are to be distinct m-place operation letters, and $\pi_1, \ldots, \pi_p$ are to be distinct m-place predicate letters. In addition, ϕ is to be a formula containing no free variables, and no nonlogical constants beyond $\zeta_1, \ldots, \zeta_n, \pi_1, \ldots, \pi_p$, and those in L; again $\zeta_1, \ldots, \zeta_n, \pi_1, \ldots, \pi_p$ are to be distinct from δ and the members of L.

For example, a possible definitional schema for the operator 'lim' (mentioned on page 440) in terms of

$$0, <, -, |\ |$$

would be the following:

$$\lim n\, A(n) = \imath x \bigwedge z(0 < z \rightarrow \bigvee k \bigwedge n[N(n) \wedge k < n \rightarrow |A(n) - x| < z]) \quad .$$

(This schema in fact reflects customary mathematical usage and will be included in theories developed below.) As another example, consider the operator '$\overset{1}{\bigvee}$' (also mentioned on page 440). The following formula is a possible definitional schema for this constant in terms of the empty set of nonlogical constants:

$$\overset{1}{\bigvee} x F(x) \leftrightarrow \bigvee y \bigwedge x[F(x) \leftrightarrow x = y] \quad .$$

Observe that the notions just introduced comprehend the case in which δ is a predicate or operation symbol, which arises when $m = 0$. Thus we can dispense with the *possible definitions* of chapter X in favor of a uniform system of possible definitional schemata.

In order to accommodate the definitional introduction of variable-binding operators, we must modify the characterization of a *definitional extension* of a theory; we now use the notion of a possible definitional schema.

Indeed, a theory U is now said to be a *definitional extension* of a theory T if (i) U is an extension of T, and, for some D, (ii) D is a class of possible definitional schemata, in terms of the constants of T, for constants of U that are not constants of T, (iii) for each constant δ of U that is not a constant of T, there is in D some possible definitional schema for δ in terms of the constants of T, (iv) each constant of U that is not a constant of T occurs in at most one member of D, and (v) the axioms of U consist of the axioms of T together with all instances within U of members of D.

As an example, we may consider a theory T_3 that closely resembles the theory T_2 of chapter X (p. 468). The *constants of* T_3 are those of T_2, and the *axioms of* T_3 consist of those of the theory of real numbers, together with all instances within T_3 of the following formulas ('A' and 'B' are here to be 0-place operation letters):

*DS*1 $\quad A \neq B \leftrightarrow \sim A = B$

*DS*2 $\quad A < B \leftrightarrow A \leqslant B \wedge \sim A = B$

*DS*3	$2 = 1 + 1$
*DS*4	$A^2 = A \cdot A$
*DS*5	$\lvert A\rvert = \imath z[(0 \leqslant A \wedge z = A) \vee (\sim 0 \leqslant A \wedge z = -A)]$
*DS*6	$A - B = A + -B$
*DS*7	$\frac{A}{B} = A \cdot B^{-1}$
*DS*8	$N(A) \leftrightarrow I(A) \wedge 0 \leqslant A$
*DS*9	$R(A) \leftrightarrow \bigvee y \bigvee z[I(y) \wedge I(z) \wedge 0 \leqslant z \wedge \sim 0 = z \wedge A = y \cdot z^{-1}]$.

It is clear that the formulas *DS*1 – *DS*9 are possible definitional schemata in terms of the constants of the theory of real numbers, and hence that *T*3 is a definitional extension of that theory. Further, *T*3 is easily seen to be equivalent to *T*2. Accordingly, in developing *T*3 and its extensions, we may employ *T*1–*T*131 of chapter X.

(The construction of *T*3 illustrates a general principle: if *U* is a definitional extension of a theory *T* in the sense of chapter X, then there is a definitional extension of *T* in the present sense that is equivalent to *U*.)

Definitional extensions continue to enjoy the properties (1) – (4) mentioned on page 462.

2. The theory of convergence. We are now in a position to extend *T*3 by introducing definitions of variable-binding operators; it is essential for this purpose to employ possible definitional schemata and not merely possible definitions. Accordingly, we construct as follows a definitional extension *T*4 of *T*3. The constants of *T*4 are those of *T*3 together with the formula-maker '⇔', which is to have degree ⟨1, 1, 2, 0⟩, and the axioms of *T*4 consist of those of *T*3 together with all instances within *T*4 of the formula:

*DS*10 $$A(n) \underset{n}{\Leftrightarrow} B(n) \leftrightarrow \bigwedge z(0 < z \rightarrow \bigvee k \bigwedge n[N(n) \wedge k < n \rightarrow \lvert A(n) - B(n)\rvert < z])$$

(This symbolism departs from our official notational style in the direction of mathematical practice, which often introduces theoretically superfluous parentheses and which, generally speaking, requires the variables accompanying an operator to be written as subscripts. Strict adherence to the style of chapter X, section 1, would convert the left side of the biconditional *DS*10 into '⇔ *n* A*n* B*n*'.)

The formula

$$A(n) \underset{n}{\Leftrightarrow} B(n)$$

is read 'A(*n*) and B(*n*) converge (to one another, as *n* approaches infinity)'.

Intuitively, the terms 'A(n)' and 'B(n)' are regarded as representing two infinite sequences of numbers,

$$A(0),\ A(1), \ldots,\ A(n), \ldots$$

and

$$B(0),\ B(1), \ldots,\ B(n), \ldots \quad ;$$

according to *DS*10, these sequences are regarded as converging if, for any positive number z, there is a point beyond which the difference between any two corresponding terms of the two sequences is less than z.

The next two theorems give simple examples of convergence and non-convergence.

*T*132

1. ~~Show~~ $\frac{n^2 + 1}{n} \underset{n}{\Leftrightarrow} n$

2. ~~Show~~ $\bigwedge z\left(0 < z \rightarrow \bigvee k \bigwedge n\left[N(n) \wedge k < n \rightarrow \left|\frac{n^2+1}{n} - n\right| < z\right]\right)$

3. $0 < z$

4. ~~Show~~ $\bigwedge n\left[N(n) \wedge \frac{1}{z} < n \rightarrow \left|\frac{n^2+1}{n} - n\right| < z\right]$

5. $N(n) \wedge \frac{1}{z} < n$

6. $0 < n$ — 3, 5

7. $\frac{n^2+1}{n} - n = \frac{n^2}{n} + \frac{1}{n} - n$ — *T*67

8. $= n + \frac{1}{n} - n$ — 7, 6

9. $= \frac{1}{n}$ — 8

10. $0 < \frac{1}{n}$ — 6

11. $\left|\frac{1}{n}\right| = \frac{1}{n}$ — 10

12. $\left|\dfrac{n^2+1}{n} - n\right| = \dfrac{1}{n}$ 9, 11

13. $1 < n \cdot z$ 3, 5

14. $\dfrac{1}{n} < z$ 6, 13

15. $\left|\dfrac{n^2+1}{n} - n\right| < z$ 12, 14

16. $\bigvee k \bigwedge n\left[N(n) \wedge k < n \rightarrow \left|\dfrac{n^2+1}{n} - n\right| < z\right]$ 4, EG

17. $\dfrac{n^2+1}{n} \underset{n}{\Leftrightarrow} n$ 2, *DS*10

*T*133

1. ~~Show~~ $\sim n + 1 \underset{n}{\Leftrightarrow} n$

2. $n + 1 \underset{n}{\Leftrightarrow} n$
3. $\bigvee k \bigwedge n[N(n) \wedge k < n \rightarrow |n + 1 - n| < 1]$ *DS*10, *T*74
4. $\bigwedge n[N(n) \wedge k_0 < n \rightarrow |n + 1 - n| < 1]$ 3, EI
5. ~~Show~~ $0 \leqslant k_0 \rightarrow \bigvee n[N(n) \wedge k_0 < n]$

6. $0 \leqslant k_0$
7. $I(n_0) \wedge k_0 + 1 \leqslant n_0 \cdot 1$ *T*54, *A*10, EI
8. $k_0 < n_0$ 7
9. $N(n_0)$ 6, 7, 8
10. $\bigvee n[N(n) \wedge k_0 < n]$ 9, 8, EG

11. ~~Show~~ $k_0 < 0 \rightarrow \bigvee n[N(n) \wedge k_0 < n]$

12. $k_0 < 0$
13. $N(0)$ *T*122
14. $\bigvee n[N(n) \wedge k_0 < n]$ 12, 13, EG

15. $\bigvee n[N(n) \wedge k_0 < n]$ 5, 11
16. $N(n_1) \wedge k_0 < n_1$ 15, EI
17. $|n_1 + 1 - n_1| < 1$ 4, 16

18.	$n_1 + 1 - n_1 = 1$	
19.	$\|1\| < 1$	17, 18
20.	$1 < 1$	19
21.	$\sim 1 < 1$	*T*76

Nonlogical operators, like the logical operators '$\bigwedge$', '$\bigvee$', and 'ι', satisfy general principles of alphabetic variance and interchange. Particular cases of these principles are given in the next two theorem schemata. (By a *theorem schema* of T_4 is understood, as before (see p. 454 of chapter X), a formula containing some additional predicates or operation symbols beyond the constants of T_4 and such that all of its instances within T_4 are theorems of T_4. In showing particular formulas to be theorem schemata of T_4, we shall consider an extension T_4' of T_4 that contains the additional 1-place operation symbols 'C', 'C_1', 'D', 'D_1', and 'E', together with the 1-place predicate 'F' (which figures in *AS*19), and whose additional axioms are the instances within this enlarged vocabulary of *AS*19 and *DS*1–*DS*10. Then each theorem of T_4' will be a theorem schema of T_4.)

*TS*134 1. ~~Show~~ $C(n) \underset{n}{\Leftrightarrow} D(n) \leftrightarrow C(m) \underset{m}{\Leftrightarrow} D(m)$

2.	$C(n) \underset{n}{\Leftrightarrow} D(n) \leftrightarrow C(n) \underset{n}{\Leftrightarrow} D(n)$	
3.	$C(n) \underset{n}{\Leftrightarrow} D(n) \leftrightarrow C(m) \underset{m}{\Leftrightarrow} D(m)$	2, AV

*TS*135 1. ~~Show~~ $\bigwedge n\, C(n) = C_1(n) \wedge \bigwedge n\, D(n) = D_1(n) \rightarrow$
$[C(n) \underset{n}{\Leftrightarrow} D(n) \leftrightarrow C_1(n) \underset{n}{\Leftrightarrow} D_1(n)]$

2.	$\bigwedge n\, C(n) = C_1(n) \wedge \bigwedge n\, D(n) = D_1(n)$	
3.	$C(n) \underset{n}{\Leftrightarrow} D(n) \leftrightarrow C_1(n) \underset{n}{\Leftrightarrow} D(n)$	2, Int
4.	$C(n) \underset{n}{\Leftrightarrow} D(n) \leftrightarrow C_1(n) \underset{n}{\Leftrightarrow} D_1(n)$	2, Int, 3

According to the next three theorem schemata, the relation of convergence is an equivalence relation, that is, reflexive (*TS*136), symmetric (*TS*137), and transitive (*TS*138). The proofs of *TS*136 and *TS*137 are very simple, and are left to the reader.

*TS*136 $C(n) \underset{n}{\Leftrightarrow} C(n)$

*TS*137 $C(n) \underset{n}{\Leftrightarrow} D(n) \rightarrow D(n) \underset{n}{\Leftrightarrow} C(n)$

*TS*138

1. ~~*Show*~~ $C(n) \underset{n}{\Leftrightarrow} D(n) \wedge D(n) \underset{n}{\Leftrightarrow} E(n) \rightarrow C(n) \underset{n}{\Leftrightarrow} E(n)$
2. $C(n) \underset{n}{\Leftrightarrow} D(n) \wedge D(n) \underset{n}{\Leftrightarrow} E(n)$
3. ~~*Show*~~ $\bigwedge z(0 < z \rightarrow \bigvee k \bigwedge n[N(n) \wedge k < n \rightarrow |C(n) - E(n)| < z])$
4. $0 < z$
5. $0 < \frac{z}{2}$ — 4
6. $\bigwedge n\left[N(n) \wedge k_0 < n \rightarrow |C(n) - D(n)| < \frac{z}{2}\right]$ — 5, 2, *DS*10, EI
7. $\bigwedge n\left[N(n) \wedge k_1 < n \rightarrow |D(n) - E(n)| < \frac{z}{2}\right]$ — 5, 2, *DS*10, EI
8. ~~*Show*~~ $k_0 \leqslant k_1 \rightarrow \bigvee k \bigwedge n[N(n) \wedge k < n \rightarrow |C(n) - E(n)| < z]$
9. $k_0 \leqslant k_1$
10. ~~*Show*~~ $\bigwedge n[N(n) \wedge k_1 < n \rightarrow |C(n) - E(n)| < z]$
11. $N(n) \wedge k_1 < n$
12. $|C(n) - D(n)| < \frac{z}{2}$ — 6, 11, 9
13. $|D(n) - E(n)| < \frac{z}{2}$ — 7, 11
14. $|C(n) - D(n)| + |D(n) - E(n)| < z$ — 12, 13
15. $|C(n) - E(n)| < z$ — *T*113, 14
16. $\bigvee k \bigwedge n[N(n) \wedge k < n \rightarrow |C(n) - E(n)| < z]$ — 10, EG
17. ~~*Show*~~ $k_1 \leqslant k_0 \rightarrow \bigvee k \bigwedge n[N(n) \wedge k < n \rightarrow |C(n) - E(n)| < z]$

    Similar to derivation of line 8

18. $\bigvee k \bigwedge n[N(n) \wedge k < n \rightarrow |C(n) - E(n)| < z]$ — 8, 17
19. $C(n) \underset{n}{\Leftrightarrow} E(n)$ — 3, *DS*10

The relation of convergence is not only an equivalence relation but also, according to the next theorem schema, a congruence relation under the operation of addition. The proof of *TS*139, which is similar to that of *TS*138, we leave to the reader.

*TS*139 $$\mathrm{C}(n) \underset{n}{\Leftrightarrow} \mathrm{C_1}(n) \wedge \mathrm{D}(n) \underset{n}{\Leftrightarrow} \mathrm{D_1}(n) \rightarrow \mathrm{C}(n) + \mathrm{D}(n) \underset{n}{\Leftrightarrow} \mathrm{C_1}(n) + \mathrm{D_1}(n)$$

If two sequences are ultimately identical (that is, differ only in an initial segment), then they converge:

*TS*140 $$\bigvee k \bigwedge n[\mathrm{N}(n) \wedge k < n \rightarrow \mathrm{C}(n) = \mathrm{D}(n)] \rightarrow \mathrm{C}(n) \underset{n}{\Leftrightarrow} \mathrm{D}(n)$$

This is a simple consequence of *DS*10.

The next theorem schema is a lemma for *TS*142; it asserts that if $\mathrm{E}(n)$ is a strictly increasing sequence of natural numbers, then, for every natural number n, $n \leqslant \mathrm{E}(n)$.

*TS*141 1. ~~Show~~ $\bigwedge n \bigwedge m[\mathrm{N}(n) \wedge \mathrm{N}(m) \wedge n < m \rightarrow \mathrm{E}(n) < \mathrm{E}(m)] \wedge \bigwedge n[\mathrm{N}(n) \rightarrow \mathrm{N}(\mathrm{E}(n))] \rightarrow \bigwedge n[\mathrm{N}(n) \rightarrow n \leqslant \mathrm{E}(n)]$

2.	$\bigwedge n \bigwedge m[\mathrm{N}(n) \wedge \mathrm{N}(m) \wedge n < m \rightarrow \mathrm{E}(n) < \mathrm{E}(m)] \wedge \bigwedge n[\mathrm{N}(n) \rightarrow \mathrm{N}(\mathrm{E}(n))]$	
3.	$0 \leqslant \mathrm{E}(0)$	2, *DS*8
4.	~~Show~~ $\bigwedge n[\mathrm{N}(n) \wedge n \leqslant \mathrm{E}(n) \rightarrow n + 1 \leqslant \mathrm{E}(n + 1)]$	
5.	$\mathrm{N}(n) \wedge n \leqslant \mathrm{E}(n)$	
6.	$n < n + 1$	*T*27, *T*80
7.	$\mathrm{E}(n) < \mathrm{E}(n + 1)$	5, 6, 2
8.	$n < \mathrm{E}(n + 1)$	5, 7
9.	$\mathrm{I}(n) \wedge \mathrm{I}(\mathrm{E}(n + 1))$	5, *DS*8, *A*17, 2
10.	$n + 1 \leqslant \mathrm{E}(n + 1)$	9, 8, *T*55
11.	$\bigwedge n[N(n) \rightarrow n \leqslant \mathrm{E}(n)]$	3, 4, *TS*121

According to *TS*142, if two sequences converge, then so do any two corresponding infinite sub-sequences.

*TS*142 1. ~~Show~~ $[\mathrm{C}(n) \underset{n}{\Leftrightarrow} \mathrm{D}(n)] \wedge \bigwedge n \bigwedge m[\mathrm{N}(n) \wedge \mathrm{N}(m) \wedge n < m \rightarrow \mathrm{E}(n) < \mathrm{E}(m)] \wedge \bigwedge n[\mathrm{N}(n) \rightarrow \mathrm{N}(\mathrm{E}(n))] \rightarrow [\mathrm{C}(\mathrm{E}(n)) \underset{n}{\Leftrightarrow} \mathrm{D}(\mathrm{E}(n))]$

2.	$[C(n) \underset{n}{\Leftrightarrow} D(n)] \wedge \bigwedge n \bigwedge m[N(n) \wedge N(m) \wedge n < m \rightarrow E(n) < E(m)] \wedge \bigwedge n[N(n) \rightarrow N(E(n))]$	
3.	~~Show~~ $\bigwedge z(0 < z \rightarrow \bigvee k \bigwedge n[N(n) \wedge k < n \rightarrow \lvert C(E(n)) - D(E(n))\rvert < z])$	
4.	$0 < z$	
5.	$\bigwedge n[N(n) \wedge k_0 < n \rightarrow \lvert C(n) - D(n)\rvert < z]$	2 (1st conjunct), *DS*10, 4, EI
6.	~~Show~~ $\bigwedge n[N(n) \wedge k_0 < n \rightarrow \lvert C(E(n)) - D(E(n))\rvert < z]$	
7.	$N(n) \wedge k_0 < n$	
8.	$n \leqslant E(n)$	2, *TS*141, 7
9.	$k_0 < E(n)$	7, 8
10.	$N(E(n))$	2, 7
11.	$\lvert C(E(n)) - D(E(n))\rvert < z$	5, 10, 9
12.	$\bigvee k \bigwedge n[N(n) \wedge k < n \rightarrow \lvert C(E(n)) - D(E(n))\rvert < z]$	6, EG
13.	$C(E(n)) \underset{n}{\Leftrightarrow} D(E(n))$	3, *DS*10

We now consider the familiar notion of the *convergence of a sequence to a number*, which emerges as a special case of the convergence of two sequences. *TS*143, which is simply an instance of *DS*10, gives a necessary and sufficient condition for a sequence to converge to a number x.

*TS*143 $C(n) \underset{n}{\Leftrightarrow} x \leftrightarrow \bigwedge z(0 < z \rightarrow \bigvee k \bigwedge n[N(n) \wedge k < n \rightarrow \lvert C(n) - x\rvert < z])$

Thus the sequence

$$C(0), C(1), \ldots, C(n), \ldots$$

is regarded as converging to the number x if, for any preassigned interval surrounding x (no matter how small), all terms occurring sufficiently late in the sequence lie within that interval.

We state the following theorems as examples of convergence to a number.

*T*144 $$\frac{n+1}{n} \underset{n}{\Leftrightarrow} 1$$

*T*145 $\quad \frac{1}{n} \underset{n}{\Leftrightarrow} 0$

The infinite sequences involved in these two theorems are respectively

$$\frac{1}{0}, \frac{2}{1}, \frac{3}{2}, \frac{4}{3}, \ldots$$

and

$$\frac{1}{0}, \frac{1}{1}, \frac{1}{2}, \frac{1}{3}, \ldots \quad .$$

The assertions *T*144 and *T*145 are thus intuitively true. (The fact that our axioms do not determine the value of $\frac{1}{0}$ does not affect the truth of *T*144 and *T*145; indeed, questions of convergence are always independent of the initial terms of the sequences involved.) We prove *T*144 and leave *T*145 to the reader.

1. ~~Show~~ $\frac{n+1}{n} \underset{n}{\Leftrightarrow} 1$

2. ~~Show~~ $\bigwedge z\Big(0 < z \to \bigvee k \bigwedge n\Big[\mathrm{N}(n) \wedge k < n \to \left|\frac{n+1}{n} - 1\right| < z\Big]\Big)$

3. $0 < z$

4. ~~Show~~ $\bigwedge n\left[\mathrm{N}(n) \wedge \frac{1}{z} < n \to \left|\frac{n+1}{n} - 1\right| < z\right]$

5. $\mathrm{N}(n) \wedge \frac{1}{z} < n$

6. $\frac{n+1}{n} - 1 = \frac{n}{n} + \frac{1}{n} - 1$ $\qquad$ *T*67

7. $\qquad = \frac{1}{n}$ $\qquad$ 6

8. $0 < n$ $\qquad$ 3, 5

9. $0 < \frac{1}{n}$ $\qquad$ 8

10. $\left|\frac{1}{n}\right| = \frac{1}{n}$ 9

11. $\left|\frac{n+1}{n} - 1\right| = \frac{1}{n}$ 7, 10

12. $1 < n \cdot z$ 3, 5

13. $\frac{1}{n} < z$ 8, 12

14. $\left|\frac{n+1}{n} - 1\right| < z$ 13, 11

15. $\bigvee k \bigwedge n \left[N(n) \wedge k < n \rightarrow \left|\frac{n+1}{n} - 1\right| < z \right]$ 4, EG

16. $\frac{n+1}{n} \underset{n}{\Leftrightarrow} 1$ 2, *TS*143

If two numbers converge, then they are identical:

*T*146 $x \underset{n}{\Leftrightarrow} y \rightarrow x = y$

An immediate corollary of *T*146, *TS*137, and *TS*138 is that a sequence can converge to at most one number:

*TS*147 $C(n) \underset{n}{\Leftrightarrow} x \wedge C(n) \underset{n}{\Leftrightarrow} y \rightarrow x = y$

Some sequences do not converge to any number; for example:

*T*148 $\sim \bigvee x\, n \underset{n}{\Leftrightarrow} x$

Proofs concerning specific instances of convergence are simplified by *TS*134 – *TS*139; for example:

*T*149 1. ~~Show~~ $\frac{n(n+1)}{n^2} \underset{n}{\Leftrightarrow} 1$

2. $1 \underset{n}{\Leftrightarrow} 1$ *TS*136

3. $\frac{1}{n} \underset{n}{\Leftrightarrow} 0$ *T*145

4. $1 + \frac{1}{n} \underset{n}{\Leftrightarrow} 1 + 0$ 2, 3, *TS*139

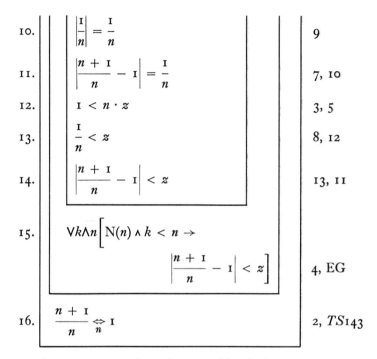

5. $1 + \frac{1}{n} \underset{n}{\Leftrightarrow} 1$ 4, *A*3, LL

6. ~~Show~~ $\bigwedge n(N(n) \wedge 0 < n \rightarrow \frac{n(n+1)}{n^2} = 1 + \frac{1}{n}$

7. $N(n) \wedge 0 < n$

8. $\frac{n(n+1)}{n^2} = \frac{n^2}{n^2} + \frac{n}{n^2}$ *A*9

9. $= 1 + \frac{1}{n}$ 8, 7

10. $\frac{n(n+1)}{n^2} \underset{n}{\Leftrightarrow} 1$ 5, 6, *TS*140

The relation of convergence is not a congruence relation under the operation of multiplication. For example,

$$\frac{1}{n} \underset{n}{\Leftrightarrow} 0$$

and

$$n \underset{n}{\Leftrightarrow} n \quad ;$$

yet it is not the case that

$$\frac{1}{n} \cdot n \underset{n}{\Leftrightarrow} 0 \cdot n \quad ,$$

for if it were, we should have

$$1 \underset{n}{\Leftrightarrow} 0 \quad .$$

However, if two sequences converge to numbers, their product converges to the product of those numbers.

*TS*150 1. ~~Show~~ $C(n) \underset{n}{\Leftrightarrow} x \wedge D(n) \underset{n}{\Leftrightarrow} y \rightarrow C(n) \cdot D(n) \underset{n}{\Leftrightarrow} x \cdot y$

2. $C(n) \underset{n}{\Leftrightarrow} x \wedge D(n) \underset{n}{\Leftrightarrow} y$

3. ~~Show~~ $\bigwedge z(0 < z \rightarrow \bigvee k \bigwedge n[N(n) \wedge k < n \rightarrow |(C(n) \cdot D(n)) - (x \cdot y)| < z])$

4.	$0 < z$	
5.	$0 < \frac{z}{2(\lvert y \rvert + 1)}$	4
6.	$\bigwedge n\left[N(n) \wedge k_0 < n \rightarrow \lvert C(n) - x \rvert < \frac{z}{2(\lvert y \rvert + 1)}\right]$	2, *DS*10, 5, EI
7.	$0 < \frac{z}{2\lvert x \rvert + z}$	4
8.	$\bigwedge n\left[N(n) \wedge k_1 < n \rightarrow \lvert D(n) - y \rvert < \frac{z}{2\lvert x \rvert + z}\right]$	2, *DS*10, 7, EI
9.	~~Show~~ $k_0 \leqslant k_1 \rightarrow \bigvee k \bigwedge n[N(n) \wedge k < n \rightarrow \lvert (C(n) \cdot D(n)) - (x \cdot y) \rvert < z]$	
10.	$k_0 \leqslant k_1$	
11.	~~Show~~ $\bigwedge n[N(n) \wedge k_1 < n \rightarrow \lvert (C(n) \cdot D(n)) - (x \cdot y) \rvert < z]$	
12.	$N(n) \wedge k_1 < n$	
13.	$\lvert C(n) - x \rvert < \frac{z}{2(\lvert y \rvert + 1)}$	10, 12, 6
14.	$\lvert y \cdot (C(n) - x) \rvert \leqslant \lvert y \rvert \cdot \frac{z}{2(\lvert y \rvert + 1)}$	13, *T*104, *T*116
15.	$\lvert D(n) - y \rvert < \frac{z}{2\lvert x \rvert + z}$	12, 8
16.	$\lvert C(n) \cdot (D(n) - y) \rvert \leqslant \lvert C(n) \rvert \cdot \frac{z}{2\lvert x \rvert + z}$	15, *T*104, *T*116
17.	$2 \leqslant 2(\lvert y \rvert + 1)$	*T*106
18.	$\frac{z}{2(\lvert y \rvert + 1)} \leqslant \frac{z}{2}$	17, 4, *T*95

19.	$\lvert x\rvert + \lvert \mathrm{C}(n) - x\rvert < \lvert x\rvert + \frac{z}{2}$	13, 18
20.	$\mathrm{C}(n) < \lvert x\rvert + \frac{z}{2}$	19, *T*112
21.	$\lvert \mathrm{C}(n)\cdot(\mathrm{D}(n) - y)\rvert < \left(\lvert x\rvert + \frac{z}{2}\right)\cdot\left(\frac{z}{2\lvert x\rvert + z}\right)$	7, 20, 16
22.	$\lvert \mathrm{C}(n)\cdot(\mathrm{D}(n) - y)\rvert + \lvert y\cdot(\mathrm{C}(n) - x)\rvert < \left[\left(\lvert x\rvert + \frac{z}{2}\right)\cdot\left(\frac{z}{2\lvert x\rvert + z}\right)\right] + \left[\lvert y\rvert\cdot\frac{z}{2(\lvert y\rvert + 1)}\right]$	14, 21
23.	$(\mathrm{C}(n)\cdot\mathrm{D}(n)) - (x\cdot y) = (\mathrm{C}(n)\cdot(\mathrm{D}(n) - y)) + (y\cdot(\mathrm{C}(n) - x))$	A9
24.	$\lvert(\mathrm{C}(n)\cdot\mathrm{D}(n)) - (x\cdot y)\rvert < \left[\left(\lvert x\rvert + \frac{z}{2}\right)\cdot\left(\frac{z}{2\lvert x\rvert + z}\right)\right] + \left(\lvert y\rvert\cdot\frac{z}{2(\lvert y\rvert + 1)}\right)$	23, *T*112, 22
25.	$\frac{\lvert y\rvert}{\lvert y\rvert + 1} < 1$	*T*106, *T*27, *T*80, *T*99
26.	$\lvert y\rvert\cdot\frac{z}{2(\lvert y\rvert + 1)} < \frac{z}{2}$	4, 25
27.	$\lvert x\rvert + \frac{z}{2} = \frac{2\lvert x\rvert + z}{2}$	*T*67, *T*68
28.	$\left(\lvert x\rvert + \frac{z}{2}\right)\cdot\left(\frac{z}{2\lvert x\rvert + z}\right) = \frac{z}{2}$	4, *T*106, 27
29.	$\lvert(\mathrm{C}(n)\cdot\mathrm{D}(n)) - (x\cdot y)\rvert < \frac{z}{2} + \frac{z}{2}$	24, 26, 28

30. $|(C(n) \cdot D(n)) - (x \cdot y)| < z$ — 29, *T*65

31. $\bigvee k \bigwedge n[N(n) \wedge k < n \rightarrow |(C(n) \cdot D(n)) - (x \cdot y)| < z]$ — 11, EG

32. ~~Show~~ $k_1 \leqslant k_0 \rightarrow \bigvee k \bigwedge n[N(n) \wedge k < n \rightarrow |(C(n) \cdot D(n)) - (x \cdot y)| < z]$

Similar to derivation of line 9

33. $\bigvee k \bigwedge n[N(n) \wedge k < n \rightarrow |(C(n) \cdot D(n)) - (x \cdot y)| < z]$ — 9, 32

34. $C(n) \cdot D(n) \underset{n}{\Leftrightarrow} x \cdot y$ — 3, *DS*10

*TS*151 and *TS*152 have straightforward proofs, which are left to the reader. The latter provides a means of expressing the convergence of two sequences in terms of the convergence of a sequence to a number.

*TS*151 $C(n) \underset{n}{\Leftrightarrow} x \wedge D(n) \underset{n}{\Leftrightarrow} y \wedge \bigvee k \bigwedge n[N(n) \wedge k < n \rightarrow C(n) \leqslant D(n)] \rightarrow x \leqslant y$

*TS*152 $C(n) \underset{n}{\Leftrightarrow} D(n) \leftrightarrow C(n) - D(n) \underset{n}{\Leftrightarrow} 0$

The last two principles of this section depend very heavily on the Continuity Schema. *TS*153 asserts that every nondecreasing sequence whose terms have an upper bound converges to a number; *TS*154 is the analogue for nonincreasing sequences whose terms have a lower bound, and can be derived simply from *TS*153.

*TS*153 1. ~~Show~~ $\bigwedge n \bigwedge m[N(n) \wedge N(m) \wedge n \leqslant m \rightarrow C(n) \leqslant C(m)] \wedge \bigvee y \bigwedge n[N(n) \rightarrow C(n) \leqslant y] \rightarrow \bigvee z\, C(n) \underset{n}{\Leftrightarrow} z$

2. $\bigwedge n \bigwedge m[N(n) \wedge N(m) \wedge n \leqslant m \rightarrow C(n) \leqslant C(m)] \wedge \bigvee y \bigwedge n[N(n) \rightarrow C(n) \leqslant y]$

3. $\bigvee m \bigvee n[N(n) \wedge m = C(n)]$ — T122

4. ~~Show~~ $\bigvee y \bigwedge m(\bigvee n[N(n) \wedge m = C(n)] \rightarrow m \leqslant y)$

Elementary, using 2nd conjunct of 2

5.	$\bigwedge m(\bigvee n[N(n) \wedge m = C(n)] \rightarrow m \leqslant z_0) \wedge \bigwedge y[\bigwedge m(\bigvee n[N(n) \wedge m = C(n)] \rightarrow m \leqslant y) \rightarrow z_0 \leqslant y]$	3, 4, *AS*19, EI
6.	~~Show~~ $\bigwedge z[0 < z \rightarrow \bigvee k \bigwedge n(N(n) \wedge k < n \rightarrow \lvert C(n) - z_0 \rvert < z)]$	
7.	$0 < z$	
8.	$\sim z_0 \leqslant z_0 - z$	7
9.	$\bigwedge m(\bigvee n[N(n) \wedge m = C(n)] \rightarrow m \leqslant z_0 - z) \rightarrow z_0 \leqslant z_0 - z$	5 (2nd conjunct)
10.	$\sim(\bigvee n[N(n) \wedge m_0 = C(n)] \rightarrow m_0 \leqslant z_0 - z)$	8, 9, EI
11.	$N(n_0) \wedge m_0 = C(n_0) \wedge z_0 - z < m_0$	10, EI
12.	~~Show~~ $\bigwedge n(N(n) \wedge n_0 < n \rightarrow \lvert C(n) - z_0 \rvert < z)$	
13.	$N(n) \wedge n_0 < n$	
14.	$C(n_0) \leqslant C(n)$	11, 13, 2 (1st conjunct)
15.	$z_0 - z < C(n)$	11, 14
16.	$C(n) \leqslant z_0$	13, 5 (1st conjunct)
17.	$C(n) < z_0 + z$	7, 16
18.	$\lvert C(n) - z_0 \rvert < z$	15, 17, *T*118, *T*115
19.	$\bigvee k \bigwedge n(N(n) \wedge k < n \rightarrow \lvert C(n) - z_0 \rvert < z)$	12, EG
20.	$\bigvee z\, C(n) \underset{n}{\Leftrightarrow} z$	6, *TS*143, EG

*TS*154 $\bigwedge n \bigwedge m[N(n) \wedge N(m) \wedge n \leqslant m \rightarrow C(m) \leqslant C(n)] \wedge \bigvee y \bigwedge n[N(n) \rightarrow y \leqslant C(n)] \rightarrow \bigvee z\, C(n) \underset{n}{\Leftrightarrow} z$

3. A sketch of further developments. The theory $T4$, with its definitional extensions, can be identified with what is generally called *differential calculus*. We offer, in partial justification of this claim, definitions of four of the most fundamental concepts in this subject.

If the sequence $A(n)$ converges to a number x, this number is called the limit of $A(n)$ as n approaches infinity. Accordingly, the mathematical notion of a limit at infinity may be introduced by the following definitional schema:

$$DS11 \qquad \lim_n A(n) = \imath x\, A(n) \underset{n}{\Leftrightarrow} x$$

(A more customary notation for '$\lim_n A(n)$' is '$\lim_{n\to\infty} A(n)$'.)

By $T148$ it is clear that the definite description on the right side of $DS11$ is not always proper; but if the sequence represented by '$A(n)$' converges to some number, then by $TS147$ the definite description is proper. The basic theorems concerning limits at infinity have essentially been obtained in the previous section; for example, $T144$, $T145$, and $TS150$ can be respectively expressed as follows:

$$\lim_n \frac{n+1}{n} = 1$$

$$\lim_n \frac{1}{n} = 0$$

$$\bigvee x\, C(n) \underset{n}{\Leftrightarrow} x \wedge \bigvee y\, D(n) \underset{n}{\Leftrightarrow} y \rightarrow$$

$$\lim_n [C(n) \cdot D(n)] = [\lim_n C(n)] \cdot [\lim_n D(n)] \quad .$$

Let '$A(x)$' represent any term of $T4$, for instance, '$(x^2 + 1)$'. Then, for each value of 'x' among the real numbers, the corresponding value of '$A(x)$' will also be a real number. It may happen that as the values of 'x' approach a fixed number l, the corresponding values of '$A(x)$' will also approach some number. In this case, we denote the latter number by

$$\lim_{x\to l} A(x) \quad ,$$

which is read 'the limit of $A(x)$ as x approaches l'. Thus, for example, choosing l as 2 and '$A(x)$' as the term '$(x^2 + 1)$', we have

$$\lim_{x\to 2} (x^2 + 1) = 5 \quad .$$

Let us examine the situation somewhat more carefully. We say that a number u is the limit of $A(x)$ as x approaches l if the values of '$A(x)$' can be brought as close to u as we wish by bringing the values of 'x' sufficiently close to l (without actually taking l itself as a value for 'x'). Thus, within T_4, the notion can be characterized as follows:

$$(1)\qquad \lim_{x\to l} A(x) = \imath u \bigwedge z(0 < z \to \bigvee y[0 < y \wedge \bigwedge x(0 < |x - l| \wedge |x - l| < y \to |A(x) - u| < z)])$$

Strictly speaking, the formula (1) is not a possible definitional schema. For simplicity, in section 2 of this chapter we excluded free variables from appearing in definitional schemata, and in (1) the variable 'l' is free. But the effect of (1) can be achieved by the following definitional schema, which introduces a constant '$\underset{\to}{\lim}$' of degree $\langle 0, 1, 2, 0\rangle$:

$$DS12\qquad \lim_{x\to B(x)} A(x) = \imath u \bigwedge z(0 < z \to \bigvee y[0 < y \wedge \bigwedge x(0 < |x - B(0)| \wedge |x - B(0)| < y \to |A(x) - u| < z)])$$

Then (1) is an instance of $DS12$ and can be used instead of the latter in developing the mathematical theory of limits at a point.

To say that $A(x)$ is continuous at a number a is to say that the number $A(a)$ is the limit of $A(x)$ as x approaches a; recalling (1), we see that the condition of continuity can be expressed as follows:

$$(2)\qquad \underset{x}{\mathrm{Cont}}\,[A(x), a] \leftrightarrow \bigwedge z(0 < z \to \bigvee y[0 < y \wedge \bigwedge x(0 < |x - a| \wedge |x - a| < y \to |A(x) - A(a)| < z)])$$

Thus we regard 'Cont' as an operator of degree $\langle 1, 1, 2, 0\rangle$. On the basis of (2) it is a simple matter to show that, for example,

$$\bigwedge a\, \underset{x}{\mathrm{Cont}}\,[2 \cdot x + 1, a] \quad ,$$

$$\sim \underset{x}{\mathrm{Cont}}\left[\frac{1}{x}, 0\right] \quad ,$$

$$\underset{x}{\mathrm{Cont}}\,[\imath y[I(x) \wedge y = 1) \vee (\sim I(x) \wedge y = 0)], a] \leftrightarrow \sim I(a) \quad .$$

Let us for the moment identify real numbers with instants of time. If $A(x)$ is understood as the distance at the instant x of a certain object from an initial position, and the object is assumed to be moving in a straight line, then the derivative of $A(x)$ at a (or $\underset{x}{\mathrm{Der}}\,[A(x), a]$) will be defined in such a way as to be the velocity of the object at the instant a. To arrive at a definition of the derivative, we consider first the familiar procedure for computing average velocities: the average velocity of an object, between two instants a and b, is the distance traveled in the interval (which may be positive or negative depending on the direction of motion), divided by the elapsed time. Thus we can characterize average velocity as follows:

$$(3)\qquad \underset{x}{\mathrm{Av}}\,[A(x), a, b] = \frac{A(b) - A(a)}{b - a} \quad ;$$

here 'Av' is to be an operator of degree ⟨0, 1, 3, 0⟩. The velocity at an instant *a* is simply the limit of the approximations obtained by taking average velocities over smaller and smaller time-intervals surrounding *a*. Thus we have the following characterization of the derivative (which in this case is interpreted as the instantaneous velocity):

$$(4) \qquad \underset{x}{\mathrm{Der}}\,[\mathrm{A}(x), a] = \lim_{h \to 0} \underset{x}{\mathrm{Av}}\,[\mathrm{A}(x), a - h, a + h]] \quad ;$$

here 'Der' is an operator of degree ⟨0, 1, 2, 0⟩. There are of course other interpretations of the derivative, depending on the interpretation assigned to 'A(x)'. Many of them have the common feature that $\underset{x}{\mathrm{Der}}\,[\mathrm{A}(x), a]$ is the *rate of change* of the values of A(x) at the instant *a*.

The formulas (2) – (4) correspond, like (1), to definitional schemata, which we may call *DS*13–*DS*15. By T_5 we shall understand the definitional extension of T_4 obtained by adding the instances of *DS*11 – *DS*14, and by T_6 the definitional extension of T_5 obtained by adding the instances of *DS*15.

The passage from differential to integral calculus is achieved by adding to T_6 the general notion of *finite summation*, that is, the operation that associates with any numbers A(0), . . . , A(n − 1), the sum of A(0), . . . , A(n − 1). This sum is usually denoted by

$$\mathrm{A}(0) + \ldots + \mathrm{A}(n - 1)$$

or

$$\sum_{i=0}^{n-1} \mathrm{A}(i) \quad ;$$

our notation will be officially

$$(5) \qquad \sum i\, n\, \mathrm{A}(i) \quad ,$$

and informally

$$(6) \qquad \sum_{i}^{n} \mathrm{A}(i) \quad :$$

We shall regard 'Σ' as a constant of degree ⟨0, 1, 2, 0⟩; thus the expressions (5) and (6) are terms in which the variable 'i' is bound and the variable 'n' is free. 'Σ' may most conveniently be introduced by two new axioms, neither of which has definitional form. Accordingly, T_7, or *integral calculus*, is to be that extension of T_6 which is obtained by adding 'Σ' to the constants of T_6 and all instances (within the present theory) of the following schemata to the axioms of T_6;

$$AS20 \qquad \sum_{i}^{0} \mathrm{A}(i) = 0$$

$$AS21 \qquad \mathrm{N}(n) \rightarrow \sum_{i}^{n+1} \mathrm{A}(i) = \left[\sum_{i}^{n} \mathrm{A}(i)\right] + \mathrm{A}(n) \quad .$$

*AS*20 and *AS*21 constitute the usual so-called 'recursive definition' of 'Σ', but it should be observed that T_7 is not a definitional extension of T_6. 'Σ' *could*, however, have been introduced by definition. In other words, there is a definitional extension of T_6 having *AS*20 and *AS*21 as theorem schemata (see Montague [3]). But the construction of the necessary definitions is rather involved, and relies on properties of the real numbers deeper than those considered here.

Before turning to the integral, it is convenient to introduce notation for the least upper bound and the greatest lower bound of a set of real numbers; we use

$$\sup_x \mathrm{F}(x)$$

and

$$\inf_x \mathrm{F}(x) \quad ,$$

after the Latin '*supremum*' and '*infimum*', to denote respectively the least upper bound and the greatest lower bound of the set of all objects having the property F. (The reader will recall from chapter X the conditions under which such bounds exist.) We regard 'sup' and 'inf' as operators of degree ⟨0, 1, 0, 1⟩ and introduce them by the following definitional schemata:

*DS*16 $$\sup_x \mathrm{F}(x) = \imath z[\bigwedge x(\mathrm{F}(x) \rightarrow x \leqslant z) \wedge \bigwedge y(\bigwedge x[\mathrm{F}(x) \rightarrow x \leqslant y] \rightarrow z \leqslant y)]$$

*DS*17 $$\inf_x \mathrm{F}(x) = \imath z[\bigwedge x(\mathrm{F}(x) \rightarrow z \leqslant x) \wedge \bigwedge y(\bigwedge x[\mathrm{F}(x) \rightarrow y \leqslant x] \rightarrow y \leqslant z)]$$

By T_8 we shall understand the definitional extension of T_7 obtained by adding the instances of *DS*16 and *DS*17.

One purpose of the integral is to assign numerical measures to such areas as that shaded below.

FIGURE I

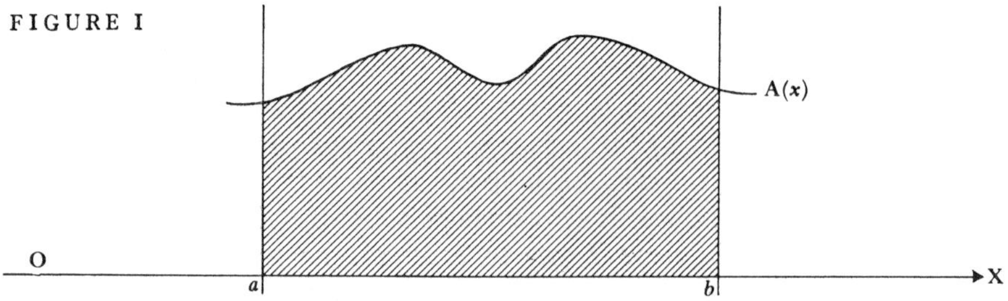

In this figure the line marked 'X' is called the X-*axis*. Each of its points is identified with a real number, in particular, with the distance (in some fixed system of units) of that point from the point marked 'O'. The curve lying above the X-axis is assumed to satisfy the following description: for any point x of the X-axis, the length of the segment joining x to the curve and perpendicular to the X-axis is the number $A(x)$. In this sense we may speak of the curve as given by the term '$A(x)$'. The shaded area may then be described as that enclosed by the X-axis, the perpendiculars to it at the points a and b, and the curve given by '$A(x)$'.

An approximation to the shaded area can be computed in the following way: divide the segment of the X-axis between a and b into three equal parts. For each of these parts, construct the largest possible rectangle with that part as base which lies completely beneath the curve. Then compute the total area of the three rectangles so obtained. In this way we arrive at the doubly shaded area in the following figure.

FIGURE II

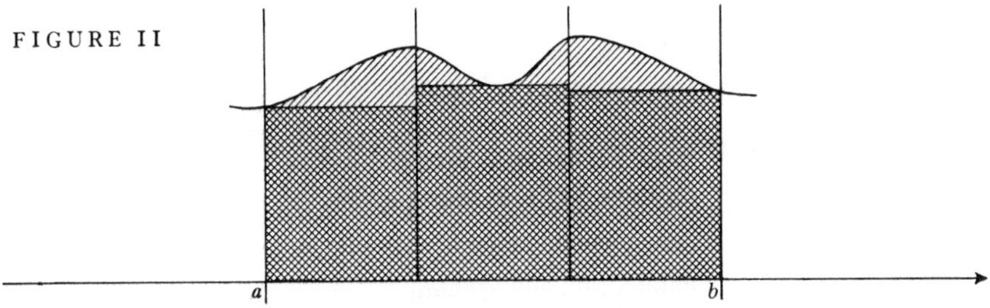

In the light of the familiar definition of area for rectilinear figures, it is seen that the doubly shaded area is given by the number

$$(7)\quad \frac{b-a}{3}\cdot\inf_{y}\bigvee x\left[A(x)=y\wedge a\leqslant x\wedge x\leqslant a+\frac{b-a}{3}\right]+$$
$$\frac{b-a}{3}\cdot\inf_{y}\bigvee x\left[A(x)=y\wedge a+\frac{b-a}{3}\leqslant x\wedge x\leqslant a+2\cdot\frac{b-a}{3}\right]+$$
$$\frac{b-a}{3}\cdot\inf_{y}\bigvee x\left[A(x)=y\wedge a+2\cdot\frac{b-a}{3}\leqslant x\wedge x\leqslant a+3\cdot\frac{b-a}{3}\right].$$

Now this approximation is not very close, but it can be improved by increasing the number of subdivisions of the interval between a and b (and hence of inscribed rectangles). For instance, if we consider six subdivisions, we arrive at the approximation in Figure III.

FIGURE III

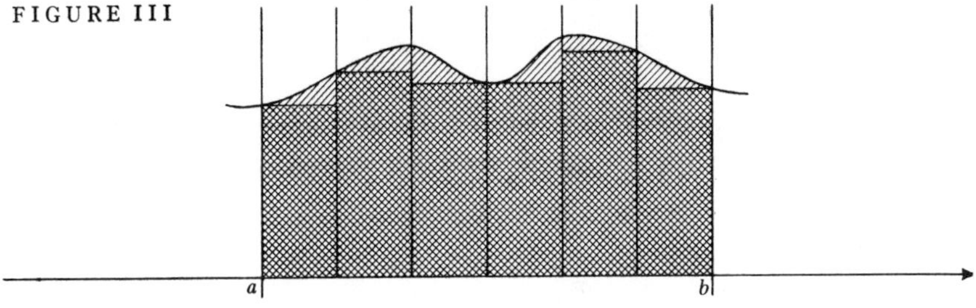

On the model of (7) above, and with the aid of 'Σ', we can express in general the area of the *inscribed approximation* resulting from n subdivisions; it will be the number

$$\sum_{i}^{n}\left(\frac{b-a}{n}\cdot \inf_{y} \forall x\left[A(x) = y \wedge a + i\cdot\frac{b-a}{n} \leqslant x \wedge x \leqslant a + (i+1)\cdot\frac{b-a}{n}\right]\right).$$

In a completely analogous way, we can obtain a family of *circumscribed* rectilinear approximations to the desired area. For instance, in the case of four subdivisions, we obtain the dotted area below.

FIGURE IV

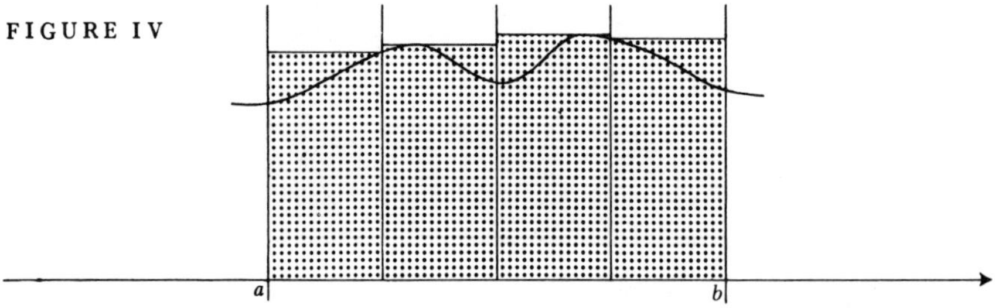

The general expression for the area of the circumscribed approximation resulting from n subdivisions is

$$\sum_{i}^{n}\left(\frac{b-a}{n}\cdot \sup_{y} \forall x\left[A(x) = y \wedge a+i\cdot\frac{b-a}{n} \leqslant x \wedge x \leqslant a + (i+1)\cdot\frac{b-a}{n}\right]\right).$$

It is intuitively clear that the shaded area, if it exists at all, is at least equal to each of its inscribed approximations and at most equal to each of its circumscribed approximations. Thus, if z is the desired area, we have:

(8) $$\wedge n\left[N(n) \wedge 1 \leqslant n \to \sum_{i}^{n}\left(\frac{b-a}{n}\cdot \inf_{y} \forall x\left[A(x) = y \wedge a + i\cdot\frac{b-a}{n} \leqslant x \wedge x \leqslant a + (i+1)\cdot\frac{b-a}{n}\right]\right) \leqslant z \wedge\right.$$

$$z \leqslant \sum_i^n \left(\frac{b-a}{n} \cdot \sup_y \bigvee x \left[\mathrm{A}(x) = y \wedge a + i \cdot \frac{b-a}{n} \leqslant x \wedge x \leqslant a + (i+1) \cdot \frac{b-a}{n} \right]\right)\Bigg]$$

Now it turns out that in case A(x) is continuous at every number between a and b (and even in certain additional cases) there will be exactly one number z satisfying (8). The shaded area can then be defined as this number; accordingly, we arrive at the following characterization of the *integral of* A(x) *between a and b*, which we identify with this area.

$$(9) \quad \int_a^b \mathrm{A}(x)\,\mathrm{d}x = \rceil z \bigwedge n \left[\mathrm{N}(n) \wedge 1 \leqslant n \to \sum_i^n \left(\frac{b-a}{n} \cdot \inf_y \bigvee x \left[\mathrm{A}(x) = y \wedge a + i \cdot \frac{b-a}{n} \leqslant x \wedge x \leqslant a + (i+1) \cdot \frac{b-a}{n} \right]\right) \leqslant z \wedge z \leqslant \sum_i^n \left(\frac{b-a}{n} \cdot \sup_y \bigvee x \left[\mathrm{A}(x) = y \wedge a + i \cdot \frac{b-a}{n} \leqslant x \wedge x \leqslant a + (i+1) \cdot \frac{b-a}{n} \right]\right)\right]$$

Here we regard the composite symbol

$$\int \quad \mathrm{d}$$

as an operator of degree $\langle 0, 1, 3, 0 \rangle$; on the left side of (9), 'a' and 'b' are free, and 'x' is bound. As usual, (9) can be replaced by a definitional schema in standard form; 'a' and 'b' would be replaced by, say, 'B(x)' and 'C(x)'. We should thus arrive at a definitional extension of T_8, and hence of integral calculus, in which the usual Riemann integral is available.

4. Historical remarks. The metamathematical notions of this and the last chapter—*definition*, *theory*, *definitional extension*, and the like—constitute an extension of the treatment in Tarski, Mostowski, Robinson [1] beyond the domain of theories with standard formalization, in particular, to theories containing variable-binding operators. The present treatment was developed in collaboration with Professor Dana Scott, and will also appear (along with its model-theoretic rationale) in Montague, Scott, Tarski [1].

For a discussion of fields and ordered fields, see, for instance, van der Waerden [1].

The Continuity Schema is due to Dedekind [1], and the present formulation of the theory of real numbers to Montague [2]. The theory of *real closed fields* (see Tarski [3]) is equivalent to the theory axiomatized by our $A1 - A15$, together with $AS19$. The addition of the predicate 'I' (denoting the set of integers), together with axioms governing it, makes a significant difference: as Tarski has shown, there is an automatic procedure for determining whether a formula is provable in the theory of real closed fields; but this is not true of the theory of real numbers, in view of Church [1]. A theory closely related to the integral calculus of the foregoing section is presented informally, without emphasis on its logical basis, in Landau [1].

It should not be supposed that, because the Principle of Archimedes ($T54$) is provable in the theory of real numbers, every model of this theory is what algebraists call an Archimedean field; indeed, A. Robinson has shown in [1] that the class of Archimedean fields cannot be characterized by any first-order theory (that is, any theory having the logical basis described in this book).

The definition of the integral given in the foregoing section, together with its intuitive justification, was strongly influenced by a conversation with Dr. J. D. Halpern.

5. Appendix: list of constants used in chapters X and XI

LOGICAL CONSTANTS	DEGREE	INTRODUCED ON
$\sim$	$\langle 1, 0, 0, 1 \rangle$	p. 439
$\rightarrow$	$\langle 1, 0, 0, 2 \rangle$	p. 439
$\wedge$	$\langle 1, 0, 0, 2 \rangle$	p. 439
$\vee$	$\langle 1, 0, 0, 2 \rangle$	p. 439
$\leftrightarrow$	$\langle 1, 0, 0, 2 \rangle$	p. 439
$\bigwedge$	$\langle 1, 1, 0, 1 \rangle$	p. 439
$\bigvee$	$\langle 1, 1, 0, 1 \rangle$	p. 439
$=$	$\langle 1, 0, 2, 0 \rangle$	p. 439
ι	$\langle 0, 1, 0, 1 \rangle$	p. 439
OPERATION AND PREDICATE LETTERS		
A	$\langle 0, 0, 0, 0 \rangle$	p. 440
B	$\langle 0, 0, 0, 0 \rangle$	p. 440
C	$\langle 0, 0, 1, 0 \rangle$	p. 440
C_1	$\langle 0, 0, 1, 0 \rangle$	p. 440
D	$\langle 0, 0, 1, 0 \rangle$	p. 440
D_1	$\langle 0, 0, 1, 0 \rangle$	p. 440
E	$\langle 0, 0, 1, 0 \rangle$	p. 440
F	$\langle 1, 0, 1, 0 \rangle$	p. 440

OPERATION SYMBOLS	DEGREE	INTRODUCED ON
$+$	$\langle 0, 0, 2, 0 \rangle$	p. 446
$-$	$\langle 0, 0, 1, 0 \rangle$	p. 446
0	$\langle 0, 0, 0, 0 \rangle$	p. 446
$\cdot$	$\langle 0, 0, 2, 0 \rangle$	p. 446
$^{-1}$	$\langle 0, 0, 1, 0 \rangle$	p. 446
1	$\langle 0, 0, 0, 0 \rangle$	p. 446
$\mathbf{2}$	$\langle 0, 0, 0, 0 \rangle$	p. 462
^{2}	$\langle 0, 0, 1, 0 \rangle$	p. 462
$\vert\ \vert$	$\langle 0, 0, 1, 0 \rangle$	p. 462
$\overline{}$	$\langle 0, 0, 2, 0 \rangle$	p. 463
$-$	$\langle 0, 0, 2, 0 \rangle$	p. 463

PREDICATES		
$\leqslant$	$\langle 1, 0, 2, 0 \rangle$	p. 446
I	$\langle 1, 0, 1, 0 \rangle$	p. 453
$\neq$	$\langle 1, 0, 2, 0 \rangle$	p. 462
$<$	$\langle 1, 0, 2, 0 \rangle$	p. 462
N	$\langle 1, 0, 1, 0 \rangle$	p. 468
R	$\langle 1, 0, 1, 0 \rangle$	p. 468

VARIABLE-BINDING OPERATORS		
$\Leftrightarrow$	$\langle 1, 1, 2, 0 \rangle$	p. 477
lim	$\langle 0, 1, 1, 0 \rangle$	p. 491
$\lim\limits_{\rightarrow}$	$\langle 0, 1, 2, 0 \rangle$	p. 492
Cont	$\langle 1, 1, 2, 0 \rangle$	p. 492
Av	$\langle 0, 1, 3, 0 \rangle$	p. 492
Der	$\langle 0, 1, 2, 0 \rangle$	p. 493
Σ	$\langle 0, 1, 2, 0 \rangle$	p. 493
sup	$\langle 0, 1, 0, 1 \rangle$	p. 494
inf	$\langle 0, 1, 0, 1 \rangle$	p. 494
$\int d$	$\langle 0, 1, 3, 0 \rangle$	p. 497

6. Appendix: list of axioms, definitions, and theorems of chapters X and XI.

AXIOMS:

*A*1 $\quad x + (y + z) = (x + y) + z$

*A*2 $\quad x + y = y + x$

*A*3 $\quad x + 0 = x$

*A*4	$x + -x = 0$
*A*5	$x \cdot (y \cdot z) = (x \cdot y) \cdot z$
*A*6	$x \cdot y = y \cdot x$
*A*7	$x \cdot 1 = x$
*A*8	$\sim x = 0 \rightarrow x \cdot x^{-1} = 1$
*A*9	$x \cdot (y + z) = (x \cdot y) + (x \cdot z)$
*A*10	$\sim 0 = 1$
*A*11	$0 \leqslant x \vee 0 \leqslant -x$
*A*12	$\sim x = 0 \rightarrow \sim 0 \leqslant x \vee \sim 0 \leqslant -x$
*A*13	$0 \leqslant x \wedge 0 \leqslant y \rightarrow 0 \leqslant x + y$
*A*14	$0 \leqslant x \wedge 0 \leqslant y \rightarrow 0 \leqslant x \cdot y$
*A*15	$x \leqslant y \leftrightarrow 0 \leqslant y + -x$
*A*16	$\mathrm{I}(0)$
*A*17	$\mathrm{I}(x) \rightarrow \mathrm{I}(x + 1) \wedge \mathrm{I}(x + -1)$
*A*18	$\mathrm{I}(x) \wedge \mathrm{I}(y) \wedge x \leqslant y \wedge y \leqslant x + 1 \rightarrow y = x \vee y = x + 1$
*AS*19	$\bigvee x \mathrm{F}(x) \wedge \bigvee y \bigwedge x(\mathrm{F}(x) \rightarrow x \leqslant y) \rightarrow$ $\bigvee z[\bigwedge x(\mathrm{F}(x) \rightarrow x \leqslant z) \wedge \bigwedge y(\bigwedge x[\mathrm{F}(x) \rightarrow x \leqslant y] \rightarrow z \leqslant y)]$
*AS*20	$\sum_{i}^{0} \mathrm{A}(i) = 0$
*AS*21	$\mathrm{N}(n) \rightarrow \sum_{i}^{n+1} \mathrm{A}(i) = \left[\sum_{i}^{n} \mathrm{A}(i)\right] + \mathrm{A}(n)$

DEFINITIONS (in the form given in chapter XI):

*DS*1	$\mathrm{A} \neq \mathrm{B} \leftrightarrow \sim \mathrm{A} = \mathrm{B}$
*DS*2	$\mathrm{A} < \mathrm{B} \leftrightarrow \mathrm{A} \leqslant \mathrm{B} \wedge \sim \mathrm{A} = \mathrm{B}$
*DS*3	$2 = 1 + 1$
*DS*4	$\mathrm{A}^2 = \mathrm{A} \cdot \mathrm{A}$
*DS*5	$\lvert\mathrm{A}\rvert = \imath z[(0 \leqslant \mathrm{A} \wedge z = \mathrm{A}) \vee (\sim 0 \leqslant \mathrm{A} \wedge z = -\mathrm{A})]$
*DS*6	$\mathrm{A} - \mathrm{B} = \mathrm{A} + -\mathrm{B}$
*DS*7	$\dfrac{\mathrm{A}}{\mathrm{B}} = \mathrm{A} \cdot \mathrm{B}^{-1}$
*DS*8	$\mathrm{N}(\mathrm{A}) \leftrightarrow \mathrm{I}(\mathrm{A}) \wedge 0 \leqslant \mathrm{A}$
*DS*9	$\mathrm{R}(\mathrm{A}) \leftrightarrow \bigvee y \bigvee z[\mathrm{I}(y) \wedge \mathrm{I}(z) \wedge 0 \leqslant z \wedge \sim 0 = z \wedge \mathrm{A} = y \cdot z^{-1}]$

*DS*10 $\mathrm{A}(n) \underset{n}{\Leftrightarrow} \mathrm{B}(n) \leftrightarrow \Lambda z(0 < z \rightarrow \mathrm{V}k\Lambda n[\mathrm{N}(n) \wedge k < n \rightarrow |\mathrm{A}(n) - \mathrm{B}(n)| < z])$

*DS*11 $\lim_{n} \mathrm{A}(n) = \imath x\, \mathrm{A}(n) \underset{n}{\Leftrightarrow} x$

*DS*12 $\lim_{x \to \mathrm{B}(x)} \mathrm{A}(x) = \imath u \Lambda z(0 < z \rightarrow \mathrm{V}y[0 < y \wedge \Lambda x(0 < |x - \mathrm{B}(x)| \wedge |x - \mathrm{B}(x)| < y \rightarrow |\mathrm{A}(x) - u| < z)])$

*DS*13 $\underset{x}{\mathrm{Cont}}\, [\mathrm{A}(x), \mathrm{B}(x)] \leftrightarrow \Lambda z(0 < z \rightarrow \mathrm{V}y[0 < y \wedge \Lambda x(0 < |x - \mathrm{B}(x)| \wedge |x - \mathrm{B}(x)| < y \rightarrow |\mathrm{A}(x) - \mathrm{A}(\mathrm{B}(x))| < z)])$

*DS*14 $\underset{x}{\mathrm{Av}}\, [\mathrm{A}(x), \mathrm{B}(x), \mathrm{C}(x)] = \dfrac{\mathrm{A}(\mathrm{C}(0)) - \mathrm{A}(\mathrm{B}(0))}{\mathrm{C}(0) - \mathrm{B}(0)}$

*DS*15 $\underset{x}{\mathrm{Der}}\, [\mathrm{A}(x), \mathrm{B}(x)] = \lim_{h \to 0} [\underset{x}{\mathrm{A}v}\, [\mathrm{A}(x), \mathrm{B}(x) - h, \mathrm{B}(x) + h]]$

*DS*16 $\sup_{x} \mathrm{F}(x) = \imath z[\Lambda x(\mathrm{F}(x) \rightarrow x \leqslant z) \wedge \Lambda y(\Lambda x[\mathrm{F}(x) \rightarrow x \leqslant y] \rightarrow z \leqslant y)]$

*DS*17 $\inf_{x} \mathrm{F}(x) = \imath z[\Lambda x(\mathrm{F}(x) \rightarrow z \leqslant x) \wedge \Lambda y(\Lambda x[\mathrm{F}(x) \rightarrow y \leqslant x] \rightarrow y \leqslant z)]$

*DS*18
$$\int_{\mathrm{B}(x)}^{\mathrm{C}(x)} \mathrm{A}(x)\, \mathrm{d}x = \imath z \Lambda n\Bigg[\mathrm{N}(n) \wedge 1 \leqslant n \rightarrow \sum_{i}^{n} \Bigg(\frac{\mathrm{C}(0) - \mathrm{B}(0)}{n} \cdot \inf_{y} \mathrm{V}x\Bigg[\mathrm{A}(x) = y \wedge \mathrm{B}(0) + i \cdot \frac{\mathrm{C}(0) - \mathrm{B}(0)}{n} \leqslant x \wedge x \leqslant \mathrm{B}(0) + (i + 1) \cdot \frac{\mathrm{C}(0) - \mathrm{B}(0)}{n}\Bigg]\Bigg) \leqslant z \wedge z \leqslant \sum_{i}^{n} \Bigg(\frac{\mathrm{C}(0) - \mathrm{B}(0)}{n} \cdot \sup_{y} \mathrm{V}x\Bigg[\mathrm{A}(x) = y \wedge \mathrm{B}(0) + i \cdot \frac{\mathrm{C}(0) - \mathrm{B}(0)}{n} \leqslant x \wedge x \leqslant \mathrm{B}(0) + (i + 1) \cdot \frac{\mathrm{C}(0) - \mathrm{B}(0)}{n}\Bigg]\Bigg)\Bigg]$$

THEOREMS:

*T*1 $x + z = y + z \rightarrow x = y$

*T*2 $z + x = z + y \rightarrow x = y$

*T*3 $\sim z = 0 \wedge x \cdot z = y \cdot z \rightarrow x = y$

*T*4 $\sim z = 0 \wedge z \cdot x = z \cdot y \rightarrow x = y$

*T*5 $-0 = 0$

*T*6	$x \cdot 0 = 0$
*T*7	$x + -y = 0 \leftrightarrow x = y$
*T*8	$x = -y \leftrightarrow y = -x$
*T*9	$x = 0 \leftrightarrow -x = 0$
*T*10	$--x = x$
*T*11	$-(x + y) = -x + -y$
*T*12	$-x \cdot y = -(x \cdot y)$
*T*13	$x \cdot -y = -(x \cdot y)$
*T*14	$-x \cdot -y = x \cdot y$
*T*15	$\sim x = 0 \rightarrow (-x)^{-1} = -(x^{-1})$
*T*16	$x \cdot y = 0 \leftrightarrow x = 0 \vee y = 0$
*T*17	$\sim x \cdot y = 0 \rightarrow (x \cdot y)^{-1} = x^{-1} \cdot y^{-1}$
*T*18	$x \leqslant x$
*T*19	$x \leqslant y \wedge y \leqslant x \rightarrow x = y$
*T*20	$x \leqslant y \wedge y \leqslant z \rightarrow x \leqslant z$
*T*21	$x \leqslant y \vee y \leqslant x$
*T*22	$0 \leqslant x \cdot x$
*T*23	$0 \leqslant 1$
*T*24	$x \leqslant y \rightarrow x + z \leqslant y + z$
*T*25	$x + z \leqslant y + z \rightarrow x \leqslant y$
*T*26	$x \leqslant y \wedge z \leqslant w \rightarrow x + z \leqslant y + w$
*T*27	$\sim y + 1 \leqslant y$
*T*28	$\sim y \leqslant y + -1$
*T*29	$x \leqslant y \rightarrow -y \leqslant -x$
*T*30	$-y \leqslant -x \rightarrow x \leqslant y$
*T*31	$x \leqslant 0 \leftrightarrow 0 \leqslant -x$
*T*32	$0 \leqslant x \wedge y \leqslant 0 \rightarrow x \cdot y \leqslant 0$
*T*33	$x \leqslant y \wedge 0 \leqslant z \rightarrow x \cdot z \leqslant y \cdot z$
*T*34	$x \leqslant y \wedge z \leqslant 0 \rightarrow y \cdot z \leqslant x \cdot z$
*T*35	$0 \leqslant z \wedge \sim z = 0 \rightarrow 0 \leqslant z^{-1}$
*T*36	$x \cdot z \leqslant y \cdot z \wedge 0 \leqslant z \wedge \sim z = 0 \rightarrow x \leqslant y$
*T*37	$y \cdot z \leqslant x \cdot z \wedge z \leqslant 0 \wedge \sim z = 0 \rightarrow x \leqslant y$
*T*38	$x = y \rightarrow x \leqslant y$
*T*39	$\mathrm{I}(y) \wedge 0 \leqslant y \wedge \sim y = 0 \rightarrow 1 \leqslant y$

*T*40 $I(y) \wedge y \leqslant 0 \wedge \sim y = 0 \rightarrow y \leqslant -1$

*TS*41 $\bigvee x F(x) \rightarrow \bigvee x F(-x)$

*TS*42 $\bigvee x F(x) \wedge \bigvee y \bigwedge x(F(x) \rightarrow y \leqslant x) \rightarrow$
$\bigvee z[\bigwedge x(F(x) \rightarrow z \leqslant x) \wedge \bigwedge y(\bigwedge x[F(x) \rightarrow y \leqslant x] \rightarrow y \leqslant z)]$

*TS*43 $\bigwedge x[F(x) \rightarrow I(x)] \wedge \bigwedge x(F(x) \rightarrow y \leqslant x) \wedge$
$\bigwedge z(\bigwedge x[F(x) \rightarrow z \leqslant x] \rightarrow z \leqslant y) \rightarrow F(y)$

*TS*44 $\bigwedge x[F(x) \rightarrow I(x)] \wedge \bigwedge x(F(x) \rightarrow x \leqslant y) \wedge$
$\bigwedge z(\bigwedge x[F(x) \rightarrow x \leqslant z] \rightarrow y \leqslant z) \rightarrow F(y)$

*TS*45 $F(0) \wedge \bigwedge x[I(x) \wedge F(x) \rightarrow F(x + 1) \wedge F(x + -1)] \rightarrow$
$\bigwedge x[I(x) \rightarrow F(x)]$

*T*46 $I(x) \rightarrow I(-x)$

*T*47 $I(x) \wedge I(y) \rightarrow I(x + y)$

*T*48 $I(x) \wedge I(y) \rightarrow I(x \cdot y)$

*TS*49 $\bigvee x[I(x) \wedge F(x)] \wedge \bigwedge x[I(x) \wedge F(x) \rightarrow F(x + 1) \wedge F(x + -1)] \rightarrow$
$\bigwedge x[I(x) \rightarrow F(x)]$

*T*50 $I(x) \rightarrow \bigvee y(I(y) \wedge x = y + y) \vee \bigvee y(I(y) \wedge x = y + y + 1)$

*T*51 $I(x) \rightarrow \sim \bigvee y(I(y) \wedge x + x = y + y + 1)$

*T*52 $I(x) \rightarrow [\bigvee y(I(y) \wedge x = y + y) \leftrightarrow \sim \bigvee y(I(y) \wedge x = y + y + 1)]$

*T*53 $0 \leqslant x \wedge \sim x = 0 \rightarrow \bigvee n(I(n) \wedge y \leqslant n \cdot x)$

*T*54 $\sim x = 0 \rightarrow \bigvee n(I(n) \wedge y \leqslant n \cdot x)$

*T*55 $I(n) \wedge I(m) \wedge n < m \rightarrow n + 1 \leqslant m$

*T*56 $x - x = 0$

*T*57 $-(x - y) = y - x$

*T*58 $x - y = (z - y) - (z - x)$

*T*59 $(x - y) + (z - w) = (x + z) - (y + w)$

*T*60 $(x + y)^2 = x^2 + 2xy + y^2$

*T*61 $1^2 = 1$

*T*62 $(x - y)^2 = x^2 - 2xy + y^2$

*T*63 $(x \cdot y)^2 = x^2 \cdot y^2$

*T*64 $y \neq 0 \rightarrow \left(\frac{x}{y}\right)^2 = \frac{x^2}{y^2}$

*T*65 $\frac{x}{2} + \frac{x}{2} = x$

*T*66 $\frac{0}{x} = 0$

*T*67 $\frac{x + y}{z} = \frac{x}{z} + \frac{y}{z}$

*T*68 $xz \neq 0 \rightarrow \frac{xy}{xz} = \frac{y}{z}$

*T*69 $y \neq 0 \rightarrow -\left(\frac{x}{y}\right) = \frac{-x}{y} \wedge -\left(\frac{x}{y}\right) = \frac{x}{-y}$

*T*70 $0 \leqslant x \wedge x \leqslant 1 \rightarrow x^2 \leqslant x$

*T*71 $0 \leqslant x^2$

*T*72 $x \neq 0 \rightarrow 0 < x^2$

*T*73 $x \leqslant x + y^2$

*T*74 $0 < 1$

*T*75 $1 < 2$

*T*76 $\sim x < x$

*T*77 $x < y \wedge y < z \rightarrow x < z$

*T*78 $x \leqslant y \wedge y < z \rightarrow x < z$

*T*79 $x < y \wedge y \leqslant z \rightarrow x < z$

*T*80 $x \leqslant y \leftrightarrow \sim y < x$

*T*81 $x \leqslant y \leftrightarrow x < y \vee x = y$

*T*82 $x < y \leftrightarrow x + z < y + z$

*T*83 $x < y \wedge z < w \rightarrow x + z < y + w$

*T*84 $0 < x \rightarrow x < 2x$

*T*85 $x < y \leftrightarrow -y < -x$

*T*86 $x < 0 \leftrightarrow 0 < -x$

*T*87 $0 < z \rightarrow 0 < z^{-1}$

*T*88 $z < 0 \rightarrow z^{-1} < 0$

*T*89 $0 < z \rightarrow [x < y \leftrightarrow xz < yz]$

*T*90 $z < 0 \rightarrow [x < y \leftrightarrow yz < xz]$

*T*91 $0 < x \wedge 0 < y \rightarrow [x \leqslant y \leftrightarrow y^{-1} \leqslant x^{-1}]$

*T*92 $x < 0 \wedge y < 0 \rightarrow [x \leqslant y \leftrightarrow y^{-1} \leqslant x^{-1}]$

*T*93 $0 < x \wedge 0 < y \rightarrow [x < y \leftrightarrow y^{-1} < x^{-1}]$

*T*94 $x < 0 \wedge y < 0 \rightarrow [x < y \leftrightarrow y^{-1} < x^{-1}]$

*T*95 $0 < x \wedge x \leqslant y \wedge 0 \leqslant z \rightarrow \frac{z}{y} \leqslant \frac{z}{x}$

*T*96 $0 < x \wedge x < y \wedge 0 < z \rightarrow \frac{z}{y} < \frac{z}{x}$

*T*97 $x \leqslant y \wedge 0 < z \rightarrow \frac{x}{z} \leqslant \frac{y}{z}$

*T*98 $x < y \wedge 0 < z \rightarrow \frac{x}{z} < \frac{y}{z}$

*T*99 $0 < x \wedge x < y \rightarrow 0 < \frac{x}{y} \wedge \frac{x}{y} < 1$

*T*100 $0 \leqslant y \wedge x^2 \leqslant y^2 \rightarrow x \leqslant y$

*T*101 $0 \leqslant x \wedge 0 < y \rightarrow 0 \leqslant \frac{x}{y}$

*T*102 $0 < x \wedge 0 < y \rightarrow 0 < \frac{x}{y}$

*T*103 $\bigvee t \bigwedge z[(0 \leqslant x \wedge z = x) \vee (\sim 0 \leqslant x \wedge z = -x) \leftrightarrow z = t]$

*T*104 $0 \leqslant x \rightarrow |x| = x$

*T*105 $x < 0 \rightarrow |x| = -x$

*T*106 $0 \leqslant |x|$

*T*107 $|x| = 0 \leftrightarrow x = 0$

*T*108 $x \leqslant |x|$

*T*109 $-x \leqslant |x|$

*T*110 $|-x| = |x|$

*T*111 $|x| \leqslant y \leftrightarrow x \leqslant y \wedge -x \leqslant y$

*T*112 $|x + y| \leqslant |x| + |y|$

*T*113 $|x - y| \leqslant |x - z| + |z - y|$

*T*114 $|x - y| \leqslant |x| + |y|$

*T*115 $|x - y| = |y - x|$

*T*116 $|x \cdot y| = |x| \cdot |y|$

*T*117 $y \neq 0 \rightarrow \left|\frac{x}{y}\right| = \frac{|x|}{|y|}$

*T*118 $|x - y| < z \leftrightarrow x - z < y \wedge y < x + z$

*TS*119 $\bigvee x F(x) \wedge \bigwedge x[F(x) \rightarrow N(x)] \rightarrow \bigvee x[F(x) \wedge \bigwedge y(F(y) \rightarrow x \leqslant y])$

*TS*120 $\bigwedge x[\mathrm{N}(x) \wedge \bigwedge y(\mathrm{N}(y) \wedge y < x \rightarrow \mathrm{F}(y)) \rightarrow \mathrm{F}(x)] \rightarrow \bigwedge x[\mathrm{N}(x) \rightarrow \mathrm{F}(x)]$

*TS*121 $\mathrm{F}(0) \wedge \bigwedge x[\mathrm{N}(x) \wedge \mathrm{F}(x) \rightarrow \mathrm{F}(x + 1)] \rightarrow \bigwedge x[\mathrm{N}(x) \rightarrow \mathrm{F}(x)]$

*T*122 $\mathrm{N}(0)$

*T*123 $\mathrm{N}(x) \rightarrow \mathrm{N}(x + 1)$

*T*124 $\mathrm{N}(x) \wedge \mathrm{N}(y) \wedge x + 1 = y + 1 \rightarrow x = y$

*T*125 $\mathrm{N}(x) \rightarrow x + 1 \neq 0$

*T*126 $\mathrm{N}(x) \wedge \mathrm{N}(y) \rightarrow \mathrm{N}(x + y) \wedge \mathrm{N}(x \cdot y)$

*T*127 $\mathrm{I}(x) \wedge \bigvee y(\mathrm{I}(y)) \wedge x^2 = 2y) \rightarrow \bigvee y(\mathrm{I}(y) \wedge x = 2y)$

*T*128 $\mathrm{R}(x) \rightarrow x^2 \neq 2$

*T*129 $0 < x \rightarrow \bigvee y\, x = y^2$

*T*130 $0 \leqslant x \leftrightarrow \bigvee y\, x = y^2$

*T*131 $x \leqslant y \leftrightarrow \bigvee z\, x + z^2 = y$

*T*132 $\dfrac{n^2 + 1}{n} \underset{n}{\Leftrightarrow} n$

*T*133 $\sim n + 1 \underset{n}{\Leftrightarrow} n$

*TS*134 $\mathrm{C}(n) \underset{n}{\Leftrightarrow} \mathrm{D}(n) \leftrightarrow \mathrm{C}(m) \underset{m}{\Leftrightarrow} \mathrm{D}(m)$

*TS*135 $\bigwedge n\, \mathrm{C}(n) = \mathrm{C}_1(n) \wedge \bigwedge n\, \mathrm{D}(n) = \mathrm{D}_1(n) \rightarrow [\mathrm{C}(n) \underset{n}{\Leftrightarrow} \mathrm{D}(n) \leftrightarrow \mathrm{C}_1(n) \underset{n}{\Leftrightarrow} \mathrm{D}_1(n)]$

*TS*136 $\mathrm{C}(n) \underset{n}{\Leftrightarrow} \mathrm{C}(n)$

*TS*137 $\mathrm{C}(n) \underset{n}{\Leftrightarrow} \mathrm{D}(n) \rightarrow \mathrm{D}(n) \underset{n}{\Leftrightarrow} \mathrm{C}(n)$

*TS*138 $\mathrm{C}(n) \underset{n}{\Leftrightarrow} \mathrm{D}(n) \wedge \mathrm{D}(n) \underset{n}{\Leftrightarrow} \mathrm{E}(n) \rightarrow \mathrm{C}(n) \underset{n}{\Leftrightarrow} \mathrm{E}(n)$

*TS*139 $\mathrm{C}(n) \underset{n}{\Leftrightarrow} \mathrm{C}_1(n) \wedge \mathrm{D}(n) \underset{n}{\Leftrightarrow} \mathrm{D}_1(n) \rightarrow \mathrm{C}(n) + \mathrm{D}(n) \underset{n}{\Leftrightarrow} \mathrm{C}_1(n) + \mathrm{D}_1(n)$

*TS*140 $\bigvee k \bigwedge n[\mathrm{N}(n) \wedge k < n \rightarrow \mathrm{C}(n) = \mathrm{D}(n)] \rightarrow \mathrm{C}(n) \underset{n}{\Leftrightarrow} \mathrm{D}(n)$

*TS*141 $\bigwedge n \bigwedge m[\mathrm{N}(n) \wedge \mathrm{N}(m) \wedge n < m \rightarrow \mathrm{E}(n) < \mathrm{E}(m)] \wedge \bigwedge n[\mathrm{N}(n) \rightarrow \mathrm{N}(\mathrm{E}(n))] \rightarrow \bigwedge n[\mathrm{N}(n) \rightarrow n \leqslant \mathrm{E}(n)]$

*TS*142 $[\mathrm{C}(n) \underset{n}{\Leftrightarrow} \mathrm{D}(n)] \wedge \bigwedge n \bigwedge m[\mathrm{N}(n) \wedge \mathrm{N}(m) \wedge n < m \rightarrow \mathrm{E}(n) < \mathrm{E}(m)] \wedge \bigwedge n[\mathrm{N}(n) \rightarrow \mathrm{N}(\mathrm{E}(n))] \rightarrow [\mathrm{C}(\mathrm{E}(n)) \underset{n}{\Leftrightarrow} \mathrm{D}(\mathrm{E}(n))]$

*TS*143 $C(n) \underset{n}{\Leftrightarrow} x \leftrightarrow \bigwedge z(0 < z \rightarrow \bigvee k \bigwedge n[N(n) \wedge k < n \rightarrow |C(n) - x| < z])$

*T*144 $\frac{n+1}{n} \underset{n}{\Leftrightarrow} 1$

*T*145 $\frac{1}{n} \underset{n}{\Leftrightarrow} 0$

*T*146 $x \underset{n}{\Leftrightarrow} y \rightarrow x = y$

*TS*147 $C(n) \underset{n}{\Leftrightarrow} x \wedge C(n) \underset{n}{\Leftrightarrow} y \rightarrow x = y$

*T*148 $\sim \bigvee x\, n \underset{n}{\Leftrightarrow} x$

*T*149 $\frac{n(n+1)}{n^2} \underset{n}{\Leftrightarrow} 1$

*TS*150 $C(n) \underset{n}{\Leftrightarrow} x \wedge D(n) \underset{n}{\Leftrightarrow} y \rightarrow C(n) \cdot D(n) \underset{n}{\Leftrightarrow} x \cdot y$

*TS*151 $C(n) \underset{n}{\Leftrightarrow} x \wedge D(n) \underset{n}{\Leftrightarrow} y \wedge \bigvee k \bigwedge n[N(n) \wedge k < n \rightarrow C(n) \leqslant D(n)] \rightarrow x \leqslant y$

*TS*152 $C(n) \underset{n}{\Leftrightarrow} D(n) \leftrightarrow C(n) - D(n) \underset{n}{\Leftrightarrow} 0$

*TS*153 $\bigwedge n \bigwedge m[N(n) \wedge N(m) \wedge n \leqslant m \rightarrow C(n) \leqslant C(m)] \wedge \bigvee y \bigwedge n[N(n) \rightarrow C(n) \leqslant y] \rightarrow \bigvee z\, C(n) \underset{n}{\Leftrightarrow} z$

*TS*154 $\bigwedge n \bigwedge m[N(n) \wedge N(m) \wedge n \leqslant m \rightarrow C(m) \leqslant C(n)] \wedge \bigvee y \bigwedge n[N(n) \rightarrow y \leqslant C(n)] \rightarrow \bigvee z\, C(n) \underset{n}{\Leftrightarrow} z$

BIBLIOGRAPHY

ACKERMANN, W.

[1] *Solvable cases of the decision problem*, Amsterdam, 1954.

ANDERSON, A. R., and BELNAP, N. D.

[1] *Entailment: the logic of relevance and necessity*, vol. 1, Princeton, 1975.

BEHMANN, H.

[1] Beiträge zur Algebra der Logik, insbesondere zum Entscheidungsproblem, *Mathematische Annalen*, vol. 86 (1922), pp. 163–229.

BERNAYS, P., and SCHÖNFINKEL, M.

[1] Zum Entscheidungsproblem der mathematischen Logik, *Mathematische Annalen*, vol. 99 (1928), pp. 342–72.

BOOLE, G.

[1] *The mathematical analysis of logic*, London and Cambridge, 1847.

[2] *An investigation of the laws of thought*, London, 1854.

BURGE, T.

[1] Truth and singular terms, *Noûs*, vol. 8 (1974), pp. 309–25.

CARNAP, R.

[1] *Logische Syntax der Sprache*, Vienna, 1934. English translation: New York, 1937.

[2] *Meaning and necessity*, Chicago, 1947.

CHANG, C. C., and KEISLER, H. J.

[1] *Model theory*, Amsterdam, 1973; second edition, 1977.

CHURCH, A.

[1] An unsolvable problem of elementary number theory, *American Journal of Mathematics*, vol. 58 (1936), pp. 345–63.

[2] A note on the *Entscheidungsproblem*, *Journal of Symbolic Logic*, vol. 1 (1936), pp. 40–41; Correction, *ibid.*, pp. 101–02.

[3] *Introduction to mathematical logic*, vol. 1, Princeton, 1956.

COPI, I. M.

[1] *Symbolic logic*, New York, 1954, 1965, 1967, 1973, 1979.

COUTURAT, L.

[1] *La Logique de Leibniz*, Paris, 1901.

[2] *Opuscules et Fragments inédits de Leibniz*, Paris, 1903.

[3] *Les Principes des Mathématiques*, Paris, 1905.

DAVIDSON, D., and HARMAN, G. (Editors)
[1] *Semantics of natural languages*, second edition, Dordrecht, 1972.

DAVIS, W. A.
[1] Indicative and subjunctive conditionals, *Philosophical Review*, vol. 88 (1979), pp. 544–64.

DEDEKIND, R.
[1] *Stetigkeit und irrationale Zahlen*, Braunschweig, 1872. English translation in *Essays on the theory of numbers*, La Salle, Illinois, 1901.

DE MORGAN, A.
[1] *Formal logic*, London, 1847.

EUCLID
[1] Book X, *The thirteen books of Euclid's elements*, translated by Sir T. L. Heath, Cambridge, 1908; second edition, 1926.

FRAENKEL, A. A.
[1] *Set Theory and Logic*, Reading, 1966.

FREGE, G.
[1] *Begriffsschrift*, Halle, 1879. English translation in *From Frege to Gödel: a source book in mathematical logic, 1879–1931*, edited by J. van Heijnoort, Cambridge, 1967.
[2] Über Sinn und Bedeutung, *Zeitschrift für Philosophie und Kritik*, vol. 100 (1892), pp. 25–50. English translation in *Translations from the philosophical writings of Gottlob Frege*, edited by Geach and Black, Oxford, 1960.
[3] *Grundegesetze der Arithmetik*, vol. 1, Jena, 1893. English translation of the initial sections and the appendix on Russell's paradox in *The basic laws of arithmetic*, translated and edited with an introduction by M. Furth, Berkeley and Los Angeles, 1964.

GARDNER, M.
[1] *The Scientific American book of mathematical puzzles and diversions*, New York, 1959.

GENTZEN, G.
[1] Untersuchungen über das logische Schliessen, *Mathematische Zeitschrift*, vol. 39 (1934–35), pp. 176–210 and 405–31.

GÖDEL, K.
[1] Die Vollständigkeit der Axiome des logischen Funktionenkalküls, *Monatshefte für Mathematik und Physik*, vol. 37 (1930), pp. 349–60.
[2] Über formal unentscheidbare Sätze der *Principia Mathematica* und verwandter Systeme I, *Monatshefte für Mathematik und Physik*, vol. 38, (1931), pp. 173–98.

HERBRAND, J.
[1] Sur la théorie de la démonstration, *Comptes Rendus des Séances de l'Académie des Sciences*, vol. 186 (Paris, 1928), pp. 1274–76.
[2] *Recherches sur la théorie de la démonstration* (Travaux de la Société des Sciences et des Lettres de Varsovie, Classe III, No. 33, 1930, 128 pp.).

HILBERT, D., and ACKERMANN, W.
[1] *Grundzüge der theoretischen Logik*, Berlin, 1928.
[2] *Grundzüge der theoretischen Logik*, second edition, Berlin, 1938. English translation: *Mathematical logic*, New York, 1950.
[3] *Grundzüge der theoretischen Logik*, third edition, Berlin, 1949.
[4] *Grundzüge der theoretischen Logik*, fourth edition, Berlin, 1959.

HILBERT, D., and BERNAYS, P.
[1] *Grundlagen der Mathematik*, vol. 1, Berlin, 1934.
[2] *Grundlagen der Mathematik*, vol. 2, Berlin, 1939.

JAŚKOWSKI, S.
[1] On the rules of suppositions in formal logic, *Studia Logica*, no. 1 (Warsaw, 1934).

KALMÁR, L.
[1] Über die Axiomatisierbarkeit des Aussagenkalküls, *Acta Scientiarum Mathematicarum*, vol. 7, 1934–35, pp. 222–43.

KAPLAN, D.
[1] What is Russell's theory of descriptions? *Bertrand Russell: a collection of critical essays*, edited by D. F. Pears, New York, 1972, pp. 227–44.

KEMENY, J., MIRKIL, H., SNELL, J., THOMPSON, G.
[1] *Finite mathematical structures*, Englewood Cliffs, 1958.

KLEENE, S. C.
[1] *Introduction to metamathematics*, Princeton, 1952.
[2] *Mathematical logic*, New York, 1967.

LANDAU, E.
[1] *Differential and integral calculus*, New York, 1951.

LINSKY, L. (Editor)
[1] *Reference and modality*, Oxford, 1971.

LEIBNIZ, G. W.
[1] Scientia Generalis. Characteristica XIX and XX, in Gerhardt's *Die Philosophischen Schriften von G. W. Leibniz*, vol. 7 (1890), pp. 228–35. English translation in *A survey of symbolic logic*, by C. I. Lewis, Berkeley, 1918, pp. 373–79 and New York, 1960, pp. 291–97.

ŁUKASIEWICZ, J.
[1] *Elementy logiki matematycznej* (Elements of Mathematical Logic), Warsaw, 1929.
[2] Zur Geschichte der Aussagenlogik, *Erkenntnis*, vol. 5 (1935–36), pp. 111–31.

Łukasiewicz, J., and Tarski, A.

[1] Untersuchungen über den Aussagenkalkül, *Comptes Rendus des Séances de la Société des Sciences et des Lettres de Varsovie*, Classe III, vol. 23 (1930), pp. 30–50. English translation: Tarski [4], Article IV.

MacColl, H.

[1] The calculus of equivalent statements and integration limits, *Proceedings of the London Mathematical Society*, vol. 9 (1877–78), pp. 9–20 and 177–86, vol. 10 (1878–79), pp. 16–28, vol. 11 (1879–80), pp. 113–21.

Mates, B.

[1] *Stoic logic* (University of California Publication in Philosophy, vol. 26), Berkeley and Los Angeles, 1953 and 1961.

[2] *Elementary logic*, New York, 1965; second edition, 1972.

[3] Leibniz on possible worlds, *Logic, methodology, and philosophy of science III*, edited by van Rootselaar and Staal, Amsterdam, 1968, pp. 507–29.

Montague, R.

[1] On the paradox of grounded classes, *Journal of Symbolic Logic*, vol. 20 (1955), p. 140.

[2] Semantical closure and non-finite axiomatizability I, in *Infinitistic Methods*, Proceedings of the Symposium on Foundations of Mathematics, Warsaw, 1959, pp. 45–69.

[3] Deterministic theories, in *Decisions, values, and groups*, vol. 2, Oxford, 1963.

[4] *Formal philosophy: selected papers of Richard Montague*, edited and with an introduction by R. H. Thomason, New Haven and London, 1974.

Montague, R., and Kalish, D.

[1] Remarks on descriptions and natural deduction, *Archiv für mathematische Logik und Grundlagenforschung*, vol. 3 (1957), pp. 50–64; vol. 3 (1957), pp. 65–73.

Montague, R., Scott, D., Tarski, A.

[1] *An axiomatic approach to set theory*, Amsterdam, unpublished.

Mostowski, A.

[1] Rules of proof in pure functional calculus, *Journal of Symbolic Logic*, vol. 16 (1951), pp. 107–11.

Pager, D.

[1] An emendation of the axiom system of Hilbert and Ackermann for the restricted calculus of predicates, *Journal of Symbolic Logic*, vol. 27 (1962), pp. 131–38.

Partee, B. H. (Editor)

[1] *Montague grammar*, New York, 1976.

PEANO, G.

[1] Sul concetto di numero, *Revista di matematica*, vol. 1 (1891), pp. 87–102, 256–67.

PEIRCE, C. S.

[1] *Collected papers of Charles Sanders Peirce*, edited by Hartshorne and Weiss, Cambridge, Mass., 1933; see various papers from 1870 to 1903 in vol. 3.

[2] On the algebra of logic: a contribution to the philosophy of notation, *American Journal of Mathematics*, vol. 7 (1885), pp. 180–202.

[3] The logic of relatives, *The Monist*, vol. 7 (1897), pp. 161–217.

POST, E. L.

[1] Introduction to a general theory of elementary propositions, *American Journal of Mathematics*, vol. 43 (1921), pp. 163–85.

QUINE, W. V.

[1] *A system of logistic*, Cambridge, Mass., 1934.

[2] *Mathematical logic*, New York, 1940; revised edition, Cambridge, Mass. (Harvard University Press), 1951.

[3] *Methods of logic*, New York, 1950; revised edition, 1959.

[4] A proof procedure for quantification theory, *Journal of Symbolic Logic*, vol. 20 (1955), pp. 141–49.

[5] *Methods of Logic*, New York, third edition, 1972.

ROBINSON, A.

[1] *On the metamathematics of algebra*, Amsterdam, 1951.

ROSSER, B.

[1] *Logic for mathematicians*, New York, 1953.

RUSSELL, B.

[1] On denoting, *Mind*, vol. 14 (1905), pp. 479–93.

[2] The theory of implication, *American Journal of Mathematics*, vol. 28 (1906), pp. 159–202.

[3] *Introduction to mathematical philosophy*, London, 1919.

SCHOLZ, H.

[1] *Metaphysik als strenge Wissenschaft*, Cologne, 1941.

SCHRÖDER, E.

[1] *Algebra der Logik*, vol. 1, Leipzig, 1890.

SCOTT, D.

[1] Existence and description in formal logic, *Bertrand Russell: philosopher of the century, essays in his honour*, edited by R. Schoenman, London, 1967, pp. 121–200.

SUPPES, P.

[1] *Introduction to logic*, Princeton, 1957.

TARSKI, A.

[1] Über einige fundamentale Begriffe der Metamathematik, *Comptes Rendus des Séances de la Société des Sciences et des Lettres de Varsovie*,

Classe III, vol. 23 (1930), pp. 22–29. English translation: Tarski [4], Article III.

[2] *Projęcie prawdy w językach nauk dedukcyjnych* (The concept of truth in the languages of the deductive sciences) (Travaux de la Société des Sciences et des Lettres de Varsovie, Classe III, no. 34, 1933, vii, 116 pp.). German translation in *Studia Philosophica*, vol. 1 (1936), pp. 261–405. English translation: Tarski [4], Article VIII.

[3] *A decision method for elementary algebra and geometry*, second edition, Berkeley and Los Angeles, 1951.

[4] *Logic, semantics, metamathematics*, Oxford, 1956.

TARSKI, A., MOSTOWSKI, A., ROBINSON, R. M.

[1] *Undecidable theories*, Amsterdam, 1953.

VAN DER WAERDEN, B. L.

[1] *Modern algebra*, New York, 1949.

VAN FRAASSEN, B. C., and LAMBERT, K.

[1] On free description theory, *Zeitschrift für mathematische Logik und Grundlagen der Mathematik*, vol. 13 (1967), pp. 225–40.

WHITEHEAD, A. N., and RUSSELL, B.

[1] *Principia Mathematica*, vol. 1, London, 1910; 2nd edition, 1925.

INDEX OF PROPER NAMES

INDEX OF SUBJECTS

K
L
M
N
O 4
P 5
Q 6
R 7